# *Because Teaching Matters*

# Because Teaching Matters

## An Introduction to the Profession

SECOND EDITION

## Marleen C. Pugach

University of Wisconsin-Milwaukee

JOHN WILEY & SONS, INC.

Vice President and Executive Publisher: *Jay O'Callaghan*
Executive Editor: *Christopher Johnson*
Acquistion Editor: *Robert Johnston*
Assistant Editor: *Eileen McKeever*
Senior Production Editor: *Trish McFadden*
Outside Project Management: *Suzanne Ingrao*
Marketing Manager: *Danielle Torio*
Editorial Assistant: *Carrie Tupa*
Senior Photo Editor: *Lisa Gee*
Senior Designer: *Madelyn Lesure*

TEXT PHOTO CREDITS:

Section 1 Opening Graphic/Commitment 1:
Digital Vision Ltd./SUPERSTOCK
Section 2 Opening Graphic/Commitment 2: Creatas
Section 3 Opening Graphic/Commitment 3:
Punchstock
Section 4 Opening Graphic/Commitment 4:
ImageSource
Section 5 Opening Graphic/Commitment 5:
ImageSource
Section 6 Opening Graphic/Commitment 6:
ImageSource
Chapter 1 Opening Graphic: Media Bakery
Chapter 2 Opening Graphic: Digital Vision
Chapter 3 Opening Graphic: Media Bakery
Chapter 4 Opening Graphic: Media Bakery

Chapter 5 Opening Graphic: David Jennings/
The Image Works
Chapter 6 Opening Graphic: Digital Vision
Chapter 7 Opening Graphic: Brand X Pictures/
Media Bakery
Chapter 8 Opening Graphic: Ellen Senisi/
The Image Works
Chapter 9 Opening Graphic: Dynamic Graphics/Creatas
Chapter 10 Opening Graphic: Media Bakery
Chapter 11 Opening Graphic: ©AP/Wide World
Photos
Chapter 12 Opening Graphic: Media Bakery

"Your Turn" box photos: Photographer's Choice
RF/SUPERSTOCK Image Source

COVER CREDITS:

Digital Vision Ltd./SUPERSTOCK          Image Source
Creatas                                 Image Source
Punchstock                              Image Source

This book was set in 11 pt. Minion by Prepare, Inc. and printed and bound by Courier/Kendallville.
The cover was printed by Courier/Kendallville.

This book is printed on acid free paper.

To order books or for customer service please, call 1-800-CALL WILEY (225-5945).

ISBN-9780470408209

Printed in the United States of America

10  9  8  7  6  5  4  3  2

*To Bill*
*for his infinite patience, support, and wisdom*

———————————————

## About the Author

 **Marleen C. Pugach** is Professor of Teacher Education in the Department of Curriculum and Instruction at the University of Wisconsin-Milwaukee, where she has been responsible for the preparation of teachers for elementary and middle schools in urban settings since 1986. Her areas of expertise include building collaborative relationships between the preparation of special and general education teachers, preparing teachers for urban schools, and sustaining school-university partnerships. She has published numerous articles, book chapters, and books on teacher education and special education. She is co-author, with Lawrence Johnson, of the book *Collaborative Practitioners, Collaborative Schools* (2002), and author of the book *On the Border of Opportunity* (1998), a study of a high school in the borderlands of New Mexico.

Dr. Pugach received her bachelor's degree from Mount Holyoke College, her master's degree from the University of Southern California, and her doctoral degree from the University of Illinois at Urbana—Champaign. She is the 2005 recipient of the Council for Exceptional Children's Teacher Education Division/Merrill Award for Excellence in Teacher Education, a 2005 Distinguished Alumni Award from the College of Education at the University of Illinois at Urbana—Champaign, and the 1998 recipient of the Margaret Lindsey Award from the American Association of Colleges for Teacher Education. In 2006 she was a Fulbright Scholar at the University of Alberta.

# PREFACE

The premise of this book is that teachers make a difference in the lives of their students. Making the decision to become a teacher is a career-long agreement to become responsible for the school lives of students, and accordingly, for the chances they will have in life once they leave each teacher's classroom. In the 25 years I have prepared prospective teachers at the university level, I have worked with countless students who fully embrace the goal of becoming teachers and who are committed both to their students and their profession. On occasion I have also had to counsel prospective teachers who believed that simply showing up in the classroom each day, or choosing to teach only some of their students well, was enough.

Today the profession of teaching is under greater scrutiny than perhaps ever before. Society has greater expectations for what teachers should know and be able to accomplish with their students than ever before, and those who prepare teachers know more about what works than ever before. Nevertheless, in some arenas ambivalence continues to exist about whether or not teachers actually need formal preparation, and in such arenas the adage that "anyone can teach" however false, actually has credence. Often those who glibly profess this position have not themselves ever taught. But ask any parent, or any student, and they will be the first to tell you that not just anyone can teach, and that teachers need to know more than content—in short, that teaching matters.

It is precisely because teaching makes such a tremendous difference in the lives of students and their families that the decision to become a teacher should not be taken lightly. Despite the external pressures to which teachers must respond, once they are in their classrooms, the individual choices teachers make directly affect the students they teach and the quality of the learning that takes place. The concept of making choices as a teacher and taking responsibility for the consequences of those choices is a central theme of this book.

The text is organized around five professional commitments that, taken together, are essential if teachers are going to make a difference in the lives of students.

Each of the five major sections of the book focuses on one of these commitments. This innovative organizing structure provides a framework for students to make sense of what it means to teach and helps readers think in a more informed way about issues that affect their initial concerns when they are making the decision to teach. In addition, it provides a structure for thinking about their career-long professional development as teachers. These five commitments are:

- Learning from Multiple Sources of Knowledge Throughout Your Career
- Using the Curriculum Responsibly
- Crossing Your Own Familiar Borders to Embrace Diversity
- Meeting the Needs of Individual Students in the Context of the Classroom and the School
- Contributing Actively to the Profession

## Organization of the Book

Chapter 1, *Teaching: A Career That Makes a Difference*, introduces readers to the concept of teaching as a career that matters and that makes a difference for children and youth. This chapter introduces the five professional commitments as well as the INTASC standards. The five sections that follow include 11 chapters.

### Commitment #1: Learning from Multiple Sources of Knowledge Throughout Your Career

Chapter 2, *Putting What You Already Know about Teaching into Perspective*, explores various sources of teaching knowledge, how teachers assign value to various sources of knowledge, the liabilities of relying on a single source of knowledge for learning to teach, and the biases that may emerge from doing so. This chapter also addresses several other influences on learning to teach. It concludes with a section on learning to observe in classrooms as an important source of knowledge, and offers guidelines and strategies for classroom observation and for interviewing practicing teachers.

Chapter 3, *Learning to Teach: What Does It Mean?*, focuses on the content and process of teacher education, how teacher preparation programs are organized, sources of experience, how one becomes certified to teach, who governs teacher education, school-university partnerships as part of teacher education, changing views of teacher education, and alternate routes to teacher certification. The chapter also addresses the professional knowledge base for teaching and how a knowledge base forms a set of criteria against which to judge how ready a teacher education student is for the classroom.

Chapter 4, *Learning from the History and Philosophy of Education*, emphasizes some of the most important foundations of education and how those foundations persist and affect the way schools are structured and the way education is carried out today. This chapter highlights critical historical developments in education, discusses specific historical issues as they relate to educating African American, Latino, and Native American children, and women in the United States. In this chapter, major philosophies of education are described and placed within the context of the historical context in which they developed.

## Commitment #2: Using the Curriculum Responsibly

Chapter 5, *Deciding What to Teach*, introduces the concept of the curriculum and how teachers make decisions about what and how to teach. It includes a discussion of varying interpretations of curriculum; the influence, benefits, and limitations of the standards-based education movement and high-stakes testing; the relationship between curriculum and instructional practices; current controversies in curriculum; and the role of textbooks in teachers' work.

Schools are more than places where students learn academics. In Chapter 6, *More Than "What Is Taught": School as a Social Institution*, the focus is on how the changing nature of society influences the role of schools and the relationship of these issues to decisions teachers make about what and how to teach. This chapter introduces the concept of the *hidden curriculum* and how the total school experience affects what students learn about the purposes of school. How schools respond to changing societal dynamics is also addressed as a form of the hidden curriculum, including, for example, responses to changing family structures, child health issues (e.g., teen pregnancy, drug/alcohol abuse), child abuse, and school violence.

## Commitment #3: Crossing Your Own Familiar Borders to Embrace Diversity

Chapter 7 examines the critical roles teachers play in ensuring that students from racial and ethnic minority groups, lower socioeconomic classes, and students whose first language is not English are fully supported as members of the school community and are served well in schools. This chapter, titled *Teaching Students Whose Race, Class, Culture, or Language Differs from Your Own*, emphasizes the centrality of a teacher's commitment to practicing culturally relevant teaching by acquiring and using cultural knowledge about students, their families, and the community in which a school is located to advance student learning. Teacher expectations, stereotypes, the effects of academic tracking, and assumptions about who can learn well are explored in relationship to the role schools can play in perpetuating inequity. The role of a social justice orientation to teaching is also discussed.

*Teaching Students with Disabilities*, Chapter 8, emphasizes historical and legal developments in the education of students with disabilities, the emergence of the inclusion movement, and the current structure of schooling relative to students with disabilities. The role of collaboration between special and general education teachers is described, as well as the role of assistive technology in meeting the needs of students with disabilities. A distinction is made between diversity of race, class, culture, and language and diversity in terms of disability. The problem of the disproportionate representation of students of color in special education is also addressed.

## Commitment #4: Meeting the Needs of Individual Students in the Context of the Classroom and the School

Chapter 9, *Organizing Good Classrooms and Good Schools*, focuses on how teachers can create classroom learning environments that meet the needs of individual students within a group context. It explores how schools and classrooms have traditionally been organized, how these patterns have or have not been successful in meeting students' needs, and how different patterns of organization and instruction are designed to better meet student needs. Topics include, for example, differentiated instruction, cooperative learning, peer mediated instruction, the role of paraprofessionals, and, at the school level, practices like block scheduling, looping, and small high schools. This chapter also includes a strong emphasis on how technology is used to meet students' instructional needs.

Chapter 10, *How Governing and Financing Schools Influence Teachers' Work,* describes the political structures that govern schooling and how decisions made within those structures influence teachers' work as they strive to meet their individual students' needs. It includes the roles of federal, state, and local government in relationship to schools with regard to both policy and funding, and emphasizes shifts in the relative influence of these three levels of government. The influence of the courts is also addressed. The chapter concludes with a consideration of the changing nature of school governance in the forms of charter schools and school vouchers and the implications of these emerging forms of governance for meeting student needs and for the role of public schooling in America.

## Commitment #5: Contributing Actively to the Profession

Chapter 11 is titled *Ethical and Legal Issues in the Work of Teaching.* One way that teaching is distinguished as a profession is in its expectations for ethical behavior. Because teachers work with children and youth, because teachers are entrusted with their education and well being, and because teachers have significant power over how they conduct themselves in their classrooms, it is critical that expectations for ethical behavior exist. Within such ethical frameworks, teachers need to be aware of legal rights and obligations in relation to their ethical behavior. Legal responsibilities are addressed both with respect to teachers' direct work with students (e.g., religious expression, reporting child abuse, corporal punishment, right to privacy) and to their own professional work lives (e.g., copyright laws, fair use regarding technology).

Chapter 12, *Becoming a Teacher: New Visions and Next Steps,* focuses on the transition that teaching is undergoing as it develops into a profession and the implications of this transition for a career in teaching. The chapter addresses the distinction between thinking of teaching as a job and thinking of it as a profession, and examines the agenda currently underway to professionalize teaching, including, for example, career-long professional development expectations, accreditation of teacher education programs, and standards-based voluntary certification of experienced teachers through the National Board for Professional Teaching Standards. An emphasis is placed on the role of teacher leadership in schools as a way of creating a more robust profession and on the evolution of teaching as a collaborative and more public form of work.

In this chapter students are also asked to engage in a self-assessment of their current thinking and their strengths and weaknesses in relationship to becoming a teacher. This chapter describes several emerging or persistent challenges for education (e.g., world language teaching) and concludes with how to prepare for finding a teaching position, how to interview, and the role of portfolios in the process.

## An Integrated Approach to Learning about Teaching

This text is designed to provide an integrated approach to topics and ideas that are critical for the development of the beginning teacher. Each chapter is focused on a major topic, but critical concepts, ideas, practices, and challenges reappear across chapters. For example, technology is discussed in relationship to teaching students with disabilities, as a critical way of transforming instruction, as an enhancement to professional interactions among teachers, and as a means of enhancing the curriculum in general. Relevant technology links and websites are identified throughout the chapters and are keyed with technology icons in the margin; relevant websites and links also appear in several end-of-chapter activities. The commitment to working with students who represent the full range of diversity, the differences across diversities, and how teachers address diversity within their classrooms are also addressed throughout the chapters. The goal is for students to begin to connect ideas and concepts across different issues in the book—and not just within a single chapter. In addition, Chapters 2 through 12 include a series of special features designed to make the connection between the ideas and concepts that are presented and the world of teaching practice.

## New Features for the Second Edition

For the second edition of *Because Teaching Matters*, the text and references have been updated to reflect changes in policy, practice, and research in teacher education and teaching since the first edition appeared in 2006. Specific new features include:

**Your turn... to reflect, Your turn... to review.** The popular **Your turn...** feature in the first edition has been modified for the second edition and is now called **Your turn... to reflect**. An additional feature using a similar format called **Your turn... to review** is included in each chapter and provides a set of short questions to allow students to review as they go along.

**Rewards and Challenges.** This new feature brings to the second edition the voices of practicing teachers. In this feature, which can be found in each chapter beginning with Chapter 2, five teachers from across the country reflect on the rewards and challenges of various aspects of teaching related to each of the book's five commitments.

**Expanded Technology Coverage.** The integrated coverage of technology has been expanded in this edition. It includes additional text, websites, end of chapter activities, and links to videos. Coverage can be identified in each chapter with a new laptop icon in the margins.

**New Chapter on Learning from the History and Philosophy of Education.** To broaden the coverage of historical and philosophical issues and to complement the historical and philosophical notes in each chapter, a new chapter on learning from the history and philosophy of education has been included as part of the first commitment, which focuses on multiple sources of knowledge for teaching.

**Why It Counts in a Diverse World.** The **Why It Counts** feature at the end of each chapter has been expanded to emphasize the ongoing theme of diversity that is addressed throughout the text.

## Features Continued from the First Edition

**Opening Dialogue:** One of the most important developments in teaching is the assumption that beginning teachers often cannot be expected to perform at the same level as experienced teachers who have mastered their profession. Rather, beginning teachers—or novices—need to work with, seek advice from, and observe their more experienced, expert colleagues as an important way of building confidence and maturity in their teaching abilities. Chapters 2 through 12 each begin with a brief dialogue between a novice and a veteran teacher. In these dialogues, the novice teacher is facing a dilemma that has no easy answer, no readily apparent course of action. Together, the novice and the veteran teacher figure out a path of action that makes sense for the situation.

**A Case in Point:** One goal of this text is to help students think about the relationship between the critical concepts in teaching that are presented and what those concepts look like in practice within classrooms and in the lives of practicing teachers. In each chapter, this case feature provides teacher, classroom, or school-based examples of the concepts.

**Historical and Philosophical Notes:** Each chapter contains both an historical and a philosophical note—an exploration of a foundational topic in education. These notes are intended to provide an historical and philosophical perspective on teaching and education, especially on the origins of some of the practices that endure today, and to reinforce and connect the historical and philosophical ideas presented in Chapter 4.

**Your Turn:** Throughout the chapters, the **Your Turn** feature asks students to stop and reflect, individually or in a small group, about an issue or topic that has been raised, often from the perspective of their own experiences as students. The **Your Turn...** feature includes both **Your turn...** to reflect and **Your Turn...** to review.

**Digging Deeper:** This feature presents the general pro and con positions for a series of education-related controversies, followed by a brief analysis of its nuances, as a means of encouraging students to go beyond the simple pro and con positions and gain a fuller, more complex understanding of the controversy.

**Why It Counts in a Diverse World:** A brief commentary is presented at the end of each chapter on the relevance of the chapter topic for learning to teach, including a discussion of how this knowledge is reflected in the actions of skilled teachers and how this knowledge is relevant for teaching diverse populations of students.

**Chapter Summary:** This feature includes a summary of the main ideas presented within the chapter.

**Critical Terms:** Central terms and concepts have been highlighted and defined in the margins of each chapter. The purpose is to assist students in acquiring a professional vocabulary that distinguishes them as developing professional teachers.

**Exploring Your Commitment:** This feature includes four types of follow-up activities:

   **In the field.** Activities to be completed in a field experience setting in the schools or in the community.

   **On your own.** Study and reflective activities for individual students.

   **On the web.** Activities that require students to investigate websites for specific information.

   **In the research.** A specific research study for students to read that is related to the chapter topic, with follow-up reflective questions that challenge students to push their thinking further regarding the issues covered in the chapter.

**Guidelines for Beginning Teachers:** These guidelines are designed to help students begin to think about making the transition from teacher education student to having their own classroom. They provide suggestions for making this transition easier and for gaining a more complete understanding of the school setting once students accept a teaching position. The guidelines provide another way of connecting the concepts and ideas in this book with the classroom.

**The INTASC Connection:** At the end of each chapter is a listing of the INTASC standards and indicators of knowledge and performances for those standards that are relevant to the issues discussed in the chapter. Standards that apply to multiple issues and concepts are repeated across chapters. This repetition illustrates connections among the various issues that are addressed in the text and provides multiple opportunities for students to consider their own growth and development in relationship to the standards.

**Reading On:** This feature includes an annotated selection of books on topics related to the chapter.

# Acknowledgments

A book that is written by one person is not at all a book that one person is responsible for producing. I have had the incredible good fortune of working with a group of smart, talented, and enlightened professionals at John Wiley & Sons, Inc., whose individual and collective efforts have made writing a text of this breadth and magnitude possible. They include Robert Johnston, who has led this project with good humor and tenacious yet gentle prodding, and the entire team at Wiley. Jay O'Callahan, Chris Johnson, Danielle Torio, Lynn Pearlman, Trish McFadden, Suzanne Ingrao, Lisa Gee, Maddy Lesure, Carrie Tupa, Melissa Kleckner, and Rachel Cirone. I am also indebted to Anne Smith, Vice President, who insisted that writing an introductory text was a good idea, and to the development editor for the first edition, Suzanne Thibodeau.

I am grateful for the feedback and suggestions provided by the many reviewers and wish to express my appreciation to each of them. My work was strengthened immeasurably by their critique and suggestions. They are:

Tempest K. Abight  *Missouri Southern State College*
Nancy Albrecht  *Emporia State University*
Debra Allen  *Nova Southeastern University*
Gloria Ayot  *Eastern Washington University*
Landon Beyer  *Indiana University*
Kathryn Birmingham  *Florida Community College*
Michael Borders  *Gordon College*
Felecia Briscoe  *University of Texas, San Antonio*
Barry Brucklacher  *Mansfield University*
John Bruno  *Florida State University*
Barbara Buckley  *Brazosport College*
Deborah Byrd  *St. Philip's College*
Roger Cleveland  *Morehead State University*
Barbara Coan  *Navarro College*
Donna Cunningham  *Texas Women's University*
Lary Duque  *Brigham Young University*
Patricia Ellis  *Florida Community College*
Kate Friesner  *College of Santa Fe*
Richard Gordon  *California State University, Dominguez Hills*
Frank Guldbrandsen  *University of Minnesota, Duluth*
Ruth Harper  *South Dakota State University*
Ashimuneze Heanacho  *Central Michigan University*
Timothy Heaton  *Cedarville University*
Dwight Holliday  *Murray State University*
Marilyn Howe  *Clarion University*
Patricia Hulsebosch  *Gallaudet College*
John Huss  *Northern Kentucky University*
Thomas Jamison  *Appalachian State University*
Kristi Johnson  *Marymount University*
Dina Laskowski  *Jamestown College*
Johan Koren  *Murray State University*
Barbara Krol-Sinclair  *College for Lifelong Learning*
Thomas Lamborn  *John Brown University*
Isabella Lindner  *St. Mary of the Woods College*
Jan Lupton  *Texas Tech University*
Andrea Malmont  *Shippensburg University*
Jeffrey Margolis  *Rowan University*

Joe Matthews *Brigham Young University*
Carol Mattson *Cypress College*
Mary Mattson-Evans *Georgia Perimeter College*
Wendy McLeish *Buffalo State College*
Denise Meister *Pennsylvania State University, Harrisburg*
Larry Mers *Houston Community College*
Mary Webster Moore *Trinity Christian College*
P. Masila Mutisya *North Carolina Central University*
Frank Orlando *Rowan University*
Marybeth Peebles *Marietta College*
Henry Pitman *Emmaus Bible College*
Jeanne Powers *Arizona State University*
Rosalie Romano *Western Washington University*
Steve Rose *Simpson College*
Elizabeth Jane Rowe *Brookhaven College*
Greg Seay *Northwestern Oklahoma State University*
Jane Spruill *Pensacola Junior College*
Theresa Stahler *Kutztown University*
Beetta Stoney *Kansas State University*
Gayle M. Turner *Appalachian State University*
James Tuttle *Shepherd University*
Gary Wakefield *Frostburg State University*
Guy Wall *Indiana University Southeast*
Barbara Walters *Ashland Community & Technical College*
Jeremy Wendt *Tennessee Tech University*
James Wenhart *Arizona State University, East*
Linda Wilson-Jones *Fayetteville State University*
Charley Wittenberg *Spalding University*
Ann Wooten *Elon University*
LaDonna Young *Southwest Tennessee Community College*

My colleagues University of Wisconsin-Milwaukee, in the Milwaukee Public Schools, and in the Milwaukee Partnership Academy, as well as my students, have continued to teach me about what it means to prepare those who hold the responsibility for educating prospective teachers, and I am grateful for the spirit of collaboration in which I am able to carry out my own work as an educator. I am particularly indebted to the talented and committed classroom teachers and teacher leaders in the Milwaukee Public Schools, whose knowledge, skills and commitment bring honor to a profession that is often misunderstood and underappreciated. I hope that through this book I have done justice to the good work and to the children and youth they teach.

I would like to recognize the work of Dr. Rosalie Romano of Western Washington University, who contributed a major portion of Chapter 4. Likewise, I would like to thank the five practicing teachers from across the country whose voices appear in the *Rewards and Challenges* feature and who managed to complete their reflections close to the end of their respective school years, when their work lives were incredibly busy: Adriana Balistreri, Mildred Boveda, Kate Flanagan, David House and Erika Stubbs. In addition, Melissa Hedges, Tyrassa Riley, and Phyllis Sanders willingly shared their stories about becoming teachers.

Several university instructors and students have contacted me about this book to share their thoughts and to provide suggestions for this revision. My virtual door is always open for communication and I would welcome hearing from any reader at my email address: **mpugach@uwm.edu**.

I am fortunate to have a longstanding friend, Corrine Glesne, who for the past 30 years has been willing to hear me out about my writing and who continues to be the other half of our two-person, long-distance writing group. Finally, I now write in a much quieter house than I did when this book was first started, but the physical distance of my children does not lessen their willingness to hear me out as I bury myself in the task of writing; Lev Rickards and Negin Toosi, and Anna Rickards, could not be more supportive. Finally, Bill Rickards, my husband, is the anchor in our complicated lives and creates the space where we can each be creative in our own ways.

Marleen C. Pugach
*Milwaukee, Wisconsin*

*Because Teaching Matters* offers a full line of teaching and learning resources to enhance the instructor's use of the text and encourage students' active reading and learning.

## Web-Based Resources for the Instructor

**Instructor's Manual**, prepared by Kim Fries, University of New Hampshire, contains chapter outlines, ideas for in-class discussion, and ideas for in-class and out-of-class activities.

**PowerPoint Presentations** offer chapter outlines and highlights from the text, prepared by Linda Wilson-Jones, Fayetteville State University.

**Test Bank**, revised by Steve Neill, Emporia State University, contains 35-50 questions per chapter, a mix of multiple choice, true/false, short answer, and essay.

**teachscape®**

**Teachscape Video Case Studies**, that may include (1) best-practice videos that show research-based practices in action in the classroom; (2) commentaries by noted researchers that are designed to provide a research-based perspective on the practices illustrated; (3) teacher reflections to promote better understanding of the featured teacher's instructional decisions; and (4) student commentary on the featured classroom processes and students' experience of the instruction.

**Instructor's Guide to accompany the Teachscape Video Case Studies** by Felicia Saffold, University of Wisconsin Milwaukee contains suggestions for using the Teachscape content as well as discussion questions and activities.

## Web-Based Resources for the Student

**Study Guide** includes pre- and post-chapter assessment questions, both short answer and essay, prepared by Rosalie Romano, Western Washington University.

**INTASC Activities** for each chapter correlate selected end-of-chapter activities with the 10 INTASC standards so they can be used as potential portfolio entries. This material was prepared by Amy Staples, University of Northern Iowa.

**"Policy into Practice"** provides discussions of current policy issues in classrooms, schools and school districts, prepared by Amy Staples, University of Northern Iowa.

**Digging Deeper** provides follow-up activities, readings, web links, and student projects for in-depth reflection on controversial issues that are introduced in each chapter's *Digging Deeper* feature. The material was prepared by Rosalie Romano, Western Washington University.

**On the Web** provides links to major websites cited in the chapter text, tables and figures, and end-of-chapter activities.

**Glossary Flashcards** offer an opportunity to drill and practice the critical terms.

## Unique organization

The text is organized around five professional commitments that provide a framework for students to make sense of what it means to teach and helps them think about issues in a more informed way.

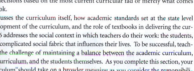

COMMITMENT #2

# USING THE CURRICULUM RESPONSIBLY

One of the most enduring challenges in education is how to decide what actually gets taught in the classroom. Curriculum is often considered to be the "stuff" of teaching. But teaching is far more than what you teach; it also involves how you teach it and to whom you are teaching it. For all teachers, novice and experienced alike, there is a constant tension among "getting through the material," making sure one has the time and skills to teach it well, and relating the material to the context of students' lives—their families, their communities, and their interests. Given these considerations, how do teachers decide what to ___ do they strike an appropriate balance? How do they know when to shift ___ whom are teachers accountable, and for what aspects of the curriculum? ___ issues affect a teacher's decisions about the curriculum?

___ we focus on how teachers make a professional commitment to creating ___ incorporates high standards but is also relevant and accessible to stu___ of the curriculum, external pressures that seek to define it, and the role ___ e drama of "what is to be taught" are all important to consider as you ___ eer as a teacher. Without a sound perspective on curriculum, you risk ___ ecisions based on the most current curricular fad or merely what comes ___ k.

___ usses the curriculum itself, how academic standards set at the state level ___ opment of the curriculum, and the role of textbooks in delivering the cur___ 6 addresses the social context in which teachers do their work: the students, ___ complicated social fabric that influences their lives. To be successful, teach___ the challenge of maintaining a balance between the academic curriculum, ___ urriculum, and the students themselves. As you complete this section, your ___ culum" should take on a broader meaning as you consider the responsibili___ r creating classrooms where students learn, not just where teachers teach.

## Teaching Students Whose Race, Class, Culture, or Language Differs from Your Own

7

Jake Harris began teaching in a small town in central Illinois a month ago. The demographic makeup of his fourth grade classroom is two-thirds white and one-third Mexican American. The Mexican American population moved here in the last decade to work in one of the local factories. Some of his students who are Mexican American have lived in the area for their entire schooling, but in the next month Jake is going to receive three students who are newly arrived from Mexico. Jake was raised in a community that was primarily white and rural: he student taught in a nearby community and has had little experience with people from other countries or cultures. He wants to teach all of his students well, but right now he is not feeling comfortable with planning for his new students. There is a special teacher to work with the new students on English language skills. Jake is fortunate to have a mentor teacher, Sally Ford, who recently retired from the district and was considered to be a highly skilled, successful teacher. He has talked with her on many occasions since he began his job.

"I just don't know how I'm going to work with them," Jake said, once he had described his concerns to Sally. "They're not going to know anything, and how will I keep them involved?"

Sally heard the concern in Jake's voice, but she was worried about how he was thinking about the situation. "Jake, let's step back a bit here," Sally said. "First, tell me what you mean when you say that your students won't know anything."

"Well, they won't know how to do the work, they won't know anything about this town or how things work, their parents won't speak English," he replied.

"Is there anything your new students do know?"

"What do you mean?" Jake asked, confused.

"Well, for starters, your new students have lived their whole lives in a country that they know a whole lot about—and that you don't know a lot about. If they've been in school in Mexico, they probably know a lot about a lot of subjects, and the challenge is communicating about it. Also, remember that your students know another language—one that you don't know," said Sally.

"I never thought of it that way," Jake said. "It's sort of like I'm only seeing what they don't have, instead of what they do have."

*Rather than think of . . . diverse students as problems, we can view them instead as resources who can help all of us learn what it feels like to move between cultures and language varieties, and thus perhaps better learn how to become citizens of the global community.*

Lisa Delpit, 1995, p. 69

## Chapter-Opening Dialogues

Brief dialogues between a novice and a veteran teacher that highlight the main focus of the chapter. In the dialogues, the novice teacher is facing a dilemma where there is no easy answer, no readily apparent courses of action. Together, the novice and the veteran teacher figure out a path of action that makes sense for the situation.

## A Case In Point

Case examples that help students think about the relationship between the critical concepts presented in the chapter and what those concepts look like in practice within classrooms and in the lives of practicing teachers.

### A Case In Point
**Current Events as the Hidden Curriculum**

Harper Lee, author of the classic 1960 novel *To Kill a Mockingbird*, weighs in on the hidden curriculum as a negative force in students' experience of school in her description of required current events in the third grade classroom of the novel's main character, Scout Finch. The unintended outcome of this seemingly innocuous, simple activity operated against students who were already at a disadvantage in school. A character wise beyond her years, Scout appears to understand a great deal about the hidden curriculum and the implicit outcomes of schooling.

Once a week we had a Current Events period. Each child was supposed to clip an item from a newspaper, absorb its contents, and reveal them to the class. This practice encouraged good posture and gave a child poise; delivering a short talk

### Historical Note
**The Influence of National Committees
on Schooling and the Curriculum**

National committees have long had an influence on the educational establishment in the United States. In the late 1800s, in the wake of great concern over the repetitive nature of the curriculum, two highly influential committees appointed by the National Education Association reviewed the elementary and secondary curriculums.

At the high school level, the general question should prepare students for college or for the world high school as preparation for college wanted a hig would prepare graduates for the rigorous academic versities, which served a small proportion of studer Education Association convened the Committee of Ter a group of influential educators, chaired by Charle

## Historical and Philosophical Notes

Historical and philosophical notes in each chapter that explore a foundational topic in education.  These notes are intended to provide an historical and philosophical perspective on teaching and education, and especially on the origins of some of the practices that endure today.

### Philosophical Note
**John Dewey and the Progressive View of Education**

How students experience the academic curriculum was a particular concern of educators who aligned themselves with the progressive education movement in the 1920s. Led by the famous educational philosopher John Dewey, progressive educators believed that teachers should put a concern for students' entire educational experience at the forefront of their planning and teaching—not just learning the material. "What the progressives shared," wrote Decker Walker and Jonas Soltis (1992), "was their opposition to prevailing school practices such as memorization, drill, stern discipline, and the learning of fixed subject matter defined in adult terms with little relation to the life of the child" (pp. 18–19). According to the famous historian of education, Lawrence Cremin (1988), several themes characterized progressive education, among them: "first, a broadening of the program and the function of the school to include a direct concern for health, vocation, and

### Your turn... *to review*
1. What is the difference between the *explicit curriculum* and the *taught curriculum*?
2. Why is it so important for teachers to assess their students' learning of the curriculum?
3. Name three different ways teachers can get information about how well their students are learning the curriculum.

### Your turn... *to reflect*
In small groups , select one content area at the high school level. In the community in which you went to school, what was included in the curriculum? What was not included or was given little emphasis? What do you think may account for what was in the explicit/taught curriculum, and what was in the null curriculum? What did you gain or lose as a result of how the curriculum was defined?

## Your Turn... to reflect / Your Turn... to review

Throughout the chapters, these features asks students to stop, reflect on and review an issue or topic that has been raised, often from ther perspective of their own experiences as students.

## Digging Deeper

A discussion of the general pros and cons of current education-related controversies, followed by a brief analysis of the nuances, to encourage students to gain a fuller, more complex understanding of the controversy.

### Digging Deeper
**The Role of Basic Skills in the Curriculum**

A recurring, contentious curriculum debate focuses on the teaching of basic skills. A basic skills curriculum is typically defined as "the fundamentals," such as phonics or grammar or mathematics facts. The purpose of schooling from this curriculum perspective is to ensure that each student acquires these basic skills.

**Pro and Con:** Proponents of a basic skills curriculum argue that learning the "3 Rs" should be the defining characteristic of good schooling. Only in a highly structured curriculum, and a highly teacher-directed classroom where each basic skill is delineated and teachers know exactly what skill they will teach next, it is argued, w                        n in the world. In      **The Nuances:** When curriculum is defined primarily as the support especially    skills, be it learning phonics, memorizing the periodic table, or m With its
              of major wars in which the United States has been involved, the   ded this
ence itself is defined narrowly as learning these skills in isolatio
elementary level, spe hose skills, but over time it is less likely to equip students for
instruction" program
skills. Increasingly, th    **Rethinking the Issue:** Teaching basic skills is an essentia
                iculum, but how teachers approach basic skills is important. Do
                urriculum, saving complex topics and discussions until stude
                he basics? Are students spending whole days drilling on the
                pending many hours completing worksheets that provide prac
                with little else? Or in contrast, do teachers motivate students to

## REWARDS AND CHALLENGES

### Making the Curriculum Meaningful

Mildred Boveda
*Miami, Florida*

My entire teaching career has taken place under the influence of the No Child Left Behind Act. Although the act contains broader notions than accountability, its restricted focus on assessing student achievement and faculty accountability in terms of what can be demonstrated statistically has had an especially detrimental effect on students who come from traditionally low performing schools. The official curriculum that is coming from the district, along with the textbooks that the district adopts, is more strongly tied to the state standards and the

With that said, when making pedagogical decisions and preparing lessons for my students, I refuse to restrict myself to only covering the tested benchmarks. The term "data-driven instruction" is frequently tossed around, but what I see is that truly effective teachers implement "student-driven" instruction. That is, teachers go beyond just using student outcomes on various measures to plan curriculum and instruction, but they also pay close attention the context in which they teach. I strive to incorporate the state standards and district curriculum by

## Rewards and Challenges

Written by practicing teachers, these personal essays reflect on the rewards and challenges of various aspects of teaching related to each of the book's five commitments.

## The Explicit Curriculum — What It Is and Is Not

We can think of the formal, written academic program of study that guides teaching as the **explicit curriculum** (Eisner, 1979). Larry Cuban (1992), another scholar of curriculum, uses the term *official* or *intended curriculum* to describe the formal academic program of study. These terms convey essentially the same message: the explicit, formal academic curriculum is a public statement of what a particular school district or state believes is worthwhile for students to know in each content area. As such, it sets the broad parameters for what you will teach. The explicit curriculum is usually a public document or series of documents, and today these documents can typically be accessed online through school district or state educational agency websites. It represents the endpoint of your teaching—what your students should know.

As a general rule, two kinds of documents usually define the formal program of study or the explicit curriculum: **academic content standards** and **curriculum guides**. Academic content standards are statements of what students should know and be able to do in each of the major content areas upon completing their PK–12 education. This knowledge is usually assessed in required standardized tests administered by the state. Building on these standards, curriculum guides give detail and resources regarding how the various subjects might be taught.

The concept of the explicit curriculum sounds simple. You are handed standards and curriculum guides, and you develop teaching plans from these materials. Districts purchase instructional materials, such as textbooks, software, and laboratory equipment, to support the course of study that has been identified as worthwhile. As a teacher, you can draw on these resources and materials to help [yo]u plan your own instruction. It is essential for all teachers to know the academic [ ]standards for their subject and grade level, and curriculum guides can help inter[pr]et those standards. But none of these documents tells you what to do each day in [yo]ur classroom. They provide a destination only, a statement of what your students [sh]ould know and be able to do as a result of the instructional program *you* create [an]d implement for *your* students. A set of standards and curriculum guides does [no]t actually tell you how to *teach* to those goals.

**Critical Term**

**Explicit curriculum.** *The formal, official, public academic program of study that defines what students are expected to know as a result of being in school.*

**Critical Term**

**Academic content standards.** *Formal, public statements of what students should know and be able to do in each of the content areas at various points in their PK–12 education.*

**Critical Term**

**Curriculum guide.** *A document prepared at the state or local district level that provides detailed information to help teachers plan instruction.*

## Critical Terms

Central concepts and terms have been highlighted in the text and defined in the margins of each chapter, to assist students in acquiring a professional vocabulary that distinguishes them as developing professional teachers.

### Why It Counts in a Diverse World

By now you probably realize that *curriculum* is a slippery term and that deciding what to teach is more complex than it may at first seem. The challenge for teachers regarding curriculum is that they are faced with a constant balancing act: there is too much that is interesting to teach; there is a need to balance content with the teaching process; there is pressure to cover the standards-based material; and the specter of annual standardized state testing is always present. In addition, local political pressures may be imposed to include—or exclude—certain topics in the curriculum.

As you think about taking on your first teaching position, the whole idea of curriculum may seem daunting. After all, it will be difficult enough to juggle all the responsibilities you will have as a new teacher. You may just want someone to hand you a textbook and tell you what to teach each day. But in reality, consid-

## Why It Counts in a Diverse World

A brief commentary at the end of each chapter on the relevance of the chapter topic for learning to teach, including how this knowledge is reflected in the actions of good teachers and how it is relevant for teaching diverse populations of students.

## CHAPTER SUMMARY

### Curriculum: A Multidimensional Term

The term *curriculum* refers to the course or program of studies for which a teacher is responsible in a particular grade and a particular content area. Curriculum is more than just the formal, or *explicit*, course that is written down and shared publicly. The explicit, formal curriculum is interpreted by teachers as they engage in the day-to-day work of teaching. What teachers actually do in the classroom relative to the explicit curriculum can be called the *taught curriculum*. What students actually take away academically from their experience of being in school is called the *learned curriculum*. The *null curriculum* consists of all of the things that are not taught in school. These various dimensions of curriculum—that which is explicit, that which is taught, and that which students learn—interact and place different kinds of pressures on teachers as they answer the question: What is worth teaching and having students learn?

### Developing the Curriculum: How Does It Work?

In today's educational environment, individual states have created academic content standards for what students should know and be able to do as a result of their PK–12 education. These standards form the backbone of curriculum development and are taken into account as states prepare curriculum guides and as local school districts use those state documents to develop their own local curriculum plans. Standards also form the basis for state testing programs. Today there is a very tight alignment, or connection, among standards, the explicit curriculum, and testing students to determine what they have learned. This alignment, which places a high value on testing, puts pressure on teachers to cover the standards whether or not they represent worthwhile ends for education. The standards can also lead to a homogenization of the curriculum across the country. Wise teachers are familiar with the standards and embed activities designed to help their students meet the standards within a meaningful curriculum.

### Curriculum—Teaching with a Purpose

Although individual variation exists among local school districts, there is still pres-

## Chapter Summary

A summary of the main ideas presented within the chapter.

## EXPLORING YOUR COMMITMENT

1. **on your own...** Select an academic content area that you are interested in teaching. Make a list of several important topics within this subject that you believe are worthwhile to learn. Then compare them with a list of state standards (available on state education agency websites) to see what that state values as being worthwhile to learn. How do you account for the difference?

2. **on the web...** What are the benefits and limitations of standardized testing? Visit the Fair Test website (http://www.fairtest.org). What issues related to standardized testing of students are addressed on this website?

3. **on your own...** Locate lists of books that are banned in local school districts near your university or in your local library. Do any of the titles that are banned surprise you and, if so, why? Use the website of the American Library Association (http://www.ala.org/alaorg/oif) to learn more about the issue of banned books nationally.

4. **on your own...** Read the 1955 play *Inherit the Wind* by Jerome Lawrence and Robert E. Lee, or view the 1960 film version starring Spencer Tracy, Fredric March, and Gene Kelly. What views of teachers and curriculum decision making are portrayed in this story?

5. **in the field...** With a principal, discuss the dominant curriculum orientation of the school. What does the school staff emphasize? What does it value as being important with respect to the curriculum it has adopted?

6. **on the web...** Locate the website for the state education agency for your home state, the state in which you are studying to be a teacher, or the state in which you think you will look for a job in teaching. Identify five different kinds of information that are available on this website. How helpful is this information to be for you once

10. **in the research...** Read Kauffman, D., S. M. Johnson, S. M. Kardos, E. Liu, and H. G. Peske. (2002). "'Lost at sea': New teachers' experiences with curriculum and assessment", *Teachers College Record, 104*, 273–300. What does this article have to offer you as you think about the role of reflection about the curriculum?

## Exploring Your Commitment

End-of-chapter follow-up activities which include:

*in the field...* Activities to be completed in a field experience setting in the schools or in the community.

*on your own...* Study and reflective activities for individual students.

*on the web...* Activities that require students to investigate websites for specific information.

*in the research...* Activities that provide a specific research study for students to read related to the chapter topic, with follow-up reflective questions that challenge them to push their thinking further.

## GUIDELINES FOR BEGINNING TEACHERS

1. You should be able to locate state-level curriculum documents for the subjects you will be teaching for whatever state in which you teach. Such documents can be used in conjunction with local curriculum guides to help you as you plan your instructional program.

2. Since you are accountable for teaching your students according to academic standards, as a beginning teacher you will want to become familiar with the standards of the state in which you are teaching. Locate the standards on the state's website.

3. As a new teacher, you will need to request the local curriculum from which you will be teaching, as well as the state documents that may provide you with additional resources. Be sure to request scope and sequence charts for the various subject areas for which you are responsible.

4. When you interview at a school, review the school or the district website to see if you can identify the curriculum orientation of the school/district. Be prepared to ask questions about the materials that are used to teach the curriculum and the kinds of units of study that have been carried out in the grade level you are interested in.

5. During your interview, ask questions about the philosophy of the school and the curriculum that is used. Try to get a sense of how much freedom you will have to mine the full potential of these materials to meet the needs of your

## Guidelines for Beginning Teachers

Practical advice for first-year teachers related to the chapter topic.

## THE INTASC CONNECTION

The INTASC standards that are most closely aligned to the issue of curriculum are Standards 1 and 7.

Standard 1 states: *The teacher understands the central concepts, tools of inquiry, and structures of the discipline(s) he or she teaches and can create learning experiences that make these aspects of subject matter meaningful for students.* The following are some relevant indicators:

● The teacher can relate his or her disciplinary knowledge to other subject areas.

● The teacher has enthusiasm for the discipline(s) she or he teaches and sees connections to everyday life.

## The INTASC Connection

A listing of the INTASC standards and statements of knowledge and performances for those standards that are relevant to the issues discussed in the chapter.

## READING ON...

Barton, A. C. (2003). *Teaching science for social justice.* New York: Teachers College Press. Angela Calabrese Barton illustrates how to teach science from a philosophical perspective that stresses connecting students to science in school and in after-school programs in low-income, inner-city communities and neighborhoods.

Horton, M. (1998). *The long haul: An autobiography.* New York: Teachers College Press. In this autobiography, Myles Horton, a famous progressive educator who was committed to social justice, reflects on how he put his philosophy of education into practice at the Highlander School in Tennessee.

Joseph, P. B., S. L. Bravmann, M. A. Windschitl, E. R. Mikel, and N. S. Green. (2000). *Cultures of curriculum.* Mahwah, NJ: Lawrence Erlbaum Associates. An analysis of major approaches to the interpretation of curriculum in schools, written from a practical perspective on what it means to teach from various philosophical perspectives on

## Reading On

A short, annotated selection of books on topics related to the chapter.

# BRIEF CONTENTS

CHAPTER 1 Teaching: A Career That Makes a Difference  1

COMMITMENT #1 LEARNING FROM MULTIPLE SOURCES OF KNOWLEDGE THROUGHOUT YOUR CAREER  17

CHAPTER 2 Putting What You Already Know about Teaching into Perspective  19

CHAPTER 3 Learning to Teach: What Does It Mean?  57

CHAPTER 4 Learning from the History and Philosophy of Education  97

COMMITMENT #2 USING THE CURRICULUM RESPONSIBLY  127

CHAPTER 5 Deciding What to Teach  129

CHAPTER 6 More Than "What Is Taught": School as a Social Institution  167

COMMITMENT #3 CROSSING YOUR OWN FAMILIAR BORDERS TO EMBRACE DIVERSITY  207

CHAPTER 7 Teaching Students Whose Race, Class, Culture, or Language Differs from Your Own  209

CHAPTER 8 Teaching Students with Disabilities  249

COMMITMENT #4 MEETING THE NEEDS OF INDIVIDUAL STUDENTS IN THE CONTEXT OF THE CLASSROOM AND THE SCHOOL  287

CHAPTER 9 Organizing Good Schools and Good Classrooms  289

CHAPTER 10 How Governing and Financing Schools Influence Teachers' Work  331

COMMITMENT #5 CONTRIBUTING ACTIVELY TO THE PROFESSION  371

CHAPTER 11 Ethical and Legal Issues in the Work of Teaching  373

CHAPTER 12 Becoming a Teacher: New Visions and Next Steps  411

# CONTENTS

## CHAPTER 1

Teaching: A Career That Makes a Difference  1

Five Professional Commitments to Guide the Choices You Make  2

Commitment #1: Learning from Multiple Sources of Knowledge Throughout Your Career  3

Commitment #2: Using the Curriculum Responsibly  5

Commitment #3: Crossing Your Own Familiar Borders to Embrace Diversity  6

Commitment #4: Meeting the Needs of Individual Students in the Context of the Classroom and the School  7

Commitment #5: Contributing Actively to the Profession  7

The Role of Reflection and Action in the Choices You Make  8

The Rewards and Demands of Making a Commitment to Teaching  8

The Rewards of Teaching  9

A Case In Point: Influencing the Lives of Students—A Teacher's Gift  10

The Demands of Teaching  11

Meeting Standards for Good Beginning Teachers  12

Teaching: Is It Really for You?  14

Making a Choice about the Kind of Teacher You Want to Be  15

## COMMITMENT #1

LEARNING FROM MULTIPLE SOURCES OF KNOWLEDGE THROUGHOUT YOUR CAREER  17

## CHAPTER 2

Putting What You Already Know about Teaching into Perspective  19

Five Kinds of Experience That Create Prior Knowledge about Teaching  20

Knowledge about Teaching from Your Own Experience of Schooling  20

Autobiographical Knowledge about Teaching  23

Rewards and Challenges: Getting Started  25

A Case In Point: Natalie's Story  26

Knowledge about Teaching from Working in Schools  27

A Case In Point: From Paraprofessional to Teacher  29

Knowledge about Teaching from Images in the Media  30

Historical Note: Catharine Beecher's Image of Teachers  32

Digging Deeper: Is Teaching a Science or an Art?  35

Knowledge from Your Own Beliefs about Teaching  36

Philosophical Note: The Role of a Philosophy of Teaching  38

Observation and Interviewing: "Making the Familiar Strange"  39

Making the Familiar Strange through Formal Classroom Observation  40

Making the Familiar Strange through Interviewing  45

Final Pointers on Observation and Interviewing  48

Why It Counts in a Diverse World  48

## CHAPTER 3

Learning to Teach: What Does It Mean?  57

The Research Is In: Good Teaching Matters  58

Who Governs Teacher Education and Certification?  60

What Do Prospective Teachers Study?  62

Subject Matter Content  62

Foundations of Education  63

Pedagogy  64

Field Experience in PK–12 Classrooms  65

Connecting the Elements of Teacher Education  66

Reforming the Preparation of Teachers: A National Commitment  67

Historical Note: Normal Schools and the Early History of Teacher Education  67

From Coursework to Standards: Increasing Rigor in Teacher Education  70

The Purpose of Standards in Teacher Education  71

The Role of Portfolios in Standards-Based Teacher Education  71

**A Case In Point:** How Portfolios Demonstrate What Teachers Know and Can Do 73

**Good Teacher Education: A Shared Responsibility between Schools and Universities** 74

**A Case In Point:** Working in a Professional Development School 76

**The New Role of Testing in Preparing Beginning Teachers—Help or Hindrance?** 76

**Philosophical Note:** An Essentialist View of Teaching and Teacher Education 78

**Accreditation of Teacher Education Programs** 79
National Accreditation 79
Accreditation and Standards: The Road to Greater Professionalization? 80

**Digging Deeper:** Do Standards and Accreditation Really Ensure Good Beginning Teachers? 80

**Preparing Enough Teachers: Responding to Teacher Shortages** 82
Shortages—A Cyclical Event in Teaching 82
Alternate Routes: A Solution to the Shortage? 82

**Rewards and Challenges:** From Teacher Education to the Classroom 85

**After Formal Teacher Education: What Comes Next?** 85
Induction—The First Stage of Your Career 86

**A Case In Point:** Mentoring a First-Year Teacher in an Urban School 87
Renewing Your Teaching License 89

**Why It Counts in a Diverse World** 90

**CHAPTER 4**

**Learning from the History and Philosophy of Education** 97

**Historical Origins of American Education** 98
Early Educational Efforts in the Colonies 99
Expanding Education, Literacy, and Civil Society 100
The Jeffersonian Ideal of Education 101
The Contested Problem of the Control of Public Education 102
Common Schools 103
The Late 19th Century: Building a System of Education 105

**Digging Deeper:** A Colonial Conflict in a Modern Setting: What High School Curriculum is Best? 105
The Limited Reach of Universal Education 108

**A Case In Point:** What Can a History of Educational Inequity Mean for Today's Students 110
Into the 20th Century 112
The Historical Record and the Current Era: Enduring Dilemmas and Persistent Controversies 113

Philosophical Views of Education 114

**Rewards and Challenges:** A New Teacher's Philosophy 115
The Map of Western Philosophical Concepts and Schools of Thought 115
Major Philosophies of Education 117
Philosophy and Purpose Revisited 120

**Why It Counts in a Diverse World** 121

**COMMITMENT #2**

**USING THE CURRICULUM RESPONSIBLY** 127

**CHAPTER 5**

**Deciding What to Teach** 129

**Curriculum: A Multidimensional Concept** 131
The Explicit Curriculum—What It Is and Is Not 131
Curriculum as What Is Taught 132
Curriculum as What Is Learned 133
What Isn't Taught—The Null Curriculum 135
Curriculum Dilemmas 136

**Developing the Curriculum: How Does It Work?** 136
How Are Academic Content Standards Created? 137
What Do Academic Content Standards Look Like? 137
What Do Curriculum Guides Look Like? 138

**A Case In Point:** Developing a Teaching Unit 141
National Influences on Curriculum Development 143

**Historical Note:** The Influence of National Committees on Schooling and the Curriculum 144

**Curriculum—Teaching with a Purpose** 145

**Philosophical Note:** John Dewey and the Progressive View of Education 146
Beyond a Technical Approach—Special Curriculum Identities for Individual Schools 147

**Digging Deeper:** The Role of Basic Skills in the Curriculum 150
Making Sense of Standards, Accountability, and the Purposes of Curriculum 152

**Rewards and Challenges:** Making the Curriculum Meaningful 153

**The Role of Textbooks in the Curriculum** 155
How Teachers Use Textbooks 155
Textbooks, Standards, and the Curriculum 158
The Textbook Industry in the United States 158

**Why It Counts in a Diverse World** 161

CHAPTER 6

More Than "What Is Taught": School as a Social Institution  167

The Power of the Hidden Curriculum  169
The Hidden Curriculum and the School as a Culture  170
Benefits of the Hidden Curriculum  172
Liabilities of the Hidden Curriculum  173

A Case In Point: Current Events as the Hidden Curriculum  175
The Hidden Curriculum as a Commentary on the Social Purposes of Schooling  176

The Current Societal Context  176

Historical Note: The Emergence of the Common School  177

Population and the Schools  179
Changing Family Structures  179
Child Abuse and Neglect  185
Violence and the Schools  187

Digging Deeper: Will Smaller High Schools Meet Students' Needs?  189
Teen Pregnancy  191
Drug and Alcohol Abuse  192

Addressing Social Dynamics by Changing the Regularities of Schooling  193
Redefining the Environment  193

Rewards and Challenges: Making School Work for Every Student  195

A Case In Point: The Salomé Ureña de Henriquez Campus, New York City  197
The Teacher's Role in Promoting Competence  198

Philosophical Note: Meeting Individual Needs through a Humanistic Philosophy of Education  198

A Brief Word about the Extracurriculum  199

Why It Counts in a Diverse World  200


COMMITMENT #3

CROSSING YOUR OWN FAMILIAR BORDERS TO EMBRACE DIVERSITY  207

CHAPTER 7

Teaching Students Whose Race, Class, Culture, or Language Differs from Your Own  209

What Changing Demographics in the United States Mean for Teachers  211

Understanding Diversity as an Asset, Not a Deficit  213

A Case In Point: Deficit or Asset?  214

How Knowing about Your Students' Lives Helps You Teach  216
Using Funds of Knowledge as a Resource for Student Learning  218

Devaluing Students in School: How Does It Happen?  219
What Teachers Communicate through Their Expectations  219

Historical Note: The Brown v. Board of Education Supreme Court Decision  221
What Schools Communicate through Academic Tracking  222

A Case In Point: A Rude Awakening about Tracking  225

Addressing Diversity of Language in the Classroom  226

Digging Deeper: What about Bilingual Education?  229

Rethinking Teaching as a Culturally Responsive Profession  231
Culturally Responsive Teaching  231
Why "Celebrating Difference" Is not Enough  233

Rewards and Challenges: Honoring Students' Cultural Differences  234
Beyond Cultural Knowledge—Multiple Perspectives and Social Transformation  235

Philosophical Note: Transforming Society through Social Reconstructionism  236

Recognizing Privilege and Power  237

"Not Seeing Color" as a Problematic Response to Diversity  238

A Special Responsibility—Teaching in a Monocultural School  239

Why It Counts in a Diverse World  241


CHAPTER 8

Teaching Students with Disabilities  249

A Broad Commitment to Equity for Students with Disabilities  251

Historical Note: Burton Blatt's Campaign to Expose Institutions for Mentally Retarded Persons  252
Federal Mandates for Equity  254

A Case In Point: Daniel Greenwood  256
From Birth to Work: Extending the Age Range of Students in School  257

Philosophical Note: The Inclusion Movement  258

Does Labeling Students with Disabilities Help or Hinder a Teacher's Work?  261
What Disability Categories Do and Do Not Provide for Teachers  264
How Disability Labels Can Lead to Inequities  264
Simplifying the Categories  267

The Teacher's Role  267

**Rewards and Challenges:** Meeting Students' Diverse Instructional Needs  268

Building Classroom Communities Where Students with Disabilities Belong  268

Being Flexible and Accommodating for Students with Disabilities  269

Collaboration Among Teachers: The Key to Success  270

The Goal: A Classroom Environment that Diminishes Differences  272

**Digging Deeper:** What Kind of Curriculum is Best for Students with Disabilities?  273

How Technology Can Help You Teach Students with Disabilities  275

Integrating Assistive Technology into the Classroom  275

Universal Design as a Strategy for Inclusion  276

A Final Point about Assistive Technology and Disabilities  277

Disability: The Same as or Different from Other Diversities?  277

What about Educating Gifted and Talented Students?  279

Why It Counts in a Diverse World  280


**COMMITMENT #4**

MEETING THE NEEDS OF INDIVIDUAL STUDENTS IN THE CONTEXT OF THE CLASSROOM AND THE SCHOOL  287

**CHAPTER 9**
Organizing Good Schools and Good Classrooms  289

What Makes a Good School? What Makes a Good Classroom?  291

In Good Schools, Students Are Motivated, Challenged, and Engaged  291

Good Schools and Classrooms Are Communities of Learners  293

Good Schools Know How Well They, and Their Students, Are Doing  295

Rethinking School Organization to Meet Students' Needs  296

The Traditional Approach: Age-Graded Classrooms and Curriculum  297

Multi-Age Classrooms  298

Looping  299

**Historical Note:** One-Room Schools  300

Class Size Reduction at the Elementary Level  301

Block Scheduling at the High School Level  302

**Digging Deeper:** Introducing Innovations into Schools  303

The Small High Schools Movement  304

Rethinking the School Day to Increase Time to Learn  307

**Philosophical Note:** Organizing Schools and Classrooms for Democracy  309

**Rewards and Challenges:** Preparing the Next Generation of Recyclers  311

A Recap: Different Organizational Patterns, Different Social Settings  311

Rethinking What Happens at the Classroom Level to Meet Student Needs  312

Differentiating Instruction to Meet Students' Needs: The Need for Flexibility  312

How Technology Helps Meet Student Needs  313

**A Case In Point:** Transforming a Sixth Grade Classroom with Technology  318

Meeting Student Needs through Peer Tutoring  320

Meeting Student Needs through Cooperative Learning  321

How Paraprofessionals Help Meet Student Needs  322

Why It Counts in a Diverse World  324


**CHAPTER 10**
How Governing and Financing Schools Influence Teachers' Work  331

Putting Governance into Perspective  332

The Influence of Local Control of Schools on a Teacher's Work  333

The Role of the Superintendent of Schools  334

The Relationship between the School Board and the Superintendent  335

Local School Board Policymaking  335

Decision Making at the Building Level  338

The Role of the Principal  338

Local School Governance through Shared Decision Making  339

Teachers' Leadership Roles in Schools  339

Negotiated Decisions: The Role of Teachers' Unions  340

**Historical Note:** Governing the Nation's Earliest Schools  342

How State Governance Influences a Teacher's Work  343

The Influence of the Federal Government in Education  344

**Rewards and Challenges:** Sharing Power in the Classroom  345

Direct Federal Involvement in Education Programs through Legislation  346

**A Case In Point:** Title IX in Action?  350

Court Decisions and Education  351

**Philosophical Note:** The Separation of Church and State and Public Education  352

The Influence of Other External Groups on Education Decisions  354

Financing Education: How Dollars Make their Way to Schools, Teachers, and Students  355

Inequities in School Funding  357

From the Federal Government, the State, and the Community to the School  358

Changing Views of the Governance and Control of Schools  359

**Digging Deeper:** Strengthening or Weakening Public Schools through Choice?  361

Home Schooling: Where Does It Fit?  363

Why It Counts in a Diverse World  365


**COMMITMENT #5**

CONTRIBUTING ACTIVELY TO THE PROFESSION  371

CHAPTER 11

Ethical and Legal Issues in the Work of Teaching  373

Trust: The Basic Moral Obligation of Teachers  375

The Multiple Dimensions of Trust  376

**Philosophical Note:** Nel Noddings and the Ethic of Care  378

Creating and Maintaining Trusting Relationships  381

The Teacher as Advocate  382

**Rewards and Challenges:** The Day-to-Day Challenges of Teaching Ethically  383

Ethical Considerations at the Teacher-to-Teacher Level  385

**A Case In Point:** Unwanted Advice  385

The School as an Ethical Community  386

**A Case In Point:** In or Out of the Teachers' Lounge?  386

Ethical Behavior, Codes of Ethics, and Standards of Professional Practice  389

The Role of Codes of Ethics for Teachers  389

The Ethics of Recommending Candidates for Teaching  389

**Historical Note:** The Moral Context in Colonial Schools  392

How Legal Issues Influence Teachers' Ethical Practice  393

Students' Rights to Free Expression of Opinions  394

Privacy and Confidentiality  395

Reporting Child Abuse and Neglect  396

Corporal Punishment  396

Search and Seizure  397

Religion in the Schools  398

**Digging Deeper:** The Persistent Debate over Teaching Evolution  399

Technology, The Internet, Fair Use, and Copyright Issues  400

The Personal versus the Professional as an Ethical Issue for Teachers  402

Personal Beliefs and Inclusivity in Public Schools  403

Personal Beliefs and the Curriculum  403

Why It Counts in a Diverse World  404


CHAPTER 12

Becoming a Teacher: New Visions and Next Steps  411

The Profession/Job Conflict  412

Defining the Tension  412

Enduring Myths about Teaching  415

Beyond the Myths: Teaching as a Profession  416

Teaching as a Collaborative and More Public Form of Work  417

Opening the Classroom Doors for Observation and Feedback  418

**Philosophical Note:** Collaboration *and* Autonomy for Teachers  420

Collaboration: A Shared Resource for Professional Dialogue  420

**Historical Note:** The Emergence of Teachers' Organizations in the United States  421

Teacher Leadership  422

Mentoring as Teacher Leadership  423

Coaching as Teacher Leadership  424

Peer Review of Teaching as Teacher Leadership  425

Teacher Leadership and the New Teacher Unionism  426

Teachers as Researchers  426

How Do Teachers Conduct Their Own Research?  427

**A Case In Point:** Yolanda's Research on Teaching Writing in a Middle School Language Arts Class  429

Why Is Teacher Research a Sign of Increased Professionalism?  430

Recognizing Accomplished Teaching through the National Board for Professional Teaching Standards  431

**Digging Deeper:** Differentiated Pay for Teachers?  434

The Role of Networking in Professional Growth and Development  435

Accountability and Control in the Profession of Teaching  437

Time to Grow, Time to Lead  439

Reflecting on Your Views and Beliefs, Assessing Your Progress  440

Reflection: An Enduring Habit  442

Incorporating New Developments in Teaching and Learning  442

School or Districtwide Professional Development  444

Setting Short- and Long-Term Goals  444

**Rewards and Challenges:** Revisiting Why We Teach  445

Becoming an Informed Professional  445

**Challenges on the Horizon in Education**  446

Global Education  447

World Languages Education  448

Resegregation of Schools  450

The Future of Public Education  450

**Finding Your First Teaching Position: Smart Preparation Pays Off**  451

Take Your Preparation Seriously  451

Make Your Portfolio Count  453

Become an Informed Job Applicant  453

Prepare for Your Job Interviews  454

**What Counts for You Now as a Teacher in a Diverse World?**  456

GLOSSARY  463

REFERENCES  469

NAME INDEX  483

SUBJECT INDEX  487

# HISTORICAL AND PHILOSOPHICAL NOTES

**HISTORICAL NOTES**    Catharine Beecher's Image of Teachers   33

Normal Schools and the Early History of Teacher Education   67

The Influence of National Committees on Schooling and the Curriculum   144

The Emergence of the Common School   177

The *Brown v. Board of Education* Supreme Court Decision   221

Burton Blatt's Campaign to Expose Institutions for Mentally Retarded Persons   252

One-Room Schools   300

Governing the Nation's Earliest Schools   342

The Moral Context in Colonial Schools   392

The Emergence of Teachers' Organizations in the United States   421

**PHILOSOPHICAL NOTES**    The Role of a Philosophy of Teaching   38

An Essentialist View of Teaching and Teacher Education   78

John Dewey and the Progressive View of Education   146

Meeting Individual Needs through a Humanistic Philosophy of Education   198

Transforming Society through Social Reconstructionism   236

The Inclusion Movement   258

Organizing Schools and Classrooms for Democracy   309

The Separation of Church and State and Public Education   352

Nel Noddings and the Ethic of Care   378

Collaboration *and* Autonomy for Teachers   420

# *Because Teaching Matters*

## *An Introduction to the Profession*

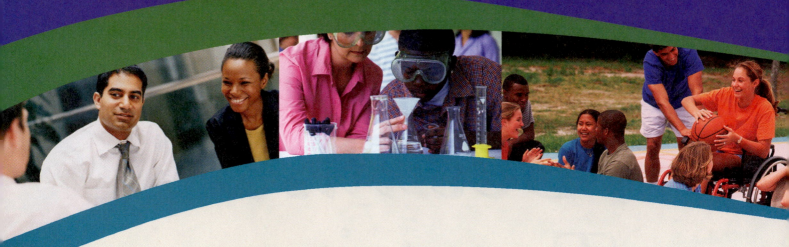

## Guiding Questions

- How do the five professional commitments in this book help you think about a career in teaching?

- How does reflecting on your own teaching help you improve your teaching?

- What are the rewards of a career in teaching?

- What are the demands and challenges of a career in teaching?

- What are the standards for good beginning teachers, and how do they influence learning to teach?

- How do you decide if teaching is for you?

- What kind of teacher do you really want to be?

# Teaching: A Career That Makes a Difference

# 1

Years after they have left school, students may forget specific lessons, but they will remember their teachers. They remember their teachers' names either because their experience in those classrooms was good or, unfortunately, because their experience was bad. Sometimes a teacher who seemed strict and harsh at the time may, over the years, be recalled with respect and admiration. For some students, a teacher is remembered as someone who turned their lives around completely. Whatever the situation, the influence teachers have on their students is long lasting and frequently it is profound.

The premise of this book is a simple one: *Good teaching makes a difference in the lives of children.* Students spend six hours a day, five days a week, in classrooms with their teachers. It is within these classrooms that students are challenged and motivated, where they can believe in the possibilities of their futures, and where they gain the knowledge and skills to pursue their dreams. When teachers do their jobs well, students from all life circumstances, in every community, attain the potential to thrive and grow and *learn.* When teachers do not do their jobs well, students irrevocably lose the opportunity schools offer for impacting their individual lives positively. The day-to-day choices and judgments teachers make directly affect the quality of learning that takes place and the very lives of their students. In other words, good teaching matters, and it matters a great deal.

It is precisely because teaching matters so much that your decision to choose teaching as a profession is so significant. Once you make the commitment to teach, you are, in essence, making the commitment to take responsibility for the quality of the experiences each of your students will have in your classroom over the entire life of your career.

What does it actually mean to *learn* to teach? What is it like to be in a classroom every day as the teacher, and how do you go about the work of making every day count for your students? What are you expected to know and be able to do as a beginning teacher, at the start of your career? How will you develop your abilities as a teacher so that you can assume your professional responsibilities with self-assurance and ensure that your students are growing and learning? What kinds of choices are you expected to make as a teacher, and what will guide you as you make these choices?

The purpose of this book is to help you begin to understand what it means to learn to teach. In so doing, you will have the opportunity to learn more about the teaching

*The purpose of education, as many have seen it, is to open the way, as the young become empowered with the skills they need and the sensitivities they require in order to be human— to create themselves and to survive.*

Maxine Greene, 1978, p. 85

profession, consider some of the most basic issues that confront the field today, and make a more informed decision about your career. More importantly, this book is designed to help you think about the real situations teachers encounter every day, the real choices teachers make, the real consequences for students, and the real difference teachers make in their students' lives.

## Five Professional Commitments to Guide the Choices You Make

Teachers make deliberate choices about the kinds of classrooms they will create and the kinds of experiences their students will have. The choices *you* make regarding your students, your classroom, and your place in the larger school, district, and community all have implications for the kind of teacher you will become—and for how you will be remembered. The concept of making choices as a teacher and taking responsibility for the consequences of those choices is a central theme of this book. Teachers certainly do not have complete control over what happens in school or over their students outside of school. Nor do they have control over certain requirements that must be met. But all teachers do have a great deal of control over what happens every day in their individual classrooms and the kind of role they themselves play within the school, the district, and the community.

This book is organized around five professional commitments that, taken together, are essential if teachers are going to make a difference in the lives of students. Within each of these commitments (see in Table 1-1), teachers make choices that affect the students they teach. These are enduring issues for teachers, and if you become a teacher, various aspects of these five commitments will be part of your decision–making throughout your career.

As a teacher, what will you do to make a difference in the lives of your students?

(Media Bakery)

2

| Table 1-1    Five Professional Commitments for Teaching | |
|---|---|

These five commitments represent career-long challenges for teachers and are areas for ongoing professional growth and learning.

| Professional Commitment | Why It Matters |
|---|---|
| Learning from Multiple Sources of Knowledge Throughout Your Career | Teachers do not finish learning when they conclude their teacher education programs. They go on learning from their own practice, from their students, and from working with other teachers, but only if they are open to learning and improvement as a career-long commitment. |
| Using the Curriculum Responsibly | The curriculum is not a static set of documents that teachers follow blindly. Within the curriculum documents that exist in any state or district to provide guidance to teachers, teachers themselves make choices about how they enact the curriculum to meet the needs of their own students. |
| Crossing Your Own Familiar Borders to Embrace Diversity | Teachers regularly teach students whose backgrounds differ from their own. Teachers are charged with creating classrooms where all students are welcomed, feel safe and secure in the classroom and school community, and are supported in learning. |
| Meeting the Needs of Individual Students in the Context of the Classroom and the School | Schools and classrooms are organized as group settings. Within these group settings teachers face the challenge of making sure they maintain attention to their individual students' needs. |
| Contributing Actively to the Profession | Teaching is not just a job where one clocks in and out at the beginning and end of the day. To keep the profession vital, teachers themselves need to contribute to and take responsibility for the profession. |

Why is it so essential to think about these five commitments both as you begin your professional preparation and throughout your career? Consider some of the important choices you will have to make regarding each of these commitments once you begin your career.

## Commitment #1: Learning from Multiple Sources of Knowledge Throughout Your Career

What you learn during your teacher education program should provide you with a sound and solid foundation for teaching—and the confidence to get started. But as is true of all professions, you cannot possibly learn everything there is to know about teaching from your formal program of teacher preparation. As in other professions, teachers are expected to begin with a certain level of competence in creating classrooms, planning instruction, and working with students to support their learning. To excel in the profession, to demonstrate that you take your work seriously, and to challenge yourself to higher levels of professional expertise, it is important to recognize that teaching is a continual learning experience over the entire course of your career. You have already learned something about teaching from your own experience as a student, but that experience is likely to look very different as you begin to view teaching from a professional perspective.

Your formal education for teaching represents only a starting point for a lifetime of professional growth and development. Highly skilled, experienced teachers know that learning how to teach did not come to an end when they completed their teacher education program. They know that they do not know everything and that working with many different students with many different needs presents ongoing challenges. To meet those challenges teachers need to continue to learn.

Where do teachers turn for credible sources of knowledge about teaching, and how do they sort through all the new ideas for "fixing" education that will inevitably encounter during their careers? Does growing throughout one's career mean shifting with every change that comes along? On what basis do strong teachers make decisions about what directions to take for their own new professional learning and development? In addition to continuing to learn from teacher educators, teachers also learn from their own teaching practice and from interacting with others about their teaching (Donovan, Bransford, & Pellegrino, 2000).

Teachers can attend classes, professional conferences, and workshops, as well as professional development activities sponsored by school districts themselves. These various sources of teaching knowledge can help teachers discover new ways of thinking about teaching. But they can also pose a dilemma for those teachers who have not developed a good strategy for figuring out why some kinds of knowledge are more useful than others or what benefits and limitations each kind of knowledge may bring. Your philosophical ideals about education—along with your professional knowledge—should help you form a set of ideas against which you judge these new sources of knowledge. So, for example, you will not adopt a new approach just because someone tells you it works, or is motivating, or is exciting. As a professional you will want to weigh new ideas against what you know and have learned about how students learn and about your specific students themselves, their families, and what will benefit them most.

The past 25 years have witnessed an explosion of research about what kinds of school environments best support lifelong professional learning and development of teachers. Teachers continue to learn when schools function as collaborative professional learning communities, when teaching is talked about regularly, when new learning among teachers is practiced, shared, and valued, and when teachers help each other learn (Hord, 2004; Fullan, 1993; Lieberman & Miller, 2004, Rosenholtz, 1989). In such an environment teachers can reflect on what they are learning from their teaching experience in collaboration with their colleagues. Understanding the

As teachers make choices about how to organize their classrooms, they need to do so in a way that makes time for groups and for individual students. (Media Bakery)

ways teachers learn and the sources of new knowledge enables you to make sound choices about how you will go on learning and improving your skills throughout your career.

What critical choices will you face regarding sources of knowledge for your own professional growth and development over the course of your career? First, teachers who view themselves as learners are ready to learn from their students. Students have much to teach teachers about their lives in and outside of school, about how they learn, about what their individual life circumstances are, and about how well teachers are teaching based on an understanding of their students' work. Second, teachers who view themselves as learners model the importance of learning for their students. Recognizing that there are significant new things to learn, that learning is to be valued, and that together with your students you may be trying out new approaches to teaching as a way of learning—all translate into the climate you create within your classroom. Finally, teachers make choices about what they are open to learning about in the first place. Is your interest in new learning focused on content only? Is it focused on new teaching methods? Are you willing to be flexible in what you will entertain as possible in your classroom—for example, a major shift to using technology? All of these issues are related to setting a course of learning throughout your career and drawing on multiple sources of knowledge to do so.

## Commitment #2: Using the Curriculum Responsibly

There is no universal agreement on the purposes of schooling. Indeed, based on varying philosophies of education, competing purposes for being in school can operate simultaneously within or across schools. As teachers make choices about the kind of professionals they wish to be, they constantly navigate within these competing purposes. The curriculum, or what to teach, is one of the most prominent places where the different purposes of schooling can play out.

The issue of what to teach is more complex than it may first appear. As a teacher, you will have access to a formal curriculum, or course of study, with formal instructional materials and textbooks to guide your work. But once you are handed these materials, you still have to make many choices about what and how you will teach. In other words, when you are handed curriculum materials, you are not handed a foolproof recipe for teaching.

For example, what topics will you decide to cover in depth, and what will you relegate to the sidelines? How will you make the curriculum, which may seem overwhelming in breadth and depth, manageable? How comfortable are you with the content you are teaching? How will you make the curriculum interesting and relevant for your students so that they are motivated to learn in the first place? Will you expect your students to learn only facts and figures, or will you challenge them to understand complex issues and ideas? What if at some point you are asked to adopt new curriculum materials that represent a different philosophy from the one upon which you have based your teaching? How will you respond in this situation? What knowledge and perspectives will you use to evaluate and respond to such changes in the curriculum?

A professional commitment to using the curriculum responsibly means that teachers not only know what is in the curriculum, but also actively think about the best way to teach that curriculum to *their* students so they can become independent, lifelong learners. Throughout their careers, teachers are faced with choices about whether to simply "cover the curriculum" or do the work of connecting the curriculum to their students' lives, giving students meaning and

To be happy in their work, teachers must enjoy being with young people every day. (Media Bakery)

reason for studying new and challenging topics and issues. Leaving the students out of the equation and opting for a focus on the content alone diminish the human, interactive nature of the teaching enterprise.

## Commitment #3: Crossing Your Own Familiar Borders to Embrace Diversity

Today in the United States teachers, in unprecedented numbers and locations, are working with students whose life experiences may not mirror their own and so, must address the challenge of bridging these divides. When teachers are unfamiliar with the cultures and languages of their students, or when teachers live outside the communities in which they teach, they must bridge cultural and socioeconomic contrasts not only with their students but also with their students' families.

It is not just cultural or economic differences that are of concern to teachers. They must also learn to work with students who have disabilities and students whose sexual orientation may differ from their own. Each of these diversities is unique and may require teachers to step outside the comfort of their own life experiences, to challenge their own beliefs and potential biases, and to create classrooms where no student will be marginalized.

What choices do teachers make with regard to working in classroom and school environments that are characterized more and more by these various diversities? Are they committed to learning about new cultures and communities? Do they view the array of differences among students and their families as assets that enrich the classroom? Do they respect and value the differences they encounter? Are they committed as teachers to believing in the potential of each of their students, to providing every student with a challenging school experience and the opportunity to grow, rather than favoring students from some backgrounds and not from others? Do they have the skills to meet their students' different needs? As teachers make such choices, they can also make the difference between a students' success and failure in school.

## Commitment #4: Meeting the Needs of Individual Students in the Context of the Classroom and the School

Schools and classrooms in the United States are by design collective, large-group settings. Within their classrooms, however, teachers are constantly concerned about meeting the needs of individual students; they work at the intersection of meeting individual needs and group needs every day. Strategies for grouping students, moving students between groups, or allocating time to provide individual attention to students who are struggling or who need advanced work, are all issues teachers face throughout their careers. These choices overlap with decisions teachers make about the curriculum itself, what is important to learn, and about what individual students and the group are interested in learning.

As part of this professional commitment, teachers must understand that teaching does not consist of just passively going into the classroom, opening the textbook, and reading the directions for the next activity to the whole class. Skilled, committed teachers actively work to figure out how to motivate and involve their students in learning. They know their students well and deliberately seek out and use teaching methods that will enable them to reach all of their students. This can often mean a judicious mix of whole class, small group, and individual work. Teaching only to the "average" student is not an option for teachers who are committed to meeting all of their students' needs.

Teachers who are serious about meeting their students' needs actively advocate for them and make the choice to seek out resources and solutions to problems so that success becomes a real possibility. They are advocates not only for individual students, but also for their classrooms as a whole—advocating for resources, for experiences, and for opportunities that enable their students to deepen their learning.

One of the great rewards of teaching is the satisfaction of watching students learn and grow. (Media Bakery)

## Commitment #5: Contributing Actively to the Profession

Long gone are the days when teachers could just go into their classrooms and shut the door—essentially shutting out the need to work with other adults. Today teachers are expected to collaborate with one another to ensure that schools and classrooms are places where students can thrive and learn. For example, beginners may be overwhelmed with the tasks before them as they start their careers, and without the help of other skilled, veteran education professionals the work would be even more challenging.

Teachers can contribute to the profession in many different ways. Throughout the course of your career, you will need to make choices about the level of commitment you will make. Will you be a passive teacher who comes in every day, gets through the day, goes home, and collects a paycheck every month? Or will you be a teacher who actively participates in the professional, intellectual life of teaching to improve what takes place in classrooms and schools for the students? In what areas might you develop special expertise, and how might you then use that expertise to better reach students and to help other teachers do the same? What kind of contribution will you make to the individual school in which you teach? Will you take on a leadership role at your local school site, for example, to build greater family participation in the school? Will you make a commitment to improve state education policy or work in professional organizations devoted to teaching in particular subjects or specialty areas? At this point you do not have to answer these questions, but as you plan for a career in teaching, it is important to recognize that becoming a productive, active member of your profession is an important goal.

**Your turn...** *to reflect*

Consider each of these commitments and identify at least two questions you have about each one. How would you go about answering your questions?

## The Role of Reflection and Action in the Choices You Make

A vital part of learning to teach is recognizing the role of teacher reflection on how to teach well. To be a teacher who makes a difference is not to do the same thing year in and year out. Teachers who are committed to their profession regularly reflect on and inquire into the quality of their work, asking themselves how much their teaching is helping students grow and learn. In this way, they work toward identifying areas of improvement and more effective practices.

Reflection also helps you to understand that teaching is not just doing what someone tells you to do or what the textbook tells you to do. As a prospective teacher, it is important to begin by asking challenging questions about what it means to teach. In so doing, you must be willing to look critically at yourself as a developing teacher—which is what reflection is about.

Teachers use reflection to inquire into all aspects of their teaching, including, for example, how to reach students who are struggling, how to teach academic subjects, how to manage relationships with students and their families, how to assess student learning, or how to integrate the arts into the academic subjects. Reflection creates a healthy tension between what a teacher knows and does well and what a teacher sets as new professional goals. It requires teachers to be actively engaged in setting goals for their own growth and development.

Asking questions and reflecting on the quality of your own teaching are not enough, however. *It is the action teachers take as a result of their reflection and inquiry that is the link to being a real professional.* As teachers ask such questions of themselves, they can begin to identify areas and issues for further learning and use these as a focus for their own professional growth and development. When they ask such questions alongside their colleagues in their school or district, the potential for improving teaching practice is even greater because it spans classrooms across educational settings.

## The Rewards and Demands of Making a Commitment to Teaching

Teaching is probably one of the most misunderstood professions—except by those who are teachers themselves. Uninformed, naive views of teaching are all too common: it is often said that teaching is easy, that all a teacher does is stand up in front of a group of students and talk, that teachers don't work "real" hours, that it's a job anyone can do well. But ask any good teacher and you will get a *very* different answer. Good teachers know that their work is both rewarding and demanding. Those who choose to teach make a commitment not only to getting great satisfaction from the rewards the profession offers, but also to meeting its demands.

## The Rewards of Teaching

Being with young people every day is one of the foremost benefits of teaching. Teachers who are committed to their profession choose to spend their days with young people and often say that they can't imagine doing anything else. As a teacher you will spend your working days with students, and your satisfaction will occur from doing so. That is one of the essential foundations of your commitment to teaching—that you enjoy and want to spend time with young people. This is true for anyone who wants to become an effective teacher.

**Managing multiple tasks at once is one of the demands of teaching.** (Michelle Birdwell/ PhotoEdit)

The greatest reward of teaching, however, is not just enjoying being with your students, but seeing them grow and learn. As a teacher, you can take pride in helping your students make progress—in specific skills, in deep knowledge of a subject, in the ability to become independent and make choices about their futures, and in their use of what they have learned. At whatever grade you choose to teach or in whatever subject, your satisfaction will come from watching your students "get it," watching the light bulbs go on in their minds, and seeing how they learn to grasp new concepts and think in more complex ways. If you teach first grade, this means you will have the satisfaction of teaching children to unlock the code of written language and learn to read. If you teach middle school mathematics, this can mean watching your students master algebra for the very first time. If you are a high school music teacher, it might mean listening to students play the first compositions they write for a class assignment—and finding a few gems among them. Such rewards drive teachers at every level—from preschool to elementary to middle school to high school.

### Your turn... *to reflect*

If you were asked to honor one of your teachers, whom would you select? Prepare a short statement for your class describing why this teacher deserves to be so honored. What is the connection between what you are saying about this teacher and your own motivation to consider a career in teaching?

Teachers also derive rewards from empowering their students both as individuals and as members of a democratic society. Teachers help students expand their views of what they can pursue and accomplish. If you teach high school, this might mean encouraging a student who may not have thought attending college was important or possible and then watching that student choose to apply to and attend college under your guidance. If you are an English teacher, it might mean seeing your students learn to write persuasive essays and then prepare letters based on those essays to a local official in the interest of improving the community. It is for these rewards that many people choose to teach in the first place. The organization *TeachersCount* supports a campaign based on the motto "Behind Every Famous Person There is a Fabulous Teacher." Their website, **http://www. teachersscount.org**, includes not only stories of exceptional teachers, but also a wide variety of information for individuals who are considering a career in teaching.

One of the hidden rewards of teaching is that you do not always know how far your influence might reach. Sometimes the positive influence you have on your students is not apparent until years or decades later. For example, a student may visit you years after graduating and let you know that your class was decisive in making a career choice. Even though at least some of the gratification you receive from your work is delayed, when you do receive it, the wait will have been worthwhile.

Teaching can also be rewarding if you seek a career where not everything is predictable and where you must be flexible to do your work well. No matter how organized or prepared a teacher may be, no teacher can predict, for example, exactly what kind of mood the students will be in each morning when they enter the classroom. "Reading" your students and making changes based on their mood may make the difference between a successful and an unsuccessful day. Furthermore, you cannot predict how well your students will do in any given lesson. Teachers have to be prepared to "read" their students' understanding while they are teaching and make adjustments to instruction along the way. Similarly, you cannot predict whether an interruption will occur that requires you to stop your teaching briefly, attend to the interruption, and pick up again—without missing a beat. This aspect of teaching gives the work vitality, and those who are comfortable with this level of unpredictability will find teaching a rewarding challenge.

Finally, teaching is rewarding because it allows you to be creative in your work—in the way you structure the semester or year, in the way you develop lessons, in how you use materials, and in the way you ask students to demonstrate what they have learned. Teaching offers you a regular opportunity to change your approach to the material you are teaching to better meet your students' needs. You can experiment, see how the changes affect your students' learning, and then try it again.

## A Case In Point
### Influencing the Lives of Students—A Teacher's Gift

A teacher's work seldom gains public recognition. Students themselves may not recognize the positive influence a teacher has had until years after they have left the teacher's classroom. In some instances, students reconnect with teachers who changed the direction of their lives. Russell Paterson, a twelfth grade student who attended elementary and middle school in a small rural community in Nebraska, moved to Chicago with his family when he entered high school. In his senior English class, students were asked to write a letter to an influential person in their lives. He chose to write to his fifth grade teacher, Eleanor Wilson.

Dear Ms. Wilson:
I'm not sure if you remember me, but I was a student in your fifth grade class not so long ago. My family moved to Chicago when I began high school. This year our English teacher asked us to choose a person who was very influential in our lives and write a letter to them, and as soon as he gave us this assignment I knew I had to write to you.

I wasn't exactly a model student in elementary school. In fact, I was a pretty rowdy kid. Looking back on it, I worked hard at doing everything I could **not** to be a good student. I was more interested in cutting up and being the class clown than I was in what we were doing in class. I didn't do my homework and I didn't like to participate in class. I also didn't have a lot of help at home. The summer before fifth grade my father was laid off and things were pretty tense around my house. None of this helped my attitude.

But there you were every morning with a smile on your face, saying hello to me like I was the best student who had ever walked into your classroom. Every day you asked me how I was doing. I didn't always answer you as nicely as you asked, but you still treated me like I was someone who mattered to you. Sometime later in the fall when I was falling further behind, you began having a bunch of kids stay in for lunch with you and you always asked us about what we were interested in. At one of those lunches I must have mentioned that I always wondered about what life was like on the other planets.

When students enter your classroom, what kind of experience will be in store for them? (Creatas/Media Bakery/ Michael Newman/Photo Edit)

After that you began bringing books and magazines for me to read about outer space, the other planets, and NASA. You let me do some special assignments about those things when other kids were doing the regular subjects. I had a little corner in your room where you kept all of those books and magazines for me. You told the rest of the class that I was the resident expert on the planets, so if anyone had questions they should come and ask me. I still wasn't a star student, but I always had something to do. It was around that time that you said to me, in a casual way, "You know, Russell, when you grow up there is a way to make a living being an expert on the planets."

At the time I didn't realize how much those words made an impression on me. I don't remember all the details about the rest of fifth grade, but I do know that I managed to get into less trouble that year, passed, moved on to middle school, and did pretty well in science all along. Now I realize that in the back of my mind I could hear you telling me much more than that I might make a living being smart about planets. What you were really saying is that I had something I could do well, that there was a way to use what I was interested in, and that what happened to me in the future was important to you. That also made it important to me.

So here I am in my senior year of high school, and next year I will be attending the state university to study astronomy. I've kept up my interest in the planets and space, and last year my counselor connected me with some people from the Museum of Science and Industry who work with high school students. I was able to get a summer job there working with the younger kids. So I'm writing to thank you for a lot of things. Thank you for not giving up on me when I was a handful, thank you for taking the time to learn about me and what I was interested in, and thank you for planting a big idea in my mind. You were a great teacher and I was very lucky to be in your class.

Sincerely,
Russell Paterson

## The Demands of Teaching

Along with the rewards of teaching come the demands of this profession. It takes skill to plan and implement motivating lessons, for example, to assess how students are progressing, and to calibrate instruction to meet students' varying needs. Teachers who are successful don't just open up the textbook each day and teach. Instead, they prepare to teach by using what they know about their students, the curriculum, and ways to instruct their students.

Teaching is also demanding because the classroom is a social environment unlike any other. Building a community that will promote learning requires teachers to establish a solid foundation of good social interaction among the students themselves as well as between students and teachers. Once that foundation is established, teachers must focus on keeping the classroom community working well. This means knowing how to make sound judgments about what students need—as individuals and as learners—in the midst of a busy day, every day. In a learning environment in which students get along well, teachers still need to maintain the community, minimize the chance of problems occurring, and manage problem behaviors when they do take place.

Being a teacher also demands simultaneously managing the students, the curriculum, instructional groups, schoolwide activities, and unintended interruptions in the classroom. In fact, the term *multitasking* could have been coined expressly to describe teaching, and good teachers do it well. Have you ever wondered, for example, how a teacher manages to work with a small group, look up at just the right time to make sure the rest of the class is doing what it is supposed to be doing, and then go back to the small group and continue the lesson? Or how a teacher knows what is going on between two students in the back of the room when she is talking with a student at her desk at the front of the room?

Teaching is also demanding because it is an inherently human profession, with all of the challenges this entails. Students have complex lives, and those lives come into the classroom whether or not you expect it. Teachers must be prepared to meet their students' needs even when they don't know from day to day what those needs might be. This demand also means that it is not enough simply to know the content you will teach. Instead, you must be able to engage in the human interaction of teaching it to your students in ways that make sense to them. If your students can't connect with what you are teaching them, they probably won't be eager to participate in what you are planning.

Another demand placed on teachers comes from the public sector. The work teachers do is not independent of the mandates of local school boards, state government, and federal government. These mandates can constrain teachers' freedom to determine what they do within their classrooms. Today, for example, through passage of the No Child Left Behind Act, the federal government is playing a much greater role in education than ever before.

Finally, teaching is demanding because of the wide range of student needs in the classroom. Some students may be victims of abuse or neglect, some may not have anyone at home to help with homework, others may struggle because they live in poverty, and still others may have material wealth but little emotional support. When you make the commitment to teach, you are agreeing to teach all the children in your classroom and to work from the problems and challenges they present in a way that will lead to their learning. More importantly, you are agreeing to find the strengths your students bring to the classroom, even in the midst of the struggles they and their families may be facing.

## Meeting Standards for Good Beginning Teachers

How will you best prepare so that you can reap the rewards and meet the demands of teaching? One way to help guide the choices you will make is to become familiar with the national and state standards for beginning teachers. INTASC—the *Interstate New Teacher Assessment and Support Consortium*—is part of an organization made up of the heads of education in every state, the Council of Chief State School Officers—and is responsible for the development of a set of national standards to define expectations

**Figure 1-1    The 10 INTASC Standards for Beginning Teachers**

**The INTASC standards represent a national perspective on what beginning teachers should know and be able to do.**

1. The teacher understands the central concepts, tools of inquiry, and structures of the discipline(s) he or she teaches and can create learning experiences that make these aspects of subject matter meaningful for students.

2. The teacher understands how children learn and develop, and can provide learning opportunities that support their intellectual, social, and personal development.

3. The teacher understands how students differ in their approaches to learning and creates instructional opportunities that are adapted to diverse learners.

4. The teacher understands and uses a variety of instructional strategies to encourage students' development of critical thinking, problem solving, and performance skills.

5. The teacher uses an understanding of individual and group motivation and behavior to create a learning environment that encourages positive social interaction, active engagement in learning, and self-motivation.

6. The teacher uses knowledge of effective verbal, nonverbal, and media communication techniques to foster active inquiry, collaboration, and supportive interaction in the classroom.

7. The teacher plans and manages instruction based upon knowledge of subject matter, students, the community, and curriculum goals.

8. The teacher understands and uses formal and informal assessment strategies to evaluate and ensure the continuous intellectual, social, and physical development of the learner.

9. The teacher is a reflective practitioner who continually evaluates the effects of his/her choices and actions on others (students, parents, and other professionals in the learning community) and who actively seeks out opportunities to grow professionally.

10. The teacher fosters relationships with school colleagues, parents, and agencies in the larger community to support students' learning and well being.

**Source:** The Interstate New Teacher Assessment and Support Consortium (INTASC) standards were developed by the Council of Chief State School Officers and member states. Copies may be downloaded from the Council's website at http://www.ccsso.org. Council of Chief State School Officers (1992). *Model standards for beginning teacher licensing and development: A resource for state dialogue.* Washington, DC: Author.

for good beginning teachers. The INTASC project was launched in the late 1980s and created a national consensus on what it means to be a well-prepared beginning teacher. From these deliberations, a set of 10 professional standards was developed. These 10 standards appear in Figure 1-1.

Although states are not required to adopt the INTASC standards, many use them voluntarily as the measure of new teachers' readiness for the classroom. Other states have adopted their own sets of standards that teacher education students must meet in order to be certified to teach. Whichever set of standards you will be asked to meet, teacher education that is based on standards requires not only that you complete courses and receive grades. You must also demonstrate that for each standard, through various activities within your teacher education program, you have the professional knowledge, skills, and personal dispositions required to teach and that you can translate that knowledge into the actions needed to perform your job well. You will be expected to perform the tasks that characterize a good teacher at a level that allows you to be recommended for teacher certification in your state. If your state uses a different set of standards from INTASC, locate your state teacher standards on the website of your state's department of education. Consider how the standards you will be asked to meet are similar to or different from the INTASC standards. The 10 INTASC standards set a high—but attainable—goal for what it means to be a good beginning teacher.

**Your turn...** *to reflect*

Review the 10 INTASC standards. Which standards seem to be a match for your idea of teaching at this point? Which surprised you? Which do you think will be the most challenging for you to accomplish?

At the end of each chapter in this book, you will find the INTASC standards listed that are relevant to the issues within the chapter, as well as some of the specific knowledge, skills, and dispositions developed by INTASC to define the standards. When a standard relates to issues in more than one chapter, you will find it repeated. This repetition shows the connections among the various issues addressed in the text and among the standards themselves and provides you with several opportunities to consider your own growth and development in relation to the INTASC standards.

## Teaching: Is It Really for You?

One of the most important purposes of this text is to help you answer the question: Is teaching really for you? Because teaching matters so much to each and every student you may teach in the future, now is the time to think about whether you can make the commitment to this profession. As you gain a deeper understanding of what teaching entails, as you obtain a more complete understanding of the dimensions of this career, and as we expose myths about the profession, you will be able to make a much more informed judgment about your career choice. If you are participating in an early field experience in a school as part of this course, you will have an even broader base of experience to draw upon in making your decision.

You are making the decision to become a teacher at a very exciting and challenging time in the development of the profession. The first few years of teaching, known formally as the period of *induction*, are now viewed as a time when teachers need and are increasingly receiving focused professional support. No longer is a new teacher expected to be able to do everything at the same level as a skilled veteran teacher. A clear understanding is beginning to emerge that the profession needs to create ways to make sure that new teachers have support and do not feel isolated within their classrooms to sink or swim on their own.

Many new avenues are opening up for teachers to provide leadership within their profession to other teachers, and increasingly there are opportunities to be compensated for taking on such leadership roles—not as principals, but as master teachers who have advanced expertise in a wide range of areas. At the same time, the expectation is greater than ever before that teachers demonstrate their abilities in the classroom so that every student in every community has the benefit of a competent, caring, and qualified teacher (National Commission on Teaching and America's Future, 1996).

**Your turn...** *to review*

1. What are one or two main purposes of having standards for the preparation of teachers?
2. How is meeting standards for teaching different from taking traditional university courses?

For many of you the decision to become a teacher is something you have thought about for a long time, whether teaching will be your first or your second career. Others of you may be considering the idea for the first time. In either case, it is critical at this point to match your initial ideas about what it means to teach with the new experiences and knowledge you will gain about the profession. Even if you have always wanted to be a teacher, now is the time to think carefully about whether you are ready to make the commitment.

Teaching is not a profession for the faint of heart. Your commitment to your students and to their learning must be unequivocal. If you find that you are not enjoying the students as much as you thought you would, now is the time to consider how this will translate into spending every day in a classroom where the students are the focus of your attention and the source of your professional satisfaction. You may learn that you cannot handle the unique and complex demands of classroom life as readily as you thought you would when you first considered teaching as a career. Some of you may find yourselves unable to juggle the many tasks teachers carry out. If you cannot cope with these demands, you have an important decision to make—not only for yourself but for the students you may be teaching. If your commitment is strong, however, then you are ready to find that balance between the excitement of moving toward your professional goal and the challenges of getting there.

**Your turn...** *to reflect*

What are three things you are most excited about or motivated about when you think about teaching? What are your three greatest concerns right now about learning to teach? Why do you think these things hold such importance for you?

## Making a Choice about the Kind of Teacher You Want to Be

As you think about the professional journey ahead of you—the journey to learn to teach—a good way to get started is to think about the kind of teacher you want to be. Every September, all over the country, families send their children to school. And every September many families are grateful that their children have been placed in the classrooms of wonderful, dedicated, caring, competent, and qualified teachers. Other families, unfortunately, are anxious or disappointed or worried because their children have been placed in the classrooms of mediocre or inferior teachers. These families realize that it will be a rough year ahead for their children.

As you envision yourself learning to teach over the next year or two, keep in mind the goal you are trying to achieve in becoming a teacher. Your future work as a teacher matters a great deal—to your students, to their families, to the school and the district in which you will teach, and to the profession itself. It is the expectations you set for yourself as a professional and the quality of the work you do as a teacher that will determine how parents and family members feel about their children being in your classroom. When you stand at the classroom door to greet your first class of students, do so with the certainty that you have made the right choice—for you and for your students.

# LEARNING FROM MULTIPLE SOURCES OF KNOWLEDGE THROUGHOUT YOUR CAREER

Throughout their careers teachers are exposed to many different ideas and sources of information about how to teach. In addition to learning from their students each day, teachers also learn about teaching from their personal background and experience, from their professional preparation, from their teaching experience, from ideas others have about teaching, from scholarly work on teaching, and from programs of professional development for practicing teachers, to name a few. These various sources of knowledge about teaching can pose a dilemma for teachers, especially if they lack a good strategy for figuring out why some kinds of knowledge may be more useful than others. As you begin to learn about teaching, you too will face a great deal of "information input." How will you make sense of all this knowledge and information? Which ideas should you keep as part of your teaching practice, which might need rethinking, and which should you discard—and why? What strategies will you use to make sure all of these competing sources of knowledge work for you in effective ways?

In this section of the book, you will be asked to think about the challenge of all of these competing sources of knowledge about teaching and how they affect learning to teach. In Chapter 2, you will explore the influence of the information, knowledge, and beliefs you already have about teaching even before you begin your formal professional preparation. You will reflect on what you already know about teaching and what you have yet to learn. In Chapter 3, you will become familiar with how teachers are prepared today, what the profession of teaching values as important knowledge and skills for every teacher, and how new teachers are assessed to see if they have learned what they need to learn to begin taking on the responsibilities of their profession. In Chapter 4, you will be introduced to ideas from the history and philosophy of education that also provide a source of knowledge for teaching. At the end of this section, you should begin to understand how teaching has evolved, the complexities of learning to teach across the career—and the rewards that come with learning to do it well.

THROUGHOUT YOUR CAREER

## *Guiding Questions*

- How does your prior experience with teaching influence how you think about teaching?

- What five kinds of experience contribute to your current views of teaching?

- How do the twelve years of experience we all have as students make learning to teach a special kind of professional learning?

- How does the media help or hinder your entering views of teaching?

- What was one of Catharine Beecher's most important contributions to the profession of teaching?

- How can observing in classrooms help you learn to teach?

- How can interviewing veteran teachers help you learn to teach?

# Putting What You Already Know about Teaching into Perspective

K ayla Jones-Martin has just been accepted into the teacher education program at the state university she attends. She has always wanted to be a sixth grade teacher, and she is thrilled that next year, as a junior, she can really begin her professional journey. A good family friend, Martha Frazier, has been an elementary school principal for 10 years, so Kayla called her to share the news.

"Martha, I made it into the program. It's really going to happen—I'm going to be a teacher! I've been planning for this for so long—I can't wait."

Martha replied, "Kayla, that's great news. I'm so happy for you. And my school is always open to you."

"I'll probably do that—I'm sure I'll need to be visiting schools for my classes. Thanks."

"Kayla, I know how excited you are and that you have a lot of terrific ideas about teaching. But remember, you haven't actually been a teacher yet. I think you'll find that even though you have a lot of great ideas already, you'll need to learn more to become a really good teacher. Things are likely to be a little more complicated than they might seem right now. So hold onto those good ideas, but remember to keep an open mind about what it means to be a teacher. I'm still learning things all the time myself."

"I never thought about it that way. And I know that's good advice. But I still can't wait to have my own classroom!"

*Teachers should ... be grounded in their own life stories but not be prisoners of their own experiences.*

Kathy Carter and Walter Doyle, 1996, p. 136

**Y**ou have decided to become a teacher. Now, as you consider entering a professional preparation program, you expect to learn all that you need so you can be effective in the classroom. But like Kayla, you are not entering this early phase of your career with a blank slate. You are already familiar with schools, and you already have many ideas about teaching. This *prior knowledge* about teaching comes from a variety of experiences you have had with schools. And although you may not be aware of it, these experiences have already influenced how you think about teaching—sometimes in profound ways.

Susan Florio-Ruane, who studies classrooms and teaching, observed that "to become a professional teacher requires reexamination and transformation of what is already known about schooling" (1989, p. 164). In this chapter, we will explore five different kinds of experiences you may have had and how these experiences may influence what you already know—and what you think you know—about teaching. Then we will suggest some strategies for using this knowledge wisely in your preparation to teach. Finally, we will introduce some critical tools that will help you develop new sources of knowledge for your teaching—namely, observing in classrooms and interviewing teachers—and help you get the most out of observations and interviews you might conduct as you are learning to teach.

## Five Kinds of Experience That Create Prior Knowledge about Teaching

At least five kinds of experiences can influence how you think about teaching:

- Your own experience as a student in schools
- Your autobiography
- Your beliefs
- Your experience working in schools
- Views of teaching you have encountered in the media

While you're probably anxious to get out there and teach now that you've made the decision to do so, it's a good idea to take some time to reflect on the **prior knowledge** you bring to your professional training as a result of your life experiences. Such reflection will make both your past and upcoming experiences much more valuable as you prepare in earnest to become a teacher.

### Knowledge about Teaching from Your Own Experience of Schooling

To most of us, what goes on in nearly every profession other than teaching is something of a mystery. But those who want to teach already have an unusual amount of experience with teachers. By the time we enter professional preparation for teaching, nearly all of us have spent at least 12 years in schools watching teachers teach. Dan Lortie, a sociologist who has studied the work of teachers, coined the term **apprenticeship of observation** to describe the knowledge we attain about teaching during the years we watch our own teachers from kindergarten to high school graduation. He believed that in many ways those school years were like "serving an apprenticeship in teaching" (1975, p. 61). But unlike a traditional apprenticeship, which usually pairs one novice with one master craftsperson for several years, as students we watch many different teachers teach. Some are wonderful models, but

**Critical term**

**Prior knowledge.** Knowledge about teaching that you already have before you enter your formal preparation, which affects how you think about teaching and what you learn about teaching as a profession.

**Critical term**

**Apprenticeship of observation.** The knowledge you have about teaching from the 12 years you spent in classrooms as a student—a term coined in 1975 by the sociologist Dan Lortie.

unfortunately others are not. Yet all of them, good and bad alike, influence the way we think about teaching. For some of us, the image of a favorite teacher is the primary motivation for wanting to become a teacher ourselves. Perhaps this is the way you always saw yourself—just like Mrs. Evans, for example, your high school social studies teacher. In contrast, for others of us, being as different as possible from a least favorite teacher is the primary motivation for teaching, and our concern is that no student go through what we went through in that teacher's classroom.

Our experiences in school also leave us with ideas about classroom procedures and routines. We have notions about what teachers look like when they stand in front of a classroom, how different subjects are taught, what teachers do while students are in their seats, how teachers develop relationships with their students, and perhaps even what the role of a teacher's aide might be. Often we pick up these images of teaching almost unconsciously and try to imitate them once we are in the classroom as teachers ourselves. These images may lead us to try out some good, effective teaching practices—but they may also lead us to try out some ineffective ones.

Because we are all so familiar with schools, we all have opinions about teaching, and we often believe that we know much of what there is to know about the work of being a teacher. Whether our ideas have credibility in the profession of teaching, we may believe that we have the answers to education. Were we to prepare for almost any other profession, we would not presume to know how to do the work. But this is not so with teaching.

As a result of the 12 years they have spent in schools watching teachers teach, students can get a false sense of confidence about what goes into good teaching. (PhotoDisc, Inc./Getty Images)

## Your turn... *to review*

1. What does the term "apprenticeship of observation" mean?
2. How does an apprenticeship of observation distinguish learning to teach from learning other professions?

The real danger from this long apprenticeship and the familiarity it provides is that we may have developed inaccurate or incomplete ideas about what it means to teach. We may believe, for example, that it is a relatively easy job. After all, how hard can it be to stand up in front of a classroom and talk to a bunch of students? Even if we had wonderful teachers as role models, we may not realize that knowledge about good teaching changes and develops over time (for example, consider the emerging role of technology in teaching). These developments constantly pose new challenges for teachers—challenges that may have been unimaginable in their own past educational experiences. In other words, we may easily confuse the side of teaching we see as students with what are clearly more complex knowledge, skills, and responsibilities that exist behind the scenes. Watching teaching and knowing what it means to teach "from the other side of the desk," as Lortie put it (1975, p. 61), are two entirely different things. Or, as Susan Florio-Ruane (1989) states, the challenge is that "the beginning teacher must try to assume a new—but familiar—role in a familiar setting" (1989, p. 167).

As students in classrooms, for example, we do not always think about the long hours teachers may put in during the evenings and on weekends preparing lessons. We probably never even see a teacher's lesson plans. We may not realize that each week for a whole academic year a certain teacher may have attended a class to learn more effective ways of teaching writing. We may not appreciate the years it may have taken for a teacher to perfect a set of routines, for example, for teaching a complex interdisciplinary unit on the history of the community in which the school is located. We may not understand that working with a small group of students in one part of the classroom, and still knowing and effectively managing what is going on in another, is an explicit skill that teachers need to learn. We may never stop to think about the hours teachers may spend after the bell rings keeping in touch with their students' families. Now is the time to view teaching from the other side of the desk.

All students bring prior knowledge to their learning—whether they are education students like yourselves or students in preschool–grade 12 (PK–12) classrooms. And all teachers are more effective once they understand the prior knowledge and ideas that students possess so that they can better connect new learning to those ideas. As you begin your formal study of teaching, one way you and your instructors can begin to understand the images and ideas that you already associate with teaching from your own prior experience is for you to create a **concept map**.

A concept map is a drawing that represents the relationships among several ideas you associate with a specific central concept, or big idea (Novak & Gowin, 1984). Figure 2-1 illustrates how a concept map works. If you were to use the

## Critical term

**Concept map.** A visual tool teachers can use to show an individual's ideas about a particular concept and how they relate to one another; concept maps can be used as a starting point for teaching new knowledge about that concept.

---

**Figure 2-1    A Visual Tool**

A concept map is a drawing that allows you to display your view of the relationships between an important, central concept, for example, *teaching*, and other subconcepts that you believe are related to teaching. Such maps are one way to show your prior understanding of a concept you are studying.

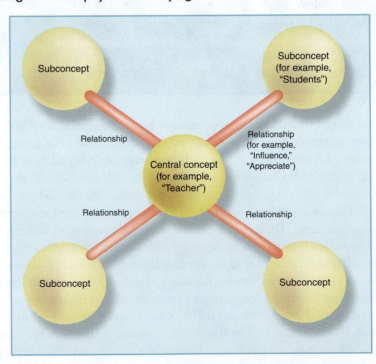

**Your turn...** *to reflect*

Create a concept map depicting your images of "teacher." Include at least six subconcepts that are connected to the concept "teacher" and the relationship between them. How does your concept map compare to those of your peers? What does your map tell you about your existing conceptions of teaching?

term *teacher* as the central concept, you would place that in the center of your map. From there you would include several subconcepts or related ideas (for example, *students*) on your map. You would then connect the terms *teachers* and *students* with a verb that shows how you are thinking about the relationship between teachers and students. You might use words such as *appreciate* or *influence*. As a result, one part of your concept map might show that in your image of teaching, teachers influence students, or students influence teachers, or they influence each other.

## Autobiographical Knowledge about Teaching

In addition to the knowledge you have accumulated as a result of your own schooling, you also know about teaching from your own personal life experiences. Your autobiography directly affects your decision to teach and the way you think about teaching. Two major influences from your autobiography are *family* and *personal commitments*.

**Family.** Prospective teachers come from many different kinds of families. Some may come from a family of teachers and, if so, may bring a different kind of understanding of the work of teachers than does someone whose only exposure to teaching has been as a student. For example, you may have seen a parent grading papers each night, or planning lessons, or talking to students' parents. Your family may be very supportive of your choice to follow in the footsteps of your mother or father and may also see itself as "a family of teachers," not only with a mother or father who teaches, but aunts, uncles, siblings, and even grandparents. It may be called "the family business." You may have spent a lot of time in the classroom of a relative, watching him or her teach or helping out. "Teacher talk" may have been common at your dinner table.

Or you may come from a family that is puzzled by your decision to become a teacher. They may think that you are considering a field that is beneath you. Or they may believe that teaching is an easy job, one that does not require a deep understanding of more than the content of the lesson you are teaching the next day. You may hear comments like "Anyone can teach." Family friends may reinforce this attitude. Or you may hear the unfortunate and absolutely inaccurate cliché, "Those who can, do. Those who cannot, teach." You may feel defensive about your choice to teach, even though you are aware that teaching is a demanding profession.

Your family may think teaching is a good career choice simply because they believe it is less stressful than other "real" jobs. They may see it as a good career because you will be finished with your work in the midafternoon each day and will have summers off or as being more compatible with family life than other career options. This, too, is an inaccurate picture of what teaching entails. If this is your motivation, it is important to understand that this is not a realistic view of teaching.

Experiences with children in nonschool settings may help you make your decision about a career in teaching, but the demands of teaching can differ in important ways from the demands of other jobs you may have held with children. (Digital Vision)

A significant life event within your family may also influence how you think about teaching. For example, you may have a sibling who has a disability. This provides you with a different perspective on the teacher's role than someone without this family experience and may lead you to a career in special education.

You may be the parent, aunt, or uncle of a school-aged child. Their experiences with their own teachers form a sort of secondhand apprenticeship of observation for you because they introduce you to another set of teachers. If you have grown children, you may recall significant events from their education that have influenced your thinking about teaching.

Finally, you may be a career switcher, perhaps with a family that is ready to support you through the next year or two of your preparation. Your goal may be to do something more meaningful in your life; you may always have wanted to become a teacher but somehow took a different path earlier in your life and now have the opportunity to make a change.

**Personal Commitments.** Personal commitments can also affect how you think about teaching and what you know about it. These commitments may lead you to form images of teaching that will also influence your preparation.

Some people are committed to teaching as a way of giving back to the community. If, for example, you have struggled to be able to attend college and are the first in your family to become a teacher, your primary commitment may be to teaching as a way of helping children in the next generation improve their life opportunities. This commitment may come about because it was challenging for you to realize your own opportunities. If you are a member of a racial, ethnic, or cultural group that is underrepresented in today's teaching force, your commitment may also be tied to the desire to become a role model for the next generation of students whose race, ethnicity, or language you share.

Many people come to teaching following a lifelong interest in becoming a teacher. You may have been the one in your neighborhood to bring together all the younger children and "play school" (and your school was probably set up a lot like the classrooms you yourself were attending). You may have been the neighborhood babysitter, and your love of children may be at the root of your desire to teach. You may have an image of yourself as a teacher, standing up in front of a classroom, or reading to students, or teaching and holding a coaching position after school.

But despite this commitment you have probably never had full responsibility for a class of 25 students all day long, five days a week. The actual responsibilities of a teacher are likely to differ greatly from your early views of them. However, the difference between your initial images of teaching and the realities of the work does not diminish the importance of your initial desire to become a part of the profession. It just means that you will need to make the transition from your love of children as a basis for teaching to your love of teaching a class of children or

# REWARDS AND CHALLENGES

Adriana Balistreri
*Milwaukee, Wisconsin*

## Getting Started

The best reward for a teacher is having students tell you that you helped them out in their learning and you made a difference in their lives. I'm a new teacher. Recently, one of my students said, "You make me love math. Math is now so easy to me. It used to be hard and I hated it." This is the best reward because this is why we teach in the frst place. As a new teacher I have the opportunity to build relationships with people who share the same passion for students and their learning as I do and to work together as a team to help all of our students be successful.

As a new teacher, the biggest challenge I face is not knowing how things work within the school, for example, the rotation schedules for art, music, computers, gym, etc. I had to learn to make a schedule for myself and plan the days carefully. Also, it can be very overwhelming learning the procedures and school rules—they are different in every school, and even though I had experience in several schools during my teacher education program, in my new school I have been continuing to learn as I have been going along. Getting to know other teachers and where you can go to find them throughout the day is another challenge. I honestly still cannot put all of the names with the faces. One last challenge of being a new teacher is learning how to stay organized as far as keeping lessons and different subject areas together. I have started to keep binders for each subject, and I am keeping my lesson plans, worksheets, and rubrics in each binder so I can find my resources easily and efficiently. ●

youth every day—and doing all the things that being a classroom teacher entails in addition to the enjoyment you derive from being with young people.

During your own apprenticeship of observation, you learned not only what teachers do; you also had specific experiences as a student that may have provided the motivation for you to teach. Both can be very strong motivators for teaching and provide strong images of what you hope to accomplish as a teacher. You may be committed to being the kind of teacher your favorite teacher was and returning to your hometown to teach, even in one of your own former schools. You may have idyllic views of what that teacher did to make your year with him or her so memorable.

Or you may be committed to moving to an urban community that is in need of teachers. This commitment may stem from your interest in fostering equity and social justice. You may view teaching as a direct way of empowering children with the skills they will need to make improvements in their own communities and within their own cultural or ethnic groups. Your family may have misconceptions about what it means to teach in urban schools. If they do not understand your commitment, they may try to dissuade you from this decision. Especially if you did not grow up in a large city, your friends may also question your decision. This questioning might strengthen your commitment, or it may cause you to rethink it.

Whatever your personal autobiography may be, it has undoubtedly influenced your decision to consider a career in teaching. The **National Education Association**, the largest teachers' organization in the United States, regularly publishes a report on the status of American teachers, including an analysis of why teachers go into teaching. Figure 2-2 illustrates the various reasons today's teachers have for choosing teaching. The case that follows shows how one student from a family of teachers dealt with her own doubts about becoming a teacher and finally resolved them.

### Critical term

**National Education Association.** The largest teachers' organization in the United States, with approximately 3.2 million members.

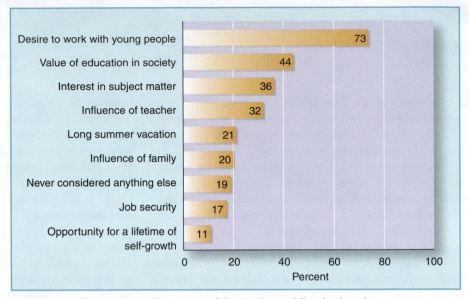

**Figure 2-2    Why Teach?**

**Teachers choose to enter the profession for many reasons, but their chief motivation is the desire to work with children and youth.**

Source: National Education Association, *Status of the American public school teacher 2000-2001:* Highlights, Figure 5. Why Teachers Originally Decided to Enter the Profession, 2001 (page 3). Retrieved from http://www.nea.org/edstats/images/statushighlights.pdf and reprinted with permission of the National Education Association © 2003. All rights reserved.

## A Case In Point
### Natalie's Story

I was a major in elementary education and Spanish. I always wanted to teach, and there are a lot of teachers in my family. But because of that I thought that maybe I should be doing something else. I wasn't so sure I wanted to fall into that family pattern. But when I was younger I was always easy with kids, I had an easy way, I did all the things that someone who wanted to teach might do. I babysat, taught Sunday school. I attended a state school, and I went to college as an education major.

But after one semester I found myself asking: Do I really want to do this? I needed to make peace with the fact that this was what *I* wanted to do—not because of my family and their expectations. So I shifted my major several times. I thought about psychology and natural resources. I always continued on with my Spanish. Then one day when I still hadn't declared a major, my stepmother sat me down and said, "You've always been interested in teaching. What's wrong with having that be your major? You can use your Spanish, you can be creative. And you can have summers off." [At this point Natalie laughs because for the past several summers she has always worked for her school district.] Also, I had a lot of work experience before I decided to go into teaching. I worked in a family restaurant, doing all of the jobs there. I worked in an electronics factory putting together transformer boards. I knew these were not things I wanted to do for the long haul. But in my teacher education program the mindset that this was actually a career—not just a job—was not communicated clearly. I was looking for a career.

Once I got into the classroom during my program, and I had that experience, I was hooked. "So this is what it can be," I said. My first field experience was in a fifth grade with a wonderful cooperating teacher. He gave me just enough guidance to get me going. I found a tremendous amount of joy in what I did.

What it is about teaching that has always drawn me is that you can't give someone knowledge, but you can help them discover it. You can take an idea, move it around, and have it fit for the kids. You have to shape it. There is a sense of comfort in that it is a profession where you help kids move forward.

It is true that you need to find your passion in teaching, and you have to hold onto that passion and let that carry you through the rougher times, the times that challenge you in the classroom—because they happen too. Some days it's that passion for teaching—whether it's for mathematics, for building a family in the classroom, for helping a new teacher along—that you bring to your work and that lets you recommit yourself to teaching and remember why you are doing this important work.

Those who are drawn to a career in teaching do so for a wide variety of reasons, but the most important reason cited is the wish to work with young people.
(Media Bakery)

Your autobiography and personal commitments constitute an important set of experiences that have influenced not only your decision to teach but also how you think about the work of teaching. These experiences may be sources of support for you or, as in Natalie's case, they may impose overt or subtle pressures on you as you move into your professional program. And like the powerful images you may have of teaching from your own experience, family and personal commitments may need to be put into perspective as you learn more about what it means to teach.

## Knowledge about Teaching from Working in Schools

You gain a different kind of knowledge from actually having worked in schools before you become a teacher. Some of you may have volunteered in schools as a tutor. Others may have worked in after-school recreation programs attached to schools. And yet others of you may have worked, for example, as paraprofessionals, assisting a teacher in the classroom. Through these experiences, you not only bring your own images of teaching; you also bring knowledge from inside the classroom gained as an adult. Paraprofessionals or other school employees who are not teachers may have a wide range of responsibilities and experiences in schools, all of which contribute to beliefs about and images of teaching.

Let's consider the case of paraprofessionals, since they probably have the most sustained classroom experience among nonteaching personnel in schools. Although most paraprofessionals work in classrooms under the direct supervision of a certified teacher, some are independently in charge of special parts of a school, such as the school library or the computer lab. In some schools every teacher may be assigned a paraprofessional for some or all of the school day. This means that paraprofessionals who have direct classroom assignments may have worked in the classrooms of excellent teacher role models or, conversely, in the classrooms of teachers who were not good role models.

As a paraprofessional, your experience will differ not only depending on the kind of situation to which you have been assigned, but also on the roles you have been asked to play. Within the classroom, for example, your major task may have been to provide support to your teacher by preparing materials, carrying out routines (e.g., attendance, lunch count, accompanying students to various special classrooms in elementary schools), or assisting students with word processing and other computer-related skills. You may also have been called on regularly to manage the classroom when the teacher was called to meetings. As a paraprofessional in special education, you may have provided specific, individually tailored support to students with special health or physical needs under the direction of a special education teacher.

Alternatively, you may have played more of an instructional role. For example, if your class was divided into small groups for learning in certain subject areas, you may have had full responsibility for one of those groups. While the teacher provided information and direction to the whole group, you may have assisted by walking around the room and providing individual explanations, or helping to keep students engaged in their work. You have probably assisted with required standardized testing.

You may have been in a situation where the teacher with whom you worked provided you with extensive explanations and instructions for why he or she made certain decisions about teaching and even asked you to watch while he or she taught—specifically so you could learn at a higher level. Then, after you had a chance to teach your own group in a similar way, you may have had the opportunity to sit down together and review what occurred during your own experience.

Paraprofessionals who decide to become teachers can draw on a much greater base of practical classroom experience than is available to other teacher education students. They may know more about how schools are run, they are more likely to be familiar with curriculum materials, they may have helped complete report cards, or they may have talked extensively with parents about student behavior.

Yet, one of the biggest challenges facing paraprofessionals is to recognize both the benefits and the limitations of their knowledge. Their experience represents a kind of apprenticeship through which they work in classrooms every day and may actually carry out instructional responsibilities. Therefore, they have been more than observers. Even so, typically they do not carry out the full range of a teacher's responsibilities. They do not perform the same level of planning that teachers do, nor do they typically have extensive knowledge about how children develop, for example, as readers, writers, mathematicians, or scientists. Although they may be familiar with some teaching methods, they may not be able to determine, based on professional knowledge, whether other methods might be more effective. And those paraprofessionals who work with teachers who are not good professional role models may not learn good teaching practices. In contrast, those lucky enough to work with a gifted teacher may acquire a tremendous amount of knowledge about good teaching.

So those who work in schools, as paraprofessionals, as substitute teachers, or even as volunteers, probably have more knowledge about teaching and a definite perspective on what the work entails. All the same, they will have to think critically about their prior experience and how their acquired classroom habits will influence them as they move into a full teaching position.

## A Case In Point
### From Paraprofessional to Teacher

Kathy Edwards is an African American woman who worked as a paraprofessional in an urban middle school for five years before deciding to complete her undergraduate education and become a teacher. Her story provides an important perspective both on her transition and on the role of paraprofessionals in the classroom.

When I decided to become a paraprofessional I didn't look at the specific duties required for this position. I was just excited to work with a diverse group of students and share my passion for mathematics. Being a paraprofessional was a job that involved instructional responsibilities without complete control over—and responsibility for—the classroom. But it also meant serving as a critical support to helping students achieve.

As a paraprofessional, I learned a lot about what type of commitment is needed for being a teacher. I also developed a deep understanding of learning and academic achievement. The students I worked with taught me a lot about how to help them succeed. For them, the most important thing was knowing that the adults in the classroom understood them as individuals. So as I observed the successes and failures of the different teachers I worked with, I saw how important it was to get to know your students—and what happens when teachers aren't good at doing that. Of course, teaching sometimes presents barriers that make it hard for teachers to get to know the students they work with. As a paraprofessional, I made sure that I had the time to speak to my students on a personal level so that they could trust me not just as an educator concerned about their academic success, but also as someone who cared about them as people.

As a paraprofessional, it was my duty to make sure all the students were on the right task, make sure behavior problems were redirected, make sure all the teachers' grades were completed, and pinch-hit as a substitute teacher when needed. Because of the rapport that I built with the students, I was able to work successfully with many students who were often labeled as "difficult." Despite my hard work, the success of these students was not often attributed to the paraprofessional. Since it was usually the teacher who was solely recognized for the success of the classroom, I decided that when I became a teacher, I would give recognition where it was due and make sure that those who served in a support staff capacity got the respect and recognition they deserved. That was certainly one reason for making the transition. But the most important reason to become a teacher was the students.

As I made up my mind to become a teacher, I had to face two big obstacles. First, I struggled to pass the required examination for admission to the teacher education program. I wasn't confident in my academic skills and it showed. Math— my academic love—was not a problem. I found a lot of support at my university and made myself take advantage of it to make sure my reading and language skills

Paraprofessionals who have worked in classrooms before becoming teachers bring valuable experience to their new position, but often discover that being the teacher of record is more challenging than it first appears. (Will Hart/PhotoEdit)

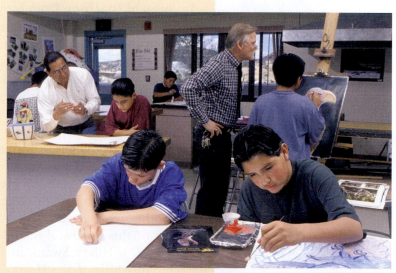

were up to par. The next obstacle was figuring out how I was going to pay the bills. As a paraprofessional, my financial situation was very limited. At times, especially during the summer, my bills tended to pile up. I was lucky to find a program that provided scholarships for paraprofessionals like me who wanted to climb the career ladder and become teachers. Without the stress of not knowing if my bills were going to be paid each month, I was able to focus more on school and the students I worked with every day.

On the whole, being a paraprofessional helped me excel in my teacher education program. I had a lot of classroom experience coming in, and this gave me an advantage. But I couldn't slack off on my university requirements—I needed what my courses offered to add to what I knew from the classroom—and to prepare me to take on all of the responsibilities of a teacher. It was time consuming, and I had to learn to balance my work, my schooling, and my family. But now that it's over, and I'm about to take on my own middle school mathematics classroom in the fall, I would have to say that my journey to becoming a teacher has been a positive one. I'm anxious to get started on my own, I'm ready, and I can't wait to have my own classroom and watch my students grow.

## Knowledge about Teaching from Images in the Media

In recent years, news about education has featured prominently in the media. Portrayals of schools and teachers have been notable in movies, television, and in print. But how realistic are these portrayals? How do they help or hinder your own development as a prospective teacher?

**Your turn... *to reflect***

What images do you have about teachers and teaching from movies or television? In a small group, identify specific movies or shows and describe the images you have from watching them. Which aspects of the teachers' roles, responsibilities, and relationships seem realistic, and which seem sensationalized? Why?

**Images of Teaching from Movies and Television.** Teachers and teaching are a relatively common theme in the movies. In her book *The Hollywood Curriculum*, Mary Dalton (2007) lists 116 movies about teachers that were released between 1936 and 2002. These films appear in Figure 2-3. In his book *Hollywood Goes Gives to High School*, Robert Bulman (2005) lists over 180 films about high schools, divided into suburban, urban, private school, and foreign films produced between 1931 and 2004.

In one category of teacher films, we see the heroic, mythical teacher who bucks the odds in challenging situations and emerges with the students victorious. Often, but not always, these heroic teachers are working in urban schools with students who are members of lower socioeconomic classes and are often members of minority groups. These teachers seem to perform brilliantly in the face of negative stereotypes about the potential of their students. Examples of this portrayal include the teacher Jaime Escalante in *Stand and Deliver* (1987), Hilary Swank in *Freedom Writers* (2007) and Meryl Streep's character in *Music of the Heart* (1999). In the case of Jaime Escalante, the Latino students in his calculus class show their abilities on the Advanced

## Figure 2-3 Hollywood's Images of Teaching, 1936–2002

**Movies provide an incomplete or partial view of what teachers really do.**

*All Over the Guy.* Dir. Julie Davis. 2001.

*American History X.* Dir. Tony Kaye. 1998.

*Animal House.* Dir. John Landis. 1978.

*Anna and the King.* Dir. Andy Tennant. 1999.

*Anna and the King of Siam.* Dir. John Cromwell. 1946.

*Arlington Road.* Dir. Mark Pellington. 1999.

*Back to School.* Dir. Alan Metter. 1986.

*A Beautiful Mind.* Dir. Ron Howard. 2001.

*Billy Elliot.* Dir. Stephen Daldry. 2000.

*Billy Madison.* Dir. Tamra Davis. 1995.

*Blackboard Jungle.* Dir. Richard Brooks. 1955.

*The Blue Angel.* Dir. Josef von Sternberg. 1930.

*Boyz N the Hood.* Dir. John Singleton. 1991.

*The Breakfast Club.* Dir. John Hughes. 1985.

*Bright Road.* Dir. Gerald Mayer. 1953.

*Carrie.* Dir. Brian De Palma. 1976.

*Cheaters.* Dir. John Stockwell. 2001.

*Children of a Lesser God.* Dir. Randa Haines. 1986.

*The Children's Hour.* Dir. William Wyler. 1962.

*A Christmas Story.* Dir. Bob Clark. 1983.

*Class of 1984.* Dir. Mark L. Lester. 1982.

*Class of 1999: The Substitute.* Dir. Mark L. Lester. 1990.

*Class of 1999 II.* Dir. Spiro Ratazos. 1993.

*Class of Nuke 'Em High.* Dirs. Richard W. Haines and Samuel Weil. 1986.

*Clueless.* Dir. Amy Heckerling. 1995.

*Conrack.* Dir. Martin Pitt. 1974.

*Cooley High.* Dir. Michael Schultz. 1975.

*The Corn Is Green.* Dir. Irving Rapper. 1945.

*Dangerous Minds.* Dir. John N. Smith. 1995.

*Dazed and Confused.* Dir. Richard Linklater. 1993.

*Dead Poets Society.* Dir. Peter Weir. 1989.

*Disturbing Behavior.* Dir. David Nutter. 1998.

*Educating Rita.* Dir. Lewis Gilbert. 1983.

*Election.* Dir. Alexander Payne. 1999.

*The Emperor's Club.* Dir. Michael Hoffman. 2002.

*The Faculty.* Dir. Robert Rodriquez. 1998.

*Fame.* Dir. Alan Parker. 1980.

*Fast Times at Ridgemont High.* Dir. Amy Heckerling. 1982.

*Ferris Bueller's Day Off.* Dir. John Hughes. 1986.

*Finding Forrester.* Dir. Gus Van Sant. 2000.

*Forrest Gump.* Dir. Robert Zemeckis. 1994.

*Goodbye, Mr. Chips.* Dir. Sam Wood. 1939.

*Good Morning, Miss Dove.* Dir. Henry Koster. 1955.

*Good Will Hunting.* Dir. Gus Van Sant. 1998.

*Grease.* Dir. Randal Kleiser. 1978.

*Grease 2.* Dir. Patricia Birch. 1982.

*Harry Potter and the Sorcerer's Stone.* Dir. Chris Columbus. 2001.

*Harry Potter and the Chamber of Secrets.* Dir. Chris Columbus. 2002.

*Heathers.* Dir. Michael Lehmann. 1988.

*High School High.* Dir. Hart Bochner. 1996.

*Higher Learning.* Dir. John Singleton. 1995.

*Hoosiers.* Dir. David Anspaugh. 1986.

*House Party.* Dir. Reginald Hudlin. 1990.

*In & Out.* Dir. Frank Oz. 1997.

*Kindergarten Cop.* Dir. Ivan Reitman. 1990.

*The King and I.* Dir. Walter Lang. 1956.

*Lean on Me.* Dir. John G. Avildsen. 1989.

*Legally Blonde.* Dir. Robert Luketic. 2001.

*Little Man Tate.* Dir. Jodie Foster. 1991.

*Looking for Mr. Goodbar.* Dir. Richard Brooks. 1977.

*Malcolm X.* Dir. Spike Lee. 1992.

*The Man Without a Face.* Dir. Mel Gibson. 1993.

*Matilda.* Dir. Danny De Vito. 1996.

*Meet the Parents.* Dir. Jay Roach. 2000.

*Menace II Society.* Dirs. Albert Hughes and Allan Hughes. 1993

*The Miracle Worker.* Dir. Arthur Penn. 1962.

*Mr. Holland's Opus.* Dir. Stephen Herek. 1995.

*Music of the Heart.* Dir. Wes Craven. 1999.

*My Girl.* Dir. Howard Ziff. 1972.

*Never Been Kissed.* Dir. Raja Rosnell. 1999.

*The Nutty Professor.* Dir. Jerry Lewis. 1963.

*The Nutty Professor.* Dir. Tom Shadyac. 1996.

*The Object of My Affection.* Dir. Nicholas Hynter. 1998.

*187.* Dir. Kevin Reynolds. 1997.

*Only the Strong.* Dir. Sheldon Lettich. 1993.

*The Opposite of Sex.* Dir. Don Roos. 1998.

*Orange County.* Dir. Jake Kasdan. 2002.

*Our Miss Brooks.* Dir. Al Lewis. 1956.

*The Paper Chase.* Dir. James Bridges. 1973.

*Pay It Forward.* Dir. Mimi Leder. 2000.

*PCU.* Dir. Hart Bochner. 1994.

*Porky's.* Dir. Bob Clark. 1981.

*The Principal.* Dir. Christopher Cain. 1987.

*Pump up the Volume.* Dir. Allan Moyle. 1990.

*The Prime of Miss Jean Brodie.* Dir. Ronald Neame. 1969.

*Rachel, Rachel.* Dir. Paul Newman. 1968.

*Raiders of the Lost Ark.* Dir. Steven Spielberg. 1981.

*Real Genius.* Dir. Martha Coolidge. 1985.

*Remember the Titans.* Dir. Boaz Yakin. 2000.

*Renaissance Man.* Dir. Penny Marshall. 1994.

*Rock 'n' Roll High School.* Dir. Allan Arkush. 1979.

*The Rookie.* Dir. John Lee Hancock. 2002.

*Rudy.* Dir. David Anspaugh. 1993.

*Ryan's Daughter.* Dir. David Lean. 1970.

*Sarafina!* Dir. Darrell James Roodt. 1992.

*Scary Movie.* Dir. Keenan Ivory Wayans. 2000.

*School Ties.* Dir. Robert Mandel. 1992.

*Searching for Bobby Fischer.* Dir. Steven Zaillian. 1993.

*Sleepers.* Dir. Barry Levinson. 1996.

*Songcatcher.* Dir. Maggie Greenwald. 2000.

*Stand and Deliver.* Dir. Ramon Menendez. 1987.

*Starship Troopers.* Dir. Paul Verhoeven. 1997.

*The Substitute.* Dir. Robert Mandel. 1996.

*Summer School.* Dir. Carl Reiner. 1987.

*The Teacher.* Dir. Hikmet Avedis. 1974.

*Teacher's Pet.* Dir. George Seaton. 1958.

*Teachers.* Dir. Arthur Hiller. 1984.

*Teaching Mrs. Tingle.* Dir. Kevin Williamson. 1999.

*These Three.* Dir. William Wyler. 1936.

*To Sir, with Love.* Dir. James Clavell. 1967.

*Top Gun.* Dir. Tony Scott. 1986.

*Up the Down Staircase.* Dir. Robert Mulligan. 1967.

*Varsity Blues.* Dir. Brian Robbins. 1999.

*Wit.* Dir. Mike Nichols. 2001.

*With Honors.* Dir. Alek Keshishian. 1994.

*X-Men.* Dir. Bryan Singer. 2000.

**Source:** Dalton, M. M. (2007). *The Hollywood curriculum: Teachers and teaching in the movies (revised edition).* New York: Peter Lang.

Placement calculus test; in the case of Hilary Swank's character, Erin Gruwell uses writing to help her students process the challenges in their lives; and in the case of Meryl Streep's character, elementary school students in low income urban schools display their talents playing violin. Bulman (2005) notes that these hero teachers are almost always white and middle class.

Dalton (2007) portrays the teachers in these films as "outsiders" who fight both societal viewpoints and often their own school administrators. In contrast to the beliefs of those in the surrounding society, these good teachers hold the highest expectations for their students' accomplishments and work with them, prod them, and do whatever it takes to help them accomplish their goals. These films create images of teachers as highly committed individuals who will let nothing stop them or get in the way of meeting their students' needs, as well as the extraordinary hard work it can take to help students achieve their goals. For prospective teachers, one important point conveyed by these films is that the students in the schools portrayed are bright and can learn challenging subjects well. The students face many obstacles, often put in place by the educational system, but they can reach their goals with the extraordinary help provided by unusually dedicated teachers. To do so, **teacher expectations** must be high, and teachers must do whatever they need to do to make sure students can meet those high expectations.

A second category of teacher in the movies demonstrates hard work, commitment, and compassion, but may not necessarily succeed with students. This teacher is dedicated to his or her students' learning, and often in these films the story focuses on an individual teacher's relationship with one or two special students. In *Dead Poets Society*, for example, the teacher played by Robin Williams works tirelessly to motivate his advantaged prep school students and to make the curriculum relevant to their lives, but ultimately he cannot protect his students from the societal pressures stemming from their privileged lives.

A far less common portrayal—but perhaps the most realistic—is the teacher as the unsung hero who is not readily recognized for the influence he or she has had on students or whose influence grows over time. An example of this portrayal is *Mr. Holland's Opus*, in which the cumulative impact of a music teacher's work is honored collectively only when generations of his students return to celebrate the end of his career. Another example of this category is the classic 1939 British film *Goodbye, Mr. Chips*. This message is not tied to any particular kind of school; it is a universal message about teachers and the potential reach of their work. It is interesting to note that movies about the arts and the power of the arts appear across categories. In addition, the highly acclaimed 2005 documentary, *Mad Hot Ballroom*, extols the virtues of the arts as a means of engaging otherwise disengaged students, as does, of course, the fictional *Sister Act II* (1993).

## Critical term

**Teacher expectations.** The expectations teachers set for what their students are capable of doing and achieving in the classroom. Teachers can treat students for whom they have set higher or lower expectations differently, often presenting lesser challenges for those whom they believe cannot achieve at high levels.

## Historical Note
### Catharine Beecher's Image of Teachers

In the nineteenth century, Catharine Beecher (1800–1878) made a major contribution to changing the image of teachers. Her well-known, influential family included, among others, her father Lyman Beecher, a highly regarded minister, and her sister Harriet Beecher Stowe, the author of *Uncle Tom's Cabin*. At a time when most teachers were men and higher education for women barely existed, Catharine Beecher argued that women should be well educated and become teachers.

Beecher based her arguments for women's education on two main ideas. First, she believed that as the primary educators of children and as the caretakers of the home, women should be well prepared for these crucial tasks—not just in the how-to's of domestic life but in a serious intellectual education as well (Dykeman, 2001). Second, she believed that both working-class and upper-class women were being held back intellectually—working-class women because they were relegated to jobs in factories or as household domestics, and upper-class women because their daily activities, such as shopping, entertaining, and light reading, were considered inconsequential (Sklar, 1973). Teaching presented an option for women that combined education with a socially useful career, which had the potential of elevating women's position in society (Hoffman, 1981). A common focus on teaching as a career could also close the gap between women in different economic classes (Dykeman, 2001; Sklar, 1973). Underlying both of these roles in the home and in schools was the need for women to have access to high-quality, rigorous, and intellectually stimulating education. As a young woman, Beecher founded the Hartford Female Seminary in Hartford, Connecticut, a school devoted to providing a serious education for women.

To accomplish her goals in the 1840s, Beecher began a campaign to raise funds to train teachers for the West—which at that time was today's Midwest. First through the Board of National Popular Education, and then through normal schools for teachers (see Chapter 3) that she helped establish in Ohio, Illinois, Iowa and Wisconsin, women were prepared to teach in the "West." Thousands made the trek under the auspices of Beecher's campaign (Hoffman, 1981). She raised funds for her cause through public speaking tours throughout the Northeast, primarily in churches (Sklar, 1973).

Through her efforts, the number of women teachers in elementary schools tripled between 1840 and 1880 (Hoffman, 1981). While today Beecher is sometimes viewed as being responsible for the feminization of teaching, or for teaching being viewed pejoratively as "women's work," she was actually a staunch advocate of women's rights and improving the image of the profession of teaching.

Teaching has also featured prominently in television shows. Notable among these is the older series, *Welcome Back, Kotter* (1975–1979), which was a comic portrayal of the ups and down of the relationship between a high school teacher and a class of students with an array of behavior and emotional difficulties. Always cutting through the comedy was the theme that Kotter cared about his students. A much more recent show, *Boston Public* (2000–2004), centers on a challenging urban high school whose teachers and administrators struggle to meet the wide-ranging needs of their students. But even though *Boston Public* does a credible job presenting what Tillman and Trier (2007) call the "everyday aspects of schooling," they also note that in just about every episode the viewer will see "more crises in one school day than typically visit a 'real' school during an entire academic year" (p. 125).

Portrayals of teachers in the visual media provide powerful images of what teaching can entail. In nearly every case, however, these images are incomplete and often sensationalize teaching in challenging schools and circumstances rather than portraying the regularities of teaching. As sources of knowledge about teaching, movies and television generally portray the extreme—and not the commonplace— challenges of teaching. In their often stereotypical and exaggerated portrayals of the most challenging high schools, they may, in fact, do more harm than good.

**Print Media.** If you read the newspaper regularly, you will inevitably come across articles about education. Newspaper staffs typically include education reporters who cover the "school beat." In small towns, local newspapers rely on the schools as a steady source of news. In addition to covering school sports events, local papers often include descriptions of special projects, print lists of students who make school honor rolls, feature unusual field trips, and spotlight teachers who are doing something unique in their classes or during the summer months. Special teacher workshops and teacher retirements, in particular stories about beloved teachers who have had long, successful careers, are also regularly reported. Teachers are a fundamental and enduring part of every community, and typically these stories create images of teachers as sources of local pride.

Other kinds of reporting can also send strong messages about the image of teachers in individual communities. In many locales, a school's scores on annual standardized tests are published in the newspapers. The variation in scores across districts is often interpreted as a measure of the quality of the teachers in a district—although no information about specific teachers accompanies such reports. Reporting of scores has intensified under current federal legislation with the **No Child Left Behind Act of 2001**, which requires annual testing for all schools that receive certain kinds of federal funding.

Media images can be powerful influences on a community's beliefs about schools in the area. From the media, individuals may believe that little good teaching takes place in urban or rural schools whose scores are low and that no bad teaching takes place in well-funded suburban schools. If a local paper is not particularly friendly to the public schools, this can create negative and sometimes very inaccurate images about teachers and the quality of the schools. Having read accounts of the schools in local newspapers, you may have biases about the quality of teaching in schools situated in different communities. These beliefs may or may not hold up once you observe the schools for yourself—and may require rethinking once you are there.

The media can also create a set of images about what constitutes best teaching practice by popularizing a particular method of teaching. For example, reporters may be biased toward a certain approach as the "best" way to teach young students to read or to learn mathematics. Their stories may therefore influence the kinds of questions parents ask teachers and principals about the instructional methods used in their child's school. Even though the public may judge the quality of teaching based on partial information from the media, this may have powerful implications for how people ultimately view what makes a good teacher, a good school, and a good school district.

In addition to the news media, stories of teachers are often the subject of literature and popular writing. Biographies and autobiographies of teachers have been the sources for many movies, or biopics, about teaching (e.g., *Conrack, Dangerous Minds, Lean on Me, The Miracle Worker*). Teachers have long published stories of their own careers and the challenges and victories they have experienced. Recent memoirs of teachers have continued in this tradition, including Rafe Esquith's 2004 book *There Are No Shortcuts* and Frank McCourt's 2005 *Teacher Man*. Memoirs such as these often inspire those who are considering teaching; in contrast to movies in which hero teachers might work with a challenging group of students for a relatively short period of time (e.g., *Freedom Writers*), these two memoirs recount the stories of a teacher in Los Angeles (Esquith) and New York City (McCourt) who had long careers in teaching.

Stereotypes about teaching and schools can also be found in children's books. Stories about the "good teacher" Miss Nelson, and her nemesis, the terrible substi-

**Critical term**

**No Child Left Behind Act of 2001.** Federal legislation applying to all schools that receive certain categories of federal funding, which increases accountability for the quality of teaching and learning through annual testing of students and which has sanctions for schools that do not perform adequately each year.

tute teacher Ms. Viola Swamp, are found in the picture book *Miss Nelson Is Missing* by Harry Allard. In another picture book, *Miss Malarkey Doesn't Live in Room 10*, by Judy Finchler and Kevin O'Malley, students begin to understand the lives of their teachers outside the classroom.

On the other hand, children's books can also provide images and stories of teachers who have made a significant difference in their students' lives. For example, the teacher in *Marianthe's Story: Painted Words and Spoken Memories* by Aliki, welcomes Marianthe, a new immigrant, and assures her that she can communicate by painting her "stories" until she masters English and can tell them herself. Another image of teaching appears in *The Landry News* by Andrew Clements, in which a teacher who has been burning out in his job is reinvigorated due to the actions of one of his students.

While works of literature for adults and children create images of teaching, in today's multimedia environment they vie with visual media. Overall, however, it seems that print media may be better at portraying the real everyday lives of teachers while visual media may tend to sensationalize and stereotype.

## Digging Deeper
### Is Teaching a Science or an Art?

One of the most important things to think about as you consider a career in teaching is what you will actually do in the classroom. How will you decide what to do during a particular lesson or in a particular subject area? How will you organize the classroom and manage the students? Often the question of how teachers carry out their profession in the classroom is talked about in terms of whether teaching is a *science* or an *art*.

**Pro and Con:** Viewing teaching as a science implies that fixed rules and procedures guide teachers in their work and that following these rules will lead to student learning (Murray, 1989). In theory, these rules are clearly stated and come from a fixed body of professional, scientific knowledge that all teachers should master. This is sometimes referred to as "outside knowledge" from experts, which can then be applied in the classroom. If you learn this body of professional knowledge, and you know how to apply it and do so consistently, the argument goes, you should be able to be a successful teacher. When teaching is viewed purely as science, teachers can be thought of as technicians who carry out methods in the classroom that are thought to represent best practice. Viewing teaching as a science, teachers can learn all the procedures they need to be successful.

In contrast, viewing teaching as an art means that what a teacher does in the classroom is not guided by a formal set of procedures and rules. The steps to success are not this clearly spelled out. Viewed as practitioners of an art, teachers have an intuition about what needs to happen. They are committed to their students and passionate about their work, and it is this moral commitment to children that drives the performance of their art—sometimes called their "craft"—in the classroom (Grimmett & MacKinnon, 1992). Teaching is less about learning the technical skills and procedures of the profession, and more about doing what seems to "feel right" in the absence of a well-reasoned, logical explanation (Yinger, 1987). In this view of teaching, teachers are born, not made.

**The Nuances:** Most good teachers do not simply follow a book of rules (for example, the teacher's manual) or implement theories and techniques of education that others have studied. Nor do they simply "wing it" in the classroom, trying out any idea that feels right intuitively. Instead, the work of accomplished, experienced teachers, which appears so effortless when you watch them in the classroom, can be regarded of as a combination of highly skilled patterns of teaching behaviors that teachers have perfected over time. For example, teachers may draw on their professional knowledge to perfect routines for discussing stories, for writing stories, for working on mathematics problems, for conducting science experiments, or for sharing current events—and then they combine these patterns into a complex "performance" in the classroom (Yinger, 1987). Over the years, good teachers can develop a whole range of highly skilled patterns in various subject areas and in classroom organization based on sound professional knowledge. So rather than plan every single step of the procedures they will use (as might be the case if teaching were pure "science"), teachers can scope out the situation, identify what is needed, draw on and combine the patterns they have mastered so skillfully, and implement them confidently—with what may appear to an observer to be minimal planning—to respond to their students' needs. This is much different, as you can see, from just doing whatever comes to mind.

Instead of calling teaching either a science or an art, then, teaching can be thought of as improvisation (Sawyer, 2004; Yinger, 1987). Good improvisation builds on a broad range of patterns actors have perfected and can call up almost at will to meet the demands of the specific performance, and this is much like what good teachers do. But the sequence and the specifics, as well as the connections between the patterns, cannot be planned out perfectly in advance, so teaching requires the flexibility that is inherent in improvisation (Sawyer, 2004) and in this sense can be considered an artistic act.

**Rethinking the Issue:** Teaching is neither pure science nor pure art. Teachers must perfect their technical skills and have a sound background of content and professional knowledge, but they must also be able to put those technical skill patterns and knowledge together in many different ways across many different subjects to respond to their students. The complexity of the classroom demands that teachers be able to figure out rather quickly whether the methods they are using are working well and how to make changes as needed.

## Knowledge from Your Own Beliefs about Teaching

Your own experience as a student, your autobiography, your personal commitments, your experience working in schools, and your contact with media images of teaching all combine and interact to form the set of beliefs you hold about teaching. Inevitably, these beliefs about teaching will influence the choices you make when you become a fully certified teacher.

For example, as an early childhood teacher, do you believe that young children should sit at a desk formally learning the alphabet or numbers during kindergarten? How much playtime should young children have during school, and why? How should science, social studies, reading, writing, and mathematics be taught? Are these disciplines always to be taught as separate subjects, or do you believe they can be combined effectively? As a prospective secondary science teacher, do you think you should correct students' writing when they hand in reports of their experiments, or is that solely the job of the English teacher? On the basis of your own experience, you may hold strong beliefs about the importance of every child completing, say, at least two hours of homework every evening starting in fourth grade. You may also believe that every student in the first grade needs to have extensive instruction in phonics every single day and cannot learn to read otherwise.

As a future middle school teacher, you may believe that the most appropriate way to manage a class of middle-schoolers is to set up a system of rewards and punishments based on earning points for good behavior and taking points away for bad behavior. You may also hold strong beliefs about the best way to teach students whose first language is not English. These beliefs come from a combination of your experiences and personal commitments. Whether a particular position is defensible may be less important to you right now than the fact that you believe it to be true and effective, and as a result, you may wish to practice it in your own classroom.

## Your turn... *to reflect*

What are the three most powerful beliefs you have about teaching? Share them with your peers. On what basis do you justify these beliefs? How are these beliefs likely to help or hinder you as you study to become a teacher?

**The Role of Misconceptions.** The images of teaching you construct out of your own beliefs, conceptions, and experiences are very durable ones. While some of these beliefs about teaching may be well founded, others may really be **misconceptions**. One goal of teacher education is to address your potential misconceptions and prepare you to justify your positions about teaching based on professional knowledge combined with reflection on professional experience. If you are going to learn to teach effectively, it will be important to question some of the beliefs you now hold about teaching and see if they hold up under the scrutiny of your own greater reflection and new knowledge.

Let's revisit some of the examples above. If you believe that all children should complete two hours of homework a night starting in fourth grade, have you given thought to what that homework would actually be? How would the homework you assign further your students' understanding of the concepts you would like them to learn? What if some of your students completed their homework in one hour? Would you force them to find something else to do for another hour? These are the kinds of questions you might reflect on with regard to your beliefs about teaching.

In the case of secondary science, you may believe that as a science teacher it is not your responsibility to correct students' writing. However, the school in which you work may expect teachers in every subject area to be involved in teaching writing as it relates to their subject. Your principal may have ample data to suggest that writing across the curriculum is a valid approach that results in better thinking and writing skills for the students in your school. Will you defend your position, or will you give yourself the opportunity to rethink it? Will you take the initiative to learn more about national projects underway that support writing in all content areas, for example, the National Writing Project (**http://www.nwp.org**)?

With regard to your entering beliefs and images, you should identify them and make them a public part of your teacher education experience. Then, as you begin to learn more in your classes and through your experiences in classrooms, you can begin to reflect on your entering beliefs—but now from

### Critical term

**Misconceptions.** Ideas you may have about teaching that are not accurate but that may represent strongly held beliefs about teaching and so may be difficult for you to discard or replace.

As a teacher education student, observing in the classroom allows you to step back from your preconceived notions of teaching and ask new questions about what it means to teach.

(Frank Siteman/PhotoEdit)

the perspective of a teacher. As you learn new concepts and new ways of thinking about teaching, consider how they compare with "what you've always imagined teaching to be."

Which of your conceptions hold true and which are you finding to be misconceptions about teaching? Some of your beliefs may be well supported by what you are learning in your professional program; others you may find conflict with some of your long-held beliefs. If this is the case, what do you think is the cause of the conflict? And, more importantly, what will you do about it? If some of your beliefs conflict with what you are learning both in schools and in the university, it will be important to question yourself— and your instructors—about them. Throughout the process of learning to teach, you need to look for evidence that will support or negate your beliefs. Are you tenaciously holding on to a belief in the absence of any substantial evidence? If you are, you might want to explore why. Certainly, it is not possible to find common agreement about everything that should happen in classrooms and schools, but as a professional your responsibility is to justify your actions in a reasoned manner, and not just because they feel right.

As you spend more time studying teaching in the university and in classrooms, you should begin to reflect on how changes in your own decisions and actions may more positively affect your students. As you begin to make real teaching choices, you will need to be able to justify your teaching decisions. A solid, robust justification should be based on your knowledge of your students, the context, the curriculum, your goals for teaching, and the professional knowledge you are gaining in your preparation to be a teacher.

## Philosophical Note
### The Role of a Philosophy of Teaching

Teacher education students are often asked to write about their developing philosophy of teaching or interview practicing teachers about their philosophy of teaching. But what exactly is a philosophy of teaching, and what is its role in the daily work of a classroom?

A philosophy of teaching is a central principle that helps guide teachers' basic choices about their students, what they teach, and how they teach it. Whether or not teachers enact their philosophy consciously and whether or not they put their philosophy into words, this basic philosophy will influence the kinds of classrooms teachers create for their students. For example, if your philosophy is based on the belief that students will learn best when what they do in school is connected to topics that interest them and experiences they have had, you will want to engage students regularly in conversation and discussion about what they know as part of planning and carrying out instruction. If your philosophy of teaching is that students should learn what is in the curriculum regardless of whether they see its connection to their lives, such discussions are less likely to take center stage in your classroom.

A philosophy of teaching is not just a lofty statement about what you believe. If you are really committed to your philosophy, any observer who walks into your classroom should be able to identify your philosophy in your actions in the classroom and see it in your everyday teaching practice. If you state a philosophy but it is not evident anywhere in how your classroom operates, it is not really a philosophy. As you learn to teach, then, you will have to focus on how to connect your philosophy directly to your choices and actions—that is, how to put your philosophy into practice.

A philosophy of teaching may not drive every single choice a teacher makes. After all, teachers make hundreds of choices every day. Because teachers work with such a wide range of individual students, they may use practices from more than one philosophical approach to meet their students' particular needs at any given time. But making the choice to draw on more than one philosophy temporarily to meet a specific individual need is not the same as adopting that philosophy as an overall approach to the classroom, or as the "big idea" that sets the tone for your classroom. Your philosophy of teaching should be visible, and you should be able to explain it, justify it, provide examples of what it looks like in the classroom to anyone who asks, and provide examples of its success.

As a teacher education student, you bring certain beliefs to your preparation. As you gain professional knowledge and experience, these beliefs may change. As a result, your philosophy of teaching is, appropriately, likely to evolve and develop over time.

In Chapter 4 and also throughout this text, you will be introduced to some of the classic philosophies of education as a way of helping you gauge the direction your philosophy is taking. By the time you complete your professional preparation, you should be able to articulate your current philosophy of education and how you are carrying it out. When you are ready to interview for a teaching position, you might think of your philosophy of teaching in terms of what a school staff can count on you to be committed to if they hire you. What kind of philosophy will your teaching express, and what will that look like in your classroom?

# Observation and Interviewing: "Making the Familiar Strange"

It is completely natural at this point in your development as a teacher to draw on your prior experience with teaching—and the knowledge that has resulted from this experience. Your familiarity with teaching is in many ways the lens through which you are likely to view what you will now begin to learn about teaching. But your prior knowledge may leave you with the impression that teaching is easy. As Munby, Russell, and Martin (2001) observe, it is probably not as easy as it seems:

> As many have noted, intending teachers' prior experience of teaching is severely restricted. Although they have observed thousands of hours of teaching behavior, they have not been privy to the profound and extensive knowledge and thinking that underlies this behavior. As with any good performance, good teaching looks easy.

When we witness a near-perfect performance in, say, the long program of a figure skating competition, we recognize the many hours of intensive work that lie behind the apparent ease of execution under demanding circumstances. But we typically do not do this of teaching. (p. 895)

Starting now, an important part of your job as a prospective teacher is to begin to understand what exactly goes into a teacher's flawless performance. This is your opportunity to step back and look at teaching from the other side of the desk. As you begin your professional preparation for teaching, your job is to learn about teaching anew, and to do that, you will need to temporarily suspend what you already know about teaching and observe teaching with a clean slate, so to speak, as a learner about teaching. How exactly *did* a particular teacher make it look so effortless?

In this section, we will explore two methods, or tools, for putting some distance between your prior knowledge and the realities of teaching: *observation* and *interviewing*. These two methods will help you to adopt the learner's stance, to look at teaching from a new vantage point, and to put your prior knowledge about teaching into perspective. Observation and interviewing will help you *make the familiar strange*.

## Making the Familiar Strange through Formal Classroom Observation

### Critical term

**Making the familiar strange.** Looking at the familiar procedures, events, and interactions in the classroom from a more objective viewpoint and treating them as something you do not fully understand. This is a way of helping you begin to analyze and ask questions about why things happen the way they do in classrooms.

**Making the familiar strange** is an idea that was developed by the educational researcher Frederick Erickson (1986). This term is used in educational anthropology to refer to taking a fresh, objective look at a situation that is familiar to you in order to learn something new about it. *Making the familiar strange* also means temporarily leaving behind any preconceived ideas you may have about the situation you are observing—in this case, teaching. Close observation is important, he states, because of "*the invisibility of everyday life.* 'What is happening here?' may seem a trivial question at first glance. It is not trivial since everyday life is largely invisible to us (because of its familiarity and because of its contradictions, which people may not want to face)" (Erickson, 1986, p. 121).

Here Erickson is reminding us that because we are so familiar with teaching, unless we observe it purposefully and with some distance we may not be able to see what is actually there. But if we do observe carefully, Erickson states, "the commonplace becomes problematic" (p. 121), and it then becomes something we can begin to ask questions about and learn from. The commonplace, in this case, is made up of all the things we already know about teaching—the things we take for granted without questioning them.

## Your turn... *to review*

1. What does the phrase "making the familiar strange" mean?
2. Why is it especially important for a prospective teacher to "make the familiar strange"?

The *commonplace* knowledge we have about teaching can only become *problematic*—and by that we mean something we can ask questions about and wonder about and reflect on and learn from—if we can step away from our everyday, casual style of observation. The goal is to become deliberate and systematic in making observations (Evertson & Green, 1986), allowing us to observe closely and carefully. In this way, we can begin to question what seems so familiar about teaching in the first place and see it from a new perspective—that of a future teacher. As Erickson noted, sometimes such careful, close observation contradicts what you think you already know. When that happens, it provides an important opportunity for professional growth and new learning through reflection.

But making what is invisible *visible* is only one purpose of close, deliberate observation. Another important purpose is to document "concrete details of practice" (Erickson, 1986, p. 121). As an observer of teaching, you will be able to identify carefully many of the specific ways teachers carry out their work. Instead of making a general statement like "The teacher conducted a lesson on multiplication," you can document exactly what is going on during that lesson, in all of its particulars. For example, when you observe deliberately and systematically, you can focus on particulars such as how teachers accomplish the following tasks:

- Start the day.
- Interact with students.
- Begin the lesson.
- Motivate students to learn.
- Distribute materials.
- Handle misbehavior.
- Keep students engaged in the lesson.
- Involve many students in discussions.
- Use specific strategies for teaching reading, writing, literature, mathematics, science, or social studies.
- Work with a team teaching partner.
- Implement classroom routines and patterns.
- Include students who have disabilities.
- Manage the whole group when working with a small group.
- Integrate technology into instruction.
- Make the transition from one activity to another, or from one location to another.

Finally, observing in the classroom gives you the opportunity to watch the **classroom as a culture**—in much the same way that an anthropologist observes distant cultures to understand them. Studying a culture includes studying customs, practices, and traditions—in this case, the customs, practices, and traditions in the classroom (Florio-Ruane, 1989).

Once you begin close observation, classrooms should start to look different from how they looked when you were a student. You can begin to think about why teachers do things in specific ways and how you would do them yourself. As a result of your observations, you should be asking questions about teaching that you probably would not have asked before. And you should start to consider your prior beliefs in relationship to the new aspects of teaching that your observations are showing you to be so important.

**Begin Observing with a Map.** When researchers observe classrooms, the first thing they may do is to draw a map. All classrooms may look somewhat alike to you, but in fact teachers usually have a great deal of control over how they set up their individual classrooms (within the constraints of available furniture and supplies).

**Critical term**

**Classroom as a culture.** The customs, practices, and traditions within a classroom that distinguish it from other organizations.

Drawing a map of the classroom allows you to ask questions about how the classroom setup influences the kind of instruction, classroom community, and classroom culture that can be developed. Questions you ask might include: What are the consequences of setting up the room in a certain way for patterns of student interaction? What would happen to movement in the classroom if the teacher arranged the furniture differently? How does the set up encourage or discourage group work?

When you draw a classroom map, you should include and label furniture, supplies, curriculum materials, teacher's work area, various sections of the room and their purpose, windows, doors, computer stations, any other unusual or important things that are present (for example, an elementary school classroom's pet hamster or lab equipment in a high school science room), and even the location of the pencil sharpener. Once you have the physical layout down, begin to look for patterns, such as traffic patterns, where the teacher is located, and whether he or she moves around the room (Glesne, 2006). After the map is drawn, consider what kind of "message" the classroom setup sends about teaching and learning.

If you are assigned to observe the same classroom over a long period of time, you might want to draw another map halfway through your time there. Then compare the two maps to see whether the physical layout and patterns have changed. If they have, how did this change affect what you observed in the classroom in terms of teacher-student and student-student interaction? How have your interpretations changed over time and why?

### Conducting a Systematic Observation.
Your goal in recording what you see during an observation is to describe in detail, in your own words, what you are seeing. You set a time frame in which you will observe, let's say, for 30 minutes, and then you begin writing. This is sometimes called **anecdotal recording**.

Deliberate, systematic observation differs from everyday, casual observation in one important way. To be a systematic observer, you will need to separate the *description* of what you see from your own judgment of it and your reactions to it. Your job is to describe what is going on, not to judge or interpret it. Separating your description of what you are seeing from your interpretation of it helps you get some distance from your commonplace knowledge about teaching. The more we can be descriptive and objective, the more we can try to understand what is going on not only from our own perspective, but from the perspective of the teachers you are observing and the knowledge these teachers have about the classroom. In summarizing the process of observation, Glesne (2006) stresses the importance of recording in detail the situations you observe and analyzing what you observe in terms of its meaning.

**Critical term**

**Anecdotal recording.** Observing and recording the specific events that occur in a defined timeframe in the classroom, without making judgments or interpreting those events.

### Your turn... *to reflect*

Write a description of your instructor after a brief period of observation. Then share that description with a partner. Evaluate how similar or different your observations are and whether you were objective or whether judgments and interpretations were included in your observational notes. What might account for your different descriptions?

Writing objective descriptions can be harder than it sounds. As you can see from this brief exercise, each of you probably observed your instructor differently and used different words in your description. To help you become more objective when you are observing, here are some guidelines suggested by Glesne (2006):

- Use concrete terms to describe what you are observing; for example, instead of *disrespectful*, provide specific examples of what the students were actually doing that made you conclude they were being disrespectful.
- Avoid vague adjectives such as *a few* or *a lot*; give exact numbers instead.
- Avoid words that imply a judgment on your part, for example, *great*, *terrific*, *terrible*, *boring*, *challenging*; aim for specific descriptions instead.
- Whenever possible, note specific dialogues between teacher and student or student and student to capture exactly what was going on between them.

Another way to help ensure that your observations are descriptive is to use a two-column format. Divide the pages into two columns: a wider column on the left (about two-thirds of the page) and a narrower column on the right (about one-third of the page). In the left-hand column write your descriptions, in chronological order. In the right-hand column write your personal comments, reactions, and questions about what you observed. Try using a different font to distinguish between description and observation, as illustrated in Figure 2-4. This way you can consciously begin to train yourself to observe more objectively and separate your precise, detailed descriptions from your comments, reactions, and questions about those descriptions. You can take the stance of being someone who is looking at the classroom objectively to learn about its specific "culture."

In Figure 2-4 you can begin to see the difference between an observation that does and does not include a lot of interpretation. The left part of the figure is Yolanda's first attempt at a classroom observation in a middle school language arts class. You can easily pick out the terms that show her interpretations and judgments. They include terms such as *interesting* and *excited*, which are judgments about the kind of work the students were doing and how they were feeling about it—with no real knowledge about whether or not that was an accurate judgment. There are terms such as *I assumed* and *this seemed more like*, which are also interpretations and are not based on the facts of the observation. In the right-hand portion of the figure you can see a more objective version of Yolanda's observation, which includes more descriptive terms and fewer interpretations. In this version you can also see the comments and questions she posed as she took notes—but on the far right-hand side of the observation record, clearly separated from the description itself.

Observing is a skill you will use throughout your career as a teacher. For example, you will rely on your observational skills to informally assess your students' progress. You may take informal notes to remind yourself about specific things you observe as you walk around the classroom when students are working. This kind of ongoing observation allows you to ask yourself a critical question: *How well is my teaching helping my students learn?* Teachers who observe their students regularly are always checking to see whether the students are "getting it," and they make midcourse corrections if students are having a great deal of difficulty. Practicing the skill of observation now will help you use it well in the future to benefit your students.

## Your turn... *to review*

1. What is anecdotal recording?
2. Why is objective description such an important tool when you observe in classrooms?
3. How does the use of objective language help you differentiate between observation and interpretation?

## Figure 2-4 Becoming an Objective Observer

A comparison of Yolanda's reports of a classroom observation for seventh grade language arts. How does the observation with and without her interpretations change your view of what is going on in this classroom?

### Report #1:

The children were in their seats when I arrived in the room at 8:45 AM. The desks were organized in a really interesting way, much different than anything I had seen before. There was a horseshoe, and inside the horseshoe were four sets of two desks each. I really liked this arrangement. All of the students were writing in journals when I got there, and they were all busy and interested in what they were writing. The teacher called individual students up to her desk and talked with them for a few minutes each while the rest of the class worked in their journals. I didn't see any directions or topics for writing, so I assumed the students could choose whatever topic they wanted. At 9:00 the teacher asked the students to put away their journals. Then she started to talk about the class writing project they were working on—oral histories of elderly people in their community who had been living in the Great Depression. This seemed more like Social Studies than Language Arts. Two students reported on their interview with Mrs. Astin, who was living in a nearby nursing home. They were excited and had a lot to say, especially about how hard it was for Mrs. Astin's father to find work and how that affected their living conditions. Several students asked questions and the teacher and the students who had interviewed Mrs. Astin all responded to the questions. After that report, the teacher asked the students to get out their materials and get to work. Some students took out a tape recorder, others went to the computer stations, and others began working in pairs to edit drafts of their reports. Most of the students were busy, but one pair was not doing what the teacher wanted. The teacher went from group to group, but spent extra time with the two students who were not doing their work. This work period continued until 10:00, when it was time for me to leave.

### Report #2: 8:45 AM

**Observation**

There were 24 students in the classroom, 15 girls and 9 boys. The room was arranged in a horseshoe shape, with eight desks inside of the horseshoe in pairs. When I arrived the students were writing in journals. The teacher sat at her desk. As the students wrote, the teacher called up individual students and spent about 10 minutes with each student. The only materials that were out when they talked were the students' journals. The classroom was quiet, and the students were all writing during journal time. At 9:15 the teacher asked the students to put away their journals. All of the students did so within a few minutes. She told the students that until 10 AM they would be working on their oral history projects about the Great Depression. She talked about the progress they had made so far and said that seven teams were done interviewing and that two more had interviews scheduled. She asked two students to report briefly on their interview from the week before with Mrs. Astin, who was living in a nearby nursing home. They talked in animated voices about the interview, emphasizing how hard it was for Mrs. Astin's father to find work and how that affected their living conditions. One student asked if Mrs. Astin had brothers or sisters. Another asked if they had trouble interviewing because they knew that Mrs. Astin's hearing was going. A third student asked if the family ever had to beg for food. After the report, the teacher asked all of the students to get out their materials and get to work. Three students took out a tape recorder to listen to their interview and took written notes on a laptop. About half of the other students went to computer stations. The rest of the class worked in pairs and seemed to be editing each other's work. During this time, one pair of students was talking about a sports event in voices that were loud enough for the rest of the class to hear. The teacher went over to them and asked them about their report. She stayed with them until they had gotten started on editing, which took about five minutes. Then she circulated around the room until 10:00 AM.

**Observer comments**

*Nice room arrangement—I've never seen this before.*

*Are they always so quiet during journal time?*

*Does the teacher give a prompt or do the students write about whatever they want?*

*Oral histories on the Depression seem like social studies to me—I wonder if the social studies teacher is working with this teacher on the project?*

*How did she arrange the interviews?*

*Are the same two students always acting out, or is this unusual today?*

**The Etiquette of Observing.** As you move through your professional pro-gram, you are likely to be asked to observe in several different kinds of classrooms. The immediate goal is to refamiliarize yourself with classrooms from the perspec-tive of a professional teacher. But eventually you will probably be asked to observe a particular student or group of students to determine their learning patterns and responses to teacher instruction. You may also be asked to observe specific teacher behaviors—for example, how a teacher adjusts his or her instruction for students whose first language is not English, or how a teacher makes the transition from one activity to another or from one subject to another, or what kind of routine a teacher uses to begin the day or the class. In each case, you will want to separate description from your own interpretation and judgment.

When you conduct an observation, remember that you are always a guest in another teacher's classroom. A few simple rules of etiquette apply:

- Be sure the teacher knows when you are coming.
- Upon arriving at the school, check in at the office.
- Sign in and get a visitor identification tag if this is required.
- When you arrive, be sure to introduce yourself to the teacher and remind him or her of the purpose of your observation. (Teachers are busy people; they might not remember the exact details of the class and assignment for which you are there.)
- Ask the teacher where you should sit.
- Find out if the teacher plans to introduce you to the class so that students know why you are in the room that day. If so, how would you like to be introduced?
- If you intend to take notes on a laptop, ask the teacher if he or she minds. (If you need to plug in your computer, bring along an extension cord. Don't ask the teacher to use valuable teaching time to help you set up.)
- If you have an observation scheduled but cannot make it, let the teacher know by leaving a message in the school office. (If you have already spoken directly with the teacher and can contact him or her directly via phone or email, do so.)
- Ask the teacher how he or she would like you to respond to the situation if students come up to talk to you during the observation.
- If you think you might complete the observation while the teacher is involved with students, let the teacher know approximately when you will be leaving.
- Convey your thanks personally or in writing.

You can practice your observation skills by clicking onto the website called *Inside Teaching* at **http://gallery.carnegiefoundation.org/insideteaching/ quest/collections.html** and watching teachers in action. As you move the mouse over the individual pictures, the name of the teacher for that website appears on the top of the picture bank. If you want to practice observing at the ele-mentary level, click on the section for elementary teachers on the right and the picture links for several website links will be highlighted. Try looking at the websites for Melissa Pedraza or Becky Pereira on literacy. If you want to practice at the secondary level, click on the secondary link and try the website for Marsha Pincus on teaching Shakespeare to students in an urban high school. There are many others to choose from.

## Making the Familiar Strange through Interviewing

Another strategy for making the familiar strange is to conduct interviews with practicing teachers. Interviewing gives you the opportunity to ask teachers to share their philosophy, to break down what they are doing, to make sense for you of what appears to be automatic, and to learn how teachers think about particular events or aspects of their work. Much as is true of observing, in a sense we engage in casual interview-like behavior all the time. We have conversations, we ask questions, we listen. But an informal, unfocused conversation is not the same as an interview. Although you may adopt a casual tone during the interview itself, you will approach it in a much more deliberate way than you would a casual conversation.

To prepare for interviewing a teacher, consider the following:

- Have six to eight questions ready to ask the person you are interviewing.
- If you have observed in the classroom of the teacher you are interviewing, pick a few issues that arose from your observation and ask questions about them.
- Come prepared with a notebook. If the teacher is willing, you might choose to record the interview using a digital recorder or MP3 player.
- Since teachers are very busy and often have little time during the day, schedule a time in advance.
- Teachers' days are often unpredictable, so be flexible if the teacher has to cancel. Above all, don't take it personally; it's probably not under his or her control.

**Constructing Interview Questions.**  Your interview will only be as successful as the preparation you put into it. First, consider how much time you have. If you are talking with a teacher during his or her planning time, the period is probably no more than 45 minutes long. If you are scheduled before school, a teacher's time is limited as well. If you are meeting after school, the teacher may be willing to stay for a longer period of time. The number of questions you will be able to ask depends on the amount of time you have scheduled.

Interviewing practicing teachers is an important way to learn about the profession. (Davis Young-Wolff/ PhotoEdit)

Second, make sure you have a focus for your interview. What is your purpose? Is it to get information about this teacher's experience or a more complete biography? Is the purpose to follow up with questions based on a previous classroom observation? Are you trying to find out what the teacher believes about current controversies in education? Are you asking questions about teaching at a particular grade level or a particular content area? The focus of your interview helps narrow the types of questions you may wish to ask.

Third, you can get the most from an interview if you take the time to construct good questions. As you do so, be sure to avoid questions that can be answered with a simple *yes* or *no*. The purpose of the interview is to get detailed information from the teacher to inform your knowledge about the profession. Since *yes/no* questions automatically limit the kind of information you will get, be sure to ask questions that encourage the teacher to talk in some depth about the issue you are raising. For example, don't ask: *Do you like your job?* Instead say: *Could you tell me three things you like about your job, and why?* Don't ask: *Do you always split the students up into small working groups?* Instead, ask: *Can you tell me the advantages of having the students work in small groups? If there are any disadvantages, what are they?*

Fourth, as you develop the questions, think about how you might probe a little deeper for more information and then jot down some possible followup questions. For example, let's say you plan to ask the teacher: *How do you develop good working relationships with the families of your students?* If the teacher answers that he or she sends a letter home at the start of the year, be prepared to follow-up with something like: *What are some other ways you connect with parents?* Or: *Can you tell me about a time you've had to work especially hard to build a relationship with a parent?*

### The Etiquette of Conducting an Interview.
Just as there is an etiquette for observing in the classroom, there is also an etiquette for conducting an interview. Some of the guidelines parallel what you should do when conducting a classroom observation, but others differ significantly.

● Be sure the teacher knows when you are coming.

● Upon arriving at the school, check in at the office.

● If you haven't already met the teacher, be sure to introduce yourself.

● Ask the teacher where he or she would like the two of you to sit.

● If you are planning to record the interview, make sure you get the teacher's permission first. If the teacher does not wish to be recorded, you will have to be satisfied with taking written notes. If you have plans to record the interview, make sure your digital recorder or MP3 player is working, and bring along an extra set of batteries or an extra battery pak, an extension cord, and an extra cassette (if applicable).

● If you are taking notes on a laptop, make sure that you are located where there is an outlet or that the battery is fully charged.

● Prepare two copies of the list of questions so that you can give one to the teacher during the interview. That way you will not have to repeat questions.

● In the course of answering one question, the teacher may also answer some of the subsequent questions before you have come to them on your list. If this occurs, there is no need, of course, to repeat the question.

● If the teacher says something that is not clear to you, ask him or her to clarify the response. Say something like: *Let me make sure I understand what you mean* (and then repeat how you understand the response). Or: *Can you repeat that? Can you tell me more about it?* Don't be afraid to show your curiosity.

● Keep track of the time. The teacher may be giving you much longer responses than are necessary. If this occurs, say something like: *Perhaps we can move on to the next question.* If the teacher is giving you a long but important response, you will have to decide whether to ask fewer questions and try to schedule a follow-up meeting.

● If you have an interview scheduled but cannot make it, let the teacher know.

● Convey your thanks personally or in writing.

## Your turn... *to review*

1. Identify three rules for constructing good interview questions.
2. Name two good behaviors to follow when conducting interviews with teachers.

## Final Pointers on Observation and Interviewing

Observation and interviewing give you an opportunity to dig deeper into teaching. If you are genuinely curious about your chosen profession, time in classrooms allows you the luxury of stepping back and considering what it really means to be a teacher. Your curiosity about becoming a teacher should lead you to want to ask many questions, to delve into how and why the things that are taking place are meaningful for students and teachers alike. Observation and interviewing are excellent ways to begin being *reflective* about teaching—something we noted in Chapter 1 as critical to good teaching.

Next, whether you are visiting a school to conduct an observation or to interview a teacher, remember that the teachers and staff are looking at you as a potential teacher. Although you may only be starting your teacher education program, you are already being sized up in terms of your overall professionalism and demeanor as you enter the building and interact with staff and students. Pay attention to the way others perceive you and your commitment to teaching.

Finally, although you may think you know the level at which you would like to teach, now is the time to keep an open mind about this important decision. Each level of teaching has its own benefits and limitations. You can use your opportunities to observe and interview teachers to broaden your understanding of the various age and grade levels and the rewards and challenges of working at each one. As a prospective teacher, you may begin your professional program set on being a high school English teacher, for example, but end up observing in an early childhood classroom and finding you love it, or vice versa. Although you may be fairly certain of the level in which you are interested, do not shut out other possibilities too early. You may be surprised at how much you like working with a particular age group that you never considered working with before.

## Why It Counts in a Diverse World

As this chapter demonstrates, prior experience and your entering beliefs about teaching almost always provide only a partial view of what teaching entails. The dilemma is figuring out how to treat your experience as *one* source of knowledge instead of treating it inflexibly as *the* source of knowledge. It is crucial to acknowledge both what you know and what you do not know about teaching. Only then can you begin to clarify what you need to learn in order to become a successful teacher.

The pull of your prior experience is strong. The influences of your own schooling and your own life experiences are significant, and they are often hard to shed. Your own years of experience in schools, and the common but inaccurate societal view that teaching is an "easy" career, may lead you to fall into the trap of believing that you know more than you actually do about the real work of teaching. If your beliefs and prior experience interact to weaken your curiosity about teaching, you may be hampered from gaining a fuller understanding of the profession. When confronted with something new, you may devalue its importance because you already have a set way of thinking about it. When you have the opportunity to observe and interview teachers, you may inadvertently fail to ask yourself important questions or to grasp the meaning of important details you may have observed. In this way, observation and interviewing can serve as weak sources of new information about teaching for you instead of being strong opportunities for new learning. You may find that you do not make the familiar strange because you lack genuine curiosity about teaching—not because you don't care but because you seem to be so familiar with it already.

If you think about other professions, you quickly realize that you would probably not make as many assumptions about how to carry out your responsibilities as you might about teaching. You would not assume that you are ready to try a case in court, or help someone who has serious mental health problems, or diagnose an illness simply based on your personal experience with the law, or therapy, or medicine. But because everyone has been to school, experience can be a pitfall (Feiman-Nemser & Buchmann, 1985) as much as it can be a benefit.

The opening quote of this chapter reminds us that experience constitutes something of a dilemma for those who wish to teach. Your own experience forms a valuable basis for your teaching; your life story is what enables you to infuse your teaching with your personal style and your personal commitments. As an individual you bring a unique perspective, idiosyncratic talents, and special areas of expertise to your work as a teacher. But as you learn to teach, your life story expands and should be enriched by the new experiences you will have in your formal preparation.

In our diverse word, expanding your experiences as you learn to teach may mean interacting with students and families whose culture and life experiences differ significantly from your own. It may mean gaining an understanding of your own misconceptions about unfamiliar communities, new cultures, schools that are much larger or much smaller than those you attended, or students and families who are recent immigrants and are just learning English.

Using your experience as a starting point, you can grow in your understanding of what it means to teach. As Carter and Doyle (1996) imply, your life story and experiences can be limiting, even imprisoning. On the other hand, if your life story and experiences form a solid foundation for your commitment to caring about teaching all children, you can build on them skillfully and complement this foundation by formal knowledge about—and new experience with—both the science *and* the art of teaching.

## CHAPTER SUMMARY

### Five Kinds of Experience That Create Prior Knowledge about Teaching

**Knowledge about Teaching from Your Own Experience of Schooling.** Teaching is the only profession for which almost everyone has at least 12 years of experience. But this experience is incomplete because it provides only a student's view of teaching—not a teacher's. This experience can provide models of good teachers and good teaching, but it can also provide negative experiences about teaching. As you move from the role of student to teacher, you should begin to take a different perspective on what you have learned from your years of experience in classrooms.

**Autobiographical Knowledge about Teaching.** Each person brings his or her own family and personal experiences to the work of teaching. These experiences provide prospective teachers with different views about teaching and different personal commitments to teaching. For example, prospective teachers whose parents were teachers are likely to have a different perspective from those who grew up with no connections to schools other than their own experience in classrooms. Having always wanted to be a teacher gives you a different perspective than that of someone who is changing careers. Your family and personal experiences are a form of prior knowledge that affect how you understand the profession of teaching.

**Knowledge about Teaching from Working in Schools.** Some prospective teachers have classroom experience beyond their own years as students. Those who have held positions as paraprofessionals or have been volunteers attain a perspective on teaching that is derived somewhat more from the teacher's side of the desk than from the student's. Many paraprofessionals are assigned to classrooms with teachers who are positive role models; others are not. In the first case, paraprofessionals may bring important knowledge to their teacher preparation; in the second, years of practicing less than optimal teaching methods can be deeply ingrained. In these cases, the prospective teacher has the job of both unlearning poor practice and learning good practice. Generally, however, the paraprofessional's classroom experience provides a helpful perspective. But in most cases, paraprofessionals still have not had the responsibility of preparing for teaching on a daily basis and all that this entails.

**Knowledge about Teaching from Images in the Media.** The media provide powerful images of teaching. Images from film can include heroic teachers working in challenging schools, individual teachers demonstrating their commitment to students who have special needs or require serious mentoring, or teachers not being recognized for the tremendous impact they have had. The print media have another kind of influence, chiefly by presenting data about school performance that can be translated into beliefs about the quality of teachers in a particular school district. Publications can also sway opinion by promoting a specific teaching method. In general, media accounts of teaching are problematic because they provide only a partial view of the real work teachers do.

**Knowledge from Your Own Beliefs about Teaching.** Your own experiences in PK–12 classrooms, your family experiences and your personal commitments, your working experience in schools (should you have it), and the images of teaching you absorb from the media all interact to form a set of personal beliefs about teaching. These may include beliefs about teachers' work, the role of certain methods in teaching, what you determine is "right" or "wrong" for students, or the role of teachers in relationship to students' personal lives, to name a few. Personal beliefs about teaching are extremely durable, and they form a powerful lens through which you are likely to view—and judge—all the new things you are learning about teaching. Some of your entering conceptions may be accurate, and others may be misconceptions. How you address these misconceptions is critical to your development as a teacher. If you persist in teaching based on misconceptions, this stance may hamper you from developing fully as a teacher.

## Observation and Interviewing: "Making the Familiar Strange"

**Making the Familiar Strange through Formal Classroom Observation.** Classroom observation provides you with the opportunity to begin to study the seemingly effortless performance of good teachers. Observation usually begins with drawing a classroom map and asking questions about the way the classroom is structured physically. When you conduct an observation, it's wise to choose a few things to focus on each time you are there. For example, you may focus on the relationship between the teacher and the students, or among the students themselves. Observation puts you in the position of becoming a student of teaching—someone who is now learning about teaching from the perspective of a professional.

**Making the Familiar Strange through Interviewing.** Interviewing practicing teachers is another opportunity to learn about teaching. Good interviewing requires you to prepare good questions beforehand, take notes or record the interview, and probe the teacher you are interviewing for more information, especially if you are not clear about the meaning of a particular response.

**Final pointers on observation and interviewing.** When you are observing or interviewing in a school, the school staff (including the school secretary and the building engineer) immediately begin to size you up as a potential member of the staff. They are looking to see whether you act professionally even in these early encounters. Do you arrive on time? If you have to cancel, do you call to let the teacher know? Are you pleasant in your interactions? Are you prepared with all the materials you need to conduct the observation or interview? The initial impression you make can make the difference in whether or not teachers and administrators in that building will welcome you back in your subsequent clinical experiences.

## LIST OF CRITICAL TERMS

Prior knowledge  (*20*)

Apprenticeship of observation  (*20*)

Concept map  (*22*)

National Education Association  (*25*)

Teacher expectations  (*32*)

No Child Left Behind Act of 2001  (*34*)

Misconceptions  (*37*)

Making the familiar strange  (*40*)

Classroom as a culture  (*41*)

Anecdotal recording  (*42*)

## EXPLORING YOUR COMMITMENT

1. ***on your own...***  Write a brief autobiography focused on your decision to become a teacher. Include reflections on your own apprenticeship of observation, your family experiences, any experiences you may have working in schools or with children, and your personal commitments and beliefs. Which of these experiences has resulted in the most powerful images and beliefs you hold about teaching? Explore these beliefs in your paper. How will your prior knowledge about teaching help you in becoming a teacher? If it might hinder you in any way, what might that be?

2. ***on your own...***  After you complete your autobiography, interview one of your peers to see how their prior experiences and knowledge are similar to and different from your own.

3. ***on your own...***  For a week, read your local newspaper with the goal of identifying all articles on education. What kinds of stories are reported? What kind of images does the reporting create? What is not reported? What kind of effect would this reporting have on someone who has school-aged children and is considering moving to the community?

4. ***on your own...***  Consider the following quotation: "Wise teachers understand the legitimacy and limitations of the diverse sources that inform teaching and they continuously draw upon them to enrich their teaching" (National Board for Professional Teaching Standards, Proposition 4). Make a table that includes the sources of knowledge we discussed in this chapter: (1) experience as a student, (2) family influences, (3) personal commitments, (4) experience working in schools, (5) media influences, and (6) personal beliefs. For each of these knowledge sources, note why they are legitimate for you and why they may be limitations for you as you begin your professional work learning to teach. How might you overcome any limitations you identify?

5. ***in the field...***  Using the guidelines in this chapter, conduct an observation in the classroom of a teacher who is neither a member of your family nor a family friend. After you have conducted the observation, see what kinds of questions the observation raises for you. Be open to Erickson's warning that some things you see may contradict what you believe. Conduct a short follow-up discussion with the teacher to gain a better understanding of what you observed. How did this observation help you understand what goes into a teacher's daily performance in the classroom?

6. ***on your own...*** With a small group from your class, develop a set of interview questions to ask an experienced teacher. Include questions about his or her career choice, what makes it satisfying, what makes it challenging, and what keeps him or her going and committed to teaching.

7. ***in the field...*** Use the interview questions you developed as a basis for preparing to conduct an interview with a practicing classroom teacher. Add other questions that might be appropriate for the specific grade level or subject for the teacher you will be interviewing. Select a teacher who is not a family friend or relative—someone you do not know already. Prepare a report on the interview, including specific comments on how this experience helped you gain a deeper appreciation for what it means to be a teacher and what questions or concerns the interview raised for you.

8. ***on the web...*** Identify two websites related to teaching that you believe can help you in your transition from being a student to being a prospective teacher—sites that can help you "make the familiar strange." Consider the following descriptors: PK–12 teaching, learning to teach, teacher education, teaching as a profession, etc. One of the sites might be a personal website of a practicing teacher. Describe the two sites, or if possible, link up to the Internet during class and share the sites with your peers and instructor. Be prepared to explain how these two sites would be helpful in your goal of becoming a teacher.

9. ***on the web...*** Visit the website for Recruiting New Teachers, an organization that, according to its website, "works to raise esteem for teaching, expand the pool of qualified teachers, and promote strategies for effective teacher recruitment, development, and retention" (**http://www.recruitingteachers.org**). What information on this website did you find most helpful? least helpful?

10. ***in the research...*** Read the 2002 article "Demystifying Reflection: A Study of Pedagogical Strategies That Encourage Reflective Journal Writing" by Elizabeth Spalding and Angene Wilson (*Teachers College Record*, October 2002, Vol. 104, No. 7, pp. 1393–1421). What questions about reflective journal writing does this article raise for you?

## GUIDELINES FOR BEGINNING TEACHERS

1. When you seek advice from other teachers in your building, make sure they are teachers who can give you good reasons for teaching the way they do. Teachers who can explain their choices have probably given them a lot of thought. "I've always done it that way," or "It's a good activity that the children like" may be an indication that a teacher has not thought much about why he or she is doing things a certain way.

2. Share enough personal information about yourself with your students so they know you are a "real person" and have a "real life" outside of school.

3.  Consider keeping a journal of your early days of teaching. It can provide you with a place to air your concerns and frustrations and also record your successes. When you are feeling stressed, make sure to read about your successes.

4.  If you are working with an educational aide or paraprofessional, make sure this individual is clear about your expectations. Demonstrate how you want things done and explain why it is important to do things in that way. Make sure this person feels like a fully valued member of your classroom's instructional team.

5.  Make a list of your fundamental philosophical commitments as a teacher. Keep this list in an accessible place and review it periodically throughout your first year to see how closely your teaching reflects these commitments. If you are keeping close to your commitments, what is supporting you? If you are not, what is making you move away from them?

## THE **INTASC** CONNECTION

The INTASC standard that most directly addresses issues regarding your professional growth as a teacher is Standard 9. It states: *The teacher is a reflective practitioner who continually evaluates the effects of his/her choices and actions on others (students, parents, and other professionals in the learning community) and who actively seeks out opportunities to grow professionally.* In this chapter, we have emphasized the need for teachers—especially beginning teachers—to be aware of the need to grow professionally, especially in relationship to ideas they may have from their own experiences as students. Indicators include the following:

●  The teacher values critical thinking and self-directed learning as habits of mind.

●  The teacher is committed to reflection, assessment, and learning as an ongoing process.

●  The teacher recognizes his/her professional responsibility for engaging in and supporting appropriate professional practices for self and colleagues.

●  The teacher understands methods of inquiry that provide him/her with a variety of self-assessment and problem-solving strategies for reflecting on his/her practice, its influences on students' growth and learning, and the complex interactions between them.

●  The teacher uses classroom observation, information about students, and research for evaluating the outcomes of teaching and learning and as a basis for experimenting with, reflecting on, and revising practice.

If you are in a state that follows a different set of teacher standards, find the state standards that most closely relate to the INTASC standards discussed here.

## READING ON...

Kohl, H. (1984). *Growing minds: On becoming a teacher*. New York: Harper and Row. Kohl reflects on what it meant for him personally to learn to teach and what he holds as most important about teaching.

Nieto, S. (2003). *What keeps teachers going?* New York: Teachers College Press. Experienced teachers reflect on what keeps them committed to their work.

Palmer, P. J. (1998). *The courage to teach*. San Francisco: Jossey-Bass. How teachers move between their love of teaching and the challenges of teaching, and retain their commitment to what is most important about the profession.

Weber, L. (1997). (Beth Alberty, Ed.). *Looking back and thinking forward: Reexaminations of teaching and schooling*. New York: Teachers College Press. An early childhood educator, Lillian Weber was a passionate advocate for open education and for teachers as vibrant, intellectual professionals.

## Guiding Questions

- Who governs the education and licensing of teachers?

- What do prospective teachers study?

- What is the role of standards in teacher education?

- How do colleges and universities and the PK–12 schools share responsibility for teacher preparation?

- How do required tests for teachers fit into teacher preparation?

- What does accreditation mean in teacher education?

- How has teacher education changed to respond to teacher shortages?

- How are new teachers supported after they complete their formal preparation programs?

# Learning to Teach: What Does It Mean?

# 3

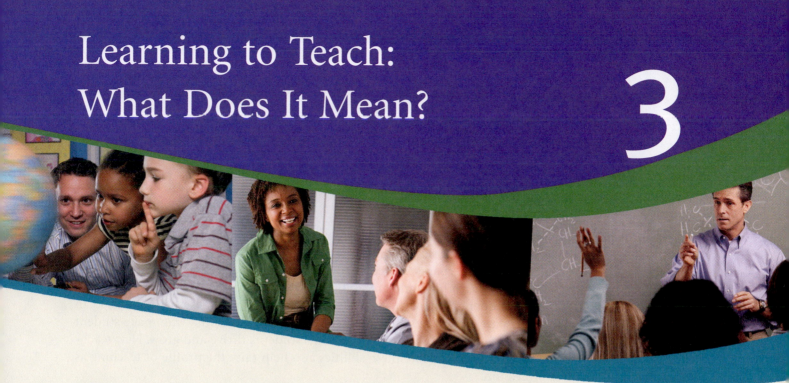

Six months have passed, and Kayla Jones-Martin has just finished her first semester, where she completed a clinical placement in a second grade. Most of her fieldwork focused on early literacy, and all semester long she tutored a student and saw a real improvement in her student's reading skills. Every two weeks she would bring in the assessments of her student's progress and discuss them with her peers and her instructors in class. Now it is December, and she is having coffee with Martha Frazier to discuss her own progress.

"You know," she began, "I never saw myself teaching young children. I had this image of my sixth grade teacher and I never gave any other grade level the least bit of thought. But I loved my work this semester. I love watching the kids learn to 'crack the code' and actually learn to read. I like thinking about what stage of development they're at and how to plan what I'm going to do with that in mind. And I'm much more patient than I ever thought I would be with them."

Martha smiled. She had started her career as a first grade teacher and stayed in that grade for 10 years, then moved to second grade for five more before she accepted the position of principal. "Well, I'm not an impartial judge since I love first and second graders too. But what comes next in your program?"

"Actually, next semester I'll be with older kids and I'll be studying math and science methods. I'm excited to be working with the upper grades and to try out some lessons with groups of students. I learned a lot last semester working with Keith, the student I tutored, but I'm feeling anxious to try some things out with a whole class, not just one child. I'm really glad I have the chance to work in different classrooms before my internship so I have a better idea of the grade level I want to focus on when that time comes".

"Every age group is a unique challenge, but you'll figure out where you're most comfortable and what the best match is. Just keep an open mind. You've already seen that you might really like the younger students, even though you never thought about that before. You might try imagining how you'll feel every morning when you walk into your classroom. What kinds of things do you actually want to be able to do with your kids? How does their age and developmental level affect what you can and can't do? You'll figure it out in plenty of time to make a decision."

*Excellent teachers don't develop full blown at graduation; nor are they just "born teachers." Instead, teachers are always in the process of "becoming." Given the dynamics of their work, they need to continually rediscover who they are and what they stand for.*

Sonia Nieto, 2003, p. 125

Every child deserves a good teacher, a teacher who can foster student learning in a safe and challenging classroom environment. The goal of teacher education, then, is not simply to let anyone who wants to become a teacher do so. Rather, it is to prepare new teachers who, like Kayla, are committed to teaching, are eager to learn how, and are well prepared to provide high-quality education to their students. Then, as they take on their first jobs, these new teachers can become part of that group of talented, committed educators who make student learning happen and in whose classrooms students thrive and grow. New teachers who can demonstrate these abilities also help raise the profile of teaching as a profession.

But what does it take to educate new teachers who are up to the task? How exactly do formal programs of teacher education operate? Is Kayla's experience typical of most teacher education students? What is the content and structure of teacher education? If you choose to become a teacher, what can you expect? How will your program draw on the prior knowledge you have already acquired about teaching? How have teacher education programs changed over time? What pressures, influences, laws, and regulations influence teacher education programs? How did the vibrant period of reform in teacher education, which began in the mid-1980s, affect how you will experience your own preparation today? These are some of the issues we will explore in this chapter.

## The Research Is In: Good Teaching Matters

In the 1990s, an influential set of research studies explored the importance of preparing high-quality teachers for our nation's schools. These studies concluded what should be obvious. If, year after year, children are placed in the classrooms of good teachers, their learning increases more than it does in classrooms of teachers who are not as highly skilled (Sanders & Horn, 1994; Wright, Horn & Sanders, 1997; McCaffrey, Lockwood, Koretz, & Hamilton, 2003). As simplistic as it sounds, if children have good teachers, teachers who consistently perform their professional responsibilities well, they learn better and they learn more. Plainly stated, good teaching matters. Today it is often said that good teaching adds value to students' lives.

Good teacher education is at the foundation of good teaching. In its 2003 report, *No Dream Denied: A Pledge to America's Children*, the National Commission on Teaching and America's Future identified six dimensions of high quality programs of teacher preparation. As Figure 3-1 illustrates, the authors of this influential report set high expectations for teacher education; these expectations raise important issues for understanding what teacher education is—and is not.

**Figure 3-1  Six Dimensions of High Quality Teacher Preparation**

The preparation of teachers entails far more than classes alone.

1. Careful recruitment and selection of teacher candidates.

2. Strong academic preparation for teaching, including deep knowledge of the subjects to be taught and a firm understanding of how children learn.

3. Extensive clinical practice to develop effective teaching skills, including an ability to teach specific content effectively, at specific grade levels, to diverse students.

4. Entry-level teaching support through residencies and mentored induction.

5. Modern learning technologies that are embedded in academic preparation, clinical practice, induction, and ongoing professional development.

6. Assessment of teacher preparation program effectiveness.

**Source:** National Commission on Teaching and America's Future. (2003). *No dream denied.* Washington, DC; Author. (p. 74).

For example, teacher education is not something that takes place solely within college or university classrooms. Instead, it takes place at the *intersection* of the formal classes you take *and* the PK–12 schools, and both are important in the preparation of new teachers. College or university classes are meant to provide critical, rigorous preparation in the content areas and in professional knowledge, supported by the use of technology. As you spend time in classrooms, you should be reflecting on what you are observing and on what you are doing, how that relates to what you are learning in your classes, and the new understandings you acquire as a result of your combined experiences. Most importantly, you should be thinking about what the students themselves are learning and what seems to account for their learning. What is the teacher actually doing? How is the teacher motivating the students? How is he or she using technology for instruction? You may only be working with one student as you begin, much as Kayla was doing in the first semester of her program. Even at this early stage of your professional development, this is your opportunity to get into the habit of reflecting on what you are doing and learning and to start taking responsibility for the quality of your own work as a teacher.

Teacher education is also not just something that happens *before* a prospective teacher takes a job in the schools. Rather, teacher education continues throughout your career, and especially in the first few years on the job, when novice teachers are consolidating their newly acquired skills. The quality of the work new teachers are able to carry out in those first few years depends on the quality of the support they receive from skilled veteran teachers.

Later on in this chapter, we will explore in greater depth the changing relationship between colleges and universities on the one hand and PK–12 schools on the other, in the service of improving teacher preparation. When both colleges and schools are strong and stable, the quality of new teachers who enter the profession should improve, which will ultimately improve the quality of teaching and the value it adds to student learning.

## Who Governs Teacher Education and Certification?

Teachers are prepared in public and private, large and small colleges and universities in every state. As does most responsibility for education in the United States, the responsibility for licensing individuals who wish to teach also falls to the states. Every state defines its own requirements for licensing teachers; these requirements reflect that particular state's values, beliefs, and expectations for what a teacher should know and be able to do.

The range of what is required is wide and varied (Darling-Hammond, 2001). Some states require a bachelor's degree to be completed before one can enter a teacher education program; others allow students to major in education at the undergraduate level. Some states place no limits on the maximum number of credits a student may take in professional education courses; others strictly regulate the number of professional credits allowed. States also vary in the levels and categories of licenses that they grant. Some states have a special license for middle school; others license teachers from grades 1 through 8 inclusively. Some states require a special license to teach early childhood students with disabilities; others license individuals to teach students with disabilities from kindergarten through twelfth grade. Some states have a bilingual education license, and others require a candidate to get a teaching license in general education before becoming a bilingual teacher. States also have different regulations governing how long a teaching license is valid and how a license is renewed. Public schools require that teachers be licensed; private schools may or may not require a valid state teaching license.

The purpose of licensing teachers is the same as that for licensing other professionals—to ensure a minimum level of acceptable performance. Licensure does not necessarily tell us that a teacher is good; it tells us, instead, that any teacher who possesses a license should be minimally "safe to teach" and "do no harm" (Roth, 1996). States work closely with colleges and universities to make sure that the teacher education programs they offer are consistent with the state's licensing requirements, and if they are, states approve teacher education programs at the various colleges and universities. When students graduate from a program approved by the state, they are eligible to apply for a teaching license in the field in which they have studied and are prepared to teach.

Because licensing teachers is a state responsibility, and because requirements and the types of licenses that exist differ from state to state, being licensed to teach in one state means that you will *not* automatically be recognized as a licensed teacher in another. Typically, when teachers are planning to move, they contact the state department of education in the state to which they are moving to find out whether their existing license is "portable" to their new state. They may have to take an additional course or two or an examination, or they may receive a temporary license rather than a permanent one, until they meet the requirements of their new state. When society was less mobile, the question of **license portability** was not a prominent concern. In today's mobile society, portability has become a much more important issue.

The Education Commission of the States, a nongovernmental organization concerned with education policy, maintains a list of state education agencies, with website information for each. This is an important resource as you consider where you will teach and what it will take to be licensed in that state (**www.ecs.org/ecsmain.asp?page=/html/statesTerritories/state_map.htm**). In addition, the National Council for Accreditation of Teacher Education (NCATE), which accredits teacher preparation programs at many colleges and universities, maintains a directory of the individuals in each state who are in charge of teacher licensing and a website that includes a section on becoming a teacher under its "Public" link (**www.ncate.org**). This section of the website, along with the "Interstate Agreement" link on the website of the National Association of State Directors of Teacher Education (**http://www.nasdtec.org**), provides information on agreements states have with each other for recognizing teaching licenses from other states. Although several states have such **reciprocity** agreements, the specifics differ from state to state regarding how easy or difficult it is to have a new state recognize your license from another state. As national efforts to set standards for high-quality teacher preparation continue to develop, greater efforts to increase the recognition of teaching licenses across state lines are taking place.

Your teaching license, however, is only as good as the preparation you receive. So although teacher education is governed at the state level, it is the quality of the program you attend that contributes to how well you are prepared. All teacher education programs minimally reflect the requirements of the state in which they are located. Beyond that, each teacher preparation program offers a unique set of courses and experiences. As long as they adhere to the basic structure and requirements set by the state for teacher education and are approved to recommend students for licensure when they complete their programs, programs can vary significantly within a state.

**Critical term**

**License portability.** The ease with which a valid teaching license from one state is recognized in another state.

**Critical term**

**Reciprocity.** Formal recognition that a teaching license that is valid in one state allows a teacher to be eligible to teach in another state.

At colleges and universities, the professional education of teachers typically begins with classes in the academic content areas they will teach to their future students. (Media Bakery)

# What Do Prospective Teachers Study?

As we have noted, the specific requirements for teacher education programs vary widely across the 50 states. Nonetheless, some broad similarities do exist in several of the general elements of teacher education programs. What tends to differ are the specific courses and the amount of coursework and related field experiences various programs require, as well as the values that define and unify them. The general elements of teacher education programs include: (1) subject matter content, (2) foundations of education, (3) pedagogy, and (4) field experience in PK–12 classrooms. Foundations, pedagogy, and classroom experience are all considered the professional part of a teacher's preparation and take place in a **professional school** on campus—that is, in a school, college, or department of education (SCDE). In college or university-based teacher education programs, you will take most of these courses before you are licensed to teach. In alternative route teacher education programs (see section on teacher shortages later in this chapter), most of your coursework will be taken while you are already teaching. But in either case it is important to understand the basic components of teacher education programs, how they are defined, and how they are related to form a sound program of teacher education.

## Critical term

**Professional school.** A unit of a college or university that prepares students for the professions, in contrast to the liberal arts and sciences, which prepare students in the academic disciplines, or subject matter.

## Subject Matter Content

To be effective, a teacher must know the subject that he or she is teaching. In recent years, there has been a great deal of criticism regarding teachers' lack of deep subject matter knowledge (Berry, Hoke, & Hirsh, 2004). A tangible result of this concern is a provision of the No Child Left Behind Act of 2001 which requires that teachers must demonstrate expertise in the subjects they teach in order to be considered "highly qualified." As a result, many states now require that, prior to being licensed, teacher candidates pass a test of content knowledge for the subject(s) level at which they will teach. The first INTASC standard also addresses the subject matter competence of beginning teachers, as do most other state teacher standards.

In colleges and universities, subject matter preparation usually takes place outside the professional school—that is, outside of the department, school, or college of education. Professors in the arts, humanities, social sciences, sciences, and mathematics prepare teachers in the content areas. If you are planning to be a high school teacher, you will take many courses in the specific content you are going to teach, for example, English or mathematics, in addition to professional preparation.

For those who are planning to become elementary school or middle school teachers, the situation is a little more complicated. Most elementary teachers are responsible for teaching all subject areas. This means that elementary teachers need to have a great deal of content knowledge across the various subjects that make up the elementary school curriculum. In some cases, particularly in the intermediate grades, elementary schools may adopt some form of departmentalization, where, for example, one teacher teaches mathematics to an entire fifth grade and another teacher teaches social studies to this same group of students. Often middle school teachers will teach at least two subjects, for example, social studies and English. Thus, elementary and middle school teachers usually must be prepared and tested in more than one academic content area, including English/language arts, science, social studies, and mathematics.

Traditionally elementary school teachers majored in education and studied, alongside their professional courses, a few academic content area courses in several of the academic areas in which they would teach. While this approach provided breadth, it has been criticized as part of the general concern that prospective teachers need greater rigor in and depth of content preparation. This criticism has led some teacher education programs to end the practice of giving an undergraduate degree in education. Instead, today an increasing number of SCDEs require a regular academic content area major. In such programs, professional courses are generally taken after the undergraduate degree is earned; a small number of introductory, pre-education courses and field experiences can be completed during the undergraduate program. In addition, some professional programs have adopted a five-year undergraduate model, with professional coursework and internships occurring primarily in the fifth year. Yet other institutions have retained the undergraduate major in education but increased the requirements in the academic content areas, which has the effect of reducing the number of elective courses a teacher education student can take.

The point of all of these changes is to strike a better balance to ensure that teachers have deep knowledge of both the academic subjects and methods of teaching. In whatever ways teacher education programs are packaged, preparation in the academic content area is crucial to good teaching. The current emphasis on content knowledge, however, has also fueled the movement to license teachers based only on their content knowledge (Berry, Hoke, & Hirsh, 2004), a topic we address later on in this chapter. Part of the challenge of designing good teacher education, of course, is successfully addressing both aspects of professional preparation.

---

### Your turn... *to reflect*

Some people argue that as long as an individual knows the content he or she is going to teach, that is enough preparation to take on the full responsibilities of a teacher. What are the benefits of this point of view? What are the pitfalls of this perspective?

---

## Foundations of Education

Another critical part of the professional preparation of teachers is the **foundations of education**, which focuses on the psychological, historical, philosophical, and sociological aspects of teaching. For example, in the realm of educational psychology, teachers need to know how children develop socially, emotionally, and cognitively, and what constitutes appropriate development at various ages and grade levels. They need to understand the various theories about how children learn. In addition, teachers need to understand and appreciate their students' different cultural, linguistic, and socioeconomic backgrounds and how to build on these backgrounds in order to foster student learning. They need to know how to recognize when student learning and behavior patterns depart from normal development, and when these departures are significant enough to suggest that a disability might exist. Finally, teachers need to understand the history of their field, the various philosophies of education, how they play out in schools and classrooms, and the role of education in our society.

Within teacher education programs, there is little argument about whether such basic knowledge is important. After all, if teachers do not understand normal human development, how would they design lessons that are appropriate for the age and developmental levels of the students they teach? How would they make informed judgments about a student who is experiencing problems and analyze whether those problems are a significant departure from normal development? If a teacher does not

**Critical term**

**Foundations of education.** The psychological, historical, philosophical, and sociological aspects of the field of education that are considered essential to the professional knowledge of all teachers.

Classes in pedagogy, or teaching methods, prepare aspiring teachers for what it means to translate content into worthwhile instructional activities for their students.
(Digital Vision)

understand the philosophy of education, how would he or she make an informed judgment about a new method or approach that represents a particular philosophy of education? What basis would a teacher have for claiming that a decision about what to teach and how to teach it, or how to respond to a particular student, is justified? Foundational knowledge in education is one area that distinguishes teaching as a profession. What has been controversial, however, is how and when these basic issues are addressed in programs of teacher education.

Until recently, courses in the foundations of education were usually taken at the start of a teacher education program, before students had field experience and had the opportunity to look at school from a teacher's perspective. Students often saw these courses as purely theoretical, with little application to the real world of teaching practice. Today issues relating to how children develop and learn, and the historical, philosophical, and sociological underpinnings of education, are discussed and learned with a view toward how they apply directly to the classroom. Therefore, today a foundations course might be offered toward the end of a teacher education program rather than at the beginning.

The relevance of these foundational perspectives is more likely to make sense to prospective teachers once they have gained some experience. For example, with regard to history, you might wonder about the history of organizing schools by grade and may want to know how long that structure has dominated. With regard to philosophy, you might begin to raise questions about what is included in the curriculum and the philosophy that led to those decisions. You might start assessing your own emerging philosophy of education against longstanding philosophies in the field. Wherever such course work and topics appear in programs of teacher education, they contain knowledge essential to the preparation of professional teachers.

## Pedagogy

**Critical term**

**Pedagogy.** The methods and activities teachers use to instruct their students.

The term **pedagogy** has its roots in the Greek word *paidagogos*, which means teacher. *Pedagogy* refers to the various methods and instructional activities teachers use to help students learn and is a critical part of their professional preparation. Academic content can be thought of as the "what" of teaching—what you teach. Instead, pedagogy refers to the "how to" of teaching, or all the ways teachers use to instruct students so that they can learn in a manner that will prepare them to live effectively in the world. Prominent among pedagogical knowledge and skills teachers need to learn include how to do the following:

● Engage students in learning.
● Organize classrooms for instruction.
● Make content meaningful for students.
● Connect content across academic areas.
● Connect students' life experiences to the content they are to learn.
● Use technology to make instruction more effective.
● Meet the needs of students whose first language is not English.
● Modify instruction to accommodate students with disabilities.
● Assess how well students are learning.

Teacher education students must also learn how to evaluate new pedagogies that develop during the span of their careers and decide if they are worthwhile given what they know about how children learn and how classrooms work.

In addition to these general pedagogical issues, prospective teachers must also learn teaching methods that are specific to the content areas they will teach. How one teaches science differs from how one teaches English or how one teaches mathematics. So in addition to the general idea of pedagogy, teachers must also possess what has come to be called **pedagogical content knowledge**. Pedagogical content knowledge is defined as knowing how best to present the knowledge in a specific academic discipline and being able to "view the subject matter through the eyes of the learner" (McDiarmid, Ball, & Anderson, 1989, p. 194). Teachers need to understand not only the content, but multiple ways to present content so that their students understand it well. For example, knowing about the Civil War does not mean a teacher necessarily has good ways of helping students understand the big concepts and historical explanations for that conflict. Furthermore, teachers must know the content well enough to be able to look at it critically—that is, to understand and present the content from multiple perspectives (McDiarmid, Ball, & Anderson, 1989). For instance, does a teacher present Columbus's arrival in the Americas as a story of discovery, or does he or she present the views of Native Americans toward Columbus, which emphasizes a story of conquest and oppression? (See Bigelow and Peterson's 1998 book, *Rethinking Columbus*, for a discussion of this issue.) A teacher has to know the subject matter well enough to present it in its full complexity, but also in such a way that students understand all of its dimensions and interpretations. Equally important, a teacher has to know the content well enough to answer the kinds of questions students at a particular age are likely to ask about the topic. All of these issues come under the concept of pedagogical content knowledge.

Classroom experience provides teacher education students with the opportunity to try out the knowledge and skills they are learning and to receive feedback on their performance. (David Young-Wolff/ PhotoEdit)

## Critical term

**Pedagogical content knowledge.** The ability to present academic content to students so they understand it well.

## Field Experience in PK–12 Classrooms

No teacher education program would be complete without some kind of direct experience in the classroom. Structured time spent in classrooms, or what is called *field* or *clinical experience*, provides a place to try out what you are learning, sharpen your skills of observation, and reflect on the decisions you are making about how and what to teach. The amount and degree of field experience are handled differently in different programs of teacher education. Some programs may require experience in the field each semester, with a gradual increase culminating in a semester- or year-long assignment that has traditionally been known as student teaching.

Historically, student teaching has been an unpaid field experience. Today there is some movement toward redefining this culminating experience as an internship or residency. In some teacher education programs, this experience may even be a paid position arranged through formal agreements between school districts and colleges or universities. Teacher education programs that have paid internships usually require at least five years to complete, with the fifth year sometimes counting toward the start of a master's degree. Finally, it should be noted that fast-track programs that emerged in the 1990s, known as *alternate routes* (which we will discuss in greater detail later in this chapter), usually immerse those who want to teach in classrooms as the paid teacher of record with minimal preparation, with formal study accompanying this initial teaching experience.

Another critical aspect of field experience is providing opportunities for prospective teachers to work with students and families whose race, ethnicity, or class differs from their own. In addition, field experience is usually the first time a prospective teacher begins to think about teaching from the perspective of the teacher rather than the student. It is the first time that teacher education students are looking at classrooms with a more critical, professional eye and identifying how what they are seeing relates to the professional concepts they are learning.

## Connecting the Elements of Teacher Education

It is important to understand how these four basic elements of teacher education programs relate to one another. Skilled teachers draw on their academic content, foundational, and pedagogical knowledge every day of their careers. The academic content a teacher education student learns is the basis the lessons he or she will learn to plan and implement, using pedagogical techniques that are a basic part of the teacher's professional repertoire. Learning to plan lessons is not useful if one does not have a place to practice those lessons, to reflect on how effective they were, and to consider how to improve lesson planning and lesson implementation in the future. Your understanding of the concepts and methods you are learning will grow over time, will be extended as you implement them in classrooms, and will be enriched by how willing you are to think about them deeply and what they represent.

### Your turn... *to review*

1. What are the four major components of a teacher education program?
2. What is the difference between *pedagogy* and *pedagogical content knowledge*?

It is not just learning technical skills—such as how to organize a reading group or how to make a long-range plan for teaching mathematics curriculum— that distinguishes good teachers. Learning to teach is not solely a matter of learning the methods of teaching. Instead, teachers must operate out of a strong sense of social responsibility to improving the lives of their students. As prospective teachers make choices about what to teach and about how to interpret the curriculum they are asked to teach, they need to bring their knowledge about the philosophy of education and education's place in our society to the choices they make about teaching. They must ask themselves why a particular topic is important, what the implications are of teaching that particular topic to their class of students, and how best to approach the topic in a way that engages the students and has meaning for them.

Learning to teach means making a commitment to using the knowledge and skills you gain in your teacher education program to help all of your students learn, reach for their dreams, and determine their own futures with confidence and pride. This means placing your students' learning and well-being first, using the professional knowledge and experiences you will gain to create exciting, motivating, and productive classrooms for those you teach.

# Reforming the Preparation of Teachers: A National Commitment

Today's teacher education landscape is complex, with some states requiring only an undergraduate degree to teach and others requiring study beyond the undergraduate years. Within states that have a minimum requirement of a four-year degree, some colleges and universities now require study beyond the undergraduate years in order to become a teacher. But whatever structure is in place, today teacher education programs are increasing the expectations they hold for their graduates. The current pressure to reform and improve the preparation of teachers goes back to the early 1980s, when American education was deemed to be in a crisis, as first presented in *A Nation at Risk* (National Commission on Excellence in Education, 1983). As we consider this issue, keep in mind the requirements for other professions in the United States. Those wishing to become lawyers or physicians, for example, must have an undergraduate degree before they pursue advanced training in professional schools, and rarely is the assumption questioned that graduate work is required to acquire the necessary knowledge and skills.

## Historical Note
### Normal Schools and the Early History of Teacher Education

Today's programs of professional education offer a dramatic contrast to the ways teachers were once trained in the United States. Although you may take it for granted that teachers should receive formal, professional education in order to carry out their professional responsibilities well, professional education for teachers did not always exist.

In the colonial period, teachers had no professional training at all. Children were most often educated at home, usually by male teachers who did this work on a part-time basis without any formal preparation other than their own schooling. Children who attended the earliest common schools in Massachusetts, which had short school terms, were usually taught by young male teachers who could take on teaching responsibilities as part-time, seasonal work. Finally, "dame schools" also existed, in which a female teacher might teach a group of students in her home.

It was not until the 1830s, when the education reformer Horace Mann successfully launched his campaign to create a publicly funded system of schools based on the emerging public school system in Massachusetts, that the professional education of teachers became a goal. Mann and his colleagues believed that if teaching were to become a true profession, teachers needed to have professional preparation. The idea of professional preparation for teachers in the United States was based on the European model of educating teachers in what were called **normal schools**. This term came from the French "*ecole normale,*" a school in which teachers learned the common practices, or "norms," of a teacher's work. The sole purpose of a normal school was to prepare teachers.

The earliest public normal school in the United States was the Lexington Normal School in Lexington, Massachusetts, which opened in 1839 with 25

**Critical term**

**Normal school.** The earliest schools that existed for the sole purpose of preparing teachers for their professional roles in the classroom.

NEW JERSEY STATE NORMAL SCHOOL, AT TRENTON.

Normal schools were the first formal institutions in the United States created for the sole purpose of preparing teachers. (Corbis Images)

female students. These were young women who had not attended high school but instead were going from their own grade school education into teaching. A few months later, a normal school at Barre, Massachusetts, opened for both men and women. As time went on, women made up the largest percentage of students in most normal schools (Herbst, 1989).

Once the idea of professional preparation for teachers was introduced with the appearance of these first normal schools in New England, similar schools began to crop up all over the country. Towns with the name Normal—such as Normal, Illinois—were where the state normal school was located. Normal schools usually had a campus grade school attached to them as a place for normal school students to practice teaching; the schools at both Lexington and Barre had such model campus schools. Normal schools were devoted to the art of teaching and to keeping an identity for the professional preparation of teachers separate from the tradition of higher education in the liberal arts and sciences. All of their resources were directed toward the education of teachers.

In some parts of the country, local residents lobbied for the establishment of a normal school. Often, especially in the Midwest, this effort was an attempt to locate an institution of higher education nearby for their children—not because they necessarily wanted their sons and daughters to become teachers but because they wanted higher education to be accessible in general. This created some tension between the goal of professional preparation of teachers and the goal of a more multipurpose institution of higher education. When normal schools were clearly devoted only to the preparation of teachers, there was no competition for resources with departments that taught other subjects. When a large institution had multiple purposes, however, the preparation of teachers could take a back seat to the traditional liberal arts and sciences. In addition, normal schools, especially those that focused specifically on preparation for teaching in elementary school, were often criticized for lacking a rigorous academic curriculum. Students who attended the early normal schools often did not have a secondary school education and thus did not have a good grasp of the content they were charged to teach.

Many of today's large state universities have roots in the normal school movement and began as two-year institutions that did not grant bachelor's degrees. The first coeducational normal school at Barre, Massachusetts, moved two years after its start to Westfield, became Westfield Normal School, then Westfield State Teachers College, and today is Westfield State College. Arizona State University in Tempe began as the Arizona Territorial Normal School, then the Tempe Normal School of Arizona, then Tempe State Teachers College, then Arizona State Teachers University, and, finally, Arizona State University. Large universities whose mission did not originate with preparing teachers also eventually began to offer teacher education programs. Often, however, the primary mission of schools, colleges, and departments of education in these institutions was to study education rather than to actually prepare teachers.

As normal schools evolved into larger, multipurpose colleges and universities, they were no longer exclusively dedicated to the preparation of teachers. Early proponents of normal schools often worried that when colleges and universities had to provide both professional preparation and a traditional education in the liberal arts and sciences, the focus on the preparation of teachers would be lost. Despite their roots in teacher education, this is precisely what happened at many large universities.

Once normal schools began to be transformed into multipurpose colleges and universities, a shift began in which those who wished to prepare teachers began to require an undergraduate degree, and usually a major in education for elementary teachers. For those who wanted to teach high school, a degree in the subject area and a minimum of pedagogy and foundations courses were usually required. This differed from the earliest normal schools, where no degree was granted at all and where students were often effectively getting the content of a high school education alongside learning how to teach. The shift to an undergraduate degree was gradual, and stand-alone teacher preparation programs existed in the United States, especially for elementary teachers, well into the twentieth century. In other countries, separate colleges for teachers continued to exist well into the twenty-first century. In New Zealand, for example, the last teachers colleges were incorporated into their universities as recently as 2006. As more and more normal schools became four-year institutions, an undergraduate degree in education became the most common route to becoming a teacher, and it was generally accepted that an undergraduate degree was sufficient for learning to teach.

Today teachers all possess at least a bachelor's degree and in many states, prospective teachers begin their professional education courses only after they have already completed a four-year degree.
(Media Bakery)

Responding to the challenge of improving the preparation of teachers, in 1986 a highly influential report called *Tomorrow's Teachers* was released. Prepared by the Holmes Group, a consortium of universities that had teacher education programs, *Tomorrow's Teachers* proposed an end to the undergraduate degree as the required degree for teaching. Instead, the report called for teachers to complete five years of higher education rather than the traditional four. This change, it was argued, would improve the quality of teacher education and also increase teaching's professional standing.

Consistent with today's concern for the academic preparation, *Tomorrow's Teachers* recommended that teachers should earn an undergraduate degree in an academic subject in which they would teach. It called for abolishing the undergraduate major in education. Alongside their academic majors, "pre-teacher education" students could also begin taking foundations courses in human development and begin some preliminary study of methods of teaching during their undergraduate years. A fifth year would be devoted to a full-time internship or residency in a school, accompanied by coursework in methods of teaching. This approach acknowledged that it takes deep knowledge *both* in academic content and methods of teaching to become a high-quality teacher. The report called on the nation's research universities to lead the way.

With the publication of *Tomorrow's Teachers*, a spirited national dialogue was initiated about the quality of teacher education and the entire profession of teaching. As a result of this report and the national debates that followed, some universities responded with five-year programs requiring an undergraduate degree in an academic major and not in education. Other universities kept their four-year programs but, as a response to the challenge created by the report, redesigned their programs to be more coherent and more rigorous.

Teacher education is still in the midst of reform—a reform that involves far more than decisions about which degree is appropriate for learning to teach. Today the debate over which degree will be required is part of a much larger dialogue about what it means to be a professional, and how to improve both the quality and the status of teaching in our society. The calls for reforms continued with the 1996 and 2003 reports of the National Commission on Teaching and America's Future; the improvement of teacher education programs based on higher expectations and higher standards is ongoing.

What does this reform movement mean for you as someone who is preparing to become a teacher? How does it affect your preparation and the world of education in which you will make your career? It means that you are becoming a teacher in a time of transition. Today's teacher education programs are being redesigned in response to past criticisms, are heeding the national call for improvement, and through increased rigor are challenging the age-old fallacy that teaching is easy and that anyone can teach.

At the start of the twenty-first century, a modest trend began to take hold among some universities to make the education of teachers a more prominent goal and to ensure that preparing teachers would become a universitywide responsibility and not just a function of the professional schools. The Carnegie Corporation of New York, for example, funded an initiative called *Teachers for a New Era*, whose aim is for university faculty to work together, across the liberal arts and sciences and education, to provide the highest quality teacher education possible (see **www.teachersforanewera.org**). It remains to be seen whether this trend will result in the allocation of more resources to preparing teachers nationwide and better alignment of the content and professional aspects of teacher education.

## From Coursework to Standards: Increasing Rigor in Teacher Education

Simply being *licensed* to teach—that is, meeting minimal expectations—is not itself a very high standard for the profession. That is why there has been a strong trend toward establishing standards of professional certification for beginning teachers—standards that raise the bar for completing your program and that are intended to improve the quality of your preparation so that you are confident, are ready to take your first classroom position, and can provide your students with a positive learning environment.

Until the early 1990s, most teacher education programs required that students seeking a teaching license pass a set of required courses and successfully complete a student teaching experience. Usually, the state defined these requirements in terms of the number of college credits needed in various courses, and the course requirements varied widely across schools, colleges, or departments of education. However, passing courses alone does not necessarily ensure that students are well prepared for student teaching or for the work of teaching. Today just taking and passing a required number of college or university courses is no longer considered sufficient for learning to teach.

## The Purpose of Standards in Teacher Education

As discussions on professionalizing teaching as a career heated up, one topic that received a great deal of attention was the need to set professional standards that beginning teachers would have to meet in order to receive a license to teach. These standards would define what *beginning teachers* should know and be able to do in order to gain a license to teach.

This is an important point; the standards you will be required to meet are not those for an experienced, veteran teacher, but rather represent what a good beginning teacher should know and be able to do. As such, standards begin to define what constitutes the **professional knowledge base** for good teaching (Reynolds, 1989). The document developed within the teaching profession to indicate what beginning teachers should know and be able to do was the 10 INTASC standards presented in Chapter 1.

As noted in Chapter 1, the INTASC standards were developed as a project of the Council of Chief State School Officers. As of July 2004, 37 states volunteered to join INTASC and adopt the INTASC standards (Council of Chief State School Officers, 2008). When states choose to adopt the INTASC standards, graduates of teacher education programs in those states have to demonstrate that they have met the 10 standards before they may apply for a teaching license. Thus, it is no longer only *input*—that is, the content of courses—that matters in preparing teachers; instead, it is the graduates' *output*, or what they are actually able to demonstrate that they know and can do. Teacher education faculty have to design their courses so as to address the standards and must assess their students' progress in the standards throughout their programs. This is a major change in the structure of teacher education programs and in the activities students must complete in order to be licensed to teach.

However, just because teacher education programs subscribe to a similar set of standards, this does not mean that all such programs are the same. A program that prepares teachers for rural schools will take up different issues and concerns than those that prepare teachers for urban schools. Programs might have different thematic emphases including, for example, technology applications, teaching for social justice, or a strong emphasis on arts integration and teaching. The standards provide a common set of expectations, but how those expectations are met and evaluated can differ significantly depending on the specific program.

## The Role of Portfolios in Standards-Based Teacher Education

Today teacher education students usually demonstrate what they know and are able to do through the development of a professional **teaching portfolio**. Such portfolios give teacher education students a chance to integrate what they are learning in their courses, in early clinical experiences, and in student teaching or internships in the schools. Portfolios allow students to document how well they are acquiring the appropriate knowledge, skills, and dispositions for teaching and the choices they are making about what it means to teach. Faculty members review these portfolios at specific points to determine whether students are making adequate progress toward meeting program standards and then provide feedback to students as a way of helping focus their continuing professional studies. Depending on specific program requirements, students may be called

**Critical term**

**Professional knowledge base.** The body of professional knowledge teachers possess that distinguishes them from what laypersons know about how to carry out the professional responsibilities of teachers.

**Critical term**

**Teaching portfolio.** A written or electronic compilation of documentation demonstrating that a teacher education student possesses the knowledge, skills, and dispositions to teach students well at the level of a beginning teacher.

Portfolios provide evidence of what new teachers know and have accomplished in their teacher education programs. (Media Bakery)

upon to discuss their portfolio orally as well as to present a written portfolio.

Portfolios that are used during teacher education to provide feedback to students and to gauge student progress are usually called *developmental*, or *working*, portfolios. Working portfolios give you a chance to reflect on your progress and to use feedback from your instructors to set goals for upcoming semesters. They provide you with a place to analyze the work your students have produced during your lessons to see how effective your teaching has been and to think about what you might need to change in future lessons. These working portfolios culminate in the preparation of a *showcase portfolio*, which is often used when interviewing for a specific teaching job at the end of a program. Showcase portfolios are not scrapbooks or collections of every exercise, assignment, and experience you have completed or every lesson you have taught. Rather, as the name indicates, they showcase your best work, the things you have accomplished during your professional preparation that best demonstrate that you are ready to take charge of your own classroom.

A good analogy for your showcase portfolio is that of editing a film. You need a lot of footage to make a good film, and a good editor selects the best footage and puts it together skillfully, with a definite plan in mind, to create the final product. To prepare a showcase portfolio, you will select your best work and put it together skillfully to demonstrate to potential employers just how good a teacher you will be. Specific requirements for portfolios will differ from program to program and from state to state. But the trend is to organize them according to the teacher education standards the state has adopted—which are often related to the 10 INTASC standards. Figure 3-2 illustrates some of the things you might find in a showcase portfolio.

A significant trend in portfolios is the *electronic portfolio*. This kind of portfolio has several benefits over "paper-and-pencil" portfolios. For example, elec-

---

**Figure 3-2    Sample Contents of a Showcase Teaching Portfolio**

The specific requirements for portfolios differ from program to program, but all portfolios allow teacher candidates to demonstrate their teaching ability.

Introductory letter to reader
Resume
Brief essay describing your philosophy of education
Examples of successful lessons taught in relevant subjects, including samples and analyses of student work completed as part of those lessons
Examples of an extensive teaching unit including student work samples
Videoclips of your teaching for any of the lessons you include
Examples of lessons that demonstrate your ability to connect the content to students' background experiences

Examples of your ability to work effectively with other teachers and education professionals
Examples of your ability to work effectively with your students' families
Examples that demonstrate your relationship with the local school community
Observations/evaluations of your teaching ability by supervisors and/or other teachers
Descriptions of any special contributions you made to the school or community that demonstrate your commitment to the profession
Description of special activities in which you have participated

tronic portfolios use software that enables students to share their work easily and regularly with faculty. Faculty can provide ongoing feedback that students can save and respond to as evidence of their professional growth and development throughout their preparation programs. Electronic portfolios need not be limited to static written descriptions of a particular lesson and its outcome; instead, prospective teachers can include videoclips of their actual teaching and their students' classroom performance. Finally, electronic portfolios are much more portable than traditional paper-and-pencil portfolios. Portfolios can be viewed on the Web, so that a school's entire interview committee can review evidence of the quality of the candidate's teaching before a formal interview. Electronic portfolios are usually password protected, which means that they will be available only to individuals who are identified by you as having permission to see them. Software for such portfolios can be developed by each institution of higher education, but many use commercial products such as Livetext© or TaskStream©.

As you think about how to demonstrate the knowledge and skills you possess, you need to make sure that you can indicate how the teaching you did during your preparation actually resulted in your students' learning. The standard for good beginning teachers is not just that they can plan lessons, but that teaching those lessons actually makes a difference in what their own PK–12 students know and can do. In addition to including lessons you have created, then, you will also need to include an analysis of samples of your students' work (see Girod, 2002) as well as some written discussion about your success in those aspects of the curriculum you had responsibility for during your final semester of student teaching or internship. (See the next Case in Point.) Prospective employers will not expect your students' results to rival those of a highly skilled veteran teacher, but a principal will expect that, during your own professional preparation, your teaching has resulted in real student learning.

## A Case In Point
### How Portfolios Demonstrate What Teachers Know and Can Do

Sometimes the value of a portfolio does not become clear until after it is completed. That was the case for Katherine Miller, a student who recently graduated from a four-year teacher education program that required a showcase portfolio organized according to the 10 INTASC standards. Katherine was asked to create an entry for each standard that included a definition of the standard, an artifact (e.g., a lesson plan and an analysis of related student work) she selected to illustrate the standard, and a written essay describing how the artifact she selected represented her ability related to the standard. She completed her final semester's internship in a sixth grade classroom in a middle school.

INTASC Standard 2 reads, "The teacher understands how children learn and develop, and can provide learning opportunities that support their intellectual, social, and personal development." To illustrate this standard, Katherine used a literacy technique called "Writer's Workshop." Students chose topics that were important to them related to the theme of their families' origins in the United States. Then they did research on the historical context of the time. They wrote initial drafts, and then revised and edited, working in pairs as peer editors. In her portfolio Katherine included her plans for the two-week period in which her students worked on this project, as well as a few samples of students' first drafts and completed papers. Her essay included a discussion of the importance of using topics that the students related to easily, her goal of creating a classroom where students understand and respect each other's origins, and the importance of developing good writing skills.

A month after completing her program, Katherine sent this e-mail message to one of her professors:

> Well, I just wanted to let you know how I'm doing, since you asked all of us to keep in touch with you. I know we all complained about the work we had to do for our portfolios. But as much work as it was, when I interviewed for a job here I was so glad I had done it. I could talk about my teaching and I feel like I really knew what I was about as a teacher—so all of those written reflections really paid off. I got the position in seventh grade. So tell the new group of interns that the work is worth it!

Your teacher education courses are extremely important in providing you with the knowledge and skills you need to be an effective teacher. They are complemented by your field experiences, which provide you with critical opportunities to connect what you are learning to real classrooms. The standards-based approach requires that you actively demonstrate your commitment, your knowledge, and your skills in the actions you have taken in those classrooms as you are learning to teach.

## Good Teacher Education: A Shared Responsibility between Schools and Universities

If teachers are to be prepared well, we have argued, they need both formal coursework and practical experience in schools that relate to one another. Neither alone is sufficient. Yet a longstanding challenge for those who prepare teachers has been how to link these two important yet different worlds. In what kinds of classrooms will you obtain your clinical experience? A significant area of transition in improving the preparation of teachers is redefining the relationship between schools and colleges or universities.

Preparing high-quality teachers, then, is a shared responsibility. When either partner—school or student—is weak, the power of teacher education is diminished considerably; when both clinical experiences and formal classwork are strong, the students in PK–12 classroom reap the benefits. Practicing teachers who are masters at their profession are needed to work alongside university faculty, with shared expectations for what it means to prepare new teachers well. This requires building strong relationships between teacher education programs and the schools.

In 1986 report *Tomorrow's Teachers*, the Holmes Group proposed that colleges and universities create special partnerships with a small number of public schools to transform them into places where people learned to teach—a parallel to teaching hospitals in the medical profession. The idea was to create an interdependent relationship between colleges and universities and schools such that improving the quality of one directly influenced improving the quality of the other. In other words, the reform of teaching in the PK–12 schools and the reform of teacher education would take place simultaneously. Schools such as these, designated as special places where teachers would learn to teach, were to be called **professional development schools**, or PDSs. In a PDS, for example, university classes might be held, faculty might conduct demonstration lessons in classrooms, and classroom teachers might co-teach university classes. University faculty might have

### Critical term

**Professional development school.** A public school that works in close partnership with a school, college, or department of education as a site for the simultaneous preparation of new teachers and improvement of teaching and learning for PK–12 students.

assigned time in the school, and skilled, veteran teachers might have part of their job description include working with and providing feedback to teacher education students. In a PDS, the pedagogy in use is meant to represent the "cutting edge" in teaching. The increase in professional development schools has led to a new professional organization, the National Association of Professional Development Schools (**www.napds.org**). In addition, the National Council on Accreditation of Teacher Education has developed a set of five standards for professional development schools (**www. ncate. org**).

This proposal marked a watershed in teacher education. Before the introduction of this concept, public schools and teacher education programs existed side-by-side, with little investment of one in the other. As teacher education programs grew larger, more and more places were needed for their students to practice within the public schools. A comfortable but benign relationship developed between the programs and local schools. Although solid relationships certainly existed between teacher education faculty and the classroom teachers who hosted their students, a serious investment in improving the quality of the whole school was not typical.

Historically, the exceptions were private campus lab schools that were often attached to normal schools. Over time, as local colleges and universities took over the responsibility for teacher education, campus lab schools tended to become educational "hothouses" that often enrolled children of local faculty members. Unlike these traditional campus schools, PDSs are designed to be public schools with typical student populations. The proposal for closer relationships launched in 1986 by the Holmes report was based on a serious, yet simple, idea: By improving the places where teachers learn to teach, we can simultaneously improve the places where children learn and strengthen the public schools.

## Your turn... *to review*

1. How does the requirement to meet a set of teacher standards change the experience of teacher education?

2. How do Professional Development Schools change the relationship between the college/university and the schools?

The emergence of professional development schools signaled the start of a new concept in education: school–university partnerships. By pooling resources, the best of both the schools and the universities could be brought to bear on improving education. Such partnerships result in closer relationships between practicing teachers and teacher education, and reduce the isolation of faculty and teachers alike. Different professional organizations may use different names for the concept of schools that partner closely with teacher education, and they may be called simply partner schools, professional practice schools, or some other similar name (American Association of Colleges for Teacher Education, 2005). Others have called for even more extensive partnerships, specifically in urban school districts, that require deeper engagement of colleges and universities. These critiques call on stakeholders in such partnerships to address not only teacher education, but the underlying inequities that exist in urban schools (Murrell, 1998) and system-to-system reform rather than just the reform of the selected professional development schools (Pugach, Post & Thurman, 2006). But whatever their name, the idea is that schools and universities are expected to work together for the collective good of teaching and teacher education. This idea is becoming more and more firmly established as part of the educational landscape.

## A Case In Point
### Working in a Professional Development School

Mary Ann Drew has been teaching high school biology for 15 years in an urban school district in Colorado. Her school was designated a PDS three years ago. Mary Ann had always had student teachers from the local university and had always been considered a model teacher for them and for her own students. When the plans for transforming the school to a PDS were being made, the principal and the university faculty member who was going to be the PDS liaison asked her if she would consider teaching one less class and working with the student teachers in a weekly seminar on site as part of her job. She would also have the opportunity to work directly with student teachers in all of the science classes.

Mary Ann loved teaching, but she had been looking for a new challenge. Although she didn't want to leave the classroom, she also knew she wanted to make a greater contribution to the profession. This seemed like a perfect opportunity. Her new position carried the title of "school–university liaison"; she would be considered a part-time faculty member at the university and, best of all, she could have an influence on more student teachers than just the one she could accommodate in her own classroom. Each week she met with the university science education professor to discuss student progress and plan the upcoming seminars. At the end of the year, Mary Ann was delighted with the progress all the science student teachers had made and was asked to continue in her special PDS role in the coming year.

## The New Role of Testing in Preparing Beginning Teachers—Help or Hindrance?

An additional development in the current trend to improve the quality of teaching is requiring teachers to pass standardized tests to demonstrate their knowledge. Whether or not the state in which you are being licensed requires such tests is important information that you should receive as part of your teacher education program.

Testing teachers was fashionable in the 1970s and is once again fashionable today. The most commonly used tests for teachers are the **Praxis™ tests**—three examinations for teachers developed by the Educational Testing Service (ETS, see **www.ets.org/praxis/index.html**). The Praxis website provides information on every state and territory that requires one or more Praxis tests. Like other such tests, Praxis is administered by ETS; applicants pay a fee directly to ETS to take the test, and cutoff scores are set by each state that requires the test. Table 3-1 summarizes the Praxis test series, including the Praxis III, which is a classroom assessment of beginning teachers based on observation rather than a written examination. Some states have developed their own examinations and do not use the Praxis tests. For example, Massachusetts requires the Massachusetts Test for Educator License (MTEL), Florida requires the Florida Teacher Certification Examination (FTCE), which tests professional education, subject area knowledge, and general knowledge.

The trend toward teacher testing is controversial. A test certainly provides another measure, in addition to a portfolio assessment, that program graduates have mas-

**Critical term**

**Praxis™ tests.** A series of tests and assessments for teacher education students and beginning teachers developed by the Educational Testing Service; in many states, passing scores on the written tests are required to apply for a teaching license.

**Table 3-1    Summary of Praxis™ Test Series**

Praxis examinations provide an additional assessment of teacher knowledge and skill.

| Test Name | Content Covered | Type of Test |
|---|---|---|
| Praxis I® | Basic academic skills in reading, writing, and mathematics<br>Three tests (states may require one or more of these): | Written, standardized |
| Praxis II® | • **Subject Assessments.** Measure subject-specific knowledge and general and subject-specific teaching skills.<br>• **Principles of Learning and Teaching (PLT) Tests.** Measure general pedagogical knowledge at four grade levels: Early Childhood, K-6, 5-9, and 7-12.<br>• **Teaching Foundations Tests.** Measure pedagogy in six areas: multi-subject (elementary), English, Language Arts, Mathematics, Science, and Social Science. | Written, standardized |
| Praxis III® | Classroom practice covering four areas:<br>• Planning for instruction<br>• Classroom environment<br>• Teaching for student learning<br>• Professionalism | Direct observation in classroom during first two years of teaching |

**Source:** Educational Testing Service. (2008). *The Praxis Series: Teacher Licensure and Certification.* Retrieved June 12, 2008 from www.ets.org.

tered a significant body of knowledge. Furthermore, many other professions have long required written examinations that students must pass to move on to higher levels of professional preparation. It is, in a sense, a rite of passage into a profession. Nevertheless, a test is just that, a written test. Whether it has applicability to a teacher's performance in the classroom has not yet been well established. It can also be argued that the standards-based approach, in which students demonstrate what they know and can do in an extensive portfolio, is a much more rigorous assessment than a test. If this is so, the argument goes, why is a test also needed?

Another issue related to testing those who wish to teach is that taking the test itself may become the sole gatekeeper into teaching in the absence of evidence of skill in the classroom working with students. For example, the federal government has provided millions of dollars of funding for the American Board for the Certification of Teacher Excellence (ABCTE), which has developed tests of academic content and professional knowledge that states can choose to adopt in place of formal teacher preparation. Founded in 2001, ABCTE bypasses formal teacher preparation altogether.

Unlike other established professions, where few would debate whether prior preparation is appropriate, questions about the value of formal preparation for teachers recur regularly. In reality most people who wish to teach really do need to learn how to do it well. If this is the case, what might account for taking the position that a test alone should be sufficient for gaining a license to teach? From a political perspective, enabling easy entry into teaching is consistent with a politically conservative national trend toward deregulation in general. By deregulating entry into teacher education, what may be perceived as simply bureaucratic requirements for becoming a teacher—translated into formal programs of teacher education—can be reduced to the barest minimum, namely, a test. From a practical perspective, requiring only a test keeps the door open to filling those classrooms where teacher shortages persist. From an economic perspective, if the status of the profession is maintained at a lower level than other professions by reducing or eliminating formal preparation, it may be easier to maintain the status quo in salaries.

Whatever the explanation, the value of teaching as a profession does not appear to be served well by failing to acknowledge both the professional knowledge and the skills needed to do the job well. If anyone can teach, then how important can education be? The stance that teaching is essentially an easy job that can be done well with no preparation does little to elevate the status of the profession.

## Philosophical Note
### An Essentialist View of Teaching and Teacher Education

One longstanding philosophy of education is known as essentialism. Those who subscribe to this philosophy believe that the main purpose of education is teaching students the basic, or essential, knowledge and skills they will need to function in the future. Essentialists are interested in defining what body of knowledge students should master; they place the learning of content at the forefront of the educational enterprise. One of the best known proponents of the essentialist philosophy of education was William Bagley (1874–1946).

In their book *Approaches to Teaching* (1986), the educational philosophers Gary Fenstermacher and Jonas Soltis used the term *executive approach* to convey the essentialist philosophy. In this approach a teacher's role is to organize the classroom for instruction and to manage students efficiently so that they will learn the core knowledge that has been identified as being important. In a strict essentialist philosophy, the teacher plays a central role in transmitting the core knowledge to his or her students and assessing their learning accordingly. Fenstermacher and Soltis believe that an appropriate metaphor for the essentialist philosophy is the school as a factory—a place where students move along the grades, learning what has been identified as the content for that grade. Because the teacher's job is defined as delivering the content efficiently to the student, an essentialist perspective on education can be regarded as a highly technical view of teaching.

The current emphasis on knowledge and skills in teacher education as represented by teacher testing is aligned with an essentialist philosophy of education. Testing places mastery of this knowledge at the forefront of what it means to learn to teach, much as the mastery of the content is at the forefront of a student's PK–12 years. The purpose of learning to teach is defined as mastering the core set of knowledge and skills as defined in the standards. As long as teachers demonstrate the knowledge and skills that are tested, they are considered to be educated teachers. Such tests were not developed, for example, for the purpose of examining teachers' motivations to teach, or their levels of interest in their students, their ability to work successfully with diverse students in their classrooms, or their creativity in getting students involved with the academic content.

Essentialism does not focus on how students use the knowledge they acquire but on how they acquire that knowledge in the first place. Making sure that students learn a basic, fundamental core of knowledge and skills as a result of being in school seems to be a legitimate goal. But the question one might ask of a teacher who is a strict essentialist is, "Is learning the content enough?" "Should there be more to education than just acquiring the basics?"

# Accreditation of Teacher Education Programs

We noted earlier that states approve teacher education programs at colleges and universities. We also described the role of teacher education standards in ensuring that each new teacher is well prepared. These represent different levels of scrutiny in the national effort to improve the quality of teaching. They are all designed to increase the likelihood that new teachers possess the knowledge and skills needed to take on their first teaching position and be successful as they do so. An additional level of scrutiny exists to ensure the quality of the teaching force. This is the *voluntary* accreditation of teacher education programs themselves.

## National Accreditation

The most prominent national organization that accredits teacher education programe is the **National Council for Accreditation of Teacher Education**, or **NCATE**. According to NCATE,

> professional accreditation of preparatory education programs is the bedrock upon which all professions (e.g., architecture, engineering, medicine, law) have built their reputations. It assures that those entering their respective fields have been suitably prepared to practice through assimilation of a body of knowledge and pre-service practice in the profession. Accreditation of schools of education indicates that the school underwent rigorous external review by professionals, that performance of a teacher candidate in the program has been thoroughly assessed before he or she is recommended for licensure, and that programs meet standards set by the teaching profession at large. (NCATE, 2003)

A second, smaller accrediting agency is called the **Teacher Education Accreditation Council**, or **TEAC**. So in addition to approval at the state level, teacher education programs can voluntarily submit to another review at the national level attesting to their quality.

NCATE assesses colleges and universities against a set of standards that form the framework for what high-quality programs of teacher education should look like. Though the dominant accrediting body for teacher education in the United States, NCATE is not the only one. The Teacher Education Accreditation Council, or TEAC, also grants accreditation. TEAC, is generally considered to be more flexible and less complex. TEAC also accredits individual education programs rather than whole college or university.

Why is voluntary accreditation an important consideration for teacher education? First, as noted earlier, all other major professions have voluntary accreditation. If teaching wants to reach the level of respect accorded to other professions, voluntary accreditation is considered to be an important part of the package. Second, institutional accreditation is essentially a professional "seal of approval." It is a signal to a future student that the college or university is recognized nationally as a

**Critical term**

**National Council for Accreditation of Teacher Education (NCATE).** The largest voluntary accreditation agency for teacher education programs nationwide.

**Critical term**

**Teacher Education Accreditation Council (TEAC).** A group that accredits teacher education programs.

program of high quality, has gone above and beyond the minimum standards required by the state education agency, and has met the more stringent expectations of the accrediting agency. Third, to meet the requirements of national accreditation, colleges and universities need to allot sufficient and appropriate resources for teacher education (for example, number of faculty, computer laboratories for instruction technology, or staff to supervise clinical experiences in the schools). Finally, some states extend reciprocity to graduates of NCATE-accredited colleges and universities in other states and recognize their teaching licenses as valid. Therefore, graduating from an NCATE-approved teacher education program increases the likelihood that your teaching license will be more easily portable should you move to a new state.

## Accreditation and Standards: The Road to Greater Professionalization?

In arguing for a national commitment to improving the quality of teaching, the National Commission on Teaching and America's Future portrayed the road to improvement as having three fundamental components: (1) standards should be established that each individual beginning teacher must meet in order to be licensed, such as the 10 INTASC standards; (2) college and university programs of teacher education should be accredited; and (3) a voluntary system of individual certification for experienced teachers should be set up. As you can see, the first two recommendations are directly related to what happens during teacher education. The National Board for Professional Teaching Standards (discussed in depth in Chapter 12) represents a voluntary certification system for experienced teachers.

Standards for beginning teachers, namely, the INTASC standards, raise the bar for what *individual teacher education students* know and are able to do. As a complement, accreditation raises the bar for *programs of teacher education and for what colleges and universities invest in teacher education*, and works to improve the quality of programs and the resources dedicated to the whole teacher education enterprise. Although there is support for these measures today, the following "Digging Deeper" discussion indicates such support is not unanimous.

### Digging Deeper
#### Do Standards and Accreditation Really Ensure Good Beginning Teachers?

Standards for beginning teachers (for example, INTASC) and accreditation for institutions that prepare teachers (NCATE or TEAC) are prominent fixtures in teacher education today. Together they set common expectations for the preparation of teachers. But how valuable are they in practice?

**Pro and Con:** Those who argue in favor of standards and accreditation believe that, without them, teaching will never reach the status of a full-fledged profession or be accorded the respect that other professions enjoy. Furthermore, those who favor a standards-based approach argue that in the past, teacher education probably did not set stringent enough goals for its graduates, and as a result too high a proportion of relatively poorly prepared students went into teaching. Standards and accreditation make demands on teacher educators to improve the quality of what they do. Supporters of standards and accreditation believe that the profession must take greater responsibility for the quality of new teachers and that achieving some level of agreement as to what beginning teachers should look like—through standards—is one way of reaching this goal.

Those who oppose standards and accreditation believe that they entail too much centralized control of teaching. Instead of allowing each program to define its own content, the INTASC and NCATE standards require a particular content as defined by their respective standards. Although this content may be important, it might also lead teacher educators to teach only to the standards (much like "teaching to the test" for school children)—and leave out what they believe to be other equally important content. Furthermore, opponents may describe the process as busywork that does not really result in good distinctions between stronger and weaker teacher education students, or stronger and weaker teacher education programs. A related argument against standards is that they are either so broad that they are not very useful in teaching, or so narrow that they fail to provide prospective teachers with a "big picture" of the purposes and commitments needed to teach well.

**The Nuances:** One way to think about standards is not simply as a set of discrete things to be learned, or as a list of narrow goals to be met, but rather as a way to think about the whole experience of learning to teach. By knowing what the standards are, students who are planning to teach can obtain direction for their professional studies. Standards invite teacher education candidates to participate in the discussion of what it means to teach, how to define various aspects of the knowledge they are acquiring, and how students' understanding squares with that of their instructors. Standards can provide teacher education students with a structure to think about their growth and development during professional preparation for teaching. Relating the standards to one another is one way to develop a better understanding of the standards and how they work together to result in growth and learning for PK–12 students under the responsibility of the classroom teacher.

For faculty members, standards can provide an opportunity to think about the quality of the various aspects of the program and identify ways to improve them. The quality of work students complete can be viewed as a reflection of how well standards are being addressed or whether they are being addressed in ways that are either too complex or too simple. When many students are having similar problems related to a particular standard, faculty can target that aspect of the program for improvement.

**Rethinking the Issue:** Used well, standards can help both teacher education students and faculty assess the quality of their work and improve it. Used poorly, they will not improve the quality of new teachers and will become just a hurdle to be overcome, a hoop to jump through. The argument may not be so much whether there should be standards, but what kinds of supports and resources are needed to create and implement sound, rigorous programs of teacher education that provide prospective teachers with ample feedback and critique to help them grow. To make a standards-based approach work well, all the stakeholders in teacher education, including students, SCDE faculty, and teachers in the PK–12 schools need to develop a shared understanding of what the standards mean in practice. It takes time, focused interaction, and sustained dialogue to make standards a meaningful force for change in teacher education. When they are treated as something to be met rather than an opportunity for program improvement, their usefulness is limited.

# Preparing Enough Teachers: Responding to Teacher Shortages

Whether there are enough teachers or not, every September America's students appear at the schoolhouse door. When teacher shortages exist, shortcuts are often taken so that each classroom has a teacher. According to Michael Sedlak (1989), this same trend has occurred throughout the history of teaching in the United States. Requirements are relaxed in times of shortages and made more stringent in times of surplus, when standards tend to be raised. When teachers are in demand, discussions of how to make teaching a more attractive profession to greater numbers of people are likely to take place.

## Shortages—A Cyclical Event in Teaching

After World War I, there was a significant teacher shortage related to the aftermath of the war and the declining number of males interested in teaching. This was followed by a surplus in the 1930s. Another shortage occurred during World War II, predictably, but this shortage lasted well into the 1960s—followed by a surplus in the 1970s. Today, in the twenty-first century, we are experiencing a shortage of teachers in certain fields (mathematics, science, special education, and bilingual education) and in certain communities, especially in urban schools. Today's shortage is also a product of the availability of more and different career paths for women and individuals of color—for whom teaching was historically one of the only ways to get ahead economically. So the traditional source of new teachers—women and minorities—is shrinking as well. According to Richard Ingersoll, however, there are actually enough teachers to fill the nation's classrooms. The problem is that licensed teachers do not stay in teaching for the long term, which forces a constant turnover in teachers, especially in hard-to-staff schools in urban and rural communities (Ingersoll, 2001).

In the current teacher shortage, as has happened in earlier eras, states and school districts are finding ways to fill classrooms with people who hold the title of teacher, whether or not they are fully prepared to teach. Districts and states can choose to confer emergency teaching licenses, requiring in some cases that those who hold such licenses enroll in a teacher education program. They may also grant emergency licenses to teachers who are certified, but in a field other than the one in which they are teaching—an "out of field" teaching assignment. Another way to fill empty teaching positions is to create *alternate route* teacher education programs—programs that place individuals in classrooms with limited professional preparation prior to doing so.

## Alternate Routes: A Solution to the Shortage?

**Critical term**

**Alternate route.** Programs that place teachers in classrooms with little formal teacher preparation prior to taking on a job. Teachers instead learn to teach on the job, often with the support of an experienced mentor.

**Alternate route** programs are often seen as shortcuts to enter the profession of teaching. Since most states require at least a bachelor's degree in order to teach, alternate routes are typically designed for individuals who already have a bachelor's degree. Alternate route programs provide a very brief period of preparation before an individual is placed in a classroom in the role of a teacher—with full teaching responsibilities. The philosophy of alternate routes is that individuals with more life experience, who have already completed an undergraduate degree, are ready to take on classroom responsibilities. Many people think of alternate routes as the "sink or swim" approach to learning to teach, a form of "on-the-job" training, where individuals learn how to teach at the same time that they carry out the full responsibilities of a teacher. Today, all 50 states, plus the District of Columbia, have some form of alternate route to teacher certification (National Center for Alternative Certification, 2007).

Once they are in the classroom, those who come to teaching via alternate routes are usually mentored by experienced teachers whose job it is to provide guidance, knowledge, support, and feedback. The amount and quality of mentoring, however, differ across programs. Alternate route programs are especially popular in urban and rural areas, which tend to experience chronic teacher shortages. *Teach for America* (**www.teachforamerica.org**) is an alternate route program that was developed specifically for recent liberal arts graduates who might want to devote two years after graduation to teaching in hard-to-staff schools in urban and rural communities—but who usually do not decide to teach for the long term. Alternate routes have also been developed for other special groups. Former members of the military, for example, can become teachers through a Department of Defense program called *Troops to Teachers* (**www.proudtoserveagain.com**).

Yet other alternate route programs have been developed specifically to increase the diversity of the teaching force and to recruit primarily from educational assistants and paraprofessionals in urban schools. These individuals are often members of racial and ethnic minority groups who live in the communities experiencing the greatest shortages. The idea of establishing alternate routes for people who already work and live in urban communities is that as teachers these individuals may be more likely to remain and teach in their communities. This outcome would reduce the teacher turnover that often plagues urban school districts and could increase the number of teachers whose race, ethnicity, or first language match those of their students.

Alternate route programs have been the source of much controversy in the past two decades. Can alternate route programs, many of which require little or no formal preparation before taking responsibility as the classroom teacher compared with college and university-based programs, ensure the quality of their graduates?

Those who enter teaching from another career, whether or not through an alternate route, may anticipate a smooth transition. Once they hit the classroom, however, they can be surprised by the challenge of the work and the energy and specialized knowledge and skill teaching requires. Those who feel secure in their content area may quickly learn that knowing content is not enough and that how to communicate that content in a way that actually helps students learn that is, how to teach the content, is harder than it seems. Individuals with strong skills—the ones we call "naturals"—may have an advantage over those whose skills need greater development. But in reality the "naturals" are few and far between, and they, too, still require time to solidify their skills and learn from their experience. Within the profession there is agreement that teachers need to demonstrate their knowledge and skills—from whatever path they enter teaching.

Not all alternate route programs are the same (Zeichner & Conklin, 2005). Some are stand-alone programs that are run entirely within school districts; others are district–university partnerships that require substantial coursework in teacher education. Some are programs that place individuals who have undergraduate degrees directly into classrooms with no prior preparation and expect these individuals to "make it," whereas others require formal classes, and sometimes enrollment in college or university-based teacher education once the teacher is in the classroom, in addition to any mentoring support that might be provided. In such expanded programs, the traditional difference between university-based

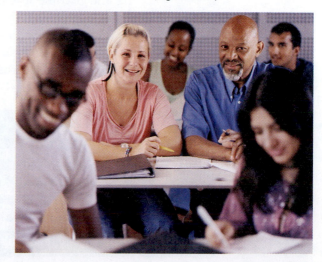

Alternate route programs often attract older, nontraditional students into the profession of teaching.
(Digital Vision)

and alternate route programs may begin to diminish. Some alternate route programs are more selective than others in terms of who is admitted. With regard to assessment, some require assessment based on state standards for teacher education and the use of portfolios for assessment, and others do not. When alternate route programs are selective, require serious coursework, and demand that students demonstrate their knowledge and skills based on accepted standards of practice, they would seem to have much greater promise than programs that simply put warm bodies into classrooms and expect them to do well. To date, no clear research evidence exists showing that teachers who enter via alternate routes are more effective than teachers prepared in college and university-based programs (Zeichner & Conklin, 2005). A well regarded study of new teaching in New York indicates that teachers prepared in alternate route programs are less likely to stay in teaching than those prepared in college or university programs. (Boyd et al., 2006)

In April 2008, on the 25th anniversary of the report titled *A Nation at Risk*, a new report, *Democracy at Risk: The Need for a New Federal Policy in Education* (The Forum for Education and Democracy, 2008), addressed the teacher shortage directly:

> "In many states, schools serving the highest-need students experience a revolving door of inexperienced and untrained teachers who undermine both student learning and school progress, contributing to the long-term failure of both. Meanwhile, higher-achieving countries that rarely experience teacher shortages have made substantial investments in teacher training and equitable teacher distribution in the last two decades. These countries routinely prepare their teachers more extensively, pay them well in relation to competing occupations, and provide them with time for professional learning. They also distribute well-trained teachers to all students—rather than allowing some to be taught by untrained novices...
>
> While we worry about the supply of doctors, engineers, and technicians, we seem to ignore the supply of teachers who will educate the highly skilled workers and thoughtful citizens of the future. We lack a national policy to increase the supply of good teachers, or to distribute good teachers to all our children. When we do not tend to those who will nurture our young in the skills and abilities that make engaged citizenship possible, we put our future as a democracy at risk." (pp. 16–17)

By whatever path teachers enter, their preparation should be rigorous and should be measured against high standards of professional practice. The profession of teaching benefits from having people from all walks of life enter its ranks. It is a worthy goal to make it possible for career-changers, young idealistic college graduates, as well as those who have always seen teaching as their calling, to study teaching and become teachers. Nevertheless, when we consider the issue of alternate routes to teaching, the age-old question must be asked: in any other profession, would people be allowed to practice without any prior preparation? One of the major recommendations in *Democracy at Risk* is to provide high quality teacher education to every prospective teacher, at government expense, with a year on clinical training in a PK-12 school connected to a university.

## Your turn... *to reflect*

By raising the standards for both traditional and alternate routes, the assumption is that the quality of all teachers will improve. Is this the only important issue relative to alternate routes? What are the implications of the fact that alternate route teachers work primarily in urban or rural communities, in high-needs schools with high-needs students? Suburban districts are less likely to hire alternate route teachers. What does this practice convey about the values of our society regarding education?

# REWARDS AND CHALLENGES

## From Teacher Education to the Classroom

Adriana Balistreri
*Milwaukee, Wisconsin*

I learned to teach in a program for urban schools at my university. The main reward from learning to teach in the urban education program is that I felt fully prepared to teach in the inner city schools of Milwaukee. I was prepared for several reasons. The first is that I was aware of the demographics of the students who attended most of the local urban schools. For example, I knew that many of my students would be living below the poverty line and receive free or reduced lunch. The reward for me is that I never lowered my standards for my students because of this. Due to my rich experience with urban teaching during my teacher education program, I was ready to teach my students with the same expectations that I would teach students at a higher socio-economic status. I did not have any biases going in and I knew, based on my field work and student teaching experience, that my new students could achieve at these high standards. Another reward is that I did not have any biases when applying to the local urban school district that I have observed that a lot of people have. My students are just as educated and enthusiastic to learn as any other population.

I love my class and my students have truly taught me more than I would have imagined. I love teaching in an urban school. Also, another reward is learning about other cultures and exposing my students to other cultures as well.

For me a challenge as a new teacher working in urban schools is teaching writing. Writing has been a challenge for me because most of my students write the way they talk and I am working on how to help my students, most of whom are African American, to learn to write in Standard American English. This is actually one of the goals for writing in my district, so my students have been working very hard on this. What I am really trying to say is that I am working hard, too—to learn how to help my students' move back and forth between their dialect in their speaking and writing and Standard American English in a respectful way, which is something we discussed in my teacher education program But I am also challenged to help them move from the language of text messaging, which has a big impact on my students' lives, to more formal writing. ●

# After Formal Teacher Education: What Comes Next?

It is tempting to think of teacher education as everything you do before you actually get into a classroom of your own and begin teaching—that once you graduate, you are done with your professional education. As we have already noted, however, learning to teach is a career-long commitment. Depending on where you are in your career, your professional learning takes on a different meaning—all for the purpose of ensuring that the students you teach learn well under your guidance.

Michael Huberman, a scholar who studies the professional careers of teachers, has identified five stages in the teacher's career (Huberman, 1993, p. 13).

● Years 1–3:   Beginnings, feeling one's way

● Years 4–6:   Stabilization, consolidation of a pedagogical repertoire

● Years 7–25: Diversification, activism, and reassessment

● Years 26–33: Serenity

● Years 34–40: Disengagement

Historically, few distinctions were made between beginning and experienced teachers. New teachers essentially have the same responsibilities as veteran

teachers from the day they start teaching; there is no staged entry into the profession. Although Huberman identified the *Beginnings* stage as a unique period in a teacher's development, only recently has this stage been recognized in more formal ways, with special designations and with special supports in many states and school districts. This *Beginnings* stage has come to be known as the **induction** period, which usually refers to the first three years of teaching and begins right after formal teacher education when, in Huberman's terms, you are "feeling your way."

During the first few years of teaching, or the induction period, novice teachers benefit greatly from working with a skilled, experienced veteran teacher, often called a mentor. (Jonathan Nourok/ PhotoEdit)

## Critical term

**Induction.** The first three years of a teacher's career, which are recognized as years requiring special support to help consolidate the beginner's skills.

## Induction—The First Stage of Your Career

Research on the beginning stages of a teacher's career has identified the induction stage as a critical period of learning—one that has the potential to solidify the knowledge and skills beginners have learned during their formal preparation and to help keep them engaged in their work (Paine, Pimm, Britton, Raizen, & Wilson, 2003). Beginning teachers' abilities are far from perfect; it is natural that they need time, experience, and guidance to strengthen their skills. Particularly during induction, teachers need special support to make the transition from a prospective teacher to an early career teacher who gains the confidence and commitment to make teaching a multiyear commitment (Johnson, 2004).

Support when you take your first position is essential precisely because as soon as you hit the classroom, you assume full responsibility for teaching. This reality can be daunting for new teachers. Once you take your first job, you must learn the ropes of the school and district and navigate them effectively, you must learn the curriculum, you must organize and plan every bit of instruction, you are on your feet and front and center with students all day long, you interact with your students' families, you deal with problems, and you must participate in all phases of the school's activities—before, during, and after school. Without support during induction, you can easily see how the first years of teaching can be overwhelming.

In some schools, principals make accommodations for new teachers, making sure they have an experienced "buddy" teacher to whom they can go for support. But buddy teachers also have full-time teaching responsibilities and are available for consultation only before and after school, and usually on a voluntary basis. This limits the range and depth of support they are able to provide. Although such buddy arrangements can be important, they are neither extensive nor systematic enough to support the needs of novice teachers.

Instead, induction is now formally recognized as the first stage of a teaching career, and districts and states have begun to create formal programs of support for new teachers by experienced teachers who are skilled in their work and whose major responsibility is to provide assistance to new teachers. Expert veteran teachers who support beginning teachers during this induction phase of the career are usually called **mentors**.

## Critical term

**Mentor.** A highly skilled, experienced teacher who has specific responsibility for supporting teachers during the induction phase of the career.

**How Does Mentoring Work?**  How do formal programs of mentoring compare with just having a reliable buddy to go to for help? Formal mentoring programs usually free up experienced teachers for part or all of the day so that their work supporting novice teachers is a formal responsibility and not another task added onto a full-time teaching job. They are often assigned to a group of novices and have a formal "caseload" of new teachers to visit. Because they have either reduced or no teaching responsibilities with PK–12 students, mentors can visit the classrooms of new teachers during the school day, observe their teaching, and do demonstration teaching in areas in which the new teacher may lack confidence or just want to see a method modeled. They may be able to take over a new teacher's classroom periodically for short periods of time so that the new teacher can observe another skilled teacher in the building or district. Mentors do not evaluate new teachers; they provide professional support.

Currently 25 states offer some kind of state supported mentoring program (Quality Counts, 2008), but only two states offer new teachers a reduced working load to ease their transition into their careers (Editorial Projects in Education Research Center, 2008). Because education is a state level responsibility, mentoring programs can differ substantially from state to state. In some mentoring programs the mentor teaches part-time and mentors part-time; in others mentors are released from their classroom responsibilities completely.

Not just any experienced teacher can be an effective mentor. Effective mentors should first and foremost to be good classroom teachers—they need to have a legitimate base of successful teaching experience on which to draw. They also need to have the ability to communicate the knowledge that underlies their experience to new teachers. It is not necessary, nor is it realistic, for all experienced teachers to become mentors. But in the absence of teachers who are able to mentor, it is difficult to retain new teachers in the profession, and to support them as they focus on how best to create a successful learning community for their students.

Mentoring new teachers is a relatively new development in the teaching profession. Acknowledging the place of mentoring in the teacher's career changes the traditional view of teaching as a flat career—that is, a career where your job on the first day you are hired is, essentially, the same as your job the last day you teach. By identifying induction as a distinct stage in a teaching career, and by developing mentoring as a response, we begin to redefine teaching as a graduated—rather than as a flat—profession, with new supports for early career teachers that should help retain them in the profession, as well as new opportunities for qualified, experienced teachers as they move through the more advanced stages of their careers.

## A Case In Point
### Mentoring a First-Year Teacher in an Urban School

Malcolm Silver completed his teacher education program in secondary English in June and landed the job he wanted teaching freshman English at a local urban high school. He had grown up in this community and was ready to give back. He had student taught in the same district but had not had any experience in the school where he would begin his career. He was asked if he wanted to participate in the district's mentoring program. At first he was not sure whether or not to volunteer, but after talking with his peers, he realized that having the extra support and help might come in handy.

Come in handy, indeed. Although Malcolm had had a very successful internship teaching freshman and sophomore English, when he got to his classroom he was completely overwhelmed. On his first planning day he found a stack of directives from the principal and the department chairperson, he had trouble finding the right number of books for his classes, and, since he was also a homeroom teacher, he had to learn a new computer system for taking attendance and lunch count. That afternoon, in walked Dale Freeman, his mentor. Dale had been a successful English teacher for 10 years in the district and now served as a full-time mentor to 12 of the district's new high school English teachers.

Dale helped him sort through the administrative tasks, showed him how to maneuver the computer system, and worked with him to arrange the classroom. Malcolm kept thinking: Will I ever get through this and think about what I will actually be teaching? Dale and Malcolm decided to meet for two hours the next morning to talk about only one thing: the curriculum. They planned out the first teaching unit, and Malcolm asked Dale to come and observe his classroom during the third week of classes. He didn't want to wait too long for the expert feedback Dale could provide. Dale visited frequently, and during the second and third units came in to demonstrate some writing techniques with Malcolm's students.

Three months into the school year, Malcolm talked about his relationship with Dale. "I would have been lost without my mentor. I thought he would be there to help me through the details, the how-to's. But as time went on, I realized that he was helping me on two levels—with the piddly, daily details and the big, important things about teaching. He always asked whether or not the students were learning, what struggles I was having meeting their needs, what changes I felt comfortable making in my original plans. He never criticized me, but he was pretty straightforward about giving me feedback and asking me questions about why I was doing what I was doing with the curriculum. When I was preparing for my first set of parent conferences, he walked me through the organizational issues and then asked, 'So, have you thought about the one or two most important things you want to talk to parents about? You only have 20 minutes with each family. What's really important here?' It was always like that— we moved between my daily needs and the big ideas. I was well prepared to be an English teacher, I knew a lot coming in and had a lot to draw on. But putting it all together for the first time was more demanding than I realized or anticipated. Dale kept me going—and I'm on my way now."

## Your turn... *to review*

1. To which stage of a teacher's career does the term *induction* refer?
2. How does mentoring change the way the career of teaching is defined?
3. Why is it important that mentors are not evaluators of new teachers?

Mentoring has special importance in alternate route programs because teachers who come to the career via this route usually have not had prior field experience and coursework in how to teach. Mentors take on the major responsibility of educating alternate route teachers while they are on the job. Without intensive mentoring, alternate programs are not really programs of professional preparation at all—but rather are "sink-or-swim" approaches to staffing classrooms.

Today mentoring programs are widely recognized as a critical means of retaining a quality teaching force. However, the financial resources required to launch and sustain these programs have not yet caught up with need. As a result, in some states, even though mentoring is mandated, it is an unfunded mandate. When this is the case, school districts may try to cobble together some sort of support for new teachers—but it may look more like the buddy system we described earlier in this section than like true mentoring. Nonetheless, the concept of mentoring during the period of induction—and its importance to the profession of teaching—are now well established.

**How Is Induction Related to Tenure?**  In most districts, tenure is granted after three successful years of teaching. Historically, tenure has been granted almost automatically as long as a teacher has not committed flagrant violations of ethics. New teachers are usually evaluated once a year by their building administrators. These evaluations are formal documents indicating the quality of teaching.

With the advent of induction, new teachers get much greater levels of feedback from their mentors—who do not serve in an evaluative position like that of the building administrator. Instead, the mentor provides consistent critique and ideas so that new teachers are constantly reflecting on their work and taking action to improve their classroom practice. This development provides the potential for tenure to take on greater meaning and reflect greater levels of achievement in a context of professional support for new teachers.

## Renewing Your Teaching License

Your first teaching license is not likely to be your last. Most states require that you renew your license regularly, but much like your initial license, what it takes to renew a license differs from state to state. Historically, many states issued lifetime licenses that required no renewal, but this has become increasingly rare.

Consistent with the general reform of teacher education, renewing one's teaching license is changing significantly. Many states are now instituting graduated licenses, with an initial license followed by a permanent or professional license that is granted based on a teacher's performance during the induction years. In the state of Wisconsin, for example, an initial educator license is granted for a maximum of five years, during which a novice prepares a Professional Development Plan focused on growth in a selected number of the INTASC standards and documents that professional growth. Once you have met the requirements for a professional license, your state may have an option for you to achieve an even high status as a master teacher—that is, recognition as a highly skilled teacher—either through meeting state requirements or meeting the voluntary requirements for certification by the National Board for Professional Teaching Standards (see Chapter 12). Wherever you receive your initial license, it is critical that you understand the requirements for renewing your initial license and take responsibility for making sure you meet whatever professional development criteria your state sets.

# Why It Counts in a Diverse World

Whether learning to teach is an easy or a difficult task is at the root of many long-standing philosophical debates about teaching, and these debates take many forms. One aspect of this debate is the question of whether teachers are "born" or "made." "She's a natural," we might hear someone say. If teachers are "born," not "made," the argument goes, then why require teacher education in the first place? Or if mastering content is all that is necessary to make a good teacher, why not allow anyone with a degree in one of the basic academic subjects, or with a passing score on a test of content, to teach—and forgo formal teacher preparation altogether?

Teacher education has undergone rigorous scrutiny over the past 25 years and continues to do so. As a result, you are entering teacher education at a time when more is expected of those who wish to teach. Consequently, your preparation should be much richer and more closely connected to the PK–12 schools. Your formal preparation as a teacher provides you with the knowledge and skills to do your job well. What you gain from your professional preparation—both in college or university classes and in the schools—is what distinguishes you from others who believe that teaching is an easy job.

But more important than all of the technical skills you acquire is your ongoing commitment to the students you will teach. Remembering why you are there, why you have chosen this particular profession, and how you can help your students grow in the time you have with them are the most crucial considerations. Fundamental to this focus on your students is the commitment to learning to teach all of your students across all racial, ethnic, language and socio-economic groups so that each child has the opportunity to succeed in life. That is why learning to teach well is so important and why the eyes of the nation are on the goal of improving teacher preparation.

## CHAPTER SUMMARY

### The Research Is In: Good Teaching Matters

How to improve the quality of teachers is part of an ongoing national debate about education and the schools. The preparation of teachers is an essential part of the goal of improving education. Reports calling for higher standards in teacher education suggest that there is wide agreement that every child deserves a good teacher and that good teaching makes a positive difference in the lives of children.

### Who Governs Teacher Licensure?

States set the requirements for becoming a teacher. Then, colleges and universities develop programs that encompass these requirements and seek state approval for their programs. Requirements differ among the states, which explains why teaching licenses are not necessarily portable from state to state without meeting additional requirements.

### What Do Prospective Teachers Study?

The four major components of most teacher education programs are subject matter content, foundations of education, pedagogy, and field (or clinical) experience. Although different teacher education programs put varying emphases on each of these components, all of them are considered important in preparing good teachers. In the past, these components were taught in isolation. Today there is a much greater effort to apply and integrate them throughout a prospective teacher's education.

### Reforming the Preparation of Teachers: A National Commitment

Part of the reform of teacher education is raising the level of education that is required to teach. Whereas the traditional degree is the undergraduate degree, today an effort is being made to move teacher education to graduate degree status. One important reason for this trend is to recognize that it takes both a solid education in academic content areas and solid preparation in the foundations and methods of education to learn to teach well. Four years is a limited time in which to learn all of these things.

### From Coursework to Standards: Increasing Rigor in Teacher Education

Simply completing coursework at a college or university has not been effective in assuring that new teachers possess the knowledge and skills to teach effectively. One of the most significant changes in teacher education is the development of professional standards for knowledge, skills, and dispositions for beginning teachers. Those who wish to teach must not only pass courses; they must also demonstrate that they meet the standards set for the profession. This demonstration usually takes the form of a professional portfolio that includes a written explanation and justification of some aspect of practice teaching related to a particular standard and accompanying documentation that represents the standard.

### Good Teacher Education: A Shared Responsibility between Schools and Universities

Schools and universities are redefining their relationships so that both teaching and teacher education benefit. The major means of reaching this goal is the creation of what are called Professional Development Schools—schools that are specially designated as places teachers learn to teach. These schools have been developed to parallel the concept of a teaching hospital in the field of medicine—a place where the newest methods are used in the most effective ways both to help PK–12 students and provide better models of teaching for new teachers.

## The New Role of Testing in Preparing Beginning Teachers—Help or Hindrance?

Requirements for testing teachers are primarily a response to the criticism that teachers are not well prepared to teach the academic subjects for which they are responsible. Testing teachers often includes not only tests of content, but also tests of basic skills and professional knowledge. Tests may help elevate the status of teaching since many other professions require passing a test prior to granting a license to practice. One outgrowth of the emphasis on testing teachers is that in some cases and in some states, passing a test is being accepted in lieu of formal preparation to teach.

## Accreditation of Teacher Education Programs

Programs of teacher education can voluntarily be considered for national accreditation to attest to their quality. The largest agency that accredits teacher education programs is the National Council for Accreditation of Teacher Education, or NCATE. NCATE sets standards for what college and university programs should do in terms of content, process, and the resources a postsecondary institution devotes to the preparation of teachers. Some states are beginning to grant reciprocity of teaching licenses to graduates of NCATE-accredited institutions in other states.

## Preparing Enough Teachers: Responding to Teacher Shortages

The country experiences shortages of teachers on a cyclical basis. Because every classroom requires a teacher, shortages usually cause gatekeepers to the profession to relax requirements and issue emergency teaching licenses. Another approach is the development of alternate routes to teacher education. Alternate routes are quicker ways to obtain a teaching license, usually by participating in an abbreviated period of preparation and learning on the job. With the rise in professional standards and expectations for increased quality of teaching, many alternate route programs are coming under greater pressure to make sure their graduates meet the same standards as those who complete university-based programs.

## After Formal Teacher Education: What Comes Next?

Learning to teach does not end with the completion of a professional program. Instead, it is recognized that new teachers enter a period of induction—defined as the first few years of teaching—when they require mentoring to strengthen their skills and gain confidence in their ability to foster student learning. Mentors are experienced, skilled teachers who not only work well with children and youth, but who also model and communicate what it means to teach well. Induction support is becoming a fixed feature in the life of new teachers.

## LIST OF CRITICAL TERMS

License portability (61)
Reciprocity (61)
Professional school (62)
Foundations of education (63)
Pedagogy (64)
Pedagogical content knowledge (65)
Normal school (67)
Professional knowledge base (71)
Teaching portfolio (71)

Professional development school (74)
Praxis™ tests (76)
National Council for Accreditation of Teacher Education (NCATE) (79)
Teacher Education Accreditation Council (TEAC) (79)
Alternate route (82)
Induction (86)
Mentor (86)

# EXPLORING YOUR COMMITMENT

1. *on your own...* Interview a graduate of your teacher education program or of another local program who has just completed his or her first year of teaching. What advice does this individual have for you that will help you take full advantage of your teacher education program?

2. *on your own...* Find out what kinds of official supports are available to first-year teachers in districts where you are interested in working. Compare your findings with those of your peers who wish to teach in other districts or states. Ask yourselves questions like: Are mentors available? What kind of experience do the mentors have? How often will they be available? Will they be able to come into my class, watch me teach, and provide me with feedback and ideas for improvement? What other induction supports does the district offer to new teachers?

3. *in the field...* Interview a mentor in a school district in your area. What kinds of support has that mentor provided to new teachers? What aspects of support does this mentor believe are most beneficial? What does the mentor consider to be his or her greatest contribution to new teachers?

4. *in the field...* Interview a teacher who is in his or her first three years of teaching. What kinds of mentoring support, if any, did this individual receive? How did the presence or absence of a mentor relationship affect this person's work and commitment to teaching?

5. *on the web...* Log onto the website for the state education agency in the state in which you think you would like to teach. Use the United States map in the States and Territories link for the Education Commission of the States to locate your state (**www.ecs.org**). What two or three important pieces of information did you learn?

6. *on the web...* Log onto a website for one of the student organizations affiliated with various professional organizations for teachers. What resources does this website provide for you? Two appropriate websites include: **www.nea.org/student-program** and **www.cec.sped.org/student**.

7. *on the web...* Check the teacher education program at your college or university to see whether it is accredited by NCATE or TEAC. Whether it is or not, log onto the NCATE website (**www.ncate.org**). Look over the entire site, but in particular review the Unit Standards, which define what colleges and universities are supposed to do to be recognized as having quality teacher education programs. From looking at this website, what does NCATE consider to be the most important aspects of teacher education?

8. *on your own...* Make a place to store assignments and materials from your work in field experiences in schools for your portfolio. Save, save, save!

9. *on your own...* Prepare a statement of your current philosophy of teaching. What do you think accounts for your current philosophy? Save this document and revisit it at the end of each semester to determine how your philosophy is changing and why.

10. *in the research...* Read the 2004 article "Are We Creating Separate and Unequal Tracks of Teachers? The Effects of State Policy, Local Conditions, and Teacher Characteristics on New Teacher Socialization" by Betty Atchinstein, Ogawa Rodney T., and Anna Speiglman (*American Educational Research Journal*, Fall 2004, Vol. 41, no. 3, pp. 557–603). This article describes the first-year experiences of six new teachers and compares them across schools. How closely do their experiences match with those you anticipate having in your first position?

## GUIDELINES FOR BEGINNING TEACHERS

1. Save your professional textbooks and use them for reference. They are likely to come in handy when you are struggling to solve a teaching problem.

2. Check out online supports. Your district's website may offer important information, but several organizational and commercial websites that are designed for teacher support are accessible on the Internet. Try these for a start:

   **www.ed.gov/pubs/FirstYear**
   **www.mightymentors.com**
   **www.nea.org/classroom/index.htmlx**
   **www.aft.org/teachers/teachertoteacher.htm**

3. Take advantage of whatever mentoring support your district offers you. If requesting a mentor is voluntary, be sure to do so. Plan to participate in new teacher support meetings or workshops your district may offer. The first year of teaching is inevitably difficult, and it is appropriate to need and get such support.

4. Contact your former professors for ideas—whether they are close or far away, whether they are professors in your professional courses or professors in the academic content areas. They are usually happy to assist you.

5. If you are facing a problem and do not feel comfortable asking someone in your school for assistance, ask someone else. Do not *ever* feel like you have to "go it alone."

6. Contact other graduates from your program. But be selective—you don't want to align yourself with whiners and those who are discontented. Find supportive colleagues who are committed professionals and can really help you.

## THE INTASC CONNECTION

All of the INTASC standards address what new teachers should know and be able to do when they complete their initial preparation and enter the classroom as licensed teachers. In this chapter, we have emphasized several kinds of knowledge and experiences you will have as you learn to teach. INTASC Standard 1 addresses knowledge of academic content. Standard 1 states: *The teacher understands the central concepts, tools of inquiry, and structures of the discipline(s) he or she teaches and can create learning experiences that make these aspects of subject matter meaningful for students.* Important indicators included in this standard are:

● The teacher effectively uses multiple representations and explanations of disciplinary concepts that capture key ideas and link them to students' prior understandings.

The INTASC standard that most directly addresses foundational knowledge is Standard 2. It reads: *The teacher understands how children learn and develop, and can provide learning opportunities that support their intellectual, social, and professional development.* Indicators include the following:

● The teacher understands that students' physical, social, emotional, and moral development influence learning and knows how to address these factors when making instructional decisions.

● The teacher is aware of expected developmental progressions and ranges of individual variation within each domain (physical, social, emotional, moral, and cognitive), can identify levels of readiness in learning, and understands how development in any one domain may affect performance in others.

The INTASC standards that address pedagogy include Standards 4, 5, and 6. Standard 4 states: *The teacher understands and uses a variety of instructional strategies to encourage students' development of critical thinking, problem solving, and performance skills.* An example of a relevant indicator includes:

● The teacher carefully evaluates how to achieve learning goals, choosing alternative teaching strategies and materials to achieve different instructional purposes and to meet student needs (e.g., developmental stages, prior knowledge, learning styles, and interests).

Standard 5 states: *The teacher uses an understanding of individual and group motivation and behavior to create a learning environment that encourages positive social interaction, active engagement in learning, and self-motivation.* Examples of relevant indicators include:

● The teacher creates a smoothly functioning learning community in which students assume responsibility for themselves and one another, participate in decision making, work collaboratively and independently, and engage in purposeful learning activities.

● The teacher organizes, allocates, and manages the resources of time, space, activities, and attention to provide active and equitable engagement of students in productive tasks.

Standard 6 states: *The teacher uses knowledge of effective verbal, nonverbal, and media communication techniques to foster active inquiry, collaboration, and supportive interaction in the classroom.* An example of a relevant indicator includes:

● The teacher knows how to ask questions and stimulate discussion in different ways for particular purposes, for example, probing for student understanding, helping students articulate their ideas and thinking processes, promoting risk taking and problem solving, facilitating factual recall, encouraging convergent and divergent thinking, stimulating curiosity, helping students to question.

If you are in a state that follows a different set of teacher standards, find the state standards that must closely relate to the INTASC standards discussed here.

## READING ON...

Bullough, R. V., and A. D. Gitlin. (2001). *Becoming a student of teaching* (2nd ed.). New York: Routledge Falmer. Explores learning to reflect and think as central elements in the preparation of teachers, including several samples of reflections from teacher education students.

Griffin, G., and Associates. (2002). *Rethinking standards through teacher preparation partnerships.* Albany: State University of New York Press. How different colleges and universities are putting standards-based teacher education into practice locally.

Johnson, S. M. (2004). *Finders and keepers: Helping new teachers survive and thrive in our schools.* San Francisco: Jossey-Bass. Susan Moore Johnson and her colleagues describe their findings on what new teachers say they need in order to stay in the profession.

Rice, J. (2001). *Teacher quality: Understanding the effectiveness of teacher attributes.* Washington, DC: Economic Policy Institute. A brief summary of research conducted on the link between various components of teacher education and the quality of teaching.

Sloan, G. D. (2004). *Tales out of school.* Portsmouth, NH: Heinemann Press. Sloan reflects on her years as a teacher from the perspective of a deep commitment to how teachers make a difference in the lives of their students.

## Guiding Questions

- What was education in the earliest schools in the colonies like?

- Whose interests did these early schools serve?

- What vision for education in a democracy did Thomas Jefferson pursue?

- When did universal public education emerge?

- What did early education look like for racial and ethnic minority groups?

- What was the effect of industrialization on education?

- What was the efficiency movement?

- What is the purpose of a philosophy of education?

- What are the major philosophies of education?

# Learning from the History and Philosophy of Education

# 4

Kayla Jones—Martin is about to successfully complete her teacher education program. Her internship in sixth grade is just about over and she has been interviewing for positions in elementary schools. Having taught across all ages during her preparation, she is hoping to find a job in third or fourth grade, years where she likes the fact that the students have the ability to be independent but are not yet so embroiled in the throes of early adolescence.

One of the last things Kayla has to do as she completes her teaching portfolio is to revise the philosophy of teaching statement she was required to keep throughout her program. As she looked over her earlier versions, she thinks about how full of clichés her first drafts were, with statements such as "I want every child to learn," "All my students should have 'hands-on' experiences," and "Children should enjoy school." Now, with four semesters of experience behind her and the reality of setting up her own classroom looming ahead, Kayla is meeting with one of her instructors, a faculty member named Barbara Lee, to talk about her philosophy statement.

"I don't think my basic beliefs have changed," Kayla began, "but what I want to write about now is *why* those statements are important and talk about the actions I can take every day to make them actually happen. I want to make sure I connect my big ideas with my teaching practice—or at least what I hope my practice will look like."

"That's a really important development for you, Kayla," Barbara said. "Your philosophy isn't really very useful unless you are thoughtful about what it means as you plan your teaching. But you also need to be thinking about how those big ideas fit together to help guide you in your overall approach. Why is it important to you that every child learn? How do you really get your students to enjoy learning and why is that so important? What do you really mean by 'hands-on learning' and how does that fit into a vision of students who are enjoying learning and for whom learning is important?"

"So I think you're saying that I need to have some kind of unifying idea that is bigger than just a bunch of disconnected statements, even if those statements are an important part of what might go on in my classroom. What do they all mean?"

"Well, that's what a philosophy of education should do, right? It should help shape and give meaning to your teaching and give you a way to explain why you do what you

*Anyone who has begun to think places some portion of the world in jeopardy.*

John Dewey

do. You've had a lot of really good experiences this semester during your internship and you should be able to include lots of examples of lessons or units you actually did, or interactions with students, that show your philosophy in practice. But to start, try writing out that big idea. You might be surprised to find that it even matches with some of the big ideas in educational philosophy and history that you studied when you first got here."

When you step into your first classroom as a teacher, the immediacy of your situation and the challenges you face will be unique in their meaning to you. And yet, as a teacher you will also be working in a longstanding, time-honored profession with a profound history and an enduring set of philosophies—philosophies that often compete with one another.

Because you are anxious to get started and get on with learning what life in the classroom will be like for you as a teacher, stopping to think about the history of education and the different philosophical approaches to it may not be the first thing on your mind. Nevertheless, it is worthwhile to take time out and do some reflecting on how education came to be the way it is today, what struggles teachers and educators have faced in the past, which ones recur and which are new, and how the various philosophies in education either co-exist or vie for power in the schools and the curriculum. The history and philosophy of education are two of the multiple sources of knowledge you can draw on as your own development as a teacher moves forward.

## Historical Origins of American Education

The philosopher George Santayana (1905) is perhaps known best for his famous and oft-quoted warning, "Those who forget the past are doomed to repeat it." For you as future educators, this is a significant motivation to read about how education has developed in the United States. The path to our 21st-century public school education system is a confounded, complicated, and contested one. The educational enterprise, even from the beginning of our nation, has always had a purpose and an aim. But whose purposes has it fulfilled? And what aims? Depending on students' gender, ethnic or racial background, or socioeconomic class, the purpose, aim, and outcome of education has often differed widely throughout history.

Contrary to popular myth, in the United States, the same education has never been delivered to everyone. The social, economic, and political context determined, and still does, the level of education students receive. As you learn about the history of education, you will begin to appreciate how many issues that are controversial today, for example, religion, curriculum, funding for schools, and more, have been wrestled with in the past.

The need for a society to educate its young is universal to all cultures. *How* we educate is what is in question. For it is in the *how* education takes place that ideologies are revealed. Who should be educated and at what level is generally decided by those in authority. Questions about *who* and *what* should be taught are accepted by the society as it seeks to maintain itself as a culture. For example, during colonial times the sons of the privileged were given access to formal education that included reading and writing. This ensured a level of knowledge and understanding for those who were destined for leadership in courts, politics and state government, and the church.

## Early Educational Efforts in the Colonies

Massachusetts Bay, New Hampshire, and Connecticut created schools that taught children to read and write so they could worship and read the scriptures. Hence, school interconnected church and the curriculum. In 1642, the Massachusetts Bay Colony passed a law that children should learn to read the Bible, lest they be ignorant of the laws of God. Religion was the reason for many Colonists to leave England and travel to America in the search of freedom to worship. For people to worship and continue in their beliefs, being able to read the Bible was considered essential.

Therefore, the first colonial schools were developed to assure that the new generation would sustain its religious beliefs and acquire the necessary basic skills to do so. Literacy was important to these new Americans in order to assure religious salvation, and reading and religion formed the basis of the curriculum. For every child in New England, some type of schooling was available. Although citizens were obligated to pay some of the expense, those too poor to pay could also send their children to school. This was an enlightened vision considering the year was 1635.

Even though, in these earliest days of the country, schools were generally available to those who wanted education, what was taught, the reason for schools in the first place, how teaching occurred, and who had access to schools differed depending on the local area. For example, African slaves in the south received no schooling except as necessary to do the labor their owners assigned them.

For boys and, in some cases, girls, New England's **dame schools** were the precursor to the primary school. Here older women, such as widows and housewives, would teach children the three R's, frequently in the kitchen area of their homes. If girls were given any education, it was at a dame school, and likely it was in sewing and homemaking skills. Rudimentary mathematics and numbers were not viewed as having importance in the early years, at least not as important as reading and some writing and it was predominantly boys who were taught this. School could last for a week, several months, or a year, depending on the needs of the community.

In all of the colonies, some boys were offered an education beyond what the Dame school and their parents could teach them. Schools for reading and writing were supported by parents, who paid some fees as they did if their children attended Dame Schools. Early textbooks for these schools were called Primers and were steeped in moral and religious teachings for boys to read, copy, memorize, and recite.

For those privileged to do well in school and who came from families that could afford to continue their child's education, **Latin Grammar schools** were founded

### Critical term

**Dame schools.** Education that was delivered in the homes of women, usually consisting of the basics of reading and writing.

### Critical term

**Latin Grammar schools.** Early schools that followed a classical curriculum consisting mainly of Latin and Latin texts, with some Greek.

In dame schools, women took children into their homes and charged a fee to teach them the three R's.
(The Art Archive/Kobal Collection)

The Boston Latin School, founded in 1635, followed a classical curriculum and educated only males until the nineteenth century.

(Boston Globe/Landov LLC)

and focused on a classical curriculum defined as the study of classical languages and literature (primarily Latin and some Greek). The boys who attended Latin Grammar schools continued into the first college, Harvard (founded in 1636), and onto leadership roles in the community, in the state, and often in government.

Learning how to read, then, was considered essential, and great importance was placed on it. If people could read, then they could both participate in their religion and be knowledgeable about the laws of the commonwealth. So early on, there was a confluence of religion, education, and leadership concerns to assure that children were educated. Whether it stemmed from religion, notions of civic participation, or preparation for leadership through attending Latin Grammar schools and the first college at Harvard, education in some kind of formal program was important to those who settled in the colonies, and particularly in New England. Education continued to be viewed early on as the best defense against sin, as a way to preserve religious belief, and as the measure of a citizen's ability to participate actively in the governance of his or her community. People who lived in the New World valued learning as a way to improve themselves and participate in civic life together. By the early 1700s, for example, such an emphasis had been placed on education that the early New England colonists exceeded the literacy rate compared to those who lived in England (Cohen, 1974).

The middle colonies, New York, Pennsylvania, New Jersey, and Delaware, took a different path than New England. People in the middle colonies came from groups such as the Irish, Scots, Danes, Germans, and other White European groups. These people being less homogeneous in terms of religion and politics than their northern counterparts, their schools reflected this diversity. Denominational schools based on the myriad religious beliefs, e.g., Quaker, Jewish, Catholic, and different Christian sects, were created so religious groups might teach their particular religious beliefs and practices to their children.

In the southern and middle colonies, schools were generally run by private authorities who were granted this status by the government; in contrast, schools in New England were more often set up by some kind of governmental authority (Butts & Cremin, 1953).

## Expanding Education, Literacy, and Civil Society

However, unregulated and mainly voluntary schools as represented in the early Colonial era were insufficient to meet the needs of a growing new society, one which increasingly would rely on common understandings among its citizens. By the mid-1700s, academies began to develop, with a shift in the curriculum from the classical study of Latin to a broader curriculum that included mathematics and science, as well as practical subject matter such as agriculture or mapping and geography. These academies became increasingly popular, and because their mission and curriculum was larger in scope began to push out Latin Grammar schools. Academies filled an important function in a new country that was developing rapidly in formal institutions such as government, trade, and economics, and required an active, participatory, and literate populace.

Benjamin Franklin first proposed the idea of an academy in 1751, initiating this shift to this more multi-faceted, practical curriculum: The Academy of Philadelphia. The following courses were advertised at the time the Academy opened in 1751:

- writing, arithmetic, and mathematics (merchants' accounts, geometry, algebra, surveying, gauging, navigation, astronomy, drawing in perspective, and other mathematical sciences)
- natural and mechanical philosophy
- Latin, Greek, English, French and German; history, geography, chronology, logic, and rhetoric (University of Pennsylvania Archives, n.d.)

Franklin argued that all subjects should be taught in the English language to all students. Moreover, he advocated for a practical nature of learning to be included, skills that would assist the young person later in life in his daily life and work.

For Franklin, education for the new society should include knowledge that would serve citizens in their endeavors. It made sense, then, to have English as the medium of instruction and to emphasize mathematics and science (then called *natural philosophy*) as the core curriculum. The schools he advocated were called **English schools** to differentiate them from Latin Grammar schools. The central struggle in creating academies was the struggle between a classical curriculum and a practical curriculum. Should the school curriculum include traditional, classical subjects or should it include the day to day wisdom and practical skills people use in their lives? Controversies over what constitutes a worthwhile curriculum continue, as we shall see in Chapter 5, and are debated about vehemently just as they were when Franklin introduced his ideas. To read more on this, see the original manuscript titled *Idea of the English School, Sketch'd out for the Consideration of the Trustees of the Philadelphia Academy* at **http://dewey.library.upenn.edu/sceti/printedbooksNew/ index.cfm?TextID=sermon_education&PagePosition=10**.

Latin Grammar schools, mainly in New England and the Middle Colonies, with some in the South, continued to evolve into these more broadly based English grammar schools. These academies were privately funded and were primarily schools for young men whose families had means, wealth, and education to support their sons going to college. As with Latin Grammar schools, English grammar schools prepared young men in mathematics, philosophy, history, geography, rhetoric, and, of course, the English language arts of literacy, recitation, writing, grammar, and so forth. They often still included, but were not limited to, classical studies in Latin and Greek languages. For a view of one student's experiences see the original document, *Memoirs of Alexander Graydon*, a student from 1760–1766 in the Academy school in Philadelphia, at **http://www.archives.upenn.edu/histy/features/ 1700s/acad_ curric.html**. This excerpt from his diary reveals an acute sense of which of his tutors were "good" teachers, and how life at this school among the students revolved around sports as well as the subjects they were learning. When Graydon left school by his own volition at the age of fourteen, he had "passed through Ovid, Virgil, Caesar and Sallust, and was learning Horace and Cicero."

## The Jeffersonian Ideal of Education

The colonists viewed education as important for maintaining their culture, including religious beliefs and traditions, but after the Revolutionary War, a now independent people had to think about the purposes of education as it applied in their new circumstance of being free from the domination of England and King George IV. Among those who were collaborating to form a new government, Thomas Jefferson argued that only with an educated populace could a free government and

**Critical term**

**English schools (academies).** Schools that followed a practical curriculum rather than a classical curriculum focused solely on Latin and Latin readings.

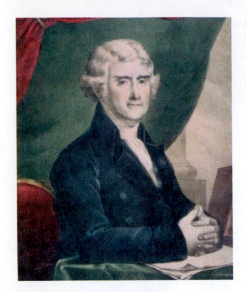

Thomas Jefferson, the third president of the United States was an early proponent of public education as a means of ensuring a well-informed citizenry able to maintain a democracy. (The Art Archive/Library of Congress/The Picture Desk)

foundation of democracy be secure. In order to participate in a self-governing democracy, its citizens had to be educated. When Jefferson stated that an informed populace safeguarded democracy, his notion rested on people having access to school, being able to learn to read, write, and, through reading and thinking, judge the worth of political ideas. Education, then, had an explicit political purpose in terms of defining and enacting the democracy.

For Jefferson, the integration of education and government became the theme of many of his writings. He submitted the following amendment to the Constitution to Congress during his State of the Union address on December 2, 1806:

> Every government degenerates when trusted to the rulers of the people alone. The people themselves are its only safe depositories. And to render even them safe, their minds must be improved to a certain degree. . . . An amendment to our constitution must here come in aid of the public education. The influence over government must be shared among all people. (as cited in Padover, 1939, p. 87)

This amendment did not pass Congress. Jefferson continued his efforts to secure public funding for education in his home state of Virginia. But why would the Congress in 1806 not pass an amendment that funded public school education for all citizens in this new nation? One reason was that the new Congress was composed of representatives from all of the thirteen new states, all of which had had experience with local control of education. To give over to the central government the responsibility to fund education in all of the states was to also give over control of what form schools, teachers, and the curriculum would take.

## The Contested Problem of the Control of Public Education

By the early 1800s, citizens were used to being able to determine what type of education they wanted. Most early schools that played a role in education were essentially private schools from the earliest part of the nation's history. We have seen that private schools were used to maintain religious beliefs, and different denominations of Christianity supported their own schools and curriculum. Privileged, wealthy parents who wanted a highly traditional, classical education for their children were willing to pay for special tutors privately or for schools that charged high tuition to provide children of the wealthy an education built on classical European traditions—even if some poorer students occasionally attended through charitable means.

But there was another reason for maintaining private control of schools beyond seeking a high classical or religious curriculum. Some citizens did not wish either a religious curriculum or a high classical one for their children. Instead, they sought alternative forms that suited what they thought their children needed in order to succeed in their lives. This laissez-faire approach to education paralleled growing economic freedoms (Butts & Cremin, 1953). The emergence of the common school challenged the core of educational practice up until this time.

## Your turn... *to review*

1. What was the driving reason for establishing the earliest colonial schools?
2. What was the major difference between Latin Grammar schools and the English school model?
3. Define Thomas Jefferson's view of the role of education in a democracy.

# Common Schools

Even as schools sprang up around the country, education was still a luxury. For most families, the daily demands of life dominated and family members had to attend to responsibilities in order to maintain necessities. Since schools were locally controlled, regions differed in how many schools were supported and in the quality of service they provided. But by the end of the 18th century it was becoming clear that not only was money needed to fund education, but the increasing population of immigrants, working people such as farmers and urban workers, brought to the forefront the desire to achieve some commonality of experience. Schools were viewed as providing a way to bring people of different backgrounds into a common experience within a participatory democratic philosophy.

In the proclamation of the Northwest Ordinance of 1787, education was viewed as being of utmost importance for the settling of the new territories which included what is now Ohio, Indiana, Illinois, Michigan, and Wisconsin. And it was viewed, in the Jeffersonian manner, as a public good. Act 3 of the Ordinance made it clear that education was integral to the society and stated: *Religion, morality, and knowledge being necessary to good government and the happiness of mankind, schools and the means of education shall forever be encouraged* (Constitution Society, 2008). Schools were seen as so important that they were subsidized by the government and supported by local taxes in order to ensure a literate public and public leadership. Specifically, land was set aside as part of the Northwest Ordinance in each township for a public school (for the original document, see **http://www.loc.gov/rr/program/ bib/ourdocs/northwest.html**).

In 1828, Andrew Jackson was elected president with a popular vote and a public demand for equality of poor and working-class people. Among the demands of the voters was access to education. It was in this context that the notion of the common school and universal education emerged.

**Horace Mann.** Horace Mann (1796–1859) is often spoken of as "the father of American education." Mann envisioned a universal public education available to all children in the country. He believed passionately that education would bring about equality, and that through a public school system available to all, the ideals of the Constitution could be realized. Through a system of public schools, all children, rich and poor, would be offered a primarily sectarian education to enlarge their view of themselves and others, and so, to build a harmonious society. Through the gateway of education, equality for all would be available and poverty would cease. Furthermore, Mann was convinced that schools should teach a common set of beliefs and moral values so as to promote harmony among different groups. Mann believed that only social good would come of public school education, and so he dedicated himself to reform education as it existed up to that point, which was characterized by a growing divide between who could afford school and who could not.

The **common school movement**, which had its start in Massachusetts, where Mann was secretary of the Massachusetts Commission to Improve Education (the state board of education), did not win easy approval. Imagine how forward thinking Horace Mann and others such as Henry Barnard of Connecticut were to foresee a robust public school system, funded by the government and available to children of both the rich and poor. The common school movement in the early part of the 1800s

## Critical term

**Common school movement.** The movement to provide universal education and schools that would serve all children at public expense.

In the 19th century, Horace Mann fought for establishing a universal system of public education and was known as the father of American Education.

(Hulton Archive/GettyImages)

was a milestone in the United States. In Europe children were educated at differing levels depending upon their social class and status. In Mann's democratic experiment, education came to be viewed as a significant way of ensuring a universally informed citizenry, people who would participate in local and national politics with understanding of broad issues. Butts and Cremin (1953) identify at least five reasons that a universal system of education was appealing:

- Promoting nationalism
- Promoting political enlightenment
- Promoting equality of opportunity
- Raising productivity to increase national prosperity
- Diminishing crime in burgeoning urban areas

Yet resistance to the idea of a common, universal education was based on many factors, including longstanding local control, objections by many religious groups to what they thought was an undermining of their religious values and beliefs by Mann's ideas of common moral values, and the local common values of each region and community reflecting local definitions of the level of education that was suited to that community.

One dispute brought to national attention by the movement for establishing common schools was a heated debate over the role religion should play in schools. The constitutional separation of church and state meant that public funding of education would not extend to religiously oriented schools. In Europe there was a history of public funding for both secular and religious schools (Butts & Cremin, 1953), but this was not Mann's vision. As an example, from 1830 to 1850 immigrants flooded into the eastern part of the United States and a large portion of these new immigrants were Catholic.

**The Catholic Issue.** Immigrants who were Catholic landed in a country that was predominantly Protestant, and where most schools taught Protestant religion to its pupils. Moreover, wherever they settled, Catholics were in the minority, and often suffered from injustice and unfair treatment. Schools taught the King James translation of the Bible, for example. Catholics began asking for their children to be taught using the Catholic Bible, but their requests were denied. In Baltimore, Catholics were discouraged by the church hierarchy from attending public schools, or even singing hymns. Eventually, Catholic populations began to see creating Catholic schools for their children as essential if they were to keep their faith.

Catholic schools were often important ways that new immigrants throughout the 1800s and into the 1900s maintained their religious and cultural identity. Immigrants from countries that were predominantly Catholic found refuge in these parochial schools. Children of Irish, Italian, German, and other immigrant groups supported parochial schools, especially in the North and in the Eastern part of the United States.

As Catholics tried to find ways of creating parochial schools, they were met with greater barriers than just funding. Tensions flared over issues such as using public funds to pay for parochial schools but also the use of public lands for the building of such schools. The "Catholic Issue" led to what today is the Catholic school system. The first Catholic parochial school was opened in Philadelphia in 1782 (National Catholic Education Association, 2008); by the late 1800s thousands of Catholic schools could be found up and down the Eastern seaboard and inland.

## The Late 19th Century: Building a System of Education

The emerging school system included mainly elementary schools; secondary schooling was still considered a luxury and was funded privately. In 1827, Massachusetts led the way for the eventual establishment of a full system of schooling by initiating the first free secondary school, but for boys only. Slow to attract students and gain public support, secondary schools spread, but in other states tuition was charged because the public did not initially see the need for post-elementary education. It was more important for youth to work.

### Digging Deeper

#### A Colonial Conflict in a Modern Setting: What High School Curriculum is Best?

As we have read, the purpose of Latin Grammar schools was to prepare young men in the classics so they could be successful in college, where the curriculum demanded a solid knowledge of Latin and Greek. In contrast, the English school approach focused on more practical matters, more science, and the actual learning of English as a school subject to prepare graduates for a practical life in society. Eventually these two curricula began to be offered together at what are now known as comprehensive high schools. What issues does this historical record regarding curriculum raise today?

**Pro and Con:** Having both a "classic" curriculum and a more practical curriculum in one school enables students of all types to engage a range of learning that might serve them well in life. The original Latin Grammar school curriculum has not survived, but today we may think of the classic curriculum as including study of authors such as Shakespeare and other primarily white male authors, the advanced study of languages, and the advanced study of mathematics and science. Students may come to these comprehensive high schools with a wide range of interests; without a comprehensive school that can offer the range of courses and programs, they may never have the opportunity to be exposed to a fuller set of ideas and choices.

In contrast, offering both a classic and a practical curriculum means a school must be large enough to hire teachers who are experts in all of these various curricular areas in order to meet the teaching demands of both aspects of the curriculum—whether all of the students are interested in studying that particular area or not. Students whose interests diverge may be attending the same school but may not attend class together across the different curricula.

**The Nuances:** A high school curriculum that views students as either preparing for a rigorous college education or for the world of work has its historical roots in this same issue. These two approaches to the curriculum persist today in the form of academic tracks, where within the same comprehensive high school some students study in preparation for college prep classes, Advanced Placement or Honors classes, and the regular track. Students do not typically move between tracks (for a more extensive discussion on academic tracking, see Chapter 7) and are often identified as college-going or non-college-going early on. Therefore, schools that offer both curricula cannot really be said to have integrated them. Rather, is it more often the case that the two exist in parallel and that many racial and ethnic minority students may have difficulty reaching and being successful in college-bound tracks.

A different but related issue that persists and that has its basis in a comparison of Latin Grammar and the English school curricula is the ongoing debate about what constitutes a "classic curriculum" in the modern world in the first place. This conflict can be best understood, perhaps, by the idea of the "canon," that is, the classic novels in English written by males that have traditionally been read in contrast to writings by racial and ethnic minority writers and women. Arguments over the canon, however, are not related only to the question of who is going to college, but often take place around decisions such as which required books should an increasingly diverse group of high school freshmen students be reading, no matter what track they are on. Which have relevance? Which are really considered to be classics in the first place?

**Rethinking the Issue:** Although the college-prep and regular curricula continue to co-exist, critics of today's secondary education regularly call for a more rigorous curriculum that will prepare all graduates for what is today's more complex world of work. What is considered essential to be able to function in the 21st century has changed, and this has implications for how the high school curriculum is defined. For example, technological literacy is a high-level skill that is expected of everyone upon graduation. Being able to understand and work with complex ideas, formerly the purview of the college-bound, is almost a basic skill for survival in today's economy. Yet high schools have not yet figured out how to redefine the curriculum for a world that is decidedly more complex. Curriculum has always been fluid, yet the historical divide between preparing students for college and for "just" the working world has persisted since the colonial era.

As cities developed, however, and industry grew, demands for more specialized labor increased and secondary schools introduced a more practical curriculum for boys. As in the past, with the development of academies, schools sought to fill the particular needs of society through a practical curriculum. Naturally, some secondary schools continued to focus on a more classical, formal curriculum, but these secondary schools were attended by those who planned on attending university. As noted above, here we can see the roots of the high school curriculum that tracks students in today's high schools in the form of college prep classes and the regular track. Eventually secondary schools became part of the elementary school movement, free and open to all. By mid-1800s, there were over five thousand secondary schools across the states, offering both college prep and vocational education courses of study. For an example of what was being read and argued about school, both aims and curricula, see the primary source document *The Means and Ends of Universal Education* ([1867]) by Ira Mayhew at **http://quod.lib.umich.edu/cgi/t/text/text-idx?c=moa; idno=AJB4672**.

**Your turn...** *to reflect*

If you were a citizen during the time of Mann's proposals for universal schooling, what position might you take? How does that debate relate to some of the current controversies in education today?

**The Effects of Industrialization.** As the new nation moved into the industrial era, rural communities became more closely tied with their urban counterparts, as more trade and the increased demand for goods and services characterized a society that was experiencing great social change. Rural areas became part of a roadway to transport agricultural goods and materials to growing towns. These rural communities were exposed to new ideas and new opportunities that shifted their once closed circle. Further, in the early 1800s, industrialization required more and more labor. Jobs for those who were willing to leave their homes and venture into factories brought new schedules and demands upon communities. What was once a closed community, where work was done in the home, and home was the place where one worked, now separated the two; work and home became distinct from one another.

New immigration in the mid-to-late 1800s fueled industrialization. The development and expansion of common schools existed alongside unprecedented levels of immigration and in a context of rapid industrialization. This meant that the numbers of students in schools was increasing rapidly as well, and this was felt perhaps most acutely in the nation's urban school systems. The increase in population, and especially in the nation's cities, had a impact on how education was viewed. Preparing for jobs in industry differed substantially in purpose from the earliest views of education in the United States, namely, as a way of fostering participation in the democracy and assuring religious knowledge.

One approach to educating large numbers of poorer students in the urban schools was known as the *monitorial system*, a method developed by the British educator Joseph Lancaster. Lancaster was committed to educating poor children by making it possible for them to attend public schools in ways that were financially efficient. The monitorial system was essentially a cross-age peer tutoring system, in which older students would instruct younger students under the guidance of an educated adult teacher (see **http://www.constitution.org/lanc**). But interest in this approach, in which class sizes could be over one hundred students, was short-lived and was replaced by the graded classroom structure that is familiar today.

Another educational development at the intersection of common schooling and industrialization was the **efficiency movement**. This educational approach emerged from the influence of Frederick Taylor, who determined that the way to make factories more profitable was to make them more efficient.

This efficiency movement influenced public schools, especially schools that had large populations of poor, working-class students, many of whom were immigrants. Students were taught in ways that would prepare them to enter the workforce; the new industries and factories required workers to follow directions, be punctual, and do the work. The express purpose was to enculturate new immigrants, to teach them to speak and understand English, to help them learn how to adapt to the customs of their new country, and, most importantly, to help them learn to be good workers. Taylor's efficiency movement was

### Critical term

**Efficiency movement.** Schooling that was designed to prepare students for life in the world of work, with an emphasis on conformity, following directions, rote learning and memorization, and strict rules of comportment.

Increased immigration to the United States during the 19th century, along with the rise of industrialization, resulted in the overcrowding of classrooms in urban schools. (The Granger Collection, New York)

applied to the schools by Elwood Cubberley, who would become Stanford University's president. Schools, particularly those schools whose students were from poor, working class backgrounds, immigrants, and second language learners, were essentially following the factory worker model, an efficiency model that emphasized conformity, following directions, rote learning and memorization, and strict rules of comportment. Clearly Cubberley's view of the purpose of schooling contrasted sharply with the purpose of education as Jefferson envisioned it.

### Your turn... *to reflect*

In today's educational climate, is there still a tension between Jefferson's education for democracy (critical thinking, powerful literacy, purposeful engagement in learning) and Cubberley's vision of schools that operate as a factory model? How does this play out in the modern world?

## The Limited Reach of Universal Education

Although universal education through the common school movement was increasing, it was actually not universally available across the population. The experiences of African American, Hispanic American, and Native American students would suggest that the Jeffersonian views of education, as well as those of Horace Mann, were limited in their reach. The concept of citizenry did not apply uniformly and this was reflected in the educational system, from which minority students and women were generally excluded.

### Education for African American Children and Youth.
African American children were generally barred from attending common schools, both in the north and in the south. Bias against African Americans was prevalent in all states, and this extended into the schools and their teachers. In the earliest days of the country's history and well into the 20th century, access to education was difficult for African American children and their parents. So where did African American children receive schooling? Wherever they could afford to, African Americans started or supported all Black schools, where their children could be taught by African American teachers. In the late 1700s and early 1800s, schools for African Americans were supported by private families or by donations and goodwill offerings by Whites.

Schools in the north were segregated, and in 1850 the Massachusetts Supreme Court ruled in *Roberts v. City of Boston* that separate, segregated schools were legal, leaving little choice for African Americans who desired their children to be educated. Some religious or philanthropic communities did open schools for African Americans. For those that had no means, Charity schools existed; they had been set up generally for poor, working class children. African American children were sent to Charity schools as well, and eventually the cost of these schools was absorbed by the state. However, segregation by race and socioeconomic class existed even within these schools, with poor, working class children who were White attending some form of Charity school and African American children, frequently poor and working-class, attending other separate Charity schools. Even in an attempt to provide education for the poorest of children, segregation prevailed.

This segregated school for African Americans was established as part of a segregated community for freed slaves in Arlington, Virginia in 1863. (Photo by Charles H. Phillips/Time Life Pictures/Getty Images)

After the Civil War, segregated schools were common in all states, but African American leaders began to argue for a more equal distribution of resources to make education for African American children possible. Two major arguments were debated. The first argument was between those who thought schools should be segregated and the opposing view, mainly held by African Americans and Whites who believed deeply in the common humanity of all, was for integration. The second debate was over the fact that as a rule African American schools received far less funding and resources than their White counterparts—so it was an argument for equality of funding.

Both of these issues continued to be challenged by a predominantly Protestant and White population, which desired to keep the races separate, but also by African Americans, who saw separate schools as a way of protecting their children from taunts and racial stereotypes and from White teachers' attitudes, which frequently were characterized by low expectations. The idea of a public school separated by race appeared to reflect a primarily racist view of African Americans as being less capable than Whites, even though strong, eloquent voices of both African American and White leaders challenged the inequality of segregation.

Nevertheless, African Americans persevered in educating their children, and also in establishing higher education. In 1837, the Institute for Colored Youth was founded, later becoming Cheyney University. In 1854, Ashmun Institute, the first school of higher learning for African American men, was established, followed in 1856 by Wilberforce University, the first African American university owned and governed by African Americans. Wilberforce University was founded by the African Methodist Episcopal Church, and its president, Daniel Payne, became the first African American university president in the country. In 1867, Howard University was founded as a coeducational university for newly emancipated slaves, with the law school added in 1869, the first all African American law school in the country. In 1881, Spelman College was founded for African American women. That same year, Booker T. Washington founded the Tuskegee Normal and Industrial Institute, which eventually became one of the leading schools of higher education for African Americans. Enrollments in these colleges and universities reflected a deep commitment to education and learning, despite often overwhelming resistance and racism. African Americans continued to fight for a high quality education for their children, but it was not until 1954 with the *Brown v. Board of Education* decision (see Chapter 7) that segregation in public schools became unconstitutional. The historical roots of educational inequity had been set at the outset of the development of the educational system in the United States.

### Education for Native American Children and Youth.

From their first interactions throughout the later settlements moving west, the early settlers believed they had to "civilize" the indigenous peoples into the English way of life. Given the overtly religious nature of the primarily Protestant society, this included conversion to Christianity. Mission schools were a common means of promoting this goal.

The treatment of the Native Americans by those who colonized the New World was

Boarding schools for Native American children systematically devalued the indigenous cultures and languages of the students who attended them.
(KRT Photo by Nebraska Historical Society/NewsCom)

based on the belief that differences, so striking in all aspects of culture, including ways of living and relating to one another, denoted the inferiority of the native peoples. For many years a curriculum known as 50/50 dominated these schools, where half the time students were taught traditional reading, writing, and arithmetic, as well as Christianity (the denomination of the sponsoring mission), and the other half was focused on vocational and farming or agricultural skills (boys) or sewing, cooking, and quilting (girls) (Hale, 2002).

Not only were missionaries committed to serving a "civilizing" role, but the eventual creation of boarding schools for Native American children, funded and administered by a governmental agency, the Bureau of Indian Affairs, had as their policy eradicating indigenous culture and languages. Children were literally sent away from their reservation homes as a matter of course. According to the historian Joel Spring (2007), boarding schools were another form of educational segregation consistent with segregated schools for African American children in the south. After the Civil War, all Native American children were sent to these boarding schools in order to assimilate them into the dominant culture and language.

As the following Case in Point demonstrates, the struggles of Native American children in schools today are heavily impacted by the historical record in education.

## A Case In Point
### What can a History of Educational Inequity Mean for Today's Students

Inequities in the American educational system are longstanding and have their roots early in the history of the country. Sherman Alexie, a highly acclaimed Native American author of adult and young adult literature, began his high school education on the Spokane Indian reservation in the state of Washington but left that school to attend a better resourced school off of the reservation. In his semi-autobiographical novel, *The Absolutely True Diary of a Part-Time Indian*, Alexie reveals the depth of his own longing for a high-quality education and the shock he experiences when he realizes what the school on his reservation cannot provide. In the following excerpt, Alexie's character has just entered his first day of geometry class:

"All right, kids, let's get cracking," Mr. P. said as he passed out the geometry books. "How about we do something strange and start on page one?"

I grabbed my book and opened it up.

I wanted to smell it.

Heck, I wanted to kiss it.

Yes, kiss it.

That's right, I am a book kisser.

Maybe that's kind of perverted or maybe it's just romantic and high *intelligent*.

But my lips and I stopped short when I saw this written on the inside front cover: THIS BOOK BELONGS TO AGNES ADAMS.

Okay, now you're probably asking yourself, "Who is Agnes Adams?"

Well, let me tell you. Agnes Adams is my mother. MY MOTHER! And Adams is *her* maiden name.

So that means my mother was born an Adams and she was still an Adams when she wrote her name in that book. And she was thirty when she gave birth to me. Yep, so that means I was staring at a geometry book that was at least thirty years older than I was.

I couldn't believe it.

How horrible is that?

My school and my tribe are so poor and sad that we have to study from the same dang books our parents studied from. That is absolutely the saddest thing in the world.

And let me tell you, that old, old, old, *decrepit* geometry book hit my heart with the force of a nuclear bomb. My hopes and dreams floated up in a mushroom cloud. What do you do when the world has declared nuclear war on you?

**Source:** Sherman Alexie, *The Absolutely True Diary of a Part-Time Indian*. Copyright 2007, Little Brown and Company, New York.

**Education for Hispanic American Children and Youth.** Patterns of segregation also characterized the educational experiences of Hispanic American children and youth. After the Mexican American war in 1848, Mexican American children, the largest Hispanic school demographic, were sent to segregated schools in order to assimilate them into White culture and language. **"English-only" rules** existed throughout the southwest, forbidding Mexican American children to speak Spanish. Rather than send their children to schools that diminished their culture, Mexican Americans in Texas established private schools for their children (Spring, 2007). The pattern was essentially the same as it was for African American students; schools were segregated within communities and substandard schooling was relegated to Mexican American students.

In California, the State Supreme Court ruled (*Mendez v. Westminster*, 1947) that separate was not equal and that Mexican American children could attend public schools along with other children. Within two years, Texas and Arizona also overturned their segregationist policy that kept Mexican American children in separate schools.

The historical roots of unequal education and the devaluing of the culture and language of Hispanic American children can be seen in these early educational practices. These roots have far-reaching effects today with continued inequities in school resources and in the presence of English-only legislation in states with large Hispanic student populations (for a discussion of bilingual education issues, see Chapter 7).

**Education for Girls and Women.** Protestant ideology fostered the belief that girls and women should have well-identified, limited roles in society, and that they should be subordinate to males, a perspective that hindered their educational progress. In the early colonies, girls' education was not seen as necessary as that for boys, and when girls were educated, it was with an emphasis on domestic skills. When we hear the term *common school*, we assume this meant schools for everyone. Yet, for girls and women, education meant learning their place in the home, in other words, staying in the domestic realm. It was considered unseemly for women to be leaders or activists, yet there were those who fought the social stigma and worked for the rights of women, both legally and educationally.

Interestingly, with the rise of academies in 1800s, some of these academies were coed, but more often separate academies for women began to spring up. Women like Mrs. Lincoln Phelps, in the late 1800s, were strongly committed to education for girls, and Phelps founded an academy that taught girls not only domestic skills but also a classically based curriculum. Emma Willard established The Troy Academy, a school for

**Critical term**

**English-only rule.** Rule barring Mexican American children from speaking Spanish in public schools.

Mount Holyoke Seminary, now Mount Holyoke College, was founded in 1836 as one of the first academies for young women in the United States and is considered the oldest women's college in the country.

women, as early as 1821. This was followed by Mount Holyoke Seminary in 1836, which was founded by Mary Lyon, and now Mount Holyoke College, considered the oldest college for women in the United States (and still a women's college). In Chapter 3 we discussed the role of Catherine Beecher, who founded the Hartford Seminary in 1828. In 1837, Oberlin College became the first institution to offer coeducation of women and men. The early education of women for work outside the home was relegated to preparing to become teachers at the elementary level—often the only way for women to get more than an elementary education themselves. The National Women's History Museum

 in Washington, DC, houses an electronic exhibit, *The History of Women and Education*, at **http://www.nmwh.org/ exhibits/Education/ 1800's.html**.

## Into the 20th Century

As public schools increased in size and scope, as immigrants from Europe and Asia came in waves into the cities, as ghettos grew alongside factories and industry, the administration of education became more formalized. With such major events putting pressure onto schools, the administration of schools became more formal and standardized. One-room schoolhouses no longer accommodated the needs of local areas and the consolidation of individual schools into school districts developed as one way of meeting educational demands. Policies were created so that schools became more consistent, resulting in mandates for what the curriculum was to be at each grade level—regulating teachers who formerly operated much more independently. A single teacher instructing a multi-aged group of children shifted into a grade level determined by age of the child, and a teacher appointed for teaching that grade level. Elementary schools became distinct from secondary schools and, in 1909, junior high schools were added. Our current 12-grade system is almost identical to this division of grades from the late 1800s. These developments, along with the passage of the 1918 Compulsory Education Act requiring all children to attend school, led to education being a focus of much debate nationwide regarding the primary aim of schools during the timespan from 1880–1930.

Recall Cubberley, who viewed schools as factories to churn out workers for the new industries. He was not alone in seeing schools as an ideal place to "train" young minds and attitudes. A new psychology was emerging through the work of B. F. Skinner and others who were known as *behaviorists*. Behaviorism hypothesized that learning is a function of change in the way one behaves. Individuals respond to events (or stimuli) that occur in the environment, a response produces a behavior, and stimulus–response patterns could be reinforced through rewards or punishments. Around this time, G. Stanley Hall, an American psychologist and educator, became interested in and developed tests to measure aptitude and achievement in children. Other psychologists began to develop ways of testing and measuring children, including their mental abilities and intellectual capacities. Research about how humans developed both physically and mentally began to be codified and led to new questions about human growth.

However, not all educators viewed children in terms of test scores, measurement, or stimulus–response. One of the best known educators who influenced schools and education was the progressive educator John Dewey (1859–1952), who was passionately committed to democratic ideals and whose entire life was dedicated to forging communities where all citizens would fully realize their power and capacities by engaging in associated living in political, social, and cultural life. For Dewey (not unlike Jefferson), democracy was a way of living together responsibly in the public realm through decision-making and negotiation, and it was through schools that democracy could be fostered and practiced. His educational philosophy of progressivism, described later in this chapter, was based on schools being laboratories of democratic associated living where children's experiences would be cultivated to learn about the world through reading and writing, hypothesizing and testing, and tackling real issues that impact their lives. Progressive education was widely practiced during this time, but existed alongside more traditional, teacher-led approaches to education where the teacher was the authority and the pupils' job was to receive information and skills as directed by the teacher.

Given the rapid development of education during this period, it is not surprising that, in 1930, a comparison between 3000 graduates of progressive and of traditional schools was undertaken. The **Eight-Year Study** attempted to ascertain the effectiveness of progressive education (see Kridel & Bullough, 2007). This study found that those who had attended and graduated from schools that were using progressive education demonstrated more intellectual curiosity and drive, revealed higher critical thinking and judgment, tended to receive more academic honors and higher grade averages, and studied the same field as those taught in traditional schools.

The findings of the Eight-Year Study might have put to rest critics who argued progressive education approaches were not rigorous or did not have academic standards and purpose. Yet, the argument between traditional approaches and progressive ones continued, and are still debated today.

### Critical term

**Eight-Year Study.** A study in the period of the 1930s that compared the progressive approach to education with the traditional approach, and found that the progressive approach produced more intellectual curiosity and drive and higher levels of critical thinking and judgment.

## The Historical Record and the Current Era: Enduring Dilemmas and Persistent Controversies

Where does the early history of education in the United States leave us today? Different specific conflicts may be in the forefront, but we can see their roots in the very arguments that began early in the development of the country.

One is the role of the federal government in controlling and funding education. The role of the federal government in overseeing and influencing public schools has increased steadily since the common school movement. Various forms of federal grants and acts have provided funding for education, with early bills, such as the Smith-Hughes Act of 1917, providing funding for teacher education programs and vocational programs at the high school level. The G.I. Bill of Rights, as it is commonly referred to (Servicemen's Readjustment Act, 1944), allowed tuition and stipends for those who served in the military. After WWII, colleges and universities took in hundreds of thousands of veterans seeking both undergraduate and graduate degrees, raising the standard of living and creating a flourishing middle class well into the 1960s. In 1958, the National Defense Act (NDEA) funded research and funding for educational programs that focused on math, science, and foreign languages, but also provided student loans for those who wanted to become teachers or school counselors. And, as we will see in Chapter 10, the federal influence has steadily increased through both funding and legislation related to issues of equity across racial and ethnic minority groups and for girls and women.

Another example of an enduring dilemma is whether federal funding should be used only for secular or also for religiously oriented education. The movement toward vouchers is starting to redefine what it means to fund education publicly, a controversy that first emerged, we have seen, during the time the common school had its start.

Becoming familiar with the how schools evolved into the public school system we have today provides a means to broaden teachers' understandings of the influences and demands that exist in today's classrooms. Schools continue to adapt and evolve in response to the demands of society. But the pull toward doing things the way they have always been done is strong. Teachers operate in the public sphere, and if schools are to challenge themselves to meet their fundamentally democratic aims for all students, not only those who have historically been served well, it is teachers who need to be active in the framing of a democratic society through their work in public school classrooms.

## Philosophical Views of Education

Successful teachers understand the principles and aims that motivate their work with their pupils. As we will note in the next chapter, successful teachers recognize that they must make difficult decisions regarding issues of curriculum (What do I teach? What do I leave out?), or behavior (How do I teach students to respect one another?), or assessment (Are tests fair to my culturally diverse students, or to my female students? What standards or criteria are best to use with my students?). It is these types of concerns that philosophy can address—concerns about what to teach, how to teach, and making decisions about how teachers relate to students.

Philosophy of education is the foundation that allows teachers to frame their work and to make decisions about teaching and learning. Therefore, it is important for you, as a new teacher, to become aware of what philosophy is and the distinctions between different traditions of philosophy as they apply to education and teaching. Developing your own philosophy of education is a continuous process of awareness and reflection as you learn what it means to become a teacher.

While successful teachers have distinct philosophies of education, these are by no means static. Successful teachers' philosophies of education continue to grow and deepen as experience in the classroom leads them to more deeply reflect upon who they are as teachers and why they choose to approach teaching in a particular way. In other words, while there is no one philosophy of education, teachers develop their own the more they grapple with issues and concerns in their classrooms. As we noted in Chapter 2, a significant reason to become aware of one's own philosophy of education is precisely because philosophy does not "solve" an issue, but rather frames the way a teacher looks at an issue and makes a decision.

Philosophies of education have emerged out of how teachers view their work. There is no one philosophy that one can say fits every teacher; teachers develop their philosophies out of their experiences and from their reading either about philosophy or about related concerns that affect teaching. Both western and eastern philosophies of education attempt to answer enduring, complex questions. But philosophy raises questions as well as tries to answer them. You will discover that no teacher is neutral about his or her philosophy of education.

Philosophy comes from the Greek words meaning "love" (*philo*) and "wisdom" (*sophos*). Philosophers are lovers of wisdom. Philosophy brings insight into the most pressing, enduring, complex issues human beings must confront in their lifetimes. What is "good" or "evil"? What does it mean to live a life? What is beauty? It is through philosophy that we come to envision a world that *could be* out of a world that *is*. How does this relate to us as teachers? Philosophy helps teachers think through opposing issues and views about how one teaches and why.

# REWARDS AND CHALLENGES

## A New Teacher's Philosophy

Adriana Balistreri
*Milwaukee, Wisconsin*

My basic philosophy of teaching is that students should be taught how to be critical thinkers and should be taught how to question what they are learning. Many times students do not question the source of information or feel comfortable disagreeing with their teacher's viewpoint or the viewpoint in their books. I want my students to develop skills that allow them to "think outside of the box" and feel confident raising such questions. The challenge I see is that many of my students automatically assume the information they are presented with is precise and correct. If my students do not have a lot of background knowledge on topics they are learning about, they are less likely to question. I have to create a classroom where they are expected to ask questions and where they are rewarded for doing so.

The reason I am committed to this philosophy is that by teaching my students to think critically, they begin to ask questions that result in great, involved discussions. These discussions lead most of my students to do additional research on their own using other books or the internet as resources. Many of my students have now developed the habit of not using only one resource and have become more aware of who is writing the information in the books they read and the biases those authors might have. ●

No teacher teaches without some framework, however hidden from view it may be. Our philosophy is deeply embedded in how we see our students and relate to them, how we approach the planning of a lesson or unit, and what we determine is the best way to instruct. A philosophy of education helps us understand questions, issues, concerns about our daily life as a teacher, often without even thinking about them. All of this and far more is animated and influenced by a teacher's philosophy of education.

Successful teachers can articulate a clearly defined philosophy of education. As you saw in the opening of this chapter, as prospective teachers you will no doubt be asked to write about your philosophy of education in an education course. Over time, as your classroom experiences begin to grow, how will your philosophy of education develop? Life as a teacher is full of conflicting issues and concerns that will affect you and your students on a daily basis. A philosophy of education is continually evaluated, revised, and then rearticulated as teachers relate it to their specific teaching situations.

Philosophy raises questions; it does not solve them. Learning about philosophy, and reading about philosophy of education can help you learn to think through complexities and to move beyond simplistic decisions and actions. But to be able to navigate through the contradictions and problems that arise in your classroom so that you are clearer about what you are teaching, how you are teaching, and why you are doing it is the benefit of having thought about and developed a personal philosophy of education.

## The Map of Western Philosophical Concepts and Schools of Thought

Aristotle, the Greek philosopher, argued that not all people value the same virtues, and because of this, education will always be contentious, with differing aims and different approaches to meet these varying aims. The schools of thought in this section examine western 20th-century philosophies of education that have influenced the formation of public school teachers and teaching. Philosophy of education is a field that continues to add to the debates educators have over the meaning and purpose of their work and takes into account these fundamental questions:

● What should the aims of education be?

● What is knowledge?

● What is the knowledge of most worth?

● What values should be taught?

● What is learning and how should it be assessed?

Questions such as these, all interesting and vital to teachers and the act of teaching, are what philosophers of education grapple with.

Every teacher has a philosophy of education that reflects his or her principles and beliefs about teaching and learning and what is necessary in order to live a good life. Philosophers everywhere wrestle with these same questions, particularly questions such as "What is a good life?" and "What does it mean to lead a good life?" Teachers are one important influence on determining what kinds of lives their students will eventually lead. In other words, teachers teach for the future, for a society and world that will be created by the young people who are being educated. How teachers carry out this essential role in society is very much a question of their philosophies of education.

Four specific areas of philosophy influence the work of teachers. Each type of philosophy illuminates a particular way of seeing the work of teachers. Each time teachers decide on what to teach, how to teach, why they teach—in fact, all decision-making in teaching—it is based upon some aspect of a teacher's philosophy of education. The four areas of philosophy are:

● *Aesthetics*: Aesthetics is concerned with issues such as "What is beauty?" "What is art?" The act of teaching is itself an aesthetic expression of art. Aesthetics extends well beyond drama, music, and art and into writing and literature. Any time a teacher or student judges any medium of expression (even technology), aesthetics comes into play.

● *Ethics*: Ethics is the never ending companion of a teacher and emerges from the branch of philosophy called *axiology*, which asks, "What is the nature of values?" Whenever questions arise regarding what is right or wrong, fair or unfair, good or bad, it is ethics that addresses such situations. Teachers are expected to make ethical decisions that include how to teach students, how to respond to disruptive students, how to justify treating one student differently from another. Ethical dilemmas, that is, situations where there are more than one way to respond, make up the daily life of teaching, as we will discuss at length in Chapter 11.

● *Logic*: Logic is the intellectual companion of teachers. Logic is the process of thinking, reasoning in a critical and disciplined way, either *deductively* or *inductively*. Based upon reasoned evidence, deductive reasoning moves from a general principle to a specific conclusion that is valid. In contrast, inductive reasoning moves from a specific principle toward a generalization, again based upon disciplined reasoning, using evidence and argumentation.

● *Epistemology*: Epistemology is concerned with the nature of knowledge itself. How do students come to know things? This question is directly related to how a teacher makes decisions about the curriculum and helps answer the central curriculum question, "What is worth knowing?" Do students come to know things by virtue of being lectured to about them, by memorizing them, or by inquiring into topics and issues? Likewise, knowing can be based on the belief that the source is an expert or authority; knowing can be based on reason and logic through evidence; knowing can be based on experiences; knowing can be based on intuition; knowing can be based on belief in a divinity. Each teaching (or pedagogical) decision is, then, also a decision about how we know things—that is, an epistemological issue.

## Major Philosophies of Education

Now let us turn to specific philosophical orientations to education in the western tradition. As you read these overviews of the major philosophical orientations, consider which seem more familiar to you, which you have experienced as a student, and which you want to learn in greater depth. Each orientation has implications for aesthetics, logic, ethics, and epistemology, and can help guide the development of your personal philosophy of education.

### Essentialism.
As you saw in Chapter 3, the philosophy of **essentialism** is based on the assumption that students should learn the basic facts regarding the social and physical world. Essentialist teachers are often called "traditional" teachers, as they teach that there is a set structure and form for all things in existence. Learning subject matter is the goal of education; reading, writing and mathematics form the main focus of an essentialist orientation. An essentialist teacher would have pupils mastering skills, moving from simple to more complex skills and knowledge.

Essentialism has dominated education in the United States from the beginning of schooling in the colonies. Teacher-centered and teacher-directed, these basic skills form the "essentials" of knowledge. Moreover, essentialism focuses on character development and the disciplining of a pupil's mind. Students are expected to listen, follow directions, read about what they are being taught, respect their teachers, and become good citizens in their communities.

The virtues essentialist teachers teach include respect for others; respect for authority, loyalty, hard work, and becoming a model citizen. The major champion of essentialism was William Chandler Bagley (1874–1946), who was a professor of education at Teachers College, Columbia University.

### Progressivism.
**Progressivism** is an orientation of philosophy of education based on the assumption that all learning is active, that learning is intellectual, social, and emotional, and that curriculum should begin with the child's interests and experiences. Progressivism elevates shared interests and shared interactions between pupils in the classroom. Each person's voice is important and one of the hallmarks of a progressive classroom is the emphasis on communication skills. There is a strong emphasis on critical thinking and problem solving within each lesson. William Chandler Bagley's commitment to essentialism stood in stark opposition to the progressive philosophy of education.

A progressive teacher, for example, will develop lessons around local issues for pupils to research. Pupils learn to discuss ideas in a way that respects but allows for disagreement with others. The work in a progressive classroom includes the experiences pupils have as well as their conceptual understanding of the world. These are starting

**Critical term**

**Essentialism.** A philosophy of education based on the assumption that students should learn the basic facts regarding the social and physical world.

**Critical term**

**Progressivism.** A philosophy of education developed by John Dewey based on the assumption that all learning is active, that learning is intellectual, social, and emotional, and that curriculum should begin with the child's interests and experiences.

The laboratory school at the University of Chicago was founded in 1896 by John Dewey to put into practice his progressive philosophy of education. (Archival Photofiles, apf2-00863, Special Collections Research Center, University of Chicago Library)

points for a progressive teacher. Another hallmark of a progressive classroom is the purposeful activity of pupils who may be engaged in research and inquiry with a group or alone. Students' questions fill the progressive classroom as the teacher builds on what the pupils are doing toward a deeper understanding of their inquiry.

The famous educator John Dewey (1859–1952) is associated with progressive education and put his progressive ideas into practice at the famous University of Chicago Laboratory School, founded in 1896. Dewey advocated for children to engage in inquiry around a compelling question so the classroom becomes an active and lively place of learning. He advocated for using the scientific method in these inquiries using the following steps:

1. Identify the problem.

2. Define it.

3. Hypothesize about it.

4. Examine consequences of each hypothesis.

5. Test the solution that seems best.

Progressive teachers view their classrooms as educative, that is, leading toward on-going understanding of the world and their place in it. Democratic principles of respect for oneself and others, classroom community, cooperation and collaboration, and discussion and dialogue are characteristics of a progressive teacher and classroom.

## Critical term

**Perennialism.** A philosophical orientation based on the assumption that all learning should be focused on unchanging principles or great ideas.

**Perennialism.** **Perennialism** is a philosophical orientation based on the assumption that all learning should be focused on unchanging principles or great ideas. The purpose of education is to expand a person's intellectual, rational power through the study of laws of nature and science, or theories of mathematics, or the accepted classical literature such as Shakespeare. Enduring ideas emerge, perennialists believe, out of a stable and unchanging body of knowledge and ideas.

Like a progressive teacher, a perennialist agrees that rote learning and drill do not lead to meaningful learning. Teaching great books and literature, and discussing the structure and meaning of these, would be compatible rather than a pencil and paper bubble test. A perennialist teacher would have a classroom that was oriented toward the teacher as the expert in relationship to this stable, well-identified curriculum.

The perennialist teacher would teach curriculum that might have little to do with students' experiences or prior knowledge, because those factors are not important to the task of learning to exercise one's intellectual capacity through reading and thinking about what has been discovered already. Perennialist teachers recognize that their pupils are rational beings, but that their work is to cultivate the "higher order" of reasoning skills, rather than the "lower order" of emotions or intuition or experiences. The perennialist classroom would be designed for seatwork; teacher-centered, guided lessons; and structured dialogue. All approaches are aimed at pupils' learning of the knowledge that has stood the test of time. The Great Books approach is a perennialist approach, where students read and analyze works by writers and thinkers who have contributed to science, the arts, and literature.

Mortimer Adler and Robert Hutchins were advocates of perennialism and designed an undergraduate curriculum called *Great Books of the Western World*. Over 100 western classical studies, from Ancient Greek philosophers such as Aristotle and Plato to mathematicians of the 20th century such as Einstein, were included. A demanding, rigorous course of study, in the Great Books curriculum pupils to read, analyze, and learn from the books and discussions. Pupils' individual interests or experiences, or even what is happening in the world on that day, have no place in a perennialist classroom.

### Social Reconstructionism.

**Social reconstructionism** is based on the belief that schools should aim to foster active participants in society through a study of social problems and an aim to create a more just society. Social reform is an integral part of a social reconstructionist curriculum. Rather than accepting society as it is, social reconstructionist teachers provide their pupils with critical thinking skills to identify, question, challenge, and try to solve the crises that beset humankind in society. Knowledge is not static to a social reconstructionist; rather, knowledge is contextual and socially constructed. The aim of education is as a vehicle for social change.

Social reconstructionism emerged during the post-World War II era, based on the ideas that we live in a period of great unpredictability and upheaval, and while human beings have the knowledge and power to destroy one another and the world, we also have the knowledge and power to create a world of peace and abundance for all humanity. In his 1932 book titled *Dare the School Build a New Social Order?*, George Counts (1889–1974) challenged schools to create curriculum and classrooms that prepare students with technology, understanding of the world, and human compassion.

Knowledge alone cannot build a new world, Counts argued, and all the skills that can be mastered are of little value without human compassion. Student experiences and a curriculum centered on social action on real life problems, such as poverty or injustice, foster awareness of the issues confronting humankind and society, as well as the cultivation of a sense of agency that a person can do something about a problem. Active engagement, critical thinking, and indisciplined and purposeful learning are linked with social justice issues through inquiry, dialogue, and complexity within the learning community of the classroom.

Problem solving and problem-based learning of specific issues bring students into the world, often to negotiate with people in positions of authority, such as elected officials or a business president. Learning about how to write letters, to address a mayor correctly, to use the computer as a tool for word processing or research, to read and analyze multiple sides of any issue, these and more are components of a social reconstructionist classroom. Teachers work with their pupils to coordinate their efforts to learn as much as they can about an issue, and then strategize together to bring it to public attention and solve it. While a topic such as poverty may seem overwhelming, social reconstructionists use a pedagogy of place, starting locally to identify an injustice or social inequality. Pupils' experiences allow them to imagine or to see the effects of poverty, define its central attributes, and find out why local people live in poverty. From that vantage point, the teacher then poses questions about the region or state or nation. This might be a stepping stone for the compelling question of why there is poverty in the world.

**Critical term**

**Social reconstructionism.** A philosophy of education based on the belief that schools should aim to foster active participants in society through a study of social problems and an aim to create a more just society.

**Critical term**

**Ethic of care.** A philosophy of education based on the commitment to caring.

**An Ethic of Care.** Nel Noddings, a philosopher of education at Stanford University, has developed a philosophy based on the commitment to caring. This relational epistemology, or way of knowing, acknowledges that all human beings are social beings. An **ethic of care** suggests we need one another, and from birth our entire life is spent moving in and out of relationships with others. Our sense of who we are as persons is developed through our relationships with others; our sense of who we are as a society is developed through our relationships with other societies. In short, we are contextual, not individual and alone.

Noddings argues that we are born with a capacity to relate and to care about and for one another. According to Noddings, caring is relational, not individualistic. Caring is life affirming, is respectful of others, and invites reciprocity with others. A caring classroom is an affirming one, an environment of inclusivity and inquiry, where teachers and pupils work together to make learning relevant and meaningful. A teacher who practices relational epistemology sees knowledge, not as static and unchanging, but as socially constructed by people who live in relation to one another. Knowledge is not handed down to us or constructed in isolation of one another; rather we build on what others have learned and experienced, learn to read and analyze and think, and proceed to construct knowledge in order to better understand ourselves and the world.

## Philosophy and Purpose Revisited

As you enter teaching, you will be asked to learn about methodologies and strategies, concentrate and read more on your subject matter discipline(s), plan lessons and units, and engage in the daily work of what it means to be a successful teacher. But all of these things can be reduced to mere activities if they are not guided by a strong sense of purpose. A philosophy of education helps you anchor your teaching with such a purpose.

Cooperating teachers have been known to ask potential student teachers to share their philosophy of education before agreeing to work with them. Employers regularly ask to read a potential candidate's philosophy of education before or during a teaching interview. They do so because it is your philosophy of education that often reveals the way you will act in your classroom with your pupils and how you will frame the decisions you make. As your teaching career moves forward, understanding the philosophy of education can also help make you aware of why you may or may not agree with a particular teaching method or strategy. What you value in education is reflected in your own philosophy.

## Why It Counts in a Diverse World

Schools and classrooms are created by people for particular purposes—whether those purposes are voiced publicly or not. They are not static and unchanging, but instead are highly responsive to what the teachers and staff inside of them choose to do. While schools have commonalities wherever they exist, each school is also different. We can generalize about education and schools, e.g., children attend to learn certain subjects, but all schools are constituted by those who are teaching and administering them. Whether children have the opportunity and means to learn in those schools is very much determined by the decisions that those in charge make.

As this chapter has demonstrated, both the history and philosophy of education can have an impact on how schools function today. Learning about the history and philosophy of education provides you with a larger, enduring sense of how public schools—and their teachers—have evolved over time to where they are today. Historical conflicts that first emerged when the country was in its infancy persist in new forms today. The historic marginalization of specific groups of citizens has not yet been overcome and whether African American, Native American, Hispanic American, and many other groups will have access to the universal education envisioned by Jefferson and Mann remains in question. Whether the prevailing philosophy of education will emphasize learning by rote and not asking questions of authority, or learning to question and actively participate in the democracy, have not been, and may never be, resolved. How do you view your own commitments in the face of education's history and its multiple philosophies?

# CHAPTER SUMMARY

## Historical Origins of American Education

### Early Educational Efforts in the Colonies

The earliest schools in New England were designed for two purposes. First, children needed to be literate in order to read the Bible and resist evils and temptations. Second, a literate society was needed in order to participate in government. These schools varied in structure and form and only extended to the elementary level. Most families paid at least some form of tuition. In New England the early schools were primarily Protestant, but in the middle colonies denominational religious schools were common.

### Expanding Education, Literacy, and Civil Society

The classical curriculum based on a knowledge of Latin and Latin texts began to shift toward a more practical curriculum that was designed to better serve the needs of the working society. Latin Grammar schools began to be replaced with what were known as academies, or English schools, first envisioned by Benjamin Franklin.

### The Jeffersonian Ideal of Education

Thomas Jefferson believed that a democracy could not function fully unless its citizens were educated. The purpose of education was to enable citizens to be informed about political issues and participate directly in a self-governing society. Jefferson tried unsuccessfully to enact legislation to fund education publicly.

### Common Schools

Horace Mann envisioned universal schooling at public expense as a means of assuring equal opportunity to all children. This ideal required the development of a system of schooling. Resistance to the idea of the common school was based on religious considerations and a tradition of local control and private funding for education.

### The Late 19th Century: Building a System of Education

As the United States developed into an industrialized nation, and as immigration increased, the nature of the education system changed. The curriculum became more functionally and practically oriented. The purpose of schooling shifted to preparing children for working in factories and other jobs where conformity rather than inquiry was desirable. Secondary education expanded and a fully functioning system of public education emerged.

### The Limited Reach of Universal Education

Although the ideals of the common school and universal education were based on high ideals for the society, in reality the same educational opportunities did not exist for African American, Hispanic American, and Native American children or for girls and women. A segregated system of schools was in place in both the north and the south for African American children, whose parents found ways to provide education despite these conditions. In the southwest, segregated schools for Mexican American children forbade the use of Spanish. Many Native American children were removed from their homes and sent to government-sponsored boarding schools where their culture and language were denied. Although girls could attend school in the colonial era, they did not typically attend secondary schools or college, except in preparation for becoming teachers.

## The Map of Western Philosophical Concepts and Schools of Thought

Four types of philosophical concepts help define the work of teachers. *Aesthetics* is concerned about issues such as "What is beauty?" "What is art?" When teachers or students judge any medium of expression (even technology), aesthetics comes into play. *Ethics* emerges from the branch of philosophy called *axiology* and is concerned with *the nature of values*. This includes issues that arise regarding what is right or wrong, fair or unfair, and good or bad. *Logic* is the process of thinking and reasoning in a critical and disciplined way about one's teaching. *Epistemology* is concerned with the nature of knowledge itself and is reflected in how teachers go about teaching so that students acquire new knowledge and ideas. It answers questions about whether students come to know things based on hearing them in a lecture, memorizing them, or inquiring into them.

## Philosophical Views of Education

A philosophical approach to education and teaching provides teachers with a framework and a set of principles to guide their practice and reflection. Philosophies of education range from students learning basic, factual knowledge; to knowing the ideas in great literature and other books; to learning through involvement in projects that demand inquiring; to taking on inequities in society; or to learning through the social context of relationships. Each philosophy has implications for how a teacher makes decisions about the curriculum and about how the classroom is constructed.

## LIST OF CRITICAL TERM

Dame schools  (*99*)

Latin Grammar school  (*99*)

English schools (academies)  (*101*)

Common school movement  (*103*)

Efficiency movement  (*107*)

English-only rule  (*111*)

Eight-Year Study  (*113*)

Essentialism  (*117*)

Progressivism  (*117*)

Perennialism  (*118*)

Social reconstructionism  (*119*)

Ethic of care  (*120*)

## EXPLORING YOUR COMMITMENT

1. *on your own...* Think back to one of your favorite teachers. Given what you have read about the major philosophical approaches to education, how would you describe this teacher's philosophy?

2. *on your own...* Now do the same for one of your least favorite teachers. What are the limitations of the philosophical perspective this teacher adopted?

3. *in the field...* Interview a practicing teacher about his or her philosophy of teaching. Try to connect this philosophy with one of the major philosophical orientations you have read about.

4. *in the field...* At your school site, walk through the hallways as if you were there for the first time. What kind of philosophy of education does this school appear to represent? What evidence can you find (e.g., how students pass through the halls, materials posted on walls, how teachers interact with students, etc.) to back up your claim?

5. *on the web...* Log onto the website of the Museum of Education at the University of South Carolina to learn about the approaches to education used in several secondary schools in the south that served African American students as part of the Secondary School Study Project (**http://www.ed.sc.edu/MusofEd/secondary_study.html**). Click on the link to Pearl High School to learn more about this study.

6. *on your own...* Select a famous individual whom you admire and who lived before 1960. What kind of education did this individual receive? What barriers, if any, did he or she face in obtaining an education? How does this knowledge affect how you view your role as a teacher?

7. *on your own...* Consider the five major philosophical orientations presented in this chapter. Identify the philosophical orientation that you seem to resonate with most. What accounts for this?

8. *on the web...* Log onto the website of the National Great Books Curriculum, a perennialist approach to education, at **http://www.nationalgreatbooks.com**. How much emphasis was given to any of these books during your high school experience? What might account for their having been either included or excluded from the curriculum?

9. *on the web...* Log onto the website of the PBS series called *School: The Story of American Public Education* at **http://www.pbs.org/kcet/publicschool/index.html**. Click onto the *Innovators* link and select one educational innovator about whom you would like to learn more.

10. *in the research...* Read the 2000 article "Love, Love, and More Love for Children: Exploring Preservice Teachers' Understandings of Caring" by Lisa S. Goldstein and Vickie E. Lake (*Teaching and Teacher Education*, November 2000, Vol., 16, pp. 861–872). How do the authors portray the role of teacher education students' ethic of care? How is it a resource? Can it be a liability?

## GUIDELINES FOR BEGINNING TEACHERS

1. Before you start planning your year, review your philosophy of education. What will you need to do in your new classroom and school to put that philosophy into practice?

2. Read the mission statement for the school and district in which you will be teaching. What philosophical orientation do these statements represent? How do they match with your own philosophical orientation? If they differ substantially, how will you begin to close the gap?

3. Learn about the history of education in the school and district in which you are working? Identify one important thing about that history that can help you in your teaching.

4. Make a date with yourself to sit down annually and revise your philosophy of education. Think about which experiences you had during the year are having the most profound impact on how you view your philosophy and how it is developing. What do you need to do in the coming year to stay truer to your philosophy?

## THE INTASC CONNECTION

In a sense, all of the INTASC standards relate to the philosophy of education, since every decision a teacher makes is somehow related to his or her philosophy. But if one thinks of historical and philosophical knowledge of education as sources of knowledge to help teachers reflect about their practice, the INTASC standard that is most closely aligned with issues related to the history and philosophy of education is Standard 9.

Standard 9 states: *The teacher is a reflective practitioner who continually evaluates the effects of his/her choices and actions on others (students, parents, and other professionals in the learning community) and who seeks out opportunities to grow professionally.* Indicators include the following:

● The teacher values critical thinking and self-directed learning as habits of mind.

● The teacher uses classroom observation, information about students, and research as a basis for evaluating the outcomes of teaching and learning and as a basis for experimenting with, reflecting on, and revising practice.

● The teacher seeks out professional literature, colleagues, and other resources to support his or her own development as a learner and a teacher.

If you are in a state that follows a different set of teacher standards, find the state standards that most closely relate to the INTASC standards discussed here.

## READING ON...

Goodlad, J. I., Goodlad. S. J. and Mantle–Bronley, C. (2004). *Education for everyone: Agenda for education in a democracy*. San Francisco: Jossey-Bass. This book re-explores the role of universal schooling in a democracy.

Greene, M. (2001). *Variations on a blue guitar: The Lincoln Center Institute lectures on aesthetic education*. New York: TC Press. Maxine Greene served in the role of philosopher-in-residence at Lincoln Center for 25 years. Her writing on aesthetic education and the role of the arts in teaching has influenced thousands of teachers.

Cusick, P. A. (2005). *A passion for learning: The education of seven eminent Americans*. New York: Teachers College Press. Cusick explores the importance of education in the lives of Benjamin Franklin, Abraham Lincoln, Jane Addams, W. E. B. Du Bois, Eleanor Roosevelt, J. Robert Oppenheimer, and Dorothy Day.

Simpson, D. J., Aycock. J. C. and Jackson, M. J. B., (2004). *John Dewey and the art of teaching: Toward reflective and imaginative practice*. Thousand Oaks, CA: Sage Publications. Simpson and his colleagues explore the practical ways teachers can implement the philosophy of John Dewey in their classrooms.

# USING THE CURRICULUM RESPONSIBLY

One of the most enduring challenges in education is how to decide what actually gets taught in the classroom. Curriculum is often considered to be the "stuff" of teaching. But teaching is far more than what you teach; it also involves how you teach it and to whom you are teaching it. For all teachers, novice and experienced alike, there is a constant tension among "getting through the material," making sure one has the time and skills to teach it well, and relating the material to the context of students' lives—their families, their communities, and their interests. Given these considerations, how do teachers decide what to emphasize? How do they strike an appropriate balance? How do they know when to shift the balance? To whom are teachers accountable, and for what aspects of the curriculum? How do all of these issues affect a teacher's decisions about the curriculum?

In this section, we focus on how teachers make a professional commitment to creating a curriculum that incorporates high standards but is also relevant and accessible to students. The sources of the curriculum, external pressures that seek to define it, and the role teachers play in the drama of "what is to be taught" are all important to consider as you envision your career as a teacher. Without a sound perspective on curriculum, you risk making teaching decisions based on the most current curricular fad or merely what comes next in the textbook.

Chapter 5 discusses the curriculum itself, how academic standards set at the state level influence the development of the curriculum, and the role of textbooks in delivering the curriculum. Chapter 6 addresses the social context in which teachers do their work: the students, their lives, and the complicated social fabric that influences their lives. To be successful, teachers must embrace the challenge of maintaining a balance between the academic curriculum, how to teach that curriculum, and the students themselves. As you complete this section, your views of "the curriculum" should take on a broader meaning as you consider the responsibility teachers have for creating classrooms where students learn, not just where teachers teach.

## Guiding Questions

- What is the relationship between what is explicitly written as the academic curriculum, what teachers teach, and what students actually learn?

- How is the curriculum developed?

- What are academic standards and how are they developed?

- How does the federal government influence the curriculum?

- How does today's accountability and standards-driven approach to education influence the decisions teachers make about what to teach?

- How do different approaches to the academic curriculum change the way students experience their education?

- What is the role of textbooks in the curriculum?

# Deciding What to Teach

**D**errick Harris has just accepted a position teaching sixth grade in an urban school that spans kindergarten through eighth grade. He is responsible for teaching language arts and social studies. The school that has hired him has high expectations for the students, who represent no fewer than 10 different cultures. Derrick was hired in May. Today, at the end of June, he was finally able to visit his classroom and collect a box of materials the principal put together to help him plan for the fall. He has started to unpack the box, has begun reading the lists of standards, the curriculum guides, and the textbooks that he has found there. Feeling overwhelmed with the sheer magnitude of what he is wading through, he has called Janice Morgan, one of the teachers he worked with last year while he was finishing his teacher education program, who promised she would be available if he needed help.

When Janice answered the phone, the first words out of Derrick's mouth were, "You've got to help me. Where do I start my planning for next year? I'm at school, sitting in the middle of a bunch of desks and I'm looking at a box of curriculum guides, standards, and textbooks" he said. "But I don't know where to start. What should I do first? I don't even know the kids I'll be teaching yet."

"OK." Janice said, "Don't read all that stuff just yet. The first thing you need to do is sit in your classroom and remind yourself why you want to be a teacher. What's important? What kind of world do you want your classroom to be for your students? You know what the answer is—I know you do—because I watched you teach all last semester."

"I know I want my classroom to be a place where the students are involved in what they are learning and even make some decisions about what's important to them to learn. I know they'll get excited about ideas that make a difference to them and make a difference in their lives. But how will I cover this whole curriculum?"

"You probably won't cover every bit of it. But the best way to get started is to recommit yourself to your own purpose for teaching. That's really where you have to start. Then you can review the state standards for Language Arts and Social Studies— you already know them from last year. Then read the curriculum guide so you know where the district wants you to go. Once you have those down, start to plan out the big

*It should be made clear that curriculum design, the creating of educative environments in which students are to dwell, is inherently a political and moral process. It involves competing ideological, political, and intensely personal conceptions of valuable educational activity. Furthermore, one of its primary components is the fact of influencing other people—namely students.*

Michael Apple, 1979, p. 111

ideas and big units you want to teach—and always ask yourself why it's important to do that specific unit. How does it fit with what you want for your students?"

"But what about these textbooks? What if they don't fit?"

"Well, you probably want to know exactly what's in those texts, because they may have some really good ideas, some good stories, and some good background material for social studies. But you can't use them well unless you know what's in them, and how you can use them to build on your own ideas. So I'd take it one document, one book at a time. Know what's in them, but they have to be part of the plan you create yourself."

"Can I do this one semester at a time? I'm not sure I can handle planning for the whole year right now."

"Sure. Let's start by planning out that first quarter together. What are you doing tomorrow afternoon?"

You have made the decision to become a teacher, you have started your first professional courses, and, depending on the kind of teacher education program in which you are enrolled, you may already be involved in early clinical experiences in the schools. At some point in your preparation, like Derrick, you will begin working with a group of breathing, thinking students, and you will want to do so in a way that unequivocally leads to their learning. Otherwise, why teach?

We have already established that learning does not happen by osmosis, that good teachers engage in purposeful planning so that students can learn. Among the many choices teachers make, however, one of the most important is deciding *what* to teach. What is worthwhile for students to study during their PK–12 education? Who is involved in making decisions about what teachers teach? Exactly how do teachers decide what to teach on a day-to-day basis? How do they set priorities? Where do new teachers go to find help in figuring out what to teach and what resources are available to assist them? What pressures are teachers under as they select what they will teach? All such questions generally fall under the topic of the school *curriculum*.

If, for example, you are planning to become a high school chemistry teacher, how do you decide exactly which aspects of chemistry to include? What will you teach by lecturing and what by independent student projects? If you are planning to become an elementary teacher, how do you decide which writing skills you should teach your students? If you are going to teach social studies in a middle school, how will you ever pick and choose among all of that interesting and important content? If you are committed to integrating the arts into your teaching, will you have enough time to explore the arts with your students without shortchanging them on their academic skills? Typically, you have only nine months each year with your students, so clearly it is not possible to teach all the content in a particular area that you think is important. And in any one of these scenarios, how will you even know where to begin? What learning will you actually be held accountable for? This is a dilemma that all teachers face throughout their careers: How to make choices about what to teach when there is so much to teach.

As we will see in this chapter, teachers do not make these choices in a vacuum. The curriculum is based on values that educational leaders, curriculum writers (who often include classroom teachers), and policymakers hold about *what is worthwhile for students to learn*. As you can imagine, defining what is worthwhile for teachers to teach and for students to learn has important philosophical implications for your work as a teacher. Because they reflect values, decisions about the curriculum can also be heavily influenced by the political environment in which teachers do their work.

# Curriculum: A Multidimensional Concept

The term *curriculum* seems like it should be straightforward enough to understand. According to Eliot Eisner (1979), a respected scholar of curriculum in education, the term originates from the Latin word *currere*, which means "the course to be run" (p. 34). The idea is that there is a set course, or program, of study that students are to complete in order to be considered well educated. As we noted earlier, the curriculum represents what is considered worthwhile for students to learn during the years they spend in school.

## The Explicit Curriculum—What It Is and Is Not

We can think of the formal, written academic program of study that guides teaching as the **explicit curriculum** (Eisner, 1979). Larry Cuban (1992), another scholar of curriculum, uses the term *official* or *intended curriculum* to describe the formal academic program of study. These terms convey essentially the same message: the explicit, formal academic curriculum is a public statement of what a particular school district or state believes is worthwhile for students to know in each content area. As such, it sets the broad parameters for what you will teach. The explicit curriculum is usually a public document or series of documents, and today these documents can typically be accessed online through school district or state educational agency websites. It represents the endpoint of your teaching—what your students should know.

> **Critical Term**
>
> **Explicit curriculum.** The formal, official, public academic program of study that defines what students are expected to know as a result of being in school.

As a general rule, two kinds of documents usually define the formal program of study or the explicit curriculum: **academic content standards** and **curriculum guides**. Academic content standards are statements of what students should know and be able to do in each of the major content areas upon completing their PK–12 education. This knowledge is usually assessed in required standardized tests administered by the state. Building on these standards, curriculum guides give detail and resources regarding how the various subjects might be taught.

> **Critical Term**
>
> **Academic content standards.** Formal, public statements of what students should know and be able to do in each of the content areas at various points in their PK–12 education.

The concept of the explicit curriculum sounds simple. You are handed standards and curriculum guides, and you develop teaching plans from these materials. Districts purchase instructional materials, such as textbooks, software, and laboratory equipment, to support the course of study that has been identified as worthwhile. As a teacher, you can draw on these resources and materials to help you plan your own instruction. It is essential for all teachers to know the academic standards for their subject and grade level, and curriculum guides can help interpret those standards. But none of these documents tells you what to do each day in your classroom. They provide a destination only, a statement of what your students should know and be able to do as a result of the instructional program *you* create and implement for *your* students. A set of standards and curriculum guides does not actually tell you how to *teach* to those goals.

> **Critical Term**
>
> **Curriculum guide.** A document prepared at the state or local district level that provides detailed information to help teachers plan instruction.

So in reality the concept of curriculum is much more complex than the sum of a set of documents, however useful they may be. To do their work well, teachers use their knowledge of the standards, the subject, and pedagogy to plan instructional units and lessons that will help them achieve the curriculum goals for that grade and content area *in relationship to the particular group of students they are teaching*. Therefore, what is stated in the explicit curriculum is not exactly the same as what is actually taught. In addition, just because teachers teach "the curriculum" does not necessarily mean that students learn it. Cuban (1992) coined the phrases the *taught curriculum* and the *learned curriculum* to describe how curriculum plays out in the classroom in terms of what is actually taught and learned.

Finally, it is also important to consider both what is and what is not included in the explicit curriculum. Eisner calls everything that is not contained in the formal, explicit curriculum—everything that is left out to begin with—the *null curriculum* (1979). The null curriculum, as we shall see, represents those things that are not valued as important enough to be part of the formal program of studies. In Chapter 6 we will take up a third dimension of curriculum, namely, the *hidden curriculum*, which is defined as all the things students learn by virtue of being in school that are not part of the explicit curriculum.

## Curriculum as What Is Taught

As soon as teachers plan what to teach, they are making choices about how they will deliver the explicit curriculum. Through their interpretations and choices, teachers begin to change the curriculum, introducing their own preferences and beliefs (Cuban, 1992)—hence, the phrase **taught curriculum**. For example, teachers may spend valuable instructional time on one aspect of the curriculum instead of another, or they may convey to their students that one feature of the curriculum is more important than another. A teacher may teach one part of the curriculum in an engaging, motivating way but another in a less motivating way. He or she may use some prescribed curriculum materials and not others. Each such choice affects the content of that curriculum for students and shapes how they understand and learn it.

Making these choices is a regular part of teaching and illustrates that teachers have some degree of autonomy in interpreting the curriculum in their own classrooms. The choices teachers make about the curriculum lets them put their own personal stamp on what and how they teach. Teachers often thrive on the freedom to emphasize the topics and projects that motivate them most—and in turn motivate their students as well—within the broad scope of the explicit curriculum. The challenge, of course—and what represents an enduring curriculum dilemma—is to make those choices in relationship *to* the goals of the curriculum in a manner that maximizes your own students' learning *of* the curriculum. As a teacher you are responsible for making sure your students learn what they are supposed to learn at any given grade level in a way that is meaningful for your students and that engages them in learning. To do that well, you are going to need to be familiar with the academic standards—the goals of the curriculum under which you are teaching.

The concept of the taught curriculum also has implications for the teachers who will work with your students in subsequent years. Teachers are responsible for preparing their students for the next level of work they will be expected to perform

The academic curriculum is not just what a teacher is supposed to teach, but also includes what the teacher actually chooses to teach and what the students learn. (Media Bakery)

in school. Those aspects of the curriculum you emphasize (or choose not to emphasize) may or may not lay the foundation for the curriculum in the upcoming grade level. In other words, you are part of a school community where ideally teachers work together, in a coordinated way, to foster all students' learning and build on what students learn in each year of school.

## Curriculum as What Is Learned

But as we stated above, what you teach is not always what your students learn. It is not enough for teachers to be concerned with presenting content; they must also be concerned with the effects of their teaching on their students. This is what makes the concept of the **learned curriculum** useful. The goal of teaching is to ensure that students learn what you set out for them to learn. How will you know if your teaching has a made a difference?

What students actually learn in relationship to the explicit curriculum is determined in large part by the choices teachers make and the events they enact in the classroom. Unfortunately, some teachers disregard the extent to which their students are actually learning, but these teachers are not carrying out their professional responsibilities well. That is why Cuban (1992) and other curriculum scholars are concerned not only with what is supposed to be taught and what is actually taught, but also with what students actually learn as a result of teaching. Today, as you will see later in this chapter, whether students are learning is a dominant theme nationally and in each state.

You probably recall at least one class during your own PK–12 education where the teacher simply stood up and lectured each day, expecting you to recall the facts in that particular content area. You probably also recall that you didn't learn all of these facts perfectly—if at all. Your teacher was likely teaching from instructional materials that were aligned with the explicit curriculum, hoping that there would be a direct transfer of factual knowledge from him or her to you, the students. Your teacher taught, but what you learned did not match what was taught.

Teachers may choose to present content in this rote manner, but if they do, their students may not always learn the material well—despite the fact that it is in the explicit curriculum. If teachers want their students to learn the explicit curriculum, standing up day after day and telling students what is in it is not a particularly effective way of teaching—and certainly not a guarantee that they will learn. To ensure that students learn, teachers must figure out ways to make the content of the curriculum meaningful to their students and connect the content to their students' lives. This might include a good lecture or teacher presentation of information now and then, but continuously relying on this approach does not engage students well. Reaching students on a daily basis requires that teachers make choices not only about what they teach, but also about how they will teach so that their specific group of students learn.

**Your turn...** *to review*

1. What is the difference between the *explicit curriculum* and the *taught curriculum*?
2. Why is it so important for teachers to assess their students' learning of the curriculum?
3. Name three different ways teachers can get information about how well their students are learning the curriculum.

The explicit curriculum is meaningless if teachers are not concerned about the degree to which their students are learning. To determine whether students have learned what they are taught, teachers continuously need to assess how their students are doing. By observing students carefully, by listening to them during discussions, by evaluating students' written work, by conferencing with students individually, and also by testing students, teachers keep track of their students' learning. The information teachers gain through ongoing assessment not only enables teachers to document their students' learning; it also provides teachers with feedback on how well they are teaching.

For example, let's say that a teacher in a middle school social studies class has just completed a unit on supply and demand. A follow-up homework essay shows that 80 percent of the class does not understand these concepts. The results of this essay provide the teacher with feedback on how well the students learned the material. Recognizing that the majority of the class did not do well, a teacher might ask him- or herself, "What can I do differently to ensure that my students 'get' these concepts?" "How can I represent these concepts more effectively?" Teachers who do not ask themselves such questions and who do not use feedback from students' work to improve their own practice are not demonstrating a reflective approach to their work and are not carrying out their professional responsibilities well. If only one or two students did not understand the material, the teacher's response might be to figure out how to provide additional support to those few students. In either case, assessing students systematically provides teachers with an understanding of how well the taught curriculum translates into what students have learned, or the learned curriculum.

Assessing students' learning is a critical factor in differentiating between what is taught and what is learned. Furthermore, it is appropriate for you as the teacher to be held accountable for what your students learn in the curriculum—accountable to the students, to their families, and to the school's administration. Regularly gathering information about how your students are doing is one of the best ways for you to know how well you are teaching the curriculum.

Over the past two decades, **accountability** for learning the curriculum has received much greater attention than perhaps at any other time in the history of education in the United States. But it is defined primarily in terms of how well students do on standardized tests, with less regard for other forms of ongoing assessment in the classroom that good teachers carry out every day—for example, informal observation of students, classroom assignments, or other assessments developed by the teacher. This view of what schools are for is aligned with the essentialist philosophical perspective introduced in Chapter 3. The goal of accountability for student learning is a worthy one, and teachers who are serious about their work have always paid careful attention to how their students are doing. However, when accountability is defined narrowly as the scores students achieve on standardized tests, teachers can feel constrained in the creativity and innovation they draw on to teach the curriculum. As we will see later in this chapter, they often feel pressured to "teach to the test."

Figure 5-1 illustrates the relationship between the explicit, the taught, and the learned curriculum and identifies the levels at which each dimension of the curriculum plays out. These three aspects of the curriculum are in constant interplay in the classroom. They reflect not only the teacher's choices about what and how to teach, but also the interactions between teachers and their students. How to balance the competing demands of the explicit and the taught curriculum in relationship to pressures to demonstrate what students have learned is a dilemma all teachers face. Moreover, the relationship among these three dimensions of curriculum can change over time. When such changes occur, they can have a profound influence on the day-to-day choices teachers make about the curriculum. For example, when the

## Critical Term

**Accountability.** Ensuring that teachers are held responsible for their students' learning; using student learning as the measure of a teacher's effectiveness.

> ### Figure 5-1    The Relationship among the Intended, Taught, and Learned Curriculum
>
> **What federal, state, and local curriculum documents represent as the intended course of study is mediated by how teachers teach and what students learn.**
>
>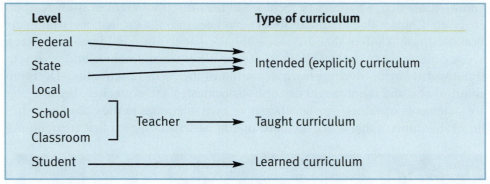
>
> **Source:** Adapted from Cuban. L. (1992). Curriculum stability and change. In P. W., Jackson (Ed.), *Handbook of research on curriculum* (pp. 216–247). New York: Macmillan.

pressure of standardized testing is great, teachers can feel constrained in what they do in the classroom and how they use their instructional time. As teachers gain greater experience, however, they can become more skilled in balancing the autonomy they have in the classroom with the requirements of the explicit curriculum.

## What Isn't Taught—The Null Curriculum

The explicit curriculum does not include everything it is possible to know, nor does it include every perspective on that knowledge. Rather, the explicit curriculum is one "take" on knowledge and on what is important to know. By necessity, much is excluded. Another way to think about what curriculum is is to consider everything that is *not* taught in school. As we noted earlier, Eliot Eisner refers to all that is not included in the public, official, explicit curriculum and is not taught as the **null curriculum**. What schools do not teach is also a statement about what is— and is not—valued in PK–12 education.

If a high school requires four years of mathematics, but music and art are taken only as electives, then for many students music and art are part of the null curriculum. If a school offers only one foreign language, then all of the other foreign languages are part of the null curriculum. The null curriculum is made up of the subjects students have no opportunity to study in school—subjects that are not deemed to have sufficient worth or value to include in the curriculum.

Similarly, if students read only literature and poetry written by European or European American male authors in their English classes, the null literature curriculum consists of all of the other works of fiction and poetry by racial and ethnic minority male and female authors and European or European American females to which students will not be exposed in school. As a result of defining the curriculum in this way, students who live in a multiethnic, multiracial society do not have the opportunity through literature as it is taught in school to gain perspective on the life experiences and issues represented by the works of a broad range of authors.

A different example of the null curriculum can be found in current views of history that students often learn relating to Christopher Columbus's arrival in the Americas. Until recent years, when teachers taught the story of Columbus, the "null" curriculum consisted of the native perspective. Today Columbus's arrival in the new

**Critical Term**

**Null curriculum.** Everything that is not included in the explicit curriculum, and, thus, is not expected to be learned during a student's PK–12 education.

world, marking the start of major European settlements in the America, is also viewed as negative because it was destructive to the indigenous people already living here.

Thus, what is *not* included in the explicit curriculum is just as much a statement of values in education as what *is* included. The concept of the null curriculum reminds us that multiple perspectives exist about what is important to know—more than what may be included in the official program of study teachers are given. Choices that are made about what goes into the explicit curriculum are simultaneously choices that are made about what is not considered important. These choices express values about what is or is not worth teaching and what is or is not worth having students learn as a result of their PK–12 schooling. Decisions about what is and is not taught can be hotly contested issues precisely because they are statements of values. Teachers face their own dilemmas in the classroom when they value content that is not included or emphasized in the explicit curriculum.

## Your turn... *to reflect*

In small groups , select one content area at the high school level. In the community in which you went to school, what was included in the curriculum? What was not included or was given little emphasis? What do you think may account for what was in the explicit/taught curriculum, and what was in the null curriculum? What did you gain or lose as a result of how the curriculum was defined?

### Curriculum Dilemmas

Now that you have a sense of the various dimensions of the curriculum, let's consider in greater detail how the explicit curriculum develops. How do decisions about it get made? What is the role of the state, and what is the role of the local school district in the development of curriculum? Just how much assistance and direction will formal curriculum documents offer you? Knowing that you cannot control all aspects of the curriculum and that you might have philosophical differences with the official curriculum, how can you nevertheless use the curriculum wisely as you plan and carry out your teaching every day? And, most important, how will you balance the competing demands between the explicit curriculum and your daily work as a teacher?

## Developing the Curriculum: How Does It Work?

In Chapter 3 you learned that the authority to govern education belongs to each state. The development of the explicit curriculum and supporting curriculum documents usually begins at the state level with the development of academic content standards, which, as we noted above, represent what the state believes students should know by the time they complete their compulsory PK–12 education. The term *academic content standards* implies that at some point students must demonstrate that they have actually mastered the standards—most often on a standardized test of achievement in that subject area. Local curriculum development at the level of the individual school district must take into account and reflect the state standards, since it is against these standards that students are tested.

In any given generation in the United States, power actually shifts, swinging back and forth between greater state control over curriculum development (a more centralized approach) and greater local control, (a more decentralized approach). We are currently in an era in which states exert a lot of control, heavily influenced, as we shall see later on, by the federal government. Because testing requirements have increased along with hefty sanctions for schools that are not performing well, academic standards play a heavier role and provide a stronger guide to the development of the curriculum. However, states have not always exerted this much power over local decisions on the curriculum.

In contrast to the educational system in the United States, most other countries have a single national curriculum. That is, education in these countries is centralized at the national level, so that teachers implement the same curriculum in every school all over the country. If a change is deemed appropriate, a national curriculum committee makes that change and all schools in that country are expected to comply. Although a national orientation to curriculum may be more efficient in terms of curriculum development, it fails to take into account the state and local autonomy that has been so prized in the U.S. educational system.

## How Are Academic Content Standards Created?

Each state has an agency with a title such as the *Department of Public Instruction* or the *Department of Education*, which is responsible for all aspects of education, including the development of academic standards. Professional educators employed by these agencies, usually along with committees of veteran teachers and other experts in the various content areas, then develop the standards for each content area. Many state agencies also rely on nationally recognized standards developed by professional organizations devoted to the major academic content areas. These organizations include, for example, the American Council on the Teaching of Foreign Languages (**www.actfl.org**), the National Council of Teachers of English (**www.ncte.org**), the International Reading Association (**www.reading.org**), the National Council of Teachers of Mathematics (**www.nctm.org**), the National Council for Social Studies (**www.ncss.org**), or the National Science Teachers Association (**www.nsta.org**), which worked under the auspices of the National Research Council in Washington, D.C., to develop academic standards for science. State committees may use these national standards in an advisory manner, or states may simply adopt the national standards, reasoning that professionals in the various content area organizations nationally possess the best knowledge to inform the development of academic standards.

State and local academic standards can provide a starting point for how teachers decide what to teach, but teachers need to be thoughtful about how they actually carry out instruction in relationship to the standards their students are required to meet. (Digital Vision)

The degree to which individual states adhere to national standards developed by professional organizations determines how similar or different academic expectations will be across the 50 states. As we noted earlier, the United States does not formally have a national education system, but when many states adhere to the same set of national academic standards (or teacher standards, for that matter), the individuality of the states begins to diminish.

## What Do Academic Content Standards Look Like?

Although across standards can have a lot in common, especially due to the influence of the national organizations identified above, each state also organizes its standards differently. Some standards may be organized by grade

level, others by topic within a school level, and others by children's general developmental levels. For example, California organizes its standards using a combination of grade levels (e.g., for English/Language Arts across all grades) and topics (e.g., high school science and mathematics courses). In contrast, Illinois organizes all of its standards by students' developmental levels, including *early elementary, late elementary, middle/junior high, early high school, and late high school.* The number of standards can also differ widely across states. Table 5-1 provides an example of how three states break down their fourth grade standards for life sciences.

As you move through your teacher education program into learning how to teach the academic areas for which you will be responsible, it will be important to become familiar with the standards for the subject and levels you will be teaching.

 Most states post their standards on the web. You can find a drop down menu to locate your state's standards at the website of Education World at **http://www.educationworld.com/standards/state/index.shtml**.

### Your turn... *to reflect*

In small groups, review Table 5-1 and consider the differences among the standards in these three states. If you moved from one state to another and were responsible for teaching fourth grade science in both settings, how much would you have to adjust your teaching?

## What Do Curriculum Guides Look Like?

Standards by themselves do not constitute a curriculum. Once standards have been set by the states, supporting curriculum materials are developed at both the state and the local levels. When the pendulum is swinging toward greater centralization of the curriculum—as it is today—state documents can exert greater influence over local curriculum development. When the pendulum is swinging toward decentralization, local curriculum development can exert greater influence. Many local school districts develop their own curriculum documents in every academic content area, even if they mirror the state documents substantially. These two levels of curriculum development are not always sequential; the state may be in a process of creating or revising curriculum documents in mathematics, for example, one year, while local districts may be revising their curricula in health in the same year.

**Curriculum Development at the State Level.** Different states use different names to describe the curriculum. California, for example, uses the term *frameworks* for the resources it offers in each of the major academic areas. These frameworks, which are book-length documents, "are the blueprints for implementing grade-level content standards adopted by the California State Board of Education" (**http://www.cde.ca.gov/be/st**). As an example, the framework for the English–Language Arts area includes the following:

- The goals and major components of an effective language arts program
- Curriculum content and instructional methods to ensure that students meet the English–Language Arts standards
- Guidance for assessing student progress
- Strategies to ensure that students with special needs access and are challenged to achieve in this area
- Professional development supports for teachers to help them carry out a "rigorous and coherent language arts curriculum"

**Table 5-1    Comparison of Fourth Grade Academic Standards and Substandards for Life Science in California, Virginia, and Wisconsin**

States break down each standard in different ways, and this affects how teachers plan the curriculum.

| California | Virginia | Wisconsin |
|---|---|---|
| Life Sciences | | |
| **Standard 2. All organisms need energy and matter to live and grow. As a basis for understanding this concept:** | **Standard 4.4. The student will investigate and understand basic plant anatomy and life processes.** | **Standard F. Students in Wisconsin will demonstrate an understanding of the characteristics and structures of living things, the processes of life, and how living things interact with one another and their environment.** |
| a. *Students know* plants are the primary source of matter and energy entering most food chains. | Key concepts include: the structures of typical plants (leaves, stems, roots, and flowers); processes and structures involved with reproduction (pollination, stamen, pistil, sepal, embryo, spore, and seed); photosynthesis (chlorophyll, carbon dioxide); and dormancy. | |
| b. *Students know* producers and consumers (herbivores, carnivores, omnivores, and decomposers) are related in food chains and food webs and may compete with each other for resources in an ecosystem. | | THE CHARACTERISTICS OF ORGANISMS |
| c. *Students know* decomposers, including many fungi, insects, and microorganisms, recycle matter from dead plants and animals. | **Standard 4.5. The student will investigate and understand how plants and animals in an ecosystem interact with one another and the nonliving environment.** | F.4.1 Discover how each organism meets its basic needs for water, nutrients, protection, and energy in order to survive. |
| | | F.4.2 Investigate how organisms, especially plants, respond to both internal cues (the need for water) and external cues (changes in the environment). |
| **Standard 3. Living organisms depend on one another and on their environment for survival. As a basis for understanding this concept:** | Key concepts include behavioral and structural adaptations; organization of communities; flow of energy through food webs; habitats and niches, life cycles; and influence of human activity on ecosystems. | |
| a. *Students know* ecosystems can be characterized by their living and nonliving components. | | LIFE CYCLES OF ORGANISMS |
| b. *Students know* that in any particular environment, some kinds of plants and animals survive well, some survive less well, and some cannot survive at all. | | F.4.3 Illustrate the different ways that organisms grow through life stages and survive to produce new members of their type. |
| c. *Students know* many plants depend on animals for pollination and seed dispersal, and animals depend on plants for food and shelter. | | ORGANISMS AND THEIR ENVIRONMENT |
| d. *Students know* that most microorganisms do not cause disease and that many are beneficial. | | F.4.4 Using the science themes, develop explanations for the connections among living and nonliving things in various environments. |

**Sources:** California State Board of Education. Grade Four science content standards. Sacramento, CA: Author. Retrieved May 16, 2008, from http://www.cde.ca.gov/be/st/ss/scgrade4.asp; Commonwealth of Virginia, Department of Education. (2000). Science standards of learning teacher resource guide, Grade Four. Richmond, VA: Author. Retrieved May 16, 2008, from http://www.do.virginia.gov/VDOE/Instruction/Sci-resource.html; Wisconsin Department of Public Instruction. (2002). Wisconsin model academic standards for science. Madison, WI; Author. Retrieved May, 16 2008, from http://www.dpi.state.wi.us/dpi/standards/sciintro.html.

● Requirements for the development of instructional materials

The English–Language Arts framework in California, for example, gives specific models for the kinds of activities teachers are expected to implement, and it states specifically that teachers are not to present lessons in which their students are merely passive listeners. Instead, teachers are directed to (1) read aloud to students, (2) structure instructional discussions with their students, (3) have students read often, and (4) have students write often. You can see that this represents a particular perspective on teaching English–Language Arts that all teachers are expected to follow, a perspective that goes beyond only having the teacher present information in a lecture-style approach.

In Virginia, state curriculum documents include sample **scope and sequence** charts. *Scope and sequence* is a common term in discussions of curriculum materials; scope and sequence charts are curriculum documents that lay out, usually in a grid or matrix format, what will be taught in a particular subject area over the course of all of the PK–12 grades. *Scope* refers to the breadth of coverage in the subject, whereas *sequence* refers to the order in which various topics and skills will be taught across the grades. In the Virginia materials, scope and sequence documents for each content area include the following:

● Essential knowledge, skills, and processes students should learn
● Reference to specific standards of learning
● Sample assessment methods
● Sample resources for teachers, including software

Scope and sequence charts can be helpful to new teachers who are unsure about how the material they are supposed to teach for their particular grade level fits into the bigger curriculum picture in their district. Textbook publishers often provide scope and sequence charts to accompany their curriculum materials across all grade levels. These charts may or may not correlate well with scope and sequence charts developed by the state. However, scope and sequence charts are not a substitute for teachers' planning their instruction based on the specific needs of their particular students.

In the Virginia curriculum documents, the standards are correlated to specific instructional activities that teachers can use, and some instructional materials are also included (see **http://www.pen.k12.va.us/VDOE/Instruction/solscope/**).

Virginia goes one step further and for certain academic areas prescribes a group of specific instructional programs that may be used. These include 13 model programs that are supposed to be effective with students who are having difficulty achieving in English and mathematics, and districts may choose among them. If you teach in a state with such mandates, you will have less autonomy with regard to curriculum choices.

In contrast, other curriculum guides can provide more in the way of a conceptual framework for teaching the subject. This is the case with the curriculum guide for mathematics in the state of Wisconsin, as illustrated in Figure 5-2. From this partial table of contents, you can see that the focus is helping teachers think differently about the teaching of mathematics so that students will be better prepared in what has long been a challenging subject in the United States, as reflected in the relatively low mathematics achievement scores of U.S. students in comparison to other countries.

These various examples illustrate that state curriculum guides can have a heavy hand in defining the kind of teaching that is expected in a particular state as a means of achieving academic standards. These documents can extend the notion of the standards and can also advocate specific instructional methods or indicate what kinds of units should be taught. The degree to which you must use highly specialized, specific programs of instruction to carry out the curriculum, however, depends on where you teach. As you identify places where you want to teach, it is important to consider how

**Critical Term**

**Scope and sequence.**
Charts that lay out the various topics within a subject that will be included, as well as what level of that topic students will study at each grade level in a particular subject.

**Figure 5-2    A Conceptual Approach to a Curriculum Guide in Mathematics for Wisconsin (partial table of contents)**

Curriculum guides can be a valuable resource to teachers as they develop lessons and units of study for their students.

**We Are All Learners of Mathematics**

Where Is Mathematics Today?

How Did Mathematics Education Get Where It Is Today?

Mathematics in Wisconsin

**Teaching and Learning Mathematics with Understanding**

Why Understanding?

What Is Understanding?

How Understanding Is Developed

Is Understanding the Same for Everyone?

Critical Dimensions of Classrooms that Promote Understanding

Structuring and Applying Knowledge

Reflection and Articulation

Classroom Norms

**Curriculum, Instruction, and Assessment**

Curriculum

What Is a Curriculum?

How Is Mathematics Knowledge Built?

What Are the Implications for Curricula?

What Are Conceptual and Procedural Knowledge?

What Is the Relationship between Conceptual and Procedural Knowledge?

What Has the TIMSS Study Found in Curricula Comparisons?

What Efforts Have Been Made to Address the Curriculum Question?

Instruction

What Is Good Mathematics Teaching?

How Is Teacher Expertise Achieved?

Professionalization or Professionalism?

What Steps Have Been Taken to Professionalize Teaching?

Assessment

Source: Wisconsin Department of Public Instruction. (2008). *Planning curriculum in mathematics.* Madison, WI: Author. Retrieved May 15, 2008, from http://dpi.wi.gov.

constrained you may or may not be by a heavily prescribed combination of standards, curriculum, mandated programs of instruction, and required statewide assessments.

The quality of these documents varies from state to state and from district to district. Within the states, guides for different subjects may also vary in quality depending on who developed them. As a teacher you will have to make informed professional judgments about how useful these various curriculum guides might be. If they are good, then such guides can help you make the transition from standards to the daily "stuff" of teaching. But remember that no matter how good these documents are, it is up to you to use them in relationship to the students you are teaching and what will work best to support their learning. The Case in Point that follows shows how a teacher can devise a special project that both accommodates standards and is in tune with students' interests.

## A Case In Point
### Developing a Teaching Unit

It's November and Derrick Harris is feeling much more comfortable in his sixth grade classroom. He's gotten through the first months with the support of his school and his teaching friend Janice, who is a sounding board for his ideas. As he plans for the second semester, he's thinking about the things his students are interested in. One of the topics that keeps coming up in different conversations is what the students are eating. There are news stories about childhood obesity, they keep hearing about problems with fast food, and some of the students come from families that are vegetarian. Derrick thinks this topic might be a good idea for a long-term project right after the winter holidays. He's playing with an organizing question such as: "How good is our food for us?"

The standards for Language Arts include writing for different purposes, organizing and making oral presentations, and writing a research paper. In social studies, the standards for his grade include understanding how the development of cities and geographic resources influence where people live. The state curriculum guide has many references that look like they would be helpful in planning. Derrick knows that his students need much more practice in taking notes for research papers and in writing persuasive essays, and he can envision some lively discussion about food. He is pretty sure that his students don't have any idea about where their food comes from, who benefits from the way the food industry is organized, and how it has changed over time.

He knows he might need some help from Sarah, the science teacher, especially if they get into the details of food chemistry, so he has a conversation with her to get some ideas as he plans. He's going to set aside a month for this project, starting with having the students analyze their own eating patterns and their relationship to family cultural practices. Then they will map where their food comes from, identify what proportion of their food is fresh versus processed, and learn about local urban gardens that are located in a few places in the community and why they were started. These and similar topics will lead to individual research projects and papers. At the end of the unit, students will prepare oral presentations for the other grade-level students and their own families as well as advertisements to be posted schoolwide. Finally, their conclusions will be posted on Derrick's classroom website.

Derrick reviewed all of his plans with Sarah, and she showed him where his plans intersected with the local science curriculum. One of the areas the local curriculum emphasized is connecting science with the other content areas, so she was happy he was making those linkages. They planned to team teach certain classes so that Sarah could demonstrate some of the lessons where Derrick felt a little less confident in the science content.

**Curriculum Development at the Local District Level.** State documents serve as resources for local efforts, where district specialists in the various content areas (or in smaller districts, a single curriculum specialist), often working side by side with teachers like Derrick's colleague, Sarah, create their own curriculum documents to interpret state standards and curriculum. Today local curriculum development efforts have two things in common. First, because of the prominence of state academic standards, they must help assure that students meet the goals in the standards that are assessed on required tests. In other words, there is great pressure to *align* the curriculum to academic standards. Second, local curriculum developers must create a local curriculum that is responsive not only to standards, but also to local expectations and values. These competing pressures may lead one district's curriculum to look different from another's even as they respond to the same set of academic content standards.

In one school district, for example, local environmental issues may be the "platform" for the study of ecology within a science curriculum. In another, literature may be chosen because it illustrates the cultural backgrounds of the students who attend school there. If you teach in District X, you might find yourself teaching a very different set of novels in high school literature classes than those taught in District Y. Specific social studies projects might be required in one district but not in another. Some schools may require that secondary students perform community service as part of their graduation requirements—essentially making it part of the explicit curriculum—and others may not. Some high schools may emphasize teaching writing across all of the curriculum areas rather than only in English class; in others, writing may be emphasized only in English class.

Local values can also fuel heated debates about what is worthwhile to teach, and they can influence the local curriculum. A school district's commitment to what belongs—and what does not belong—in a local curriculum can create bitter rivalries. These rivalries usually reflect strongly held values for some or all of the citizens in the community, and defending local curriculum practice has sometimes been a flashpoint for controversy.

Debates about what should and should not be included in the curriculum are often fueled by strong philosophical or religious beliefs. (©AP/Wide World Photos)

One of the best known, longstanding examples of curriculum rivalry that continues to reverberate today occurred in the 1925 Scopes trial in Tennessee, immortalized in the classic play *Inherit the Wind* (Lawrence & Lee, 1955). In this trial, a local high school biology teacher disregarded the explicit science curriculum defined by state law (the Butler Act) as creationism and instead made a decision to enact, in the *taught* curriculum, the theory of evolution. This particular argument—that is, creationism versus evolution—is driven by deep-seated values regarding the relative roles of secular versus religious interpretations of scientific phenomena. It has been played out over and over again as a local curriculum issue, and the disagreements continue to surface today. School districts in Georgia, Pennsylvania, Kansas, and Ohio, among others, have engaged in curriculum debates that pit the teaching of evolution against teaching about "intelligent design," which is principally based on the belief that "some structures or processes in nature are irreducibly complex and could not have originated over long periods of times (American Association for the Advancement of Science, 2008).

The balance between the explicit curriculum at the state and local levels is always in play for teachers. In addition, as we will discuss shortly, your own philosophy always affects the daily choices you make about how to construct the curriculum that you actually teach.

## National Influences on Curriculum Development

Earlier we noted that the development of state academic standards is often influenced by national professional organizations. However, national events themselves can also influence what is considered important for students to learn. Perhaps one of the best known examples of national influence on curriculum development occurred in the early 1960s, when, with the launch of Sputnik in 1957, the Russians beat the United States into outer space. This single event caused a remarkable surge in federal funding for science and mathematics education—over $100 million between 1958 and 1968 (Eisner, 1979). This funding was based on the belief that the United States had to invest in education—especially in mathematics and science—so that the Russians would not continue to gain the upper hand. As a result, districts scrambled to redesign their curriculums in accordance with new, higher expectations for achievement in science and mathematics; parallel levels of activity took place among university scholars in these fields. National efforts at curriculum development translated into new activities at the local level and also influenced the content of textbooks.

### Your turn... *to review*

1. What is the purpose of academic standards?
2. What role can curriculum guides play in helping teachers plan their work?
3. How can national events influence the curriculum?

Another such example was the 1983 report, *A Nation at Risk: The Imperative for Educational Reform*, published by the National Commission on Excellence in Education. Beginning with the somber statement, "Our nation is at risk" (p. 5), this report counseled that the country was failing to educate its children well and that education was endangered by "a rising tide of mediocrity" (p. 5). The report recommended strengthening high school graduation requirements, adopting standards, lengthening the school day, and increasing the rewards in and respect for the profession of teaching. It led professional organizations to develop national academic standards in each of the content areas and prompted states to adopt academic standards. These actions contributed to today's tighter alignment among standards, the curriculum, and standardized tests, or assessment. Today there is again heightened interest in how well the United States is doing in relationship to other countries in science and mathematics-related fields. The Science, Technology, Engineering and Mathematics Education (STEM) coalition works provide support for STEM education (**www.stemedcoalition.org**).

National events have exerted—and continue to exert—a strong homogenizing influence over much curriculum development. When many states adopt academic standards developed by national professional organizations, this effect is heightened. Further contributing to this homogenization is the national impact of textbooks, which we will discuss in detail later in this chapter. National commissions such as the one that produced *A Nation at Risk* can have the effect of reducing variability at the state and local level. So although no formal national curriculum exists, a de facto national curriculum is sometimes said to exist as national reports and curriculum developments exert their influence and as national standards are adopted and adapted at the state level. The influence of national bodies on state and local curriculums has a long history, as the following Historical Note describes.

## Historical Note
### The Influence of National Committees on Schooling and the Curriculum

National committees have long had an influence on the educational establishment in the United States. In the late 1800s, in the wake of great concern over the repetitive nature of the curriculum, two highly influential committees appointed by the National Education Association reviewed the elementary and secondary curriculums.

At the high school level, the general question was whether high school should prepare students for college or for the world of work. Those who saw high school as preparation for college wanted a high school curriculum that would prepare graduates for the rigorous academic programs at selective universities, which served a small proportion of students. In 1893, the National Education Association convened the Committee of Ten on Secondary Education, a group of influential educators, chaired by Charles Eliot, the president of Harvard University, to consider the secondary school curriculum.

Members of this committee recommended a high school curriculum of nine academic subjects, including geography, history/government/political economy, biology, physical science (physics, astronomy, chemistry), mathematics, modern languages, English, Greek, and Latin. Their intent was to ensure that high schools taught a strict academic curriculum to prepare graduates for college. To influence the common schools, the committee recommended that students begin their studies of some of these subjects as early as elementary school. The Committee of Ten also recommended that the curriculum should not be differentiated for those who were or were not planning to attend college. Rather, everyone would study these classical subjects. As a result of this highly uniform academic curriculum, many students dropped out since it did not address vocational education.

In the same year that the Committee of Ten was appointed, 1893, the National Education Association also appointed the Committee of Fifteen on Elementary Education. This committee supported the basic academic subjects of grammar, literature, arithmetic, geography, and history. However, the elementary curriculum they developed also included music, manual training, physical culture, and drawing. This committee recommended restructuring the elementary school years and reducing the number of grades from 10 to 8. The plan did not include kindergarten. According to educational historians Butts and Cremin (1953), the recommendations of the Committee of Fifteen "faced backward rather than forward and . . . completely ignored individuality in education" (p. 384).

Although the recommendations of these two committees were not uniformly supported, their work was influential. Their curriculum recommendations and recommendations for how schools should be structured were widely adopted. These two highly visible committees, whose members were among the elite of the country, commanded a national platform for recommending curriculum and structural reform. It is apparent now, however, that their recommendations served only a small proportion of elementary and secondary students and was not meant to serve all students.

## Curriculum—Teaching with a Purpose

The dominant philosophy in education today is teaching to academic standards that are tested regularly on a statewide basis. Standards drive the curriculum, and teaching to the standards defines what is valued. This approach to education is closely related to the philosophy of *essentialism* discussed in Chapter 3. Earlier scholars of curriculum such as Eisner and Vallance (1974) identify this philosophy as a *technical approach to education*, in which curriculum is defined as whatever means teachers use to ensure that students meet the standards. In other words, what is worthwhile for students to know and for teachers to teach is defined narrowly as the standards themselves, which become the endpoint, or purpose, of education.

As a general operating principle for teaching, it seems reasonable enough to assume that the curriculum—that is, what you teach—should be aligned with standards for academic performance in the various subject areas. When teachers have a clear picture of what their students should learn, this should help them make decisions about the taught curriculum. And teachers certainly need to be able to demonstrate that their teaching has resulted in student learning. At the same time, however, the more public pressure there is on teachers to make sure their students perform well on standardized tests, the more likely it is for curriculum decision making to be based only on preparing students to do well on those standardized tests and not on any larger or more meaningful curriculum goals. The standards can all too easily become the curriculum.

Other approaches to curriculum represent different purposes and provide unique departure points for developing a school's unique identity and answering the question "What's worth knowing?". When a whole school purposefully orients its curriculum in a particular way, that school is taking a stance on what it believes is worthwhile to teach and have students learn. Evidence of its curricular stance should be apparent across the school, thus giving a particular focal point and character to the school, and a sense of direction and commitment on the part of the teachers, students, and families. Different philosophical approaches to education representing different purposes can dominate at different times in history. A substantial body of thought in education that emerged and dominated in the early part of the twentieth century, for example, argued vehemently against a strictly technical view of education, as the following Philosophical Note describes.

## Philosophical Note
### John Dewey and the Progressive View of Education

How students experience the academic curriculum was a particular concern of educators who aligned themselves with the progressive education movement in the 1920s. Led by the famous educational philosopher John Dewey, progressive educators believed that teachers should put a concern for students' entire educational experience at the forefront of their planning and teaching—not just learning the material. "What the progressives shared," wrote Decker Walker and Jonas Soltis (1992), "was their opposition to prevailing school practices such as memorization, drill, stern discipline, and the learning of fixed subject matter defined in adult terms with little relation to the life of the child" (pp. 18–19). According to the famous historian of education, Lawrence Cremin (1988), several themes characterized progressive education, among them: "first, a broadening of the program and the function of the school to include a direct concern for health, vocation, and the quality of family and community life; second, the application in the classroom of more humane, more active, and more rational pedagogical techniques…, third, the tailoring of instruction more directly to the different kinds and classes of children who were being brought within the purview of the school" (p. 229).

Rather than seeing a teacher's role simply as "pouring in" academic knowledge, John Dewey and his followers believed that the purpose of education was to promote individual growth and intellectual development as a means of preparing students to participate actively and creatively in the democracy (Tanner & Tanner, 1980). In this view, when children and youth interact with the academic curriculum in meaningful ways, they will grow intellectually and be prepared for addressing the pressing problems of society. Dewey was concerned with children's overall development not only for the sake of their individual growth, but as a specific means of enriching the democracy. In contrast, having children sit still and simply receive academic knowledge passively from their teachers—having it "poured into their heads," so to speak—is known as the transmission model of education.

This transmission model of teaching is usually thought of as a relatively conservative educational philosophy based on the belief that children's minds are essentially empty vessels waiting to be filled with academic knowledge. Teachers transmit this body of knowledge from their own minds to those of their students, usually by highly teacher-directed activities such as lecturing. Teachers may deliver essential knowledge fundamental to each of the academic disciplines—essentialism. Or they may teach from time-honored, classical texts from the liberal arts which are considered to be perennially appropriate for developing students' intellect; this approach is known as perennialism. Both of these approaches are more focused on the content of the curriculum and on what students need to master, and less on the child as a developing individual (Tanner & Tanner, 1980).

You can imagine that very different messages are communicated by the actions of a teacher whose philosophy is aligned with students sitting and absorbing academic information compared with a teacher who communicates that learning in an exciting, meaningful interaction among the students, the ideas and knowledge in the academic curriculum, and the teacher. If a school subscribes to a transmission-oriented philosophy, it can readily communicate to students that their job is to sit, listen, and give back the knowledge to the teacher in rote format in workbooks, on worksheets, and on tests. When the transmission model dominates, students themselves have little say about what and how they learn and about the relevance of the knowledge they are supposed to master. Furthermore, current advances in educational psychology suggest that students do not simply sit and absorb knowledge. Instead, they filter and process new knowledge that teachers may deliver through the background knowledge and experience they already possess.

The two extremes of the philosophical spectrum in education—the transmission model often represented by essentialism versus the progressive child-centered model—are rarely seen in their pure formats. There is a constant philosophical tension in education between the need for students to learn important content and the need for them to be highly engaged in their learning so that the content is meaningful and useful. Highly skilled teachers are often masters at embedding the learning of content itself within an educational environment in the classroom in which students are motivated to learn and have ample opportunities to use what they are learning in meaningful ways.

John Dewey, the famous philosopher of education, was a passionate advocate for child-centered, progressive approaches to teaching and learning.
(Corbis Images)

## Beyond a Technical Approach—Special Curriculum Identities for Individual Schools

Despite the pressure schools are under to conform to standards and standardized testing, which can easily lead to a highly technical approach to education or to an emphasis on teaching only "basic skills" (see below), several different orientations to curriculum exist in schools all over the United States today. The different curriculum identities individual schools adopt may range widely across different purposes for education. Many schools frame their curriculums in specific ways as a means of attracting students to their school, its special identity, and its special sense of purpose—for students and teachers alike.

For example, special schools for the arts, such as New York City's High School of the Arts made famous in the 1980 movie *Fame*, exist in many major cities. Arts schools emphasize the philosophy that artistic activity is a worthwhile way of knowing and learning about the world that is not widely accessible in a conventional academic curriculum. In addition, schools whose curriculum emphasizes science and mathematics are increasingly popular. The state of Illinois sponsors the residential Illinois Mathematics and Science Academy (http://www2.imsa.edu/), and North Carolina sponsors the North Carolina School of Science and Mathematics, also a residential school (http://www.ncssm.edu/).

Not all specialized schoolwide curriculums focus on a specific academic content area. A school could organize its curriculum according to a set of specific values that define a school's character. If the school's curriculum centers on globalization, one might expect value to be placed on world social studies and world languages and on how individuals and nations can work together in a global context. A school might also orient its curriculum to technology and place value on learning to use technology in order to advance student learning across all of the academic content areas.

Other schools orient their entire curriculum around the value of promoting **social justice**. In this curriculum, students explore topics associated with fostering equity; reducing oppression; building tolerance and understanding across people from different cultural, language, racial and economic groups; or promoting peace in the world. Students in a school with this curriculum orientation can be expected to engage in projects in their neighborhoods and communities specifically designed to address the goals of social justice and to read sources that promote a vision of the world as a more equitable one. The goal is not simply to study these issues, but rather to develop a commitment to critique the status quo and engage actively in social change (Sleeter & Grant, 2002). In response to the crisis precipitated by Hurricane Katrina, a social justice curriculum project was undertaken in conjunction with Spike Lee's film *When the Levees Broke*. This curriculum, entitled *Teaching the Levees: A Curriculum for Democratic Dialogue and Civic Engagement* (Crocco, 2007), consists of DVDs of the film and a complete set of lessons and activities to engage students directly in an inquiry into issues of race and class related to Katrina (see also http://www.teachingthelevees.org). Schools with this orientation are often found in urban school districts, where issues of discrimination and the absence of equity are prominent and pressing concerns. Teachers at schools that focus on social justice may be affiliated with activist educational organizations such as *Rethinking Schools* (http://www.rethinkingschools.org/ index.shtml) or the *National Coalition of Education Activists* (http://www.nceaonline.org).

Yet other schools may emphasize a particular instructional approach. **Project-based learning** requires students to draw on several content areas to systematically inquire into authentic problems. For example, a school could launch a project on reducing toxic waste runoff into waterways. This kind of project would integrate the use of science, mathematics, social studies, and, of course, reading and writing. A different project might be created around the question: *What does it mean to leave your country and move to another one?* Although many schools use projects as part of their curriculum, some schools rely on integrated projects as the major organizing

**Critical Term**

**Social justice.** A curriculum orientation that organizes education around understanding the problems of society and working toward equity and justice in the society.

**Critical Term**

**Project-based learning.** Studying a particular question, problem, or theme in depth over time that requires the use of several academic content areas.

Arts specialty schools integrate the arts into every subject throughout the curriculum. (Tom Carter/ PhotoEdit)

framework for the entire curriculum, adopting different questions, problems, or themes each semester or year.

A project-based approach to the curriculum is based on the following principles (Mergendoller, Markham, Ravitz, & Larmer, 2006):

● Relevance to the real world

● Learning in depth with complex tasks sustained over time

● Helping students learn not just content, but how to make use of their knowledge

● Extended inquiry process that is influence by students and demands their engagement with ideas

● Enabling a range and diversity of outcomes for the project

Because project-based learning has multiple facets and multiple outcomes (rather than a one-dimensional measure of a student's knowledge on a test), technology is especially well-suited to allow students to collect and analyze data, learn about the topics for the project from multiple perspectives, and demonstrate what they have learned through multimedia presentation formats. The George Lucas Foundation sponsors a free e-newsletter on project-based learning that demonstrates the relationship between this approach to curriculum and the use of technology at **http://www.edutopia.org/project-learning**.

Some urban schools have adopted an Afro-centric curriculum (Pollard & Ajirotutu, 2000), which emphasizes the accomplishments of African American and African people as a basis for creating pride in the African American community and for encouraging higher levels of educational achievement among African Americans. Schools committed to this orientation emerged in the late 1980s, when renewed criticism began to be voiced about the poor outcomes of desegregated education for African American students.

Other specialized curriculum orientations take their cue (and usually their title) from the person who founded them or the location at which they originated. For example, Montessori schools, which can be found in nearly every state, are named for the famous Italian educator Maria Montessori, who advocated a highly child-centered curriculum that integrated the various content areas (**http://www.montessori.org**). Montessori schools are usually early childhood and elementary schools; they use specialized instructional materials to carry out the curriculum. They are typically independent private schools that offer their own teacher preparation, although a small number of public Montessori schools exist as well. The Reggio Emilia curriculum for early childhood education began in the Italian city of Reggio Emilia in 1963 and is based on the belief in the infinite potential of each child, and of children's rights (Reggio Emilia, n.d.).

Many specialty schools had their origins during the height of school desegregation efforts in the late 1960s and 1970s, when urban school districts were attempting to stem the flight of white, middle-class families and wanted to offer specialized programming that would attract white families. These schools were called **magnet schools** (Metz, 1986) because, magnet-like, they were meant to draw students to them through their unique character and curriculum. Today we can see these specialized curriculums at work not only in urban public schools as extensions of efforts that began in the era of desegregation, but also in a wide spectrum of schools across the country, including as the focal point for many charter schools (see Chapter 10). In all of these schools, specialized curriculums provide the school with a distinct identity; this identity communicates to students and families alike what will be emphasized during a student's educational experience and often attracts families to them.

**Critical Term**

**Magnet schools.** Schools with a unifying theme designed to attract students because of the special opportunities associated with the curriculum designed around that theme, often developed following Brown decision to retain middle-class students in inner-city urban schools.

Schools that have a social justice curriculum emphasize teaching students to take action to improve their community, city, state, or nation. (Jeff Greenberg/PhotoEdit)

Schools that adopt specialized orientations to curriculum usually do not advance a purely technical view of teaching as the purpose and organizing framework for their schools and for their students' learning. Instead, they have adopted a perspective that gives special meaning and purpose to their teachers' work—and to their students' learning. Nevertheless, adopting a schoolwide curriculum orientation does not mean that a school ignores students' learning of knowledge and skills related to the standards; rather, it places that learning within a context that is defined by the overall curriculum orientation that gives meaning and authenticity to students' learning experiences. Teachers and administrators in public schools with specific curriculum orientations must still ensure that their students meet state standards as assessed on standardized tests. Their challenge, then, is to determine how they can include all of the subject areas that are tested from the perspective of the curriculum emphasis the school has adopted. This requires teachers to use their knowledge about state standards to integrate specific, focused instruction on those standards in the context of the curriculum framework—that is, the purpose —operating in their school.

### Your turn... *to reflect*

Conduct a brief, informal survey in class among your peers to identify the range of curriculum orientations in the PK–12 schools you attended. What orientation predominated? How did these orientations influence the purpose of your educational experiences?

## Digging Deeper
### The Role of Basic Skills in the Curriculum

A recurring, contentious curriculum debate focuses on the teaching of basic skills. A basic skills curriculum is typically defined as "the fundamentals," such as phonics or grammar or mathematics facts. The purpose of schooling from this curriculum perspective is to ensure that each student acquires these basic skills.

**Pro and Con:** Proponents of a basic skills curriculum argue that learning the "3 Rs" should be the defining characteristic of good schooling. Only in a highly structured curriculum, and a highly teacher-directed classroom where each basic skill is delineated and teachers know exactly what skill they will teach next, it is argued, will students gain the fundamentals they will need to function in the world. In the recent past this "3Rs" view has gained some additional support especially in districts and schools where student achievement is low. With its emphasis on annual testing, the No Child Left Behind legislation has fueled this debate and drawn attention to persistent low achievement among particular groups of students, including many racial and ethnic minority students and students who have disabilities.

Pitted against the basic skills view are those who argue that the goal of schooling ought to be defined more broadly: a curriculum should be designed so that students are challenged to think about issues, solve problems, and engage in debate and dialogue about important issues. In short, students should be fitted with educational experiences that will help them navigate in today's complex world. The work students do in schools, the problems they solve, and the books they read and discuss should all represent what are called authentic experiences, as opposed to small bits of isolated information, for example, a spelling rule.

**The Nuances:** When curriculum is defined primarily as the acquisition of basic skills, be it learning phonics, memorizing the periodic table, or memorizing the dates of major wars in which the United States has been involved, the educational experience itself is defined narrowly as learning these skills in isolation. Particularly at the elementary level, specific programs for mathematics and reading, known as "direct instruction" programs, have been developed that focus on the teaching of basic skills. Increasingly, they constitute the main curriculum in many schools whose students are not achieving. Often these instructional programs are highly controlled, and several provide a script that tells teachers exactly what they must say and do in each lesson every day—even illustrating required hand signals the teacher is to use. When this happens, not only is the explicit curriculum itself specifically defined, but the taught curriculum is explicitly prescribed as well. Teachers working from a highly prescriptive basic skills curriculum do not need to plan instructional activities for their students; rather, they simply open the text and teach the next lesson exactly as it is written. This affects the ability of teachers to be creative as they move from the explicit to the taught curriculum.

Nevertheless, students do need to master basic skills in order to engage in more complex curricula and, eventually, complex jobs. After all, it would be difficult to read about complex issues in social studies or biology without mastering reading, or to write a research paper about literature without mastering writing. However, limiting the curriculum to the acquisition of basic skills will not help students reach the more complex goals that they will inevitably be called upon to do in an advanced technological world.

Some children need more explicit instruction in basic skills than do others; this difference may explain part of the support for a basic skills approach. In any classroom there are likely to be students who are ready for more complex tasks and those who have to work harder, and with more directed teaching, to master basic skills so they can learn more complex tasks. The problem comes when a teacher pitches the entire curriculum to those who need the most explicit, teacher-directed instruction; this is likely to lower the bar and the expectations for all students. Using a basic skills approach may result in short-term gains on those skills, but over time it is less likely to equip students for the future.

**Rethinking the Issue:** Teaching basic skills is an essential part of the curriculum, but how teachers approach basic skills is important. Do teachers limit the curriculum, saving complex topics and discussions until students have learned the basics? Are students spending whole days drilling on the basics? Are they spending many hours completing worksheets that provide practice in the basics with little else? Or in contrast, do teachers motivate students to learn the basics so that they can use them to participate in interesting, exciting work in school? Do they provide adequate practice in skills, explicitly teaching students the basics but not making the basics the goal of education? What appears to be problematic is teaching basic skills in isolation from any larger goals and processes of education and viewing the acquisition of basic skills alone as a sufficient goal for education.

## Making Sense of Standards, Accountability, and the Purposes of Curriculum

Today standardized testing functions as an extremely high-stakes event for teachers, schools, and school districts. Test scores are public events, and the scores for individual schools or school districts are often published in local newspapers. With the passage of the No Child Left Behind Act (see Chapter 2), federal funds given to school districts to support education for low-income students are now tied to annual testing, with an accompanying set of sanctions for schools that do not perform well.

When standardized testing is such a high-stakes event, the message to teachers and principals is that getting students ready for the tests is one of the most important and highly valued aspects of teaching. What is valued is usually what is taught. Teachers can feel extraordinary pressure to make sure their students meet every standard that appears on the state tests—no matter how many standards there are. When standards and testing are aligned in such a tight manner, this can influence teachers' choices as to which aspects of the explicit curriculum they will emphasize.

So how will you navigate this complex world of standards, curriculum, and the purposes of education? How will you take this all into consideration as you plan your year, specific units of study, and daily lessons? How will you go beyond merely "covering the material" to make education meaningful to your students? And how will you do all this while keeping in mind that you are accountable for your students' learning and, whether or not you are a strong proponent of testing, how they perform on standardized tests?

Knowing the academic standards for a particular subject at a particular grade level does not necessarily mean that teachers limit themselves to teaching only the narrow slices of information that standardized testing may require. Instead, skilled teachers typically draw on much more challenging and interesting ways of teaching than merely preparing their students for the tests, but embed what is tested into that teaching. When they are planning units of instruction and lessons, teachers may first ask themselves important questions such as: Why is this a good unit to teach? How is this important to my students? How does it connect to what I've done before and what I'm planning afterwards? What do I know about my students that will help me develop the unit and the lessons in it? Then, because they are familiar with the academic standards for their subject and grade level, they can integrate them into the larger purposes of their instructional planning—rather than make the standards the sole focus of their teaching.

As an example, if standards and state tests at the elementary level contain items testing students' knowledge of punctuation, teachers can teach writing skills based on writing assignments that concern situations and issues related to their students' lives or to the subjects they are studying. In the process they can also provide focused instruction on the use of various forms of punctuation. As students write more and more, teachers can assess their students' work to gauge how well they are able to use punctuation in the context of writing that captures their interest. They can teach short, directed lessons ("mini-lessons") on punctuation that are directly related to the specific

Standardized testing has become a high-stakes event in schools, especially since the passage of the No Child Left Behind Act, but its widespread use is still controversial. (David Jennings/ The Image Works)

# REWARDS AND CHALLENGES

## Making the Curriculum Meaningful

Mildred Boveda
*Miami, Florida*

My entire teaching career has taken place under the influence of the No Child Left Behind Act. Although the act contains broader notions than accountability, its restricted focus on assessing student achievement and faculty accountability in terms of what can be demonstrated statistically has had an especially detrimental effect on students who come from traditionally low performing schools. The official curriculum that is coming from the district, along with the textbooks that the district adopts, is more strongly tied to the state standards and the state test than ever before. Schools that have not performed well on state exams in the past are often lauded by the state and federal government for devoting large chunks of time to a "back to basics" approach. Often, the heavily regulated schools—such as the one that I currently teach in—are schools in which the student population is mostly made up of minorities and students from low socioeconomic backgrounds. In Florida not only are learners retained if they can't pass the test, but local schools are given letter grades that have a real effect on the property values for the neighborhoods in which the schools are located. Consequently, I am obligated to ensure that my students meet the standards, in part to avoid the stigma that is associated with failing the test.

With that said, when making pedagogical decisions and preparing lessons for my students, I refuse to restrict myself to only covering the tested benchmarks. The term "data-driven instruction" is frequently tossed around, but what I see is that truly effective teachers implement "student-driven" instruction. That is, teachers go beyond just using student outcomes on various measures to plan curriculum and instruction, but they also pay close attention the context in which they teach. I strive to incorporate the state standards and district curriculum by engaging my students in integrative projects that are meaningful to them. I asked one of my students who is in special education whether she liked working from the textbook or working on projects. She replied, "When I have to read from the textbook I forget the information by the end of the day, but working on projects I get to go over important information more than once and I see why it is important to my life."

Working on projects, having classroom dialogues, and working with novels definitely requires more work and dedication on my part than simply following the textbook. I am confident, however, that my students are not only able to demonstrate their knowledge of isolated standards but that they are developing a positive disposition toward learning. ●

problems students are having, rather than hour-long lessons solely on punctuation. For teachers who view their work in this way, the curriculum is not defined by the need to learn punctuation, although that specific goal might certainly be located in a curriculum document related to writing. Rather, learning punctuation is a strategic by-product of the writing students do on subjects meaningful to them. Thus, one can create a *taught curriculum* that embeds the standards into the larger purposes of education.

By themselves, then, academic standards are not necessarily a negative influence either on the development of curriculum or on teachers' decision making. Depending on how they are used, academic standards can help focus the curriculum planning in which all teachers engage. Table 5-2 reminds us of the opposing ways standards can be used. As you can see from the table, standards can help teachers focus their work. But when standards become the sole focus of how teachers view their responsibilities, they have the potential to turn teaching into a technical, skills-only endeavor—which is seldom the way to keep students engaged and motivated in school. The current pressure from NCLB to raise test scores has put teachers in the uncomfortable position of placing undue attention on the standards alone.

The narrow use of standards as an approach to the curriculum has often been criticized on the basis that when curriculum planning begins with the end-point (i.e., meeting the standards), most educators rarely question whether

## Table 5-2    Positive and Negative Uses of Academic Standards

Academic standards can provide useful benchmarks for teachers as they plan instruction and assess student learning, but they can also narrow the scope of teaching if they are used in isolation.

| Helpful Standards | Harmful Standards |
|---|---|
| Improve the quality of teaching by directing it toward worthy goals: meaningful problem solving, application of knowledge, and the pursuit of deeper understanding. | Equate *harder* with *better*, without changing the quality of how things are taught, calling for "tougher" expectations that focus on acquiring "more" and "harder" skills/knowledge. |
| Articulate core ideas and critical skills, in and across disciplines, in a way that is sufficiently pointed to be meaningful for guiding practice without being overly prescriptive. | Focus on retention of prescribed, disconnected facts and skills for each discipline. |
| Formulate "reasonable expectations" within an age span for a range of intellectual competencies and skills that children need to acquire. | Require achievement of specific skills and competencies that children must acquire in order to move on to the next grade. |
| Serve as a means for educational stakeholders to develop shared meanings and common expectations about what are considered the essentials of learning. | Serve as a means for disciplinary experts to assert the importance of their respective fields by focusing on such detailed and encompassing aspects of each discipline that what a reasonable and full education entails is lost sight of and the combined expectations of all the different standards in all the different fields become humanely impossible to achieve. |
| Are assessed through multiple standards-based performance tasks and processes that examine the degree to which students are progressing toward important ideas and skills. | Are assessed through multiple-choice, norm-referenced, standardized tests that emphasize skills and facts out of the context of real-life application and that evaluate student achievement primarily in relation to the performance of other test takers. |
| Are supported by teaching and assessments that value diverse ways of pursuing and demonstrating knowledge. | Are accompanied by teaching and assessments that emphasize one "right way" and one "right answer." |
| Promote teaching that is responsive to how students learn, that connects to students' understandings, that guides, sustains, and focuses practice and study in the context of clear images of excellence and the potential of all to learn. | Promote teaching that emphasizes conveying information and covering content and that is thought to be received better by some more than by others because intelligence is inherently "fixed." |
| Use assessment results as one of many sources of evidence to inform instruction, to keep students and parents apprised of progress, to trigger special supports for students who need them, to analyze how teaching practices can be improved, and to make decisions about where resources should be allocated. | Use assessment results as the sole basis for making decisions about what group or track students should be placed in, whether students should be promoted or retained in grade, whether students should graduate from school. |
| Are accompanied by standards for the opportunities to learn—standards of access and standards of practice— that are needed for all to achieve desired goals. | Focus exclusively on content and performance standards for students with little attention directed at addressing the broader contexts that enable or prohibit school improvement efforts. |

**Source:**  Reprinted by permission from *The Heart of the Matter* by Beverly Falk. Copyright © by Beverly Falk. Published by Heinemann, a division of Reed Elsevier, Inc., Portsmouth, NH, 2000. All rights reserved.

these outcomes represent good, worthwhile things for students to learn (Eisner, 1979). Instead, the standards are often accepted automatically as the most appropriate goals for education. Efforts to develop the curriculum are focused on teaching to the standards efficiently and effectively (Eisner, 1979), putting constraints on teachers' creativity and restricting their choices. When this more harmful use of standards drives education, what is worth knowing—and teaching—assumes a restricted place in professional discourse about education.

To emphasize the problem that occurs when what is important educationally clashes with what standardized tests often demand of students, one of veteran teacher Rafe Esquith's fifth grade classes created their own reading test, which they believed was a better measure of reading proficiency than any packaged examination. It consisted of three items:

1.  Have you ever read secretly under your desk in school because the teacher was boring you and you were dying to finish the book you were reading?

2.  Have you ever been scolded for reading at the dinner table?

3.  Have you ever read secretly under the covers after being told to go to bed? (Esquith, 2007, p. 33)

---

**Your turn...** *to reflect*

After reading Table 5-2, discuss the helpful and harmful uses of standards. Reflecting on your own education, how do you think your own teachers viewed the goals of teaching in relationship to academic standards?

---

## The Role of Textbooks in the Curriculum

No discussion of the curriculum would be complete without addressing one of the most familiar aspects of education—textbooks. The textbooks you are given as a new teacher will undoubtedly have an impact on your teaching. But what is the relationship between textbooks and the curriculum? What kind of impact will textbooks have on your teaching the curriculum? The answer depends on how you use them.

### How Teachers Use Textbooks

Imagine that you are getting ready to begin school in your first year of teaching. You are handed a curriculum document for the grade or subject you will teach, and you are also given the teacher's guide for your textbooks. How will you use these materials?

**The Textbook as the "Teacher-Proof Curriculum."** As you well know (and probably wish to forget), some teachers simply follow the textbook every day ("Open up to page 124 and begin reading…"). Rather than think about who their students are and what specifically they need, teachers who blindly adhere to the textbook relinquish their control over how they teach the curriculum. They treat the textbook as the sole authority over the curriculum (Ben-Peretz, 1990) and have no alternative if the textbooks are not available or if the teacher's manual is missing. When teachers use textbooks in this uncritical, highly dependent manner, the textbook itself becomes the taught curriculum.

**Critical Term**

**Teacher-proof curriculum.**
Highly prescriptive curriculum or instructional materials that can be implemented without independent thinking or decision making on the part of the teacher.

Some textbook and curriculum materials, like the highly prescriptive basic skills programs described earlier, are actually developed so that teachers need not make any decisions at all—what is known as the **teacher-proof curriculum**. This term denotes a lack of trust in teachers to make good curriculum decisions for their students and deprofessionalizes teaching. When the curriculum is "teacher-proofed," it is created in such a way that anyone can teach it and, in theory, get it "right." However, if all there were to teaching was following the commercially prepared textbook, there would be no need for professional preparation. Obviously, we know this is not the case. How teachers use the textbooks and other instructional materials in relationship to the goals of the curriculum determines how successful they will be in fostering their students' learning.

You do not want to become the teacher who reads from the teacher's guide each day or the teacher who could turn an extra page in the teacher's guide and not know that a page had been skipped. But actions like these, which are not characteristic of good teachers, are what lead to ideas such as "teacher-proofing" the curriculum and a lack of trust in teachers to do the job well.

### The Textbook as Curriculum Potential.
The other extreme in terms of the materials you use to teach would be teaching with no textbooks at all and creating all of your classroom activities from scratch. If you were a high school history teacher, for example, you might develop instructional materials based solely on primary documents such as historical letters, or use biographies or fictionalized novels of historical events. Not using textbooks provides teachers with complete freedom to develop materials, activities, and resources, but it requires much work from teachers.

Between these two extreme views of curriculum is another concept, namely, the *curriculum potential* of textbooks. The curriculum scholar Miriam Ben-Peretz (1990) explored this idea in her book entitled *The Teacher-Curriculum Encounter: Freeing Teachers from the Tyranny of Texts*. Obviously, even when teachers are teaching from good, high-quality textbooks and using curriculum materials, the textbook developers cannot anticipate the specific needs of a particular group of students in a particular year—or the preferences of an individual teacher. In her book, Ben-Peretz presents textbooks and other commercial curriculum materials as representing **curriculum potential** for your teaching. She believes that teachers must deliberately engage in efforts to *interpret* the curriculum materials for their particular teaching situations, using "the materials in ways which go beyond the explicit intentions of their developers" (p. 47). If we consider textbooks and supplemental materials as a source of potential for teaching—rather than a complete package in need of no interpretation—we are making the shift from treating the textbook as the explicit, teacher-proof curriculum to taking professional responsibility for the taught curriculum. By doing so, the end result of our teaching—that is, what students learn—should be more satisfactory than if we merely taught exactly what is in the textbook without any interpretation. Figure 5-3 portrays the continuum of teachers' roles in relationship to the curriculum and textbooks.

**Critical Term**

**Curriculum potential.** Using textbooks and other instructional materials by interpreting their potential to meet the needs of a specific class of students.

Another reason the concept of curriculum potential is so important is that many textbook companies include far more resources, ideas, and activities than a single teacher could ever use. Teachers' guides are usually full of ideas and extended resources far beyond what you will need. Your goal should be to make deliberate choices that support the goals of the curriculum and the students whom you are teaching.

## Figure 5-3 Teachers' Roles in Relationship to the Curriculum and Textbooks

One of the important decisions teachers make in terms of curriculum is the role of textbooks and how much they allow textbooks to drive what they do each day.

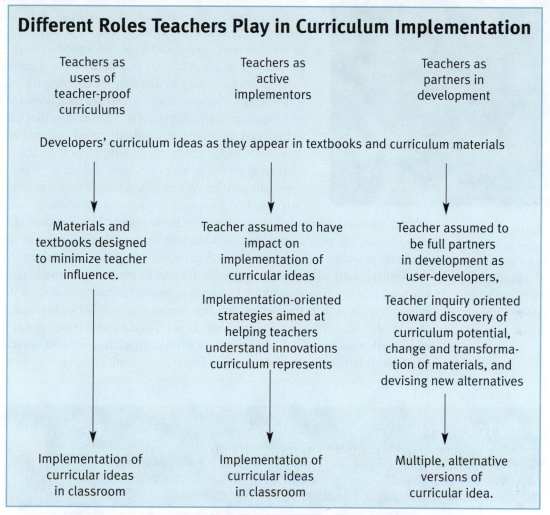

**Different Roles Teachers Play in Curriculum Implementation**

| Teachers as users of teacher-proof curriculums | Teachers as active implementors | Teachers as partners in development |
|---|---|---|
| | Developers' curriculum ideas as they appear in textbooks and curriculum materials | |
| Materials and textbooks designed to minimize teacher influence. | Teacher assumed to have impact on implementation of curricular ideas | Teacher assumed to be full partners in development as user-developers, |
| | Implementation-oriented strategies aimed at helping teachers understand innovations curriculum represents | Teacher inquiry oriented toward discovery of curriculum potential, change and transformation of materials, and devising new alternatives |
| Implementation of curricular ideas in classroom | Implementation of curricular ideas in classroom | Multiple, alternative versions of curricular idea. |

**Source:** Adapted from Connelly, F. M., and M. Ben-Peretz. (1980). Teachers' roles in the using and doing of research and curriculum development. *Journal of Curriculum Studies*, 12 (2), 95–107. © by Taylor & Francis Ltd.: http://www.tandf.co.uk/journals.

As a new teacher, you may lack the confidence to stray far from the textbook. It may serve as a safety net as you learn the ropes and put together meaningful lessons every day, five days a week. However, there is danger in adopting the habit of depending too much on the textbook. If you get accustomed to letting the teacher's guide do the work for you, if you fail to seek the potential of the curriculum materials you have, you may never be able to tailor your teaching to the needs of the students who are sitting in front of you. Adopting the philosophy of teacher as interpreter of curriculum materials means you need to be familiar with the textbook and other commercial materials available to you so that you know what the textbook can and cannot do, what students' needs it can and cannot meet. You will have to make judgments about the usefulness of the particular curriculum materials available to you.

Rather than letting textbooks guide instruction, skilled teachers use them as a resource and tool to help make choices about what and how to teach. (Media Bakery)

## Textbooks, Standards, and the Curriculum

Textbook publishers are keenly aware of the development of standards for the academic content areas from the various professional organizations. But there will never be a one-to-one match between the standards a particular state adopts and the nationally oriented textbooks from which you will no doubt be asked to teach. States and local districts often work to identify the sections in adopted texts that address the standards so that teachers can easily see whether they are covering the material that will be tested. These sections of texts are then linked to the scope and sequence curriculum charts. The result is that teachers who feel pressed to cover the standards-based material and prepare their students for the tests can simply look to these charts for what sections of the textbooks they will teach. This approach is essentially another version of teaching from the teacher's guide— only now the day-to-day sequence is coordinated and organized around the standards and not the sequence of the textbook. This approach does not take into account the specific students one is teaching or the specific context in which one is teaching. In reality, it is simply another form of teacher-proof curriculum.

Another critical issue with regard to the use of textbooks is the biases they may contain. Just because a textbook has been approved for adoption does not mean it is free from bias. It is important that teachers review textbooks for multiple forms of potential bias. This includes not only bias related to who is and is not represented in textbooks, but also bias in terms of what perspectives are and are not presented. What is left out of textbooks is another way to think about the null curriculum.

## Your turn... *to reflect*

Select a textbook from the classroom in which you are completing your field experience. Look through the table of contents. Review the photographs. Then read at least two chapters. What kinds of biases, if any, can you identify in the textbook? How would you use the textbook in planning your curriculum given these biases, if they exist?

The potential of the curriculum as represented by textbooks lies in your ability as a professional teacher to make wise, informed professional decisions about what aspects of the text fit your goals for your students as well as the standards your students are expected to meet. Then you can fashion a taught curriculum that is not defined entirely by standards and textbooks, but rather that draws on standards and textbooks as your professional tools. Curriculum materials are an important part of teaching, but only if they are used well by teachers who know what their goals are and how they can help their particular group of students meet them.

## The Textbook Industry in the United States

In 2007, the estimated sales of textbooks and related products at the elementary and high school levels combined totaled $6.4 billion (Association of American Publishers, 2007). Clearly, textbooks are an institutionalized feature of the educational landscape and represent big business in education. How does a specific district decide what textbooks it will purchase?

For the purposes of selecting textbooks, states are considered either *adoption states* or *open territory states*. Figure 5-4 shows that 22 states are adoption states and that the remaining 28 are open territory states. In *adoption states*, decisions about textbooks are made centrally by the state education agency. Textbooks for the various subject areas are selected on a regular rotation or adoption cycle—usually every five to six years. A state-level committee selects a small number of textbooks, or a short list, for a particular content area, and school districts choose from those on the list adopted by the state. This means that in selecting textbooks, the state exerts a high degree of control over the curriculum as represented in the textbooks. In contrast, in *open territory* states, local school districts can select whatever texts they wish. Typically, a district also selects a short list of texts, and teachers have the opportunity to look them over and pilot-test their use before a final adoption decision is made. In this decision-making process, local selection committees can also evaluate supplemental materials that publishers offer, which can include teacher's guides, student workbooks, student materials for duplication, kits of manipulatives for mathematics instruction (e.g., counting cubes, geoboards), class sets of books of children's literature, and, increasingly, technology supplements (e.g., CDs). Most publishers automatically develop scope and sequence charts across grade levels for their textbook programs as well.

---

**Figure 5-4    Methods of Textbook Adoption by State**

Some states adopt specific textbooks on a statewide basis, whereas others are "open territory" states where individual school districts make their own decisions about what textbooks they will use.

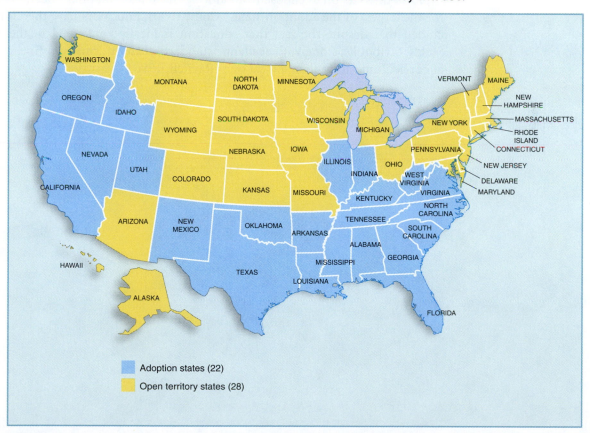

Adoption states (22)

Open territory states (28)

**Source:** Association of American Publishers. Retrieved May 14, 2008 from http://www.publishers.org/school/index.cfm.

In an education system driven by academic standards, textbook developers try to respond to the need to include material directly related to state standards. Textbook publishers are knowledgeable about the state of education in the country and work hard to be aware of the issues that will affect the books they develop (Cody, 1990).

As Figure 5-4 illustrates, some of the largest states, for example, California and Texas, are adoption states. Because of their large populations, these two states are considered important textbook markets and exert a disproportionate influence on the kinds of textbooks publishers develop. Recall that the California curriculum frameworks explicitly direct textbook publishers to orient their textbooks in a certain fashion to conform to these frameworks. To win adoption of their books, which results in considerable profits for them, textbook publishers want to please education officials in these states and can look to them for guidance in developing their materials. Large urban school districts are also significant sources of potential revenue, even if they are in open adoption states. These school districts can also be of great importance to publishers as decisions are made about what textbooks contain (Squire & Morgan, 1990), but they are not nearly as important the states of California and Texas.

This dual system of textbook selection —adoption and open territory—means that teachers have very different levels of input in choosing textbooks. If you teach in an adoption state, your books will be chosen by a small number of teachers from the entire state who serve on a statewide committee. If you teach in an open territory state, you are likely to have the opportunity to be selected as a member of a textbook adoption committee for your district and have direct input into these critical decisions. However, because the largest publishers are motivated to invest in the development of texts for the largest adoption states, and because the development of textbooks is an expensive proposition for any publishing company, local districts often choose from among those texts that have been developed for the largest of the adoption states (Cody, 1990). Educators have therefore concluded that despite the fact that education is locally controlled in the United States, textbooks, along with academic standards, can informally define a national curriculum rather than a local one (Ravitch, 1996).

## Why It Counts in a Diverse World

By now you probably realize that *curriculum* is a slippery term and that deciding what to teach is more complex than it may at first seem. The challenge for teachers regarding curriculum is that they are faced with a constant balancing act: there is too much that is interesting to teach; there is a need to balance content with the teaching process; there is pressure to cover the standards-based material; and the specter of annual standardized state testing is always present. In addition, local political pressures may be imposed to include—or exclude—certain topics in the curriculum.

As you think about taking on your first teaching position, the whole idea of curriculum may seem daunting. After all, it will be difficult enough to juggle all the responsibilities you will have as a new teacher. You may just want someone to hand you a textbook and tell you what to teach each day. But in reality, considerations about the curriculum should be one of the first things you think about. Curriculum is what gives meaning to your teaching—it represents the essential question: What is worth teaching and what is worth having your students learn?

Without a perspective on curriculum and the worth of the goals you are trying to meet, you may fall into two traps. First, you may adopt a pattern of teaching only from the text or teaching only activities that satisfy the state standards, whether or not the standards are valuable goals for your students. Second, you may plan daily activities in the absence of well-thought-out goals for the longer term, and in the process you may deprive your students of a taught curriculum that makes sense, adds up to something meaningful, and is more than the sum of what you do every day in class. Although every good teacher struggles to figure out how to balance the competing demands of the various dimensions of the curriculum, good teachers always ask themselves questions such as: Why are we doing what I have planned for today? Why is this a worthwhile activity, and how does it fit into a larger goal for my students?

Finally, in planning the curriculum, teachers need to consider how to make the curriculum relevant to their students. When teachers' backgrounds differ from those of their students, teachers need to become familiar with students' cultures and communities so that they can make meaningful connections between what the students bring to the classroom and already know and the goals of the curriculum in terms of students' new learning. Good teachers can answer these questions not only for themselves but also for their students and families.

As a new teacher, you will probably find yourself more dependent on curriculum materials and textbooks at first than you will be as you gain experience. But at any level, teachers need to become familiar with the curriculum, the standards that drive the curriculum, and the textbooks that hold curriculum potential. As a more experienced teacher, you might even volunteer to work on curriculum development and write new curriculum for your grade level and content area when a change is warranted.

Being accountable for student learning does not mean simply teaching material. Instead, it means having a profound respect for the relationship between the curriculum and the students you are teaching. It means understanding the relationship between the purposes of the curriculum, the explicit curriculum, what you teach, and what your students learn.

# CHAPTER SUMMARY

## Curriculum: A Multidimensional Term

The term *curriculum* refers to the course or program of studies for which a teacher is responsible in a particular grade and a particular content area. Curriculum is more than just the formal, or *explicit*, course that is written down and shared publicly. The explicit, formal curriculum is interpreted by teachers as they engage in the day-to-day work of teaching. What teachers actually do in the classroom relative to the explicit curriculum can be called the *taught curriculum*. What students actually take away academically from their experience of being in school is called the *learned curriculum*. The *null curriculum* consists of all of the things that are not taught in school. These various dimensions of curriculum—that which is explicit, that which is taught, and that which students learn—interact and place different kinds of pressures on teachers as they answer the question: What is worth teaching and having students learn?

## Developing the Curriculum: How Does It Work?

In today's educational environment, individual states have created academic content standards for what students should know and be able to do as a result of their PK–12 education. These standards form the backbone of curriculum development and are taken into account as states prepare curriculum guides and as local school districts use those state documents to develop their own local curriculum plans. Standards also form the basis for state testing programs. Today there is a very tight alignment, or connection, among standards, the explicit curriculum, and testing students to determine what they have learned. This alignment, which places a high value on testing, puts pressure on teachers to cover the standards whether or not they represent worthwhile ends for education. The standards can also lead to a homogenization of the curriculum across the country. Wise teachers are familiar with the standards and embed activities designed to help their students meet the standards within a meaningful curriculum.

## Curriculum—Teaching with a Purpose

Although individual variation exists among local school districts, there is still pressure to conform based on the standards. Districts may adopt their own approaches to curriculum, for example, using local community situations to study environmental issues, but teachers are still accountable for preparing their students to meet the standards. Individual schools can also adopt particular curriculum orientations, such as a social justice philosophy. Such philosophies provide teachers with support for embedding the standards in a curriculum that has a more meaningful purpose rather than defining curriculum simply as covering all the material related to the standards.

## The Role of Textbooks in the Curriculum

Textbooks and supplements are a nearly universal tool in teaching, but they are not to be used without thought. Teaching word-for-word what is written in the textbooks or relying exclusively on the teacher's guide fails to represent the teacher's professional knowledge and judgment about the relationship among the textbook, the curriculum, and the students he or she is responsible for teaching. Rather, the goal is to learn how to use textbooks as tools in relationship to the purposes of and their relationship to the curriculum.

## LIST OF CRITICAL TERMS

Explicit curriculum  *(131)*

Academic content standards  *(131)*

Curriculum guide  *(131)*

Taught curriculum  *(132)*

Learned curriculum  *(133)*

Accountability  *(134)*

Null curriculum  *(135)*

Scope and sequence  *(140)*

Social justice  *(148)*

Project-based learning  *(148)*

Magnet schools  *(149)*

Teacher-proof curriculum  *(156)*

Curriculum potential  *(156)*

## EXPLORING YOUR COMMITMENT

1. *on your own...*  Select an academic content area that you are interested in teaching. Make a list of several important topics within this subject that you believe are worthwhile to learn. Then compare them with a list of state standards (available on state education agency websites) to see what that state values as being worthwhile to learn. How do you account for the difference?

2. *on the web...*  What are the benefits and limitations of standardized testing? Visit the Fair Test website (**http://www.fairtest.org**). What issues related to standardized testing of students are addressed on this website?

3. *on your own...*  Locate lists of books that are banned in local school districts near your university or in your local library. Do any of the titles that are banned surprise you and, if so, why? Use the website of the American Library Association (**http://www.ala.org/alaorg/oif**) to learn more about the issue of banned books nationally.

4. *on your own...*  Read the 1955 play *Inherit the Wind* by Jerome Lawrence and Robert E. Lee, or view the 1960 film version starring Spencer Tracy, Fredric March, and Gene Kelly. What views of teachers and curriculum decision making are portrayed in this story?

5. *in the field...*  With a principal, discuss the dominant curriculum orientation of the school. What does the school staff emphasize? What does it value as being important with respect to the curriculum it has adopted?

6. *on the web...*  Locate the website for the state education agency for your home state, the state in which you are studying to be a teacher, or the state in which you think you will look for a job in teaching. Identify five different kinds of information that are available on this website. How helpful is this information to you in your preparation for teaching, and how helpful will it be for you once you begin teaching? Did anything surprise you about the website? If so, what and why?

7. *on the web...*  Locate the websites of at least two schools that have special curriculum orientations (for example: Montessori Schools, Waldorf Schools, Reggio Emilia). What can you learn from reading these websites about what these schools believe is worth knowing?

8. *in the field...*  Review the curriculum materials in one subject area in one grade. Include textbooks and any other supplemental materials for that subject. What broad topics are covered? What do you notice about the breadth and depth of coverage? What did you learn from reviewing these materials?

9. *in the field...*  Interview a teacher or administrator to discuss how he or she balances the demands of meeting the state standards with the curriculum that is used in the school. What role do the standards play in this teacher's planning for lessons and units of study?

10. *in the research...*  Read Kauffman, D., S. M. Johnson, S. M. Kardos, E. Liu, and H. G. Peske. (2002). "'Lost at sea': New teachers' experiences with curriculum and assessment", *Teachers College Record, 104*, 273–300. What does this article have to offer you as you think about the role of reflection about the curriculum?

## GUIDELINES FOR BEGINNING TEACHERS

1. You should be able to locate state-level curriculum documents for the subjects you will be teaching for whatever state in which you teach. Such documents can be used in conjunction with local curriculum guides to help you as you plan your instructional program.

2. Since you are accountable for teaching your students according to academic standards, as a beginning teacher you will want to become familiar with the standards of the state in which you are teaching. Locate the standards on the state's website.

3. As a new teacher, you will need to request the local curriculum from which you will be teaching, as well as the state documents that may provide you with additional resources. Be sure to request scope and sequence charts for the various subject areas for which you are responsible.

4. When you interview at a school, review the school or the district website to see if you can identify the curriculum orientation of the school/district. Be prepared to ask questions about the materials that are used to teach the curriculum and the kinds of units of study that have been carried out in the grade level you are interested in.

5. During your interview, ask questions about the philosophy of the school and the curriculum that is used. Try to get a sense of how much freedom you will have to mine the full potential of these materials to meet the needs of your particular students, or whether you will be expected to follow the curriculum exactly.

## THE INTASC CONNECTION

The INTASC standards that are most closely aligned to the issue of curriculum are Standards 1 and 7.

Standard 1 states: *The teacher understands the central concepts, tools of inquiry, and structures of the discipline(s) he or she teaches and can create learning experiences that make these aspects of subject matter meaningful for students.* The following are some relevant indicators:

● The teacher can relate his or her disciplinary knowledge to other subject areas.

● The teacher has enthusiasm for the discipline(s) she or he teaches and sees connections to everyday life.

● The teacher can create interdisciplinary learning experiences that allow students to integrate knowledge, skills, and methods of inquiry from several subject areas.

Standard 7 states: *The teacher plans and manages instruction based upon knowledge of subject matter, students, the community, and curriculum goals.* Indicators include the following:

● The teacher understands learning theory, subject matter, curriculum development, and student development and knows how to use this knowledge in planning instruction to meet curriculum goals.

● The teacher values both long-term and short-term planning.

If you are in a state that follows a different set of teacher standards, find the state standards that most closely relate to the INTASC standards discussed here.

## READING ON...

Barton, A. C. (2003). *Teaching science for social justice.* New York: Teachers College Press. Angela Calabrese Barton illustrates how to teach science from a philosophical perspective that stresses connecting students to science in school and in after-school programs in low-income, inner-city communities and neighborhoods.

Horton, M. (1998). *The long haul: An autobiography.* New York: Teachers College Press. In this autobiography, Myles Horton, a famous progressive educator who was committed to social justice, reflects on how he put his philosophy of education into practice at the Highlander School in Tennessee.

Joseph, P. B., S. L. Bravmann, M. A. Windschitl, E. R. Mikel, and N. S. Green. (2000). *Cultures of curriculum.* Mahwah, NJ: Lawrence Erlbaum Associates. An analysis of major approaches to the interpretation of curriculum in schools, written from a practical perspective on what it means to teach from various philosophical perspectives on curriculum.

Thornton, S. J. (2005). *Teaching social studies that matters.* New York: Teachers College Press. The author provides strategies for how to make the social studies curriculum exciting and engaging for students.

## Guiding Questions

- What is the "hidden curriculum" and how is it related to the school as a culture?

- What are the benefits and liabilities of the hidden curriculum?

- Who are today's students?

- What problems and challenges do today's students and their families face?

- What is the role of smaller schools in addressing social issues?

- How are schools attempting to change the social environment to be more supportive of students and families?

- How do teachers promote students' competence in the face of challenging life situations?

- What is the role of extracurricular activities in the schools?

# More Than "What Is Taught": School as a Social Institution  6

In the first month of school, Derrick Harris has made a point of getting to know each of his sixth grade students. He knows his success as a middle school teacher depends on it. He has had his students start writing personal journals during the Language Arts period, and he writes back to them each week. Every morning he greets each student at the door of the classroom, and he makes sure he has an informal conversation with all of his students at least once a week. He has been learning about their interests, their likes and dislikes, the music they listen to, the movies they see, their families, and their different living situations. One thing he has learned is that two of his students, Monique and James, both live in homeless shelters. Monique has lived in the shelter with her mother for six months. James just moved to a shelter over the summer, when his mother was laid off from her job and could no longer afford the rent.

Although Derrick tried not to show it, having students in his classroom who did not have a real home upset him. He had not worked with homeless students before and had not really thought about what it meant. He was also not sure how to talk about this with Monique and James. One day after school, during his fourth week on the job, Janice Morgan stopped by to see how he had set up his classroom and how things were going. The first thing Derrick wanted to talk about was Monique and James.

"I just wasn't ready for this. I don't know why I didn't think about it before, but somehow the reality is harder than I realized. It's not like my life has been exactly easy—you know that. But we always had a place that was our home—even if it was very small and very plain."

"But it's what they have to deal with right now," said Janice. "How much do you really know about their circumstances yet?"

"Not as much as I'd like. I haven't been comfortable asking them too much. They have both gotten their homework done so far, and they both seem interested in school. But they haven't told me much more than that they are living in the shelter."

"You're going to have to talk with them about where they live just as you'd talk with your other students. If you don't talk about it, they won't feel comfortable

*If we don't stand up for children, then we don't stand for much.*

Marian Wright Edelman

talking about their situation with you. And you don't want to send the message that you're not interested in them. Maybe you could start by asking them where they do their homework, if there's anyone to help them with it, and when they go to bed. Then you can start talking with the school social worker about other things you need to know."

"I'll take a deep breath tomorrow and try to have those conversations with them. And you're right. I know I'll feel much better once I can talk with them more."

Even though we generally think of schools as places where children learn academics, students learn a lot more in school than just what is in the explicit curriculum. Simply by virtue of being in school every day, students learn many "lessons" beyond the academic curriculum—lessons about the purposes of schools, what students need to do to please teachers, what is important in schools and to teachers, who is recognized, and much, much more. Schools are social institutions, and since students spend at least 12 years of their lives in schools, they are not oblivious to how these institutions operate. In fact, they are often quite astute observers of their schools. We considered the classroom as a culture in Chapter 2. We can also think of the school as a culture, with its own traditions, practices, and values. The unanticipated "lessons" students learn by participating in this culture, these "by-products" of being in school, can be either a positive or a negative force in a student's school experience.

Because schools teach more than just the academic curriculum, teachers need to be aware not only of their obligations regarding academic content and the explicit curriculum, but also the ways the organization and structure of the school and their classroom affect their students. Are the students happy in school? Are they involved? Are they productive? Do students get along? When students encounter problems, are these handled in a way that supports students? Teachers must take responsibility for the kinds of teaching and learning environments they create both at the school and at the classroom level, and for the messages students take away from these environments. To do this, they must first realize that "as teachers, all the decisions we make, no matter how neutral they seem, may impact in unconscious but fundamental ways the lives and experiences of our students" (Nieto, 1996, p. 318).

In order to teach the academic curriculum well, teachers must place a high value on the overall well-being of their students. All students are individuals who live in specific social and economic circumstances and attend school in a specific social context. Some students, like James and Monique, may live in particularly difficult circumstances. Therefore, it is not enough to consider your students neutrally, that is, simply as learners. Being in school can strengthen or diminish students' well-being, and for this reason all education professionals are obligated to work toward making schools places where students thrive.

From Chapter 5 you already have a sense of where the academic curriculum comes from. In this chapter, we will explore a much broader definition of curriculum—that is, curriculum defined as the sum total of a student's experience in school. We will consider this issue from two perspectives: (1) the hidden messages students get while attending school, and (2) how schools as institutions respond to students' changing social needs in a changing social context. Finally, we will see how these dimensions affect the lives of teachers and the decisions they make.

**Your turn...** *to reflect*

Make a list of 10 things you learned as a result of being in school in addition to academic content. Does your list include positive and negative types of learning? What do you think accounted for these outcomes of your PK–12 education? Compare your list with those of your peers. Which aspects of your lists are similar, and which are different? What might account for the differences?

## The Power of the Hidden Curriculum

The unarticulated lessons students learn and the messages they receive as a result of attending school do not appear in the formal academic curriculum. Yet their collective impact has been deemed so important by educators that it has acquired its own name: the **hidden curriculum** (Jackson, 1968). The hidden curriculum can be thought of as everything students learn in schools that is not explicitly laid out in the academic curriculum—whether these lessons are intended or unintended (Tanner & Tanner, 1980). Although the hidden curriculum was initially defined as the unintended results of schooling, today many would argue that what at first appear to be unintended outcomes are often intended ones—that is, outcomes that may systematically benefit different groups of students.

The hidden curriculum is a companion concept to the terms *explicit curriculum* and the *null curriculum* discussed in Chapter 5. It represents real learning but not the kind one may readily associate with conventional notions of what schooling is for—that is, academic learning. The concept of the hidden curriculum is a powerful way of understanding the total experience children and youth have in school. It is a vital concept mainly because once we realize that this "curriculum" also exists, we accept that in addition to academic outcomes, an unofficial, unvoiced set of other outcomes also result from attending school, outcomes for which teachers and administrators have a great deal of responsibility.

**Critical term**

**Hidden curriculum.** The unstated outcomes of education that students experience and learn by spending time in schools. These outcomes may be intended or unintended, positive or negative.

Students learn more than just academics when they spend time in school.
(Digital Vision)

## The Hidden Curriculum and the School as a Culture

Much like a classroom can be thought of as a culture with its own set of customs, assumptions, and expectations, schools, too, can be regarded as cultures. If you think of schools from this perspective, you can begin to understand the concept of the hidden curriculum. In the same way that the official academic curriculum is a statement of values about what is important to learn, the atmosphere and expectations that exist in a school also represent a statement of values. We do not usually question the assumed values and expectations that fall outside the academic curriculum, but they represent enduring features of schooling nevertheless. Precisely because they are so embedded in how schools operate, we rarely question or discuss them. This is why they function as a *hidden* curriculum.

The hidden curriculum, though unspoken, operates so regularly in schools that it would be nearly impossible for students to miss its message. Eliot Eisner (1979) prefers the term *implicit curriculum* (1979) to hidden curriculum, signifying that these expectations, or outcomes, are implicit in the act of attending school. He describes the phenomenon as follows:

> Thus, the implicit curriculum of a school is what it teaches because of the kind of place it is. And the school is that kind of place through the ancillary consequences of various approaches to teaching, by the kind of reward system it uses, by the organizational structure it employs to sustain its existence, by the physical characteristics of the school plant, by the furniture it uses and the surroundings it creates. These characteristics constitute some of the dominant components of the school's implicit curriculum. Although these features are seldom publicly announced, they are intuitively recognized by parents, students, and teachers. And because they are salient and pervasive features of schooling, what they teach may be among the most important lessons a child learns. (Eisner, 1979, pp. 82–83)

For example, one common feature in most schools is grouping students in classes with peers of the same age. This fact of schooling provides a lesson to students about the value of working with those of your own age—and devalues the potential of cross-age peer learning and tutoring. Nowhere in the formal curriculum is it stated that students are better off in same-age classes or even that such classes are desirable. But that is what most schools assume. So it is, in effect, a "hidden" outcome learned as a result of spending time in school—an example of the hidden curriculum. As we will see in Chapter 9, some schools defy this cultural norm by practicing multi-age grouping and so send a different hidden message than that communicated in most schools.

In most schools it is assumed that teachers have greater power than students. After all, teachers organize the curriculum, develop activities and projects, construct and grade tests, and generally run the show. Frederick Erickson, the scholar of classroom culture mentioned in Chapter 2, commented on this assumption as follows: "Classrooms are characterized by marked asymmetry of form and informal rights and obligations among participants. Formally and informally the roles of teacher and student are asymmetric" (Erickson & Shultz, 1992, p. 469). Year after year students learn that this asymmetrical relationship is a regular part of the schooling and that only rarely do students themselves have greater say than their teachers. It can be done otherwise, and schools and philosophies exist in which there are less hierarchical definitions of the teacher-student relationship. But common practice in the United States is hierarchical.

What about the seemingly simple question of furniture that Eisner raises as an issue related to the hidden curriculum? The arrangement of a classroom sends a message to the students you teach. If each desk stands in isolation, this conveys the idea that working in isolation is valued. When desks are paired or arranged in groups, a different message is sent, creating the possibility for shared tasks. If you have movable desks but students always face the teacher and never regroup for purposes of class discussion, it's likely that fewer students will participate, especially those who sit in the back rows, without heavy prodding by the teacher. This also sends a particular message—that students who sit in the back of the classroom may not be expected to participate regularly or to be fully engaged in the lesson. And if the furniture is screwed to the floor, as it often is in large lecture halls, the instructor is, in essence, stuck with the message that instruction is to proceed in lecture format in front of a large group.

Big decisions about how to interact with students or organize the classroom, as well as smaller decisions such as seating patterns and the arrangement of furniture, all communicate messages to students about why they are at school.
(Michael J. Doolittle/The Image Works)

As another example, until the advent of cell phones, teachers could communicate with families only after school hours and at appointed conference times. Most schools had only a single telephone line teachers could use, and it was typically located in a public place, so that holding a private conversation was nearly impossible. The message this arrangement sent was that teachers could not easily contact the parents and families of their students and that doing so was not a high priority. In contrast, cell phones and email enable teachers to keep in touch with family members and even, on occasion, to have students talk with their family members during the day in relationship to problems that may arise. The context of schooling changes significantly when students call their families with a teacher standing right there, in close proximity, rather than waiting to see if their teacher might call home in the evening. This creates a very different set of relationships between teachers and parents or guardians.

The hidden curriculum is the result of decisions made by educators regarding how schools should work—even if those decisions were made a long time ago and continue simply by force of tradition and custom. Seymour Sarason (1982), an astute observer of schooling, calls the unexamined practices that have resulted from these past decisions and traditions the **regularities of schooling**. He states that recognizing these regularities, or patterns, is critical because if they are not acknowledged in the first place, we cannot even begin to imagine changing them. If some of these regularities of schooling are not the best way to support student learning, then recognizing them and talking about them are the first steps to creating new regularities with more beneficial outcomes.

The hidden curriculum operates at every level at which decisions are made and directly influences how students experience school. Every decision, regardless of whether it has been thought through, explicitly represents some kind of purpose. What patterns exist in enrolling students in Advanced Placement classes in high school? Which students are represented in leading roles in school plays? Are those elected to student council year after year representative of the entire student body or rather of a narrow group? If there are separate classes for students who are identified as gifted and talented, who ends up in those classes, and who does not? These are all examples of the hidden curriculum.

**Critical term**

**Regularities of schooling.** A term coined by Seymour Sarason to describe the traditions and practices of schooling that are taken for granted and are not questioned—even though schooling could be organized and carried out in other ways.

As a new teacher, you will find many of the regularities of the school culture already determined for you. However, within your own classroom you do have control over many of the choices you make about what kind of experience, that is, the classroom culture, you create for your students. Whether or not these choices are directly related to the academic curriculum, they influence how your students experience school. Every choice you make about how you organize and deliver the academic curriculum carries with it implicit messages about the kind of place your classroom is.

For example, if you are planning to be an upper elementary or middle school teacher, you may decide to structure your curriculum around a series of contemporary problems (e.g., environmental protection or segregated housing patterns) and integrate reading, mathematics, social studies, and science as you address these problems. This is a curriculum approach that may not be dictated at the school level. If you make this choice, the hidden message you are sending is that the traditional academic subjects are useful for studying complex problems. Similarly, if you are a high school physics teacher, you may choose to teach chapter by chapter in the book with few demonstrations, or you may elect to make demonstrations of physical phenomena a centerpiece of your teaching. If you choose the latter, you are communicating the hidden message that as a teacher, you value having the students observe and interact with the phenomena they are studying.

As another example, if you are a first grade teacher, you may choose to teach your students to take responsibility for retrieving materials from around the classroom or for choosing activities for specific times in the day. When you teach your students to take on these responsibilities (and you will have to teach them specifically how to do this at this age), you are communicating the idea that in your classroom, you trust them to take on this level of responsibility. If you pass out all materials yourself and control all choices for the students, the message they receive is that they are not ready to exercise any freedom of choice within the classroom.

## Your turn... *to review*

1. What is the difference between the explicit curriculum and the hidden curriculum?
2. Name two examples of what students can learn from the hidden curriculum.
3. How can the hidden curriculum become a liability for students? A benefit?

As Sarason points out, many of the regularities and hidden outcomes of PK–12 schooling can be changed, depending on the political pressure that operates in a school or local district. When various people in powerful positions are wedded to the fundamental purposes of the hidden curriculum, it may be difficult to change. However, we cannot assume that all implicit, or hidden, outcomes of schooling are problematic. Some may be beneficial to students, whereas others may be detrimental.

## Benefits of the Hidden Curriculum

What benefits might accrue to students as a result of spending time in schools? Obviously, the answer to this question depends on the particular school and school district the students attend. But we can identify some general factors that are often said to have a positive effect on students.

School provides the opportunity to learn and practice the social skills associated with being part of a group. This opportunity arises naturally since students go to school with lots of other students and interact directly with them every school day. Social learning includes learning to listen, share, take turns, and work with others. Depending on the demographic makeup of the school, education also includes learning to be part of a classroom community with students of different backgrounds and life experiences. In any individual classroom, the proportion of group interaction, and thus the potential for social learning, depends on how a teacher chooses to organize the work. The "hidden" social learning outcomes of schooling are diminished when parents choose to school their students at home (for a detailed discussion, see Chapter 10). Parents who choose home schooling are opting for academic over social interaction benefits, and also over interaction with a diverse group of students.

Every day they are in the classroom, teachers convey messages about who they believe can or cannot learn rigorous material in school.
(Radius Images/Media Bakery)

Some would argue that another beneficial lesson of schooling is learning to take responsibility. In the early grades students may take responsibility for smaller aspects of their education, while as they progress to high school they take much greater responsibility for their assignments, long-term projects, and so on. Completing homework may also be interpreted as an example of students' learning to take responsibility. As we will see in the next section, some educators believe that students are not given enough responsibility for their own learning.

Eisner (1979) identifies some additional potential benefits of being in school: "punctuality, working hard on tasks that are not immediately enjoyable, and the ability to defer immediate gratification in order to work for distant goals" (p. 81). To this list one might add learning to follow directions and to get one's work done in a timely fashion. Depending on the quality of the teaching to which they are exposed, students may also, and arguably should, learn that learning is exciting, that the study of various subjects is stimulating, and that academic skills can be applied to many problems and situations both inside and outside of schools.

## Liabilities of the Hidden Curriculum

The hidden curriculum is more often seen as a liability than a benefit. Two issues are usually raised with regard to the hidden curriculum as a negative force in education: (1) the issue of the passive nature of much educational practice, and (2) the issue of whether schooling differentially favors those who already come to school with social and economic privileges. Both have long histories as political critiques of schooling.

### Education as a Passive Experience.
The typical organization of schooling has long been seen as teaching students to be passive consumers of a not-too-interesting education. Instead of motivating students to explore academic areas in which they are passionately interested and to engage them in authentic problems in which they are invested, schools are said to lock students into a life of rote, boring encounters with the curriculum. The structure of the explicit curriculum itself and its ubiquitous presence in the classroom can potentially have a detrimental impact on how students think about the process of learning—and on what they actually learn. As a result, the hidden message students may come

away with is that learning is boring and that any excitement they may feel about academic subjects occurs outside of school. Erickson and Shultz (1992) use the comical metaphor of the school lunch to capture students' passive consumption of the curriculum:

> In ordinary classroom practice in American schools it appears that the reigning conception of curriculum and pedagogy is that of school lunch. It is as if the job of the teacher were to take packages of mind-food from the freezer (the curriculum), thaw them in a microwave (instruction), and see to it that the students eat it until it is finished (classroom management to maximize time on task). It is not the teacher's responsibility (nor that of the student) to decide what or how much should be eaten or when and how long mealtime should be. Not only is the food served entirely prepackaged but much of each student's daily portion is chopped into small bits, boiled, or mashed in an attempt at predigestion that lowers its basic nutritional content. Moreover, large amounts of sugar, salt and fat are found in the food. Although these substances enhance palatability somewhat, they are deleterious for the students' long-term health and well-being. (p. 467)

In this ironic view of students' experience of schooling, Erickson and Shultz (1992) raise serious questions about the structure of the curriculum when teachers merely follow it explicitly and deliver it without consideration of how to teach it well to their particular group of students. This view also raises questions about what messages students are receiving when teachers choose to follow the explicit curriculum narrowly. These authors also lampoon the "dumbing down" of the curriculum and the tendency to teach specific aspects of it as isolated, small segments of information rather than in a context of meaningful classroom experiences. Their metaphor seeks to imply, of course, that no student should be subjected to the "school lunch" philosophy of experiencing school. Schooling should not result in students disliking learning, but instead should be rich with experiences that convey the message that learning is exciting, motivating, highly integrated across subjects, and meaningful.

Certainly, not all teachers and all schools provide a "school lunch" learning experience. However, through this metaphor Erickson and Shultz are pointing out that given the demands of the academic curriculum and additional pressure to meet curriculum standards, it is all too easy to create this kind of educational experience.

### Your turn... *to reflect*

Think back to your own high school experience. Pinpoint a specific class, for instance, your required freshman English class or government class. What kinds of hidden lessons did you learn in this specific class? Whom did the class benefit most? Whom did it benefit least? For those who benefited least, what changes might the teacher have made to create a more supportive learning environment for every student?

**The Hidden Curriculum and the Question of Privilege.**  One of the most contentious issues related to the hidden curriculum is whether schools are intentionally designed to promote the academic achievement of every student, or whether by design some groups of students systematically have much less chance of achieving well. The argument that schools are not created to ensure that everyone learns at high intellectual levels is based on the belief that the purpose of school is to reproduce the existing, dominant economic system. From this perspective, which is called

**critical theory**, the idea is that those who come to school privileged continue to be privileged, receiving better education and better opportunities for advancement than those who are not so privileged to begin with. Instead of leveling the playing field, these critics argue, schooling reinforces existing socioeconomic divisions among students, fails to serve all students well, and makes it difficult, if not impossible, for students in lower socioeconomic classes to gain the education they need to move up the economic ladder. We will explore this issue in much greater depth in Chapter 7.

Kenneth Sirotnik (1991) cites some essential questions he believes critical scholars of education must ask: "Whose interests are, and are not, being served by the way things are?" and "How did it come to be this way?" (pp. 250–251). By asking questions about "the way things are," Sirotnik invokes the concept of the hidden curriculum and challenges the reader to make the hidden, implicit purposes of schooling visible. For example, if urban and rural schools consistently receive less funding than suburban schools, the inequitable distribution of resources disadvantages urban and rural students. If teachers do not believe that racial and ethnic minority students, or students whose first language is not English, are capable of high levels of intellectual challenge, these teachers can contribute to a cycle of poverty and low-level jobs and aspirations for their students. If guidance counselors often advise racial and ethnic minority students and students from low socioeconomic levels to consider the military or technical school upon graduation, but often advise middle- and upper-middle-class students to pursue a college track, then that school is differentially advancing the interests of students from higher socioeconomic classes. These are all instances of how the hidden curriculum operates as a powerful negative force every day in schools. By maintaining a cycle of low achievement for some students and high expectations for the already privileged, schools and the teachers in them help reproduce the socioeconomic structure of society.

In a famous study comparing working-class, middle-class, and upper-class elementary schools, Jean Anyon (1981) described how schools in poorer areas did not challenge students intellectually and exposed them to a much more rote approach to learning than was used for students in higher income neighborhoods. Depending on where they attend school, students may learn that their teachers care a great deal about their achievement or that their teachers believe they are not capable of learning complex material. As the following Case in Point illustrates, even a seemingly neutral lesson may carry a powerful negative message from a teacher.

**Critical term**

**Critical theory.** Analysis of education that focuses on understanding and changing structural inequities that systematically advantage certain groups of students over others.

## A Case In Point
### Current Events as the Hidden Curriculum

Harper Lee, author of the classic 1960 novel *To Kill a Mockingbird*, weighs in on the hidden curriculum as a negative force in students' experience of school in her description of required current events in the third grade classroom of the novel's main character, Scout Finch. The unintended outcome of this seemingly innocuous, simple activity operated against students who were already at a disadvantage in school. A character wise beyond her years, Scout appears to understand a great deal about the hidden curriculum and the implicit outcomes of schooling.

Once a week we had a Current Events period. Each child was supposed to clip an item from a newspaper, absorb its contents, and reveal them to the class. This practice encouraged good posture and gave a child poise; delivering a short talk

> made him word-conscious; learning his current event strengthened his memory; being singled out made him more than ever anxious to return to the Group.
>
> The idea was profound, but as usual, in Maycomb it didn't work very well. In the first place, few rural children had access to newspapers, so the burden of current events was borne by the town children, convincing the bus children more deeply that the town children got all the attention anyway. The rural children who could, usually brought clippings from what they called The Grit Paper, a publication spurious in the eyes of Miss Gates, our teacher. Why she frowned when a child recited from The Grit Paper, I never knew, but in some way it was associated with fiddling, eating syrupy biscuits for lunch, being a holy-roller, singing Sweetly Sings the Donkey and pronouncing it dunkey, all of which the state paid teachers to discourage. (pp. 279–280)

While Scout Finch certainly understood how the experience of schooling for white town children differed from that of white rural children and how the same educational setting can hold profoundly different meaning for students in different socioeconomic groups, it is likely that Miss Gates did not think twice about what she was communicating to the poor rural students in her classes.

**Your turn... *to reflect***

How could Miss Gates have changed the hidden curriculum around current events in her classroom? Can you think of a similar example from your own schooling? From schools in other areas in your state or region?

## The Hidden Curriculum as a Commentary on the Social Purposes of Schooling

The choices teachers make about how to structure their classes have profound social consequences for students. Every choice a teacher or a school or a school district makes affects how students feel, how they believe they are valued, and what they believe they can do academically and socially. Every choice sends messages to students about the purpose of their time in school. If teachers challenge students wisely, then students learn that their teachers wish to develop their intellects. If teachers extend a hand to help struggling students, then students learn that their teachers want everyone to learn, and not just those to whom learning comes easily. The hidden curriculum reminds teachers that they are responsible for creating a total school experience that is fair, safe, and responsive—in short, classrooms in which every student is motivated to learn.

The hidden curriculum also sends messages to students about how the school responds to their particular social circumstances outside of school. It is this topic we explore next.

## The Current Societal Context

In any given era, different social dynamics prevail, and the hidden curriculum can reflect the ways teachers, educational leaders, and policymakers respond to these prevailing social dynamics and issues. Sometimes responses are mandated at the state or district level because the need to address a specific problem is felt so strongly—or the political pressure to respond is so great. Special programs may then be funded that become part of the formal curriculum, and sometimes formal curriculum materials are developed to help districts with implementation. For example, a state may mandate that all middle and high school students participate in drug and alcohol abuse awareness activities. Individual districts, schools, and teachers might decide to respond to local social issues themselves, taking a proactive stance on what they value and what they believe needs attention. How schools respond to the social needs of their students, and what issues they choose not to respond to, send important messages to students—and their families—about how the schools view their particular social circumstances.

For example, if a school is experiencing increased instances of bullying, the school might work with the students involved and at the same time assess the school-wide environment and redesign it to begin to prevent bullying. In contrast, a school might instead respond solely by cracking down on the individual students and not examine whether the school's environment generally might be contributing to the problem. These two responses send different messages to all students—bullies and victims alike. Similarly, when students experience problems of a personal social nature, teachers and educational staff may respond in different ways—some being supportive, others not—resulting in different learning environments for students. Schools cannot control the social circumstances of students' lives, but education professionals do have control over their response to these changing circumstances. You can see how one high school in Anchorage, Alaska, met the challenge of addressing its diverse students' social and emotional needs in the video at **http://www.edutopia.org/anchorage-social-emotional-learning-video**.

Teachers are obliged to teach all the students who enter their classrooms, no matter what their social circumstances. Universal, compulsory schooling did not always exist in the United States, as the following Historical Note illustrates. The emergence of the common school signaled the intent to educate every student, a commitment that created challenge for teachers and schools. Whether the hidden curriculum of schools promotes or hinders meeting every student's needs is an important consideration as you think about how you will create your own classroom community.

## Historical Note
### The Emergence of the Common School

The more heterogeneous the student population, the greater are the challenges of providing an adequate education to all students. In a universal system of public schooling, where all students are given a free public education during their PK–12 years, educational policymakers, curriculum developers, and teachers are challenged to make schools work well for all economic, racial, ethnic, and language groups. However, children and youth in the United States did not always have access to publicly funded education. It was not until the emergence of the common school movement, which eventually led to universal compulsory education, that education was considered a right for all citizens.

In the colonial era, only the children of the elite were educated, and students were taught in a range of private schools as well as in private homes. Typically, only boys attended school. Religion was a regular part of the curriculum, and often the rationale for education was to enable students to read the Bible. In fact, the oldest legal mandate for educating children was the work of the Massachusetts Colony in 1642, requiring that all children learn to read to ensure that they were not deluded by Satan and, thus, fail to learn the Bible (Johnson, 1963). This law, which required that a selectman in each locale take responsibility for making sure children were learning to read (but not necessarily in formal schools), was known as the Old Deluder Satan Act.

The notion of universal education was introduced in colonial times, but it was not widely accepted (Butts & Cremin, 1953). Thomas Jefferson was one of its earliest proponents, and his concept of the common school was intimately connected to his ideas about democracy. Put simply, Jefferson believed that an educated citizenry was the best way to assure good government. As Butts and Cremin characterized this perspective, "If people were going to rule, they ought at least to rule well" (p. 191). Reaching this goal meant that every child deserved to be educated without regard for the family's ability to pay. If common schooling were going to exist, public funds would have to be set aside for this purpose.

Once schooling became a function of the public trust, arguments about the curriculum developed. What should the role of religion be in publicly funded schools? Should the curriculum remain focused on the basics of reading, writing, and mathematics? Should it be expanded to include subjects such as geography, law, physical education, drawing, and government, for example? The question of curriculum also extended to whether practical subjects such as simple book-keeping, or vocational subjects such as agriculture, should be included. What about moral education, which immediately raised the issue of the role of religion in the newly conceptualized, publicly funded schools?

Despite deep disagreements about these issues—disagreements that continue today in debates about the purposes of education—the idea of the common school began to take hold beginning around 1830. Its acceptance was incremental, but nevertheless the idea prevailed, in no small part owing to the persistent political work of its greatest champion, the educator Horace Mann. Mann, who lived in Massachusetts, believed that education was the single most important means of helping people improve their status in life. He worked tirelessly to convince politicians that his vision of the common school was the means to realizing the true meaning of a democracy. He argued for a secular curriculum for the common school. Once such schools were established, states began to pass compulsory attendance laws, reasoning that if common schools existed for the public good and at public expense, children and youth should be attending them.

As immigrants poured into the nation's cities, another argument for compulsory attendance at common schools developed: to hasten immigrants' acculturation to their new homes and their new nation. Furthermore, because children in many cities were living in poverty and were spending their time on the streets, social reformers such as Jacob Riis in New York called for compulsory schooling. Riis believed that a partnership between schools and social service agencies would help meet the needs of students who came from homes marked by poverty (Butts & Cremin, 1953).

The system of common schools expanded steadily to accommodate growing numbers of students, and by the turn of the twentieth century, 32 states, mostly in the North and West, had passed compulsory attendance laws, assuring the place of universal, common education in America. In the year 1865, 57 percent of American children attended common schools. By the turn of the century, enrollment had risen to 90 percent (Cremin, 1988).

At its inception, the rise of the common school as a means to protect democracy and provide opportunity for equity among all citizens represented a unique development. Theoretically, the common school allowed individuals to move up in social class by virtue of receiving a public-funded education, and at the same time it helped ensure an educated citizenry to promote democratic practice. This noble goal of providing a common educational system—rather than one system for the elite and another for those who were not well-to-do—set the American system of education apart from education in all other parts of the world. However, the promise of universal common schooling of uniformly high quality for every child remains a national challenge.

Social trends affect students and families everywhere. In the next section we examine major current social issues and trends, how schools address these issues, and the explicit and implicit messages schools convey depending on how the social issues are addressed.

## Population and the Schools

According to the last U.S. Census, taken in 2000, there were approximately 72 million persons under the age of 18 living in the United States; of these, 60 million children and youth were enrolled in schools ranging from nursery school/kindergarten through twelfth grade (Day, 2003). Of the children and youth enrolled in schools, 9.2 million attend preschool/kindergarten, 33.7 million attend grades 1–8, and 16.4 million attend high school in grades 9–12. Of the total students enrolled in grades 1–12, about 90 percent attend public schools (Day, 2003). National data also indicate that half of all family households in the country included children under the age of 18 (Fields & Casper, 2001), which means that nearly one out of every two family households has a school-aged child.

Although school enrollments fell during the 1970s and 1980s, the school-aged population has steadily increased since then. The 2000 Census Bureau report also indicates that the number of elementary and high school students peaked in April of 2000 to an all-time high, with an increase of 8 million students between 1990 and 2000 (Day, 2003). Enrollments at the preschool/kindergarten level have also increased. In 1964, approximately 5 percent of students attended preschool; in 1999, this figure had risen to 50 percent, signaling a profound change in how society views the role of preschool. From 1969 to 1999, the number of children attending kindergarten increased from 11 percent to 58 percent. Today, 95 percent of all five-year-olds are enrolled in school, with 74 percent in kindergartens, 15 percent enrolled in preschool (nonpublic), and an additional 6 percent in first grade. These population changes bode well in the near term for prospective teachers.

Compared to the 1960s, when only 5% of young children attending preschool, today over 50% of young children attend preschool. (Media Bakery)

### Changing Family Structures

If you were teaching in the 1950s, most of your students would have been living in traditional nuclear families, with both parents and with children who all had the same family name. Today this model is quite changed. In any school district, you will teach students who live with both parents, one parent, stepparents, grandparents, other related adults, or gay or lesbian parents.

**With Whom Do Children and Youth Live?** No matter where you teach, your students' family structures are not likely to be homogeneous. Figure 6-1 illustrates the percentage of children by state who are under the age of 18 and who are not living with married parents. In addition, we know that 27 percent of children who are under the age of 18 live in a single-parent household; another 5 percent live in a nonparent household (Lugaila & Overturf, 2004). Poverty rates are highest for single-mother households across all racial and ethnic groups, as illustrated in Figure 6-2.

The role of grandparents as primary caregivers is also shifting. U.S. Census data indicate that from 1970 to 1992, the increased number of children living with grandparents was due to single parents residing with grandparents. Between 1992 and 1997, however, the situation shifted, and the increase was in grandchildren living with grandparents in the absence of a parent (Bryson & Casper, 1999). Today, of the 5.8 million co-resident grandparents in U.S. households, 2.4 million were the primary caregivers of children under the age of 18 in those

---

**Figure 6-1    Map, by State, of Children Who Are Not Living with Married Parents**

Because many of their students will not be living in traditional two-parent families, it is up to teachers to identify the various support structures students have for whatever family arrangement in which they live.

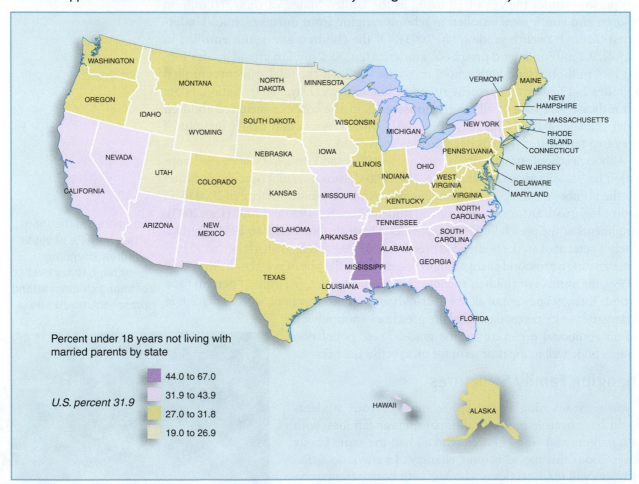

Percent under 18 years not living with married parents by state

*U.S. percent 31.9*

- 44.0 to 67.0
- 31.9 to 43.9
- 27.0 to 31.8
- 19.0 to 26.9

**Source:** Lugaila, T., and J. O. Verturf. (2004, March). *Children and the households they live in: 2000*. Census 2000 Special Reports, Report CENSR-14. Washington, DC: U.S. Census Bureau. Retrieved August 19, 2008, from http://www.census.gov/population/www/cen2000/briefs.html.

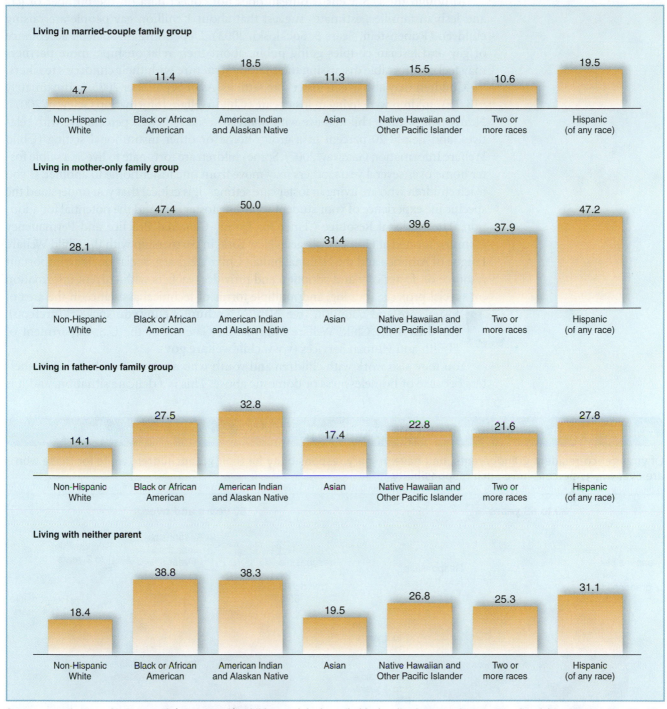

**Figure 6-2    Poverty Rates for Children Under 18 by Living Arrangement**

Poverty rates increase for students who do not live in a married-couple family, but making assumptions about students' abilities to learn based on their income status can set up low expectations on the part of their teachers.

**Living in married-couple family group**

| Non-Hispanic White | Black or African American | American Indian and Alaskan Native | Asian | Native Hawaiian and Other Pacific Islander | Two or more races | Hispanic (of any race) |
|---|---|---|---|---|---|---|
| 4.7 | 11.4 | 18.5 | 11.3 | 15.5 | 10.6 | 19.5 |

**Living in mother-only family group**

| Non-Hispanic White | Black or African American | American Indian and Alaskan Native | Asian | Native Hawaiian and Other Pacific Islander | Two or more races | Hispanic (of any race) |
|---|---|---|---|---|---|---|
| 28.1 | 47.4 | 50.0 | 31.4 | 39.6 | 37.9 | 47.2 |

**Living in father-only family group**

| Non-Hispanic White | Black or African American | American Indian and Alaskan Native | Asian | Native Hawaiian and Other Pacific Islander | Two or more races | Hispanic (of any race) |
|---|---|---|---|---|---|---|
| 14.1 | 27.5 | 32.8 | 17.4 | 22.8 | 21.6 | 27.8 |

**Living with neither parent**

| Non-Hispanic White | Black or African American | American Indian and Alaskan Native | Asian | Native Hawaiian and Other Pacific Islander | Two or more races | Hispanic (of any race) |
|---|---|---|---|---|---|---|
| 18.4 | 38.8 | 38.3 | 19.5 | 26.8 | 25.3 | 31.1 |

**Source:** Lugaila, T., and J. O. Verturf. (2004, March). *Children and the households they live in: 2000.* Census 2000 Special Reports, Report CENSR-14. Washington, DC: U.S. Census Bureau. Retrieved August 19, 2008, from http://www.census.gov/population/www/cen2000/briefs.html.

households (Simmons & Dye, 2003). Of these grandparent caregivers, 34 percent lived in households without the child's parent. In the majority of living situations where grandparents are the primary caregivers, 33 percent have been the primary caregiver for five years or more, as illustrated in Figure 6-3. For students reported to be living with no parent, over one-third are living with grandparents (Simmons & Dye, 2003). It is critical that teachers have this information because they must communicate regularly with the relative who is the primary caregiver.

Although the U.S. Census Bureau does not collect data on the number of gay and lesbian families, estimates suggest that about 1 million gay people are raising children (Rubenstein, Sears & Sockloski, 2003). Depending on societal acceptance of gay and lesbian couples going public about their relationships, more partners may feel comfortable discussing their family structure with their children's teachers.

Children may also live in foster care settings. As of September 2005, approximately 513,000 children were living in foster care (Child Welfare Information Gateway, 2007). Nearly half of these children live with nonrelatives; another 25 percent live with relatives, and nearly 20 percent in a group home or other institutional setting (Child Welfare Information Gateway, 2007). Some children are fortunate to live in a stable foster home over several years; others may move from one foster home to another. If you teach children who are living in foster care settings, it is critical that you understand the specific life experience of your student regarding foster care and the potential for adoption. The National Resource Center for Family-Centered Practice and Permanency Planning located at Hunter College in New York, in partnership with the Child Welfare League of America and the National Indian Child Welfare Association, is an important resource on foster care and adoption and provides teachers with current information on special projects, training, and multiple forms of technical assistance in the area of foster care and adoption (see **http://www.hunter.cuny.edu/socwork/nrcfcpp**). Another is the Child Welfare Information Gateway of the U.S. Department of Health and Human Services (**www.childwelfare.gov**).

You may also work with children and youth who are temporarily living in shelters because of homelessness or domestic abuse. This is a delicate situation, and it is

## Figure 6-3    Co-Resident Grandparents as Primary Caregivers

Of younger co-resident grandparents, half have primary responsibility for their grandchildren, while for those who are over 60, 31 percent have such responsibility.

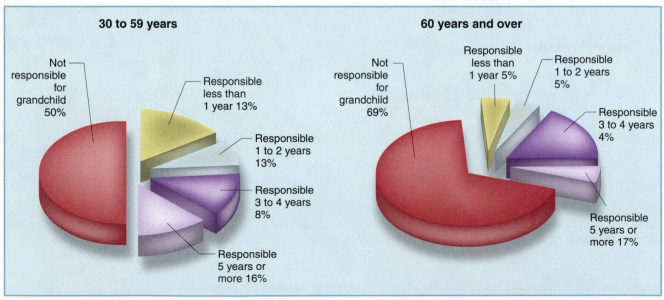

**Source:** Simmons, T., and J. L. Dye. (2003, October). *Grandparents living with grandchildren: 2000.* Census 2000 Brief. Report C2KBR-31. Washington, DC: United States Census Bureau. Retrieved August 19, 2008, from http://www.census.gov/population/www/cen2000/briefs.html.

essential to work with the school's support staff to help your students feel secure at school. It is also important to recognize that family and living structures are changeable and that during a single year some of your students' family and living situations may shift. Students may be in and out of shelters, or they may move between family members. In addition to changing the adults with whom they reside, or the place where they live, students may also experience the death of a parent, grandparent, sibling, or other family members who are primary caregivers.

### Responding to Changing Family Structures.

When teachers do not know about a student's family structure or feel uncomfortable about it, they can readily communicate the idea that they are not interested in the student. Teachers must be conscious of the words they use when referring to adults at home who are responsible for students. For example, saying, "Have your parents sign this" is not appropriate language in today's classrooms, because students may live with only one parent, grandparents, or other family members. Insensitivity to students' individual home structures can easily be interpreted as a sign of disrespect or unconcern.

Today children are more likely than ever before to live in nontraditional family structures, for example, with a grandparent rather than a parent. (Corbis Digital Stock)

Teachers must be sensitive to—and equally comfortable with—every type of family with which they may come into contact. Teachers also need to be careful not to make assumptions about the resources families provide for their children. Although some family configurations may put greater stress on the family unit than others (for example, single parenting), this does *not* automatically translate into a lack of commitment to a child's education. Nor does it necessarily represent an inability to support a child who is struggling. Each situation requires you to know the family, the assets within that family's situation that support the children, as well as the challenges the family may be facing. For example, a student may have a single parent but in addition may have a very supportive extended family that provides great stability. An African American child who lives in a challenging urban environment may have strong ties with his or her family's local church. Failing to know the details, you may communicate incorrect assumptions to your students about their lives. Such messages are part of the hidden curriculum and provide students with implicit perspectives as to how school personnel value their students' family structures.

There are important legal reasons to be familiar with each child's family structure as well. For example, you must know which adults have the legal right to take a child out of school or pick a child up from school. This information is generally collected at the start of every school year. Once you have received it, you should review each student's situation and be sure you get to know the person who has legal custody or guardianship.

Finally, as a teacher you may not feel comfortable with or agree with the family lifestyles of all of your students. Your responsibility is not to judge the families, but rather to work respectfully with every family to create and strengthen the circumstances in which your student—their child—can be successful in school.

Teachers are not the only school personnel responsible for meeting students' needs. School counselors, social workers, or school psychologists may create support groups for students who are experiencing divorce or the death of a parent, grandparent, or sibling. Counselors and school psychologists can also direct families to other, outside supports in the local community, region, or state. Special programs typically exist, for example, for families who have lost members due to cancer. Special camping programs, sometimes as short as a single weekend, are available for families in which a parent has died. Teachers who are aware of these potential supports can be proactive in securing the best services possible for their students.

Authors of children's and young adult literature have responded to changing family structures with works of fiction and nonfiction alike. These can be important resources for teachers, whether they are used in the classroom as a whole or are suggested to students and their families. Figure 6-4 includes a sample of book titles related to different family structures that you can use with your students. Teachers who use such literature are sending implicit messages that all family structures are valued enough to be represented in the literature in their classrooms.

Across the social and economic spectrum, families may experience stress that affects children. Many children respond to stress by developing adjustment

---

**Figure 6-4    Examples of Books for Children Representing Different Family Structures**

Authors of children's literature have written and illustrated books that address the full range of family structures, which provide teachers with another way to communicate the value of every child's living arrangement.

**Living with Grandparents**

*Stone Fox* by John Reynolds Gardiner
*Visiting Day* by Jacqueline Woodson
*The Rain Catchers* by Jean Thesman

**Gay and Lesbian Parents**

*From the Notebooks of Melanin Sun* by Jacqueline Woodson
*Heather Has Two Mommies* by Leslea Newman
*Daddy's Roommate* by Michael Willhoite
*My Two Uncles* by Judith Vigna

**Foster Homes/Group Homes**

*The Christmas Promise* by Susan Campbell Bartoletti
*The Fire Pony* by Rodman Philbrick
*Georgie* by Malachy Doyle
*Heaven Eyes* by David Almond
*Surviving the Applewhites* by Stephanie Tolan
*The Great Gilly Hopkins* by Katherine Paterson
*Holding up the Earth* by Dianne Gray

**Homeless Shelters**

*Homeless* by Bernard Wolff
*Monkey Island* by Paula Fox

**Adoption**

*White Swan Express* by Jean Davies Okimoto and Elaine M. Aoki
*How I Was Adopted* by Joanna Cole
*Our Baby from China* by Nancy D'Antonio

**Living with other Relatives**

*Our Gracie Aunt* by Jacqueline Woodson

problems (Meyers & Nastasi, 1999), whereas other children may be comparatively invulnerable to the negative impact of the stressors in their lives, exemplifying the concept of **resilience** (Garmezy & Rutter, 1983). Children can be resilient for a variety of reasons. For their part, teachers should not make assumptions about students' levels of stress or support, but rather should get to know the child and his or her family situation well and make decisions based on accurate knowledge. At the same time, teachers must be ready to solicit resources for students who need them through the auxiliary services available at school and in the community.

## Child Abuse and Neglect

The abuse and neglect of children is a national tragedy that crosses all socioeconomic, racial, and ethnic lines. Reports of **child abuse** and neglect increased over a thirty-year period from 150,000 per year in 1963 to about 3 million in 1993; part of this increase can be ascribed to the passage of federal and state laws that mandate reporting of suspected maltreatment of children (Lowenthal, 2001). In 2006, the total number of referrals was 3.3 million, involving 6 million children; of these reports, approximately 905,000 cases were substantiated, a rate of nearly 12 victims per every 1000 children (U.S. Department of Health and Human Services, 2006). However, many believe that cases of child abuse and neglect are seriously underreported and that only one out of every three people who suspect child maltreatment reports it (Childhelp USA, 2006).

Teachers, like medical, law enforcement, and human services personnel, are mandated to report suspected child abuse and neglect. Thus, every teacher must be familiar with the laws of the state in which he or she is teaching, the signs of suspected abuse and neglect, and the steps to be taken when abuse and neglect are suspected. Teachers do not investigate suspected child maltreatment themselves, but rather report it to the designated person within their school—typically a counselor, social worker, psychologist, or the school principal. The reporting laws are structured so that mandated reporters cannot be held personally liable for making such reports as long as they are made in good faith (Lowenthal, 2001). This encourages reporting, ensuring that as many children as possible are protected. Although all state laws must subscribe to a basic federal definition of child abuse and neglect, these laws differ; in some states, every single citizen is obliged to report suspected cases of child abuse and neglect.

The most prevalent form of child maltreatment is **child neglect**, accounting for approximately 60 percent of all victims in 2006; 80 percent of those who maltreat children are parents (U.S. Department of Health and Human Services, 2006). Another 16 percent were cases of physical abuse, 9 percent were sexual abuse, and 7 percent emotional abuse.

The most important federal legislation on this issue is the Child Abuse Prevention and Treatment Act (CAPTA), which was passed in 1974 (Public Law 93-247) and amended in 2003 as the Keeping Children and Families Safe Act (P.L. 108-36). This law provides minimum definitions of child neglect and abuse. However, each state has its own laws and definitions using federal legislation as its basis, and states themselves are responsible for carrying out activities to prevent and investigate suspected cases of child neglect or abuse. The federal legislation also supports the Child Welfare Information Gateway at **www.childwelfare.gov**.

**Critical term**

**Resilience.** A characteristic of some children who are exposed to stressors from the social conditions of their lives but who appear to be invulnerable to the negative effects of those stressors.

**Critical term**

**Child abuse.** The federal definition is "any recent act or failure to act on the part of a parent or caretaker which results in death, serious physical or emotional harm, sexual abuse or exploitation; or an act or failure to act which presents an imminent risk of serious harm."

**Critical term**

**Child neglect.** Failing to provide for the basic needs of children, including physical, medical, educational, or emotional needs and, in many states, abandonment.

## Table 6-1    Signs of Child Maltreatment

Teachers should be alert to the following signs.

| Types of Child Maltreatment | Signs of child maltreatment: Consider the possibility of abuse when the child: |
| --- | --- |
| **Physical Abuse** | Has unexplained burns, bites, bruises, broken bones, or black eyes |
| | Has fading bruises or other marks noticeable after an absence from school |
| | Seems frightened of parents and protests or cries when it is time to go home |
| | Shrinks at the approach of adults |
| | Reports injury by a parent or another adult caregiver |
| **Neglect** | Is frequently absent from school |
| | Begs or steals food or money |
| | Lacks needed medical or dental care, immunizations, or glasses |
| | Is consistently dirty and has severe body odor |
| | Lacks sufficient clothing for the weather |
| | Abuses alcohol or other drugs |
| | States that there is no one at home to provide care |
| **Sexual Abuse** | Has difficulty walking or sitting |
| | Suddenly refuses to change for gym or to participate in physical activities |
| | Reports nightmares or bed wetting |
| | Experiences a sudden change in appetite |
| | Demonstrates bizarre, sophisticated, or unusual sexual knowledge or behavior |
| | Becomes pregnant or contracts a venereal disease, particularly if under age 14 |
| | Runs away |
| | Reports sexual abuse by a parent or another adult caregiver |
| **Emotional Maltreatment** | Shows extremes in behavior, such as overly compliant or demanding behavior, extreme passivity, or aggression |
| | Is either inappropriately adult (parenting other children, for example) or inappropriately infantile (frequently rocking or head banging, for example |
| | Is delayed in physical or emotional development |
| | Has attempted suicide |
| | Reports a lack of attachment to the parent |

**Adapted from:** U.S. Department of Health and Human Services. Child Welfare Information Gateway (2006), *Recognizing Child Abuse and Neglect: Signs and Symptoms Factsheet*. Washington, DC: Author.

Given the prevalence of child abuse and neglect in the United States today, at some point in your career as a teacher you may likely be working with victims of such maltreatment. As an ethical professional—and as a mandated reporter—you have a job to protect children and youth by reporting suspected cases of abuse or neglect to the designated person in your school. If you suspect a case of neglect or abuse during one of your early field experiences or as a student teacher or intern, you should report your suspicions first to the teacher with whom you are working. Many teacher education programs include training to help you carry out your responsibilities as a mandated reporter. If this is not the case, you should seek out a workshop or training session to provide you with this information.

## Violence and the Schools

School violence can range from bullying, threatening remarks, and physical fights to assaults with or without weapons and gang violence (National Youth Violence Prevention Resource Center, 2005). Because of the media attention it attracts, school violence, and especially school shootings, are a dominant topic in discussions of schools despite the fact that schools are actually relatively safe places (Gladden, 2002). Between the mid-1990s and 2000, the incidence of violence in schools actually declined but has now plateaued (Mayer, 2008). But youth violence remains a pressing national concern. Of violent deaths among children, less than 1 percent of the total takes place at school (National Youth Prevention Resource Center, 2005). Although some schools are safer than others, school violence crosses racial, cultural, and economic lines. It occurs in suburban schools, rural schools, and urban schools alike. Therefore, all teachers need to be aware of how to make schools safe places.

Following a high school shooting in Oregon, in 1998 the U.S. Department of Education published *Early Warning, Timely Response: A Guide to Safe Schools* (Dywer, Osher, & Warger, 1998), issued to help prevent violence in schools. Figure 6-5 identifies 12 specific measures schools can take to be proactive in their prevention of violence.

Students are more likely to feel comfortable in school when they can have an honest conversation with an adult at school about their problems. (Media Bakery)

---

### Figure 6-5    Twelve Strategies for School Violence Prevention

**Schools can take deliberate measures to become places where violence is minimized and where students feel supported to do their best work.**

1. Focus on academic achievement
2. Involve families in meaningful ways
3. Develop links to the community
4. Emphasize positive relationships among students and staff
5. Discuss safety issues openly
6. Treat students with equal respect
7. Create ways for students to share their concerns
8. Have in place a system for referring children who are suspected of being abused or neglected
9. Offer extended day programs for children
10. Promote good citizenship and character
11. Identify problems and assess progress toward solutions
12. Support students in making the transition to adult life and the workplace

**Source:** Dwyer, K., D. Osher, & C. Warger. (1998). *Early warning, timely response: A guide to safe schools.* Washington, DC: U.S. Department of Education.

What do these measures mean for you as a teacher? As the figure suggests, a safe school functions as a community in which all students feel welcome and respected, are confident in sharing problems with the teachers, staff, and administration, and feel secure so they can learn. In such a school, the professional staff works together to create an atmosphere in which students do not see violence as their only option if they have a problem. Creating safe schools takes an active commitment. As you can see, because it is directly concerned with the atmosphere in schools, creating safe schools is definitely related to the hidden curriculum—the total experience students have in school.

If a school has a history of being unsafe, if fighting and threatening occur often, it will take strong, consistent leadership to change the character of the school. Installing metal detectors, while a deterrent, will not on its own change a school that is not safe without a school-wide effort to change the school's culture. Those who staff schools need to make a serious commitment to creating safe places—for students and teachers alike. Schools that do make this commitment send an important message to their students—that the school staff is dedicated to making school a place where students feel respected, safe, and supported as learners.

In *Early Warning, Timely Response*, the authors point out that the early warning signs of violence may include actions such as social withdrawal, feelings of isolation, a sense of rejection, uncontrolled anger, expression of violence in writing and drawing, patterns of chronic hitting and/or bullying, and others (for a complete list, see Dwyer, Osher, & Warger, 1998, pp. 8–11). How schools respond to such early warning signs is one of the most important messages schools send to their students. Those school staff members who misinterpret early warning signs may exacerbate the situation. One of the most important principles these authors set forth is to avoid making judgments about potential violence based on false stereotypes—that is, race, socioeconomic status, cognitive or academic ability, or physical appearance. Judgments about a child's capacity for violence should be based on actual behavior, not assumptions. Another critical principle they emphasize is that students who are potentially aggressive usually display multiple signs of problematic behavior.

You can readily see that teachers or school staff members who ignore either of these principles may send messages that students are violent when in fact they are not. In doing so, teachers fail to treat students respectfully and risk losing their trust. Teachers who fail to build a solid, respectful, trusting relationship with their students are likely to have difficulty providing support to students who need encouragement to avoid engaging in violent behavior in the future. The hidden curriculum in schools and classrooms that are not sufficiently proactive in preventing school violence using the guidelines offered here is that schools are not places that need to be made safe for students.

Bullying is a specific form of school violence that is defined as "*intentional* actions *repeated over time* that *harm, intimidate,* or *humiliate another person (the victim)*, and occur within the context of an *imbalance of power*, either real or perceived, between the bully and the victim" (Bear & Blank, 2008). A single instance of teasing would not be considered bullying. As is the case with other forms of violence, the best practice a school can engage in is creating a school environment that is based on mutual respect and dignity. This will not completely prevent bullying from occurring, but it can go a long way toward reducing it.

A more recent form of bullying can take place on the internet and is called *cyberbullying.* Cyberbulling includes email, instant messaging, chat rooms, or messages on cell phones (Kowalski & Limber, 2007). It seems to escalate in fifth grade and reaches its peak by eighth grade (Worthen, 2007). Internet technologies can have great benefits in improving education, but they also pose great risks and problems as represented by developments such as cyberbullying. The Center for Safe and Responsible Internet Use includes materials for parents: *Cyber-safe Kids, Cyber-savvy Teens* (**http://cyberbully.org**), and a guide for teachers, *Educator's Guide to Cyberbullying and Cyberthreats* (**http://cyberbully.org/cyberbully/docs/ cbcteducator.pdf**). As is the case with other forms of violence prevention, preventing cyberbullying takes a schoolwide effort coordinated with parents, families, and the community.

A specific population of students who are disproportionately targeted negatively in schools are lesbian, gay, bisexual, or transgendered (LGBT) students or students whose parents are LGBT. In a 2008 report on the school experiences of LGBT parents and students (Kosciw & Diaz, 2008), 42% of LGBT students reported being verbally harassed, with only about half of these students reporting the incident to a school official or teacher. LGBT parents report that when schools have comprehensive safe schools policies, the frequency of such incidents is reduced. Having students feel safe reporting such incidents is critical, as LGBT students often choose not to attend school in the face of these problems (Kosciw & Diaz, 2008).

Is it easier for a school staff to build relationships with students if the school population is smaller? Indeed, some educators think one way to enhance relationships is to reduce the size of schools. The movement toward creating smaller high schools might hold this potential.

## Digging Deeper
### Will Smaller High Schools Meet Students' Needs?

One trend in secondary education is establishing small high schools—usually no more than about 400 students. Small high schools can provide a more personal setting for students, make learning meaningful, make sure students are not anonymous in school (as can easily happen in a large high school), and improve high school graduation rates. In small high schools, the argument goes, students' individual social, emotional, and academic needs have a much greater chance of being met.

**Pro and Con:** Supporters of the small high schools movement believe that such schools can be more effective than large, comprehensive high schools, which often have thousands of students. In such large schools students can get "lost," they may associate with only one small group or clique of students during their entire high school career, or they may drop out before anyone realizes that they are gone. In large high schools, teachers often see their students for only 45 minutes a day, and during that time they are often focused on delivering the content of the subject they teach. In small high schools, teachers and students can more easily collaborate to structure in-depth projects that are carried out over a long period of time each day, for several weeks. The Bill and Melinda Gates Foundation has donated nearly $1.5 billion to create small high schools based on rigor, relevance, and relationships.

Those who are skeptical about small high schools do not believe that size is the most important consideration. Specific characteristics of good high schools, such as the commitment of the teachers and staff, the school environment, and an emphasis on the serious study of academics, are elements that separate high schools with lower dropout rates from those with higher ones (Bryk & Thum, 1989). When school staff members are committed, they connect with the students and recognize their needs. Moreover, the budgets of small high schools may not be able to support teachers with expertise in all of the disciplinary content areas required. Finally, small high schools cannot offer the diversity of course offerings or extracurricular activities available in a large high school. The trend toward small high schools is taking place primarily in urban communities, leading some to question why the benefits of larger, comprehensive high schools are so easily discarded (see Kozol, 2007).

**The Nuances:** To the extent that size makes it possible for teachers to spend more time with their students and build strong relationships with them, small high schools may have an advantage over their larger counterparts. However, the quality of the educational staff is an issue in every school, no matter what its size. It takes teachers who are committed to their students and who see their students as individuals in relationship to the subjects they teach. If students experience school as a series of classes where teachers are only interested in their subjects—and not in the students who are learning those subjects—students are likely to fail to connect and then will "vote with their feet" by skipping classes or dropping out.

Small schools offer greater flexibility of scheduling, with teachers having more freedom to spend extended time on projects across different subject areas. Teachers in small schools need to be willing to engage in this kind of teaching and to collaborate with teachers from other content areas to create projects that motivate students and that demand solid content knowledge to make those projects worthwhile. To ensure expertise, small schools may seek teachers who are licensed in more than one subject area.

Finally, small schools need to consider what kinds of extracurricular activities they can offer. Will they partner with other small schools for sports teams, large drama productions, band, or debate? Or will these activities be scaled down, even though they may interest individual students and motivate them to stay in school?

**Rethinking the Issue:** No matter what their size, it takes a great deal of hard work for high schools to be effective. One of the greatest challenges for large and small high schools alike is preparing teachers at the secondary level not only to be knowledgeable in their content area, but also to be committed to knowing who their students are and taking into account their students' development in relationship to the content. Traditionally, secondary teachers have been prepared with a heavy emphasis on their content area, or academic discipline, but with less attention to how to teach that content well to adolescents. The small high schools movement is based on the belief that relationships between teachers and students, rigor in the academic curriculum, and connections across the curriculum are all essential ingredients for success. What distinguishes smaller high schools is that teachers are expected to develop relationships with their students and to worry about their well-being, whereas in large, impersonal high schools the structure itself can work against building such relationships.

## Teen Pregnancy

Another societal issue that affects schools is teenage pregnancy. Birth rates for girls ages 15 to 19 declined from 111 pregnancies per 1000 teens during the 1990s to 75 such pregnancies in 2002. In 2005, teen births rate were 40 births per 1000 teen girls aged 15–19 (National Campaign to Prevent Teen and Unplanned Pregnancy, 2008). The United States still has the highest level of teenage pregnancy in the developed world (National Campaign to Prevent Teen and Unplanned Pregnancy, 2008). At the turn of the twenty-first century, the teenage pregnancy rate in the United States was two times greater than Great Britain's teenage pregnancy rate and ten times greater than that of the Netherlands (Kirby, 2001).

Teenage pregnancy and its prevention provide a good example of how schooling and society interact. Teenage pregnancy is linked to welfare dependency, poverty, and the poor well-being of children; teen mothers are less likely to finish high school and less prepared to compete for better paying, more stable jobs (National Campaign to Prevent Teen and Unplanned Pregnancy, 2008). However, efforts to prevent teen pregnancy—and the school's role in that campaign—are fraught with political tensions that are often opposed to one another. Most students are taught about how to prevent pregnancy—whether through sex education or abstinence education (National Campaign to Prevent Teen and Unplanned Pregnancy, n.d.). This issue has become very politicized. Many conservative politicians wish to fund only prevention programs that promote abstinence, whereas progressive politicians may wish to fund programs that minimally include education about contraception and responsible sexual behavior in addition to abstinence.

Recent research on the prevention of teen pregnancy documents some interesting findings with regard to these conservative versus progressive tensions. First, the majority of Americans believe that abstinence should be encouraged *and* that contraception should be taught and be available to sexually active teens (Bleakley, Hennessy & Fishbein, 2006). Next, abstinence education and sex education curriculums are not mutually exclusive. Although some pure abstinence-only programs exist, others are comprehensive and include discussions of contraception; similarly, programs of sex education often address abstinence (Kirby, 2007). Effective programs always address the issue of how to deal with pressure to engage in sexual behavior and provide opportunities for students to practice how to negotiate and how to refuse to engage in sex (Kirby, 2007). Programs that use a sexuality-based curriculum with explicit discussions of contraception and HIV, for example, do not result in increased sexual activity (Kirby, 2007). In addition, abstinence-only programs have not proved to be effective in delaying teenagers' sexual activity (Trenholm et al., 2007).

Perhaps most important, however, is the growing evidence that involving teens in after-school service-based learning programs contributes to the reduction of teen pregnancy (Kirby, 2007; Manlove et al., 2004). Programs like these, also known as *youth development programs*, provide structured time for teenagers to think about their experiences and contributions as they participate in service activities, and as a result can promote personal growth in self-esteem, resilience, and school achievement. Therefore, in addition to specific pregnancy prevention programs, schools can provide structured extracurricular activities that involve students in service projects—and all teachers can be involved in promoting these possibilities for their students. However, schools cannot be expected to do the work of prevention by themselves. Community activities and opportunities outside of school—as well as supports outside of school—must also exist (National Campaign to Prevent Teen and Unwanted Pregnancy, 2008; Kirby, 2007).

With the rise of technology, the effectiveness of video and computer-based programs to prevent teen pregnancy has come into play. Kirby (2007) found that short videos on this topic which do not require any interaction by the viewer are not effective interventions. However, longer videos and computer-based programs that do require interaction, and that are viewed more than once, may be a positive influence.

## Drug and Alcohol Abuse

Another social issue that affects schools is the abuse of drugs and alcohol by children, particularly by adolescents. The report *Monitoring the Future* (Johnston, O'Malley, Bachman, and Schulenberg, 2008), an annual survey of drug and alcohol use among eighth, tenth, and twelfth grade students, indicates that in 2007 nearly 22 percent of all eighth graders, 40 percent of all tenth graders, and 51 percent of all twelfth graders have used illicit drugs during their lifetime. In 2007, a modest decline occurred in the use of marijuana and stimulants (except cocaine). The use of ecstasy showed an increase. The use of other hallucinogens (e.g., LSD, heroin, cocaine, and crack) was stable during 2007. Increases were identified in the use of inhalants among tenth graders (Johnston et al., 2008).

Along with the modest decline in the use of many illicit drugs, the number of teens who smoke cigarettes has continued to decline significantly. Levels of smoking declined for all three age groups included in the survey over the past ten years, but nearly half of all twelfth graders have tried smoking cigarettes and about 22 percent currently smoke (Johnston et al., 2008). Therefore, the trend is in the right direction, but since about one-fourth of all high school seniors are regular smokers, a tremendous amount of work remains to be done in reducing teen smoking levels.

Although its use has declined since the 1990s, alcohol consumption continues to be problematic, with 72 percent of students reporting drinking more than a few sips of alcohol by the time they graduate from high school—and 39 percent of these students report having done so by the eighth grade (Johnston et al., 2008). Furthermore, 55 percent of twelfth graders and one-fifth of all eighth grade respondents said that once during their lives they had been drunk (Johnston et al., 2008).

As in many other cases, schools have been viewed as the most appropriate place to provide education on the prevention of drug and alcohol use. Packaged programs such as the highly popular Drug Abuse Resistance Education (DARE) Program, which is taught by local police officers, has not historically resulted in prevention, but it does build positive relationships between police officers and students (University of Akron, 2006). The new revised curriculum, however, is showing some more positive results (University of Akron, 2006). Today that view is changing and there is some recognition that schools alone, with all of their other responsibilities, cannot do the job themselves (Anderson, Aromaa, & Rosenbloom, 2007). When schools do provide programs on drug and alcohol prevention, it is critical that they select programs that have a track record of leading to such prevention. Organizations such as Join Together (**www.jointogether.org**) include lists of promising programs.

## Addressing Social Dynamics by Changing the Regularities of Schooling

Schools cannot solve all social problems, nor should we expect them to. But being the places where most children spend a great deal of their time, it is not surprising that schools have become a focal point for programs aimed at responding to the social dynamics of our society. Even the best school programs cannot compensate for a completely dysfunctional family, a parent who does not have good parenting skills, the effects of a family tragedy like a death or serious illness, and the like. Nevertheless, the school and its teachers do play a critical role in addressing these issues. How each school chooses to do so illustrates its own hidden curriculum.

### Redefining the Environment

Once we define curriculum as the total school experience, we begin to see that a school's staff must ask itself whether its practices are providing the most positive, supportive environment possible for students who may, for a wide variety of reasons, be struggling—socially as well as academically. Is the school a place where students find adults whom they trust? Do all students feel welcomed? Is there a commitment to preventing problems from escalating? Do students have legitimate outlets for resolving conflicts? What signals does the social organization of the school send to students about their relationships with each other and with their teachers and administrators? What kind of social atmosphere is created and sustained on a daily basis? In short, is the school as a social environment creating stress unnecessarily, or is it organized to prevent or reduce stress in the first place? Being aware of the degree to which a school does or does not create stress for students means entering the arena of the hidden curriculum. Modifying the school environment in order to reduce stress is in reality a way to reduce and prevent school problems (Meyers & Nastasi, 1999).

**Peer Mediation.** One thing schools can do is to implement structured programs of **peer mediation**, in which students learn to resolve conflicts and become mediators for their peers when disagreements occur. During a typical peer mediation session, an adult in the building is with the mediator and the students who are not getting along. Peer mediators also meet periodically as a group to process and discuss their experiences and fine-tune their skills. Schools that adopt peer mediation communicate several important messages that are not part of the typical hidden curriculum:

● The school recognizes that students do not always get along.

● Not getting along does not mean getting into a fight.

● You can get perspective on your problem by talking about it to someone else your own age.

**Critical term**

**Peer mediation.** Structured programs of problem solving in which students are trained to work with their peers to solve problems between students.

Peer mediation is a technique where students themselves are trained to help each other solve social problems at school. (Media Bakery)

**Critical term**

**Developmental guidance.** Classroom program or curriculum that addresses personal and social aspects of learning and that sometimes includes career awareness.

**Critical term**

**Full-service schools.** Schools that include social and health services in the same building or complex, reducing the need for families to go to several locations to receive services.

Peer mediation modifies the traditional school environment in several important ways: it provides the resource of peer mediation itself for all students; it creates a cadre of students, namely, the peer mediators, for whom the idea of mediation is important to their lives in school; and it provides a resource for teachers whose students are experiencing problems. Educators for Social Responsibility (2007) is one of several national professional groups that include information about peer mediation on their website (**www.esrnational.org/es/peermediation.htm**). Peer mediation has become such an important practice that the Association for Conflict Resolution has published a set of recommended standards for peer mediation in the schools (**www.mediate.com/acreducation**).

**Developmental Guidance.** Another way to modify the school environment to reduce stress is through developmental guidance programs. When the word "guidance" is used in the context of schools, you may think of a guidance counselor in high school who helped you with your schedule and with college applications or other postsecondary plans. **Developmental guidance** is a different concept completely.

Developmental guidance refers to classroom-based programs that address many, if not all, of the social dynamics we have discussed in this chapter. These programs are implemented by school counselors, school psychologists, or school social workers, who teach specific lessons within a teachers' classroom on, for example, social skills, problem solving, drug and alcohol abuse, child neglect and abuse, individual differences, prejudice, or, at the appropriate ages, sex education. Other issues mandated at the state level might also be included. Sometimes there is a formal, structured curriculum for these lessons. Developmental guidance works best when classroom teachers participate in these lessons and carry the messages into the day-to-day routines and language of the classroom.

Developmental guidance, then, raises difficult social issues in a safe environment. It communicates the message that it is all right to talk about these issues and that they are not invisible to the school staff. In addition, one of the most important features of developmental guidance programs is that students have the opportunity to build a safe relationship with an adult in the school building other than the teacher. Even when students have very good relationships with their teachers, they may be experiencing specific problems they would prefer discussing with another individual at school.

**Full-Service Schools.** Another development that radically changes the regularities of schooling is locating social and health services in or near schools, combining and collaborating to form what are called **full-service schools**. These schools are generally developed in communities where students and their families do not have the resources to obtain the social or health services they may need. In the full-service model, schools are reconceptualized as centers that house multiple services within the community and for the community. This is why full-service schools are sometimes known as *community schools*.

Traditionally, school buildings have not been used in the early morning and late afternoon or evening hours; this represents an inefficient use of publicly owned buildings that are located in every community. Once we begin to think of schools as buildings that can be used before and after school hours, full-service schools are

# REWARDS AND CHALLENGES

## Making Schools Work for Every Student

**Mildred Boveda**
*Miami, Florida*

I became acquainted with the work of Paulo Freire when I had the opportunity to study abroad in Brazil. The introduction to Freire had a profound effect on my career choice as I explicitly studied and learned about the connection between social change and education. I myself am a prime example of how schooling can potentially serve as a means out of poverty for those who come from traditionally underprivileged and marginalized sectors of society. Unfortunately, as the post-NCLB achievement gap rhetoric indicates, a vast disparity exists between the achievement of middle class white students and their poor, Black and Latino counterparts. Consequently, as an educator I am fully cognizant of the fact that there must be a shift in the methods that teachers use to engage students from historically disenfranchised settings.

Although my current socioeconomic status and level of education is worlds apart from that of most of my students and their parents, I attempt to be aware and sensitive to their needs and voices—especially when deciding what and how I teach in my classroom. With the support of my administration, my school has begun a series of after school meetings where dialogues with parents and students are resulting in positive transformations at our school. I have personally seen the amazing progress that students have made as a result of their parents and teachers collaborating. While we are located in a lower socioeconomic community, I realize that all of our parents and students are a source of rich knowledge and abilities. It is exactly that source that I am attempting to tap into in order to make my students' educational experience an authentic one, thus ensuring their success. ●

a natural development. Services that can be provided might include health, mental health, dental, daycare, recreation, adult education, cultural activities, drug and alcohol prevention, dropout prevention, welfare services, crisis intervention, and economic services and job placement (Dryfoos, 1994; Warger, 2002).

The Coalition for Community Schools describes partnerships that are essential to building successful community schools as follows: "Boiled down to the basics, a community school is both a set of partnerships and a place where services, supports and opportunities lead to improved student learning, stronger families and healthier communities. Using public schools as a hub, inventive, enduring relationships among educators, families, community volunteers, business, health and social service agencies, youth development organizations and others committed to children are changing the educational landscape—permanently—by transforming traditional schools into partnerships for excellence" (Coalition for Community Schools, n.d.).

Early efforts to establish full-service schools often began by locating health clinics in or near schools (Dryfoos, 1994). Getting to a health clinic can be difficult for some families, and full-service schools reduce the need for transportation to health services. From the teacher's perspective, the ready availability of health services can meet the immediate, short-term health needs that may be preventing students from focusing in school. If these needs can be met at an on-campus clinic, children can return to class and concentrate on their studies.

Increasingly schools are staying open in the late afternoon and evenings to serve all members of the community. (Media Bakery)

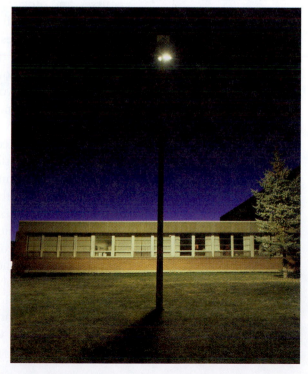

---

**Figure 6-6    Essential Qualities in a Community School**

The Coalition for Community Schools defines five qualities of a community school. They include:

- **Quality education:** High-caliber curriculum and instruction enable all children to meet challenging academic standards. The school uses all of the community's assets as resources for learning and involves students in contributing to the solution of community problems.

- **Youth development:** Young people develop their assets and talents, form positive relationships with peers and adults, and serve as resources to their communities.

- **Family support:** Family resource centers, early childhood development programs, coordinated health, mental health and social services, counseling, and other supports enhance family life by building upon individuals' strengths and skills.

- **Family and community engagement:** Family members and other residents actively participate in designing, supporting, monitoring, and advocating quality programs and activities in the school and community.

- **Community development:** All participants focus on strengthening the local leadership, social networks, economic viability, and physical infrastructure of the surrounding community.

**Source:** Coalition for Community Schools, *Frequently Asked Questions about Community Schools.* Retrieved May 6, 2008, from http://www.communityschools.org.

---

In making the transition from providing health services to creating a true center of family activity in the community, schools often team with other social agencies, such as the YMCA, Boys and Girls Clubs, or the Children's Aid Society, to provide onsite before- and after-school care for students whose parents work beyond school hours. A full-service school can also offer GED courses, computer courses, and other family supports in the late afternoons and evenings to meet the needs of families, often in conjunction with local institutions of higher education. This model requires that school personnel and outside service providers work together to provide the range of services needed to support students and families. A high level of coordination and interagency cooperation is essential for full-service schools to work smoothly and effectively. To achieve this level of cooperation, the school principal and a lead onsite service provider must work together as full partners (Dryfoos, 2007).

The full-service, community school concept, described in Figure 6-6, represents a comprehensive transformation of how we think about the use of schools in relationship to the community. According to the Coalition of Community Schools, "A community school is both a place and a set of partnerships between the school and other community resources. Its integrated focus on academics, health and social services, youth and community development and community engagement leads to improved student learning, stronger families and healthier communities. Schools become centers of the community and are open to everyone – all day, every day, evenings and weekends. Using public schools as hubs, community schools bring together many partners to offer a range of supports and opportunities to children, youth, families and communities." (http://www.communityschools.org). The following Case in Point describes a community school in New York City. It is one of 21 community schools sponsored by the Children's Aid Society.

## A Case In Point
### The Salomé Ureña de Henriquez Campus, New York City

The Salomé Ureña Henriquez Campus includes three public middle schools in New York City, and is a community school in partnership with the Children's Aid Society of New York City. The campus, which is located in a neighborhood populated mainly by immigrants from the Dominican Republic, is named for Salomé Ureña de Henriquez, an educator in the Dominican Republic who was the founder of the first school for girls there in 1881, as well as a feminist poet.

Between 85 and 90 percent of the students on the campus qualify for free lunch, and about 30 percent speak a language other than English as their first language. The student body is 95 percent Latino. The campus sets high standards for all of its students. The schools emphasize different curricula but share many components of the community school partnership.

A new school building opened in 1992; for several years before its opening, school leaders, Children's Aid Society staff, and members of a local community organization for immigrants from the Dominican Republic worked together to plan for the new community school. In 2005 it became a three-school campus.

Students and their families have access to health and mental health onsite services:

- A medical and dental clinic
- A mental health unit with expertise in depression counseling
- A crisis intervention team
- An orthodontic clinic
- Regularly scheduled "town hall" meetings that provide students with a forum for sharing their opinions and concerns about relevant topics such as dating, domestic violence, gangs, and sexuality.

In addition, students and families can be referred to other hospitals and/or agencies if their needs cannot be met on site. Registration for the state health-care program can also be completed on campus.

Working with its community service partner, the campus has established before- and after-school programs that are offered not only during the week, but also on weekends, during school holidays, and in the summer. These include regular tutoring, homework help, and several activities designed to enrich students' lives after school. In addition to sports and an open gym, extended programs also include dance, orchestra, band, and fine arts classes.

Adult education courses are offered onsite including classes in English as a Second Language, computers, and citizenship for new immigrants. Parent Literary Circles are also offered.

Recognizing the importance of the relationship between families and school success, the school has issued a fact sheet noting that "the full service approach of Children's Aid community schools addresses the multiple needs of children by recognizing that learning is influenced by ongoing experiences within families, schools, and communities." One of the most important characteristics of this community school campus is that the teachers and staff treat everyone with respect. This respect appears to pay off in the campus's high attendance rates, which hover around 90 percent.

**Sources:** Community School Fact Sheet, http://www.childrensaidsociety.org.

## The Teacher's Role in Promoting Competence

When their lives are in stress, students may be vulnerable to feeling a lack of competence. Yet competence is one of the key factors in children's ability to cope with difficult life circumstances (Meyers & Nastasi, 1999). Teachers can help create the circumstances that promote their students' competence at both the classroom and the school levels.

At the classroom level, teachers promote competence by creating learning environments that are respectful of students, of their life circumstances, and of the differences among them. Good teachers are sensitive to their students' needs but do not allow those needs to be used as an excuse for not taking learning seriously— by students or by teachers themselves. Teachers are also knowledgeable about the programs a school sponsors to serve its students, and they draw on those programs for the benefit of their students.

At the school level, teachers must consider whether the environment of the school promotes students' competence. In general, how do teachers talk about their students? How do they interact with their students? All teachers are citizens of their schools and are professional colleagues with their peers. If a school environment is not supportive of the students—that is, if the hidden curriculum is sending messages to students that not all students are valued or that handling challenging social issues is not really the school's responsibility—then teachers have the responsibility for advocating with the administration and the local community to change the school environment.

Schools that are considered to be failing can turn around by focusing on changing the way students interact. The video *Peace Helpers, PS24* illustrates how a school in Brooklyn, New York, did just that. See the video at **www.edutopia.org/peacehelpersvideo**.

Teachers need not have the same level of skills as their colleagues who are school counselors, psychologists, or social workers. These support personnel are trained specifically to provide interventions concerning problems related to students' social lives. However, neither can teachers simply ignore the reality of their students' social contexts and teach as if their students are not experiencing problems and stress, if in fact they are. Teachers do have the power to influence their students during school, create supportive environments for them, and meet their individual needs. But they must wield that power responsibly.

Meeting students' individual needs is emphasized in an educational philosophy known as *humanism*. This philosophy applies to all students, not just to those who are experiencing difficulty. Its focus on the affective, or emotional, side of a student's growth has relevance for the idea that schools should be places where students sense that they are valued, feel like they belong, and find school an important place to be.

### Philosophical Note
#### Meeting Individual Needs through a Humanistic Philosophy of Education

Humanism is an educational philosophy that emphasizes the development of students as individuals. Its goal is to help each student develop his or her personal interests and engage in learning because of an intense personal interest in it and because it has meaning. In a school or classroom that is oriented toward humanism, a teacher would be concerned with how students view their own development. Gary Fenstermacher and Jonas Soltis (1986) state that to a humanistically oriented teacher, "filling the student's head with specific knowledge that has been selected, packaged, and conveyed by others only keeps the student from grasping himself as a human being" (p. 26). Teachers who subscribe to a purely humanistic philosophy would provide students with the freedom to choose what they would like to learn, rather than imposing their view of what is important to learn.

The humanistic approach to education has a long history and is rooted in the philosophy of Jean Jacques Rousseau, who lived in the latter part of the eighteenth century. Rousseau believed that education should never get in the way of a child's development. Rather, education should enable that development to take place. This philosophy got a boost in the 1960s with the emergence of a school of humanistic psychology led by advocates such as Abraham Maslow and Carl Rogers. Maslow made a major contribution to a humanistic approach by positing a hierarchy of human needs, starting with fundamental needs such as food, clothing, and shelter and ending with the highest need—self-actualization. The teacher's role is to provide an environment that is responsive to students' emotional, affective, and psychological needs, thus allowing them to grow and move toward higher and higher levels of needs being fulfilled. Maslow's hierarchy is a reminder that teachers interact on a daily basis with people—students who have individual lives, needs, wishes, and goals—and that unless they attend to those needs, learning is likely to be difficult to accomplish.

The freedom to choose what one wishes to study is critical to a pure humanistic philosophy of education. A teacher would encourage students to choose what they would like to learn and then work with them to learn it—all for the purpose of providing learning that is meaningful to the student and authentic with respect to his or her interests. In a standards-based educational environment, allowing for student choice about what is important to learn is not an easy task, and so it is a challenge to adhere to a truly humanistic philosophy of education. Nevertheless, this philosophy can serve as a reminder for all teachers to attend to their students as individuals, to respond to their affective needs, and to create classrooms in which students are motivated as much as possible by their own interests and aspirations.

## A Brief Word about the Extracurriculum

A different aspect of schools as social institutions comes about as a result of the extracurriculum. The extracurriculum is made up of the after-school activities in which students participate voluntarily, and in which academic instruction is not the primary goal (Eccles & Templeton, 2002). We usually think of these extracurricular activities at the middle and high school levels as sports, band, choir, clubs, drama, service projects, newspaper, yearbook, student council, and the like. These are valuable activities that enable students to pursue their interests and special talents. However, some extracurricular activities may be considered more valuable than others in a particular school, and that is when the hidden curriculum operates. Participating in specific extracurricular activities—or not—may send clear messages to students about their worth.

For example, in many high schools the highest status is assigned to athletics. The hidden curriculum operates in how a school addresses the competition to make certain teams, how teachers respond to athletes who are struggling academically, whether cliques among athletes or cheerleaders are encouraged or discouraged, and so on. At the middle school level, where the tone for upper-level athletics is set, is everyone allowed to play on sports teams, or does heavy competition to make certain teams begin in sixth or seventh grade? In other schools, the tradition might be that drama students have high status owing to their greater visibility. In yet others it may be a science or mathematics competition that is valued. Schools make choices when their teachers and staff differentially value various extracurricular activities. Think, for example, how the regularities of a school would change if the highest value were placed on community service instead.

## Your turn... *to reflect*

In pairs, discuss the value the teachers and administrators in your middle and/or high school placed on various extracurricular activities. What specific actions by the teachers and/or administrators communicated the level of value of those activities to you? How did your recognition of their valuing make you feel?

Activities that are sponsored by affiliated agencies, such as Boys and Girls Clubs, the local YMCA/YWCA, community arts programming for youth, and so on, such as constitute a parallel extracurriculum and are sometimes called "positive youth development" activities. Agencies such as these can support choirs, athletic teams, and drama productions, offering an important alternative source of constructive after-school activities. Such activities have a positive effect on youth, and can also lead to higher academic achievement and increased high school graduation rates (Eccles & Templeton, 2002). Teachers need to be aware of students' participation in these activities in the same way they are about students' participation in extracurricular activities directly sponsored by the school.

## Why It Counts in a Diverse World

Students do not simply arrive at school each day with their heads a blank slate, ready to have a teacher pour knowledge into them. Your job might be easier if this were the case, but the passion of teaching does not lie with teaching the academic curriculum in isolation. Instead, it lies at the intersection of the academic curriculum and the students themselves. Teachers and school administrators create the conditions in which students learn, and either those conditions lead to exciting, stimulating, and meaningful learning experiences, or they do not. Students, as we have noted, are keen observers of both the explicit and the hidden curriculum that operate within every school. They know what their experiences are, and they can give anyone who asks about them specific examples—often parodying their teachers and administrators in the process.

Chances are you, as a new teacher, may focus disproportionately on delivering the academic curriculum, on establishing the pace and sequence of the year's lessons, and on analyzing how well your students are doing under your tutelage. This is a normal stage in your professional development as a teacher. However, whether or not you focus your energy on your students' total school experience in your classroom, you are going to create a classroom atmosphere, and the choices you make in creating that atmosphere result in students' learning many implicit lessons about what school is for and their place in it. How children experience your classroom will have a decided impact on how they view the formal curriculum they are supposed to master.

When they enter your classroom, students do not leave their individual life experiences and individual needs at the door. The dilemma of the curriculum that we have raised in this section is how to place the academic curriculum in the context of students' lives, which are diverse indeed. Learning academics and the everyday realities of students' lives, are intertwined and inseparable. The challenge is to create a classroom community that fosters students' feelings of competence so that they can be successful in their academic learning. This is an issue for every school in every community. How does a school staff work together to reduce students' stress and make them feel valued? What kinds of supports exist in school to help teachers with students who are experiencing problems? How much does the school take responsibility for its own hidden curriculum and use this powerful school dynamic to build places where every student feels safe and comfortable in order to concentrate on learning?

Although as a classroom teacher you may or may not have responsibilities in programs that directly address students' personal needs, the existence of such programs at your school means that you have a professional obligation to consider their role in relationship to the full range of students you will be teaching. If you do not teach in such programs directly, your knowledge of them is critical because it will enable you to better meet the needs of your students. Furthermore, these may be areas in which you will take a personal and professional interest and in which you may choose to develop expertise in the future.

# CHAPTER SUMMARY

## The Power of the Hidden Curriculum

The hidden curriculum encompasses all the things students learn as a result of being in school that are not part of the explicit academic curriculum. Understanding the impact of the hidden curriculum sensitizes teachers to the fact that different schools create different kinds of atmospheres. Some argue that the hidden curriculum contains "lessons" that are beneficial, such as learning to be on time and to work within a group setting. Others argue that the hidden curriculum's "lessons" are harmful and can purposely disadvantage certain groups of students, namely, those who are already disadvantaged when they come to school. In this view, the hidden curriculum fails to support students who for a variety of reasons may struggle with learning and in so doing recreates the current social order.

If teachers are to have any control over the hidden curriculum, it has to be made public and become a focus of professional interaction and action. Teachers need to be aware of the consequences to their students of being in school and to engage in dialogue about the kind of place their classroom is—as well as the school as a whole.

## The Current Societal Context

Several developments in society have resulted in changes that can place stress on students and make learning difficult. Changes in family structure mean that more students live with single parents or with grandparent caretakers. Students from all socioeconomic groups, races, and ethnicities can, unfortunately, experience child neglect and abuse. Although drug and alcohol abuse, teen pregnancy, and school violence have decreased somewhat in the very recent past, these dynamics are still at work in the population under 18. Therefore, all teachers are likely to teach students, at some point in their careers, who are experiencing some or all of these stressors.

Teachers need to be aware of the life circumstances of each of their students and to be sensitive to individual needs that might result from a family's social dynamics. At the same time, teachers must also guard against making stereotypical judgments about students based on their family circumstances. Teachers must also recognize that despite the challenging social situations in which they may live, some children are resilient to the stressors they experience at home.

The messages teachers send to students about their family circumstances are a powerful part of the hidden curriculum. Whatever the life circumstances or family structures of their students, when teachers strive to develop healthy working relationships with all of their students and their families, they ensure that students have the best possible opportunity to have a productive, challenging, and successful experience in school.

## Addressing Social Dynamics by Changing the Regularities of Schooling

Schools can either exacerbate the stressors on their students or diminish them. Schools can do a number of things to create less stressful learning environments, including peer mediation, programs to reduce and prevent violence, programs to educate students about the dangers of drug and alcohol use, or age-appropriate developmental counseling for all students. Teachers are not expected to do this kind of work alone, and can be supported by educational specialists such as school counselors, psychologists, or social workers, who may run specialized groups for students who are experiencing similar personal difficulties. Schools can also extend their reach and become full-service schools for the entire community.

When schools take deliberate steps to create safe places for their students, they are sending messages about how they value their students' needs. Supporting students' needs related to their life circumstances does not mean ignoring the academic curriculum. When schools make sure that they are supportive places in which to learn, students can gain feelings of competence that can serve them throughout their lives.

## LIST OF CRITICAL TERMS

Hidden curriculum (*169*)

Regularities of schooling (*171*)

Critical theory (*175*)

Resilience (*185*)

Child abuse (*185*)

Child neglect (*185*)

Peer mediation (*193*)

Developmental guidance (*194*)

Full-service schools (*194*)

## EXPLORING YOUR COMMITMENT

1. *on your own...* Read Chapter 2 of Harper Lee's 1960 novel, *To Kill a Mockingbird*. Prepare a brief written reflection on the hidden curriculum that is operating in this chapter with regard to reading.

2. *in the field...* Walk through the hallways of an elementary, middle, or high school. As you walk, observe as carefully as you can. What clues do you observe that give you a sense of what the culture of this school is like? What makes you interpret the clues this way?

3. *in the field...* Observe an informal situation at a school, such as the lunchroom, the playground in an elementary school, or the hallways in a middle or high school. Consider the way the teachers and staff interact with the students in these informal circumstances. What hidden messages are students being sent during these less formal times of the day? How are these messages creating—or not creating—supportive learning environments for students?

4. *in the field...* Interview a school counselor, psychologist, or social worker about the kinds of programs their schools have to support students who are experiencing stress in their lives. Find out who initiated the programs, whether there is a formal curriculum for them, and who takes the lead responsibility for them. What is the role of the classroom teacher, if any, in these programs?

5. *on your own...* Obtain the mission statement and goals for a particular school. What does this statement tell you about the purposes of the school? How do you see those purposes manifested at the school, for example, when

you enter the school, the office, or the classrooms? Compare mission statements from several schools in which you and your peers are completing your field experiences.

6. *on the web...* For one of the major social issues raised in this chapter (e.g., violence, alcohol and drug abuse, child neglect and abuse, teen pregnancy), find at least three websites that provide useful information about this topic for families and teachers. Identify three specific ideas from each website that are useful to you as a prospective teacher. How did you judge whether or not the information was valuable? Whether the website presented a balanced view of the issue?

7. *on the web...* Log onto the website of the Coalition for Community Schools at **http://www.communityschools.org**. Study the different approaches to community school building that are described. Go to the website for a specific community school linked to these different approaches. Does one approach have more merit than another? Why or why not?

8. *on your own...* Prepare a brief written reflection on the degree to which you are aware that your own elementary, middle, or high school did or did not provide support for students who were struggling with personal issues— including support for issues you yourself may have been dealing with during your school years. What did the school do well, and what could it have done better to provide support?

9. *in the field...* Investigate the sex education program that exists in a local school or district. What is the philosophical orientation of this program? Who teaches this material? Has this program been the source of any controversy in the district? If so, why?

10. *in the research...* Read Amatea, E. S., H. Daniels, N. Bringman, and F. M. Vandiver, (2004). "Strengthening counselor–teacher–family connections: The family–school collaborative consultation project". *Professional School Counseling, 8* (1), 47–56. This article describes a school-based intervention to implement new strategies for creating much stronger relationships among counselors, teachers, and families. How easy or difficult would it be to implement these strategies in your future classroom?

## GUIDELINES FOR BEGINNING TEACHERS

1. Understand how your actions and decisions can result in implicit, or hidden, outcomes for your students. Every decision you make represents some kind of purpose—whether or not you have thought it through explicitly. As you organize your classroom, think carefully about the messages your decisions and plans might convey to your students. Are they the messages you want to convey? If not, how can you change your approach?

2. Be aware of the kind of social institution the school in which you work represents to your students. Know what messages the school sends in relation to students' social needs.

3. Plan an early meeting with the school social worker, psychologist, or counselor. Ask him or her to describe the services provided and any advice for a new teacher.

4. Ask your principal to clarify the chain of command should you suspect a case of child neglect or abuse.

5. How you teach, the stance you take toward your students, and the degree to which you are responsive to your students and their full experience of schooling are all implicated in the success—or failure—of your work as a teacher. Take this responsibility seriously.

## THE INTASC CONNECTION

The INTASC standards that address school as a social institution include Standards 2, 5, and 10.

Standard 2 states: *The teacher understands how children learn and develop, and can provide learning opportunities that support their intellectual, social, and personal development.* Indicators include the following:

- The teacher is aware of expected developmental progressions and ranges of individual variation within each domain (physical, social, emotional, moral, and cognitive), can identify levels of readiness in learning, and understands how development in any one domain may affect performance in others.

- The teacher appreciates individual variation within each area of development, shows respect for the diverse talents of all learners, and is committed to helping them develop self-confidence and competence.

Standard 5 states: *The teacher uses an understanding of individual and group motivation and behavior to create a learning environment that encourages positive social interaction, active engagement in learning, and self-motivation.* Indicators include the following:

- The teacher understands how social groups function and influence people, and how people influence groups.

- The teacher takes responsibility for establishing a positive climate in the classroom and participates in maintaining such a climate in the school as a whole.

- The teacher helps the group to develop shared values and expectations for student interactions, academic discussions, and individual and group responsibility that create a positive classroom climate of openness, mutual respect, and support.

Standard 10 states: *The teacher fosters relationships with school colleagues, parents, and agencies in the larger community to support students' learning and well-being.* Indicators include the following:

- The teacher understands how factors in the students' environment outside of school (e.g., family circumstances, community environments, health and economic conditions) may influence students' life and learning.

- The teacher values and appreciates the importance of all aspects of a child's experience.

- The teacher is concerned about all aspects of a child's well-being (cognitive, emotional, social, and physical) and is alert to signs of difficulty.

- The teacher participates in collegial activities designed to make the entire school a productive learning environment.

- The teacher talks with and listens to the student, is sensitive and responsive to clues of distress, investigates situations, and seeks outside help as needed and appropriate to remedy problems.

If you are in a state that follows a different set of teacher standards, find the state standards that most closely relate to the INTASC standards discussed here.

## READING ON...

Evans, R. (2004). *Family matters: How schools can cope with the crisis in childrearing.* San Francisco: Jossey-Bass. Evans explores contemporary trends in parenting, arguing that parents are not taking enough responsibility for childrearing in our society.

Freire, P. (2000). *Pedagogy of the oppressed.* New York: Continuum. A classic volume on the empowering potential of education.

Koplow, L. (2002). *Creating schools that heal: Real-life solutions.* New York: Teachers College Press. Koplow explores the role of every educator in a school in developing close relationships with students and preventing stress and violence in children.

Phillips, R. J. Linney, & C. Pack. (2008). *Safe school ambassadors: Harnessing student power to stop bullying and violence.* San Francisco: Jossey-Bass. A focus on how students themselves can be instrumental in building a safe school community.

Raider-Roth, M. (2005). *Trusting what you know: The high stakes of classroom relationships.* San Francisco: Jossey-Bass. Raider-Roth presents her research on how students view the importance of having trusting relationships with their teachers.

Wessler, S. L. (2003). *The respectful school: How educators and students can conquer hate and harassment.* Alexandria, VA: Association for Supervision and Curriculum Development. Wessler describes how to create a school culture based on positive relationships among students, teachers, and families.

# CROSSING YOUR OWN FAMILIAR BORDERS TO EMBRACE DIVERSITY

Given the changing demographic patterns in the United States, teachers are now, in unprecedented numbers and locations, teaching students whose life experiences often do not mirror their own. At the same time, a persistent achievement gap continues to separate many racial and ethnic minority students, low-income students, and students with disabilities from their peers. How teachers make the connection between their own experiences and those of their students is central to students' success in the classroom. Do teachers wish to engage with their students, their students' families, and the communities in which their students live—even when they are not familiar? Are teachers prepared to take the risks involved in acknowledging a lack of knowledge—about a student's race, ethnicity, family cultural practices, or community? The relationship between teachers' and students' experiences also has implications for how teachers work with students with disabilities—whose race, ethnicity, or socioeconomic class may or may not differ from those of the teachers.

To meet the obligation of closing this gap in achievement, teachers must commit themselves to making sure every student they teach benefits from school. To do so, teachers must first focus on their own self-knowledge and self-awareness. Teachers can respond to their own lack of knowledge and familiarity regarding issues of race, class, culture, or disability in several ways. They are proactive in educating themselves about their students, and they use their newly acquired knowledge to create classrooms where they connect with their students.

Chapter 7 addresses working successfully with students whose race, class, culture, or language differs from that of the teacher and the repercussions that take place when the teacher fails to do so. Chapter 8 discusses working with students with disabilities and the relationship of that responsibility to issues of race, ethnicity, language, and social class. The challenge for teachers is to ensure that each of their students has the opportunity—and the support—to learn.

## Guiding Questions

- What do the changing demographics in the United States mean for teachers?

- What does it mean to understand diversity as an asset, not a deficit?

- How does knowing about your students' lives help you teach?

- How do schools make some students feel valued and others devalued?

- What do schools communicate through academic tracking?

- How can teachers use students' language diversity to foster learning the curriculum?

- What is culturally responsive teaching?

- Why are the limitations of a "celebrating diversity" approach to education?

- What is the role of privilege in teaching in diverse classrooms and schools?

- Why is "not seeing color" a problematic response to diversity?

- What special considerations apply to teachers in monocultural schools?

# Teaching Students Whose Race, Class, Culture, or Language Differs from Your Own

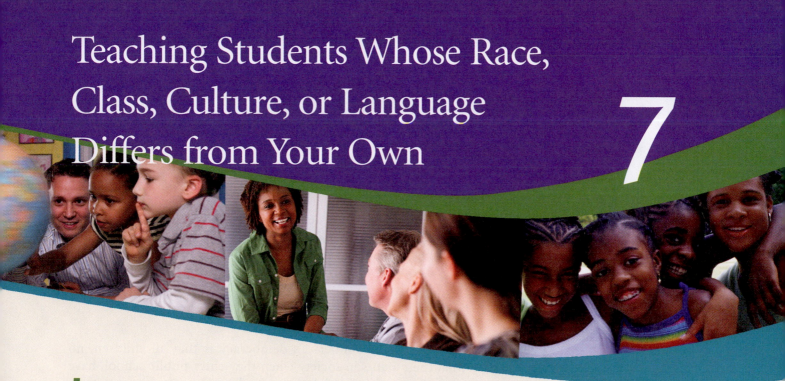

Jake Harris began teaching in a small town in central Illinois a month ago. The demographic makeup of his fourth grade classroom is two-thirds white and one-third Mexican American. The Mexican American population moved here in the last decade to work in one of the local factories. Some of his students who are Mexican American have lived in the area for their entire schooling, but in the next month Jake is going to receive three students who are newly arrived from Mexico. Jake was raised in a community that was primarily white and rural: he student taught in a nearby community and has had little experience with people from other countries or cultures. He wants to teach all of his students well, but right now he is not feeling comfortable with planning for his new students. There is a special teacher to work with the new students on English language skills. Jake is fortunate to have a mentor teacher, Sally Ford, who recently retired from the district and was considered to be a highly skilled, successful teacher. He has talked with her on many occasions since he began his job.

"I just don't know how I'm going to work with them," Jake said, once he had described his concerns to Sally. "They're not going to know anything, and how will I keep them involved?"

Sally heard the concern in Jake's voice, but she was worried about how he was thinking about the situation. "Jake, let's step back a bit here," Sally said. "First, tell me what you mean when you say that your students won't know anything."

"Well, they won't know how to do the work, they won't know anything about this town or how things work, their parents won't speak English," he replied.

"Is there anything your new students do know?"

"What do you mean?" Jake asked, confused.

"Well, for starters, your new students have lived their whole lives in a country that they know a whole lot about—and that you don't know a lot about. If they've been in school in Mexico, they probably know a lot about a lot of subjects, and the challenge is communicating about it. Also, remember that your students know another language —one that you don't know," said Sally.

"I never thought of it that way," Jake said. "It's sort of like I'm only seeing what they don't have, instead of what they do have."

> *Rather than think of . . . diverse students as problems, we can view them instead as resources who can help all of us learn what it feels like to move between cultures and language varieties, and thus perhaps better learn how to become citizens of the global community.*
>
> Lisa Delpit, 1995, p. 69

Sally continued: "That's what I'm trying to help you see. And as you think this through, remember that every time you talk about the students in a group, using words like "them" and "they," it sounds like you are really thinking about it as an "us" and "them" situation. When you do that, you're putting a real distance between yourself and the new students—but also between yourself and the Mexican American students who are already in your classroom. I'm pretty sure that's not the kind of classroom you want to have or the kind of teacher you want to be. So let's start thinking about how you can connect to your students, and all the things the new students do know and bring to your classroom. You also have students in your class who have been here a while and speak both languages—what a great resource!"

## Critical Term

**Achievement gap.** The gap between African American or Latino students and white middle-class students in terms of school achievement, usually reported based on the results of standardized tests.

A fundamental promise of America's democracy is that all children, no matter what their status in society when they enter public school, have the opportunity to receive a good education and, as a result, improve their capacity to be successful adults. But throughout the history of public schooling in the United States, specific groups of children have not received the full benefits of public education and, as a result, have had difficulty being successful in school (Cremin, 1988). Students who most often experience school in this negative, harmful way are children who are members of racial and ethnic minority groups and/or children from the lower socioeconomic levels of our society. Today the term **achievement gap** is commonly used to describe the difference in achievement in school. This term usually refers to the disparity in learning between African American or Latino students and white middle-class students.

Many dynamics in society contribute to the systematic disadvantaging of specific groups of students. Some practices that contribute to the low achievement of students from racial and ethnic minorities or from low-income families unfold in individual classrooms between particular teachers and students—and are under the direct control of teachers. Other practices are part of the larger organizational structure and policies that govern schooling. Still others reflect problems in the larger society. The actions of an individual teacher certainly cannot solve, for example, widespread social problems such as generational poverty or segregated housing patterns. But individual teachers and individual schools *can* and *do* make a difference in the lives of their students every day. Teachers and schools can have a profound positive effect on the achievement of racial and ethnic minority and low-income students. Schools do exist that are beating the odds.

Despite these individual successes, the achievement gap persists (Hendrie, 2004). In too many schools and classrooms, racial and ethnic minority students continue to fail in unacceptable numbers. For example, students who are Black, Latino or American Indian have only about a fifty-fifty chance of completing high school and graduating with a diploma (Urban Institute, 2004). The purpose of this chapter is to explore this persistent, troublesome pattern in the nation's schools and to discuss what teachers can do in their own classrooms and schools to promote the school success of students who represent the full range of racial ethnic, cultural, and language diversity.

# What Changing Demographics in the United States Mean for Teachers

As it was at its founding, the United States continues to be a nation of immigrants. Unlike immigrants in earlier years, however, who mostly flooded urban areas, the new immigrant groups that are populating our nation's schools are dispersing across the country not only in cities, but also in suburbs, small towns, and isolated rural communities. Although the greatest multiplicity of racial and ethnic groups often exists in our cities, immigration patterns are widely distributed in the nation so that today teachers in communities all over the country are working with students from the far reaches of the globe. Increasingly, teachers have students in their classrooms and schools whose cultural, language, or economic experiences differ significantly from their own. Figure 7-1 illustrates the percentage of people 5 years or older in the United States who speak a language other than English at home (Shin & Bruno, 2003) The most commonly spoken home languages other than English are Spanish and Chinese (National Heritage Language Resource Center, 2008).

| Figure 7-1 | Distribution of Persons Who Speak a Language Other Than English at Home, by State |
| --- | --- |

**In states across the country, today's teachers are likely to work with a wide range of students whose race, ethinicity, or language differs from theirs.**

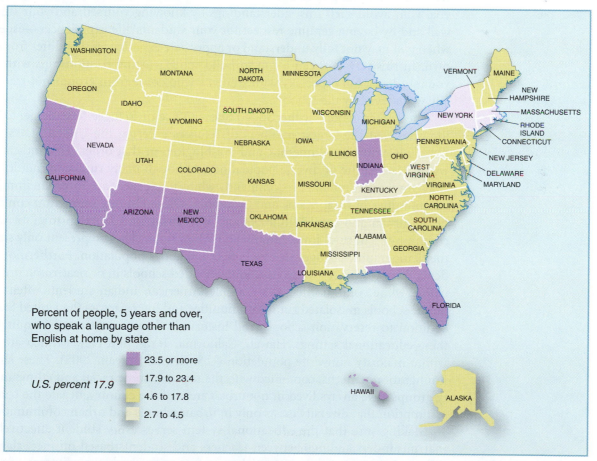

Percent of people, 5 years and over, who speak a language other than English at home by state

*U.S. percent 17.9*

- 23.5 or more
- 17.9 to 23.4
- 4.6 to 17.8
- 2.7 to 4.5

**Source:** Shin, H. B., and R. Bruno. (2003, October). *Language use and English speaking ability: 2000.* Census 2000 Brief, Report C2KBR-29. Washington, DC: United States Census Bureau. Retrieved July 21, 2008 from http://www.census.gov/prod/2003pubs/c2kbr-29.pdf.

Today's teachers must create a positive classroom environment for a diverse student population. (Bob Daemmrich/The Image Works)

Whether it is one student, or a large group of students, or the whole class that differs from the teacher—as well as from other students—teachers must bridge the gap. They must identify and overcome any personal biases they may have about a particular group of students. On another level, they must make sure their classroom provides a supportive environment for all of their students, one in which everyone is respected, feels comfortable and confident, and can learn. In other words, teachers must create strong classroom communities among students from many different backgrounds.

Why are these issues so critical to you as a prospective teacher? It is because any time teachers are not familiar with their students' backgrounds and life experiences, the potential for problems exists. Discontinuities or incompatibilities based on racial, ethnic, or socioeconomic differences between teachers and their students can result in inequities in the way teachers interact with and instruct their students, and thus negatively affect achievement (Nieto, 2004). In addition, according to Jacqueline Jordan Irvine, "cultural misunderstandings between teachers and students result in conflict, distrust, hostility, and possible school failure" (1990, p. 26). As you learn to teach, your goal is to avoid such misunderstandings by knowing yourself and your students well and by having genuine respect for your students' life experiences—especially when you may not fully understand or appreciate experiences that differ from your own. In this way, you can begin to build solid, trusting relationships with all of your students, but especially with students who come from groups not traditionally well served by the schools.

The annual report of the United States Office of Refugee Resettlement (2005) indicates that the largest numbers of refugees entering the United States are in Florida, California, Minnesota, and Washington, in that order. This indicates the widespread nature of diverse populations. Although many rural communities and small towns may remain predominantly white, today there are Somalian immigrant communities in rural Maine and Columbus, Ohio; Hmong immigrant communities in urban and rural Minnesota and Wisconsin; and Mexican migrant worker communities in rural Iowa, Illinois, and Washington. These represent only some of the demographic changes that can affect a school's population. Furthermore, students from yet other groups have long attended schools in or near rural, predominantly white communities. For example, American Indian students often attend public schools in isolated rural communities and towns across the United States in addition to reservation schools, and historically have been treated inequitably in these educational settings. Hawaii, California, Texas, and New Mexico are states with a majority nonwhite population (U.S. Census Bureau, 2005). These shifts in immigration patterns, combined with the fact that some racial and ethnic minority groups have always lived in nonurban areas of the country, negate the common assumption that diversity exists only in urban schools and urban communities.

Making sure that the educational system serves every student effectively and that misunderstandings between teachers and students based on race, class, and culture do not occur is an essential part of every teacher's commitment—in every single community whether rural, urban, suburban, or small town. Especially if a student is one of an isolated few from an unfamiliar racial, ethnic, or language group in a remote community or a suburban school, a teacher can model how to create a harmonious, tolerant, and bias-free community within the classroom and the school. Shifts in immigration and housing patterns, combined with traditional minority populations who live and attend school outside of urban areas, illustrate how critical it is that each person seeking to become a teacher be prepared to work effectively with the full diversity of students.

Prospective teachers also need to recognize that social class differences can likewise lead to misunderstandings between teachers and students. Middle-class teachers might misunderstand the cultural traditions and practices, for example, of low-income, white rural Appalachian students from communities in places such as southern Ohio and Kentucky and, in so doing, can disadvantage them as learners.

Teachers who respect their students' cultural strengths, life experiences, and community resources, and are able to draw on this knowledge to strengthen connections to their students and families and to anchor the curriculum are better positioned to meet their students' needs. When teachers legitimize their students' life experiences and see them as essential to the success of the educational process, they increase their students' opportunities for educational achievement and future success. One of the first steps in this process is valuing students' diversity as an asset in classrooms and schools.

## Understanding Diversity as an Asset, Not a Deficit

A longstanding, erroneous assumption has been made in this country that in order to learn, racial and ethnic minority and low-income students must overcome deficits associated with their culture, community, or social class (Delpit, 1995; Nieto, 2004). This **deficit model** of diversity places the focus on what students and their families *do not* have and *cannot* do. When this perspective prevails, teachers—and others who work in schools—may fail to see the assets children and families do possess that form the basis for their future learning. This can occur because teachers and other school-based professionals are unfamiliar with or do not understand the cultural knowledge—or assets—within their students and families and within the community, or simply do not value these assets. Teachers and other school professionals who "buy into" this deficit model may believe that students bring nothing of substantial value to their formal schooling. Accordingly, the erroneous belief may be that students need to be taught everything, and have no resouces within their families or communities that can support or be connected to their schooling, as Jake Harris was doing in the opening of this chapter.

What teachers who adopt the deficit model are really saying is that because their students' knowledge and background are not the same as their own, they view this knowledge and background as having little value. These teachers may also fail to understand the importance families and the community place on getting an education. Teachers may assume that because the knowledge students bring does not match the knowledge they must have to be successful in the school curriculum, it is unimportant in school. But to be successful, teachers need to use the knowledge and background students have from their cultures and communities as a basis for new learning—rather than hold onto the idea that students have little useful to build upon in school.

Unfortunately, many teachers fail to value the assets within racial, ethnic, or low socioeconomic communities whose practices they are either unfamiliar with or do not understand. For example, a teacher who is unfamiliar with the African American community but teaches African American students may not understand the central,

**Critical Term**

**Deficit model.** Assuming, inaccurately, that students from low-income families or racial and ethnic minority families lack substantial, useful knowledge or resources upon which to build and support a student's education.

stabilizing role of the church in most African American communities. Like Jake at the start of this chapter, a teacher who has a new immigrant from Nicaragua may believe this student "doesn't know anything," when in reality the student knows a great deal about life in Nicaragua and may have attended several grades of school in Nicaragua—even if he or she cannot communicate that knowledge readily because of a temporary language barrier. In comparison, the teacher may not know much about Nicaragua and will have a lot to learn from this student and his or her family. Or a teacher might assume that because students live in an economically depressed neighborhood in the community their families are completely unable to help them in school, and have nothing to offer. These beliefs all represent the deficit model— seeing only what is *not* there, ignoring what *is* there and making assumptions about a community in the absence of real knowledge about it.

In contrast, if teachers make a commitment to identifying and valuing the assets children and their families do possess—however unfamiliar they may at first be— they can draw on these assets to create educational programs that result in student success. To do so, teachers need to place themselves in the position of being learners about their students' cultures, communities, and life experiences. What do their students know, and how can that knowledge be used? What do their students' families know by virtue of their life experiences and their occupations that can help students? It is up to teachers to make these connections. Good teachers are skilled in using students' existing knowledge as a bridge to helping then gain new knowledge.

## A Case In Point
### Deficit or Asset?

Erika Thompson is a 45-year-old African American woman who recently took her first teaching position as an elementary teacher in a large urban school district. She worked for 10 years as a paraprofessional in this same district, attending a local university part-time to complete her undergraduate degree and teaching certification. Erika grew up in a poor neighborhood in her city. However, as she writes in this essay, what others may have perceived as deficits were, for her, assets. Her essay reveals how those who are outsiders to low-income neighborhoods can misjudge the quality of life that goes on in families within those same neighborhoods.

I have experienced the advantages and disadvantages of privilege in my life growing up as a poor black female. I grew up the fourth oldest in a large family with nine siblings. I went to St. Cecelia's Catholic School. My family attended the open housing marches with a local civil rights leader nightly. Politics and social issues were always discussed in my home. I learned at an early age that neighborhoods and schools were segregated based upon race and class.

I learned that segregation was wrong. By the fifth grade I understood the concept of separate but equal—understanding that "equal" was not a true part of the concept. Yet, as a young child, I was amazed to see people from all races working together to help black people get better housing conditions and equity in their schools.

I was disadvantaged during these times because we were extremely poor and could not collect welfare because my father was in the home. I lived in condemned houses, and many of us suffered from malnutrition. Studies show, however, that if children have some type of organization to give them a collective cause they fare better in school. I feel privileged to have experienced the open housing marches, because I learned about the world and my community at a young age. I feel privileged that I could watch and help my father attempt to change the situation in our schools. He was one of the co-founders of a local effort to create independent community schools at that time.

It was a privilege to have gone to a special camp every summer. It was my first experience with people of different races without my parents. There were rich and poor children of different races. I saw rich white children with lots of things. I understood that I could not have these things. I was raised to know that if mama didn't buy it, I should forget about it. She would say, "Get your education and you can buy anything you like." I did. Instead, I learned to concentrate on the activities and to enjoy all of the campers' company.

My high school was a community boarding school in a small rural community. This was another mixed community. I had to do lots of community service work because my parents could not afford the tuition. Yet, I consider this experience to be a privilege. I continued to learn to work with people of different backgrounds.

Two years ago I observed a case of race and class privilege in the classroom where I worked as a paraprofessional. I watched the white teacher I worked with rush poor drug-addicted, black parents out of the classroom when they showed up announced or unannounced. I watched this teacher allow white parents in unannounced to talk to her. One white parent was a newspaper editor. She was allowed to work with the children. Her son was a well-loved, privileged, high achiever. I watched this happen over and over. I noticed how happy this child was when his mother was in the room. I began to wonder what other black students might be feeling as they watched this happening over and over again. It disturbed me. I finally talked to the teacher.

I realize that it has been functional for mainstream society to maintain segregated housing patterns, with people in dilapidated buildings and confined areas, for people to be redlined by insurance companies, for keeping great schools to themselves, and for being afraid simply because someone looks different. Many students in our community are affected by poverty and the biases of the teachers and the institution. I believe that poverty and discrimination can have a negative effect on children as they attempt to learn in school. But it is up to teachers to understand that teaching students who live in poverty does not give teachers license to ignore students and their families, or to take less interest in them, or to overlook the family structures that support students even if they are poor. As an urban educator, I would continue to have the highest expectations for my students. It is important for me, as a black educator, to show students how to get back up and work around the poverty and the biases they encounter.

In her classic 1983 book *Ways with Words*, a highly respected educational researcher, Shirley Brice Heath, studied the oral language and literacy patterns of children and families in two very small, rural communities in the Piedmont mountain region of the Carolinas, which she named Trackton and Roadville. In her renowned study, she provided a detailed picture of how teachers in nearby towns who would teach children from these very small communities could gain knowledge of their students' local, rural language and community to improve their own success as teachers. In the epilogue of her book, Heath asks: "Will the road ahead be altered for the students from Trackton and Roadville who have, through the efforts of some of their teachers, learned *to add to their ways of using language* learned at home?" (p. 362, italics added). By interpreting rural students' home language patterns as an asset to be built upon, rather than as a deficit to be overcome, the teachers in Heath's work demonstrate their own commitment to an asset view of diversity of language and community.

# How Knowing about Your Students' Lives Helps You Teach

Teachers who are actively committed to making meaningful connections between the aims of school and their students' lives are using what is called **contextualized teaching and learning** (Tharp, Estrada, Dalton, & Yamauchi, 2000). By using the knowledge they gain about their students, their students' families, and their students' communities, teachers can increase their students' motivation to learn the curriculum. Reviewing what is known about contextualizing teaching, Tharp and his colleagues (2000) noted that "students are willing to struggle with unfamiliar language and abstract notions in science, math, and other content areas when they are motivated by *interesting activities they and their families value*" (p. 26, emphasis added). Describing one study of first and fourth grade students, Tharp and his colleagues (2000) state that "tapping into students' relevant individual and familial experiences always elicited more lively, attentive participation. Indeed, this strategy often brought a tangential or vague discussion back into focus" (p. 26).

You might ask yourself, "But isn't it a good idea to contextualize teaching and learning for all students?" The answer is yes. However, in schools where teachers and students are from similar backgrounds, teachers may not think about the context because it is equally familiar to them and their students. When the context of the students does not match that of either the teacher or the school, a conscious effort needs to be made to make the connections, and it is teachers who have to do this work, illustrated in Shirley Brice Heath's study mentioned above. This is true for teachers of all ethnic, racial, or socioeconomic groups.

Two things need to be in place for teachers to be successful in contextualizing teaching and learning. First, teachers must genuinely believe that students who differ from themselves can learn and teachers must set high expectations for what they expect their students to achieve. Second, teachers must be proactive in making sure they gain knowledge about their students' lives, family experiences, and interests as well as their communities. Learning about their students shows a deep and abiding respect for the students' racial or ethnic identity or social class. It also creates a base of information from which teachers can plan and implement lessons and units starting from the perspective and interests of their students and the issues they see as important (Barton, 2003).

## Your turn... *to reflect*

How much knowledge do you have about racial, ethnic or socioeconomic groups that differ from yours? What kinds of experiences do you think you will need to engage in to learn more about your students' cultures, families, and communities when they differ from yours?

If teachers are serious about contextualizing their teaching effectively at the classroom level—that is, connecting with their students across a racial, ethnic, or socioeconomic divide—they must first make it a priority to gain an understanding of and appreciation for their students' cultures and communities. One of the first things a teacher can do to gain this important contextual knowledge is to *ask the students*. Sometimes teachers, not wanting to appear ignorant, will neglect to ask their students or family members questions about culture and the community. But in many cases the teacher *is* in fact ignorant about the specific culture and community in question and needs to develop allies in the school and in the community to build an understanding of it. These allies may be teachers or other staff members in the school who themselves are members of the cultural groups about which another teacher needs to learn, parents and family members of the students, or other community members. While it may at first be uncomfortable to ask for assistance, it is crucial to the success of your students' learning that you do so. In asking for assistance, you begin to establish personal relationships with your students, their families, and other individuals in the school and community as well.

When teachers' backgrounds differ from those of their students, it is teachers who become learners about the cultures and communities of their students and families.
(Thinkstock/Media Bakery)

Developing into a teacher able to help assure the educational achievement of low-income and racial and ethnic minority students is likely to be a greater challenge for those teacher education candidates who may have never interacted with individuals different from themselves. For example, prospective teachers who attended monocultural schools—that is, schools populated by students only from their own cultural and socioeconomic group—may not have had opportunities to interact with students from other backgrounds.

Such cultural learning is necessary for all teachers whose background differs from those of their students. Korean American teachers who teach Mexican American students in Los Angeles, Puerto Rican teachers who teach Chinese students in New York City, African American teachers who teach Laotian students in Milwaukee, middle-class white students who teach in rural Appalachia, to name a few, all must engage in self-reflection regarding how they view this diverse range of

---

### Figure 7-2    Contextualizing Teaching

**The Center for Educational Research on Equity, Diversity and Education identified eight ways teachers can contextualize their teaching, or connect lessons to their students' lives. You will see that funds of knowledge are an important part of making these connections.**

- Begin activities with what students already know from home, community, and school.
- Design instructional activities that are meaningful to students in terms of local community norms and knowledge.
- Acquire knowledge of local norms and knowledge by talking to students, parents or family members, and community members, and by reading pertinent documents.
- Assist students to connect and apply their learning to home and community.
- Plan jointly with students to design community-based learning activities.
- Provide opportunities for parents or families to participate in classroom instructional activities.
- Vary activities to include students' preferences, from collective and cooperative to individual and competitive.
- Vary styles of conversation and participation to include students' cultural preferences, such as co-narration, call-and-response, and choral, among others.

**Source:** Adapted from: The Center for Educational Research on Equity, Diversity and Education. (2002). *The five standards for effective pedagogy.* Retrieved May 10, 2008, from http://crede.berkeley.edu/standards/standards.html.

students. But demographic analyses of the teaching force indicate that for the foreseeable future, the teaching force will continue to be made up primarily of white, middle-class women (National Center for Educational Statistics, 2007), many of whom will teach ethnic or racial minority students or low-income students. Therefore, the majority of the nation's teachers will face the challenge of crossing cultural boundaries and will need to address their own lack of familiarity with their students' cultures and communities if they are to be successful contextualizing their teaching. They cannot be "out of cultural sync" with their students (Irvine, 1990, p. 61) and be successful. It is not just a matter of learning about their students; rather, it is an issue of whether or not teachers value what they are learning and can use this new knowledge effectively to help their students learn.

## Using Funds of Knowledge as a Resource for Student Learning

**Critical Term**

**Funds of knowledge.**
Knowledge students and families possess from their own cultural and community experiences that enables them to operate successfully in their own cultures and communities but that often is a mismatch with knowledge required to be successful in school and is often, therefore, devalued.

Luis Moll and his colleagues (Moll & Gonzales, 2004) applied the concept of **funds of knowledge** specifically to describe the knowledge that students and their families possess from their own cultural and community experiences. Knowledge from their own households and communities enables students and families to operate successfully in them, but this same knowledge may not be valued or understood by those outside of the community. Often there is a mismatch between the knowledge required at school and the funds of knowledge students from racial and ethnic minority , or low socioeconomic communities possess. As a result, these funds of knowledge are often treated as unimportant in school, rather than as an asset.

Roseberry, McIntrye, and Gonzalez (2001) describe how the concept of funds of knowledge plays out in schools. They note that children who are not from white, middle-class homes experience a prominent discontinuity between

> the worlds they know at home [i.e., their funds of knowledge] and the world of school. To varying degrees, these children may find that they do not know how to show the teacher what they know in ways she can recognize. They may be asked to engage in activities they do not fully understand. And they may find that the teacher talks in ways that are unfamiliar and confusing. Children from middle-class homes, where the funds of knowledge correspond nicely to those of school, experience much less discontinuity. For example, they know what the teacher is talking about most of the time, and if they don't, they know how to ask for help in ways the teacher recognizes. (pp. 3–4)

## Your turn... *to review*

1. What is the difference between an asset approach to diversity and a deficit approach to diversity?
2. Given the current demographics of the teaching force, why is an asset approach important in schools?
3. What are *funds of knowledge*?
4. How might a teacher use the concept of *funds of knowledge* in planning a lesson or unit of study?

As we noted earlier, whether they do so intentionally or not, teachers who ignore these funds of knowledge communicate to students that the knowledge they and their families possess, which is so vital to their lives within their own homes and communities, is neither valued nor useful in school. This gap between the student's knowledge and what school requires creates discontinuities that contribute to the persistent achievement gap we discussed earlier in the chapter.

The idea of funds of knowledge is that teachers can build on them as a starting point for connecting what students are already familiar with to new knowledge from the curriculum (Tharp et al., 2000). For example, let us say that a fifth grade Mexican American student, Graciela, comes from a low-income family in the border community of Nogales, Arizona. Graciela's father is a gardener for several wealthy families. The topic in an upcoming science unit is plant growth. Rather than assuming that Graciela's father is "just a gardener," a teacher who wishes to draw on the funds of knowledge Graciela's father actually possesses might meet with her father to discuss the unit, see if he would like to help, find out what aspects of plant growth he would be comfortable talking about, and perhaps ask him to agree to be interviewed in front of the class. Depending on Graciela's father's English language skills, the teacher may need to arrange for an interpreter. This approach not only honors Graciela's family's knowledge, but it also demonstrates to the other students the respect the teacher has for the work Graciela's father does. In other words, it is what teachers *do* with the knowledge they gain about their students' lives *in relationship to instruction* that is important in closing the achievement gap.

You can observe funds of knowledge at work in the video *The Classroom Mosaic: Culture and Learning*, which is session 6 of the program called *The Learning Classroom: Theory into Practice* (**www.learner.org**). In this video, you will observe teachers who are clearly placing value on the cultural knowledge of their students and their families.

## Devaluing Students in School: How Does It Happen?

Whether students experience schools as places where they are valued or devalued depends on what teachers, administrators, other professionals, and the entire school staff communicate to students and their families about their cultures, communities, and abilities, as well as on how students and families are treated. Those who work in schools make choices about how they interact with students and families—whether these are conscious choices or not. Becoming conscious of these choices and making choices that consistently value students and their families is one of the teacher's most important jobs.

Students will not be engaged in school if they believe that their teachers do not value them and care about them and the knowledge and experiences they bring to school. Such students become disadvantaged in school. For students who may already be at some disadvantage because of larger societal and economic forces, and in particular because of poverty, school should not be a place that makes the situation harder. Instead, school should provide opportunity and support, and teachers are on the front line for providing this structure on a daily basis.

### What Teachers Communicate through Their Expectations

One of the most important things teachers communicate to their students is whether or not they actually believe their students are capable of succeeding in school. Many teachers do this well and make sure that their students from all racial, ethnic, and socioeconomic groups succeed. They set high expectations for their students and believe that their students' challenging life situations are not an

A teacher's job is to encourage each student in the classroom to participate rather than favoring students from one particular background. (Monkey Business Images/Media Bakery)

excuse for low achievement. They organize their classrooms and construct their teaching so that all students learn.

Other teachers, however, believe "failure is inevitable for some" (Ladson-Billings, 1994, p. 25). Teachers who hold this bias against their students may act repeatedly in ways that let students know they are not "supposed" to succeed. As we noted in Chapter 6, when a teacher's behavior is based on the erroneous belief that some students cannot learn well, those behaviors can systematically disadvantage a particular group of students. In such circumstances students may suffer the consequences of low *teacher expectations* (see Chapter 2).

For example, teachers may interact differently with students from particular racial, ethnic, or socioeconomic groups in some of the following ways:

● Calling on students less frequently during class discussions, which diminishes students' opportunities to talk about the topics under study and/or share their viewpoints

● Not encouraging students to try hard, which communicates the idea that "you can't do it anyway"

● Not allowing students the same amount of time to think about and construct their responses to teacher questions as other students are allowed, which limits students' ability to try out their newly developing knowledge

● Identifying and correcting misbehaviors more frequently than for the same misbehaviors in other students, which sets different and inequitable standards for behavior within the same classroom

● Correcting misbehaviors more harshly than for other students, which also sets different and inequitable standards for behavior within the same classroom

● Giving students lower grades for comparable work than other students receive, which lets students know their teacher is not evaluating their work fairly

● Not listening to or acknowledging students' attempts to communicate about a particular situation, which tells students their attempts to communicate are not valued

Teachers may also establish different interpersonal relationships with students whose race, ethnicity, or social class differs from theirs and, as a result, fail to get to know them as well as students from their own group. They may do this in the following ways:

● Engaging less in informal talk with students from particular racial, ethnic, or socioeconomic groups, which communicates that teachers are not really interested in the students and their lives

● Greeting students from some groups with a smile and conversation as they enter the room in the morning while ignoring others, which communicates that not all students are equally welcome in the classroom

● Demonstrating closer physical proximity to some students than to others, which communicates that the teacher wishes to maintain distance from certain groups

● Establishing closer relationships with families who come from their own racial/ethnic/socioeconomic group compared with families who do not, which limits the teacher's ability to gain the family's trust and support in working together to benefit the student.

When teachers do not believe in the first place that their students can succeed in school by virtue of their race, ethnicity, or social class, and when they engage in behaviors such as those described above, the result can be a **self-fulfilling prophecy** in education. Anita Woolfolk, a noted educational psychologist, defines this concept as "a groundless expectation that comes true simply because it has been expected" (2001, p. 415). The self-fulfilling prophecy can occur when teachers believe certain students will not do well and then systematically treat these same students in ways that create discomfort, lack of respect, and lack of motivation for learning. They are likely to ignore improvement or any student behaviors that indicate the students' ability or effort. As a result, these same students are more likely to end up doing poorly with that teacher in that classroom—fulfilling the teacher's original bias against the students.

As the effects of such systematic actions on the teacher's part accumulate, it is easy to see how they can create negative experiences for students who are on the receiving end of these teacher behaviors. When this occurs, students can readily recognize that it is their group in particular that is being singled out for unfair treatment on the part of the teacher.

Sonia Nieto (2004) makes the important point that most teachers do not consciously engage in these negative behaviors. The fact remains, however, that teachers, although they are professionals, do not always act in the best interests of their racial and ethnic minority and low-income students. Teachers may hold onto a deficit view of their students rather than a view that values and builds on their student's assets. Unfortunately, once low expectations have been set, teachers typically look for evidence of student behavior that confirms their low expectations.

Reaching out to family members and gaining their trust and respect, especially families whose background differs from that of the teacher, is one of the most important responsibilities teachers have. (Ellen B. Senisi/ The Image Works)

### Critical Term

**Self-fulfilling prophecy.**
A teacher's expectations about a student which may come true whether or not there is evidence to support that expectation.

## Historical Note
### The *Brown v. Board of Education* Supreme Court Decision

In 1954 the Supreme Court ruled on a case that is considered a turning point in the history of education in the United States: *Brown v. Board of Education*. At that time, segregation of schools by race was the norm in communities all over the country, and schools for African American students were substandard in terms of the buildings themselves and the instructional materials and budgets available to teachers (Walker, 1996).

The practice of segregated schooling was supported and protected legally by the 1896 "separate but equal" ruling by the U.S. Supreme Court in *Plessy v. Ferguson*. In reality, however, separate schools for racial and ethnic minority children were not equal. Ending "separate but equal" schools and achieving equality of education was one of the longstanding goals of the National Association for the Advancement of Colored People (NAACP).

Lawyers associated with the NAACP had long been working toward a case that would test the *Plessy v. Ferguson* decision. The specific issue they contested was whether separate but equal schools—which the NAACP argued were not equal but rather were detrimental to the education of African American students—deprived minority students of their rights under the Fourteenth Amendment of the Constitution, which requires equal protection under the law. When *Brown v. Board of Education* was brought before the Supreme Court beginning in 1952, there were actually four similar cases representing other parts of the country (*Briggs v. Elliot* in South Carolina, *Davis v. County School Board of Prince Edward County* in Virginia, *Bolling v. Sharp* in the District of Columbia, and *Bulah (Belton) v. Gebhart* in Delaware) (Howard University School of Law, 2004). The *Brown v. Board of Education* case was a consolidation of these five cases. The NAACP lawyer who argued the case before the Supreme Court was Thurgood Marshall, who later became the first African American justice of the U.S. Supreme Court.

The specifics of *Brown v. Board of Education* are well known. In the segregated schools of Topeka, Kansas, an African American student named Linda Brown had to cross town to attend a segregated school, even though an all-white school was located a few blocks from her home. The lawsuit named on her behalf and filed against the Topeka Board of Education was based on the argument that segregated schools were inherently unequal and provided inferior education to minority students—even if the school buildings were equivalent—and that segregation itself was "dehumanizing." It took two years for the Court to render a decision; on May 17, 1954, the justices voted unanimously to overturn the 1896 *Plessy v. Ferguson* decision, thus rendering the segregation of schools by race unconstitutional as a violation of the Fifth and Fourteenth Amendments to the Consitution (Motley, 1996). In the Southwest, similar patterns of school segregation existed for Mexican American Students, who regularly attended substandard schools (Guajardo & Guajardo, 2004).

This historic decision meant that school systems all over the country began to grapple with ways to overcome segregation. Fueled by a follow-up decision know as *Brown II*, active school desegregation efforts were undertaken (Brown, 1996). The force of law itself, however, was not enough to overcome deeply entrenched attitudes about schooling, and the effort to desegregate schooling represented one of the most contentious periods in the country, especially in the nation's large, urban school districts. De jure segregation—that is, segregation by force of law—was no longer permitted. But de facto segregation, or segregation that took place despite laws prohibiting it, continued to be practiced in subtle and not so subtle ways, resulting in the persistence of an achievement gap between white and minority students. So although the *Brown v. Board of Education* decision achieved the protection of the law, the work of creating and sustaining equal education for racial and ethnic minority students remains a significant challenge today (Ladson-Billings, 2004).

## What Schools Communicate through Academic Tracking

In addition to the potential to be treated inequitably by individual teachers, racial and ethnic minority students and low-income students are also devalued by decisions regularly made about how schools are organized and about how opportunities are made—or not made—available to students. Furthermore, society itself creates the conditions under which certain groups of people seem to be valued more highly than others. So to understand the persistent problem of low achievement for racial and ethnic minority and low-income students, we must also consider the way school itself is organized and the larger societal dynamics that result in negative educational experiences for specific groups of students. Segregated schools, which existed before *Brown v. Board of Education* and still exist today, are one form of stratification. Another example of this practice is **academic tracking.**

Academic tracking is a prevalent, systematic, and institutionalized practice that can result in low academic achievement among racial and ethnic minority and low-income students. It is an organizational strategy based on the concept of teaching homogeneous groups of students; students are divided into groups based on their perceived abilities and instructed in those groups. In elementary schools this division shows up most often in organizing low, middle, and high reading groups based on achievement and skill levels—which might be named or numbered by the teacher. In high school, tracking shows up in the form of Honors and Advanced Placement courses for some students and a vocational, nonacademic track for others. Some school districts create special classes for students who are labeled "gifted and academically talented," which is another form of tracking. When students are tracked into classes and schools, they typically remain in the original groups to which they were assigned and rarely "jump tracks" during their school experience. In other words, "once in the lower track, always in the lower track."

At first glance, tracking might seem to be an efficient way for teachers to teach; after all, isn't it easier to teach students who are on the same academic level together? But when tracking is used as a grouping strategy, it nearly always contributes directly to the marginalization and low achievement of students in the lower tracks. In schools with diverse student populations, middle- and upper-class white students are typically found in the higher level groups and classes, and racial and ethnic minority students and low-income students are typically found in the lower level groups and nonacademic classes. When this occurs, and it nearly always does, the message that is communicated for that particular school is that few if any racial or ethnic minority students, or students who are poor, are smart enough to be in the most challenging groups or classes.

Tracking is widespread nationally, and so this same faulty message is communicated in schools all over the country, creating pervasive stereotypes about who can succeed in school. Because higher and lower groups are often divided by race, ethnicity, and class, tracking also limits interaction among these groups of students, creating unequal academic status and diminishing the possibility that students who are not white will view themselves as capable, challenged learners (Schofield, 1995). But clearly it is *not* the case that *no* ethnic and racial minority students, or low-income students, are capable of achieving in the highest level classes. What is it about tracking that *systematically* results in the consistent exclusion of racial and ethnic minority students from the higher tracks, once they are placed in lower tracks?

In schools where tracking is prevalent, minority students are often prevented from participating in challenging, rigorous academic classes like this one. (Digital Vision)

## Critical Term

**Academic tracking.** Grouping students homogeneously by academic ability for purposes of instruction.

---

### Your turn... *to reflect*

What do you recall about instructional grouping in your own elementary school experience? In your own high school experience, who was encouraged to take the most challenging classes? Who was not? How do you think this affected the experience you had and that of your classmates?

One well-documented aspect of tracking is the effect on the curriculum itself: in the lower tracks the curriculum is less challenging, less interesting, and less motivating than that in higher tracked groups and classes. In summarizing this large body of research on tracking, Linda Darling-Hammond (2004) notes the following:

- In lower tracks, students are more likely to have a curriculum that is rote-oriented and to achieve at lower levels compared with students who have the same abilities but are not placed in lower academic tracks.

- Teachers in lower tracks are not as demanding, do not support students well, and do not motivate students well. They are likely to criticize students for their behavior rather than to engage in an academic interaction.

- It is these differences in teacher behavior in the classroom that can account for a good deal of the achievement gap. If a more challenging curriculum is used, students with the same abilities do better than those in a lower track.

Therefore, *the system of tracking itself* sets up students in lower tracks for low achievement and failure. Starting out in a low academic group sets into motion the dynamics described above, and low expectations are nearly always built into the tracking system, regularly depriving minority and low-income students of opportunities that are afforded to white middle-class students. In the end, then, tracking appears to ensure that students' learning opportunities are limited and can serve to segregate schools (Le Tendre, Hofer, & Shimizu, 2003). For example, the effects of tracking can be reinforced by high school guidance counselors when they view students in the lower tracks as lacking the ability to attend college, to do well in college, or to plan for a professional career. As a result, guidance counselors can fail to give students in lower tracks information about college preparation, required testing for admissions, or high school course sequences required for college admissions, reasoning that "they won't be going to college anyway." The phenomenon of low expectations can then extend across a student's whole school career, following the student around like a shadow.

Another important question about tracking is: Who gets into which groups in the first place and why? When we examine this question, we begin to see how the role of the larger society figures in matters of low school achievement. Racial and ethnic minority or low-income students, who are likely to have less access to resources that prepare them for school, are more likely to be placed in lower groups at the start of their school careers. When teachers do not understand or value the funds of knowledge students bring to school, they may fail to see them as "smart" when students are assessed for group placements. Thus, even though students may be very smart in the context of the knowledge of their own family, culture, and community values, teachers may place them in a lower group.

When a tracking system is in place early in a student's educational career, teachers are forced to divide students into groups based on limited and sometimes faulty knowledge about those students. And when tracking results in the systematic segregation of racial and ethnic minority and low-income students, it becomes a systematic instrument of inequity in the schools, as the next Case in Point shows. Because of the lowered curriculum expectations in lower tracks, the problem is compounded over time. The cumulative effects of tracking are perhaps best characterized by Lisa Delpit (1995) in her discussion of how power issues play out in schools and classrooms. Among the power issues she describes is "the power of an individual or group to determine another's intelligence or 'normalcy.' Finally, if schooling prepares people for jobs, and the kind of job a person has determines his or her economic status, and, therefore, power, then schooling is intimately related to that power" (pp. 24–25). In Chapter 9 we will introduce some alternatives to academic tracking.

## A Case In Point
### A Rude Awakening about Tracking

Carol Werner, now a professor of education, recalls her own school experiences with tracking.

I attended elementary school in the late 1950s in a small suburban bedroom community outside of New York City. Our community had a population of about 24,000, of which about one-third were white and Catholic or Protestant, one-third white and Jewish, and one-third African American. I came from a middle-class white Jewish family; my grandparents were immigrants and neither of my parents attended college, but they attained middle-class economic status through the modest success of my grandfather's—and then my father's—small family business.

Our neighborhoods were segregated, and so the five neighborhood elementary schools in my community were completely segregated as well, which was typical of the times. But because our community had only one junior high and high school, once we reached seventh grade everyone went to school together. Issues of race were prominent in our community, which saw some of the first sit-ins in the country. The first steps to integrate the elementary schools through bussing were taking place at the time I began seventh grade.

The first day of junior high school in September of 1961 was an auspicious one for our class; we were the first to attend a newly built school. Nervous about the move up, anxious to make new friends, everyone milled around the hallways until homeroom, talking and introducing ourselves. Our homeroom classes were randomly assigned, and so white and African American students were assigned together, talked, and began to make acquaintances. When the first hour bell rang, we all scrambled to find our next classrooms.

My first hour class was social studies with Mrs. Taylor, who to my 12-year-old self appeared to be about 70 years old. The class was Social Studies 201. When passing time was over and the classroom door was closed, I looked around the room. Not a single student in the room was African American. Minutes before, we had been together in the same class for homeroom. Suddenly, we were not. I vividly remember thinking: "Where did everyone go?" As the day went on, I realized that all of my major academic classes had the same number: Social Studies 201, English 201, Math 201, Science 201. Except for Home Economics and Physical Education, every class I attended that day was nearly all white. As the week went on, I began to understand the system. I realized that there were three or four sections of each class, numbered consecutively from 201 to 204. The students in classes that were numbered 204 were almost all African American. The students in classes that were numbered 201 were all white; a few Asian students were enrolled in these class sections as well. At the time, I understood that something was very wrong with this picture, but I was powerless to address it at that point in my life. So although my junior high was "integrated," this was true only in the most limited sense, and it was certainly not a school where everyone had an equal chance to be challenged academically and succeed. The memory of the door closing on my Social Studies class that September morning has stayed with me all of these years as the epitome of inequity in education.

# Addressing Diversity of Language in the Classroom

Teachers can also devalue students because their first language is not English, or because they speak a dialect other than standard English. Students whose first language is not English and who are learning English are often identified as **English Language Learners** (**ELL**). Teachers also encounter language issues regarding dialect for African American students who speak **African American Vernacular English**, or **AAVE** (also known variously as Black English, Black Language, Ebonics, or African American Language), and who may not have mastered standard English. Standard English is usually defined as the English that is taught in the schools and that is used in print media, and in the mass media (Perry & Delpit, 1998).

Later in this chapter we will address the often bitter debates in some states about the value of formal programs of bilingual education. But despite those conflicts, many teachers all over the country instruct students whose first language is not English or who speak **AAVE**. How might teacher–student interactions related to the issue of language disadvantage students in school and contribute to their low performance? Teachers who do not value their students' first language or dialect may demonstrate the following behaviors:

- Forbid students to use their first language or dialect in school, or punish students using it in school
- Assume that students who do not speak English well are not intelligent
- Assume that students who do not speak English well need to be referred to special education
- Tell students who speak AAVE that they are speaking "slang"
- Refer to standard English as "proper English" compared with AAVE
- Assume that parents and other family members are not intelligent because they do not speak English or because they speak AAVE
- Become impatient with family members whose first language is not English or is AAVE
- Fail to solicit input from families whose first language is not English
- Fail to have written notices and letters that are sent home translated so that families have access to important school information
- Fail to welcome interpreters that family members may bring to conferences (Often a family member will serve in this role, usually a young family member such as a sister or brother of the student.)

## Critical Term

**English Language Learners (ELL).** Students whose first language is not English.

## Critical Term

**African American Vernacular English (AAVE).** The language, or dialect of English, that is used by many African American people in the United States.

## Your turn... *to review*

1. Define the term *self-fulfilling prophecy* and discuss why it is important for a teacher to be aware of how this operates in classrooms and schools.
2. Name three reasons that tracking can be detrimental to a child's experience in school.
3. Why is it important for a teacher to be able to demonstrate respect for a student's native language or dialect but also help him or her learn standard English?

When teachers act in these ways, they communicate disregard and disrespect for the home language used by students and their families. For example, if teachers imply that the only "proper" English is standard English, they communicate the belief that the student's first language or dialect is not "proper" at all—when it in fact is in the context in which it is used. If teachers refuse to allow Latino students to speak any Spanish at all at school, at any time and in any place, they are negating the value of the student's first language completely—and that of their family and community as well. In so doing, teachers can create a gulf between themselves, their students, and their students' families. Sonia Nieto (2004) sums the situation up well, noting that "the language dominance of the student is not the real issue; *rather, the way in which teachers and schools view their language may be even more crucial to student achievement*" (p. 216). Thus, the attitude a teacher has toward students whose first language is not English or who speak a dialect of English shapes how those students experience school and how those students are supported (or not supported) as learners.

This is not to say that some students do not have real language learning needs in school that require attention and instruction. They do, and students who do not speak English need to master the language to be successful in this country. Students who speak only AAVE will be limited in their ability to take advantage of opportunities if they do not learn standard English. How do teachers successfully address language in the classroom, and what might be an appropriate stance with regard to a student's first language or dialect?

Perhaps most important, teachers need to be clear about when it is appropriate for students to use their first language. Teachers need to set parameters for when they expect a student to use (or try to use) standard English and when it is appropriate to use their first language. They need to let their students know what these expectations are and why they are important. In order to communicate this idea in the classroom, teachers must be comfortable talking about language-related issues with their students and have a clear awareness of what these parameters are.

Teachers should recognize that forbidding students to speak their first language at all in school is both unrealistic and unnecessary. Students regularly participate in informal conversations in the classroom, on the playground, in the lunchroom, and in other informal situations. Students who, for example, speak Spanish at home will often naturally gravitate toward using it in informal situations. If students are told they may never speak their first language or dialect in school, they will likely do so on the sly. Setting up these unrealistic expectations can lead to distrust because the teacher is not displaying sensitivity toward the reality of the student's language use. Instead, students are likely to learn to hide and cover up the fact that they are speaking their native language or dialect. The teacher therefore needs to set clear expectations for when standard English is expected for both speaking and writing.

In the southwestern United States, school district regulations in the mid-twentieth century commonly forbade the use of Spanish; students were actually punished for speaking Spanish, including "Spanish detention," in which students were required to stay after school if they spoke Spanish (Crawford, 1991). Yet teachers would regularly identify students who could serve as

Students whose first language is not English bring cultural and linguistic richness to the classroom.
(Bob Daemmrich/The Image Works)

interpreters within their classrooms for students whose English was limited or nonexistent (Pugach, 1998). Teachers knew that it was not possible for them to work effectively without acknowledging their students' first language and allowing its use, even in the face of a school district's regulations against the use of Spanish. Similarly, in boarding schools for American Indian children who were removed from reservations, native languages were systematically prohibited to promote "civilization" of American Indian people (Spring, 2007).

In their book *The Real Ebonics Debate*, Theresa Perry and Lisa Delpit (1998) report on an interview they conducted with Carrie Secret, a fifth grade teacher in Oakland, California. This interview demonstrates the direct manner in which Ms. Secret approaches her students' use of language in her classroom, how she sets expectations, and how she supports her students in moving back and forth from using African American Vernacular English (Ebonics) and standard English as they work to master standard English:

> When writing, the students are aware that finished pieces are written in [standard] English. The use of Ebonic structure appears in many of their first drafts. When this happens I simply say, "You used Ebonics here. I need you to translate this thought into English." This kind of statement does not negate the child's thought or language. … Some days I simply announce, "While you are working I will be listening to how well you use English. In your groups you must call for a translation if a member of your group uses an Ebonic Structure."
>
> I once had some visitors to my class and they said, "We don't hear Ebonics here." But that is because I had explained to my children that company was coming, and when company comes, we practice speaking English. Company is the best time to practice because most of the visitors are from a cultural language context different from ours.
>
> Students talk. They bring their home language to school. That is their right. If you are concerned about students using Ebonics in the classroom, you will spend the whole day saying, "Translate, translate, translate." So you have to pick times when you are particularly attuned to and calling for English translation.
>
> When the children are working in groups together, say three or four of them, I try to keep them in an English-speaking mode, but I don't prevent them from using Ebonics. I want to give them time enough to talk through their project in a comfortable language. It's like a prewrite to me. But at some point, they have to present their project to me, and these are required to be presented in their best English. (Perry & Delpit, 1998, pp. 81–82)

Respecting a student's first language is critical for building a solid classroom community; this includes African American Vernacular English (AAVE), the first language of many African American students. (Brand X Pictures/Media Bakery)

Ms. Secret seems comfortable addressing issues of language use in a direct, upfront, and consistent manner with her students. She has set clear expectations for the use of AAVE and for the use of standard English, and she expects her students to learn and use standard English well so that they have the skills they need to be successful in the cultural world of education and work. At all times she is respectful of the students' first language.

Teachers can successfully set similar parameters for students whose first language is not English. These parameters, however, obviously need to take into

## Your turn... *to reflect*

How comfortable would you be talking with students whose first language is not English, or who speak AAVE, about the role of standard English in their lives? What accounts for your own particular comfort level, or lack of comfort, about this topic? Compare your response to those of your peers in a small-group debriefing.

account how much English a particular student is capable of using and for what purpose. If students can function well in their regular classroom, then the use of their second language should parallel the kinds of expectations Ms. Secret set around the use of their first language: make clear distinctions, make sure the students know when they must use English, and support the students in gaining competence in written and oral standard English.

Lisa Delpit (1995) talks about the importance of being direct with students who are not members of the dominant, powerful group in a society. Standard English is the language of power in our society; those who can speak it can participate in the structures of society where decisions are made and resources are allocated. As Delpit (1995) states: "If you are not already a participant in the culture of power, being told explicitly the rules of that culture makes acquiring power easier" (p. 25). Regarding issues of power as they relate to language use, teachers need to be explicit with their students about gaining competence in standard English at the same time they respect their students' first languages.

Compared with students in other countries, American students do not acquire second languages readily, and the teaching of second languages is not a strong aspect of the education system. Sonia Nieto (2004) notes the irony that students who speak a language other than English—and who are often from low-income families—are considered to be "problems" in school because of their language status at the same time their middle-class peers may be struggling to learn a second language down the hall in a formal classroom setting. Classroom teachers can do much to build respect for second language and for the broader cultural understanding that speaking a second language or dialect represents. In the absence of such a commitment, teachers may instead view the fact that students speak a language other than English as a deficit rather than an asset. Not recognizing language as an asset can contribute to their students' failure to achieve well in school.

## Digging Deeper
### What about Bilingual Education?

Bilingual education is one of the most controversial issues in American education today. The legislative foundation for bilingual education programs was the 1968 Title VII legislation under the Elementary and Secondary Education Act, which supported bilingual education for all language minority students but which gave preference to students of lower socioeconomic status (Crawford, 1991). The legal foundation for bilingual education followed with the 1974 *Lau v. Nichols* decision, which addressed bilingual education as a civil rights issue. The *Lau* decision resulted in what have come to be known as the Lau Remedies, which provide specific guidance in meeting the needs of language minority students (Crawford, 1991; Hakuta, 1986).

**Pro and Con:** In broad brushstrokes, pro and con positions regarding bilingual education are as follows. Those in favor of bilingual education argue that it is a civil rights issue, that language minority students deserve equality of educational opportunity, and that developing the educational potential of language minority students is an investment in the country's future economic well-being (Hakuta, 1986). Those against bilingual education argue that English is the language of the United States and everyone should learn it, that bilingual education will slow the integration of immigrants into the American culture, and that immersing new immigrants into English-speaking classrooms (the "sink-or-swim" method) worked in the past and should work now as well (Crawford, 1991; Hakuta, 1986). Groups such as English for the Children, founded by businessman Ron Unz in California, have sponsored active political efforts to eradicate bilingual education through state referendums, which have been successful in California and Arizona.

**The Nuances:** First, as a matter of educational policy the American education system is decidedly weak among the industrialized countries in educating its students to speak a second language, which suggests a general devaluing of that ability. Failure to value speaking a second language means that the opportunities for cultural learning that accompany the learning of a second language are also diminished. Given this policy landscape, whether Americans are interested in learning to speak a language other than English well is fundamentally at question.

Second, there is an inaccurate perception that the fundamental purpose of bilingual education is to maintain a student's first language. In reality, most bilingual education programs exist to help students make the transition from their first language to English, but without eradicating their first language (Hakuta, 1986). Rather, the first language is used as a resource from which to build English language skills and is seen as valuable to maintain. This is an important point, because it affirms that learning English is valued by immigrant communities and that the transition to English-speaking classrooms is important. Immersing students in English with no eye toward helping them maintain their first language devalues their abilities in their first language and works to eradicate students' abilities to speak it. Because it subtracts the original language students speak, the immersion approach has been dubbed "subtractive bilingualism."

Third, when students learn skills in one language, they transfer those skills into their second language. So, if students are learning mathematics in a classroom where Spanish is spoken, they are likely to transfer those content skills into English when they make the transition into classes where English is the dominant language of instruction. They do not lose their academic skills in the transition.

Fourth, it is difficult to separate the issue of bilingual education from the socioeconomic status of immigrant groups. Whether bilingual education is valued depends on the community in which it is taking place and the status of the first language students speak. For example, most bilingual education programs are launched in low-income communities to support new immigrants who need to learn English. In these communities such programs can be viewed as government support to poor immigrants and interpreted through the lens of stereotypes and biases about those immigrant groups.

When two-way bilingual education programs are launched in middle-class communities, however, where native English speakers learn, for example,

Spanish, and native Spanish speakers learn English, they are viewed as important educational assets for all students. This was the case with a successful bilingual education program in Miami, Florida, at the Coral Way Elementary School starting in 1963, which had a population of middle-class Cuban Spanish-speaking students who learned English and middle-class white English-speaking students who learned Spanish (Hakuta, 1986). Learning a second language is what was valued in this program—and it was seen as advantageous for both groups of students. Programs like these are called "additive bilingualism." In other words, when middle-class students gain the benefit of learning a second language, the educational program is generally valued. "Bilingualism becomes an educational 'extra' that will pay social, academic, and economic dividends in the future" (Crawford, 1991, p. 117). But when low-income students are supported in learning a second language (i.e., English for new immigrants) it is valued less.

**Rethinking the Issue:**  From these nuances, you can see that a simple "pro" and "con" approach leaves out many important considerations for teachers who work with students whose first language is not English. Bilingual education is the most visible program in the United States around which language learning is discussed. Yet its very discussion is fraught with issues related to immigration, socioeconomic status, what it means to be an American, and whether we, as a country, value learning more than one language.

# Rethinking Teaching as a Culturally Responsive Profession

The negative experiences of students who are devalued in school because of race, class, culture, or language, as well as the persistent achievement gap between middle-class students and many students from these groups, make it crucial for teachers to be responsive to their students. How can teachers be responsive to their diverse student populations?

## Culturally Responsive Teaching

In Figure 7-3, Villegas and Lucas (2002) identify six characteristics of teachers who are responsive to student differences in a way that fosters success in school—characteristics that constitute what today is known as **culturally responsive teaching**. This list serves as a summary of many of the important concepts we have introduced in this chapter thus far. Villegas and Lucas (2002) embrace the importance of contextualized teaching and learning, but they also emphasize the personal commitments teachers must make regarding issues of diversity and interaction across various groups.

As Figure 7-3 illustrates, becoming a culturally responsive teacher is not a simple matter. It entails taking seriously the responsibility for closing the achievement gap between primarily white middle-class students and racial and ethnic minority students and/or students in lower socioeconomic classes who are not achieving well in school. Culturally responsive teachers practice these multiple actions together to create classrooms where students from all ethnic, racial, language, and income groups are successful. Their actions are rooted in a deep professional and personal commitment to the belief that students from all backgrounds are capable of high achievement in school.

**Critical Term**

**Culturally responsive teaching.** Teaching that is continuously responsive to the race, class, culture, ethnicity, and language of each student. It is based on the knowledge and active use of students' backgrounds and cultural experiences to create and implement curriculum, ensuring that all students are successful in school.

**Figure 7-3    Six Characteristsics of Culturally Responsive Teaching and What They Mean for Prospective Teachers**

Teachers who are responsive to their students' different cultures and life experiences engage in many positive behaviors to provide their students with powerful and meaningful educational experiences.

| Characteristics of Culturally Responsive Teaching | What This Means for You as a Prospective Teacher |
|---|---|
| 1. Teachers "recognize that the ways people perceive the world, interact with one another, and approach learning, among other things, are deeply influenced by such factors as race/ethnicity, social class, and language. This understanding enables teachers to cross the cultural boundaries that separate them from their students." | 1. You are committed to engaging fully with people who are different from you and to gaining a deep understanding of how culture—your own as well as that of your students—legitimately affects the way people interact. |
| 2. Teachers "have affirming views of students from diverse backgrounds, seeing resources for learning in all students rather than viewing differences as problems to be solved." | 2. You consistently view your students' cultural experiences, language, and knowledge as *assets* that enrich the learning environment, rather than as *deficits.* |
| 3. Teachers "have a sense that they are both responsible and capable of bringing about educational change that will make schooling more responsive to students from diverse backgrounds." | 3. You take a proactive, public stance that consistently supports students whom the educational system may otherwise shortchange. |
| 4. Teachers "are familiar with their students' prior knowledge and beliefs, derived from both personal and cultural experiences." | 4. You are committed to deep learning about your students' cultural experiences, those of their families, and those of the community, and you view these as resources for your teaching. |
| 5. Teachers "see learning as an active process by which learners give meaning to new information." | 5. You involve your students in their own learning that is connected to how they view the world, rather than simply delivering information to them. |
| 6. Teachers "design instruction that builds on what students already know while stretching them beyond the familiar." | 6. Because you are familiar with your students' backgrounds, and you respect those background experiences, you can effectively draw on them as a legitimate starting point for instruction. |

**Source for left column:** Villegas, A. M., and T. Lucas. (2002). *Educating culturally responsive teachers: A coherent approach.* Albany: State University of New York Press, p. xiv.

Culturally responsive teaching is also known by several other similar, related terms: *culturally compatible teaching, culturally congruent teaching, culturally appropriate teaching,* and *culturally relevant teaching* (Nieto, 2004). Each of these terms signifies teaching that overcomes the discontinuities or incompatibilities between teachers and their students based on issues of race, class, or culture (Nieto, 2004).

**Your turn... *to reflect***

Read the first four practices that appear on the left-hand side of Figure 7-3. For each of these practices, rate yourself using a scale of high, medium, or low in terms of your current comfort level in carrying out this responsibility. What accounts for your own comfort level? What do you think you might need to do to gain a greater comfort level? Share your responses with your peers.

## Why "Celebrating Difference" Is not Enough

In the previous section, we described several dynamics that can contribute to the achievement gap between racial and ethnic minority or low-income students and their teachers—who are often, but not always, white and middle class. We argued that contextualized, culturally responsive teaching and learning are critical in fostering academic achievement. But sometimes the efforts teachers make to address issues associated with diversity of race, culture and class—however well-intentioned—only scratch the surface and are in reality not effective in helping to close the achievement gap. One example of a surface-level commitment is the idea of "celebrating difference."

A popular way for teachers to recognize the varied backgrounds of their students is to implement activities such as holiday folk fairs, sharing foods and traditions, and identifying of famous figures from particular racial or ethnic groups. Celebrating events like Black History Month (February) or Hispanic Heritage Month (September 15 to October 15) falls into this category. In a related fashion, teachers may develop and implement specific units of study on particular cultures or introduce ethnic themes into the study of various content areas (Sleeter & Grant, 2002). For example, a teacher may plan a unit on Asian cultures in social studies. Teachers may also create units on famous minority inventors for social studies or science or include in their instruction historical information about mathematics and mathematicians in Egypt. James Banks (1995), a scholar of multicultural education, uses the term *content integration* to describe cultural activities such as these, activities that are added onto the existing curriculum—whether they be celebrations or specific units of study. You might often hear teachers talking about the importance of "celebrating difference" or "celebrating cultural diversity" when referring to activities that represent such cultural activities.

Implementing content integration activities can be a good way to help students and teachers learn more about each other and can no doubt contribute to students' pride in their own backgrounds. These activities may also open up dialogue about different cultures and, when families participate, contribute to building a more solid community between the school and the families. At the same time, because these kinds of activities do not necessarily address the complex classroom and school dynamics that actually lead to students being marginalized, this approach has limited ability to help students reach the goal of achieving success *in their studies in school*. Nevertheless, teachers who implement activities designed to "celebrate difference" and increase multicultural awareness and knowledge among their students may erroneously view their actions as adequately fulfilling their responsibilities to their students' racial, ethnic, and socioeconomic diversity.

For example, teachers may celebrate Martin Luther King Day each year by having students read King's *I Have a Dream* speech and by studying King's life, but may not realize that they do not call on their African American students to participate in discussions nearly as often as they call on others, thus diminishing their opportunity to participate fully in learning. Teachers may celebrate Cinco de Mayo and have their Latino students talk about the significance of the holiday, but may fail to create responsive

Ethnic festivals can create a shared understanding of students' cultures, but teachers must go beyond such celebrations to make sure that students from all backgrounds have the opportunity to learn and succeed in the academic curriculum. (Michael J. Doolittle/The Image Works)

# REWARDS AND CHALLENGES

## Honoring Students' Cultural Differences

Kate Flanagan
*San Francisco*

I began teaching fifth grade in the San Francisco Public Schools five years ago, and this is the first year that I have had a student who was of my same ethnicity, Caucasian. The make-up of my student body is primarily first generation Chinese American immigrants. In addition, I have a few Latino and African American students. All notices home, all daily announcements, and all parent-teacher conferences are translated into Cantonese and Spanish. Almost all of the parents at my school come to conferences and Back to School nights, but most are working one or more jobs to stay afloat in San Francisco's expensive economy. Our parents believe in the importance of an education, and pass along a strong work ethic to their children. Most parents have not been to college and work at minimum wage jobs. Since they are so busy working, they can rarely come to school or help out in the classroom. At home, most of my children do not speak English and their parents can only help them with their math homework. I quickly learned to assign homework that the students could truly do independently.

Each year when we study immigration, we go to Angel Island in the San Francisco Bay, and on that field trip, I have the most parent volunteers of the year. They take the day off from work to see the Immigration Station, where Chinese immigrants were detained upon entry to San Francisco, for months or even years. In class, we learn a lot about each other through our immigration interviews, and we always have about five or six students in the class who can share their own experiences. It is a challenge for the few African American students at my school, as they are in such a minority. There are usually only one or two African American students in each class, and the school yard is often a place where racist comments are heard. As a teacher, I try to honor the cultures of all of my students and to teach about discrimination in all of its forms.

Each year that I have taught, I have had newcomers who have just arrived from China, with little or no English. It is quite challenging to teach a fifth grade science or U.S. history text to a newcomer. The newcomers at my school are lucky to arrive at a school where so many of their classmates speak their native language. My students have always been eager to help out the newcomers by translating or showing them the lay of the land. My teacher education program in San Francisco had a strong emphasis on teaching English Language Learners. By the end of the school year, I am always amazed at how much language my newcomers and ELL students have gained, how much they have started volunteering, and how quickly they have progressed.

It is a challenge to teach students who are outside of my ethnic, linguistic, and socioeconomic background. But it is rewarding for me to learn from their different cultures and to honor the knowledge that my students bring to the classroom. ●

relationships with the parents and families of their Latino students compared with those of their other students. Teachers and schools may sponsor holiday folk fairs representing multiple cultures and share ethnic foods, costumes, songs, and dances, but may never make the effort to reach out to various cultural communities at any other time of the year. Teachers may put up posters of famous Latino, African American, or Southeast Asian figures but may fail to incorporate the students' various cultural life experiences in a writing assignment. Thus, teachers can easily adopt a content integration approach that "celebrates differences" without really engaging *on a personal level* in what it means to make sure that every single student is treated equitably in terms of his or her potential to be successful in school ("I celebrate all the holidays. I include Christmas, Hanukkah, and Kwaanza in December. Isn't that enough?").

As we noted above, teachers who rely exclusively on the content integration approach to diversity typically do so with positive intentions and with a genuine desire to build a more tolerant, respectful classroom community. But as a dimension of multicultural education, content integration alone is problematic because it does not focus on fostering students' achievement and because it keeps issues of cultural diversity on the periphery of the curriculum (Sleeter & Grant, 2002).

Content integration does not require a real change in the curriculum. Nor does it necessarily mean that teachers view their students' cultures and communities as assets for learning, or that they contextualize their teaching and learning in a way that leads to student learning and closing the achievement gaps. In short, content integration can actually function as an excuse for not addressing the central issues of whether the teachers' pedagogy is effective in instructing students well.

## Beyond Cultural Knowledge—Multiple Perspectives and Social Transformation

Other characteristics of multicultural education are also critical in creating classrooms that are responsive to racial and ethnic minority and low-income students. First, teachers must actively help their students understand that concepts and events can be interpreted from different perspectives depending on the various racial, ethnic, or socioeconomic groups that are doing the interpreting (Banks, 1996; Nieto, 2004). For example, a teacher may present the story of the first Thanksgiving and discuss whether the perspective of American Indian people is taken into account. A different example of what it means to acknowledge multiple perspectives on events occurred in the week after the 9/11 tragedy at the World Trade Center in 2001. At an urban middle school in a midsized city, the principal and teachers were discussing the event with their students and talking about the need to protect the community and the country from terrorists. In the course of this discussion, a 14-year-old boy who lived in one of the roughest neighborhoods in the city remarked, "You know, I live in a neighborhood where there is gunfire almost every day, and where people are getting killed all the time. Why hasn't anyone been caring all this time about how safe me and my family are?" This remark represents the lived experience—that is, the perspective—of this student and raises some difficult societal issues that cannot be ignored in classrooms.

Another example of how teachers acknowledge different points of view may occur in relationship to the use of multicultural literature (see, for example, the Cooperative Children's Book Center in Madison, Wisconsin, **www.education.wisc.edu/ccbc/**). The field of child and adolescent literature has grown exponentially in the past decades, and several prominent racial and ethnic minority authors have emerged who have written consistently high-quality fiction about racial and ethnic minority characters, families, and communities. Teachers can use such multicultural literature in several ways. A sensitive teacher who is trying to acknowledge the perspectives of her students will encourage discussion and dialogue about the issues raised in the literature and will be prepared to answer difficult questions that students may raise regarding inequities in our society as they relate to the story. Such teachers would expect that students would raise challenging issues regarding race, class, culture, or language and would be prepared to discuss them. Teachers who may be less fully committed may answer questions about the plot itself, but ignore or shortchange any discussion of more difficult aspects of the book—usually because they do not feel comfortable talking about the issues themselves. Teaching Tolerance is a program of the Southern Poverty Law Center that provides resources to help teachers build classrooms that embrace diversity. On its website (**www.tolerance.org**) you will find a link to *The ABC's of Culture in the Classroom.* This link includes a short video of a high school English teacher talking about the need to select literature that reflects the diversity of his classroom and his students' interests.

From these examples, we see that teaching students that issues can be addressed from multiple perspectives often leads to discussions of larger inequities in our society and in the world. When teachers actively and purposefully work with their students on issues such as these, we often say that a teacher is implementing a social justice orientation to education. The following Philosophical Note describes a social justice, or social reconstruction, approach to the curriculum. Whether or not you implement a social justice orientation to teaching and to the curriculum, as a teacher you will be called upon to respond to students' concerns, opinions, and perspectives. If your students' race, ethnicity, language, or social class differs from yours, your students are likely to raise challenging issues that you may or may not feel comfortable addressing. A teacher who respects his or her students and takes their concerns seriously will, over time, make it a goal to become increasingly comfortable engaging in a discussion of these issues, as challenging and as difficult as it might seem.

## Philosophical Note
### Transforming Society through Social Reconstructionism

What approaches should be taken by those who subscribe to a philosophy of education based on social reconstructionism? This philosophy is based on the belief that the purpose of education is to prepare students to contribute to reducing inequities, power differences, and problems within society. The goal is greater social justice for those in society who are oppressed.

To achieve this goal, teachers first must work with their students to help them become conscious of problems in society. Teachers can do this by making the study of social problems a central part of the curriculum (McLaren, 2003; Sleeter & Grant, 2002). Class work can then emphasize an activist approach to social problems, involving students in projects and activities that contribute directly to improving society. These activities seek to develop not just a consciousness of social problems but a social conscience as well (McLaren, 2003). By making these issues the focus of education, social reconstructionists would say that they are preparing the next generation to become social activists and to address these problems in their adult lives.

Social reconstructionism is based on taking a *critical perspective* on education. A critical perspective views society in the context of the problems and inequities inherent in the society and the need to take action to solve them. As teachers whose philosophy is based on social reconstruction choose what to teach in the academic subject areas, they look for ways to introduce a critical perspective on problems related to that subject (Eisner, 1979). In science this might include the location of toxic waste sites in rural communities, the safety of the food supply, or the effects of lead paint in urban areas. In social studies this might include an analysis of local voting patterns or local housing patterns, the location of public libraries, or racial profiling by police officers. A math teacher might ask students to study and manipulate statistics related to these or other issues that illustrate social inequities. An English teacher might select literature that would help his or her students understand the perspective of those in society who are oppressed.

Teachers who are advocates of a social reconstructionist philosophy also work to practice justice and equity in their own classrooms. They endeavor to develop healthy democratic classroom communities in which students feel comfortable addressing social issues not only in society at large and in the local community, but in their own school and classrooms as well.

A second additional characteristic of multicultural education is that teachers can teach lessons directly that actively contribute to affirming diversity and reducing prejudice and bias (Banks, 1996; Nieto, 2004). Taking this step requires a different level of personal commitment than content integration. It may require more risk-taking and personal growth to create an environment where issues of prejudice and bias, whether on a personal, classroom, schoolwide, or societal level, are addressed. Because of the nature of our society, racial and ethnic minority students in particular often experience prejudice and bias in their daily lives. All students' experiences spill out into the classroom in many ways. If teachers do not acknowledge the life experiences of students who experience prejudice, it will be difficult to create a classroom community in which students feel valued, respected, and motivated to learn. This does not mean that it will be easy to address the concerns students raise. But teachers who ignore these issues also ignore the reality of their students' lives. Teachers and students alike have the responsibility to challenge practices that lead to racism and discrimination (Nieto, 2004).

And third, one of the most important goals of multicultural education should be for teachers to work toward transforming schools so that equity is achieved throughout the school as an organization and society at large (Banks, 1995; Nieto, 2004). For example, has the local high school addressed the issue of racial and ethnic minority group representation in Advanced Placement classes? What about the representation in various after-school extracurricular activities? Are the teachers schoolwide looking at their school in terms of whose needs are being met and working to empower all students across racial and ethnic lines? To ensure that equity is provided in our schools for every student, these more complex levels of multicultural education, which may represent more complex challenges for teachers, must be in place.

## Recognizing Privilege and Power

We began this chapter by talking about schools that are populated by a wide range of students from many racial and ethnic groups or from low-income families. We also stressed the nature of the relationships teachers need to establish with students, families, and the community in which the school is located as a basis for building a solid relationship and for gaining information to help connect the students to the curriculum.

To extend our consideration of what it means to teach students whose race, ethnicity, language or class differs from that of their teacher, we also need to explore the concept of privilege, and in particular, **white privilege**. This term, coined by Peggy McIntosh (1989), refers to the advantages white persons experience simply by virtue of being white compared with individuals from racial or ethnic minority groups. This issue is critical because a large proportion of the teaching force is white and may not be aware of how privilege operates in the lives of students and in society.

McIntosh (1989) argues that even if one does not acknowledge or recognize such privilege, it nevertheless accrues to people who are white because of the overall dispersal of power and privilege in our society; privilege is an "unearned advantage" (p. 11). Some of the examples she cites of privilege include:

> I can go shopping alone most of the time, pretty well assured that I will not be followed or harassed.
>
> I can turn on the television or open to the front page of the paper and see people of my race widely represented.

**Critical Term**

**White privilege.** The advantages white persons experience by virtue of being white, whether they seek the privileges out or not, compared with individuals from racial or ethnic minority groups.

Whether I use checks, credit cards, or cash, I can count on my skin color not to work against the appearance of financial reliability.

I can swear, or dress in second-hand clothes, or not answer letters, without having people attribute these choices to the bad morals, poverty, or illiteracy of my race.

I can do well in a challenging situation without being called a credit to my race.

I am never asked to speak for all the people of my racial group.

I can be pretty sure that if I ask to speak to "the person in charge," I will be facing a person of my race.

If a traffic cop pulls me over or if the IRS audits my tax return, I can be sure I haven't been singled out because of my race.

I can be sure that if I need legal or medical help, my race will not work against me.

If my day, week, or year is going badly, I need not ask of each negative episode or situation whether it has racial overtones. (McIntosh, 1989, pp. 10–11)

Events such as these can be daily experiences for racial or ethnic minority persons in our society that persons who are white do not experience. Not having these negative experiences is what makes being white a privilege that is conferred simply by the fact of not being a member of a racial or ethnic minority group. Teachers who are white and who are teaching racial and ethnic minority students may have difficulty connecting to their students without an understanding of the differential role privilege plays in society.

The existence of privilege does not mean that white teachers may not have struggled in their lives, experienced hardship, or had to overcome disadvantage. Nevertheless, McIntosh's concept constitutes a particular, persistent kind of privilege that does exist in our society but often is not acknowledged.

Because they can experience its negative effects so regularly, racial and ethnic minorities have no choice but to acknowledge privilege and its attendant power. According to Gary Howard, "members of the dominant group in any society do not necessarily have to know anything about those people who are not like them. For our survival and the carrying-on of the day-to-day activities of our lives, most white Americans do not have to engage in any meaningful personal connection with people who are different. This is not a luxury available to people who live outside of dominance and must, for their own survival, understand the essential social nuances of those in power" (Howard, 1999, p. 12). To be an effective teacher in a multiracial, multiethnic school, it is critical to recognize the "luxury" Howard speaks of and deliberately engage with students, families, and community members—people who can help white teachers gain a deep understanding and appreciation of the lives of their students, families, and the community.

## "Not Seeing Color" as a Problematic Response to Diversity

Sometimes well-intentioned teachers may take the position that they treat all of their students as individuals and that they "don't see color." When teachers make such statements they are usually trying to convey the importance of being consistent with all of their students and are describing their attempts to make sure that each student has the same opportunity as the next, regardless of race, class, culture, or language.

Although teachers should look at all of their students as individuals, a student's individuality does not exist in a vacuum of race or ethnicity or class. Instead, a student's individuality is affected and shaped *both* by individual differences and by the culture and community to which he or she belongs. Racial and ethnic minority students do indeed "have a color," and this fact is central to their life experience—along with who they are as individuals. Persons who are white also "have a color," namely, white, but it is rarely talked about in this way. When teachers claim that they "don't see color," what they are really communicating is that they don't see a fundamental reality of the lives of their students. "Not seeing color," then, can negate who the students actually are. It also means that the teacher who professes this stance does not have to talk about color—that is, race or ethnicity—and is thus freed from self-examination about issues that he or she may find uncomfortable.

Vivian Gussin Paley, who writes poignantly about her experiences as an early childhood educator in Chicago, addresses this issue in her book *White Teacher* (2000). She recounts how she learned to embrace her students' diversity in the newly integrated preschool where she taught in Chicago. If you do not talk about difference, Paley reflects, in effect you are judging students only from the vantage point of what you know. And what you know best is your own culture, race, or ethnicity—and not that of your students who differ from you. Thinking about her own education as a young Jewish student in a public school that was primarily populated by Gentile students, she writes that her teachers "insisted we were all just children, which meant that we were all Gentile children since that was the only kind of child they thought about or talked about. The more my parents provided me with roots in my own culture, the more I felt my differences from the culture of the school. Failing to be recognized as a Jew, and knowing I was not a Gentile, I did not know what I was at school." (pp. 11–12).

Paley goes on to describe a conversation with an African American parent of one of her preschool students about the idea of "not seeing color." Recounting a meeting with this parent, Paley (2000) writes:

> Mrs. Hawkins told me that in her children's previous school the teacher had said, "There is no color difference in my classroom. All my children look alike to me."
>
> "What rot," said Mrs. Hawkins. "My children are black. They don't look like your children. They know they're black, and we want it recognized. It's a positive difference, an interesting difference, and a comfortable natural difference. At least it could be so, if you teachers learned to value differences more. *What you value, you talk about.*" (p. 12, emphasis added)

Valuing difference is precisely the commitment we have been talking about in this chapter. When teachers learn about difference, they can use their knowledge to create the conditions in which students who are different from their teachers all have the opportunity to achieve well in school.

## A Special Responsibility—Teaching in a Monocultural School

What about teachers who teach in schools where the students are of the same race, ethnicity, and social class? How do the ideas, concepts, and issues discussed in this chapter apply when this is the case?

Every teacher has responsibility for creating a classroom in which students have the tools and skills to engage in reducing discrimination and building a tolerant and harmonious classroom community. Although classroom dynamics may not involve interactions among students from different racial, ethnic, or social class groups, teachers make deliberate choices about how they address conflict and difference within their classrooms and how students are expected to deal with conflict and discord. In a monocultural classroom, for example, differences in religion may surface that require lessons in tolerance. Biases about racial or ethnic groups who are not represented within the classroom may also surface, and teachers must address these biases. No matter where they teach and no matter how diverse or similar their student populations are, teachers have a responsibility to create and sustain classrooms that are models of tolerance and inclusiveness and to support students' development in their ability to live in a multiracial, multiethnic society.

Specifically regarding race and ethnicity, teachers who work in monocultural schools whose students are white may be using a content integration approach, thereby enriching the curriculum with multicultural topics. But what does it mean to transform the curriculum for a monocultural group of students? How are issues of equity embedded throughout the curriculum, rather than merely being added periodically? This is where it becomes important to teach students about multiple perspectives on knowledge and the role of social justice in the curriculum. As teachers make choices about the taught curriculum, to use Cuban's term from Chapter 5, they need to decide how they will address multiple perspectives on, and interpretations of, the curriculum, as well as issues of social justice. What perspectives will they introduce? How will they plan for their students to have authentic experiences with racial and ethnic minority persons that will help to break down any stereotypes and biases the students (and the teacher) may have? What perspectives on history are taught? What perspectives on the Civil Rights era are presented? What choices will teachers make about multicultural literature? And, most important, if these topics do become a part of the curriculum, as they should, how prepared are teachers to address students' responses—especially any misconceptions or biases students may have about the issues?

When an African American teacher works in a school with an African American student population, or a Mexican American teacher in a Mexican American school in the Southwest, students will no doubt often talk about issues of equity because of their ongoing experiences with prejudice, bias, and the lack of equity their group faces in the society. As a result, issues of social justice will more naturally permeate classroom conversation, and overcoming the hardships associated with socioeconomic status is also likely to be a critical ongoing issue for discussion and action. But what is the teacher's obligation to teach about other racial and ethnic groups in a school that is monocultural and minority? About prejudices and biases that may exist within their own minority group with respect to other minority groups? The point is that whether a school has a multicultural population or a monocultural one, if we wish to achieve a more harmonious and tolerant society, teachers are obliged to work toward greater tolerance across groups wherever they teach.

## Why It Counts in a Diverse World

Students come to school with different life experiences, different family traditions, different languages, and different cultural experiences. How successful they are in school depends, in large part, on the way teachers and schools build on the particular configuration of their experiences prior to attending school as a basis for teaching and learning. Teachers who accept their students' many differences and view these differences not as deficits but as assets from which to build are in a much better position to help their students achieve success in school than are teachers who do not so value these differences.

In a democracy, school is supposed to function as an equalizer across different groups. The record of American education today, however, suggests that school is not fulfilling this equalizing function for many groups of students. When teachers themselves make the commitment to understand their students' life experiences, cultures, communities and languages—and the **funds of knowledge** these represent—they help schools to serve this equalizing function. When they do not, they diminish the potential of schooling to serve all students well, and they contribute to the role the educational system plays in perpetuating inequities.

When you receive your teaching license, you are licensed to teach all children—not just those who are like you and not just those whom you like. As a prospective teacher, you have an obligation to do everything you can to break patterns of low achievement and help close the achievement gap within your classroom and your school. Teachers, therefore, can make a real difference in the lives of their students and in the role school plays in their students' future accomplishments.

## CHAPTER SUMMARY

### What Changing Demographics in the United States Mean for Teachers

Today multiracial, multiethnic student populations attend school all over the United States. The educational system is not serving this diverse student population well, and a persistent achievement gap exists between middle-class white students and many racial and ethnic minority students, as well as low-income students. Further complicating this picture is the fact that the majority of teachers are white and come from middle-class homes, which means their backgrounds and life experiences can differ substantially from those of their students. Because they are charged with the learning of all of their students, teachers have a special responsibility to cross racial, ethnic, language, and socioeconomic borders. This applies to all teachers whose students' race, ethnicity, or income status differs from their own.

### Understanding Diversity as an Asset, Not a Deficit

Diversity is often thought of as a deficit in our society that places children at risk of failure in school. When teachers view children's cultures, communities, or first languages and dialects as deficits, they fail to value the knowledge students and their families have. This usually occurs because there is a mismatch between the knowledge that is valued in school learning and the knowledge that exists within racial and ethnic minority or low socioeconomic communities. Although societal dynamics such as inequities of wealth and power have a profound impact on peoples' lives, in the microcosm of schools, teachers have an enormous influence on their students' success.

### How Knowing about Your Students' Lives Helps You Teach

When teachers take an active role in gaining knowledge about the students' cultures, families, and communities, they can use this knowledge as a starting point for instruction and connect students' existing knowledge to the new things they are learning. Families possess *funds of knowledge*, or knowledge that they need to be successful in their own communities or occupations, that can enhance instruction and increase student motivation for learning.

### Devaluing Students in School: How Does It Happen?

Teachers' behaviors communicate to students whether or not they are valued—as individuals and as members of their cultures and communities. When teachers systematically devalue their students through their behaviors, students are not likely to be engaged in school and may not believe there is a good reason to be involved in education. Teachers must monitor the expectations they set for students to ensure that they are not setting lower expectations for students whose race, ethnicity, or socioeconomic status differs from theirs. Schools often organize instruction using homogeneous groups, or *academic tracking*, which can also place racial and ethnic minority and low-income students at a disadvantage. Students in lower tracks tend to receive less challenging, motivating instruction, use a less interesting curriculum, and are likely to do less well academically. Teachers may make erroneous judgments about their students' abilities by virtue of group membership, rather than seeking examples of students' behavior and achievement that signal their ability to do more complex, challenging, and interesting work.

## Addressing Diversity of Language in the Classroom

As teachers interact with students whose first language is not English or who speak a dialect of English, they must create classroom conditions that respect the students' first languages/dialects but that also convey the purpose and goal of mastering standard English. Wrongly assuming that students have deficits simply by virtue of group membership or first language/dialect can negatively affect students' experiences in school and can contribute to lowered achievement.

## Rethinking Teaching as a Culturally Responsive Profession

An important concept in overcoming the achievement gap is *culturally responsive teaching*. This concept refers to teaching that is continuously responsive to the race, class, ethnicity, and language of each student and that is based on the knowledge and active use of students' backgrounds and cultural experiences to create and implement curriculum, ensuring the success of all students in school. To be a culturally responsive teacher, the teacher must not only learn about students' lives, families, and communities, but must also take responsibility for ensuring students' learning, reject the deficit view of racial and ethnic minority and low-income students, understand the multiple perspectives and interpretations held by different groups, and actively foster student achievement across all groups.

## Why "Celebrating Difference" Is Not Enough

The responsibility for addressing diversity is not met by including special activities that celebrate cultural difference, such as holiday celebrations or special units of study on specific cultures. These are appropriate activities in a classroom, but they are not sufficient. To fulfill their responsibilities to a multiracial, multiethnic class of students, teachers need to incorporate teaching that acknowledges multiple perspectives on interpreting the curriculum, engage in activities that lead to reduction in bias, and actively plan and implement instructional approaches that ensure that all students learn well.

## Recognizing Privilege and Power

The gap between a primarily white, middle-class teaching force and a student population that is increasingly multiracial and multiethnic means that white teachers in particular must be aware of the privileges and power they hold by virtue of being white. The term *white privilege* denotes not having to endure daily experiences that call into question one's place in society, as is usually the case if one is a member of a racial or ethnic minority group. Although individuals who are white may not ask for the privileges that the fact of being white confers on them, these privileges nevertheless exist and can create a divide between teachers and their students if this fact goes unacknowledged.

## "Not Seeing Color" as a Problematic Response to Diversity

In an attempt to treat all students equally, sometimes teachers say that they "do not see color." Racial and ethnic minority students are in fact individuals of color. Group membership based on race and ethnicity does influence who students are and the assets they bring to the classroom, as do students' individual differences. When color is ignored in the classroom, students get the message that the differences among them are not valued.

## A Special Responsibility—Teaching in a Monocultural School

Addressing diversity is not just a responsibility for teachers who work in multiracial, multiethnic schools and classrooms. Teachers whose race, ethnicity, or income status is similar to that of their students also have an obligation to address issues of equity, bias, and tolerance. Whether a school has a multicultural population or a monocultural one, if we wish to achieve a more harmonious and tolerant society, teachers are obliged to work toward greater tolerance across groups wherever they teach.

## LIST OF CRITICAL TERMS

Achievement gap  *(210)*

Deficit model  *(213)*

Contextualized teaching and learning *(216)*

Funds of knowledge  *(218)*

Self-fulfilling prophecy  *(221)*

Academic tracking  *(223)*

English Language Learners (ELL) *(226)*

African American Vernacular English (AAVE) *(226)*

Culturally responsive teaching  *(231)*

White privilege  *(237)*

## EXPLORING YOUR COMMITMENT

1. *in the field...*  In your field experience site, analyze the demographics of the school to which you are assigned, both for the student population and for the teachers/administrators. What racial, ethnic, and language groups are represented among the students? the teachers? What do you notice about interaction patterns among the students of different racial and ethnic groups? What do you notice about the teachers' interactions with the students?

2. *on your own...*  How familiar are you with the racial or ethnic groups that are represented in the school? How will you learn about the groups that are represented in a way that will help you teach well? Develop a plan.

3. *in the field...*  As you walk through the school, what evidence do you see that the school practices culturally responsive teaching? Using Figure 7-3 as a guide, what practices associated with culturally responsive teaching have you observed? What practices have you not observed?

4. *in the field...*  In the classroom in which you are observing, how are issues of race, class, culture, and language addressed? What dimensions of multicultural education do you observe?

5. *in the field...*  Look at the child and adolescent literature in your classroom or the school library. How well does it represent multiple cultures? Does it represent the cultures of the students who attend the school? Interview someone at the school who is responsible for selecting and ordering literature. How is the issue of multicultural representation addressed in the book selection process?

6. *on your own...*  What groups in your community might you say are marginalized? What evidence exists to back up your claims?

7. ***on your own...***  Explore what agencies exist in your community to address the needs of racial and ethnic minority groups and low-income groups. How are these services funded? As a teacher, why might these services be important to your work?

8. ***on the web...***  Log onto the website of the *Brown v. Board of Education* National Historic Site (**www.nps.gov/brvb/**). The National Historic Site is located in Topeka, Kansas. How might viewing this website help you gain a greater understanding of the *Brown* decision?

9. ***on the web...***  Log onto the Teaching Tolerance website at **www.tolerance.org/teach/**. How might this website help you as you strive toward a classroom free of prejudice and bias?

10. ***in the research...***  Read McAllister, G. (2002). "The role of empathy in teaching culturally diverse students." *Journal of Teacher Education*, 53, 433–443. Why is empathy an important issue in the classroom?

## GUIDELINES FOR BEGINNING TEACHERS

1. When you get your first school assignment, drive around the neighborhood of the school to become familiar with the community and the resources and assets it contains.

2. Find out the demographic statistics for your school and classroom. Analyze the kinds of differences that exist between you and your students and their families. How will you learn about these differences?

3. Establish relationships with your students' families from the start of the year. Keep a log of the *funds of knowledge* you learn about as you get to know the families of your students.

4. Identify resources that will help you gain knowledge about your students' cultures and begin to use those resources to enhance your understanding.

5. Monitor your own behavior toward students whose group membership differs from yours. Each week, focus on five students and keep mental "tabs" on your interactions with them compared with other students. Are you treating all students as capable learners?

6. Keep a list of the various characteristics of multicultural education you plan to incorporate in your classroom. Are you focusing more on one characteristic than another? Are you leaning toward activities that are more comfortable to you than others, for example, cultural celebrations rather than social justice and equity? If so, set goals for shifting the balance.

7. Regularly analyze the progress of your students by group membership. What do you notice about their patterns of achievement? If a particular group is always lower in achievement than another, analyze your practice and set specific goals for improving the situation.

8. Plan to establish a working relationship with adults in the community whose race, ethnicity, or income status differs from your own. How can this relationship help you grow as a professional?

## THE **INTASC** CONNECTION

INTASC Standards #3 and #5 are related to the issues of diversity. Standard #3 is a general standard covering diversity. It states: *The teacher understands how students differ in their approaches to learning and creates instructional opportunities that are adapted to diverse learners.* Indicators include the following:

- The teacher knows about the process of second-language acquisition and about strategies to support the learning of students whose first language is not English.
- The teacher has a well-grounded framework for understanding cultural and community diversity and knows how to learn about and incorporate students' experiences, cultures, and community resources into instruction.
- The teacher believes that all children can learn at high levels and persists in helping all children achieve success.
- The teacher is sensitive to community and cultural norms.
- The teacher brings multiple perspectives to the discussion of subject matter, including attention to students' personal, family, and community experiences and cultural norms.

Standard #5 states: *The teacher uses an understanding of individual and group motivation and behavior to create a learning environment that encourages positive social interaction, active engagement in learning, and self-motivation.* Indicators include the following:

- The teacher understands how participation supports commitment, and is committed to the expression and use of democratic values in the classroom.
- The teacher helps the group to develop shared values and expectations for student interactions, academic discussions, and individual and group responsibility that create a positive classroom climate of openness, mutual respect, support, and inquiry.

If you are in a state that follows a different set of teacher standards, find the state standards that most closely relate to the INTASC standards discussed here.

## READING ON...

Obidah, J. E., and K.M. Teel. (2001). *Because of the kids: Facing racial and cultural differences in school.* New York: Teachers College Press. Obidah and Teel, an African American and a white teacher, worked together over three years to confront their own beliefs and biases about race and culture.

Spring, J. (2007). *Deculturalization and the struggle for equality: A brief history of the education of dominated cultures in the United States.* (5th ed.) Boston: McGraw-Hill. In this short book, Spring provides a historical perspective on the education of Native Americans, African Americans, Asian Americans, and Hispano/Latino Americans and also places their experiences in the context of the Civil Rights movement of the 1960s.

Thompson, G. L. (2004). *Through ebony eyes: What teachers need to know but are afraid to ask about African American students.* San Francisco: Jossey-Bass. In a direct but sensitive manner, Thompson lays out many issues that prospective teachers who are not

African American may not be comfortable discussing in terms of working effectively with African American students.

Walker, V. Siddle. (1996). *Their highest potential: An African-American school community in the segregated south*. Chapel Hill: University of North Carolina Press. Vanessa Siddle Walker describes the enduring strengths of a segregated school in the pre-*Brown v. Board of Education* South and the high expectations teachers set for students at this school.

Valenzuela, A. (1999). *Subtractive schooling: U.S.-Mexican youth and the politics of caring*. Albany: State University of New York Press. In this award-winning book, Valenzuela portrays the educational experiences of Mexican American students in a Houston high school and illustrates what happens when educators fail to create supportive, caring environments for their students.

## Guiding Questions

- What is the broad commitment that has been made to educating students who have disabilities?

- How did Burton Blatt change the view of educating individuals with cognitive disabilities?

- What are the major principles that guide the federal law for educating students who have disabilities?

- How does labeling students with disabilities help or hinder a teacher's work?

- How do teachers build classroom communities that embrace students who have disabilities?

- What is the role of collaboration between teachers in working with students who have disabilities?

- What is assistive technology and how does it help teachers provide learning opportunities for students who have disabilities?

- How is disability the same or different from other diversities?

- What are the essential issues in educating students who are labeled as gifted and talented?

# Teaching Students with Disabilities

# 8

Jake Harris's fourth grade class has been making steady progress as he continues to improve his teaching skills and learn how to carry out all of the responsibilities of a teacher. He continues to meet with his mentor, Sally Ford, at least every two weeks for advice and support, and just to share the successes he is having—which are increasing all the time. Jake has gained confidence over the past several months. But today he's facing a challenge. He just learned that a new fourth grade student, Sharla Ryan, will be arriving in two weeks, a student who has a significant hearing impairment. Sharla will be accompanied at all times by an interpreter.

"I have some students with learning disabilities and I've gotten pretty good at accommodating their needs—which aren't all the same, by the way," he told Sally. "But I've never worked with a student with a hearing problem—let alone someone who needs an interpreter. It's one thing to be flexible—but it's another to have to work through an interpreter all the time!"

"What do you know about Sharla?" Sally asked.

"Well, I met with Joanna Willis once already. She's the special ed teacher for students who are deaf and hard-of-hearing for our area. She met with Sharla and her family a few weeks ago. Sharla's been in public school since kindergarten, and before that she went to a special ed preschool program. The most important thing Joanna told me is that Sharla uses oral language and sign language—but I'm going to have to get used to her speech."

"And what about her achievement so far? Is she on grade level?"

"She's on level for fourth grade in most subjects. Her favorite subject is social studies, according to Joanna. She also seems to make friends easily and gets along with the other students."

"Okay," said Sally. "So you don't have to worry about a student who is far behind academically. And it sounds like you aren't facing a student who'll be difficult in terms of behavior. Did Joanna talk about any technology that Sharla uses? It seems like what you have to figure out first is how you're going to get comfortable working with an interpreter in your classroom. So, what do you think you should do?"

*There is nothing inherent in disability to produce handicap, i.e., a belief in one's incompetency.*

Burton Blatt, 1984, p. 298

"Well, I'm not sure what's next, but I think I need to meet with Joanna again right away just to talk about what it's like to work with a student who has an interpreter. I guess I need to know what my relationship is supposed to be with the interpreter. I'm just not sure. Who do I look at when I have a question? Who repeats things to me—or to Sharla—if one of us doesn't understand? What about the students' relationship to the interpreter? It's a lot to figure out."

"Yes," said Sally. "But it sounds like Joanna will be a big help, so you're not in this alone—and that's very important. It will be a challenge, but I have a feeling that once you get used to working with Sharla and her interpreter, it will just seem like part of your job. And I'm sure you and your students will all be learning sign language along the way. So think about it as an opportunity for your whole class."

You may take for granted accommodations such as interpreters for students with hearing impairments, Braille signage on elevators, curb cuts on sidewalks, public restrooms with access for those in wheelchairs, ramps to enter schools and college or university buildings, special parking places, and the right to a free public education itself for people with disabilities. But these are relatively recent developments in the United States. They are the result of several decades of political and legal activity at the state and national levels. Advocacy by and for individuals with disabilities culminated in the passage of landmark federal legislation in the 1970s that guaranteed educational services and resources for students with disabilities and the subsequent recognition of broad civil rights for all persons with disabilities.

You are beginning your career when educating students who have disabilities is both a national commitment and a legal obligation. Whether you are considering teaching in general education at the early childhood, elementary, middle school, or high school level, students with disabilities will surely be among those

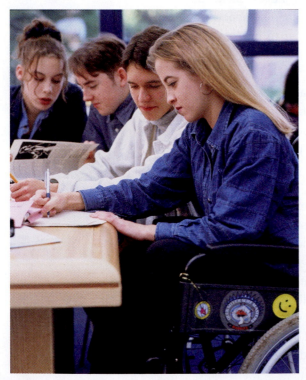

Today the majority of students with disabilities attend regular schools and participate in general education classrooms with students who do not have disabilities. (Ian Shaw/Stone/Getty Images)

you teach—as was the case in Jake Harris's class. How will you, as a novice teacher, know what to do to ensure that all of your students—including those with disabilities—learn to their maximum capacity and are challenged to reach their fullest potential? If you are thinking of becoming a special education teacher, then teaching students who have disabilities will be your primary responsibility, but you will share this responsibility with general education teachers like Jake Harris.

This chapter begins with a discussion of the evolution of the broad commitment to students with disabilities in this country, legal considerations, the roles teachers play in providing an appropriate education for students with disabilities, and the special relationships that must be forged between general and special education teachers as they work together to educate students with disabilities. We will also explore the role of technology in helping students with disabilities. In addition, although several of the issues discussed in Chapter 7 apply to students with disabilities, disability is a particular kind of diversity. We will explore similarities and differences among these different kinds of diversity in this chapter as well.

# A Broad Commitment to Equity for Students with Disabilities

Assuring an appropriate education for students with disabilities is part of a broad national commitment to civil rights and equity for individuals with disabilities. Coming on the heels of the Civil Rights era, federal legislation protecting the educational rights of students with disabilities was first passed in 1975, bringing to an end their systematic segregation in the educational system.

As you begin to think about what it might be like to work with students with disabilities, it is important to understand that as the segregation of students with disabilities has diminished, a close relationship has evolved over the past 30 years between general and special education teachers. In earlier generations, and especially before 1975, classroom teachers did not interact regularly either with special education students *or* with their teachers. Instead, students with disabilities, especially those with significant disabilities, usually attended segregated classes that were often located in the basement of the school or at the end of the hallway—if such classes even existed. Often students attended segregated schools in completely separate buildings from regular public schools. Or they attended special schools sponsored by a county or a regional special education center, or state residential schools for visually or hearing-impaired students, students with cognitive disabilities, or students with multiple disabilities. Parents might have kept their children at home altogether with some form of home-based instruction or paid for private teachers or tutors themselves. Students who attended special facilities often faced long bus rides or, in the case of state residential schools, moved away from home entirely. Some parents, having few other choices or resources, placed their children with disabilities in institutions or hospital settings.

Special education functioned much like another low, homogeneous academic track in the education system (Iano, 2004). When special education teachers did work in regular schools, they often went about their teaching quietly, separate from that of other teachers. If special education teachers worked in segregated facilities, they had virtually no interaction with general education teachers. Students with disabilities rarely studied the academic curriculum used by their peers in regular schools or classrooms and rarely interacted with students in general education classrooms who did not have disabilities. Teachers and parents rarely pushed to have students with more significant disabilities educated in general education classrooms. Students with mild disabilities that had never been identified participated in regular schools and classrooms (Sarason & Doris, 1979), without the supports and assistance afforded by today's laws and often without success.

## Your turn... *to reflect*

What personal experiences have you had with people who have disabilities? What specific challenges do you believe individuals with disabilities face in school? in social situations? in the workplace? How do these experiences contribute to your thinking about your own role as a teacher working with students with disabilities? If you have a disability yourself, how have your experiences influenced your thinking about your future work as a teacher?

Today the participation of and support for students who have disabilities is no longer considered unusual. In 2006, approximately 6 million students aged 6 through 21 received special education services; the majority spend part or all of their education in general education classrooms in our schools (United States Office of Special Education Programs, 2006). So you can see why it is so important for all teachers to think about what it means to work with students who have disabilities. In today's schools, special education and general education teachers are expected to collaborate as a matter of course, sometimes teaching together in the same classroom as they figure out the best way to support students.

As a result, it is not enough for teachers to be skilled in working with their students; they also need to be ready to work actively with other education professionals, sharing ideas, information, and solutions to problems. As you consider a career in teaching, it is important to think about the skills you will need to interact effectively with your professional peers. Later in this chapter we will explore collaboration and teamwork in greater depth, but for now you need to focus on the idea that neither special nor general education teachers work in isolation in educating students with disabilities.

## Historical Note

### Burton Blatt's Campaign to Expose Institutions for Mentally Retarded Persons

Burton Blatt was a vigorous advocate for the humane treatment of individuals with disabilities. (Syracuse University Archives)

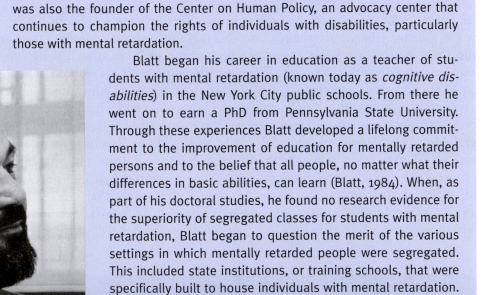

One of the foremost champions of the rights of individuals with disabilities was Burton Blatt (1927–1985). Blatt was a professor at Syracuse University from 1960 until his death and served there as the dean of the School of Education. He was also the founder of the Center on Human Policy, an advocacy center that continues to champion the rights of individuals with disabilities, particularly those with mental retardation.

Blatt began his career in education as a teacher of students with mental retardation (known today as *cognitive disabilities*) in the New York City public schools. From there he went on to earn a PhD from Pennsylvania State University. Through these experiences Blatt developed a lifelong commitment to the improvement of education for mentally retarded persons and to the belief that all people, no matter what their differences in basic abilities, can learn (Blatt, 1984). When, as part of his doctoral studies, he found no research evidence for the superiority of segregated classes for students with mental retardation, Blatt began to question the merit of the various settings in which mentally retarded people were segregated. This included state institutions, or training schools, that were specifically built to house individuals with mental retardation. Blatt was a regular visitor to institutions such as these as part of his work preparing special education teachers.

Along with his overriding belief that mentally retarded individuals could be educated, Blatt began to question the purpose of these institutions and wondered whose needs they really served. He believed that many mentally retarded persons were so labeled as a result of growing up in poverty, and, if this was the case, why was institutionalization the appropriate response? He was especially concerned about the "back wards" of these institutions, where life for residents was bleak and hopeless and, in his view, subhuman. "We began to understand," he noted, "that 'back ward life' is an invention of the nonretarded and a reflection of their character rather than a necessary concomitant to severe mental retardation. As we grew to appreciate the certainty that back wards could be eradicated, some of us learned with ever increasing anxiety and torment how truly evil these monuments to inhumanity were" (Blatt, 1984, p. 273). Blatt could find little justification for perpetuating these institutions which, by isolating those who were retarded, existed to make life easier, he believed, for those who were not.

The horrors of institutional life, combined with his passionate belief that persons with mental retardation could be educated and lead productive, if sheltered, lives, led Blatt to continue this line of study throughout his career, most of which was spent at Syracuse University. He conducted studies on the effectiveness of segregated special education classes in regular schools, questioning basic practices and identifying pitfalls, such as the following:

● The curriculum and materials were watered down versions of the regular curriculum.

● Teachers often paid greater attention to establishing control than they did to actual instruction and learning.

● Teachers and students alike demonstrated a lack of understanding of the purpose and goals of their education and were often unclear as to what came next and why (Blatt, 1984).

Blatt understood these pitfalls many years before they were accepted as a standard critique of segregated classrooms. Interestingly, it was not until the reauthorization of the federal law requiring public education for students with disabilities, in 1997, that the question of the quality of the academic curriculum finally received public attention—over 30 years after Blatt had first raised the same concerns.

In 1965, conditions surrounding mental retardation were receiving a great deal of public attention, largely as a result of the work of the Kennedy family and the very public visits Robert Kennedy was making to state institutions. During that year, Blatt teamed with photographer Fred Kaplan and gained permission to photograph the dreaded "back wards" of several of the institutions he had come to believe should not exist. Their book based on these visits, which was published in 1966, was called *Christmas in Purgatory* (Blatt & Kaplan, 1966) and was followed by a story and photographs in *Look* magazine the next year. With its publication, the story of these institutions finally broke. Their book "widely exposed the American public to the decrepit netherworld that constituted the lives of hundreds of thousands of forgotten citizens" (Kliewer, 2000, p. 59).

Blatt went on to continue his distinguished career as a passionate advocate for individuals with disabilities. He gave testimony in court cases that contributed to the passage of the first special education legislation, wrote widely to create a vision of responsible alternatives to institutionalization, and worked tirelessly in the arena of public mental health policy to support the changes he believed were essential to provide people with mental retardation with dignified lives that maximized their potential to live well in the world. He continued his work until his premature death at the age of 57.

Burton Blatt was one of the great humanitarians in the history of special education. He was a visionary for what special education could be: humane, individualized, progressive, and based on the fundamental belief that every human being is worthy of respect. He understood that large institutions, by their very nature, were warehouses for human beings and could not be humane places. Instead, he advocated community-based residential programming to meet the needs of individuals with mental retardation.

In his years at Syracuse, Blatt taught many students who are now leaders in special education and who carry on his legacy of advocating for the rights of individuals with disabilities across the country. Those who were not privileged to work with him often lamented their lost opportunity. Christopher Kliewer (2000) writes:

> I wish I had known Burton Blatt, the researcher, philosopher, essayist, poet, theologian, journalistic muckraker, advocate, and above all, teacher. His death in 1985 eliminated the possibility that I might join him in an earthly discussion—there in the early morning hours when he would arrive at his office, the sun just beginning to rise, the smell of pipe tobacco surrounding him, pen in hand, as he exchanged countless correspondence with children, colleagues, and friends around the world. I would have liked to lean forward and asked him, "How have we improved, if at all? Where do we go from here?" More selfishly, "Am I making a difference?" (p. 59)

### Critical Term

**Individuals with Disabilities Education Act (IDEA).** Federal legislation protecting the rights of students with disabilities to receive a free, appropriate education that meets their needs.

### Critical Term

**Americans with Disabilities Act (ADA).** Federal legislation protecting the rights of children and adults with disabilities in society at large, rather than only in educational settings.

During the late 1960s and early 1970s, families of school-aged students with disabilities, as well as adults with disabilities, lobbied tirelessly for the passage of legislation protecting their civil and educational rights.
(Corbis Bettmann)

## Federal Mandates for Equity

In 1975, Congress passed Public Law 94–142, the Education of All Handicapped Children Act, which mandated equity in education for children with disabilities from birth through age 21. Over time, the name of this legislation was changed to the **Individuals with Disabilities Education Act** (**IDEA**), the title by which it is known today. IDEA was reauthorized in 1997, at which time Congress for the first time paid special attention to ensuring that students with disabilities had access to the same academic curriculum that students without disabilities were expected to learn. This was an important change in the law; it raised expectations for what students with disabilities could achieve in school. The law was again reauthorized in 2004, with particular attention being paid to, among other issues, improving the quality of special education teachers.

In 1990, Congress passed a second far-reaching piece of legislation, known as the **Americans with Disabilities Act** (**ADA**), which guarantees civil rights to individuals with disabilities beyond the realm of education and prohibits discrimination against them. The ADA is meant to ensure reasonable accommodations for people with disabilities to enable them to participate in the everyday life of the society. These two laws, IDEA and ADA, combined to set a new standard for the place of individuals with disabilities within our society and provided definition to the work of special and general education teachers alike.

The IDEA legislation is based on several important principles. These principles represent legal obligations; if parents and families of students with disabilities, or the school, disagree with the way a student's situation is handled, the rights of due process according to the law must be applied. The principles include the following:

- Students with disabilities must be given a free, appropriate education; everyone must be included.
- Their education should be provided in the **least restrictive environment (LRE)** so that students with disabilities can interact with their peers who do not have disabilities and, as much as possible, learn the general education curriculum.
- Students with disabilities must receive educational and related services (e.g., occupational therapy) stated in a formal document known as an **Individualized Education Plan (IEP)**.
- Parents and families must be included in planning for the education of students with disabilities.
- When evaluating students for a possible disability, that evaluation must not be biased and must be conducted in a manner that does not discriminate against students owing to their race, ethnicity, or language.

But what do these principles mean for teachers? Table 8-1 identifies several implications of the law that apply to general education and special education teachers alike. Both have responsibilities related to carrying out these principles, though from different perspectives. Together they work to ensure that they provide a high-quality education for students with disabilities.

**Critical Term**

**Least restrictive environment (LRE).** Students with disabilities are to be educated in the learning environment that poses the fewest restrictions on their lives as students and that provides the most opportunities for interaction with nondisabled peers.

**Critical Term**

**Individualized Education Plan (IEP).** A legal document defining the educational program and related services for a specific student who has a disability.

## Table 8-1    The Major Principles of IDEA and Their Implications for Teachers

Special education legislation creates certain specific responsibilities for general and special education teachers in their work with students who have disabilities.

| IDEA Principle | Implications for Teachers |
| --- | --- |
| Nondiscriminatory evaluation | If you're thinking of referring a child to be evaluated for a possible disability, have you asked yourself the following questions: (1) If English is not this child's first language, might I be confusing his or her need to learn English with a real learning problem? (2) Could this child be displaying behaviors that are appropriate to his or her cultural background—but that I may not understand because I'm unfamiliar with them? As a special education teacher, am I using evaluation tools that are not discriminatory? |
| Free, appropriate education | For my students who are identified as having a disability, have I looked at their IEPs? Am I familiar with the educational goals and related services? Have I set high expectations for this student's learning? Have I talked with the special education teacher (or if you are a special education teacher, to the general education teacher) so our work is coordinated to best help the student? |
| Least restrictive environment (LRE) | Are my students who have identified disabilities full members of my classroom? Are they included—not just tolerated—in all classroom activities and events? Have I helped establish friendships between students who do and do not have disabilities? If you are a special education teacher, are you familiar enough with the general education curriculum to make learning it meaningful and possible for students with disabilities? |
| Parent and family participation | Do I stay in close contact with the families of my students with disabilities? Do I coordinate family meetings with the special/general education teacher? Do I listen to the concerns of the family and learn about the student from them? |

One of the most familiar terms with regard to special education—and one of the most hotly debated topics—is *inclusion*. The least restrictive environment (LRE) principle is the basis of the preference for including students with disabilities in general education classrooms. This preference stems from the belief that general education classrooms provide the greatest opportunity for interaction among students with and without disabilities, as well as the greatest chance for students with disabilities to have access to and learn the general education curriculum. LRE does not mean that all students with disabilities *must* be educated in general education classrooms. Reasonable people both within and outside of special education disagree on this issue, as we will see later in this chapter. The preference for the general education classroom is also not intended to mean that students with disabilities are placed into general education classrooms without the support of special education teachers and other professionals who work with students with disabilities.

What is important is that no longer is the only readily available choice for students with disabilities a highly restrictive or segregated educational setting. Instead, a continuum of possibilities exists, ranging from full-time enrollment in a general education classroom with support as needed, as we shall see in the Case in Point below, to special facilities for students with more significant, complex disabilities. Despite the existence of the full range of educational environments, a preference—but not a requirement—does exist for the general education classroom as the optimal educational setting for most students with disabilities.

## A Case In Point
### Daniel Greenwood

To understand the tremendous impact of changes in special education over the past 30 years, consider the situation of Daniel Greenwood, a middle school student who is paraplegic but has no cognitive disability. He uses a wheelchair but has full use of his arms. Daniel is fully capable of participating in all of the learning activities in the classroom with no special accommodations other than needing to move around the classroom in his wheelchair and to have access to appropriate locations in the school with occasional assistance (i.e., office, restroom, cafeteria, nurse's office, etc.). He attends his neighborhood middle school, participates in all general education classes, and is a member of the school's choir and student council. He travels between the floors of his school in an elevator that was installed during the school's last renovation as required by the ADA, and he enters the school through wide doorways that were similarly installed at that time.

Before IDEA and ADA, schools were not required to accommodate students who were in wheelchairs. Because most schools were inaccessible to all students in wheelchairs, parents who wanted their children to attend a school and participate in the general education school curriculum were rarely able to have them do so. Before 1975, Daniel would not likely have had any access to equal education—not to the curriculum, not to the able-bodied peer population, not to general education classroom teachers, not to the extracurricular activities sponsored by the school—with his able-bodied peers, the regular teaching staff, and the day-to-day activities in his school. Even after the law was passed, students who needed schools to be accessible structurally often could choose only from among a handful of a district's schools that could accommodate wheelchairs and could not often attend their neighborhood school—a restricted form of accessibility.

Daniel is now able to take full advantage of the educational resources afforded to his able-bodies peers and to contribute to his school as well. Not only does he have the opportunity to participate in the social, intellectual, and extracurricular life of his school, but his peers also can develop relationships with Daniel as a friend, classmate, and peer in after-school activities. In earlier generations, interaction with individuals with disabilities usually occurred only within the family, often hidden from the day-to-day activities of society. The possibilities for creating friendships and for enriching one another's lives was restricted by institutional barriers that prevented interaction between individuals who did and did not have disabilities. For Daniel and his friends, this is no longer the case.

Chances are that you yourself attended public school after passage of the 1975 legislation and perhaps also after passage of the ADA. If so, you probably do not find it remarkable that students with and without disabilities attend school together. Like Daniel Greenwood and his friends, you and your friends may represent a generation in which students with and without disabilities interacted readily and developed friendships both inside and outside of the classroom.

## From Birth to Work: Extending the Age Range of Students in School

Typically, public education begins at age 4 or 5 and ends at age 18. For students with disabilities, a free, appropriate education begins at birth and extends to age 21. Beginning at birth, special education provides **early intervention** services to ensure that children get a strong start. For students aged 18 to 21, special education provides **transition services** to plan for what will happen once the student leaves school.

**Early Intervention.** Young children with disabilities benefit from intervention at the earliest of ages, and often from birth, to improve their level of functioning. The majority of early intervention services for infants and toddlers who have disabilities, nearly 80 percent, take place in the home with the assistance of special education professionals (United States Department of Education, 2007). Preschool programs served approximately 680,000 children between the ages of 3 and 5 during 2003; of these, 34 percent attended a regular early childhood program, 32 percent attended an early childhood special education program, and 16 percent spent time in both settings (United States Department of Education, 2007).

If you are planning to be an early childhood teacher, it is especially important to understand the benefits of early intervention. Early childhood education teachers in preschools and kindergartens increasingly work with students who have disabilities and have the opportunity to contribute directly to providing early intervention programs.

> **Critical Term**
>
> **Early intervention.** Special education services for young children from birth to age 5.

> **Critical Term**
>
> **Transition services.** Special education services to help adolescents and young adults with disabilities make the transition from the school setting to the "real world" of work and living away from home, whether in a protected or a completely independent living or work situation.

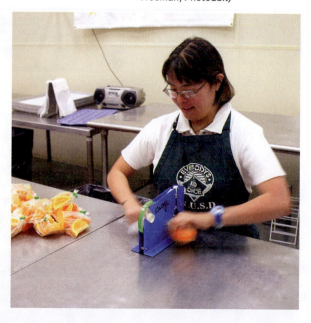

Students with disabilities can attend school until the age of 21 and, during their high school years, often are prepared for the transition to the world of work. (Tony Freeman/PhotoEdit)

**Transition Services.** Students with disabilities usually require special support to make the best transition possible from the relatively sheltered world of schooling to the more challenging adult world of work and independent living. Depending on the nature of the disability, students who are leaving high school, together with their families, require different kinds of support. If the student can live independently, transition support might involve finding an appropriate job. If the student cannot live independently, transition planning might involve finding a group-living situation and a work environment that provides support for adults with disabilities.

## Your turn... *to review*

1. What are the names of the two major pieces of federal legislation protecting the rights of individuals with disabilities?
2. What was the main focus of Burton Blatt's criticism of services for people with cognitive disabilities?
3. What does the term *least restrictive environment* refer to?

If you are planning to be a high school teacher, you may be working with students who are over the typical high school graduation age of 18. Although your job will not involve providing direct support for transition, you may be collaborating with special education teachers who work with students and their families on the transition from school to adult living and work.

Early intervention and transition services are part of the broad legislation that was enacted to ensure that people with disabilities would no longer be marginalized in our society—whether in the schools, the workforce, transportation, or social, cultural, and entertainment opportunities. As a result, our expectations as a society have changed, and we now assume that people with disabilities will be participating in our society and in our schools. In the schools, however, the question of how much inclusion is enough—or too much—continues to be debated.

## Philosophical Note
### The Inclusion Movement

With passage of the first federal special education legislation in 1975, the philosophy of educating students with disabilities changed radically from a philosophy of segregation to a philosophy of integration. The original term used to describe this new philosophy was "mainstreaming," which meant that students with disabilities were entering the mainstream of American schooling. Under the mainstreaming philosophy, increasing numbers of students began to spend at least part of their day in the general education classroom and continued to receive a portion of special education services in part-time segregated classrooms. Others continued being educated in segregated settings. The trend toward placing students with disabilities in general education classrooms was beginning to be established.

Today the term used to describe the integration of students who require special education in our schools is " inclusion," or "inclusive education," which signifies a preference for most, if not all, special education services to be delivered in the general education setting, with special education teachers often working directly in the general classroom setting. Two important philosophical goals are foundational to the inclusion movement: first, students with disabilities should be educated with their peers who do not have disabilities, and second, the academic goal should be to learn the general education curriculum as much as possible.

The overarching theme of the efforts that have led to today's emphasis on inclusion is the increased participation of those with disabilities as members in a community of learners and in society (Sailor, 2002). Few would argue that the goal of integrating individuals with disabilities into society and guaranteeing their civil rights is anything but appropriate. However, inclusion as an educational philosophy continues to divide special and general education teachers alike and the families of students who require special education. These divisions occur in regard to questions such as: Just how much inclusion is appropriate? Is full inclusion the goal for all students, that is, spending all day, every day, in general education classrooms with appropriate supports? Is it appropriate for any student with a disability to receive some of his or her education in a segregated setting? Can the philosophical goals of inclusion be met if we persist in educating students with disabilities apart from their nondisabled peers?

At one end of the philosophical spectrum are those who believe that anything that diminishes the participation of students with disabilities in general education is unacceptable. For example, the goal of having all students with disabilities attend their neighborhood school, which has long been viewed as a hallmark of a normalized place for students with disabilities in education and society, has not yet been realized. When students with similar disabilities are grouped together in particular schools, which is practical administratively, their presence is typically disproportionate to their presence in the population at large. Those who support full inclusion are committed to ensuring that students with disabilities do not experience the hardship, shame, and discrimination often associated with segregated settings, as well as the lowered expectations for achievement in academics or in life skills that have historically accompanied these segregated educational experiences. Supporters of full inclusion press for general education teachers to acquire greater skills and comfort levels in providing educational services to students with disabilities, with support from a special education teacher. The goal is to put all of the necessary supports in place within the general education setting, including all of the related services that a particular student with disabilities might require.

On the other end of the spectrum are those who believe that inclusion will result in the demise of special education services as represented by special part- and full-time classrooms, as well as the services of special education teachers, for students with disabilities. Proponents of this position do not want to see a return to the days of segregating students with disabilities in substandard institutions and classrooms. But they are concerned about preserving the hard-won gains that have finally resulted in specially designated special education services and a strong special education identity (e.g., Fuchs & Fuchs, 1994). If inclusion in general education is deemed good public policy, is it not possible, they argue, that many schools and school districts might systematically reduce the number of special education teachers needed to support students with disabilities and instead assume that general education classroom teachers will be able to provide these same services alone? This is not the intent of the federal legislation, which definitively states that special education and related services should be provided. However, in tight fiscal times school districts might assume that students with disabilities can be well supported in general education with fewer special education services and resources.

A second argument raised by opponents of full inclusion is that general education teachers may not be up to the challenge of providing good instruction to students with disabilities (Fuchs & Fuchs, 1994). Therefore, is it not better to pull students back into part- or full-time special education classrooms where, it is argued, they will receive the same high-quality education they have always received? This argument is based on the contested assumption that the quality of education within segregated special education classrooms was uniformly high before the inclusive education movement started. It is also based on the contested assumption that general education classroom teachers are not prepared to be flexible and accommodating in their classroom organizational and instructional decisions or are not willing to work collaboratively with special education teachers. Some believe that this is a paternalistic position, based on the belief that only special education teachers really care about students with disabilities and are the only ones who are committed to providing the kind of educational environment that is required.

Although most students with disabilities can be well educated in general education settings, at times special assistance may be required and may be beneficial. How does this fit in with the philosophy of inclusion? Students with disabilities must be full, participating members of a classroom and school community, a community in which all members, at one time or another, based on their individual needs, may receive some type of special service to enable them to succeed—either inside the general education classroom or with specialized help. That service may be provided by a special education teacher, by a school psychologist, or by a school technology specialist. Students who have other needs, for example, the services of a specialist in English as a Second Language, may also leave the classroom for short periods of time. First and foremost, it is critical that the student be treated as a fully participating member of the classroom community, not a periodic visitor whose "real" education happens only when a special education teacher is present.

An important challenge for teachers and schools, then, is to reflect on the kind of community and education the school is providing. Are students with disabilities regularly interacting with their nondisabled peers? Are accommodations made in all areas for students with disabilities? If a student leaves to get special assistance, how do the other students and the teacher view the student who leaves? How do they welcome that student when he or she returns? How do they respond when an accommodation is made? For example, in a suburban high school an accommodation was made for a member of the boys' volleyball team so that a student who had a mild physical disability remained on the junior varsity team for all four years and served as team captain in his senior year, even though the general rule was that seniors could not play on the JV team. He was realistic about his physical limitations but loved the game and wanted to play throughout his high school career. He was an accepted member of his sport, and both the school and the coach believed this accommodation was good for the student, the team, and the school. This student required an accommodation but otherwise no special attention. What he did require was a high level of acceptance for the accommodation.

Many proponents of inclusion argue that the reform of schools for all students is essential to achieving the goals of inclusion (Brantlinger, 1997; Iano, 2004). How does the school approach issues of community and belonging for all of its students, not just those with disabilities?

It was not that long ago that teachers didn't even have to think about teaching students with disabilities—it just didn't happen. Today, as a society, we have begun to accept the responsibility for integrating people with disabilities, and specifically for educating students with disabilities in the public schools. Whether society will achieve the goals of those who favor full inclusion, completely eradicating the need for any segregation for people who have disabilities, is not clear. But the movement toward inclusivity continues and presents a challenge for special and general education teachers alike. How successful educators are in advancing this goal depends on the efforts of every teacher and administrator who is committed to educating students with disabilities.

## Does Labeling Students with Disabilities Help or Hinder a Teacher's Work?

When we talk about teaching students with disabilities, who exactly are we talking about? Of the wide range of students teachers work with, who exactly is included under the federal laws governing special education?

Every child who receives special education services goes through a formal process in which he or she is identified as a student with a disability and is assigned to a specific disability category. It is on this basis that the federal government calculates the amount of additional funding states receive to help support special education. The 6.7 million students aged 3 through 21 who were served under the IDEA law in 2005–2006 represented approximately 14 percent of the total school population; of these, white students made up about 60 percent of the students served; 20 percent were African American; 16 percent Hispanic; 2 percent Asian/Pacific Islander; and 1 percent American Indian/Alaska Native (United States Department of Education, 2007). Table 8-2 shows the changes in the number of students served in special education between 1995 and 2006. Specific categories of disability that are recognized in the federal law are listed and defined in Table 8-3.

Nearly forty-one percent of all students who were identified as needing special education services in 2005–2006 were in the category of specific learning disabilities; approximately 22 percent more fell into the category of speech and language impairments (United States Department of Education, 2007). Along with mild forms of mental retardation

The type of disability a student has can tell you some important things about how to educate that student, but that information doesn't take the place of a teacher learning about each student as an individual person and learner. (Ellen Senisi/The Image Works)

**Table 8-2    Changes in the Number of Students aged 3–21 Served in Special Education Between 1995 and 2006 (in thousands)**

From 1995 to 2006 there has been an increase in nearly every category of disability.

| Disability | 1995–1996 | 2005–2006 |
|---|---|---|
| Specific learning disabilities | 578,000 | 735,000 |
| Speech or language impairments | 1,022,000 | 1,468,000 |
| Mental retardation | 571,000 | 556,000 |
| Emotional disturbance | 437,000 | 477,000 |
| Other health impairments | 133,000 | 570,000 |
| Multiple disabilities | 93,000 | 141,000 |
| Hearing impairments | 67,000 | 79,000 |
| Orthopedic impairments | 63,000 | 71,000 |
| Visual impairments | 25,000 | 29,000 |
| Autism | 28,000 | 223,000 |
| Traumatic brain injury | 9,000 | 24,000 |
| Deaf-blindness | 1,000 | 2,000 |
| Developmental delay | — | 339,000 |
| All disabilities | 5,572,000 | 6,713,000 |

**Note:** Reporting for development delay began in 1997.
**Source:** United States Department of Education. (2007). Digest of Education Statistics. *Children 3–21 years old served in federally funded programs for the disabled, by type or disability: Selected Years.* Washington, DC: U.S. Department of Education Institute of Education Sciences. Retrived May 13, 2008, from www.nces.ed.gov.

**Critical Term**

**High-incidence disabilities.** Disabilities that occur with relative frequency in the population, for example, learning disabilities and speech and language impairments; often referred to as mild disabilities.

**Critical Term**

**Low-incidence disabilities.** Disabilities that occur with relative infrequency in the population, for example, cerebral palsy or deafness.

and emotional disturbance, these four categories account for most students served under IDEA—roughly 80 percent in 2005–2006 (United States Department of Education, 2007). These disabilities are sometimes referred to as mild or **high-incidence disabilities** because compared with other disabilities such as vision or hearing impairment, they occur relatively frequently in the population. Most mild disabilities are not apparent until students are in school and encounter the school curriculum and the school's academic and behavioral expectations. Statistically speaking, 1 out of every 10 students is likely to have some kind of disability, though usually a mild disability.

In contrast, disabilities that occur infrequently in the population are often referred to as **low-incidence disabilities**. In 2007, the nine other categories of disability that appear in Table 8-3 and that may be considered low incidence together constituted only roughly 20 percent of the remaining students who were identified and received special education.

How helpful are these categories of disability for you as a prospective teacher? What kind of information do they provide you with as you plan your instruction? To what extent are these labels useful, and to what extent might they actually be a hindrance to teachers and students?

**Table 8-3    Categories of Disability as Defined in the Individuals with Disabilities Education Act (IDEA. Part 300.7)**

The categories used by individual states may not reflect the specific language of these federal categories of disability.

| Disability Category | Definition of Disability |
|---|---|
| Autism | A developmental disability significantly affecting verbal and nonverbal communication and social interaction, generally evident before age 3. |
| Deaf-blindness | Hearing and visual impairments that in combination cause such severe communication and other developmental and educational needs that they cannot be accommodated in programs solely for children with deafness or blindness. |
| Deafness | Hearing impairment that is so severe that the child is impaired in processing linguistic information through hearing, with or without amplification. |
| Speech and language disorder | A communication disorder, such as stuttering, impaired articulation, a language impairment, or a voice impairment. |
| Hearing impairment | An impairment in hearing, whether permanent or fluctuating, that is not included under the definition of deafness. |
| Mental retardation | Significantly subaverage general intellectual functioning, existing concurrently with deficits in adaptive behavior and manifested during the developmental period. |
| Multiple disabilities | Impairments that occur together, the combination of which causes such severe educational needs that they cannot be accommodated in programs solely for one of the impairments, not including deaf-blindness. |
| Orthopedic impairment | A severe orthopedic impairment, including impairments caused by congenital anomaly, disease, and other causes. |
| Other health impairment | Having limited strength, vitality, or alertness, including a heightened alertness to environmental stimuli, that results in limited alertness with respect to the educational environment, due to chronic or acute health problems. |
| Serious emotional disturbance | One or more of the following characteristics over a long period of time and to a marked degree that adversely affects a child's educational performance: inability to learn that cannot be explained by intellectual, sensory, or health factors; inability to build or maintain satisfactory interpersonal relationships with peers and teachers; inappropriate types of behavior or feelings under normal circumstances; general pervasive mood of unhappiness or depression; tendency to develop physical symptoms or fears associated with personal or school problems. Includes schizophrenia but not children who are socially maladjusted, unless they have an emotional disturbance. |
| Specific learning disability | A disorder in one or more of the basic psychological processes involved in understanding or in using language, spoken or written, that may manifest itself in an imperfect ability to listen, think, speak, read, write, spell, or do mathematical calculations; learning problems are not the result of other disabilities or environmental, cultural, or economic disadvantage. |
| Traumatic brain injury | An acquired injury to the brain caused by an external physical force, resulting in total or partial functional disability or psychosocial impairment, or both. Does not apply to brain injuries that are congenital or degenerative, or to brain injuries induced by birth trauma. |
| Visual impairment including blindness | An impairment in vision that, even with correction, adversely affects a child's educational performance; includes both partial sight and blindness. |

**Source:** Individuals with Disabilities Education Act, 1997, 34CFR Part 300.7.

## What Disability Categories Do and Do Not Provide for Teachers

Disability categories are important to school districts because to receive federal funds, districts must count and report their special education student population annually according to the federal categories. They therefore have an important fiscal and administrative purpose. When it comes to helping teachers make specific decisions about how to instruct their students, however, categorical labels are less helpful to teachers than it would first appear. That is, knowing a student's disability label does not necessarily give a teacher much help in planning instruction.

A disability category provides teachers with a general idea of the challenges a student might face. It points you as a teacher in a general direction, and it gives you an idea of the general scope of the adjustments you may have to make. For students with more significant disabilities, a teacher can make some early judgments about what modifications might be needed. You can anticipate, for example, that a student with a visual impairment might require seating adjustments, large computer fonts, or print-to-voice software programs to facilitate responding to and completing written work. For a student who has a physical disability and uses a wheelchair, you will have to rethink the arrangement of the room. For a student with a hearing impairment who uses the services of an interpreter, as we saw in Jake's classroom when his student Sharla was about to arrive, it may take some adjustment to become comfortable working together. If a child struggles with a specific aspect of the curriculum owing to a learning disability, you will likely need to make some accommodations in how you teach and assess the curriculum. Students with significant multiple disabilities—especially when impaired cognitive functioning is part of the disability—may need a heavily adapted general education curriculum or a different curriculum altogether—one that emphasizes daily functional tasks and skills.

These general understandings of what you may need to do to enable a student with disabilities to be a full member of your classroom community and achieve in the curriculum are just that—general understandings. They tell you very little about the specific needs of the students in terms of who they are as unique individuals and as learners, which is the starting point for planning instruction. What students may need as a result of a disability will be influenced not only by their disability, but also by their unique intellectual ability, personality, style, likes and dislikes, ethnicity, culture, language, and life experience. A student's disability is only one part of his or her identity and personal makeup. A disability label does not tell you how smart students are, their friendship patterns, what sports they like, what they like to eat, what movies they like, what their dreams are for the future. It also does not tell you how students learn and how the classroom and the curriculum may have to be modified to help them learn. Furthermore, within each category of disability, the degree of a student's difficulties related to the disability differs for every child.

Lukas Bratcher is a high school student who happens to have a disability—but what impresses his teachers most is his commitment to a career in music. You can  find Lukas' story at **http://www.edutopia.org** under the Video Library link and see how technology—and the support of his teachers—enabled him to be a full member of his high school's music program.

## How Disability Labels Can Lead to Inequities

A teacher's first responsibility to all students in the classroom is to get to know every student well in order make informed judgments about students' learning needs and to establish a positive social environment in the classroom. The problem with labels arises when teachers—either special education teachers or general education classroom teachers—think of students only or chiefly in terms of their disabilities, rather than in terms of who they are as individuals who also happen to have disabilities. Thinking about the disability label first—instead of the student—can lead to serious inequities that can easily disadvantage students with disabilities.

Unfortunately, the history of education for students with disabilities has too often been based on teachers making generalizations about what students need socially and academically, as well as about their capacities for learning and participation based solely on their disability label. Teachers may, for example, set lower expectations for what students are capable of achieving—socially as well as academically—based on their disability label. They may assume that they themselves are incapable of working effectively with a student who has disabilities based on the label. Or teachers may be swayed by the negative reactions or opinions of some of their peers who themselves feel uncomfortable or unwilling to welcome and work with a student who has disabilities. These responses can easily lead to negative school experiences for students with disabilities. At the extreme, some critics of special education have argued that if schools in general were more adaptable to all students, special education itself might not be needed (Skrtic, 1991).

For example, when a teacher does not actively facilitate friendships between students with and without disabilities, that teacher is operating on the basis of a hidden curriculum that communicates to every student that some of them are more valued in the classroom than others. In this way the teacher is isolating students with disabilities. When teachers simply "tolerate" the presence of a student with a disability but do not plan instruction to include the modifications a student needs, the student's chances for success are diminished. Attitudes like these are not healthy for a teacher to communicate about any student, but for students who may be marginalized anyway because of a disability, the consequences may be even more harmful. The message teachers send to their students with and without disabilities in this case may be, "I'm not particularly interested in having a student with a disability in my class."

In addition to providing only limited information to teachers, relying on category labels presents several other problems, as illustrated in Table 8-4. As this table indicates, the use of categories is not neat and clean. That is, categories of disability are not mutually exclusive; sometimes characteristics overlap, and what is good practice for a student with one kind of disability may also be effective for students with other kinds of disabilities (or students with no disabilities at all). Sometimes, too, children with the same disability will have different characteristics. Labels also change over time as new disabilities are identified.

Despite strict definitions under IDEA, the process of identifying students within categories of mild disabilities can be inconsistent. For example, a racial or ethnic minority student may be identified as having an emotional disorder in one school or school district but not in another, which can lead to the disproportionate representation of racial and ethnic minority students in special education. Even though the law is meant to protect students from discrimination in the identification process, the disproportionate representation of racial and ethnic minority students in special education persists (Donovan & Cross, 2002). This problem reinforces the need for teachers to practice culturally responsive teaching.

**Your turn...** *to reflect*

Divide your class into groups and have each group carefully read the limitations of the use of labels for making teaching decisions and the implications for teachers as illustrated in Table 8-4. Are some arguments more convincing than others? Why?

**Table 8-4** **The Limitations of Disability Labels for Helping Teachers Make Instructional Decisions**

Categories and labels can point teachers in a general direction, but it is essential to consider each child as an individual to determine what approach is appropriate.

| Problems with Disability Labels (Council of Chief State School Officers, 2001, p. 8) | Implications for Teachers |
|---|---|
| A specific disability can manifest itself in individual children in a tremendous range of ways and across a continuum from mild to severe. | The same disability may look different for each student with that label, so it is not possible to make generalizations about what kinds of teaching may work best. All students are individuals even though they may have the same disability label. |
| Students with different disabilities often have characteristics that overlap, making identification more complex. | Knowing that a specific student has a specific characteristic does not necessarily mean that he or she has a particular disability. Making judgments about categories of disabilities based on one characteristic is not appropriate. |
| Students may have multiple disabilities and specialized needs that cross disability categories. | If a student has more than one disability, decisions about what to teach need to take into account not only the two disabilities separately, but also how they interact and how this affects the student's needs. |
| The operational definitions of specific disabilities vary from state to state and district to district. | Even though there is a set of federal definitions for disability categories, states can develop their own classification systems that can be similar to or very different from federal definitions. What qualifies as a disability in one state may not qualify in another state. This means that definitions are not consistent. |
| Educational practices may be similar for individual students with different disabilities. | What works well instructionally for a student with learning disabilities may also work well for a student with mild mental retardation. The category label does not provide a mutually exclusive set of instructional practices that can be counted on to work effectively only with that disability. |
| Certain minority groups are disproportionately represented in specific disability categories. | When members of certain minority groups are overrepresented in categories of disability, one has to ask whether it is a disability or whether the identification procedures are unduly biased against students in those groups. Teachers must ask themselves whether the student actually has a disability or not. |
| An increasing number of students have disabling conditions that do not fit well within the traditional disability categories. | The original set of categories developed by the federal government does not account for new manifestations of disabilities that may develop within the school-aged population. Teachers need to be flexible in responding to the development of new categories that may require new instructional approaches. |

**Source:** The Interstate New Teacher Assessment and Support Consortium (INTASC) standards were developed by the Council of Chief State School Officers and member states. Copies may be downloaded from the Council's website at http://www.ccsso.org. Council of Chief State School Officers. (2001). *Model standards for licensing general and special education teachers of students with disabilities: A resource for state dialogue.* Washington, DC: Author. http://www.ccsso.org/content/pdfs/spedstds.pdf.

## Simplifying the Categories

Because of the problems associated with labeling, some states have moved away from the use of the federal disability classification system and toward a system that provides only a few general disability categories or a single category denoting that a student will require special education services. Each state decides the kind of classification system it wishes to use. Many states have selected systems that downplay categorical labels as a way to encourage teachers to focus on individual students' needs rather than needs that are presumed to exist because of a particular disability label. States still have to report students by federal disability categories, but for practical purposes, states may use many different systems.

As a result, in some states a child may be seen as a child with a *learning disability*, while in another state this same child might be said to have a *mild disability* (a more general term), and in yet another state the same child might simply be identified as a *child with special needs*. In Missouri and Iowa, students are identified by the educational environment or classroom setting they need, and not by a disability label at all. In Missouri a student might be in a classification indicating that he or she is educated outside of the general education classroom for less than 21 percent of the day. This information gives a teacher some idea of the degree of special assistance the student might require outside of the general education classroom.

States also decide the kinds of licenses they will issue to special education teachers. In some states, a special education teacher might be licensed to teach students across several disability categories in grades PK–12. In other states, licenses may be organized strictly according to disability category and age (for example, an elementary license for learning disabilities). States may follow a two-category system of licensing, one for teachers of students with mild disabilities and another for teachers of students with more severe disabilities. In some states, you need a general education teaching license before you can obtain a special education license, and in others you do not.

The federal government is also starting to move away from a strict reliance on specific categories of disability. Since 1997, it has been possible to identify young children with disabilities who need special education services as having a **developmental delay** rather than belonging to a specific disability category. A developmental delay means that a young child is not reaching typical developmental milestones and requires early intervention services to help in his or her development. When young children are identified as having a developmental delay, they can be eligible to receive special education services but they do not have to be identified as belonging to a specific category of disability, and perhaps avoid being judged prematurely or stereotypically by doing so. Children through age 9 can be identified as developmentally delayed and still receive the benefits of federal funding for special education services.

**Critical Term**

**Developmental delay.** A term used to describe children who are not reaching typical developmental milestones and who may, based on such a delay, be eligible to receive special education services.

## The Teacher's Role

The mere passage of legislation, however great a landmark in society, does not in and of itself solve the problems of the marginalization of people with disabilities, much as neither the decision in *Brown v. Board of Education* in 1954 nor the civil rights legislation passed in the 1960s ended the marginalization of African American students or racial discrimination. The culture of our schools has improved significantly for students with disabilities in terms of access to public schools and to general education classes. The challenge for teachers and administrators is to

# REWARDS AND CHALLENGES

## Meeting Students' Diverse Instructional Needs

Kate Flanagan
*San Francisco*

Each year that I have taught fifth grade, I have had students with disabilities in my classroom. I have had "resource students" who were pulled out of class a few times a week to get extra help, and "inclusion" students who had a paraprofessional with them almost the whole day in my classroom to help modify their work and give them one-on-one assistance. I have also had "emotionally disturbed" students in my classroom.

It is often a challenge to reach the needs of all the learners in the classroom. It can be just as challenging to reach the needs of the gifted student as it can the student who struggles because of a disability. Harder still is the challenge of addressing the needs of all students at once, from the student who reads far below grade level, to the student who reads far above grade level.

I have found that differentiating instruction and providing a classroom climate of acceptance and appreciation for all learners have been the most helpful tools for success. I often use cooperative groups in my teaching, where every student has a job to do, one that I know they will be able to succeed at. In addition, I modify the core curriculum for my students with disabilities and my gifted students, to encourage high expectations and success for both groups.

It is important to create the type of classroom community where all learners feel safe and respected. At the beginning of the year, I spend a lot of time building this type of climate,

through partner and group work, with much cooperation and sharing. My school is a TRIBES school, which means that we spend a lot of time community building. We take our agreements about treating each other with mutual respect very seriously. We find each other's strengths and create opportunities to appreciate these strengths. Once this type of community is created, the students are happy to help each other and to work together. They know that their personal goal is not necessarily the goal of another student.

It can be very challenging reaching the needs of all students in a classroom. Still, with each challenge, there is a reward. This year, I often worried about one of my lowest level students, as he came into my fifth grade reading at first grade level. I worried about how I would meet his needs and be able to teach him fifth grade standards. Luckily, he had a para-professional to work with him and help to modify the curriculum for him. By the end of this year, with increased independence, he was able to read, research, write a draft, and type a five paragraph biography of his hero and then read this out loud to the class. He was glad to be doing what the other students were doing. Hearing the appreciations for his work from his classmates made him very proud. He even asked for a copy of his paper to give to both of his grandmothers. At times like this, the rewards of teaching students with disabilities easily outweigh the challenges.  ●

guarantee that students with disabilities are not simply *present* in the educational system, but that they receive a high-quality education that meets their needs and challenges them educationally. What must general and special education teachers do to make this happen?

## Building Classroom Communities Where Students with Disabilities Belong

Your first responsibility as a general education classroom teacher will be to welcome students who have disabilities into your classroom and make sure they are fully integrated into your classroom community. This responsibility challenges you to think about how you, and your students who do not have disabilities, interact with students who do. What friendship patterns exist in your classroom between your students with and without disabilities? What leadership roles do you make available to students with disabilities? How do your students learn to work together and support each other across the differences they each bring to the classroom? This commitment means that you, as the classroom teacher, understand that students with disabilities are *your* students—even if they work with both you and a special education teacher. They are not guests or occasional visitors in your classroom; rather, they are students who may receive additional help from other teachers from the home base of your (and their) classroom.

And if you are a special education teacher, one of your roles will be to work with the general education classroom teacher to support students with disabilities in their social interactions, to know the students in their classrooms, and to build their confidence in the classroom as a social setting.

## Being Flexible and Accommodating for Students with Disabilities

Your second responsibility is to be flexible in making accommodations and modifications in all aspects of your classroom operation in order to help students with disabilities access and learn the curriculum. In each class, you will have students who will need varying amounts of individual assistance with issues of learning and/or behavior in order to be successful—whether or not these students have disabilities. So you need to be prepared to adjust the kinds of support you provide to meet the range of student needs in every class you teach. Some students will learn easily and will need only you to set the stage; these students will "run" with the work you have structured for them. Other students will need you to break down the learning task in more detail and provide explicit directions on how to perform each aspect of the task. Some students will be able to work independently for long periods of time and will require less frequent feedback from you than other students; others will need to know exactly how they are doing each step of the way.

Building a classroom that welcomes students with disabilities as fully participating members of the community is essential for the success of inclusive teaching. (Robin Sachs/ PhotoEdit)

The same is true with your students who are formally labeled as having a disability. Some will require minor accommodations or modifications and will then be able to learn successfully, and others will require more complex interventions because their disabilities are more complex. For those who need more complex interventions, the expertise of the special education teacher may be critical.

The use of a device to amplify sound for a student with a hearing impairment or the need to rearrange the physical environment to accommodate classroom traffic patterns that include a wheelchair are two examples of relatively easy adjustments. On the other hand, when students with disabilities are struggling with learning and behavior (these represent the larger proportion of students identified as having disabilities), teachers have to make different kinds of accommodations, perhaps including changing instructional methods and classroom management strategies.

In Chapter 9 we will explore an idea called differentiated instruction. This is a way of teaching that takes into account students' differences from the very start of a teacher's planning for instruction. Rather than assume that all students are the same, effective teachers plan for the variation among their students, including students who have disabilities. By carefully using a mix of approaches, they are able to accommodate a wider range of students than is possible when the teacher expects students to be performing close to each other academically.

Many—but not all—students who are struggling with learning and/or behavior owing to mild disabilities may require more explicit instruction from the teacher in academics or in practicing social skills and will need these tasks to be broken down in order to be mastered. Teachers need to be thoughtful about how to break down complex learning and social tasks in ways that help students be successful and not just assume that students with disabilities are capable of mastering only simple learning tasks. Different accommodations are needed when students are not able to function academically at the same level as the other students in the class. Then the challenge is how to include students in the substance of class activities, keeping expectations high without making unrealistic demands.

## Collaboration Among Teachers: The Key to Success

If you are preparing to be a general education teacher, you may be wondering how you will be able to meet the needs of your students with disabilities. You are not, after all, preparing to be a special education teacher, and as such you are not expected to have specialized knowledge about every type of disability. You may at first be cautious, especially working with a student who has a disability you may not have encountered before. That is precisely why you will work as a member of a team with the special education teachers and other specialists. The majority of students with disabilities today receive most of their education in general education classrooms. The challenge to provide equitable education is played out in classrooms every day as general and special education teachers continue to forge new relationships to support students with disabilities. So another responsibility related to teaching students with disabilities is to work collaboratively with the special education teacher. Figure 8-1 lists five characteristics of collaborative professionals.

How does collaboration among teachers actually work in schools and classrooms? Schools organize collaboration between general and special education teachers in many different ways, depending on the number of specialists available, the number of students with identified disabilities, and the preferences of the local school and school district.

**Working Together to Solve Students' Problems.**  Special education teachers provide a crucial form of collaboration with classroom teachers by providing advice and specialized knowledge, which is sometimes called consultation. A relative-

### Figure 8-1    Qualities of Collaborative Professionals

**Learning how to work well with each other is now a basic responsibility for all education professionals in the schools.**

1.  People who are effective at collaboration recognize that the goal is complex and requires a joint effort to be achieved.

2.  People who are effective at collaboration acknowledge and honor the creativity generated by working together with others. It is not just that working together makes the task more manageable; collaborative interactions lead to results that are more creative than what any single person could have designed alone.

3.  People who are effective at collaboration enjoy the social nature of joint problem solving. Part of the responsibility of working well together is the ability to respect other participants in the collaboration—even if you don't always agree with them. When collaborative interactions begin, there is a need to establish trust among the participants; with this trust established, disagreements that occur do so within a context of respect for others.

4.  People who are effective at collaboration value the growth they experience as a result of participating in the collaboration.

5.  People who are effective at collaboration are reflective about their own professional practice. People who invest the time and energy in collaborative efforts are not satisfied with the same routine of teaching practice day in and day out. Instead, they challenge themselves to grow and improve their practice at the same time they contribute to the improved practice of the whole.

**Source:**  Pugach, M. C., and L. J. Johnson. (2002). *Collaborative practitioners, collaborative schools* (2nd ed.). Denver: Love Publishing.

ly simple accommodation or modification that the general education teachers may implement through discussion with the special education teacher may help the student improve. Indeed, when special and general education teachers collaborate before a student is ever labeled as having a disability, they may be so successful that formal special education services are not required. The special education teacher might also come in and observe the class to gain a new view of the situation and some new ideas.

When special and general education teachers team and problem solve together, they bring their joint expertise to the education of students with disabilities. (Will Hart/PhotoEdit)

Because of the problems associated with the identification process noted in Table 8-1, the referral process is not completely objective. Formally referring a student to be tested for special education is a serious step and should be made only after a teacher has tried to intervene with a student and has assessed the impact of those interventions, has worked extensively with the special education teacher, and has also worked with the student's family.

For example, some teachers may frequently communicate with special education teachers for ideas but rarely refer students. These teachers have created classroom environments that support a wide range of learners, and they flexibly accommodate the instructional variations needed to make sure all students learn. When these teachers initiate a formal referral, the special education teacher knows it must be a serious situation. Other teachers may be less flexible and create classrooms that are not equally supportive of a wide range of learners. They may frequently refer students for special education because the range they are comfortable teaching is narrow to begin with. For these teachers, making a referral to special education is easier than making changes in their classroom community and style of instruction. This practice can be interpreted as a form of "blaming the victim," or the student, for the teacher's shortcomings.

Because of the subjectivity of several categories of disability, and especially the category of learning disabilities, a practice called *response to intervention* (Rti) has recently been introduced that requires teachers to document their systematic attempts to work with students who are having difficulty—as a way of reducing unnecessary referrals to special education. This approach is based on the belief that too many students are referred to, and end up in, special education more because of poor teaching rather than because they actually have a disability. Teachers are encouraged to intervene using what are thought to be high quality teaching approaches and to frequently check on their students' progress. While some view Rti mostly in relationship to special education, others view it as what all teachers should be doing. You can learn more about Rti at **www.rti4success.org**.

**Sharing Teaching Responsibilities.** Another form of collaboration occurs when a special education teacher spends a period of time each day—or the whole day—working in the general education classroom to support specific students who have disabilities. This kind of collaboration is known as *co-teaching*. A special education teacher may be present working in a general education classroom for a single subject area each day or several times per week, or a specific time period each day without regard for the subject that is being taught. In some schools special and general education teachers work as members of a permanent team, sharing the classroom and the students on a full-time basis.

When teachers team within the general education classroom, they must make several important decisions about how they will divide the labor of teaching. Will the special education teacher work with small groups of students who need more individualized attention? Will the two teachers split the class in two so that each has responsibility for a smaller number of students? Who will deliver the main lesson on a particular topic? Co-teaching is more difficult than it sounds because teachers who co-teach must agree on their shared goals, forge a set of common beliefs, achieve parity, and work cooperatively for the good of their shared students (Villa, Thousand, & Nevin, 2004).

In some schools special education teachers pull students out of class to work in small groups at different times of the day in what are often called *resource rooms*. This is less common today than it was in the past. Even so, you as the general classroom teacher still need to develop a strong, positive, collaborative working relationship with the special education teacher, to confer regularly, and to make sure that if your students are pulled out, they are getting a fully coordinated set of learning experiences that maximize the time they spend in both settings. This is especially important today since most students with disabilities are expected to learn the general education curriculum and will usually be tested in it as well—no matter whether they receive part or all of their education in general education classrooms.

## Your turn... *to reflect*

Using Figure 8-1 as a guide, rate yourself on your readiness and willingness to engage in collaboration in your future work as a teacher. Which aspects of collaboration will be easy for you? Which will be a particular challenge? How will you get beyond the challenges collaboration may pose for you?

Collaboration and teamwork among teachers will be useful in your future work as a teacher, and not just in relationship to teaching students with disabilities. But it is especially crucial in the case of educating students with disabilities because general and special education teachers alike are expected to interact with each other and often work side-by-side in the same classroom. Special and general education teachers might also work with speech and language therapists, occupational therapists, audiologists, psychotherapists, or physicians—each of whom might be working with a particular student who has a complex disability and helping provide that student with an appropriate, high-quality education. As a general or special education teacher, you will also be expected to work closely with the families of students with disabilities, who often are in the best position to share important knowledge about their children's special needs. As a team, you and your colleagues can make decisions about what is best educationally for a particular student with disabilities and share responsibility for helping students achieve their goals.

Students who have disabilities significant enough to require them to have an educational aide, or paraprofessional, with them throughout the day require a different form of collaboration. A paraprofessional, for example, may help position a student with significant physical disabilities or may work individually within the classroom to support a student who has autism. They may provide direct support to students with disabilities to enable the students to remain in the classroom for all or part of the day.

## The Goal: A Classroom Environment that Diminishes Differences

The more your class is designed as a learning environment where you expect individual differences to exist, the easier it will be for you to implement a curriculum and modifications for any student who needs assistance to be successful—

including your students with disabilities. In a classroom environment where difference is considered to be normal, teachers consciously choose organizational and instructional strategies that diminish the gulf other teachers may create, whether consciously or unconsciously, by focusing on the difference itself rather than on what needs to be done to support all students' learning. Teachers with a flexible approach to teaching in the first place will find making accommodations for students with disabilities less problematic than those who are not.

Classrooms that provide accommodating environments and are inclusive are more supportive of students with disabilities than those that are not. Thus, another difference in teaching students with disabilities is the conscious way a teacher chooses to design his or her classroom and learns whether these decisions provide enough support for students who are likely to struggle. An accommodating classroom environment is a place where all students are welcomed equally, where their differences are respected, and where the teacher makes a conscious effort to create and sustain harmonious relationships among all of them. Classrooms that include students with disabilities are also classrooms where students are challenged and where they have access to and can learn the general education curriculum. As we explore in Digging Deeper, students with disabilities can learn complex material in the general education curriculum.

## Digging Deeper
### What Kind of Curriculum is Best for Students with Disabilities?

Today the general education curriculum is viewed as the optimal academic curriculum for most students with disabilities, and only some students with significant disabilities may have a special curriculum that focuses on functional living and working skills. If the majority of students with disabilities are to be taught the general education curriculum and to be tested in this curriculum under the No Child Left Behind Act, how will this work? How can students with disabilities learn more complex concepts and skills? Do they need highly specialized forms of instruction to be successful? Can they succeed in higher level curriculum activities? Is it even realistic to expect students with disabilities to master complex curriculum topics?

**Pro and Con:** Beginning with the emergence of modern special education practice during the late 1960s and early 1970s, the official curriculum for students with disabilities generally consisted of the basic skills, with pared-down content so students would master the basics before attempting anything more complex. These highly structured programs, which were often based on behaviorist approaches to learning, were thought to represent the best hope for improving the skills of students with disabilities. As a result, students struggling the most in school received a curriculum that was the least interesting or motivating. The curriculum was also typically limited to reading and mathematics, and rarely exposed students to science, social studies, or writing. Because students with disabilities were usually educated in segregated classes or schools, whether they could handle a more challenging, interesting curriculum was rarely considered.

It was not until the 1980s, when the integration of students with disabilities was well under way, that several special educators began to question whether an approach based on decontextualized, basic skills-only instruction was the most appropriate form of instruction for students with disabilities. They began to experiment with more challenging ways of teaching reading and writing and a more interesting, motivating curriculum that created an authentic context for learning. This work challenged special educators to determine whether their students could reach higher levels of learning and participate in more complex instruction. This important research demonstrated how new methods of teaching, not only in reading comprehension and writing instruction, but also in science and social studies, might benefit students with disabilities (e.g., Cawley, Hayden, Cade, & Baker-Kroczynski, 2002; Feretti, MacArthur, & Okolo, 2001; Morocco, Hindin, Mata-Aguilar, & Clark-Chicarelli, 2001; Palincsar, Magnusson, Collins, & Cutter, 2001).

To illustrate the position against more complex curriculum and instruction, it is useful to recall the relationship between the official, intended curriculum and the taught curriculum, concepts discussed in Chapter 5. Today the intended curriculum for most students with disabilities is, without question, the general education curriculum. In practice, however, the "taught curriculum" may still represent a more traditional approach. Given the national debates that pit basic skills against a more complex curriculum, special education students may still work primarily in basic skills programs, based on the continuing belief that these skills must be mastered before students with disabilities can do more complex and challenging work in school. However, most students who have disabilities are now tested in the general education curriculum under the No Child Left Behind Act, ensuring their complex learning is more important than ever before.

**The Nuances:**  Students who have disabilities often need explicit instruction in some higher level skills. In the same way that teachers are explicit in the teaching of basic skills, they may need to be just as explicit in the teaching of complex skills that will help students with disabilities succeed in the general education curriculum. Moreover, when teachers use small groups for instruction in the content areas, they must make sure that students with disabilities are fully integrated into the social norms of small-group work (Anderson & Fetters, 1996). Finally, it is important to find multiple ways for students to reflect their accomplishments than a paper-and-pencil test. Technology applications that allow students to display their work in innovative ways, for example, may be appropriate for some students with disabilities.

Therefore, special and general education teachers alike are challenged to learn teaching methods that invite students with disabilities to participate fully, that provide them with the explicit instruction they may need to participate in complex curriculum, and that allow them to express what they have learned in new ways. In this way, continuity can be achieved between the official, general education curriculum and the taught curriculum.

**Rethinking the Issue:**  Choices about what curriculum students with disabilities can handle are influenced by two important issues. First, it is no longer appropriate to assume that students who are struggling owing to disabilities cannot handle complex ideas and topics, or must master "the basics" before they participate in activities that are interesting and motivating. Second, decisions about what curriculum is appropriate should not be based on unfounded assumptions about what students with disabilities can accomplish. As we discussed earlier in this chapter, each student is an individual, and a disability label does not change this basic fact. To find out what a student can accomplish, teachers need to work individually with students and let their behavior and performance guide the expectations teachers set and the curriculum they provide.

# How Technology Can Help You Teach Students with Disabilities

Some of the most important advances in the use of technology in schools have been made on behalf of students with disabilities. Eager to find ways to enable students to communicate, to be mobile, and to participate in general education classrooms to access the general curriculum, special educators have been leading advocates for the increased use of technology in the schools. They have created new and more powerful technologies to enable greater integration of students with disabilities (Woodward & Cuban, 2001), and these new technologies often determine whether a student with disabilities can participate easily in general education classrooms. Technological advances now give students with more significant disabilities the ability to communicate their needs, wants, and interests. For students with sensory impairments (vision and hearing impairments), new technologies can literally open up the world to them, giving them the ability to find and use information and communicate in settings where this was unimaginable in the past. Technology as it applies to people with disabilities is called **assistive technology**, or AT.

## Integrating Assistive Technology into the Classroom

Assistive technology can make the difference between gaining the self-confidence that comes with academic success or experiencing persistent feelings of failure that can result when students with disabilities are unable to achieve well at school. For example, a high school student who has a learning disability that includes very poor fine motor skills and who struggles with handwriting will almost certainly have difficulty taking notes in class. This same student, however, may be skilled with a laptop and take notes easily on it, using the spellcheck and grammarcheck functions. As a teacher, how comfortable are you going to make it for this student to use a laptop in your class? Some teachers may believe that using a laptop to take notes gives the student an unfair advantage, even though a student's IEP may require that a laptop be allowed.

Teachers who feel this way might only begrudgingly allow use of a laptop—a subtle but powerful form of marginalizing the student who needs this tool. In contrast, other teachers may recognize the usefulness of laptops for all students and may encourage other students who do not have disabilities to do the same.

For some students with disabilities, assistive technology may be the best way for them to have consistent access to the curriculum and/or to communicate with everyone else in the classroom—whether it is in a general education classroom, a special education classroom, or a special facility. More important, such technologies may make it possible for students to interact with each other in social situations.

To appreciate the crucial role technology can play for students with disabilities, we need only think about the simpler and more primitive tools we now take for granted that enable many of us to function in the world. We use these simpler "technologies" daily and never question whether their use should be "allowed." For example, eyeglasses enable people with imperfect sight to experience the world visually; a stool or ladder enables a person who is short in stature to reach items in high places (Staples & Pittman, 2003). Cell

**Critical Term**

**Assistive technology.**
Technology developed to give individuals with disabilities the ability to have access to the curriculum and other resources and to communicate easily and regularly.

Assistive technology enables students with disabilities to participate much more easily in general education settings and can also have applications for students who do not have disabilities. (Bob Daemmrich/PhotoEdit)

**Table 8-5    Three Categories of Assistive Technology**

Assistive Technology can range from low to high-tech devices.

| Low-Tech | Mid-Tech | High-Tech |
|---|---|---|
| • Reading frames (cardboard frame to show one line of text at a time)<br>• Sticky notes to mark important words/sections<br>• Graph paper<br>• Small white or blackboards<br>• Communication books with pictures to help a nonverbal student communicate<br>• Timers<br>• Line magnifiers<br>• Seat cushions | • Recorded books<br>• Tape recorders<br>• Amplication systems for students with hearing impairments<br>• Specialized calculators (e.g., large displays)<br>• Hand-held talking dictionaries<br>• Electronic organizers<br>• Switches to allow physically disabled students to activate other devices<br>• Talking switches for nonverbal students | • Alternative computer keyboards<br>• Mouse emulators to enable physically handicapped students to operate computers<br>• Scanners<br>• Digital whiteboards to save things that are written on whiteboards<br>• Text-to-speech software<br>• Talking wordprocessing software<br>• Screen reading software<br>• Word prediction software<br>• Speech recognition software<br>• Augmentative communication software to allow nonverbal students to communicate<br>• Graphic organizers<br>• Braille translation software<br>• Electronic math templates to align numbers correctly |

**Source:** Adapted from Massachusetts Department of Education. *Assistive technology guide for Massachusetts schools*. (2002, November). Malden, MA: Author.  Retrieved May 13, 2008, from http://www.doe.mass.edu/edtech/assistive/ATguide.pdf.

phones are a more recent means of communicating with others; before cell phones, our access was restricted to where phones were located. We are so used to the ease of communication they provide that we no longer think of them as special. The goal with AT is to reach a point where teachers and students use it effortlessly, it loses its novelty, and children's learning is advanced as a result. Table 8-5 illustrates the full range of AT.

## Universal Design as a Strategy for Inclusion

**Critical Term**

**Universal design.** Design of architecture and learning environments that is based on a consideration of all individuals, including those with disabilities, from the outset rather than as an afterthought.

With the passage of the Americans with Disabilities Act in 1990, the **universal design** of architectural elements was initiated to provide full access for people with disabilities (Pisha & Coyne, 2001). Universal design means that all buildings and public places should be designed with the needs of all citizens in mind, including those with disabilities. As we noted in the opening section of this chapter, introducing universal design in architectural planning resulted in changes that benefit the general population as well as people with disabilities and that are now taken for granted. For instance, elevators in schools benefit those who are temporarily disabled due to accidents, notably, injured athletes who are temporarily in a wheelchair or use crutches; curb cuts benefit families with babies in strollers as well as adolescents who are bike riding or roller blading.

The challenge with regard to education is to extend the concept of universal design to the Universal Design of Learning, or UDL, so that all students, including those with disabilities, can have increased access to the general education curriculum through better design of all instructional materials using multimedia technologies (Center for Applied Special Technology, 2007; Pisha & Coyne, 2001). Technology holds the key to making the curriculum maximally accessible to all learners by making it possible to build flexibility directly into the original design of these materials. Several projects to create these technologies are sponsored by the Center for Applied Technology at **www.cast.org**. But what technological advances can help move us toward the Universal Design of Learning?

A good example is text-to-speech software. Text-to-speech software allows students to hear their texts as oral speech rather than to read them. Screenreading software, for example, reads the text aloud to students. Screenreading software is a support to students with visual impairments who cannot read written text, but it also enables students who read below the reading level of their textbooks to participate fully in the content of instruction even as they work to improve their reading skills. Screenreading software can also help young students use books on topics that interest them, even when the books are beyond their reading level; it can also be used to read webpages.

These examples illustrate that software originally viewed as assistive technology for students with visual impairments can be helpful in the classroom far beyond this particular disability, providing teachers are creative and flexible enough to allow students to use it. As more and more curriculums and instructional materials are developed with flexibility for students with disabilities built in, the notion of assistive technology as "something special" should diminish considerably.

## A Final Point about Assistive Technology and Disabilities

Just as a disability label does not provide specific direction for the kinds of instruction a specific child might need, a disability cannot always be matched to a specific kind of assistive technology. Students' individual needs determine what technology is best for them. Some students with the same disability label may need more or less help from assistive technology to succeed, depending on their specific intellectual, emotional, and physical characteristics. So be cautious not to assume that a child with a particular disability will need a particular kind of technology—or that a child without a formally identified disability will not benefit from a particular kind of technology. At the same time, you need to be familiar with the general kinds of technologies that are likely to be helpful to students with particular categories of disability. Your goal is to locate—with help from a special educator if necessary—the technology tools that will best help the individual students you will be teaching.

> **Your turn...** *to review*
>
> 1. What is one way a disability label can be useful to a teacher? One way it can be detrimental?
> 2. What is assistive technology?
> 3. What does the term *universal design of learning* refer to?

# Disability: The Same as or Different from Other Diversities?

Many fundamental civil rights issues that affect ethnic and racial minority groups also apply to people with disabilities. For example, the goal of reducing the segregation of people with disabilities, according to Sarason and Doris (1979), was helped by the climate established by the *Brown v. Board of Education* decision in 1954. Decreasing the marginalization of traditionally powerless groups, reducing

Students with disabilities come from all backgrounds, but teachers can sometimes misinterpret the behaviors of racial and ethnic minority students and assume there is a disability when none exists. (Bill Aaron/PhotoEdit)

oppression, providing equity in education, and establishing workplace rights are some of the common goals shared by those who fought for the civil rights of both racial and ethnic minorities and people with disabilities.

This is not to say, however, that diversity of race and ethnicity and diversity based on disability are exactly parallel. Placing all kinds of diversities under one umbrella without consideration of how they differ can cause difficulties in understanding how complex the concept of diversity is. Beyond the question of fundamental civil rights, which are similar across diversities, what differences should you consider and what implications do these differences have for you as a prospective teacher?

In Chapter 7, we emphasized the importance of learning about your students' backgrounds. Once identified, these family, cultural, or community assets bring an important perspective to how you think about teaching students whose backgrounds and communities may differ from your own. The goal is to move away from a biased, deficit view of students and their communities toward an appreciation of their assets. Understanding and building on these assets can strengthen a teacher's approach to any problems a student may be experiencing. This applies to teachers who work with students from racial and ethnic minority groups or from lower socioeconomic groups—regardless of whether students have a disability.

This is an important issue because every student with a disability also belongs to a racial, ethnic, and socioeconomic group. In contrast, unless you are a special education teacher, you will *never* teach a whole class of students with disabilities. It may well be, however, that as a classroom teacher you will teach in a classroom where your students' race, ethnicity, or socioeconomic background is different from yours.

The goal of our discussion in Chapter 7 was to encourage you to think about the role teachers play in closing the achievement gap across racial, ethnic, and socioeconomic class lines and how society and the schools often perpetuate the gap. Your role as a teacher is to set high expectations, to know your students and their potential, and to connect your teaching to your students' cultures and communities—all for the purpose of ensuring your students' growth and learning. If students who have disabilities are not white and middle class, they are also likely to be subjected to bias and stereotypes based on race, ethnicity, and class. You must therefore view your students' needs through both their individual cultural backgrounds *and* their disability. As you interact with students and their families, it is important to consider these various diversities in relationship to one another.

For example, working with students who have disabilities usually requires a teacher to construct an individual educational intervention, accommodation, or modification in the classroom to meet a student's needs; such individual accommodations are not required based on students' race, ethnicity, and social class (Pugach & Seidl, 1998). The educational issue for students with disabilities is the individual educational need of the student because of that disability—as defined in the student's IEP. In contrast, the educational issue related to racial and ethnic minority students is to challenge the societal dynamics and stereotypes that lead to devaluing language and culture in the first place. By equating disability with diversity, these larger systemic inequities may be masked (Ball & Harry, 1993; Rueda, 1989).

Finally, teachers need to have a clear understanding of different kinds of diversity so that they can avoid making the assumption that a disability exists when it does not—and not use special education inappropriately as a dumping ground for racial and ethnic minority students. Study after study (Donovan & Cross, 2002; Heller, Holtzman, & Messick, 1982) has documented that disproportionate numbers of students from racial and ethnic minority groups are inappropriately labeled as having disabilities. Despite attempts to ensure its objectivity, the special education identification process is still subjective for categories of mild disability, which contributes to the overidentification of many students from racial and ethnic minority groups, especially African American and Native American students (Harry & Klinger, 2006). Interestingly, Latino students tend to be underrepresented in special education rather than overrepresented, and states with high Latino populations are represented proportionally to their overall presence in the population (Perez, Skiba & Chung, 2008).

For example, a teacher may misinterpret a student's struggle to learn English as a learning disability. Or a teacher may misinterpret the exuberant behavior of a young African American male as a behavior disorder. The teacher who uses the special education system to explain away students' behaviors, rather than seeing the behaviors in their larger sociocultural context, may be confusing diversity of race and/or ethnicity with disability, with potentially very harmful effects on students.

When schools and teachers fail to make clear distinctions between disability on the one hand, and diversity associated with race, ethnicity, language and social class on the other, they may fail to create educational environments that serve all students well. It is critical that you, as a prospective teacher, are familiar with these distinctions and that you regularly address the challenges posed by these multiple diversities.

## What about Educating Gifted and Talented Students?

The education of students identified as gifted and talented does not fall under the laws that define education for students with disabilities, and states do not receive federal funds as part of IDEA for this purpose. Programs for these students are funded at either the state or the local school district level (Donovan & Cross, 2002). In addition, the federal government provides some funding for state and local programs and for research on the education of gifted and talented students through the Jacob K. Javits Gifted and Talented Students Education Program. The focus of this funding is to identify srategies for supporting gifted and talented students in underrepresented groups.

Some state and local programs emphasize a talent development model, which is based on assuring that students in all classrooms are exposed to challenging and rigorous learning opportunities (Neag Center for Gifted Education and Talent Development, 2008). This approach gives all students the chance to stretch themselves. Other programs identify students who achieve certain scores on tests of intelligence from general education classrooms and provide segregated programs within public schools—either part or full time. This approach limits who gets exposed to the high end of the academic spectrum.

As a classroom teacher, you need to recognize which of your students requires a real challenge beyond what you are providing to the class. Some of these students may also have identified disabilities. The goal of teaching should be to provide meaningful learning experiences for *all* of your students. The same flexibility teachers need to exercise to meet the needs of their students who struggle should be extended to students who need to be challenged academically.

## Why It Counts in a Diverse World

Until recent decades students with disabilities were denied the right to a free public education. Now that this right has been established, the teacher's responsibility is to see that students with disabilities are not simply included but are full members of the classroom community. Some teachers carry out these responsibilities willingly and genuinely improve the lives of their students. Others do not make their classrooms welcoming, positive communities, and in the process they disadvantage students with disabilities. Teachers can also disadvantage students from minority groups when they refer them for special education based on cultural or language characteristics rather than on actual indicators of a disability.

It is crucial for you, as a new teacher, to take your responsibilities toward students with disabilities very seriously, not only because you are legally mandated to do so, but also because you have an obligation to meet the needs of all your students. By doing so, you may recognize special talents in your students with disabilities, even if you have to look a little harder and structure your classroom a little differently to enable those talents to surface. In doing so, you also model for your nondisabled students what it means to be part of an inclusive community.

## CHAPTER SUMMARY

Today students with disabilities receive most of their education in general education classrooms with their nondisabled peers. All teachers therefore need to be prepared to work well with this student population and to help them reach their potential. Teachers can do so by (1) welcoming students with disabilities, (2) making the accommodations and modifications necessary to enable students with disabilities to be successful, and (3) collaborating with professionals and family members to be as responsive as possible to the needs of students with disabilities.

## A Broad Commitment to Equity for Students with Disabilities

Students with disabilities are protected by federal laws that guarantee a free, appropriate public education. These laws mandate that, as appropriate, students with disabilities must be educated with their nondisabled peers and be taught the general education curriculum. Efforts to achieve this commitment to equity emerged shortly after the Civil Rights era of the 1960s, culminating in the 1975 Education of All Handicapped Children Act, today known as the Individuals with Disabilities Education Act, and the 1990 Americans with Disabilities Act.

## Does Labeling Students with Disabilities Help or Hinder a Teacher's Work?

Federal legislation recognizes 13 categories of disability. These categorical labels, though important for obtaining federal funds to support special education, are of only minimal help to teachers as they make the individual instructional decisions tailored to their students' needs. Regardless of categories, teachers must get to know their students as individuals and learn exactly how a student's particular disability interacts with his or her intellectual abilities, personal interests, culture, language, and family experiences. Students with disabilities are individuals first, and their capacities should not be judged solely on the basis of the disability label they carry.

## The Teacher's Role

One of the most important things teachers can do to meet the needs of students with disabilities is to plan the classroom from the outset as a place based on high expectations for all students and that provides the supports and flexibility to help students achieve those expectations. In the case of students with disabilities, this may mean adjusting the physical environment or making changes in how teachers structure the curriculum and organize instruction. Teachers who successfully create classroom communities where differences among learners are supported in the first place generally have fewer difficulties accommodating students with disabilities.

## Collaboration: The Key to Success

Collaboration between general and special education teachers is one of the hallmarks of successful educational programming for students with disabilities. In some cases, general classroom teachers consult with special education teachers about students who are having difficulties but who are not labeled as having a formal disability. In other cases, special and general education teachers team within the general education classroom setting and work together each day to meet the needs of all their students. Collaboration takes work, but it also provides the rewards associated with pooling resources to meet the needs of students with disabilities.

## How Technology Can Help You Teach Students with Disabilities

Special technologies have been developed to support students with disabilities in the area of communication and access to the general education curriculum. Technology as it is applied to people with disabilities is known as *assistive technology*, or AT. The kinds of technologies that may be needed to assist a particular student will depend on the combination of his or her disability, individual interests, intellectual capacity, and background. Decisions about what kind of AT may be appropriate must be made considering all of these factors. Universal Design of Learning (UDL) refers to creating curriculum materials with built-in features that make them accessible to all students.

## Disability: The Same as or Different from Other Diversities?

Diversity as it relates to race, class, culture, and language is not exactly the same as diversity based on disability. Although fundamental similarities exist in terms of the struggle for civil rights, access, and an end to marginalization, important distinctions exist as well. Students with disabilities usually require a special, individualized intervention to support their success in school. Students who are members of racial and ethnic groups require an understanding of their culture and/or language and the resource it represents as a legitimate background for learning rather than an individual intervention. Students with disabilities always have a culture, language, race, or ethnicity in addition to their disability. Finally, teachers can fall into the trap of thinking a racial or ethnic minority student who is struggling with learning and/or behavior has a disability, when in fact the student may be acting within an acceptable range of behaviors within his or her culture or is making adequate progress toward learning to speak English but is not yet ready to engage in all the academic tasks required.

## What about Educating Gifted and Talented Students?

Programs to meet the needs of students who are gifted and talented vary widely across states. The goal of all such programs is to challenge a students to their greatest potential. Programs for this group of students are not funded by IDEA, but a large research center on programs for gifted and talented students has been funded for many years.

## LIST OF CRITICAL TERMS

Individuals with Disabilities
    Education Act (IDEA)  (*254*)

Americans with Disabilities
    Act (ADA) (*254*)

Least restrictive environment
    (LRE) (*255*)

Individual Education Plan (IEP)  (*255*)

Early intervention  (*257*)

Transition services  (*257*)

High-incidence disabilities  (*262*)

Low-incidence disabilities  (*262*)

Developmental delay  (*267*)

Assistive technology  (*275*)

Universal design  (*276*)

## EXPLORING YOUR COMMITMENT

1. *on the web...*  Log onto the website for the International Council for Exceptional Children at **www.cec.sped.org**. What resources can you find on this website to help you in your future work with students with disabilities? The link to the National Clearinghouse for Professions in Special Education will be a resource for those who wish to pursue a career working with individuals with disabilities.

2. *on the web...*  Log onto the website for The Association for Severe Handicaps, or TASH, at **www.tash.org**. Locate the section on the history and mission of TASH. Then review the section on public policy. How does this organization differ from what you learned reviewing the website for the International Council for Exceptional Children?

3. *on the web...*  The assistive technology website at **http://connsensebulletin.com** provides several resources about this aspect of technology. Check at least two links on this website and identify how they can help you in your work teaching students who have disabilities.

4. *on your own...*  What resources exist on your own college or university campus for students who have disabilities? What specific services are provided? What percentage of students on your campus are being served by this unit?

5. *in the field...*  Meet one or more of the special education teachers and interview them about how they engage in collaboration with general education classroom teachers. How much do they collaborate? on what topics and for what purposes?

6. *in the field...*  Identify all of the students in the class in your field site who are formally labeled as having a disability. Are there other students in the classroom who also struggle with learning or behavior but who are not formally labeled? How do you account for the differences? How does the school provide special education services to students with disabilities?

7. *in the field...*  Observe the students in your class in an informal setting such as recess or lunch. What do you notice about the social interactions between students who are labeled as having a disability and those who are not so labeled?

8. *on the web...*   Locate the classification system for disabilities that is used in your state. Select two other states near yours and review their classification systems. How do they differ? How are they similar? How might these various approaches to categorizing students with disabilities affect your teaching?

9. *on your own...*   For a period of a week, keep a journal documenting observations of individuals who have disabilities in your community. Where did you observe these individuals? What accommodations or modifications did they use? How did others respond to them? Write a short reflection on how your observations relate to your preparation as a teacher.

10. *in the research...*   The following study describes the experiences of general education classroom teachers as they first begin to include students with disabilities in their classrooms: Giangreco, M. F., R. Dennis, C. Cloninger, S. Edelman, and R. Schattman. (1993). " 'I've counted Jon': Transformational experiences of teachers educating students with disabilities." *Exceptional Children, 59,* 359–372. Which of their experiences seems most meaningful for you?

## GUIDELINES FOR BEGINNING TEACHERS

1. Resist the use of labels to describe your students. Even if other teachers talk about "My LD student" or "My blind student" ask a question like, "I'm not sure whom you're talking about. What's the student's name?" Demonstrate your interest in your students as individuals first.

2. Once a week, make sure you observe your students with disabilities to assess how well they are integrated into your classroom community.

3. Know what is in your students' Individualized Education Plans. If you do not know where they are or what is in them, meet with the special education teacher to make sure you have the appropriate access to and information about your students' needs as reflected in their IEPs.

4. Recognize that special education can be used inappropriately to segregate racial and ethnic minority students and students from lower socioeconomic classes. Use the referral system to special education sparingly—only when you are certain that the difficulties a student is exhibiting cannot be accounted for by any other reason but a potential disability.

5. Welcome students with disabilities into your classroom.

6. Make decisions about the capabilities of students with disabilities based on who they are and what they are able to do—not on false expectations based on the particular disability label they have.

7. Create a unified classroom community where students with disabilities feel comfortable, are welcomed as full members of the class, and are supported as learners.

8. Be open to adapting and modifying the curriculum and your instructional approaches to accommodate the needs of your students, including the use of technology to make the curriculum accessible.

9. Meet the special education teachers in your school early on and work with them to gain the knowledge you will need to be successful with the particular students you have. If you are planning to be a special education teacher, meet each classroom teacher who works with students you teach.

10. Work as partners with families of your students with disabilities.

## THE **INTASC** CONNECTION

INTASC Standard 3 is a general standard covering diversity, and includes the issue of working with students with disabilities. This standard reads: *The teacher understands how students differ in their approaches to learning and creates instructional opportunities that are adapted to diverse learners.* Indicators include the following:

● The teacher knows about areas of exceptionality in learning—including learning disabilities, visual and perceptual difficulties, and special physical or mental challenges.

● The teacher appreciates and values human diversity, shows respect for students' varied talents and perspectives, and is committed to the pursuit of "individually configured excellence."

● The teacher makes appropriate provisions (in terms of time and circumstances for work, tasks assigned, communication, and response modes) for individual students who have particular learning differences or needs.

● The teacher can identify when and how to locate appropriate services or resources to meet exceptional learning needs.

In addition, Standard 10 reads: *The teacher fosters relationships with school colleagues, parents, and agencies in the larger community to support students' learning and well-being.* Indicators include the following:

● The teacher understands and implements laws related to students' rights and teacher responsibilities (e.g., for equal education, appropriate education for handicapped students, confidentiality, privacy, appropriate treatment of students, reporting in situations related to possible child abuse).

● The teacher is willing to work with other professionals to improve the overall learning environment for students.

● The teacher makes links with the learners' other environments on behalf of students, by consulting with parents, counselors, teachers of other classes and activities within the schools, and professionals in other community agencies.

An additional set of INTASC standards was developed and published in 2001 (**http://www.ccsso.org/pdfs/SPEDStds.pdf**) that deal explicitly with preparing all teachers to work with students who have disabilities. These standards use the 10 original INTASC standards and extend their interpretation for preparing teachers to work with students with disabilities in great detail (Council of Chief State School Officers, 2001).

If you are in a state that follows a different set of teacher standards, find the state standards that most closely relate to the INTASC standards discussed here.

## READING ON...

Haddon, M. (2003). *The curious incident of the dog in the night-time.* New York: Random House. A novel whose protagonist is a 15-year-old, Christopher Boone, who has Asperger Syndrome, a form of autism.

Harry, B., M. Kalyanpur, and M. Day. (1999). *Building cultural reciprocity with families: Case studies in special education.* Baltimore, MD: Paul Brookes. Cases of students with disabilities who are from diverse racial and ethnic backgrounds, illustrating how teachers worked with their families to provide, in a culturally responsive manner, a supportive environment for growth and learning.

Harry B., and J. Klingner. (2006). *Why are so many minority students in special education?* New York: Teachers College Press. An examination of the teaching practices that result in referring culturally diverse students to special education.

Taylor, D. (1991). *Learning denied.* Portsmouth, NH: Heinemann. Taylor poignantly describes what happens when the drive to identify a student, Patrick, as having a disability overpowers the school's ability to see Patrick as an individual.

# MEETING THE NEEDS OF INDIVIDUAL STUDENTS IN THE CONTEXT OF THE CLASSROOM AND THE SCHOOL

Teachers work in a unique setting: the classroom. The structure of classrooms, as well as of schools themselves, means that teachers must figure out how to meet the needs of their individual students within a social, group environment. Within the classroom, the choices teachers make about how to organize instruction—and the classroom community as a whole—have implications for how well teachers are able to address their students as learners, as individuals, and as class members. How teachers balance the demands of meeting their students' wide-ranging individual needs with the demands of the group represents a continuing professional challenge. Every teacher faces some variation on these questions: How do I get maximum time with individual students? How do I create a sense of community in the classroom that helps both individuals and the group? How do I structure groups when students need more instruction?

In Chapter 9, we explore how different organizational structures and instructional formats influence the climate for student learning. Chapter 10 discusses how schools are governed and financed at the local, state, and federal levels and how the decisions made at these levels also affect teachers' efforts to create classrooms that work both for the group and for individual students.

This section should stimulate your thinking about the images you already have about classrooms and provide you with alternative images of the ways in which instruction can be organized to better meet students' individual needs. With these alternative ideas in mind, you can begin to challenge yourself to consider what it will take to become skilled in implementing such approaches to your classroom and your work as a teacher.

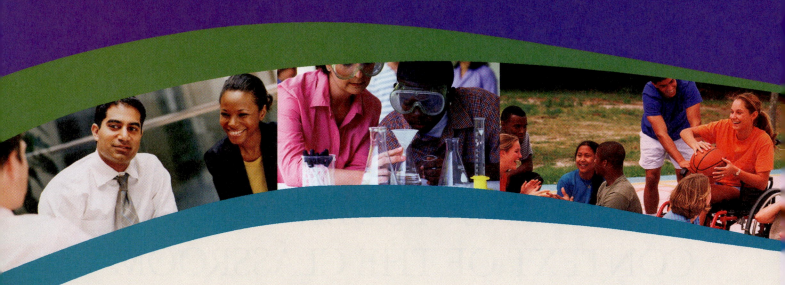

## Guiding Questions

- How do teachers motivate, challenge, and engage students?

- How do teachers create a thriving classroom community?

- How do teachers communicate with students about their progress?

- What are the purposes of the traditional age-graded classroom and curriculum?

- How do multi-age grouping and looping change the way teachers approach their work and their students?

- What are the benefits and limitations of block scheduling at the high school level?

- What are the challenges of implementing class size reduction?

- How can technology be used to improve student engagement and learning?

- How does differentiated instruction help create better learning experiences for students?

- What is the role of cooperative learning in meeting students' academic and social needs?

- How does peer tutoring provide improved conditions for learning?

- What is the role of paraprofessionals in the classroom?

# Organizing Good Schools and Good Classrooms

# 9

Lucy Richards is finishing her last semester in teacher education. With one month left to complete her internship in a third grade classroom, she is hoping to be hired as an elementary school teacher in the local suburban district. After interviewing at several schools, she spends much of her time at home staring at the phone, waiting for it to ring. Finally, Ms. Martinez, the principal of Driscoll Elementary, calls to offer her a position. Ms. Martinez is delighted to hire Lucy but wants her to know that Driscoll will be moving to a looping model in the fall. Should she accept the position, Lucy will begin with her students as a first grade teacher and move up with them for two more years through third grade.

Lucy has read about looping but has never seen it in action. She asks for a few days to think it over and immediately calls her cooperating teacher, Janet Daniels, a 20-year veteran. "Janet, they've offered me a job at Driscoll. The thing is, they are moving to looping in the fall. I'd teach the same kids in first, second, and third grade. But I don't know if I can do it."

Janet asks, "Well, what exactly are you worried about?"

"I'm not sure," Lucy responds. "I always imagined myself teaching at one grade level for a few years so I could get that grade's curriculum straight. I never thought seriously about moving up with my students, but it actually sounds like it has some advantages."

"I think you're right to give it a real chance. You've already worked with students who are above and below the third grade level—so you have some idea of what comes before and after. And since you'll know what your students have learned the previous year, you'll be able to jump right into teaching as soon as school begins. I think this system has a lot of advantages—for both you and the kids. And you'll really get to know the families over three years. I do wonder what would happen if you and a kid had a personality clash—but that's a good question to ask Ms. Martinez. Give it some thought—and let's talk more as soon as you get to school in the morning."

Lucy puts down the phone. "Well" she says to herself, "maybe I can handle this after all."

*Never forget these kids watch you constantly. They model themselves after you, and you have to be the person you want them to be. I want my students to be nice and to work hard. That means I had better be the nicest and hardest-working person they have ever met. Don't even think of trying to deceive your kids. They are much too sharp for that.*

Rafe Esquith, 2007

Schools are, by their very nature, places where students are gathered together into various groups for the purpose of learning. The size of these groups, their composition, the way students are selected to be in them, and how long students—and teachers—stay in them all affect how education works and how students experience school. For Lucy, a different approach to grouping students was an unexpected consideration as she thought about her first job.

School districts make choices about how children are grouped in school buildings, for how many years, and with what other students. Within classrooms, teachers also make decisions about how to group students. Most elementary schools follow the conventional structure of moving students to a different teacher each year, and most high schools generally have students move to a different teacher nearly every hour. Other schools may use different kinds of organizational patterns as a way of improving the quality of teaching and learning.

In the classroom, it is the teacher's job to balance the group context with the needs of each individual student regardless of the organizational pattern the school follows. One of the skills you as a professional teacher will need to possess is precisely this: the ability to be effective with groups of students so that each individual student learns. Teachers are not individual tutors; rather, they are responsible for making learning take place for individuals within a group. That is why the successful experiences you may have had with individual children or with very small groups of children, as we noted in Chapter 2, may not directly translate to success in the classroom. Taking responsibility for the academic learning of a large group of students is much more complex.

Another way to think about classroom organization is to consider that in schools and classrooms, learning takes place in a social setting. Different organizational strategies represent different social settings for students and teachers alike. To create successful schools and classrooms, it is critical for teachers, administrators, and all staff members to recognize the importance of the social setting and understand how the organization of learning within it affects how students learn. In the past two decades, schools have attempted unprecedented levels of reform, all directed toward the goal of better meeting students' needs and improving student learning at a time when the student population is more diverse than ever. For many schools, these reforms include trying out different patterns of student and teacher interaction and different options for how instruction takes place in classrooms.

In this chapter, we take up the issue of how classrooms and schools are organized to support students' growth and learning. What makes one school rather than another a good place to learn? What are some of the things they have in common? How do different organizational structures help or hinder teachers in their efforts to be responsive to their students within the overall structure of schools and classrooms?

**Classrooms are social as well as academic settings.**
(Media Bakery)

## Your turn... *to reflect*

Do you think you attended a "good school" as a student in elementary or secondary school? What characteristics made it a good school? Do you also think this was true for other students? Why might it have been a good school for some but not for others? Now think about the classrooms you have been in. What made them good or not? Were they good classrooms for all students? some students?

# What Makes a Good School? What Makes a Good Classroom?

We know that schools can be very different from one another, can subscribe to different educational philosophies, have different themes, and emphasize different areas of the curriculum. We also know that good schools exist in all kinds of communities, including communities that are urban, wealthy, rural, suburban, or poor. Despite all of this variation, in all schools and classrooms that work well, certain characteristics seem to be present that make them work—for students and teachers alike.

As a general rule, schools that work well are places where students are motivated to learn and learn to think in complex ways, which is necessary for success in today's complex world (Tharp, Estrada, Dalton, & Yamauchi, 2000). They are strong communities in which students feel that they have a place—as human beings, as learners, and as members of their school; they are also professional communities for teachers and supportive communities for families. In such schools, teachers and administrators value improving the quality of their practice and take action to do so. They are places where teachers themselves are engaged in learning. In these schools, students are motivated to learn, with the result that students actually do learn well.

## In Good Schools, Students Are Motivated, Challenged, and Engaged

Good schools are places where students are *motivated* to learn, and it is up to teachers to know how to create classrooms that provide that motivation. Students want to spend time in such schools and classrooms because they are exciting places to be. In classrooms that are motivating, teachers encourage all members of the class to do their best work. Classrooms that support students' efforts, classrooms where students believe they have a chance of succeeding, classrooms where teachers assist students in their learning on a continuous basis are classrooms where students are engaged and tend to learn well.

### Motivating Students through High Expectations.
Students know whether a teacher does or does not expect a lot of them academically and behaviorally. Schools and teachers that set high expectations for all students, not just for those who appear to have the ability to achieve or who come to school with greater readiness than others, are good places for students to learn. They are places where all students have the opportunity to achieve because, as a starting point, their teachers believe in their capacity to do so and create the conditions that will promote their intellectual and emotional growth.

In schools where high expectations prevail, teachers encourage all students to engage in complex thinking about the curriculum, developing rigorous assignments that push students toward high-level thinking. Teachers ensure not only that students have the basic skills, or tools, they need to engage in more complex work, but also that students think and manipulate information as they communicate about and solve problems. Students do not merely sit all day and listen to teachers—the transmittal approach to learning we discussed in Chapter 5. Rather, they engage in discussion with their teachers and their peers, in a dialogue designed to foster student growth and understanding of the work at hand (Tharp, Estrada, Dalton, & Yamauchi, 2000). They also engage in inquiry into the issues they are learning about. That does not mean that a teacher will never lecture or never provide very focused, explicit instruction, but a teacher's expectations of her students cannot be viewed as high or challenging if the students are asked to do only rote, low level work each day.

Teachers also set clear expectations in order to motivate students. If students do not know what is expected of them, or if a teacher's expectations are ambiguous, students are less likely to be eager to participate in school. Therefore, good teachers know not only what they are teaching, but also why they are teaching it—and they can communicate their reasons to students in ways that make sense to them. When students view what they are being asked to do as authentic and having value, they are more likely to be engaged.

Motivation, then, depends on the kinds of activities students are asked to do in school in the first place. How teachers decide to implement the curriculum, what to emphasize, and what approaches to instruction they provide can work in a way that is motivating or not motivating to students. When students are treated as passive learners and are only expected to sit still and listen, they will likely not be motivated because they may not see the point of being in school in the first place. In such situations students may not pay attention, may be bored, or, especially at the high school level, simply may not show up.

### The Relationship between Teacher Knowledge and Student Engagement.

One of the most important things teachers can do to engage their students in learning is to know their subject matter *and* know how to explain it to students well. In Chapter 3 we talked about the concept of pedagogical content knowledge—that is, the special knowledge teachers possess by being able to convey the content in ways that make sense to their students. When teachers do not deal with students' questions about the content authentically, students can easily tune out.

This happens in at least three ways. First, teachers might simply provide an answer that is incorrect, not wanting to appear as if they can't answer the question. Obviously, all teachers have moments where they might say to their students, "You know, I'm not sure, but I'll check and let's talk about it tomorrow." But if this recurs on a regular basis, teachers can quickly get a reputation for "getting it wrong" or just not knowing their material. Next, teachers can simply shut down the sense of community that enables students to ask questions and feel comfortable doing so. When teachers are not knowledgeable about the content and are not sure how to explain it, they themselves feel a lack of confidence and students easily pick up on this. Teachers such as these might follow the textbook and be uncomfortable diverging from it.

Teachers can also display their discomfort by ignoring students' questions altogether, by providing a partial answer that does not satisfy the student's question or their interest, or by creating a classroom environment where students do not feel comfortable or safe even asking questions in the first place. And this does not occur only with topics that might be controversial, for example, complicated current events or issues in science such as stem-cell research or evolution. Have you ever seen teachers shy away from answering a question in mathematics or from providing a scientific explanation because they simply did not know how to address it?

### Intrinsic and Extrinsic Motivation.

Motivation can be intrinsic or extrinsic, but to foster lifelong learning among their students, teachers need to help their students develop internal or **intrinsic motivation** to learn. That is, students develop the desire to learn primarily because they are interested in what they are learning and value it, and not just because they will receive an external reward or grade (Stipek, 2002). To foster intrinsic motivation, teachers need to create interesting lessons and units of study, as well as projects and assignments that students consider engaging and meaningful.

**Critical Term**

**Intrinsic motivation.** Motivation to do something without external rewards or consequences.

In contrast, **extrinsic motivation** is characterized as working for an external reward or reinforcement for learning. Rewards such as candy or points toward a prize, or negative outcomes such as taking away classroom privileges, represent *extrinsic motivation* to learn. When students are motivated primarily by external forces, they are much less likely to be interested in engaging in school tasks or to see learning as an important goal in itself (LePage, Darling-Hammond, & Akar, 2005). Rather, they may only work to gain the material reward that a teacher offers—or to avoid an unpleasant consequence. Teachers often use extrinsic rewards that are social rather than material, for example, student choice time once a week. In schools and classrooms where students are intrinsically motivated to learn, teachers may use systems of external rewards and consequences, but only sparingly and strategically in order to promote an individual student's sense of efficacy (LePage et al., 2005).

Why do some teachers rely almost exclusively on extrinsic systems of motivation? One explanation is that their lessons and instructional approaches may not be interesting enough to capture their students' attention, so they may be relying on extrinsic motivation to control their classes as a replacement for providing challenging instruction. Another is that teachers may not have developed sufficient confidence in their skills for managing classrooms for learning. For some new teachers, extrinsic systems of motivation provide them with a sense of security—that students will do what the teacher asks if they can receive a reward. Finally, teachers may rely on extrinsic motivation because they have not established positive, trusting relationships with their students. When such relationships are missing, students are less likely to be engaged in learning.

**Critical Term**

**Extrinsic motivation.** Motivation to do something because one receives a reward or one wishes to avoid a punishment.

## Your turn... *to review*

1. What is the major difference between intrinsic and extrinsic motivation?
2. What are the benefits and limitations of extrinsic motivation?
3. What is the relationship between teachers' pedagogical content knowledge and students' engagement in the classroom?

## Good Schools and Classrooms Are Communities of Learners

Because school is a social phenomenon, principals and teachers need to consider how student interactions with each other and with the teachers and staff affect and support student growth and learning. Yes, school is about learning, but it is also a deeply social setting that provides opportunities for students to get to know each other, learn how to work collaboratively, and take on responsibility. Directly related to the issue of motivation, then, is the sense of community that is intrinsic to good schools.

**Creating a Strong Classroom Community.** One way the teacher facilitates student growth and learning is by creating a strong classroom community in which all students are affirmed as individuals and as learners. Classrooms that are strong communities exhibit a high degree of mutual respect among students and between students and the teacher. In these classrooms, things run smoothly and management problems are diminished and often prevented to begin with (LePage, Darling-Hammond, & Akar, 2005).

Motivation plays a major role in creating classroom communities. Teachers who motivate students acknowledge the good work of all class members regularly, both publicly and privately, providing *specific* feedback to students on the quality of their work. Such teachers support individual students who may not feel confident, and recognize the accomplishments of students who struggle—however small their accomplishments may be. These teachers also know that embarrassing and belittling students are not ways to motivate them to learn.

Strong classroom communities are learning communities in which students are clear about the teacher's goals and are responsive to the teacher's high expectations for their learning and behavior. Students and teachers, being "in it together," take mutual pride in the accomplishments of the community's members. A classroom in which students share responsibility for the quality of the community makes a strong statement about what role the school should take in the social development of its students.

Students are quite aware of what qualities the classrooms of good teachers should have. Figure 9-1 illustrates the opinions of some urban middle school students about the good teacher's classroom.

**Connecting to the Local Community.** Successful schools draw on the community as a source of knowledge and resources for their students' education (Comer, 1997; Gonazalez, Moll, & Amanti, 2005). Teachers know the students and the community well and value that knowledge by using it to extend the community that supports student learning (LePage, Darling-Hammond, & Akar, 2005). Families and community members feel comfortable at school and participate in the life of the school. In schools where these connections do not already exist, teachers and administrators can take purposeful action to build strong relationships between the community and the school—attesting to their commitment to make community an important part of the school and to make the school an important part of the community.

Teachers who make strong connections between the lives of their students and classroom instruction, especially when the community of the teacher differs from that of the student, also promote student learning (Banks, et al., 2005).

**A Community for Teachers.** Strong school and classroom communities depend on the quality of their teachers. You cannot have a thriving school without capable teachers, so schools must be learning communities for teachers as well. Teachers and administrators should work toward sharing a vision of the purpose

| **Figure 9-1    What Middle School Students Say about the Classrooms of Good Teachers** |
|---|

**All good teachers share certain characteristics, and students readily recognize them.**

| |
|---|
| Good teachers push students. |
| Good teachers maintain order. |
| Good teachers are willing to help. |
| Good teachers explain until everyone understands. |
| Good teachers vary classroom activities. |
| Good teachers try to understand students. |

**Source:** Corbett, D., and B. Wilson. (2002). What urban students say about good teaching. *Educational Leadership,* 60, 18–22.

of the school, with shared responsibility for improving the quality of the community and the achievement of its students (Fullan, Bertani, & Quinn, 2004).

Such schools are places where teachers are given the opportunity, and the support, to continue developing their skills and capacities. New teachers bring considerable skill to a school when they take their first positions—but being new, they need time and support to develop confidence. In strong schools veteran teachers support new teachers, and skilled teachers model instruction to help new teachers to develop greater capacity in the classroom (Humphrey, Wechsler, Bosetti et al., 2008). Supporting new teachers is the responsibility of the entire school, not just a designated mentor. They are places where teachers can talk about their work, share ideas, and find colleagues to support them as they try out new approaches with the goal of improving their teaching practice.

Teachers who are satisfied in their professional teaching communities and believe their professional expertise and experience are valued are more likely to be motivated to do their job well. Further, when teachers feel secure in their workplace, they are more likely to be creative and innovative. They are also more likely to demonstrate a willingness to try new pedagogies and to organize instruction in different ways to maximize student learning.

## Good Schools Know How Well They, and Their Students, Are Doing

In good classrooms teachers continually assess the progress of their students and use those assessments to evaluate the quality of their own teaching (Shepard, Hammerness, Darling-Hammond, & Rust, 2005). This does not mean giving tests daily. Rather, teachers assess their students' performance using multiple methods: observation, informal class work and projects, student portfolios, as well as through formal tests. All serve as tools that can inform a teacher's work.

One of a teacher's most important responsibilities is to provide meaningful feedback to students on the quality of their work. (Corbis Digital Stock)

In such classrooms, assessment becomes a learning tool for teachers and students alike. Teachers regularly provide useful, meaningful feedback to their students based on their assessments (Falk, 2000). A paper with a grade but with no comments or with only a generalized statement like "Good" or "Nice job" is insufficient; students need specific ideas about what they are doing well and where they need to improve. That teachers should provide specific feedback seems obvious, but it is not always provided in a way that helps students. Without it students are often left wondering what they have done incorrectly or which aspects of their work they need to improve. In many ways, it is much more important to provide feedback on work in progress than it is to comment extensively about a grade once the work is finished and the student is beginning a new task or project. If students do not know how they are doing and how to improve their work, they will not have a clear idea of how to meet their teacher's expectations.

Good schools also assess their own effectiveness. Administrators and teachers gauge the success of their teaching by considering how well their students are learning. It has always been important for teachers and schools to look toward evidence of how their students are learning as a way to improve their instruction. By reflecting on the data students produce in whatever assessments a teacher might use, teacher planning is grounded in their students' learning, and assessments are used to form new teacher approaches to instruction (Stiggins, Arter, Chappuis, & Chappuis, 2005). In other words, assessment, learning and teaching go hand in hand. Unfortunately, in the era of the No Child Left Behind legislation, the pressure for students to achieve on standardized tests has spawned a frenzy of attention to only one kind of data—that generated by standardized tests. Schools need to be attentive to multiple forms of data, and the data generated by classroom teachers as they go about their daily work are one of the most important sources of knowledge for improving the quality of teaching. Based on their analyses, teachers and administrators can work together to make decisions about how to improve the quality of their work. For example, at the school level they may review student assessments, consider absentee and truancy rates, look at the range of students in Advanced Placement classes at the high school, or analyze rates of family participation in conferences.

Just as individual teachers reflect on their own performance based on what they learn from their students' work, the school staff as a whole can reflect on the school's performance based on what they learn from the data that describe the school's effect as a whole.

## Rethinking School Organization to Meet Students' Needs

When teachers and administrators implement practices that characterize good schools, they are already putting the needs of individual students first. They are focusing on how to create healthy places for children and youth to learn, schools that motivate, support, and facilitate students' intellectual and emotional growth and development. But how much does the traditional organization of schools help or hinder creating schools that work for students—even when good teaching is taking place? In this section, we consider the traditional organization of schools and compare it with several organizational patterns that create different grouping structures.

When you think of the word "school," the image many of you conjure up is the traditional school—long hallways filled with classrooms, little interaction between classrooms or the teachers, a separate school for the elementary grades, another one for grades 6 through 8 or 7 through 9, and a comprehensive high school. You may think of classes as having about 25 or 30 students of the same age. If you grew up in a rural area, your image may be slightly different. You may have gone to an isolated small rural school for grades K through 8, followed by a regional high school serving several communities, with long bus rides every day to get there and back. School was generally in session from about 8 AM to 3 PM.

But whichever schools you attended, in all of them students were usually assigned to classes based on their age. This organizational scheme, known as the *age-graded* classroom model, predominates in U.S. schools, with students moving up in grade each year with their peers of the same age. Depending on the size of the school, several class sections may be provided for a single grade.

In the age-graded model, elementary school students traditionally stay with their teacher for only one year. That teacher usually teaches all subjects, although a specialist teacher might be provided for music, art, or physical education. In middle schools and high schools, students usually go from class to class, with a different teacher for every subject. This structure is known as **departmentalization**. Sometimes, in the upper elementary grades, some departmentalization also takes place.

**Critical Term**

**Departmentalization.** An organizational structure where teachers with academic content expertise teach only the subjects in which they are experts, and students move from teacher to teacher and class to class during the school day. Departmentalization can take place for every subject, or a single teacher might teach two subjects (for example, language arts and social studies).

The age-graded approach represents what we have come to think of as a well-organized school: classes of comparably aged-children learning with their same-aged peers, moving up from grade to grade year after year, with a new teacher every year. As we learned in Chapter 5, the curriculum is organized and divided by these same age and grade considerations, all the way from kindergarten to twelfth grade. As we learned with regard to the concept of the "hidden curriculum" in Chapter 6, we take grouping by age for granted. It is one of the assumptions that is made about schooling in the United States that often goes unquestioned.

## The Traditional Approach: Age-Graded Classrooms and Curriculum

In the **age-graded school** model, school districts usually establish a cutoff date to determine when students are eligible to attend a certain grade. Sometimes this date falls at the end of the summer, for example, at the end of August, and sometimes it falls at the end of the calendar year. In a district where the cutoff comes at the end of August, all children who are 5 at the end of August might be eligible for first grade starting in September, and all children who are 12 by the end of August might be eligible to begin grade 7.

> **Critical Term**
>
> **Age-graded school.**
> A school with classrooms organized by age, with students moving up to a new grade each year with a new teacher.

Why do we group children by age? The underlying assumption is that all children of the same age will learn at the same pace and have the same needs. Under this organizational plan, teachers are supposed to be able to meet individual students' needs because all of the students in a particular classroom are thought to be at approximately the same level precisely *because* they are all close in age. The curriculum is also organized in the same way, by grade, to meet the needs of children who are supposed to be functioning at that level. So not only are students grouped by age, but also textbooks, workbooks, and supplemental materials that students use are organized to meet age-graded classes.

Age-graded grouping, then, is designed to be an efficient way of organizing schools and classrooms, a way that makes it easier for teachers to teach and children to learn. Because in theory students in the same grade should be functioning at similar levels of intellectual and social development in a graded-level organizational structure, teachers are not supposed to have to differentiate their instruction much to meet the needs of their students. The age-graded classroom is assumed to be an efficient model because it limits the range of what a teacher needs to know and simplifies teachers' work and narrows the curriculum range for which teachers are responsible.

Historically, age-graded grouping in large schools was a product of demographic shifts and a move toward what is often called a factory model of education. As population centers moved from rural to urban and suburban areas, it was necessary to figure out a way to educate large numbers of children and move them through the system in an orderly fashion. Age-graded schooling developed as one solution to this problem, and, obviously, it has had a powerful, sustained impact on schooling.

> ## Your turn... *to reflect*
>
> Think back to your own schooling. Were you always in age-graded classrooms? What were the advantages of this structure for you? for your classmates? the disadvantages? If you were in another kind of situation, what was it like?
>
>

But is the age-graded, 8AM-3PM model necessarily the best way to organize schools for learning and for meeting students' individual needs? What other forms of school organization and grouping might serve students better than the traditional pattern? What other forms of organization are possible, and how much are they used in the United States? What promise do they hold for improving education?

## Multi-Age Classrooms

One alternative is **multi-age classrooms**, where students of various ages are enrolled in the same classroom and taught simultaneously by the same teacher. Multi-age classrooms are nongraded; they most often include students in a two- to three-year age range and are often, but not exclusively, found in elementary schools. Students learn together across the different developmental ranges they represent. You might find that one multi-age classroom includes students from traditional grades 1, 2, and 3, whereas another has students from traditional grades 4, 5, and 6.

Simply putting children of varying ages together will not ensure that the benefits of multi-age grouping will result. Instead, teachers must be prepared to organize their classes and instructional materials so that children's individual needs can be met (Katz, Evangelou, & Hartman, 1990). And, obviously, they must be teaching in schools where this approach is supported. When this occurs, proponents of multi-age grouping are often passionate about its benefits.

### Your turn... *to reflect*

Brainstorm a list of benefits of multi-age grouping for teachers and students. What challenges might this approach present for a teacher?

Because multi-age classrooms are nongraded, the basic assumption is that all students have individual needs that teachers must meet—no matter what their age (Walser, 1998). Teachers in multi-age classrooms do not expect to be able to teach to only one level of student development. Instead, multi-age classrooms are organized from the outset to meet students' individual needs and to provide instruction to make this happen. In contrast to age-graded classrooms, teachers in multi-age settings have always assumed that students are not on the same level. This situation is not viewed as a problem, but rather as a common condition of schooling and a regular part of a teacher's work. Annual standardized testing by grade under the No Child Left Behind Act is not compatible with multi-age classroom arrangements, but proponents continue to support these arrangements because of their benefits (Walser, 1998).

In multi-age classrooms, teachers group their students according to their various levels of development rather than by their age. Those groups are likely to change during the course of a day and over the year as teachers continuously assess their students' progress, which is also a hallmark of multi-age classrooms (Walser, 1998). Teachers can take advantage of the natural relationships children develop across different ages and have older students assist younger ones. Finally, in multi-age classrooms students do not have to compete with one another to get to the top of their class; rather, students compete against themselves and their own level of development.

Some studies comparing the achievement of students in traditional age-graded classes versus multi-age classrooms suggest that achievement is equivalent (Lloyd, 1999; Veenman, 1995). Others have found superior achievement in multi-aged classrooms (Pavan, 1992). Teachers in these classrooms expect to provide curriculum at a level that meets each child's needs and thus may be more likely to meet the needs of students at the high end of the achievement spectrum (Lloyd, 1999).

## Looping

Another way of organizing schools, **looping**, is the practice of keeping students of the same age together with the same teacher for more than one year; it is also sometimes known as *multiyear grouping*. At the elementary level, classes usually loop for two or three years, and then the teacher returns to the lowest grade in the loop. For example, let's say that as a fourth grade teacher you loop with your class for three years, taking them from fourth grade through the end of sixth grade. At the end of sixth grade the students would get a new teacher, and you would return to fourth grade to work with a new group of students for another three years. Looping is not the norm in the United States. It is more commonly found in elementary schools and has been used successfully in high schools as part of a program for students who are at risk of school failure (Yamauchi, 2003). In contrast, looping is practiced regularly in Waldorf Schools (Association of Waldorf Schools of North America, n.d.) as well as schools in Japan and Germany (Nichols & Nichols, 2002).

One important advantage of looping is that it gives teachers and their students an opportunity to establish a solid, family-like relationship over a long period of time (Reynolds, Barnhart, & Martin, 1998; Simel, 1998). This is crucial for the relationships not only between teachers and students, but also among students themselves. Similarly, looping affords parents and families the opportunity to develop an ongoing relationship with their child's teacher over a long period of time. Parents whose children have been in looping arrangements beyond one year have significantly more positive attitudes than those who were not in looping situations (Nichols & Nichols, 2002). Establishing a long-term relationship means that teachers, students, and families have continuity from year to year, as well as over the summer.

With looping, students do not have to get used to a new teacher, new routines, new expectations, and new ways of "doing business" at school every fall. This can significantly reduce students' anxiety about the start of a new school year. And teachers do not have to spend the first several weeks of school getting to know their new students—their developmental levels; their likes, interests, and dislikes; and the way they learn best. Thus, everyone can start right in on the process of learning as soon as they return to school, without wasting valuable time as is necessary in traditional age-graded classes (Black, 2000). In looped classrooms, an entire month is "saved" at the start of the second year that teachers and students are together, a month that is virtually "lost" in the traditional age-graded classroom.

Another benefit of looping is that teachers can begin to think about their students not in terms of "What can I teach them in nine months?" but rather, "How are my students developing over time, and how can I meet their individual needs to make sure that at the end of our third year together, they are ready to move into the next level?" This approach forces teachers to be very familiar with children's patterns of development for the entire age range they teach. The ability to work with a child over time can also reduce the pressure a teacher may feel to accomplish everything in a short nine-month period. At the same time, it increases the teacher's responsibility for what a student learns during the several years they are together.

Sometimes schools interested in moving toward multi-age grouping first begin with several years of looping (Northeast and Islands Regional Education Laboratory at Brown University, 1997). This allows teachers to get used to thinking about a wider range both of student development and the curriculum, as well as plan for multiple levels within a single classroom. Then, as teachers move into multi-age settings, they are used to thinking of children less in terms of tightly defined age ranges and more in terms of their development over time.

### Critical Term

**Looping.** Keeping students of the same age together with the same teacher for more than one year; students move up with their teachers to the next grade.

## Historical Note
### One-Room Schools

Today only about 400 one-room schoolhouses exist in the United States; at the start of the twentieth century about 200,000 such schools were in operation. (Corbis Images)

In the early history of schooling in the United States, one-room schools dominated the educational scene in all areas except urban centers. As the twentieth century dawned, approximately 200,000 one-room schools existed; toward the end of the century, the number had dropped to approximately 800 (Rose, 1997). In 2006, fewer than 400 one-room schools remained in at least 24 states but are found primarily in Pennsylvania, Nebraska, and Montana (www.theoneroomschool.org).

Historically, rural schoolhouses always had multi-age groupings and one teacher. This organizational arrangement was born of necessity, and the range of ages was often quite wide. Students helped each other across age and grade levels as a matter of routine, and teachers expected to teach multiple age and developmental levels together. Although those who recall their education in rural schools do so with a sense of nostalgia, wistfulness, and a romantic view of the past, the reality of what it meant to teach in a one-room school was far from romantic. Small buildings served as schoolhouses, and in the Southwest, old train cars were sometimes converted into schoolhouses. As Mike Rose observed during his travels around the country:

> Depending on era and region, they were built of sod, adobe, or logs, stone or clapboard. By and large, they were harsh, uncomfortable places. School life met the demands of the farm calendar, with some schools open for seven or eight months, some for three or four. A plaque on that schoolhouse in Tennessee noted that some children went for six weeks. The one-room school typically included 1st through 8th grades; ages and attendance varied widely, and class size ranged from half a dozen to 40 or more. For all their variety, and given the minimal centralized regulation—they epitomized local control—they were surprisingly uniform in their organization (young children in front, older in back), pedagogy (grammar, spelling, penmanship), arithmetic, U.S. history, physiology, geography. (Rose, 1997, p. 36)

In these rural schools, teachers were nearly always young unmarried women who worked for exceedingly low salaries. Their responsibilities included not only teaching, but firing up woodstoves and cleaning the schoolhouse. They taught all subjects at all grade levels. Rose continues:

> The teacher walks to the door, about to call the children in for the morning. She's young, she works for one-third less pay than a man, has most likely a high school education or less, perhaps barely out of the country school herself. If she's not from here, she boards with one of the families of her pupils or lives in a small, minimally appointed teacher-age [living quarters], open to the scrutiny of the community. Her letters may well reflect what many from the time reflect—the loneliness and vulnerability, the frustration over discipline and inadequate supplies, the challenge of so many lessons, all those kids. Still, the work offered one of the few avenues to independence and authority. It was a chance, as one young woman put it, to "try myself alone and find out what I am." (Rose, 1997, p. 36)

Today small rural one-room schools are the exception. For those who teach in them, and for those families whose children attend them, one-room schools are still valued for their unique ability to provide each child with a highly personal kind of education. But financial considerations pressure communities to close such schools and consolidate them with surrounding districts. In December of 2005 National Public Radio presented a series of broadcasts on seven one-room schools from across the country, ranging from Alaska to New Hampshire. The stories of these schools can be heard at www.theoneroomschool.org.

## Class Size Reduction at the Elementary Level

Another way to better meet students' individual needs is to reduce class size. Each school district sets class size; this number is extremely important because it determines the number of teachers a district needs to hire. Traditionally, the younger the students, the greater the effort to keep class size as small as possible to make sure that the youngest students get a strong start in school and are prepared for the increasing complexity of the curriculum. **Class size reduction** enables teachers to spend more time with each student.

In 1998, in an attempt to reduce class size in kindergarten and grades 1, 2, and 3 to no more than 18 students per class, federal legislation called *Class Size Reduction*, or CSR, was enacted that provided $2.5 billion to reduce class size. In the No Child Left Behind (NCLB) Act of 2001, funds for class size reduction were folded into the overall NCLB funding plan (see Chapter 10 for details of the NCLB legislation). Many states have also enacted and funded their own class size reduction legislation. The earliest experiment using CSR involved kindergarten students in Tennessee; it showed that especially for students in central city schools, smaller classes were associated with higher achievement (Finn, 2002). Following this experiment, large-scale CSR efforts were initiated in California and Wisconsin for grades K–3. Today, efforts to reduce class size in the early grades have been made in at least half of the states (Finn, 2002).

When a state undertakes a CSR initiative, two immediate things happen that have serious financial implications for school districts. First, there is a need for more classroom space for the new classes that are created as a result of reducing the size of each existing class. If the original class size was between 25 and 30, CSR could easily result in doubling the number of classrooms needed for grades K–3. An alternative to needing so many classrooms is to have two teachers team within the same classroom—often two teachers for 30 students. When CSR is based on a team teaching model, teachers must learn to work together for the good of their students, thus stretching them professionally.

### Critical Term

**Class size reduction.**
Usually refers to funding to ensure small class sizes from kindergarten through third grade; funding may be federal or state, or both.

---

## Your turn... *to review*

1. Identify three important ways schools can motivate students.
2. What are three ways that looping changes the way schools and education function?
3. Name one benefit and one limitation of class size reduction.

Second, CSR creates an immediate need for new teachers to staff the new classrooms. If enough teachers are not available, then districts may have to hire teachers who are not fully qualified and may be entering teaching via an emergency teaching

Class-size reduction is an effort to keep the student-to-teacher ratio at 15–1 in the early elementary grades. (Media Bakery)

license. If the point of CSR is to improve student achievement by improving the teacher–student ratio, giving teachers the opportunity to focus their instruction more intensely and meet individual students' needs, it is not logical to place teachers who have inadequate or limited qualifications in those classrooms. However, that is precisely what happened in California when that state moved to a CSR model (Stecher, Bohrnstedt, Kirst, McRobbie, & Williams, 2001). The California experience underscores the importance of anticipating needs in terms of teachers and infrastructure (i.e., buildings and classrooms) before beginning CSR initiatives.

When districts or states decide to introduce CSR, they also need to tie reducing class size to providing professional support to teachers about which teaching approaches best benefit students in small classes. Although CSR represents a real opportunity for good teachers to focus their work and increase the amount of attention they can pay to each child, poor teachers will not become good teachers just because they have fewer students to teach. This includes professional development in preparing teachers who will team under CSR to work effectively with another teacher.

Research on CSR has demonstrated that it is most effective in kindergarten and first grade; in later grades its value is a bit ambiguous. For CSR to work, classes need to be reduced to between 13 and 17 students. Finally, CSR appears to be more effective in improving the achievement of students from ethnic and racial minority groups (American Educational Research Association, 2003). Anecdotal reports by teachers and parents who have experienced CSR also suggest that teachers are less stressed, are better able to focus on individual students, and can work more effectively with students' families (Gilman & Kiger, 2003). CSR's positive effects suggest that it is one important alternative as schools restructure to meet student needs.

## Block Scheduling at the High School Level

**Critical Term**

**Block scheduling.**
Organizing the high school schedule to allow for longer class periods that meet fewer times a week.

In the typical high school, students move from class to class in 45- or 50-minute blocks, with teachers often teaching more than 150 students a day. **Block scheduling** was developed to address two pitfalls of this approach: (1) the inability to delve deeply into a subject and engage in projects that require substantial class time, and

(2) the difficulty a teacher has in getting to know students when teaching so many of them for such short time periods.

The traditional 45- or 50-minute schedule does not provide adequate time for a teacher to involve students in complex projects or for teachers and students to develop a good sense of community in the classroom. Barely have teachers begun class when they must think about ending it and preparing for a new class. In block scheduling, the schedule is rearranged so that classes meet every other day for twice the amount of time as in a typical daily schedule. Increasing the amount of class time a teacher has with students creates the opportunity to rethink instruction.

With block scheduling, teachers must be prepared to offer a stimulating, motivating class for double the time they used to teach—usually about 90 minutes—on an every other day schedule. This transition can be difficult. Teachers who are not skilled in the first place and do not provide a good learning environment for 45 minutes will likely encounter even greater difficulty for 90 minutes. In some schools, block scheduling is introduced without attention to improving the quality of instruction, weakening its potential to support reform and instructional improvement for students (Hackmann, 2004).

Introducing block scheduling and preparing for its implementation can help high school teachers rethink their approach to instruction and facilitate students' work on more complex projects, experiments, and research. With longer periods available, teachers can construct their classes so that while some groups of students are engaged in independent project work, others are working in small skill or review groups with the teacher. Or teachers can conference with individual students while others are working. They can also set up peer tutoring programs that might take place during one of the extended class periods each week. These kinds of interactions often occur at the elementary level but have not usually been implemented widely, if at all, in a traditional high school setting.

Obviously, when teachers have extended time with their students, they can get to know their students well. Close relationships are also possible in traditional high schools, though teacher–student interaction is more difficult in the traditional setting with teachers and students alike rushing around and moving from class to class. Block scheduling cuts into the traditional structure and may enhance a teacher's ability to be more responsive to student needs.

## Digging Deeper
### Introducing Innovations into Schools

Introducing change in organizing schools is not always easy. Many scholars of education lament the fact that the basic structures of schooling and teaching seem so resistant to change (Sarason, 1982; Tyack & Tobin, 1994). They portray the deep-seated practices, or regularities, that characterize most schools—established patterns of behavior that are accepted as the norm and are rarely questioned. Such patterns are hard to change because, according to Sarason, "it is extraordinarily difficult to see how they [the regularities of schooling] restrict the universe of alternatives we permit ourselves to think about" (p. 28). Larry Cuban, who has written widely on the implementation of technology in schools, discusses how slowly this innovation has been accepted. He also argues that innovation for the sake of innovation is not helpful (Cuban, 2001). Often people who are critical of schools dismiss new alternatives as impossible to achieve. Innovation seems to be valued, but what does it mean to move from the idea to actual implementation?

**The Nuances:** Innovation in schools is nearly always more complex than it at first appears. Although individual teachers may be committed to making changes within their classrooms, changing the structure (and by extension, the culture) of the school is a big undertaking. It requires that the administration and the teachers all be willing to work toward a common goal (Fullan, 1993). The ability to achieve this common goal depends in large part on the credibility of the person introducing it and the extent of teacher "buy-in." Once change is decided on, sufficient planning time is required to consider all of the potential problems and challenges the change demands. Administrators, teachers, and paraprofessionals require sustained professional development to prepare for the innovation.

For example, if a high school is moving toward block scheduling, the school needs to rethink the entire time frame of the day. A representative group of teachers and other staff members—as well as students—might visit a school or schools in another part of the country that have implemented block scheduling to get ideas on how it works and to get advice regarding pitfalls. Planning also includes not only changing the actual schedule, but also redesigning the technology that creates student schedules. Clear communication with families is essential and requires another level of planning. Teachers also need to consider how their instruction will change when class periods are doubled in length. Some teachers may be ready for this change; others may need extended professional development to gain confidence in how to implement intensive, extended instructional activities. Teachers may also request time to observe one another when they are using new these new instructional strategies.

Time and professional development demand financial resources. Furthermore, consideration needs to be given to teachers who may not be supportive of the shift. Will they be permitted to transfer to another school? If the district is small and no transfer is possible, how will the teachers who are most resistant be addressed?

**Rethinking the Issue:** Innovations in school structure can represent critical opportunities for schools to create new patterns of teacher–student interaction. When innovation is mandated without adequate attention to the details of its implementation, however, and when insufficient resources are invested in the initial stages of the change, it is not surprising that an innovation may not be implemented well. Teachers may be wary of innovation if there is inadequate support. But with adequate planning and ongoing support, and based on a change that is justifiable, teachers are often willing participants in any endeavor to improve teaching and learning.

## The Small High Schools Movement

Another major effort to reorganize and restructure American schools is the trend toward creating smaller schools, especially smaller high schools. During the latter half of the twentieth century, however, many rural school districts were consolidated to become larger districts as a way of making education more efficient (Hampel, 2002). With school consolidation, one-room schoolhouses and other rural schools became feeders for large, comprehensive high schools that could offer a much wider range of courses by centralizing resources for course offerings and extracurricular activities (Hampel, 2002). Teachers could specialize, become experts in their subjects, and teach only those subjects to their students.

This centralized approach gave students from rural communities access to a broader range of academic subjects that would otherwise not have been available—for example, foreign language instruction. A small rural school might not be able to afford a foreign language teacher on its own, but if communities consolidated their funding to create large high schools, they could afford a foreign language program. Similarly, a small isolated school might not support a marching band or a drama program, but a large high school could. Consolidation was also a solution for school districts experiencing declining enrollments.

## Your turn... *to reflect*

In a small group, discuss the size and scope of your own high school. What were the benefits of your high school? the drawbacks?

Despite the opportunities afforded students in large high schools, dissatisfaction especially with large urban high schools grew at the beginnning of the 21st century. High school dropout rates, which hover between 25 and 30 percent, are a major cause of concern in the United States (Sum & Harrington, 2003). In urban districts the problem is even greater; for every 100 students who enter ninth grade, only 67 graduate, with even lower rates for African American and Hispanic students (Armstrong, 2005). Many high schools students are not connecting with school and with their teachers. Size is thought to play an important part in this situation; teachers in large urban schools systematically report higher frequencies of absenteeism and dropping out (National Center for Education Statistics, 2003).

In small high schools, a personal approach replaces the anonymity students may experience in large, factory-like high schools.
(Media Bakery)

But perhaps more important is that in many large urban high schools, students may feel that learning is not connected to them and their lives. As we noted in Chapter 7, rather than just teach the academic content in a manner that is entirely decontextualized from the students, their lives, and their communities, teachers need to place learning within the context of the students' lives. They need to focus on motivating students and on connecting new knowledge to what the students already know and value. This approach is even more critical when students face challenges in their lives outside school that are beyond their control. Although there has been some modest reduction in the dropout rate, it is higher for African American and Hispanic students compared with white students (Armstrong, 2005).

Developing relationships between teachers and students that build a community is also a problem in large suburban high schools. School shootings such as those in Columbine, Colorado, and Paducah, Kentucky, have become emblematic of the disaffected, disconnected suburban high school student. Students may form cliques to create an identity for themselves, and these cliques can define their high school experience much more than anything else related to school. The organization of the school day, with students moving from class to class and teachers

often teaching hundreds of students a day helps create the conditions in which students can too easily become anonymous. Large comprehensive high schools do indeed appear to have some limitations.

The modern inception of small schools was initiated in New York City in 1985 under the leadership of Deborah Meier, who started a successful small schools movement in East Harlem, including Central Park East Elementary and Central Park East Secondary schools (Meier & Schwartz, 1995). Located within some of the lowest performing of New York City's schools, Meier and her staff envisioned these schools as small, intimate learning communities, where students, families, and teachers could work closely to ensure that students were engaged and were learning. The curriculum was based on a progressive educational philosophy, with high levels of student engagement in challenging projects. Using this approach, Meier and her staff turned around achievement rates for the city's most disadvantaged group of students, lowered dropout rates for high school students, and saw many of them attend some of the nation's most prestigious colleges and universities.

Two general models have been presented for these new, small high schools. In the first, schools usually of no more than 400 students are created in new spaces that are dedicated to new small schools. In the second, large, existing high school buildings are turned into what are known as multiplexes—that is, a set of small "schools within a school" that have individual identities and curriculums, but that share the same building and facilities. These new, smaller high schools (1) have a clear identity, theme, or focus; (2) put a high value on teachers, administrators, and students developing close working relationships; (3) are committed to high levels of student engagement in their work; and (4) emphasize student achievement and preparing students for college and the world of work. Student learning is clearly at the center of the work of small high schools. To support the creation of smaller schools, the Bill and Melinda Gates Foundation launched an extensive initiative and by 2003 the foundation had granted over $400 million to restructure high schools, primarily in urban areas.

How small high schools will deal with issues such as extracurricular activities is still emerging. This is an important issue because small high schools are not able to hire specialist teachers in as wide a range of areas as is possible in comprehensive high schools. Because staff size is smaller than that in the traditional comprehensive high school, small schools may have to share teachers who possess high levels of expertise in the traditional content areas as well. Others do not have adequate teacher expertise across all subjects.

What does the small high school trend mean if you are planning to be a high school teacher? You will teach fewer students, but you will be expected to develop stronger relationships with those students. You may be called on to teach more than one subject area, requiring that you have expertise in those subjects. You will, no doubt, be working closely with other teachers in other subject areas, so collaboration will be an essential part of your job. Students are likely to engage in project-based learning in smaller high schools, projects that demand a high level of application of academic knowledge. High levels of teacher involvement will be expected in all aspects of the school. Thus, neither teachers *nor* students can remain anonymous or uninvolved in small high schools. Figure 9-2 presents a list of common features of good small high schools.

Small high schools are viewed as one solution to the problem of low achievement and low graduation rates among high school-aged youth. Like the other structures we have described (e.g., multi-age classrooms, looping, year-round schools, etc.), breaking up large high schools and forming small high schools alone

## Figure 9-2   Common Features of Successful Small High Schools

**Small high schools represent one effort to connect students with their schools, to engage students in learning, and to increase high school graduation rates.**

- A clear delineation of goals and standards that help focus curriculum, learning, and instruction.
- A distinctive educational approach, such as a theme or a special focus.
- Strong outreach to families of students and high levels of involvement with the families.
- An orientation toward active learning in the classroom and in the community, including service to the community.
- Extensive partnerships with community and business groups (which might include having a school share space with a community agency or business partners).
- Regular monitoring of student achievement, using multiple measures of learning to refine and improve schools.
- Students' and educators' choice of the school is a voluntary one.
- A strong principal or other leadership structure, such as a teacher leader or group of leaders, to ensure that there is follow-through on implementing decisions, programs, and practices that the school community agrees should be implemented.

**Source:** Adapted from North Central Regional Education Laboratory. (n.d.). *Small by design: Resizing America's high schools*. Retrieved July 25, 2008, from http://www.ncrel.org/policy/pubs/html/smbydes/index.htm.

will not change how students experience high school (Noguera, 2002). Instead, these structural changes create the potential for teachers to rethink how they teach and what they ask students to do, and to expand student involvement in their own learning.

## Rethinking the School Day to Increase Time to Learn

A different way of creating new opportunities for students is reconsidering the typical, longstanding approach to the length of the school day and the school year, as well as the structure of the school year itself. Increasing the way time in schools is conceptualized is the focus of considerable discussion. A national organization devoted to this topic has been created, the National Center on Time and Learning (**www.timeandlearning.org**).

**Lengthening the School Day and Year.** A different way to increase time to learn is to extend the school day and the school year themselves. Given the pressures to close the achievement gaps not only among groups within the United States, but also between the United States and other countries, the question of how much time is actually devoted to learning in our schools is an important consideration.

Further, the pressure created from No Child Left Behind and its emphasis on standardized testing has often narrowed the subjects that are offered, with a primary focus, especially at the elementary level, on reading and mathematics and reduced time even for social studies and science. This leaves little room for extremely important non-core subjects such as the arts and physical education (American Educational Research Association, 2007; Gabrieli & Goldstein, 2008). By extending the school day, it is argued, schools do not have to make difficult decisions about cutting out programs that are highly motivating and that often capture the interest and commitment of students to their schools, especially in the arts (see The Arts Education Partnership at **www.aep-arts.org**).

Not only can more time be devoted to more subjects, but teachers would have more time to provide individual support to students, especially students who are learning English at the same time they are learning academics (American Educational Research Association, 2007; Silva, 2007). Another important consideration regarding the length of the school day is that it would provide teachers with much needed time to engage in professional development to improve the quality of their teaching and their students' learning (Gabrieli & Goldstein, 2008; Silva, 2007).

Finally there is the question of extending the school year itself. The typical school year in the United States is 180 days, but it is longer in several European countries as well as in Japan. The old style calendar, with three months of vacation, is called into question when issues of time to learn are raised. One way to reconsider the structure of the school year is *year-round schools*.

## Critical Term

**Year-round schools.**
Schools with a calendar organized so that students attend over the course of the entire calendar year, with shorter vacations interspersed across the year.

**Year-Round Schools.**  **Year-round schools** are schools that follow a nontraditional calendar. Historically in the United States schools are in session for roughly 9 or 10 months of the year—from late August or early September through May or June. In year-round schools, students attend over the course of the entire calendar year, with shorter vacations interspersed across the year—rather than a single long summer vacation. The most common year-round calendar is one in which students attend school for 9 weeks (45 days) and then have a 3-week vacation (15 days), often known as the 45–15 plan (Everhart, 2003).

In rural areas, the traditional school calendar was often a response to family and community labor needs. Children would be home to help with the summer farmwork. In areas of the country that depend on summer tourism, having additional workers available during the summer months for restaurant and other service sector jobs was—and continues to be—an important source of labor. In urban areas, this calendar was adhered to as a way of providing a long summer respite for urban populations eager to escape the city (Weiss & Brown, 2003). Summers off became a fundamental organizing principle of schooling and extended to all kinds of schools—rural, suburban, small town, and urban alike. Thus, a combination of economics and lifestyle dictated the traditional school calendar.

In the late 1960s, several schools in California began shifting to a year-round calendar. Beginning in the 1970s, with the rise of school reform initiatives, the idea of year-round schools began to be explored more widely across the country. During the 2006–2007 academic year, over 3000 schools across 46 states were on year-round calendars, and approximately 2.2 million students in the United States attended these schools (National Association of Year Round Education, 2008).

What are the advantages of a year-round calendar? Proponents argue that when students are in school across the entire calendar year, with shorter vacations, school is a more consistent and continuous experience. Students are less likely to forget material and skills over shorter breaks than they are during the long summer break. Many schools, especially in California, embarked on the year-round calendar to alleviate overcrowding. This is called a multi-track approach. Groups of students can rotate in and out of the building depending on their vacation schedule, which can be staggered to maximize the use of the building. However, many schools simply elect to move to a year-round calendar because of its benefits to the students. In these schools, all students attend on the same year-round calendar.

How does the year-round calendar affect the day-to-day life of a teacher? On the practical side, teachers have several vacations during the year rather than only one and can take advantage of traveling during off-peak times. Frequent vacations have been identified as a way of reducing teacher fatigue. Because school is in session during some portion of the traditional summer vacation, the availability of advanced summer school coursework may be affected. However, some colleges and universities tailor courses for practicing teachers in particular schools or districts, a trend that can alleviate this problem.

Studies comparing the achievement of students in year-round versus traditional calendar schools have typically indicated that students in year round schools do neither better nor worse than their peers who attend school with a full summer off. Year-round schools may improve the achievement of disadvantaged students because they provide a more consistent educational experience over time (McMillen, 2001). However, in general, the argument in favor of year-round schools cannot reliably be made on the basis of superior achievement.

While there has been increased interest in shifting the calendar to a year-round schedule, the traditional calendar has shown great resistance to change (Weiss & Brown, 2003). To use Sarason's (1982) term, the traditional calendar represents one of the most dependable regularities of schooling.

## Philosophical Note
### Organizing Schools and Classrooms for Democracy

The Jeffersonian ideal of education (see Chapter 4) was based on the belief that education was central to a well-functioning democracy; it takes an educated citizenry, Jefferson observed, to participate in a democracy. But educating citizens for democracy does not necessarily mean that they experience democracy in schools or in the classroom. Ironically, many schools and classrooms do not seem to be based on a democratic philosophy at all: teachers tell students what to do; students have little to say about what they believe is important to learn or what they would like to learn. What does it mean to organize schools and classrooms for democracy?

The idea of democratic schools has a long history and can be traced back to the influence of John Dewey. In his book *Democracy and Education* (1916/1966), Dewey set forth a vision of students as participants in a community where each student is valued, where each student's interests are honored and the perspective of each is heard, where each student contributes to and interacts with the group, but where the interests of the individual and the interests of the group are negotiated within the community through discussion. Extending Dewey's philosophy, a contemporary educator, Amy Guttman (1987), suggested that it was important to state specifically that classrooms and schools can really be said to be democratic only if they are committed to nondiscrimination.

In describing of modern democratic schools, James Beane and Michael Apple (1995) identify the following characteristics:

● Democratic schools are communities that prize diversity but also have a common purpose.

● Democratic schools value collaboration and cooperation rather than competition.

● In democratic schools, the school does not erect barriers to participation in any aspect of school for its students; this would make tracking and other forms of exclusion unacceptable.

● Democratic schools are committed to building a more democratic world and improving the real conditions of life in the school, the community, and the nation at large; the curriculum supports this goal.

● Democratic schools are schools where teachers are active participants and fully valued members in decision making about the school.

But what does a philosophy of democratic education mean for the organization of classrooms on a day-to-day basis? In democratic classrooms, students' voices are heard and respected. The curriculum is organized in a way that enables students to have some level of choice in what they study or in how they study a predetermined subject or theme. They may not make every single decision about what to study, but they work collaboratively with their teachers and clearly have some ability to determine important decisions.

A high value is placed on student interaction and discussion as a means of fostering a community within which all opinions are heard and valued. Teachers might hold regular daily or weekly meetings with the class to discuss important issues and to model how the classroom community participates in such discussions. They may use these meetings to try to reach consensus on issues that are important to the class, to discuss how to support students who are struggling, or to identify projects the class may want to launch. If there are problems in the classroom community in terms of getting along, these meetings might be used to address the situation and find a solution.

In the democratic classroom, students and teachers alike are encouraged to accept the diversity of viewpoints that are expressed. They are ready and willing to participate in discussions about challenging issues—the same issues they may be working on in their projects and activities. Teachers in democratic classrooms and schools have an obligation to teach about issues from multiple perspectives so that students are exposed to diverse viewpoints, in particular viewpoints that may not regularly be heard.

Teachers in democratic classrooms are also willing to share power with their students, though the teacher does not relinquish all of his or her responsibility. However, teachers who wish to support democracy in the classroom are comfortable with some degree of shared participation and decision making. There is a conscious effort on the part of the teacher to make student participation and decision making a goal.

A democratic philosophy is compatible with a social reconstructionist philosophy of education. As Beane and Apple's list illustrates, the curriculum in a democratic school is one in which students take on projects whose focus is improving conditions in the world. Students would be expected to master the skills to participate in debate and dialogue—broadly interpreted as being skilled in speaking, in reading about contested issues, and in writing about them, as well as having the quantitative skills to analyze data they may collect. When students are committed to working on an authentic school, community, state, or national problem, they may be more likely to communicate clearly about the problem and about possible solutions to elected officials.

To prepare their students to participate responsibly in a democracy, teachers who subscribe to this philosophy make deliberate choices about how they organize their classrooms, the communities they create within those classrooms, the issues their students study, and their own roles in their schools. Although democratic schools are not the norm, teachers in schools all over the country are committed to these principles and practice them on a daily basis.

# REWARDS AND CHALLENGES

## Preparing the Next Generation of Recyclers

David House
*Athens, Ohio*

Living in such a beautiful area as Athens, Ohio, our view, sheds, watersheds, and public spaces of beauty are extremely important to many community members and to me. I wanted to work with my students in some way to help protect this beauty. So five years ago, I started a school-wide recycling effort in which the sixth graders in my homeroom class organize, manage, and implement a weekly recycling plan. With this project-based approach to curriculum, we have managed to save thousands of pounds of recyclables from finding their way to our local landfill. We have also been empowered to inspire younger students to become "recycle wise." All this work progresses as we master our state and locally mandated curriculum standards. With this project-based framework, my students and I have been more inspired in our own work and have accomplished much more than "making it through our sixth grade curriculum." I am very proud of this program and the students share fond reflections with me about their time working on the recycling team. As an environmentalist, I keep this project and its success close to my heart.

The recycling project begins week one with our training program. The students are taught the various roles they will work to master in the future. These roles include a supervisor who, with the help of a pre-made checklist, actually supervises the weekly recycling by employing the check sheet to insure all areas of the weekly work flow smoothly. Next is the manager, whose charge is to answer directly to the supervisor about suc-

cesses, problems, and other general feedback on the weekly operations. In addition, our collection team members work room to room collecting the recyclables and transporting them to our main recycling area (the cafeteria). In the café, our sorter team members are hard at work organizing the recyclables collected throughout the week and managing the flow from the collecting team members. All of this is overseen by the student supervisor and manager. After the weekly tasks are completed, we weigh, average, document, and display our records in various spreadsheets and graphs so the rest of the school can view our successful endeavors.

To promote the program at the beginning of the year, our class goes room to room performing a unique skit for each K-6 classroom. In this student-generated drama, they act out the important aspects of the program entertainingly to insure success while teaching younger students the impacts they can make by recycling. To end the year, we have a "Recyclebration," in which we highlight the successes of the year's program and focus on improvements for the next year through writings, debates, and public viewings of our yearlong efforts. We create a recycled art display while publishing our records for the community; parents and community members are invited to browse the art creations and read the results of our yearly work. This work has shown me that a project-based approach that engages my students, and the entire school and community, can accomplish much more than merely covering our curriculum. ●

## A Recap: Different Organizational Patterns, Different Social Settings

Each of these different organizational patterns share one common goal: to improve students' educational success. Multi-age classrooms, looping, year-round schools, class size reduction, block scheduling, small high schools and extended time to learn all address different aspects of some of today's most pressing problems in education. They seek to improve schools primarily by questioning some of the most common assumptions about how schools are organized for learning and by restructuring schools according to a different set of assumptions. In this way, they seek to create a different set of social circumstances within which children and youth attend school, different social settings, and different patterns of interaction between students and teachers—in short, different expectations for how school is experienced. Several of these trends address improving education by connecting students and their families more intimately to their schools. By building stronger relationships among teachers, students, and families, the assumption is that individual students will become more engaged and more successful in school.

But these approaches all depend on one critical thing: teachers knowing how to teach well and how to use the opportunities these reconfigured educational settings provide to support their students' learning. In other words, teachers must always possess a high level of professional knowledge in the methods of teaching and apply that knowledge in whatever school structure exists. A school's organizational structure cannot make up for an incompetent teacher or a teacher who is not committed to teaching students well. What it can do is to create a new set of expectations for the level of skill and commitment teachers demonstrate as they engage their students in learning.

# Rethinking What Happens at the Classroom Level to Meet Student Needs

The collective purpose of the many different organizational structures described in the preceding section is to change the conditions under which teachers teach and students learn. Ask any teacher, however, and you will find that in any given classroom, no matter what the structure of the school, levels of student development actually vary widely. Seldom are all students of the same chronological age in the same classroom functioning at the same level of cognitive development or readiness for learning.

As a result, teachers must be ready to organize their classrooms and use curriculum materials so that they can work with students whose levels of learning differ, who have different starting points, and who require different amounts of teacher attention. You may or may not take a position teaching in a school that has participated in a structural redesign. Within your own classroom, however, there are different ways you can organize for teaching and learning, structure groups and group activities, and determine the format of the day to better meet your students' individual needs.

These structures and approaches enable teachers to set up different patterns of interaction between teachers and students, between students and students, and between students and curriculum materials. They provide greater opportunities for students to participate and more opportunities for them to receive feedback on their progress.

## Differentiating Instruction to Meet Students' Needs: The Need for Flexibility

Recognizing that variation across students is the norm rather than the exception, one of the ways teachers can think about organizing their instruction is to prepare to differentiate it from the outset. **Differentiated instruction** is a commonly used term that refers to a way of teaching in which a teacher's entire approach to curriculum and instruction takes into account these differences instead of expecting all students to be working at the same level.

So rather than planning a lesson and being frustrated that all students aren't "getting it," teachers rely on instructional procedures that are intended to respond to the full range of students in their classrooms. Tomlinson and McTigue (2006) describe a U.S. History class where, in studying the Constitution, the teacher, for example; (1) is clear about the essential understandings he wants his students to gain; (2) provides vocabulary lists for students who require them; (3) provides a

**Critical term**

**Differentiated instruction.** Approaching instruction from the belief that students' abilities differ and that it is the teacher's responsibility to organize instruction to account for those differences on an ongoing basis.

choice of related questions so students can participate in the topic from a point of their own interests, divides the class time into thirds, with one third always being devoted to teacher teacher-directed instruction to build various student skills, and two-thirds split between two specific topics on the Constitution; (4) provides resources at multiple reading levels to support students in their work; and (5) gives students various ways of demonstrating how well they understand what he has set out for them to learn.

You can see how adopting a differentiated instruction perspective is related both to the curriculum and also to an educational philosophy that is more student-centered and less traditional than just relying on teacher lecture and worksheets. It is both a mindset of teachers and schools and a specific set of practices teachers can use to plan and implement their curriculum. You can also see how an approach like project-based learning, which we discussed in Chapter 5, is compatible with (but not the same as) differentiated instruction.

Differentiated instruction requires that teachers be flexible in their views of what it means to organize instruction and move well beyond adopting a one-dimensional approach to teaching that at its foundation disallows for the real variation among students that exists. It requires grouping students flexibly rather than creating a static grouping system at the start of the year and maintaining it no matter what the topic, project, or student ability. It is a means for addressing the curriculum in a way that makes it accessible. As Tomlinson and McTigue (2006) remind us: "If we had at our grasp the most elegant curriculum in the world and it missed the mark for students with learning disabilities, highly advanced learners, students with limited English proficiency, young people who lack economic support, kids who struggle to read, and a whole host of others, the curriculum would fall short of its promise."

## How Technology Helps Meet Student Needs

In Chapter 8 we discussed *assistive technology*, or technology designed to support students with disabilities. Technology can help all students, however, and has the potential to transform teaching and learning.

Classrooms that use technology to enhance learning the curriculum can provide wide-ranging opportunities that are not otherwise available to students. (Dynamic Graphics/Creatas)

**Critical Term**

**Instructional technology.**
Technology that supports
students' learning the
school curriculum.

**Instructional Technology in Today's Classrooms.** An important distinction exists between technology in general and **instructional technology**. Instructional technology is used to enhance students' learning of the school curriculum. It is broader and more sophisticated than software programs that allow students to practice specific skills or get immediate feedback on whether or not they have the correct answer, or "skill and drill" programs. Its real potential, and the one that can transform the way we think about education, rests with its ability to motivate and engage students in research, writing, and thinking, as well as presentation skills, using multimedia software and the Internet.

Technology can broaden students' educational horizons, providing them with access to places and people that were unavailable in the past. It creates the opportunity for serious, expanded study of a huge variety of topics far beyond what a textbook could ever offer. This availability lets students—especially those who may not be able to travel beyond their own rural or urban neighborhoods—begin to think about the larger world and see a broader range of possible future jobs, professions, and contributions to the world.

Through technology, for example, students can take field trips to locations and museums around the world, or participate in an ocean voyage with scientists to study the condition of the oceans (**http://www.pbs.org/odyssey**) or with other classrooms to track the

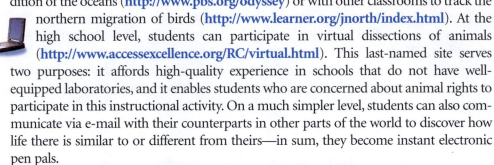 northern migration of birds (**http://www.learner.org/jnorth/index.html**). At the high school level, students can participate in virtual dissections of animals (**http://www.accessexcellence.org/RC/virtual.html**). This last-named site serves two purposes: it affords high-quality experience in schools that do not have well-equipped laboratories, and it enables students who are concerned about animal rights to participate in this instructional activity. On a much simpler level, students can also communicate via e-mail with their counterparts in other parts of the world to discover how life there is similar to or different from theirs—in sum, they become instant electronic pen pals.

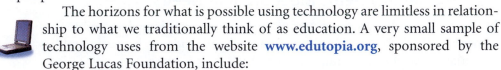 The horizons for what is possible using technology are limitless in relationship to what we traditionally think of as education. A very small sample of technology uses from the website **www.edutopia.org**, sponsored by the George Lucas Foundation, include:

- Providing resources in the world languages students are studying, for example, daily newspapers or websites
- Integrating streaming video and photographs into oral history projects
- Using digital temperature probes to study natural environments in a Minnesota prairie
- Having first graders follow the progress of an endangered sea turtle
- Videoconferencing with scientific experts
- Using global positioning systems to build a trail on an island school in Maine

A different example comes from the BioKIDS project at the University of Michigan, in which elementary school students use Cyber Tracker, a program that allows them to track animals in their schoolyards using PDAs. Once these data are collected, students can use the data to study the diversity of animals species and to conduct experiments (for more on this project, see **www.biokids.umich.edu**).

As Figure 9-3 illustrates, 94 percent of all classrooms are connected to the Internet, which enhances a teacher's ability to integrate the Internet into the curriculum (Wells, 2006).

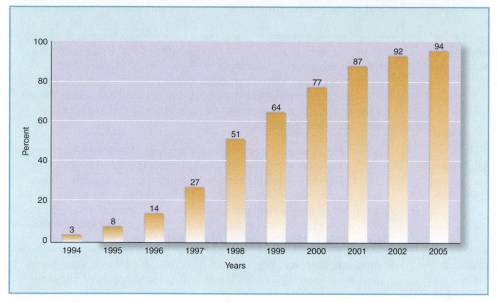

**Figure 9-3    Accessibility to the Internet in Public School Classrooms, 1994–2005**

The widespread availability of the Internet in public school classrooms makes it possible for teachers to plan to integrate greater technology resources into the curriculum.

**Source:** United States Department of Education. (2006). *Internet access in U.S. public schools and classrooms: 1994–2005.* National Center for Education Statistics, Report 2007-020. Washington, DC: Author. Retrieved May 22, 2008, from http://nces.ed.gov/pubs2004/2004011.pdf.

In terms of distribution of computers, the highest percentage exists in towns (98%) and the lowest in urban schools (88%), with schools in urban fringe communities at 96% and rural communities at 95% (U.S. Department of Education, 2006). Nearly half of all public schools with Internet access also have wireless access, and the ratio of students to computers designated for instructional purposes is approximately 4 to 1, down from 12 to 1 in 1998 (U.S. Department of Education, 2006). What these statistics do not tell us is how powerful or current the computers that are available may be, or what kinds of software are available to teachers and students. Also, other technologies may or may not be available that expand a teacher's ability to build a technologically advanced curriculum (e.g., digital cameras, laptops, MP3 players, and PDAs).

The new technologies also redefine one of the most basic roles of teachers by redefining what it means to be literate. In the past the term *literacy* referred exclusively to print materials. Today the term *multimodal* literacy is used to denote the various literacies that students must master and can use, many of which are technology-based. As illustrated in Table 9-1, multi-modal literacy is an accepted part of literacy learning as evidenced by the position of the National Council of Teachers of English in its guidelines for multimodal literacies.

**Your turn...** *to reflect*

How was technology used in your own PK–12 education? Did it help support your own learning? If yes, why? If no, why not?

**Table 9-1    Selected Issues Multimodal Literacy from the National Council of Teachers of English and Implications for Teachers**

Multimodal literacy exists in relationship to other literacies and resources in the schools.

| Multimodal Literacy Issue | What It Means for Teaching |
|---|---|
| Integration of multiple modes of communication and expression can enhance or transform the meaning of the work beyond illustration or decoration. | It is the interplay of meaning-making systems (alphabetic, oral, visual, etc.) that teachers and students should strive to study and produce.<br>Art, music, movement, and drama are also ways of knowing and should not be considered curricular luxuries.<br>All modes of communication are codependent. Each affects the nature of the content of the other and the overall rhetorical impact of the communication event itself. |
| Young children practice multimodal literacies naturally and spontaneously. They easily combine and move between drama, art, text, music, speech, sound, physical movement, animation/gaming, etc. | Children who grow up in impoverished or repressed literacy environments may not experience this important early literacy foundation.<br>The over emphasis on testing and teaching to the test may deprive many students of the kinds of multimodal experiences they most need.<br>An exclusive emphasis on digital literacies is not what most advocates of technology rich composition advocate. Such an emphasis would limit students' access to other modes of expression. |
| The use of different modes of expression in student work should be integrated into the overall literacy goals of the curriculum and appropriate for time and resources invested. | In personal, civic, and professional discourse, alphabetic, visual, and aural works are not luxuries but essential components of knowing. |
| Because of the complexity of multimodal projects and the different levels of skill and sensitivity each individual brings to their execution, such projects often demand high levels of collaboration and teamwork. | Teachers of the English/Language Arts already have models for this type of collaboration, such as those for producing a play. Any dramatic production includes speech, movement, costumes, props, sets, lighting, and, sometimes, music and dance. Beyond the performance itself is the need for producing appealing programs and advertising. And, beyond that are the persuasive verbal skills needed to raise funds to produce the production.<br>Other kinds of more traditional multimodal projects also require this type of collaboration. When students produce brochures, literary magazines, books, videos, or greeting cards, collaboration improves the product and helps all students involved learn more. |
| The use of multimodal literacies has expanded the ways we acquire information and understand concepts. Ever since the days of illustrated books and maps, texts have included visual elements for the purpose of imparting information. The contemporary difference is the ease with which we can combine words, images, sound, color, animation, video, and styles of print in projects so that they are part of our everyday lives and, at least by our youngest generation, often taken for granted. | Readers in electronic environments are able to gain access immediately to a broad range and great depth of information that not 15 years ago would have required long visits to libraries or days of waiting for mailed replies.<br>The techniques of acquiring, organizing, evaluating, and creatively using multirnodal information should become an increasingly important component of the English/Language Arts classroom. |
| From an early age, students are very sophisticated readers and producers of multimodal work. They can be helped to understand how these works make meaning, how they are based on conventions, and how they are created for arid respond to specific communities or audiences. | Students should be invited to collaborate with their teachers in the study of new literacies and in the practical aspects of integrating those literacies into the curriculum. |

**Source:** Adapted from "A Summary Statement Developed by the Multimodal Literacies Issue Management Team of the NCTE Executive Committee." Approved by the NCTE Executive Committee, November 2005. Retrieved May 23, 2008, from www.ncte.org.

Technology also provides new and different modes of communicating what students know. Rather than writing traditional reports in social studies or science, students can create multimedia presentations that demonstrate their understanding of material. Rather than simply studying a period in recent history, students can videotape oral histories of important people in their communities and create multimedia presentations that include the interview, student narration about the period of study, and research presented as the textual part of the presentation.

Technology can also be an extremely strong motivator. Students who have trouble writing conventionally on paper might be quite willing to complete their essays, stories, and projects via word processing or multimedia presentations. Reluctant students might be willing to engage in research on the Internet. Technology can also extend opportunities for student participation, with course software that provides an electronic structure for student discussions and sharing of work both in and out of school. As a motivator, technology can provide students with a legitimate way to gain status in their school and community. Schools can develop technology groups, or clubs, for students with advanced skills, as well as for students who want to learn higher-level technology. Technology club members can help teachers troubleshoot equipment, take digital videos or photos, upload those images to other documents, or help students and teachers prepare multimedia presentations. Technology club members can also document important school events and share those presentations at occasions such as open houses or parent conferences. Students skilled in technology can teach teachers—as well as other students—how to use technology tools, at the same time gaining valuable experience as teachers themselves.

As we discussed in Chapter 8, technology has also made possible the creation of curriculum materials that can provide greater individualized instruction and specific feedback to students than was possible before. CD-ROMs now exist (e.g., Pair-It Books from Steck-Vaughn, 2004) that allow students to preview a book, predict what they are about to read, and record and review those predictions to compare them with the story. Finally, this CD enables students to choose whether they would like to read the book or have the book read to them. If the students are reading, the program provides them with prompts and cues to assist them.

In addition, technology can help teachers track student learning and share their assessments with students and families. Teachers can keep track of students' grades electronically and use technology in other ways to increase their professional productivity. When students complete their work in an electronic format, teachers can keep samples of student work and projects electronically, retain their own comments/feedback, review that work with students and families, and rely on that work as the basis of end-of-semester or end-of-year presentations of student achievement.

On a practical level, technology can support students by facilitating communication among teachers, students, and families. Teachers and families can communicate via e-mail, though electronic communication is not a substitute for face-to-face relationships between families and teachers. All the same it can help increase the frequency of communication so that teachers and families are working together more closely for the students' benefit.

Much like the school structure reforms that we discussed earlier in this chapter, however, technology can be implemented well or poorly. Technology is not merely a means for students to play video games, to surf the Internet for sites unrelated to school, or to use instructional software that provides only low-level "skill and drill" activities. It is only meaningful in relationship to a well thought out curriculum. Additionally, teachers need to be careful, thoughtful consumers of instructional software, to be cautious about what Internet sites they allow their students to explore, and to control the use of computer time. It is critical for teachers to understand their legal obligations with regard to Internet use, an issue we will discuss in Chapter 11. But used judiciously, technology is a rich resource for teachers and students and should be an essential part of any teacher's repertoire of skills.

To meet the challenge of preparing teachers to use technology well, in 2000 the International Society for Technology in Education (ISTE) developed the National Education Technology Standards, or NETS (www.iste.org), with a version for students and for teachers. The standards for students were revised in 2007 and those for teachers in 2008. These revised NETS for teachers, listed below, emphasize several critical issues to guide teachers' implementation of technology as a way of engaging students in learning the curriculum. They include:

- Teachers use their knowledge of subject matter, teaching and learning, and technology to facilitate experiences that advance student learning, creativity, and innovation in both face-to-face and virtual environments.

- Teachers design, develop, and evaluate authentic learning experiences and assessment incorporating contemporary tools and resources to maximize content learning in context and to develop the knowledge, skills, and attitudes identified in the NETS's.

- Teachers exhibit knowledge, skills, and work processes representative of an innovative professional in a global and digital society.

- Teachers understand local and global societal issues and responsibilities in an evolving digital culture and exhibit legal and ethical behavior in their professional practices.

- Teachers continuously improve their professional practice, model lifelong learning, and exhibit leadership in their school and professional community by promoting and demonstrating the effective use of digital tools and resources. (ISTE, 2008)

## A Case In Point
### Transforming a Sixth Grade Classroom with Technology

When you walk into Kenisha Carter's sixth grade classroom in an urban school district in California, the first thing you notice is that every student has a laptop computer. The 25 students in her classroom sit in groups of 5 around trapezoidal tables. Since this is a wireless technology environment, there are no worries about students tripping over wires and cords. A videoconferencing unit sits on one side of the classroom. The teacher's computer station is at the front, with a few desktop computers to one side. Although Kenisha is no computer guru, technology has transformed the way she teaches.

Five years ago when she began her teaching career, Kenisha was interested in technology, but she never imagined a classroom like the one she has now. When her district announced a school technology conference during her second year of teaching, she applied to attend, and it was there she learned about the potential for laptop use in the classroom. After she returned from the conference, she met with her principal to discuss the possibility of applying for a grant to be a demonstration site for laptops and other forms of technology. Early in the summer she learned that her grant application had been approved. Although the school used some technology for administrative purposes and had a computer lab, technology use was not common among the teachers. When the grant was approved, Kenisha's principal was willing to support her. The school already had videoconferencing equipment but it was rarely used, so it was moved into Kenisha's classroom. Kenisha had participated in two required workshops over the summer and was ready to begin in the fall.

Today laptops are such a regular part of her teaching that she doesn't consider them unusual, and neither do her students. Arriving each morning, the students sit down and begin working on their electronic journals. Each entry is automatically sent to a folder where Kenisha can read them and provide feedback. Then students begin silent reading time; as it nears an end, they record their reading on a chart in their electronic reading folders. To assess reading comprehension, students create "story maps" using the Inspiration software program, which demonstrates their understanding of major structural features of the story such as character or plot. Once they have completed a book, they prepare a book report online that can be read by all of their classmates, who are expected to provide them with feedback in their electronic book report folders.

Kenisha teaches social studies and science using a project-based approach. Students select a subtopic within the general topic they are studying (for example, World War II), learn to take notes on the topic using an electronic notetaking program, and prepare multimedia presentations using presentation software such as PowerPoint or HyperStudio. They conduct much of their research on the Internet. Sometimes Kenisha chooses specific websites and organizes them for the students through a special software program designed for this purpose. But as a general rule she has learned that once she has set expectations and worked with students at the start of the year regarding Internet use, they do not usually surf the net for sites that are not related to their studies. Kenisha has begun to use the videoconferencing equipment to have her students make their presentations to other fifth grade classes in the metropolitan area and across the country who are studying the same topics.

For mathematics, Kenisha uses a combination of approaches. Because many of her students are still rusty on some of their basic facts, she uses a program that provides direct practice, alters the speed with which students need to work, and records student progress. Her main approach to mathematics is a problem-solving one, and she uses the district's curriculum. Many of the curriculum units come with software for collecting and analyzing data, for example, and for making tables and graphs as a means of interpreting the data. She uses these mathematics skills for social studies and science projects.

When you ask Kenisha if she would return to what teaching was like before laptops, she responds with an emphatic "No!" Technology makes her work more efficient and reduces the amount of time she spends on noninstructional tasks. For example, with laptops there is no time wasted passing out and collecting papers. Kenisha prepares assignments and sends them to electronic folders that are on each laptop. All students have the assignments and do not need to shuffle through desks to find materials. They submit most of their homework online, so she does not have to cart papers back and forth—just her own laptop.

The easing of administrative and "housekeeping" tasks is extremely useful, she observes. But without question, the most important thing about laptops, Kenisha believes, is that her students are pushed toward greater independence as learners. Since Kenisha can observe their work so readily, students take a great deal of responsibility, for example, for monitoring their work. They are highly involved in their projects for social studies and science—often because they have selected the topic and are responsible for presenting it. They must apply their skills in reading—and especially in comprehension—as they conduct research and prepare presentations. They must learn to "multitask" online when they are both conducting research and taking notes. For most students, Kenisha says, technology is a great motivator. Finally, Kenisha believes that by using laptops and other forms of technology, she is preparing her students—who are not advantaged socioeconomically—to do the level of work that will prepare them for high school, postsecondary education, and their future careers.

**Virtual Schools.**  In the past decade, a small movement has developed outside of conventional schools, made possible entirely by developments in technology. This is the movement toward **virtual schools** (also called cyberschools), or schools that are conducted partly or entirely online for students of traditional PK–12 school age. Courses that are offered online may be developed by the school district, or the district may rely on the courses and curriculum developed by a for-profit company.

Most virtual courses are supplemental to regular education (The Peak Group, 2002) and represent high school courses (Clark, 2001). By the end of 2002, between 40,000 and 50,000 students at the PK–12 level had taken at least one online course (United States Department of Education, n.d.). High school students who have exhausted advanced courses offered by their own schools can tap into online courses at the next level of study in that subject—thereby meeting their individual needs. Another use of virtual high schooling is providing education in isolated rural areas where budget restrictions may result in closing high schools.

A different population of students who are served by virtual schools are students who are home-schooled (see Chapter 10 for discussion of home schooling). One of the challenges of home schooling is having access to curriculum materials. Online courses and curricula can be a useful tool for families that participate in home schooling.

Virtual schools are not without their challenges. They require a sound technology infrastructure to support online courses. Students who participate must have the ability to learn independently, high levels of parent involvement, and teachers to monitor the quality of student work. Finally, there is no guarantee of the quality of the courses, which can affect the quality of a student's learning in virtual classes.

## Meeting Student Needs through Peer Tutoring

**Peer tutoring** refers to having students tutor other students to improve their learning. Tutoring can take place among same-age students—peers—within the same grade, or it can take place across different ages and grades and classrooms—when it is known as cross-age tutoring. Peer tutoring provides students with extra help in learning specific academic skills, while increasing the time students spend in academic work during the school day.

The value of peer tutoring is well established in the research literature on education. Peer tutoring programs can result in improvements in academic skills, social

**Critical Term**

**Virtual schools.** Schools that are conducted partly or entirely online for students of traditional PK–12 school age.

**Critical Term**

**Peer tutoring.** Structured programs in which students are trained to tutor other students.

interaction behaviors, classroom discipline, and student self-esteem; it is critical to note that both the student being tutored and the student tutor realize these benefits (Kalkowski, 1995). It has been especially successful for elementary students (Rohrbeck, Fantuzzo, Ginsberg-Block, & Miller, 2003). The quality of the experience peer tutors and their "students" have depends largely on how well the teacher trains peer tutors for their jobs and how closely the teacher monitors the learning that results from a peer tutoring program. Student tutors need to know exactly what they are expected to do, and tutoring sessions need to be well structured. Just putting students together in pairs and asking one of them them to tutor will not work, nor will it have the same results as a carefully crafted, structured program where the teacher develops the model, trains the students, and keeps track of student progress.

Teachers need to be very clear both with themselves and with their students about the specific expectations for a peer tutoring program and what it can and cannot accomplish. Peer tutoring programs can succeed, and they are often as productive for the tutor as they are for the person who is being tutored. Tutoring provides increased opportunities for students to practice carefully identified skills and therefore creates a useful way to give students greater individual attention. Such programs can complement—but are not a substitute for—a curriculum that is rich in meaning and that requires students to stretch their thinking and build complex new understandings facilitated by a teacher.

## Meeting Student Needs through Cooperative Learning

**Cooperative learning** is a set of strategies that combines social goals for students with academic goals (Cohen, 1986; Johnson & Johnson, 1987). In cooperative learning, mixed-ability, or heterogeneous, groups of students work together on well-defined tasks, sharing various aspects of the responsibility for learning the material. They learn to work together at the same time that they work on learning academic content.

Cooperative learning was developed as a means of helping teachers instruct heterogeneous groups of students within a single classroom rather than relying strictly on academic tracking. Although teachers have always taught heterogeneous groups, the goal of many of the earliest cooperative learning efforts was to create deliberate grouping patterns in the classroom in which students with disabilities and their peers without disabilities could interact in meaningful tasks without sacrificing student learning.

In cooperative learning, students learn to take on various roles within a group and take responsibility for carrying out those roles. The goal for each group member is to learn the material. At the end of the group activities, students are encouraged to assess not only their learning of the academic material or their completion of the academic task, but also how well they interacted as a group and carried out their responsibilities as group members. Finally, the teacher must hold individual students accountable for what they were supposed to learn, rather than having one student represent the entire group's achievement. In this way, all students ensure that all other students in their group are learning.

Teachers need to practice cooperative learning techniques so that they can serve the twin goals of social and academic

**Critical Term**

**Cooperative learning.** A set of organizational strategies that combines social goals with academic goals for mixed-ability groups of students.

When teachers use cooperative groups to foster student learning, it is important to assess the quality of the group's work as well as that of individual students. (Gabe Palmer/Corbis Images)

growth. Those who are skilled in this technique often spend the first month of school teaching their students the routines of working in groups, of moving their chairs, of carrying out their social roles in the group, and so on. Investing in this set of organizational skills should be accomplished early in the year so that the teacher can rely on this approach throughout the year without having to reteach students how to participate in a cooperative group.

## How Paraprofessionals Help Meet Student Needs

Many schools employ classroom assistants, or aides, to provide direct support to teachers and students within the classroom. These are paid positions in schools and are designed specifically to assist teachers with a wide variety of tasks within the classroom and in the school as a whole. These assistants are called *paraprofessionals*, and are sometimes known as *paraeducators*. During 2003–2004, schools employed nearly 700,000 paraprofessionals in various capacities (U.S. Department of Education, June 2007).

### A Career Ladder for Paraprofessionals. Paraprofessionals in education often live in the community in which the school is located. In urban areas, where teachers are predominantly white and middle class and often do not live in the immediate community, paraprofessionals are often members of racial and ethnic minority groups who do live in the community. The paraprofessionals' intimate knowledge of the community can be a distinct advantage in their work with children and youth. For this reason, paraprofessionals represent a potential pool of new teachers and, if they become licensed teachers, can increase the diversity of the teaching workforce.

Many colleges and universities nationwide have developed programs to support paraprofessionals who wish to become teachers. Such programs can capitalize on the paraprofessionals' classroom experience and build on that experience as they work toward full licensure for teaching. Programs that view the paraprofessional experience as preparation for teaching represent a purposeful career ladder approach to the preparation of teachers. In this approach, classroom experience is valued as a basis for becoming a teacher but not as a substitute for formal teacher education.

The No Child Left Behind legislation of 2001 raised the standards for paraprofessionals who carry out instructional roles. This law requires that they have a high school diploma and must complete 48 credits of postsecondary education, hold an associate's degree from a two-year college, or demonstrate their instructional skills through a formal assessment of their abilities.

### What Paraprofessionals Do. Paraprofessionals perform a wide range of tasks in schools. They assist teachers in nonteaching duties in order to free them to focus on student learning. Specifically, they can prepare instructional materials, take attendance or lunch count, monitor the lunchroom, be on duty at outdoor recess at the elementary level, or be on hall duty when classes are changing at the high school level. Many paraprofessionals also participate in teaching tasks under the guidance of the certified classroom teacher. Table 9-2 provides examples of the kinds of activities identified by the National Resource Center for Paraeducators (http://www.nrcpara.org) as appropriate for paraprofessionals as well as those responsibilities that should be carried out only by a licensed teacher.

Clear lines should be drawn between the role of a paraprofessional and the role of a classroom teacher. It is up to the classroom teacher to provide clear and direct

## Table 9-2    Differentiated Roles for Paraprofessionals and Teachers

**Paraprofessionals and teachers work as members of a team, but also have different roles in the classroom.**

| Appropriate Tasks for Paraprofessionals | Tasks not to Be Delegated by Teachers to Paraprofessionals |
|---|---|
| When working with individual or small groups of students, implement instructional activities developed by teachers. | Diagnose individual students' needs. |
| Implement behavior management or disciplinary plans that the teacher has developed. | Consult with colleagues to plan specialized instruction for all students who need and can profit from it. |
| Provide assistance to teachers in assessing student progress. | Create and sustain student-centered environments. |
| Provide documentation of students' progress to help the teacher plan and modify curriculum and instructional activities to respond to student needs. | Align instructional strategies with the curriculum. |
| Help teachers organize instructional activities and maintain a productive and supportive learning environment for students. | Plan lessons based on student needs. |
| Help teachers involve parents and families in their children's education. | Make accommodations and modifications to content and instructional activities to meet the needs of individual students. |
| Carry out clerical tasks. | Facilitate learning outcomes. |
| Make or duplicate materials. | Assess students' progress |
| Supervise students in nonclassroom settings in the school. | Involve parents and families in every aspect of the students' education. |

**Source:** Adapted from Pickett, A. L., M. Likins, and T. Wallace. (2003). *The employment and preparation of paraeducators: The state of the art.* New York: National Resource Center for Paraprofessionals, Center for Advanced Study in Education, City University of New York. Retrieved May 23, 2008, from http://www.nrcpara.org.

guidance to paraprofessionals in terms of how to perform tasks that are directly related to the learning process—for example, assisting with instruction or assessment.

Paraprofessionals continue to play an important role in helping meet the needs of students with disabilities. In fact, the majority of paraprofessionals in schools are hired to work with students with disabilities (Katsiyannis, 2000). Because so many students with disabilities now receive their education in general education classrooms, paraprofessionals often accompany students, particularly those who may have more significant disabilities, to these classrooms. Their services are sometimes written directly into the IEP to ensure that this resource will be available to students who need it.

According to a study conducted in Minnesota (ERIC Clearinghouse on Disabilities and Gifted Education, 2003), teachers need the following skills to do this work:

● Ability to communicate well with paraprofessionals
● Ability to manage the tasks of paraprofessionals, including planning and scheduling

● Ability to model the instructional tasks the teacher wishes the paraprofessional to carry out

● Ability to provide appropriate training for the paraprofessional

We might add to this list the ability to provide feedback and constructive criticism to paraprofessionals as a means of improving their skills and abilities.

## Why It Counts in a Diverse World

By this time it should be obvious: teaching is more than just standing in front of a classroom lecturing students. Instead, it is more like a sophisticated juggling act in which the teacher must keep all of the parts moving in a finely tuned rhythm: the students as individual learners, the students as a group, the curriculum goals, and the classroom as a community. A good teacher cannot drop anything, or the whole juggling act may fall apart.

Teaching is also more than just teaching to the average student, which is often where teachers aim their teaching. By knowing how to use grouping strategically and purposefully, teachers can increase the time and opportunity students have to learn in ways that are sensitive to whom they are as individuals. The structures, strategies, and approaches we have discussed here represent some of the ways teachers can organize their classrooms to maximize student engagement and learning. The point of this chapter is to emphasize that the organizational structures within which teachers teach and students learn have considerable influence on how education is conceptualized and delivered in our schools, and that different structures provide different opportunities for teachers and students alike.

How schools are organized and how they group students impact how teachers meet students' needs. Today the range of student needs is wide and it is critical that teachers are committed to implementing instructional strategies that will help close the achievement gaps so persistent in our society. Even if a school is organized traditionally with an age-graded curriculum, it may be possible to begin some experiments with innovations on a smaller scale, across a classroom or two, to introduce new ideas about how the school is organized. Sometimes a small experiment is the catalyst a school needs to try a new way to organize its teaching and learning. But in whatever situation, good teachers know how to use the group context in positive ways both to build students' social skills and to ensure their learning. Finally, within any organizational pattern of schooling, teachers make critical choices every day about how to implement the curriculum. These decisions influence how well teachers motivate students and keep them engaged in learning.

As you begin your teacher education program, it may often seem to you that successful veteran teachers manage the learning of individual students within the group effortlessly. But veteran teachers who are good at their work have developed these skills through practice. As a teacher education student—and soon to be a beginning teacher—you will find that the skill develops over time. What may look effortless to you as a novice is something that you can master through your own practice, feedback, and reflection.

# CHAPTER SUMMARY

One challenge of teaching is to determine how to meet individual needs within the structure of the school. The organization of schools and the choices teachers make within their own classrooms all affect a teacher's ability to meet students' needs.

## What Makes a Good School? What Makes a Good Classroom?

Certain characteristics of good schools must be present in any organizational plan. Good schools motivate students to learn. In good schools, high expectations are set for student accomplishments, and teachers consistently support students' efforts. The curriculum itself is motivating to the students and is connected to their lives.

Good schools are also good communities for students, teachers, and families. They reflect a sense of belonging and interdependence that work together to support student learning. In such classrooms and schools, students know what they are to learn and have multiple opportunities to practice various skills and strategies, and they receive specific feedback on the quality of their performance.

## Rethinking School Organization to Meet Students' Needs

The traditional school structure is based on the belief that students of the same age will be at the same developmental level. But in age-graded classrooms, teachers always have to teach a wide range of students, and several alternative structures exist to assist teachers in meeting this wide range of student needs.

These alternatives—multi-age classrooms, looping, year-round schools, class size reduction, block scheduling in high schools, and small high schools—increase the amount of time teachers spend with students and also allow greater depth of exploration of the curriculum. For such organizational changes to be maximally effective, they must be accompanied by ongoing professional development for teachers so that they can master the more complex instructional strategies such structures require.

## Rethinking What Happens at the Classroom Level to Meet Student Needs

Other structural changes are focused more on the individual classroom. Some of these changes include differentiated instruction, technology to enhance students' learning of the curriculum, virtual classes to provide access to courses otherwise not available, peer tutoring for specific skills, and cooperative learning that enables a heterogeneous grouping of students.

Another way teachers can get additional help to meet students' needs is through working with a paraprofessional. Paraprofessionals can take on a wide variety of tasks, but most often they carry out well-defined instructional duties under the direction of the classroom teacher. To be successful managing the work of a paraprofessional, a teacher needs to be deliberate in how he or she prepares the paraprofessional for these roles.

## LIST OF CRITICAL TERMS

| | |
|---|---|
| Intrinsic motivation (*292*) | Block scheduling (*302*) |
| Extrinsic motivation (*293*) | Year-round schools (*308*) |
| Departmentalization (*296*) | Differentiated instruction (*312*) |
| Age-graded school (*297*) | Instructional technology (*314*) |
| Multi-age classrooms (*298*) | Virtual schools (*320*) |
| Looping (*299*) | Peer tutoring (*320*) |
| Class size reduction (*301*) | Cooperative learning (*321*) |

## EXPLORING YOUR COMMITMENT

1. *on your own...* Interview someone in your neighborhood or on your campus who has school-aged children. Ask him or her what makes a good school. Compare these responses with a small group of your peers and look for patterns in the responses.

2. *on your own...* Interview a school-aged child and ask him or her what makes a good teacher. Write a short reflection including the results of this interview and the implications of this child's perspective on your own decision to teach.

3. *in the field...* In the school where you are completing your field experience, describe the patterns by which students are grouped. How are they similar to or different from those in the classrooms of your peers? Your own classroom experiences?

4. *in the field...* Interview a teacher whom you have selected because of his or her reputation for meeting individual students' needs. How does this teacher account for his or her success? What strategies does he or she use to organize the classroom to meet student needs? What technology, if any, does he or she use?

5. *on the web...* Visit the Technology Integration link on **www.edutopia.org** and locate the *How to Integrate Technology* module. This module includes a self-assessment survey and related resources to items on the survey for which you might need support to improve your ability to integrate technology into your teaching.

6. *on the web...* Explore the website of the Apple Learning Interchange at **http://edcommunity.apple.com/ali**. Identify at least two projects that give you new ways of thinking about teaching at the grade level/subject in which you are interested.

7. ***on the web...*** Explore the *Educator Resources* link of the website of the International Society of Technology in Education at **www.iste.org**. Identify at least two resources from this link that will help you in your work as a teacher.

8. ***in the field...*** Form a small group from your class to study the organizational structures of the schools in your area. Select at least five schools. How many, if any, use looping, multi-age grouping, class size reduction, virtual schools, small high schools, and so on? Interview a principal or a long-time teacher who is involved in one of these organizational structures to discuss the benefits and limitations of the approach that has been adopted.

9. ***in the field...*** Identify an educational aide or paraprofessional in the schools in your area. Interview this person to see the kind of responsibilities he or she has on a daily basis. Has this person ever considered becoming a fully licensed teacher? Why or why not?

10. ***in the research...*** Read Donovan, L., Hartley, K., & Strudler, N. (2007). "Teacher Concerns during Initial Implementation of a One-to-One Laptop Initiative at the Middle School Level." *Journal of Research and Technology in Education*, 39 (3). This study documents the concerns teachers have as they implement this technological reforms.

## GUIDELINES FOR BEGINNING TEACHERS

1. Find out whether paraprofessionals work in your building and whether you will have the services of one of them. Talk to an experienced teacher about how to establish a positive working relationship with a paraprofessional in your classroom.

2. When you interview at a school, ask about the philosophy of grouping students. Does the school have classrooms that rely on multi-age grouping or looping? At the high school level, is there block scheduling? Schools that are implementing these approaches may be more flexible in general about innovation.

3. Conduct informal interviews with the other teachers in your grade level to find out what strategies they use to make sure they are meeting the needs of their individual students.

4. Make a multiple-purpose record sheet with the names of all of your students. When students are working at their seats or in small groups, circulate to take brief notes on their work. Review this sheet a few times a week to determine which students might need additional assistance.

5. Meet the technology support staff member in your building. Have him or her show you the technology resources available to you so that you can incorporate them into your regular teaching.

6. Visit **DonorsChoose.org**, an organization that provides teachers with resources for their classrooms based on the submission of a grant.

## THE **INTASC** CONNECTION

The INTASC standards that most directly address the organization of classrooms are Standards 4 and 5. Standard 4 states: *The teacher understands and uses a variety of instructional strategies to encourage students' development of critical thinking, problem solving, and performance skills.* Indicators include the following:

● The teacher understands principles and techniques, along with advantages and limitations, associated with various instructional strategies (e.g., cooperative learning, direct instruction, discovery learning, whole-group discussion, independent study, interdisciplinary instruction).

● The teacher knows how to enhance learning through use of a wide variety of materials as well as human and technological resources (e.g., computers, audiovisual technologies, videotapes and discs, local experts, primary documents and artifacts, texts, reference books, literature, and other print resources).

Standard 5 states: *The teacher uses an understanding of individual and group motivation and behavior to create a learning environment that encourages positive social interaction, active engagement in learning, and self-motivation.* Indicators include the following:

● The teacher understands how social groups function and influence people, and how people influence groups.

● The teacher knows how to help people work productively and cooperatively with each other in complex social settings.

● The teacher recognizes factors and situations that are likely to promote or diminish intrinsic motivation, and knows how to help students become self-motivated.

● The teacher values the role of students in promoting each other's learning and recognizes the importance of peer relationships in establishing a climate of learning.

● The teacher recognizes the value of intrinsic motivation to students' lifelong growth and learning.

● The teacher creates a smoothly functioning learning community in which students assume responsibility for themselves and one another, participate in decision making, work collaboratively and independently, and engage in purposeful learning activities.

● The teacher organizes, allocates, and manages the resources of time, space, activities, and attention to provide active and equitable engagement of students in productive tasks.

● The teacher maximizes the amount of class time spent in learning by creating expectations and processes for communication and behavior along with a physical setting conducive to classroom goals.

If you are in a state that follows a different set of teacher standards, find the state standards that most closely relate to the INTASC standards discussed here.

# READING ON...

Berge, Z. L., and T. Clark, (Eds.). (2005). *Virtual schools: Planning for success*. New York: Teachers College Press. Practitioners in online education talk about their experiences working in virtual, online education environments.

Boss, S., and J. Krauss, (2007). *Reinventing project-based learning: Your field guide to real world projects in the digital age*. Washington, DC: International Society for Technology in Education. A practical resource for technology integration through projects.

The George Lucas Educational Foundation, (2002). *Edutopia: Success stories for learning in the digital age*. San Francisco: Jossey-Bass. Describes innovative uses of technology in a variety of classrooms.

Ginsberg, M. B., and R. J. Wlodkowski. (2000). *Creating highly motivating classrooms for all students*. San Francisco: Jossey-Bass This volume focuses on motivational strategies and choices in schools and classrooms that support culturally responsive teaching.

Meier, D., N. F. Sizer, and T. R. Sizer. (2004). *Keeping school: Letters to families from principals of two small schools*. Boston: Beacon Press. Through letters, principals of small schools explain their philosophy and commitments to the small learning communities their schools represent.

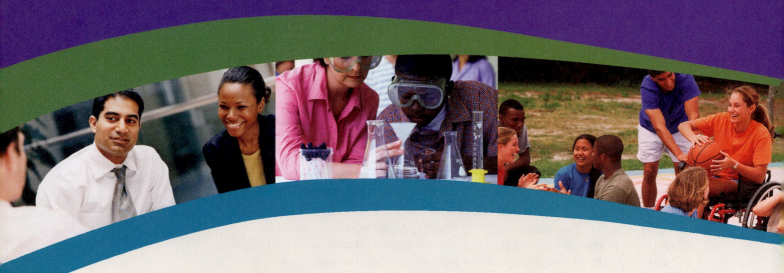

## Guiding Questions

- How does the local control of schools affect a teacher's work?

- What is the role of the local school board?

- What is the role of the superintendent?

- How does governance and administration of the school building affect a teacher's work?

- What role do teachers' unions play in decision making?

- How does state governance of schools work?

- What influence does the federal government have in the schools?

- What influence comes from legislation?

- What influence comes from decisions made by the courts?

- How do other external groups influence educational decision making?

- How are schools financed?

- How is school governance changing with the introduction of school choice?

- How does home schooling fit into school governance issues?

# How Governing and Financing Schools Influence Teachers' Work

# 10

One of the things Lucy Richards did not know—and did not ask about—was that her school controlled its own budget. Each year in February the principal, Ms. Martinez, called together the school-based council, which included teacher, parent, and staff representatives from the school, to deliberate on how to allocate funds for the next school year.

All teachers and staff in the school were invited to attend these meetings, and Lucy had started sitting in on them in January to see what they were about. As the council began deliberating about the budget for the next year, it became clear that the school could not again afford both a full-time librarian and a full-time network support/technology coordinator. Arguments for and against these positions were heated, and many people were just plain upset that the funds were not there for both positions.

"Well, that's the reality of our situation for next year," said Ms. Martinez, the principal. Funding is down this year. It's a combination of lower enrollments and the new voucher program. We don't have to make this decision today, but we do have to be thinking about it. We meet again in a week. Let's all think about it hard between now and then."

That evening Lucy called Janet Daniels, her cooperating teacher from the previous year, to discuss the situation.

"It's a very hard decision," Lucy said. "My kids need both kinds of support, and I need the technology support for sure, especially because I'm really trying to get my kids ready for more advanced technology work for next year."

"Well," Janet responded, "the school needs to look at all the positions and see if there are other places that make more sense in terms of cutting back. Were any others mentioned at your meeting? Maybe you can use the rest of this year to start building up some strength in technology among the teachers. It won't replace network support, but it will help."

"Those are good ideas and I can bring them up. I guess I didn't realize how much responsibility comes with making these budget decisions at the school."

*Much of the controversy brewing about public education is found in the debate over who should have ownership or control of public schools.*

Good & Braden, 2000, p. 10

"But consider the alternative," Janet replied. "Your teachers, staff, and parents know your school best, so it's really a benefit to make those decision yourselves, as hard as they are. Not all schools have that opportunity."

"I know, and I'm glad to be able to sit in on the discussions and offer some suggestions as a new teacher. But I guess at this point I'm also glad not to be an official member of the council yet."

The topic of how schools are governed and financed may seem to be remote in importance at this point in your preparation to teach. But as Lucy's experience illustrates, decisions about such issues affect teachers each day of their working lives. Decisions about governance and finance translate into policies, procedures, and practices that make a difference in how teachers do their jobs and in the resources that are available to them as they strive to meet their students' needs. Teachers do have a lot of latitude once the classroom door is closed and instruction begins. Nevertheless, there are countless ways in which local, state, and federal entities, including the courts, other external groups, and financial forces, all exert influence—directly or indirectly, formally or informally—on a teacher's day and on the environment in which teachers do their work.

This chapter addresses the roles of federal, state, and local government in relationship to schools with regard to both policy and funding, as well as the influence of the courts and the role and influence of organized groups, such as professional organizations, parent organizations, and business groups. Influences on education—and so, on your work as a teacher—come from all of these levels of government and constituencies that are concerned about education. Their relative influence shifts over time, changing the balance of power and the educational landscape.

The chapter concludes with a discussion of charter schools and school voucher programs, which are emerging as new forms of schooling that challenge traditional governance and funding patterns in education, and that have important implications both for meeting student needs and for defining the role of public schooling in the United States. Home schooling as an emerging option is also addressed.

## Putting Governance into Perspective

Because it is not explicitly identified as a federal power, the responsibility for education, according to the Tenth Amendment of the Constitution, is reserved to the individual states. Essentially, this means that every state makes its own decisions about education, which explains, for example, the wide range of requirements across the 50 states for becoming a teacher. As such, the educational system in the United States contrasts with that of most other countries, where unified national systems prevail. For example, in France and England—and in countries whose educational systems are the legacies of French and English colonialism—decisions about curriculum, testing, and teacher preparation are controlled centrally by a national Ministry of Education or a similar national agency. Decisions made by such agencies guide educational practice throughout the country. In the United States, despite the states' governing authority, the federal role in education has increased substantially over time, to the point that federal legislation and federal policy increasingly drive much education decision making.

Besides the federal and state level, there is a third level of governance for education in the United States: local school boards. Local school boards have day-to-day responsibility for education at the district level as well as budgetary authority over the schools. Whereas local school boards must follow both federal and state policies, they have historically had a great deal of control in defining education locally.

What actually happens in the school building in which you teach is influenced by all three levels of authority. But whether you teach in a federal system like that in the United States or in a national system like that in Europe or other countries that have adopted the European model, each individual school also has its own character, its own organizational culture, and its own personality that directly influence your work and your success in meeting your students' needs. A school's individual culture is defined largely by the tone the principal sets and by the teachers who work in it, as well as by the norms and policies of the local school district. Yet principals and teachers do not work in a vacuum, and they must be responsive to the policies of the larger agencies that govern education.

Decisions about education are made in both a political and a professional arena. But the mandates and directives from the federal, state, and local governing bodies, however well intended, may not always be in the best interests of the students once they are implemented. Teachers, administrators, parents, families, and students may not agree with what these three bodies mandate. When this happens, teachers and administrators are placed in the challenging position of maintaining a balance between meeting external mandates and obtaining the best possible education for their students. A healthy school organization cannot control everything that comes its way, but it can put pressure to do things a certain way into perspective in relation to the goals it values. That is why it is so critical for you to take an active role within your school and provide input into the decision-making process.

Despite the increasingly powerful federal and state roles in education, local school boards and superintendents still maintain a great deal of influence on a teacher's daily life. For example, the state sets academic standards, but it is local decisions that most often influence how those standards will be met, what instructional programs will be adopted, what teaching materials will be available, what supports teachers can count on to help their students meet the educational goals, and how schools are organized. But exactly what does the tradition of local control of schools mean for you as a teacher?

# The Influence of Local Control of Schools on a Teacher's Work

Local school districts are known as the **local education agency (LEA)**. At the district level, schools are controlled by a school board made up of community members who are either elected or appointed to their positions, with an average of between five and seven board members. Local policies set by these boards are carried out by the superintendent of schools, an education professional who is hired by and serves at the pleasure of the local school board. There are approximately 15,000 local school boards in the United States (National School Boards Association, 2008). Local school boards are, in theory, designed to be nonpartisan entities and to function outside the traditional political party structure. In the interest of preserving this level of independence, school board elections are often held separately from other partisan elections (Butts & Cremin, 1953). In practice, however, individual school board members can be quite partisan in the positions they take.

Among their many responsibilities, school boards have the authority to tax the community to raise funds for schools and to develop the school district budget,

**Critical Term**

**Local education agency (LEA).** A term used to describe the local school district.

both of which directly influence teachers' lives. Another fundamental board decision is to set class size, which determines how many teachers a district will need. Class size is an enduring feature of schools that has obvious implications for any teacher's ability to meet students' needs. Class size is usually a direct function of the district's budget, since the largest portion of all school budgets goes to support the salaries and benefits of teachers. When a policy decision to reduce class size is made at the state or federal level (see the discussion of class size reduction initiatives in Chapter 9), this has implications for how a local district must allocate its funds.

Nationally, school board members are typically white and usually work in the professions or own their own businesses (Bennett & LeCompte, 1990; Land, 2002). So although a locally elected school board should provide all families with the opportunity to participate in making education decisions, control is correlated more with income and status (Rufo-Lignos & Richards, 2003). Most often school board members are not professional educators, although they certainly can be. In many ways the role of the school board is paradoxical: the board is charged with responsibility for setting local education policy, but its members usually do not have professional backgrounds in education. Nevertheless, the school board is a major gatekeeper in terms of implementing new ideas and practices in a school district designed in theory to help the district meet its students' educational needs. These new policies, ideas, and initiatives come from many sources, including the superintendent of schools. Therefore, the school board's relationship with the superintendent is a critical consideration.

## Your turn... *to reflect*

Have you voted in a local school board election? If so, how did you decide for whom to vote? If you have not voted in such an election, do you know when school board elections are held in your community? What do you think accounts for your choice not to vote?

## The Role of the Superintendent of Schools

The superintendent of schools is the chief education professional in a school district. Although superintendents carry out the local school board's policies, in reality they themselves can have significant influence on how schools operate. As the lead district administrator, the superintendent hires the district-level instructional staff (e.g., directors of curriculum or special education), the administrative staff (e.g., head of human resources), and building principals. If the district is small, the superintendent may also be directly involved in hiring teachers—although this is typically the responsibility of building principals. In larger districts, Human Resources departments are charged with the hiring process. Superintendents may hire principals who agree with them and will not challenge their decisions, or they may look for creative principals who will bring fresh new ideas to the district. Hiring decisions are usually approved by the local board of education, but board members do not normally have a direct role in hiring the professional staff although they formally approve such decisions. The major exception is, of course, selecting the superintendent of schools, which is always the job of the school board.

Superintendents set the overall tone of a district and communicate their vision to both the teachers and public. They work directly with boards of education to "sell" ideas and initiatives for improving the district, and they seek the board's approval for the direction in which they wish to take the district. At the same time, they must negotiate with the school board regarding initiatives proposed by board members and provide professional insight into the strengths and liabilities of these initiatives.

Superintendents can also make significant curriculum decisions. They can mandate, for example, that all schools use a particular approach to teaching a particular subject. Or they may decide that a district will require teachers across all grades and subjects to emphasize writing—often called *writing across the curriculum*—as a districtwide initiative. Such an initiative requires that all teachers take responsibility for fostering writing competence among their students. A teacher in such a district may not say, "But I'm not an English teacher," and ignore the quality of students' writing. If you are planning to be a high school mathematics teacher, for example, and you want to teach in this district, you need to be prepared to view your work in a broader context than you might initially have envisioned depending on a curriculum decision made by the superintendent. Similarly, superintendents may decide to begin a foreign language program at the elementary school level or integrate the arts across the entire school curriculum. Each new initiative is likely to mean reallocating dollars from other programs to fund the new ones. If existing district programs are working well, new initiatives proposed by a new superintendent may seem like a burden. If they are not, new initiatives may make sense.

How much will you, as a new teacher, interact with the district superintendent? If the district in which you teach is large, the answer is: probably very little. In large districts, superintendents administer large staffs at central offices, are usually highly visible public figures, and interact with and are accountable to many constituencies in the community. If you work in a small district with few school buildings, however, you may see and interact with the superintendent more regularly. But whether or not you see the superintendent often, the preceding examples illustrate that superintendents make significant decisions about many aspects of education that influence your life as a teacher.

## The Relationship between the School Board and the Superintendent

The superintendent–school board relationship is critical to the smooth operation of the local school district and, more importantly, to the learning environment. Ideally, board members and the superintendent have a good working relationship that reflects a healthy balance between input from the board and decision making by the superintendent.

In reality, however, local school boards can differ significantly in how they define their relationship with the superintendent. At one end of the continuum, a school board can view its role mainly as setting broad policy, leaving the professional decision making to the superintendent, whose influence then predominates. At the other end of the continuum, a school board can exert a great deal of direct control and micro-manage how the superintendent runs the district, which weakens the superintendent's influence. Superintendents may find that the directives mandated by a "controlling" school board may not always be guided by sound knowledge of educational practice or be in the students' best interests. Instead, new ideas and initiatives may be driven more by political positions and the political ambitions of various school board members.

## Local School Board Policymaking

Exactly what kinds of policies do school boards set, and which decisions affect your life as a teacher? School board members may advocate for certain favorite projects. For instance, a board member may be a passionate supporter of arts education and may therefore lobby strongly to retain arts programming in the face of budgetary constraints. Another board member may advocate for expanding the science

Local school boards are responsible for setting local policies that are sometimes very controversial. (©AP/Wide World Photos)

curriculum. Whoever prevails during these discussions will affect your students' choices as they move through the school system, as well as the distribution of resources to the range of instructional programs.

School board members may also promote specific programs or features of instruction. Such decisions may be based on the way they were taught or on personal belief. Or they may be projects that are well supported by research. One board member may, for example, support teaching only "the basics." Another may believe that students should not use calculators in mathematics and may propose policies to ban their use. Another may not support programs of bilingual education. Decisions such as these also directly affect the teachers' choices about instruction.

School board members may use their office to promote a specific political or educational agenda. For example, school board members have actively promoted the censorship of books. Challenges to books in schools and school libraries have increased in the past decade, which can lead to banning certain books in libraries and the curriculum. The American Library Association (ALA) documents challenges to books annually. Figure 10-1 shows the 10 books that were most

| Figure 10-1 | 10 Most Frequently Challenged Books of 2007 in Order of Frequency |
| --- | --- |

Challenges represent documented requests to have specific books removed from school libraries or from the curriculum.

1. ***And Tango Makes Three***, by Justin Richardson/Peter Parnell.
   Reasons: Anti-ethnic, sexism, homosexuality, anti-family, religious viewpoint, unsuited to age group

2. ***The Chocolate War***, by Robert Cormier.
   Reasons: Sexually explicit, offensive language, violence

3. ***Olive's Ocean***, by Kevin Henkes.
   Reasons: Sexually explicit, offensive language

4. ***The Golden Compass***, by Philip Pullman.
   Reasons: Religious viewpoint

5. ***The Adventures of Huckleberry Finn***, by Mark Twain.
   Reasons: Racism

6. ***The Color Purple***, by Alice Walker.
   Reasons: Homosexuality, sexually explicit, offensive language

7. ***TTYL***, by Lauren Myracle.
   Reasons: Sexually explicit, offensive language, unsuited to age group

8. ***I Know Why the Caged Bird Sings***, by Maya Angelou.
   Reasons: Sexually explicit

9. ***It's Perfectly Normal***, by Robie Harris.
   Reasons: Sex education, sexually explicit

10. ***The Perks of Being A Wallflower***, by Stephen Chbosky.
    Reasons: homosexuality, sexually explicit, offensive language, unsuited to age group

**Source:** American Library Association. Banned Books Week. Retrieved May 24, 2008, from http://www.ala.org.

---

**Figure 10-2    Ten Most Challenged Books of the 21st Century (2000–2005)**

The ten most challenged books of the century include the following titles.

1. **The Chocolate War** by Robert Cormier
3. **Alice** series by Phyllis Reynolds Naylor
4. **Of Mice and Men** by John Steinbeck
5. **I Know Why the Caged Bird Sings** by Maya Angelou
6. **Fallen Angels** by Walter Dean Myers
7. **It's Perfectly Normal** by Robie Harris
8. **Scary Stories** series by Alvin Schwartz
9. **Captain Underpants** series by Dav Pilkey
10. **Forever** by Judy Blume

All but three of these books were also listed in the top 10 of the most challenged books of the 1990s. The ALA reports there were more than 3,000 attempts to remove books from schools and public libraries between 2000 and 2005. Challenges are defined as formal, written complaints filed with a library or school requesting that materials be removed because of content or appropriateness.

**Source:** Adapted from the American Library Association. Retrieved March 24, 2008, from http://www.ala.org.

frequently challenged in 2007; Figure 10-2 identifies the 10 authors whose books were most frequently challenged in 2000–2005. The ALA takes a position against censorship based on the provisions of the First Amendment, and since 1982 it has continuously sponsored an annual "Banned Books Week" in September to honor the right to express one's opinion and allow unorthodox or unpopular opinions to be available in print.

Challenges to books are raised for a variety of personal and political reasons. Recently, however, fundamentalist Christian religious groups or school board members have often promoted censorship efforts. For example, in 2004 the Charles County, Maryland, school board members challenged a book by the African American author Zora Neal Hurston and simultaneously supported a proposal to recommend having the Gideons International hand out Bibles to each student in the schools (Partlow, 2004).

**Your turn...** *to reflect*

Review the books and authors that have been challenged over the last decade. Which of these authors/books have you read? Do you think it is appropriate for these books or authors to be banned from school libraries or the school curriculum? Why or why not?

Whether or not the longstanding tradition of local school board governance should continue is being debated today. Particularly—but not only—in urban schools, successful attempts have been made to take control of the district away from the school board for the purpose of working directly with failing schools (Land, 2002). In these situations, city or state officials may work with an existing school board or replace the board completely (Education Commission of the States, 2005b). Twenty-nine states now have some form of legislation or policy that allows them to take over whole school districts if they are not deemed to be performing well, and 15 have policies that permit them to assume control over individual schools (Education Commission of the States, 2005). The passage of the No Child Left Behind Act, discussed later in this chapter, has impacted the whole issue of school takeovers, as it requires that schools whose students do not reach a certain level of achievement over a five-year period must be reconstituted.

## Decision Making at the Building Level

Many critical decisions are also made by the building principal at the building level. These decisions directly affect your work environment.

### The Role of the Principal

The traditional, historical view of a principal is that of an individual, often a male, who authoritatively makes decisions on behalf of teachers and asks teachers to implement them. This top-down view of school leadership stems historically from the tradition of having largely male principals and largely female teachers. This paternalistic system has existed especially at the elementary school level. Over time, however, theories of school leadership have changed so that today it is not uncommon to talk about collegial, collaborative models of leadership, in which the principal supports and empowers teachers themselves to share ideas for school improvement (York-Barr & Duke, 2004).

Just as a superintendent sets the tone for a school district, principals do the same for the school. They define the patterns of communication and interaction that exist in the school. They create organizational cultures within their schools that either enable teachers to participate in decision making or require them merely to follow through on decisions made at the top. Principals can also foster a climate of professional collaboration or, alternatively, a climate that inhibits such interaction. Although in general the movement has been toward more participatory forms of school leadership, with teachers often having input into important decisions at the school (Lieberman & Miller, 1999; 2004), a principal can choose to honor this kind of participation to a greater or lesser extent. Principals may also create what has been called "contrived collegiality," in which teachers are mandated to work together but no real spirit of collegiality exists (Hargreaves, 1994). Good school leaders, aware that ideas for improving schools often come from the ranks of teachers, create open communication so that good ideas can surface and be translated into practice in the schools.

Principals set a tone not just for teachers but for students, clarifying expectations and patterns of acceptable behavior. And, like teachers, principals are more successful when they create strong relationships with teachers, students, the students' families, and the surrounding community. These relationships have been formalized in the development of local school councils.

### Your turn... *to reflect*

You probably attended at least two or three schools during your own PK–12 education. If you moved a lot during your school years, you may have attended several more. Think about the principals of the buildings you attended. What impact did the principals have on the school? What do you remember about any of the principals that is positive? negative? Do you recall at all whether the relationship between the principal and the teachers was cordial?

## Local School Governance through Shared Decision Making

Although in theory school boards represent the community, the interests of all families may not be well represented by the school board. Furthermore, school boards take a districtwide perspective, so that while they certainly have responsibility for each individual school, they may not be focused on schools as individual entities.

In an effort to give families and community members a greater say in the education of their children, many districts have created an additional level of authority in each individual school—a local school council. A term frequently used to describe this form of shared leadership, authority, and governance at the local school site is **site-based management**. Site-based management gained favor in the 1980s as a means of reforming schools (Holloway, 2000; Dounay, 2005). The intent of these local councils is to bring together representatives of students' families, community and/or local business representatives, teacher and staff representatives, and the school administrator to collaborate in making decisions about the individual school (Leithwood & Menzies, 1998). At the high school level, students themselves might participate as members of the council. Seventeen states require some form of site-based management (Dounay, 2005).

The local school council can deliberate on nearly all aspects of the school and can share decision-making authority with the principal—including developing and approving the local school budget. One of the most radical forms of local school governance occurred in the Chicago Public Schools beginning in 1988, where such councils were introduced as a major vehicle for school reform and had the authority to hire and fire principals (Easton & Storey, 1994; Rau, Baker, & Ashby, 1999). This form of school governance differs significantly from the traditional view of a school, with a strong principal who "runs the show" with little input from anyone else. In some cases principals can run such councils without fostering real collaboration, but then it becomes just a rubber stamp for the principal. This is hardly the intent of such a council, and it is up to council members to make sure it functions as a collaborative decision-making body rather than as an example of "contrived collegiality".

If you are in a school that has local governance through a school council, you will want to learn which teachers serve on the council, how often the council meets, over what issues it has authority, and what challenges it is addressing. As a new teacher, you will not likely be expected to participate in this role, but that depends on the dynamics of your school; you may wish to participate or you may be asked to participate. Regardless of whether you participate directly during your early years of teaching, you should become familiar with how decisions are made at your school. Only then can you provide input, offer constructive criticism, and help shape your school's policies and practices—which in the end determines how your school meets the needs of the students you will teach.

**Critical Term**

**Site-based management.** Individual management of schools where principals share decision-making authority with teachers, staff, and community members.

In many schools, a local school council works with the principal, sharing responsibility for decisions made at individual school buildings. (Peter Chen/ The Image Works)

## Teachers' Leadership Roles in Schools

In some schools, teachers, rather than a formally appointed school principal, are in charge of the building. These schools, which are the exception, are usually small and often have a leadership team made up of a small group of teachers (McGhan, 2002) who are in charge of all administrative responsibilities for the building. In some situations teachers may sometimes take on part-time classroom and part-time administrative responsibilities.

What differentiates teacher-led schools most from schools with a traditional structure is that everyone charged with administrative responsibility brings the classroom perspective to the decision-making process.

Teacher-led schools have to deal with the same issues that principal-led schools do, but unlike principal-led schools, the teachers are empowered to make the decisions needed to improve instruction and learning for their students. Teacher leadership teams are emerging on two fronts: in the small high schools discussed in Chapter 9 and in charter schools.

## Negotiated Decisions: The Role of Teachers' Unions

State education agencies, state superintendents, local school boards, school superintendents, and building principals all have a great deal of decision-making power that affects your work as a teacher. These entities or individuals do not make all the decisions, however. Many decisions are forged between the teachers' union and the school board through the process of negotiating the teachers' contract.

Over 90 percent of teachers in the United States belong to one of the major teachers' unions, the American Federation of Teachers (AFT) or the National Education Association (NEA) (Johnson & Boles, 2001). Local branches of these unions bargain at the school district level. The collective bargaining process is regulated by law at the state level. These regulations specify the issues that may be part of the collective bargaining process. In other words, some issues can be negotiated, others cannot be negotiated, and for some issues it is permissible to negotiate but negotiation is not mandated. As Table 10-1 indicates, in 35 states teachers have the right to collective bargaining; the remaining 15, located mostly in the southern and southwestern portions of the United States, do not (Education Commission of the States, 2008b).

Teachers' unions do not negotiate only salaries and benefits; they also negotiate working conditions, including in many districts class size (Johnson & Boles, 2001). The determination of working conditions has a direct impact on your ability as a teacher to meet your students' needs. For example, although the students' school year is usually determined by the state, the teacher's work year is typically negotiated by teachers' unions. In many districts teachers have a few paid days before and after the mandated dates for students. Unions may negotiate these and other issues, such as how much professional development will take place as a regular part of the school calendar and how teachers are compensated for participating in district-sponsored professional development after regular school hours or on the weekend. They may negotiate how much preparation time a teacher will have, if any, during the school day; when parent/family conference days occur; and, depending on the state, class size as well. In addition, if a district has a local school governance council or site-based management team, the conditions of these entities can also be negotiated through the bargaining process.

One of the most important things unions negotiate is how teachers get jobs in specific schools and how they move from job to job within the district. Do more senior teachers always get the first pick of jobs, despite their abilities? Or can schools interview and hire any potential teachers for their school, selecting the teachers they believe will best complement their existing staff, whether they are more or less senior in status? These kinds of decisions, which are negotiated ones, have serious implications for how schools function. They make the union a powerful partner in determining some of the most important decisions that affect teachers' work on a daily basis.

## Table 10-1    Status of Collective Bargaining for Teachers by State

In states that permit collective bargaining, teachers' unions negotiate with local school districts on salaries, benefits, and working conditions.

| Collective Bargaining States | States without Collective Bargaining |
|---|---|
| Alaska | Alabama |
| California | Arizona |
| Connecticut | Arkansas |
| Delaware | Colorado |
| Florida | Georgia |
| Hawaii | Kentucky |
| Idaho | Louisana |
| Illinois | Mississippi |
| Indiana | North Carolina |
| Iowa | South Carolina |
| Kansas | Texas |
| Maine | Utah |
| Maryland | Virginia |
| Massachusetts | West Virginia |
| Michigan | Wyoming |
| Minnesota | |
| Missouri | |
| Montana | |
| Nebraska | |
| Nevada | |
| New Hampshire | |
| New Jersey | |
| New Mexico | |
| New York | |
| North Dakota | |
| Ohio | |
| Oklahoma | |
| Oregon | |
| Pennsylvania | |
| Rhode Island | |
| South Dakota | |
| Tennessee | |
| Vermont | |
| Washington | |
| Wisconsin | |

**Source:** Education Commission of the States. (2008). *State notes: State/collective bargaining policies for teachers.* Retrieved May 24, 2008, from http://www.ecs.org/clearinghouse/77/27/7727.pdf.

Teachers unions have long been faulted for making seniority, rather than demonstrated skill, the basis of staffing decisions. Many unions are starting to find ways to move away from this practice, under pressure from the reform environment. Finally, unions can also negotiate peer assistance and review teams. The function of such teams is to identify teachers who are not performing well in their jobs, offer professional development support, and counsel teachers to leave the profession if it is in the best interests of the students to do so (see Chapter 12 for an extended discussion of peer assistance and review teams). This type of program directly affects the well-being of students by placing a high priority on the quality of teaching students receive and not solely on protecting all teachers' jobs.

## Historical Note
### Governing the Nation's Earliest Schools

During the colonial period there was a strong interest in establishing schools, but schools were not governed by the system that exists today. In early America, states did not have units of government devoted to education. Who organized these early schools, and how were they governed?

In the colony of Massachusetts, town meetings established the first schools in the 1630s. Towns often designated a schoolmaster and in many cases a location for a school. These early schools primarily served upper-class male children and were not meant to provide universal education. In 1642 Massachusetts established a law requiring that parents and children's caretakers provide for the education of their children. This legislation allowed town officials to fine families that did not educate their children, but it did not establish actual schools. Instead it enacted the principle that education was critical to the strength of the colonies as they broke away from England. Most of the other New England colonies followed with similar laws requiring that parents and families educate their children in the basics.

A breakthrough came in 1647, when Massachusetts passed the "Old Deluder Satan Act." This act required that every town that had 50 families or more had to employ a teacher for its children, who would be paid either by the families or, if the town chose to do so, by levying taxes. Towns of 100 families or more had to establish actual schools. In addition to teaching reading and writing, these schools were required to teach Latin grammar so that boys could be prepared for higher levels of education. This started the tradition of naming schools "Latin Grammar Schools," and in New England there are still public schools that carry vestiges of this title. For example, Boston Latin School is the oldest continuously operating public school in the United States, founded in 1635.

Students were taught reading and writing in these early schools primarily so that they could do two things: read the Bible and understand the colony's laws. As a mandated activity, education served both a public function in terms of fostering informed adult citizens and a religious function. The strange name of this legislation, the Old Deluder Satan Act, refers to the importance of being able to read and write so that children would not be deluded by Satan, but would instead have a strong understanding of their religion, adhere to it, and not be swayed to follow inappropriate paths of behavior.

Many different forms of schooling existed in the colonial period to meet the requirement that children be educated. Children of poor families were often apprenticed and might learn the basics as part of their apprenticeship. Wealthier parents might hire a tutor for their children. Families who could afford it might send their children—usually their daughters—to study with a widow in what were known as dame schools. Or students might attend a school built by the town itself. In whatever school environment children learned, education had become an important feature of colonial life.

According to R. Freeman Butts and Lawrence Cremin (1953), the patterns established in the New England colonies represented four essential beliefs about governing and administering education: "the state could require children to be educated; the state could require towns to establish schools; the civil government could supervise and control schools by direct management in the hands of public officials; and public funds could be used for the support of public schools" (p. 103). Thus, the idea took hold early in the history of the United States that the responsibility for education reached beyond individual decisions at the family level, but rather was a public good that required public stewardship.

## How State Governance Influences a Teacher's Work

The authority for making decisions about education is centralized at the state level, and it is at this level that many policies are set. Every state except Wisconsin and Minnesota has a state board of education, which is either appointed or elected, and all states have some kind of **state education agency (SEA)** that governs education and carries out the policies of the state board. The state agency is a department of the state government and has a title such as *Department of Education* or *Department of Public Instruction*. A link to the terminology and units in each state is available at **http://www.statelocalgov.net/50states-education.cfm**.

SEAs set policies that can influence your career and work as a teacher. For example, this agency decides what is required in order for an individual to become a licensed teacher—what professional content and what field experiences are required, and sometimes how much of each, and what standards need to be met. SEAs set policies regarding the professional examinations prospective teachers may be required to pass, such as selecting tests and setting pass scores. They also determine what kind of professional development practicing teachers must complete in order to retain their teaching licenses.

SEAs are also responsible for major policy decisions related to the curriculum, particularly the development of academic content standards, which define the knowledge and skills your students will be required to know and be tested in at various points in their PK–12 education. State agencies also determine which standardized tests will be used and set annual schedules for the administration of the tests. If the state is a textbook adoption state (see Chapter 5), the state determines the text selection. Each of these policy decisions has a direct impact on your daily work in the classroom. SEAs set the length of the school year, a consideration that has a direct bearing on what teachers can reasonably expect to attain with their students during the year. In addition to setting policy, the state agency also carries out regulatory tasks. For example, the state collects information from each school district on students' daily attendance; this information can be used to determine how many dollars flow from the state to the local district.

**Critical Term**

**State education agency (SEA).** The agency at the state level that makes educational policy and ensures that districts within the state comply with regulations governing education.

The actual makeup of the state agency, its title, and the title of its head vary from state to state. The agency head is known generically as the chief state school officer and in many states holds the title State Superintendent of Public Instruction. Chief state school officers are the principal advisers to governors about education issues. They play the same basic role in every state: to help formulate and carry out education policy at the state level. They use the power of their office to build public support for various education initiatives. The basic structure of the state educational agency, with a chief officer, dates to the years following the Civil War (Butts & Cremin, 1953).

In 36 states chief education officers are appointed by either the state board of education or the governor, and in the remaining 14 they are elected. To identify the model in your state or the state(s) in which you would like to teach, go to the States Notes link at **www.ecs.org**. Whether chief state school officers are appointed or elected has ramifications for the policy decisions they may make, decisions that are usually tied directly to the political agenda of the governor who made the appointment when the position is appointed.

SEAs also play an important role in relation to the federal government's education policies. SEAs interact directly with the federal education establishment to receive funds, establish guidelines consistent with federal policy, and monitor local districts for compliance with federal regulations. When state boards of education or governors take issue with federal policies and legislation, the chief state school officer is often the one who negotiates with the federal government about how to interpret federal policy and regulations.

At the state level, governors themselves have become much more active in setting educational policy than perhaps ever before. Assisting in these efforts is a nonpartisan, nongovernmental organization, the Education Commission of the States, (ECS), which was created in 1965 to help governors shape education policy and to provide a forum for governors and education policymakers to discuss and debate critical educational policy issues and initiatives (Education Commission of the States, 2008b). Today every governor belongs to the ECS. Chaired alternately by a Democratic and a Republican governor, the ECS provides state-by-state data on the implementation of educational policies—for example, charter schools, the No Child Left Behind Act, citizenship, or literacy.

## The Influence of the Federal Government in Education

Until the 1960s, few decisions about education were made at the federal level; instead, control, authority, and decision making were concentrated at the state and local level. Funding for education was largely a local and state concern, and schools were regulated almost completely by the states, with few, if any, federal regulations applying to them.

There were two prominent exceptions to this limited federal role. The first was the pivotal U.S. Supreme Court decision, *Brown v. Board of Education*, which struck down separate but equal schools in 1954 (see Chapter 7). The second was the policy decision to fund science and mathematics curriculum development with federal dollars following the former Soviet Union's launch of Sputnik in 1957 (see Chapter 5). These decisions, for the first time, began to create a substantial role for the federal government related to education.

# REWARDS AND CHALLENGES

## Sharing Power in the Classroom

David House
*Athens, Ohio*

From the beginning, working with rural students in southeastern Ohio has shown me that potent learning is grown in environments where empowered individuals are the catalysts for empowered communities. With this lens, I have worked to foster a learning environment where individual voices exchange ideas to build democratic communities. I believe teachers should work to shift the power of the educational experience over to the students. With this shift of power, teachers can establish and strengthen our students' voices in their daily school experiences. Modeling and teaching listening that initiates action is very impacting. We can build community around the notion that each student's voice will be heard and acted upon. When our voices are heard, we become more powerful, individually and communally.

Trust must be nurtured to support the building of community. Teaching the democratic principle of shared trust and implementing experiences to nurture trust helps my students appreciate the power of trust in their lives. Highlighting the power of trust in others specifically helps build community abd leads to interdependent responsibility. If the notion of common responsibility can be grown in the classroom, the community will be strong. Taking ownership of one's own life and how it impacts others' lives allows members of shared communities to truly make a difference. In my classes, these foundations in interdependent responsibility help my students gain access to powerful learning through our concern for shared goals.

Respect is the key element for building community in democratic ways. Without respect, my students—all students—feel devalued and communities are disconnected and lost. If I want my classroom to be a true community, respect for all individuals is crucial. Building and maintaining respect in our classrooms should be our number one goal each day. Students who are respected respect others and establish common feelings, and it is these shared feelings that build communities. By shifting the power to students, richer learning can take place for everyone. The power shift helps communities flourish by empowering individual voices, building trust among members sharing common goals, and most importantly always upholding respect for each individual in the community. These are lessons that reach to the heart of what it means to be involved in decision-making in one's classroom, school and community—hopefully not only as children, but as adults who will participate in and lead public decision-making in the future. ●

This situation changed radically in the 1960s with President Lyndon Johnson's "War on Poverty." Federal legislation designed to diminish the effects of poverty focused principally on the role of the schools in achieving this goal. As a result of these programs, the relationship between local school districts, the state, and the federal government would undergo a fundamental change. The importance of education at the federal level changed again dramatically in 1979 during the administration of President Jimmy Carter, with the passage of legislation creating the U.S. Department of Education, a cabinet-level position. Before that time, education was administered as part of the Department of Health, Education and Welfare. The creation of a cabinet-level position with a separate secretary of education appointed by the president was evidence of increased support for a federal role in education, sending a message to states that they would now be sharing the responsibility for this critical aspect of society. Elevating education to a cabinet-level position also politicized education at the federal level in a more public way than ever before. Today this department has a budget of nearly $69 billion (U.S. Department of Education, 2008). According to its mission statement, the purpose of the Department of Education is to:

● Strengthen the federal commitment to assuring access to equal educational opportunity for every individual;

- Supplement and complement the efforts of states, the local school systems and other instrumentalities of the states, the private sector, public and private nonprofit educational research institutions, community-based organizations, parents, and students to improve the quality of education;
- Encourage the increased involvement of the public, parents, and students in federal education programs;
- Promote improvements in the quality and usefulness of education through federally supported research, evaluation, and sharing of information;
- Improve the coordination of federal education programs;
- Improve the management of federal education activities; and
- Increase the accountability of federal education programs to the President, the Congress, and the public. (U.S. Department of Education, 2003)

## You turn... *to review*

1. What is an SEA? An LEA?
2. Name two ways local school boards directly affect your teaching.
3. Name two major issues a teachers' union can negotiate related to the conditions of work.

## Direct Federal Involvement in Education Programs through Legislation

The federal government has increased its involvement in education largely through legislation. Such legislation often has funding attached to it, and in order to receive funding, states must comply with federal regulations associated with the law. One such landmark piece of legislation, discussed in Chapter 8, is the Individuals with Disabilities Education Act, or IDEA (first passed as Public Law 94-142 in 1975), which provides specific rules and regulations regarding how the education of students with disabilities is to be carried out. IDEA had as its initial goal the funding of 40 percent of the additional dollars required to provide a free and appropriate education to students with disabilities above and beyond what it cost to educate students who do not have disabilities. This goal was never reached, and today the federal contribution has leveled off at approximately 18 percent of the additional cost of educating a student with disabilities. Three other examples of significant legislation include the Elementary and Secondary Education Act of 1965, Title IX of Education Amendments of 1972 prohibiting discrimination in education based on gender, and the No Child Left Behind Act of 2001.

The programs championed by President Johnson provided federal funding to support a variety of education programs targeted at schools whose students lived in poverty. The **Elementary and Secondary Education Act (ESEA)** of 1965 was designed specifically to bring federal dollars to these school districts as a means of leveling the education playing field. Passage of the ESEA made the federal government a major player in education. According to Lawrence Cremin (1988), the ESEA was also an important antipoverty measure that set the stage for the schools to be viewed as a central institution by which the effects of poverty were to be eradicated. Title I of the ESEA provided direct funding for schools with high populations of students from low-income families in the form of additional personnel, materials, and professional development for teachers.

**Critical Term**

**Elementary and Secondary Education Act (ESEA).** A major piece of federal legislation that provides federal direction to education and federal funds for schools, first passed in 1965.

Other federal legislation passed during this era also provided funds for education. For example, the 1964 Economic Opportunity Act funded Head Start, the prominent community-based early childhood program. Head Start was based on the concept that the earlier the intervention in the lives of children living in poverty, the better their chances for success in school and as adults in society. During the George W. Bush administration, funding to Head Start has been cut and when increases were proposed, they did not cover inflation (National Women's Law Center, 2008).

The ESEA and programs such as Head Start have been a feature of federal education legislation for decades and represent the continuous involvement of the federal government in education. Virtually every urban school district in the country has Title I funding, which is one kind of **categorical aid** because it can be used only for specific categories of services delineated by the federal government. The ESEA has been reauthorized several times by Congress, and as a result, the federal government is playing a larger role in education than ever before. In each successive reauthorization of this legislation, the federal government called for greater accountability of states and local school districts in terms of how they use federal dollars and how children are achieving as a result of this national investment. The most demanding legislation in terms of accountability is the No Child Left Behind Act.

Vice-President Hubert Humphrey visits with students from a Head Start program in 1967. Head Start was one of the first federally funded education programs that provided early education to young students from low socio-economic backgrounds.
(Corbis Images)

### The No Child Left Behind Act.

The most recent reauthorization of the ESEA in 2001 was the No Child Left Behind Act (NCLB). The NCLB goes further than any other piece of federal legislation in exerting a variety of federal controls over local schools, including the requirement that students are tested annually in reading and mathematics. These regulations have a direct effect on teachers' work. This act has been extremely controversial because schools that do not demonstrate what is called adequate yearly progress (AYP) on required standardized testing for student achievement are subject to a series of sanctions and can eventually be closed.

NCLB is based on four principles:

- accountability for results
- more choices for parents
- greater local control and flexibility
- an emphasis on doing what works based on scientific research

Accountability is based on annual scores on each state's system of student assessment. If a school does not meet AYP after five years they must undertake one of the following restructuring approaches:

1. Close and reopen as a public charter school.
2. Replace all or most of the school staff that are "relevant" to the school's failure.
3. Contract with an outside entity to operate the school.
4. Turn school operations over to the state, or a state take-over.
5. Undertake other major restructuring changes in school governance that lead to fundamental reform.

**Critical Term**

**Categorical aid.** Federal funding to school districts to support a specific category of federal education program.

You can see that although the intentions of increasing the accountability of each school for its students' achievement is a worthy goal, the principles and sanctions of NCLB are far-reaching and are inextricably tied into the contested territory of the control and governance of public education. Further, because NCLB tests only in reading and mathematics, this has impacted how schools choose to spend their instructional time, a topic we took up in both Chapters 5 and 9.

Supporters of the NCLB argue that its accountability measures pressure school districts to focus on increasing student performance and building the capacity of its teachers and staff to improve the quality of instruction, especially for racial and ethnic minority and low-income students (U.S. Department of Education, 2004). Critics pose two different arguments regarding NCLB. One set of critics takes the position that while attention to accountability and especially to the achievement of low-income students is appropriate, the time frames for achieving the goals are highly unrealistic (Center on Education Policy, 2005). A second set of critics suggests the following:

● The law was poorly conceived in the first place, especially in terms of motivation for learning (Noddings, 2005).

● It places too much emphasis (and therefore wastes precious classroom time) on test preparation (Noddings, 2005; Public Education Network, 2005).

● The curriculum has been narrowed (Noddings, 2005), and "many schools have abandoned earlier, more ambitious learning experiences in order to achieve short-term goals on test scores" (Public Education Network, 2005, p. 4).

● The pressure on test results may actually encourage schools to cheat on tests that measure adequate yearly progress (Noddings, 2005).

Both sets of critics are in agreement that the government has failed to provide school districts with the resources to help reach its central objective, that is, to develop the capacity of teachers to improve student achievement.

As is the case with other federal legislation, school districts are subject to the regulations of NCLB only if they choose to accept federal funds. Urban school districts and isolated rural school districts, which are the target of the law, tend to be underfunded to begin with and cannot easily afford to bypass these federal dollars. Therefore, the restrictions related to this legislation result in greater pressure on urban and rural districts than they do on wealthier districts, which may have far fewer low-income students and may actually opt out of the law by rejecting its funding.

**Gender Equity under Title IX Legislation.** The federal government also enacted legislation to ensure gender equity, known as **Title IX** of the Education Amendments of 1972. For schools that receive federal funds (and nearly all public schools do), this legislation mandates equity among males and females in education programs. Probably the biggest direct impact of Title IX in the public schools has been equity in athletics. Before its passage in 1972, schools were not required to provide opportunities for females to participate in athletics or to fund girls' and women's sports teams at the same level as those for boys and men. As a result of Title IX, schools are obliged to provide funding for girls' and women's sports teams. In the 30 years it has existed, the number of females participating in high school sports has increased tenfold. Nevertheless, in 2003–2004 there were only 2.9 million female high school athletes compared with 4.2 million male high school athletes (Women's Sports Foundation, 2008).

**Critical Term**

**Title IX.** Federal legislation designed to ensure equity between men and women in education.

## Your turn... *to reflect*

In a small group, reflect on your high school experiences. What aspects of your high school, if any, showed responsiveness to the issues mandated under Title IX legislation? What aspects of your high school failed to provide equity to male and female students? What do you believe perpetuated the lack of equity? How did your high school experiences differ in this regard based on the years in which your group members attended high school?

Title IX applies beyond athletics. Gender inequity has historically taken place in the curriculum areas of science and mathematics, which have traditionally been male-dominated. Although females may have been enrolled in classes over the years, often they were not expected to do well, were not supported by their teachers, or were not encouraged to consider careers in the sciences and mathematics. Title IX draws attention to this issue even though academics has received less attention than athletics.

This legislation has been in effect for over 30 years. After 25 years of Title IX funding, a report prepared by the federal government documented the following accomplishments (U.S. Department of Education, 1997):

● Increased participation of females in athletics

● Increased athletic scholarships for women

● New professional opportunities for employment

● Increased opportunities in mathematics and science

● Lowered dropout rate for young women who are pregnant or are mothers

Title IX has indeed made this issue more visible, but educational inequity continues. Questions of gender equity surfaced very loudly early in 2005 when the president of Harvard University, Lawrence Summers, implied that women may not be as well suited to careers in mathematics and science as are their male counterparts. With this in mind, what are your day-to-day responsibilities as a teacher with regard to Title IX?

As a middle or high school teacher, for example, you may have advisory responsibilities within a homeroom or "advisory" group. You may be expected to discuss careers or to talk about course choices with the students in your group. If you are a mathematics or science teacher, it is critical that you think about how you are interacting with your male and female students and whether you are giving your female students the same support and encouragement as your male students. In a related matter, does your school have a "hidden curriculum" as to who gets counseled to take advanced science and mathematics? Who is encouraged to join the mathematics club or participate in science competitions? If you observe such gender preferences at your school (or any other preferences), you will want to raise this issue with your colleagues.

The National Science Foundation, which is the major federal agency to promote the progress of science, has an ongoing program of research on science and gender especially

Federal legislation known as Title IX resulted in much greater funding for female athletic programs in the schools. (Media Bakery)

focused on careers in science, technology, engineering, and mathematics (STEM). Here are four of the myths about girls and science they have identified:

**1. Myth:** *From the time they start school, most girls are less interested in science than boys are.* **Reality:** In elementary school about as many girls as boys have positive attitudes toward science.

**2. Myth:** *Classroom interventions that work to increase girls' interest in STEM run the risk of turning off the boys.* **Reality:** Actually, educators have found that interventions that work to increase girls' interest in STEM also increase such interest among the boys in the classroom. When girls are shown images of women scientists and given a greater sense of possibility about the person they could become, the boys get the message too–"I can do this!"

**3. Myth:** *Science and math teachers are no longer biased toward their male students.* **Reality:** In fact, biases are persistent, and teachers often interact more with boys than with girls in science and math. A teacher will often help a boy do an experiment by explaining how to do it, while when a girl asks for assistance the teacher will often simply show how to do it.

**4. Myth:** *When girls just aren't interested in science, parents can't do much to motivate them.* **Reality:** Parents' support (as well as that of teachers) has been shown to be crucial to a girl's interest in science, technology, engineering, and math. Making girls aware of the range of science and engineering, careers available and their relevance to society works to attract more women (as well as men) to STEM careers (NSF, 2008).

If your school holds career days (these are usually held beginning in the upper grades in elementary school), who is invited to represent various careers, and is an effort made to promote the idea that all careers are equally attainable by both sexes? And if you are interested in coaching along with teaching, you will need to determine whether the girls' teams get the same level of support as the boys' teams. Are there subtle inequities—for example, do boys have newer uniforms? In the case that follows, a relatively new high school teacher faces a situation that shows the school still has a way to go to address the problem of equity.

## A Case In Point
### Title IX in Action?

Joe Ellis is a high school mathematics teacher in a small town in the West that is located about 50 miles from a large city. He has been teaching for a year. His responsibilities include teaching geometry and one class of Algebra II. He knows it is important for his students to gain confidence in mathematics, and he is committed to this goal. Joe was familiar with Title IX legislation from his teacher education program, and he had hoped that his school was a place that encouraged all students to study higher level mathematics. Throughout his first year of teaching, however, he noticed that very few girls participated in the upper level mathematics courses or in the math club. Joe was careful in his own classes to encourage his female students, but he was not sure how to raise this concern before his whole department. His department was made up of three male teachers.

The summer before his second year of teaching, the mathematics teachers met to do some joint planning for the coming year; these were paid staff development days in August. At these meetings, all the mathematics teachers talked about setting goals for their department for the coming year. Feeling more confident than he had a year before, Joe raised the question of girls' participation in mathematics and asked whether the upper level classes and the math club had always attracted so few girls, or whether this was a recent development. His colleagues answered that it was pretty typical but that they really hadn't paid much attention to it. Joe asked one of his colleagues to observe his teaching a class to see if he was doing anything to discourage his female students from moving ahead in mathematics. One of his colleagues, Tim Heller, volunteered— and also asked if anyone would be willing to watch him and give him similar feedback. By the end of their planning days, each of the three teachers had agreed to have someone come in and at least count how many times they all called on the girls and boys. Although this was a meager beginning, Joe was glad he had spoken up.

**The Paradox of Federal Legislation.** Federal involvement can clearly set the bar higher for significant societal issues that states and local school districts might otherwise choose not to address, such as in gender equity; equity in schooling across diverse racial, ethnic, language, and socioeconomic groups; or educational rights for individuals with disabilities. Federal legislation can be a double-edged sword, however. On the one hand, it can set this bar and may provide funding to support groups of students that are marginalized in education. On the other hand, the bureaucracy and other demands associated with meeting the regulations of legislation can cause schools to spend countless hours and resources on bureaucratic details that do not directly contribute to the instructional process.

In addition, legislation—whether at the federal or the state level—can mandate educational change without providing adequate funding to implement those changes. This sets up a situation where, given their already tight budgets, it is difficult for states and local school districts to meet the goals of federal legislation. This is the case with IDEA, where the early federal promise to fund at 40 percent has never been accomplished. With regard to NCLB, the lack of adequate funding continues to be a challenge as states not only try to keep up with the requirements, but, more important, try to fund the improvement of instruction so that students can meet the achievement goals of the law. In times of diminished funding, the leverage of federal legislation can become a frustration for schools despite the legislation's good intentions for students and society.

## Court Decisions and Education

Another major source of federal authority and influence on the schools is the U.S. Supreme Court. When the Court rules on cases related to education, these decisions in effect set policy. Despite the tradition that combines state control of education with local control by local school boards, federal influence has grown as a result of judicial decisions. The *Brown v. Board of Education* decision, for example, changed the course of education nationwide, led to significant policy decisions to support desegregation, and, as such, directly affected state and local school district practices and the lives of teachers and students alike.

Another major decision came in 1974, when the Supreme Court ruled on the question of the assistance to be given to students whose first language is not English. This decision, known as *Lau v. Nichols,* ruled that schools were required to use students' home language to support them in learning standard English. This case originated with a class-action suit brought against the San Francisco Board of Education on behalf of students whose first language was Chinese. According to Pang, Kiang, and Pak (2004):

> Like Brown v. Board of Education, the Supreme Court decision in the Lau case fundamentally reformed U.S. educational policy. Because of the leadership of Chinese American students and parents, the educational rights of limited-English speaking students of all nationalities were formally recognized and protected. (p. 552)

When it rules on such cases, the Supreme Court in effect sets education policy on a national level, usually as a means of ensuring the rights of groups who have not enjoyed the equal protection of the law in the realm of education.

State court decisions can also influence subsequent federal policymaking. For example, the original 1975 legislation protecting the rights of students with disabilities developed largely out of several state court cases that affirmed the right of students with disabilities to equal protection under the law. The rights established under these state court decisions eventually influenced federal policy that guarantees students with disabilities a free and appropriate public education.

## Philosophical Note
### The Separation of Church and State and Public Education

The First Amendment to the Constitution prohibits establishing religion as an instrument of the state. This has been interpreted as the separation of church and state, and has distinguished the United States from many other nations. With regard to education, this philosophy has meant that public schools are not to be instruments of any specific religious group or denomination. As much as the United States is a nation that values the separation of church and state, it is also a society that takes religion—and religious freedom—quite seriously. As Joel Spring points out, "there is a thin line between not allowing the establishment of religion and interfering with the free exercise of religion" (1998, p. 257). Often the schools have been caught in the middle of these competing goals.

But how exactly should the schools go about separating themselves from religion? What influence, if any, does and should religion have in how schools operate? This issue will undoubtedly come up in your work as a teacher. For example, how much, and in what ways, should you talk about religion in your classroom? How will you address religious holidays? Will you "celebrate" Christmas by decorating your room? set up a Secret Santa gift exchange for students? participate in such an exchange among the school staff? If you were asked to direct a winter holiday program in your school, what would your response be? How would you think about this in relationship to your students who do not celebrate the typical holidays, and perhaps have no winter holiday tradition? If you were a coach, how would you respond to students who might wish to say a denominational prayer before a football game? And what is the relationship between your responsibilities as a teacher and your own religious beliefs? How will you learn about your students' various religions?

The philosophy behind the separation of church and state in the schools has received various interpretations over time, in part with the guidance of the courts. For example, a primary aim of the first schools in the New England colonies was to teach children so that they could read the Bible. Ministers were often the schoolmasters in both the northern and the southern colonies. And religious denominations established schools during the earliest settlement of the country. From these beginnings, religion continued to play at least some role in the public, secular schools well into the twentieth century, when a much stricter separation of church and state began to be practiced. The role of religion as it relates to education has long been a contentious issue, but the focus ebbs and flows in different eras. Two major points of contention today are the focus of the church–state debate as it relates to the schools. First, what, if any, role does religion have within the public schools? Second, should public funds generated from tax dollars be used to support parochial schools?

A strict separation of church and state, it is argued, does not support a place for religion in the public schools, whose purpose is to promote a society that is tolerant of religious plurality. In today's educational context, there have been many attempts to promote specifically Christian religion in the public school, for example, reading the Protestant Bible in public school classrooms on a daily basis. Other attempts have included posting the Ten Commandments in every elementary and secondary public classroom in particular states. These efforts have been ruled unconstitutional as they clearly do not have a secular purpose (Colasanti, 2008).

One question that is often asked with regard to religion and the public schools is: What is the difference between teaching religion in the service of a particular faith and teaching about religion as a topic of study? In other words, what is the purpose of the activity? Activities sponsored by schools and mandated for all students at the school that are aimed at propagating a particular religious belief, whether in the formal academic curriculum or extra curricular activities, are usually interpreted as being inappropriate under the First Amendment. For example, prayers at events such as commencement or before football games have been the focus of several court cases and have often been ruled unconstitutional if they are part of a school-sponsored event and thus forced on the entire student body of a public school.

Often principals and teachers will argue that holidays such as Christmas have essentially become so secular that it is not inappropriate to celebrate them in the schools. However, not all students celebrate Christmas, some students are prohibited by their religion from celebrating any holiday (e.g., Jehovah's Witnesses), and the line between Christmas as a religious holiday and Christmas as a secular celebration is often not clear. As a result, teachers must be extremely careful to honor the religious traditions of all of their students and not allow one tradition to be privileged over others. Teachers are not prohibited from teaching students about religious traditions across different faiths, but teachers in public schools cannot promote a specific religion or celebrate any holiday as a religious event.

## The Influence of Other External Groups on Education Decisions

Many nongovernmental interest groups also influence educational policy and practice. Although nongovernmental organizations do not have the power to legislate, they can have a powerful influence on the way states and the country think about educational policy and issues, and can use their power to lobby directly for changes in policies and mandates in the field of education.

Some of these groups may be considered "booster groups" whose primary purpose is to benefit schools in terms of human and material resources. These may include, for example, parent groups or local school–business partnerships. Organizations such as the Parent Teacher Organization (**www.ptotoday.com**) or the National Parent Teacher Association (**www.pta.org**) not only provide direct support to schools at the local level, but also represent the interests of parents and schools politically and work to influence education through lobbying efforts. Parents of children and youth with disabilities have been extremely successful in advocating for special education services in the schools and were instrumental in gaining support for the IDEA legislation. The lead professional organization in special education, the Council for Exceptional Children, sponsors a public policy and legislative information site on its homepage (**http://www.cec.sped.org/pp/**).

Teachers' unions themselves continue to be extremely influential in a broad arena of educational and political areas. Their lobbying arms both within individual states and nationally have the potential to influence education legislation and funding. In individual states their strength and influence vary widely, but nationally they are highly visible in a wide range of political spheres.

Other nongovernmental groups study education issues, generate reports on education, and lobby for education legislation and policy changes. In Chapter 5, for example, we discussed the influence of national committees on the school curriculum. Groups such as the Education Commission of the States is another example of an organization that is heavily committed to improving education. Yet another current example is the National Commission on Teaching and America's Future (NCTAF, **www.nctaf.org/home.php**). In addition to preparing policy reports on improving the quality of teaching and learning, NCTAF assists no fewer than 22 state partnerships in reform efforts.

Finally, groups that are committed to improving education can join together to form coalitions, or partnerships, to influence improving education. The Holmes Partnership, for example, supports collaborations between schools and universities to work together toward the reform of education (**www. holmespartnership.org**). This organization networks such partnerships across the country. The National Commission on Teaching and America's Future (**www.nctaf.org**) brings together a policy coalition of key stakeholders, including, for example, state policymakers, higher education officials, teachers' unions, business leaders, and elect-

Parent–teacher organizations, teachers unions, and other independent organizations can lobby for important state and federal legislation related to education. (© AP/Wide Word Photos)

ed state and local officials to work across organizations for the purpose of improving education (NCTAF, 2008).

The current interest in reforming public education has brought into the policy environment the ever greater involvement of the business community as well. The interest of the business community may be interpreted as a commitment to improving the quality of the future workforce through improved education. With the rise of for-profit schools, the interest of some members of the business community in educational reform can also be interpreted as an issue of potential gain from establishing schools that are profit-driven.

## Financing Education: How Dollars Make their Way to Schools, Teachers, and Students

Public schools receive their funds from three sources: property taxes levied in local communities, state allocations, and federal dollars. In 2005–2006, the United States spent a total of approximately $520 billion on education (U.S. Census Bureau, 2008). Figure 10-3 shows the total revenue generated from each of these sources for 2005–2006.

Dollars spent for education in a local school district are usually reported as **per pupil expenditure**, which refers to the total amount of money an individual school district spends to educate each individual pupil who is enrolled. Per pupil expenditures vary widely within and across states. As Figure 10-4 indicates, the average per pupil expenditure is $9,138 annually (U.S. Census Bureau, 2008). The state that spent the most per pupil during 2005–2006 was New York at $14,884, and the state that spent the least was Utah at $5,437 per pupil. These figures include salaries, wages, and benefits, as well as pupil support, staff support, general administration, and school administration.

**Critical Term**

**Per pupil expenditure.** The average total amount of money that is spent per pupil each year, which varies greatly from state to state.

| Figure 10-3 | Revenues for Public Education Generated by Local, State, and Federal Sources for 2005–2006 |

**State and local revenues account for the majority of school funding, with federal sources playing a much smaller role.**

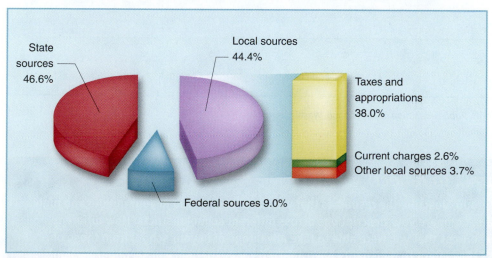

**Source:** U.S. Census Bureau. (2008, April). *Public education finances 2006.* Washington, DC: Author.

**Figure 10-4    Average Per Pupil Expenditure, by State, 2005–2006**

Per pupil spending for education differs widely across the states and the District of Columbia.

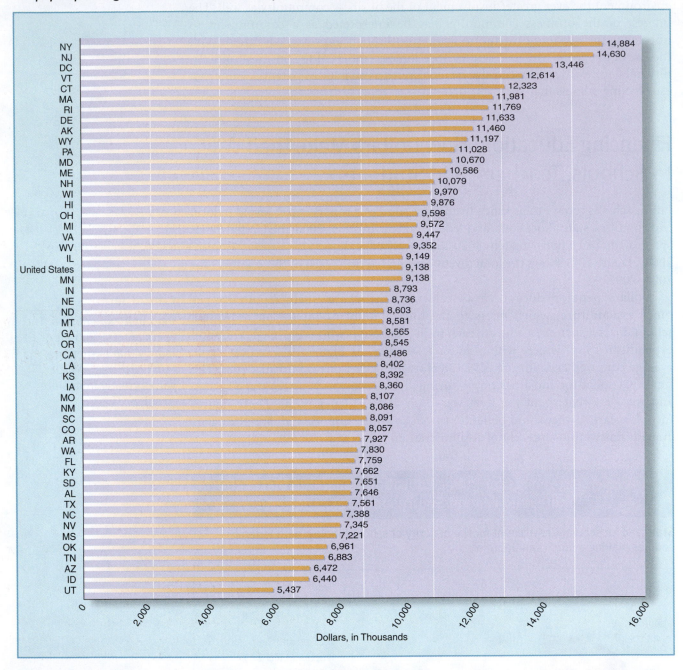

| State | Dollars |
|---|---|
| NY | 14,884 |
| NJ | 14,630 |
| DC | 13,446 |
| VT | 12,614 |
| CT | 12,323 |
| MA | 11,981 |
| RI | 11,769 |
| DE | 11,633 |
| AK | 11,460 |
| WY | 11,197 |
| PA | 11,028 |
| MD | 10,670 |
| ME | 10,586 |
| NH | 10,079 |
| WI | 9,970 |
| HI | 9,876 |
| OH | 9,598 |
| MI | 9,572 |
| VA | 9,447 |
| WV | 9,352 |
| IL | 9,149 |
| United States | 9,138 |
| MN | 9,138 |
| IN | 8,793 |
| NE | 8,736 |
| ND | 8,603 |
| MT | 8,581 |
| GA | 8,565 |
| OR | 8,545 |
| CA | 8,486 |
| LA | 8,402 |
| KS | 8,392 |
| IA | 8,360 |
| MO | 8,107 |
| NM | 8,086 |
| SC | 8,091 |
| CO | 8,057 |
| AR | 7,927 |
| WA | 7,830 |
| FL | 7,759 |
| KY | 7,662 |
| SD | 7,651 |
| AL | 7,646 |
| TX | 7,561 |
| NC | 7,388 |
| NV | 7,345 |
| MS | 7,221 |
| OK | 6,961 |
| TN | 6,883 |
| AZ | 6,472 |
| ID | 6,440 |
| UT | 5,437 |

Dollars, in Thousands

**Source:**  U.S. Census Bureau. (2008, April). *Public education finances 2006.* Washington, DC.

## Your turn... *to reflect*

In a small group, describe the resources that were available to you in your middle and high school years. Compare your descriptions across different school districts. How different were the resources that you were able to take advantage of in your school from those of your peers? How might that disparity have affected your experience in secondary school?

## Inequities in School Funding

In traditional school funding patterns in the United States, the majority of funds for education are raised in local communities through property taxes, based on the value of local property. Therefore, the wealthier the community, the more dollars collected in local property taxes to fund the schools. But as the achievement gap between students in high and low socioeconomic groups and also that between middle-class white students and racial and ethnic minority students (who are concentrated in urban schools) has widened, efforts have been made to allocate funding in a more equitable manner across all school districts. Is it appropriate, critics ask, to fund schools primarily on the basis of property taxes, which inevitably means that urban and rural schools will always lag behind schools in wealthier suburbs, where more dollars can usually be raised owing to the greater value of property in their communities?

### Your turn... *to review*

1. What are the benefits and limitations of the No Child Left Behind Act?
2. What group does IDEA protect? Title IX?
3. What was the Lau decision and to which group of students does it pertain?
4. What are the different origins of funds to support the public schools?

Frustration with these disparities has led to multiple legal challenges to conventional approaches to funding schools in states across the country, with the goal of equalizing funding across school districts. In 31 states low-income families have sued states on this issue. The most famous of these cases is the *Serrano v. Priest* suit in California, which ruled against the existing funding system based on the Fourteenth Amendment (Cooper, Fusarelli, & Randall, 2004). Although many such suits have not been successful, the press to equalize school funding is a high-visibility issue nationally and the challenges that have been raised have begun to contribute to states increasing the proportion of funding to schools and a subsequent reduction in reliance on property taxes alone. As a consequence, states are now responsible for funding, on average, about 47 percent of school costs; local sources of revenue fund approximately 44 percent of the cost, down from about 47 percent in 1989–1990; and federal dollars make up the final contribution, with an increase from about 6 percent in 1989–1990 to about 9 percent of the total today (U.S. Census Bureau, 2008). Obviously, local revenues remain a critical factor in financing schools. But in an effort to speed the equalization of funding, some states restrict the amount of funding that can be raised through local property taxes.

When school districts wish to build new schools or make major repairs and renovations to existing schools, they are required to raise the necessary money if adequate funds are not available in the budget. This is accomplished through a vote, usually called a referendum, by local residents. In approving a referendum, a community is sanctioning the local school board's request to borrow funds or to float bonds for the purpose of capital improvements in the schools, which is passed on to the taxpayers in the form of increased school taxes. When the economy is weak, referendums for schools usually are not successful, except in very high-income communities where residents may believe they can easily absorb the added tax burden. In large, financially strapped urban areas, such referendums have not usually been successful in the recent past.

In a centralized school budgeting process, a district might decide to budget for a library/media specialist for each school; in a decentralized budgeting process, the individual school staff decides whether it will spend funds on this position, or whether another use of the funds would be more advantageous for its students. (©O'Brian productions/Corbis Images)

**Critical Term**

**Centralized budgeting system.** A system in which budgetary decisions are made at the school district level with little budget authority at the local school level.

**Critical Term**

**Decentralized budgeting system.** A system in which schools get a certain amount of money to spend each year and the school principal—sometimes in conjunction with a teacher or community advisory group—develops a local budget based on the individual needs and goals of the school.

In the report *Tough Choices, Tough Times*, a report of the New Commission on the Skills of the American Work Force (National Center on Education and the Economy, 2006), its proposed redesign of the entire system of American education called for complete state funding of the schools. So that high-functioning schools in advantaged communities do not have to reduce the quality of their education, the commission also proposed an infusion of at least $19 billion so that all schools can upgrade their programs.

## From the Federal Government, the State, and the Community to the School

Once funds reach the local school district, they are apportioned according to the budget developed by the local school board. Most often budgets are developed by district superintendents and their staff members and presented to the school board for review, revision, and approval. Certain funds that come to school districts from federal and state sources, however, are restricted to specific uses, such as federal categorical aid, and local districts may use those dollars only for the purposes for which they were allocated. Federal funds cover many purposes, including improving technology in schools. States can apply for funds under the Enhancing Education Through Technology Program, or EETP, which enable states to provide LEAs with subgrants to help improve student learning through the integration of technology. The majority of a district's budget is allocated to paying for teacher and staff salaries and benefits, which are listed as part of the *cost of instruction*. In 2005–2006, instruction accounted for 62 percent of spending in public schools (U.S. Census Bureau, 2008), with support services (e.g. administration, pupil support services, etc.) accounting for another 35%.

Individual districts rely on either a **centralized budgeting system** or **decentralized budgeting system** to allocate funds. The kind of budgeting that is practiced has direct implications for how much flexibility an individual school and its teachers have in funding programs.

In a centralized system, decisions about how to spend money are made at the district level by the superintendent or other district-level administrators. Under this kind of system, district administrators may set aside dollars for professional development activities and organize them all at the district level, determine how many dollars are allocated for substitute teachers and hold those dollars in a central pool, decide how many field trips a particular school is allocated, order textbooks on a districtwide basis, buy computers for each school, or decide what other supplemental books, if any, can be ordered. Some districts may order all school supplies and send a prescribed amount to each school for the semester or the year. With regard to personnel, in a centralized system the district may decide whether to provide each school with a library/media specialist, a nurse or health aide, or a full-time art or music teacher. In a centralized system, principals and teachers have less influence on how money is spent. Rather, control is concentrated at the district level, giving the superintendent and other district administrators a great deal of authority.

In a decentralized budgeting system each school principal gets a certain amount of money to spend in a given year and draws up his or her own budget for the school. In schools that have a local community council, that group often provides input on designing the annual school budget. Similarly, if there is a strong collaborative working relationship between the teachers and the principal, teachers' input on the budget will be sought and valued. Decentralized budgeting means that critical decisions are made mostly at the school level about personnel, curriculum materials, field trips, technology, and so on. In a decentralized system, teachers may also control a small budget for a grade level or classroom and use it to purchase instructional materials of their choice.

Districts may also centralize major budget functions for activities determined to be important by the district administration but decentralize others. For example, a district may provide centralized training in the use of technology, but it may be up to an individual school to buy computers and software and to hire a teacher or other professional to provide network support or leadership regarding the application of technology to instruction. The district may make decisions about how many classroom teachers will be assigned to a specific school, but the school may hire teachers in special areas, parent and family coordinators, or other professionals and classroom aides.

As a new teacher, you are not expected to have detailed, complex knowledge about your school's budget and how it works. But it is important for you to know how much input and authority you and your peers have to influence how dollars are spent. If you work in a school where the budget is decentralized, you should have the opportunity to help decide whether the money allotted to your building is being spent in a way that best benefits your students and best helps you meet their educational needs. If you choose not to be involved in budgetary deliberations, you are agreeing to let your peers and the building administrator decide how the school's money will be spent. You may trust their decision making completely and have great confidence in the way they develop the school's budget. But if you are not so confident in the existing budget, it will be important for you to take an active role in contributing to its development.

How public schools are financed is a contentious issue because of the inequity across communities and the low achievement of many students in urban and rural schools. Equalizing funding across public schools is seen as one way of improving the schools that are not serving students well. Such changes in how funds are generated and distributed are taking place within the public schools themselves, under the control of public agencies and public local school boards. Another development that is affecting how the country thinks about improving the quality of education and how education dollars are allocated is the question of school choice, which involves a fundamental redefinition of how education is governed and controlled in this country.

## Changing Views of the Governance and Control of Schools

Traditionally, most school-aged children have attended public schools in their own neighborhoods at public expense. If families chose to send their children to private schools, whether secular or parochial, they bore responsibility for paying the tuition. Support for public schooling has been based generally on the philosophy that a strong public education system is foundational to a democracy and its ability to educate its citizens and to foster democratic values. This system has been one of the most durable ones in the United States, and its structure has assured a steady stream of students and funding for the public schools.

Not all public schools are high-quality schools, however, and in some cases they do not enable students to learn well. In the 1980s, the concept of choice was introduced into the contemporary educational landscape, based on the philosophy that families should

## Critical Term

**Charter school.** A nonsectarian, publicly funded school that is usually not bound to the regulations of a typical public school or the restrictions of the collective bargaining agreement between a school district and a teachers' union.

## Critical Term

**Vouchers.** An arrangement whereby parents can enroll their children in a private school and can apply a specific amount of public dollars toward the tuition for that school.

be able to choose the school they would like their children to attend and not be limited to what may be an ineffective public school. Families that have the means to move to communities where schools are considered to be more effective, it was argued, already have a choice about where their children attend school—a choice they make by moving into a particular community so that their children can attend a particular public school system. Families without the means to choose a community with high-performing schools, the argument goes, do not have such a choice and may be relegated to low-quality schools. Giving lower income families a choice, proponents argue, introduces greater equity in terms of ensuring the quality of their children's education.

The two prominent forms of choice operating in today's educational context are **charter schools** and **vouchers**. Charter schools are publicly funded entities that enable the creation of schools with greater autonomy and freedom from bureaucratic restrictions. They are special schools within the public school system, but they operate outside of the bureaucratic rules of the public system. Charter schools often have a specific identity or theme. Rather than having the public school district alone create and manage schools, the authority to found, or charter, a school can be located within a public school district or be extended to other entities in a community, for example, the city council or a local college or university. Legislation regarding charter schools differs from state to state. Regulations often, but not always, permit charter schools to be operated by for-profit companies (e.g., Edison Schools). States can also legislate who can be permitted to start a charter school. They can be started by individuals who have no educational experience, or they can be started by teachers or other educators who want the freedom to create a new kind of school. Standards for accountability for charter schools also differ across states. In 2005–2006, over 1 million students were enrolled in about 3,800 charter schools (U.S. Department of Education, 2007b).

Vouchers represent a different form of school choice. Voucher programs allow families to choose a private school and use public funds to pay the tuition; in other words, money that would have been spent in the public schools follows the child to whatever school he or she attends, moving funds directly out of public schools on a per-child basis. Vouchers were initially started to provide choice to low-income families. Advocates of vouchers are not limited to residents in low-income communities, however. In some states, conservative politicians have proposed legislation that would enable all children in the state, regardless of income level, to use a voucher to attend any school they wish. In some voucher programs, notably in Milwaukee and Cleveland, vouchers for education can be used at either sectarian or parochial schools. When vouchers are used at parochial schools, public funds directly support religious education. The majority of students in the Milwaukee voucher program attend parochial schools.

School voucher programs, which are highly controversial, were first developed to assist low-income families in sending their children to private schools using public dollars to pay tuition. (Bob Daemmrich/ The Image Works)

The concept of school choice challenges the longstanding approach to school governance and funding in the modern United States. It is based on the assumption that the public schools as they have always existed may be unable or unwilling to successfully reform themselves. It reallocates funds directly out of the public school system to support either new charter schools or to provide subsidies for students to attend private schools, often parochial schools, through vouchers. Needless to say, and as the next section illustrates, school choice is a hotly contested issue.

# Digging Deeper
## Strengthening or Weakening Public Schools through Choice?

School choice is ostensibly a way of improving the public schools by introducing competition from private schools. Does introducing choice strengthen or weaken public schools?

**Pro and Con:** Proponents of choice believe that in addition to providing low-income families with choices, introducing competition into the education system will stimulate the reform and redesign of public schools and thus lead to their improvement (Good & Braden, 2000). This approach is assumed to strengthen public schools by forcing them to compete for students. Rather than assume that they have a ready population each fall from the local neighborhoods, schools will have to prove themselves to families as they make choices about where to send their children to school. Another assumption is that schools that develop in the private sector will model innovation.

Those who argue that school choice will weaken the public schools are concerned about the flow of dollars out of the public schools, especially at a time when the federal government is placing extreme pressure on the public schools to perform under the NCLB legislation, which requires substantial funding. Concern also exists that when charter schools are run by for-profit companies, for example, the Edison Company, the bottom line will not be the best interest of the students, but rather that of the company's profits. Opponents' further concerns include the erosion of the church–state separation, especially with school vouchers. Opponents also argue that choice will lead to the development of a two-tiered system of public education in this country—a private school system for those who can afford it and for low-income parents who are effective in accessing school choice options, and a public school system for the children of families who are not.

**The Nuances:** School choice does not reflect a traditional alignment of political views. In contrast, its varied stakeholders exemplify the saying "politics makes strange bedfellows." On the one hand, some families in urban communities whose choices are limited and whose children do attend failing schools support school choice. Without question, all failing schools, no matter where they are located, need to be improved. Some low-income parents in urban areas have been proponents of choice and voucher programs because of the immediate relief it provides to them and their children by enabling them to leave schools that are failing. However, not all urban schools are failing schools, and within the urban context, schools exist that can be models for other schools that are not doing well. Schools that are thriving in urban communities may have had their roots in the magnet school movement of the 1970s, which introduced the idea of schools with specific identities, themes, or curriculums.

On the other hand, conservative politicians and policymakers, and also religious leaders whose denominations have parochial school interests, are also proponents of choice. Their perspective is typically rooted in a deep belief in privatization and deregulation, often with the goal of ending all controls over public schools, including the certification of teachers—and often the demise of teacher's unions as well. Revenues would be redistributed in support of private sectarian and parochial schools. Proposed legislation to support universal voucher programs for families of all income levels suggests that some voucher proponents have as their ultimate goal enabling any parent to take funds from public schools and use them for any private school, whether they are low-income parents looking for a real choice and who have no other means of doing so, or high-income families who can already afford to send their students to a private day or boarding school and may already be doing so. Communities where vouchers can be used at parochial schools are supporting what often have been church–related schools that have been struggling financially. For example, the Catholic school system does not have the large supply of nuns and priests to teach as it has in the past. This is a very different perspective on vouchers than the original arguments related to low-income communities alone.

In spite of the differing commitments of these different constituencies favoring school choice, the repercussions are serious for the institution of public schooling in the United States. These are not limited to questions of reallocation of funds. For example, charter schools are not always required to accept students who have disabilities or students who are English language learners, which creates a disproportionate representation of students from these groups in public schools—students who require special services and additional resources to succeed. Some states have loose or nonexistent accountability standards for schools that accept vouchers, but not for public schools. If charter or choice schools prove to be highly ineffective or engage in illegal financial practices, as has been the case with some voucher schools in the state of Wisconsin, public schools—whether or not they have the resources—must always provide the safety net and scramble, often at the last minute, to find places for students whose schools have been closed. When vouchers are used for parochial schools, issues related to the separation of church and state are a major consideration since public funds are used in schools that are clearly committed to establishing a specific religion.

**Rethinking the Issue:** School choice may encourage creativity and innovation in education. But it does not enable a system of public schools to be strong—either as a societal entity or as a force for promoting democracy. It directly reduces funds for public schools. School choice blurs the lines between public and private education on many counts. Charter schools can be public or private. Vouchers that are used for parochial schools force the issue of the separation of church and state in public education. Charter schools that operate outside of the school district and do not need to adhere to negotiated salary schedules, but are publicly funded, often offer lower salaries and benefits to teachers. Teachers and administrations in charter schools and private schools that accept vouchers are not always obliged to be certified, as public school teachers are.

In the United States private schools—sectarian and parochial alike—have traditionally existed outside public control and without the support of public dollars. Once public dollars for education go to private and parochial schools, control over education shifts from being solely a function of public institutions to public and private institutions, including religious instruction. Thus, the values of public schooling are called into question by the trend toward school choice. The question remains whether school choice has as its goal the strengthening of public schools or reshaping the entire enterprise of school governance and funding. Ultimately, a critical question is whether or not the country desires or needs a strong public school system to support its historical commitment to upward mobility through public education.

School choice has real implications for you as a teacher. What kind of school do you wish to teach in as you begin your career? If you choose to teach in a school that does not require teachers to be certified, how does that affect your view of teaching as a profession? How will you feel if you, as a public school teacher, are suddenly asked to receive students whose school of choice has been closed? Perhaps you are thinking that in the future you may wish to form a charter school. Will you limit your efforts to creating a charter within the public school system, or will you move outside the system? These issues represent only a few examples of the dynamics that may occur as the educational system grapples with school choice.

## Home Schooling: Where Does It Fit?

"Going to school" is usually viewed as compulsory attendance at a school building. It can be private or public, it can be parochial or secular, it can be urban or rural or suburban, but traditionally, at least during the twentieth century, children nearly universally attended school. In contrast, a recent trend in the United States is home schooling.

Home schooling exists outside of the traditional governance system of education. When parents elect to school their children at home, they are in essence bypassing the governance and decision making of either public or private schools and are making virtually all decisions about their children's education on their own.

Home schooling is legal in all 50 states, but it has only been so since 1993 (Basham, 2001). States do require some accountability for home schooling, but the degree varies widely from state to state. Figure 10-5 indicates the various levels of regulation across the 50 states according to the Home School Legal Defense Association (**http://www.hslda.org/laws/default.asp**). As this figure illustrates, the levels of regulation of home schooling are evenly divided across the states, ranging from literally no requirement to report anything at all to the state to extensive requirements for accountability, including approval of the curriculum and requirements to report test scores.

In 2003, approximately 1.1 million students were being educated at home, representing about 2.2 percent of school-aged students; this compares with about 850,000 home-schooled students in 1999. Eighty percent of home-schooled children are entirely home schooled, and the remaining 20 percent attend either public or private schools part of the time (National Center for Education Statistics, 2004).

Parents may choose to home school their children for a variety of reasons. Thirty-one percent of families reportedly choose to educate their children at home because they are dissatisfied with the school environment; the second most common reason has to do with religious considerations. An additional 30 percent choose home schooling in order to provide religious or moral instruction (National Center for Education Statistics, 2004). According to the U.S. Census Bureau (2005), 77 percent of children who are home schooled are white, 81 percent are from two-parent households, and in 54 percent of those households, only one parent was in the labor force.

Although in the 1960s home schooling was practiced primarily by members of the counterculture, today the largest percentage of families who home school their children, 75 percent, are affiliated with the Christian Right; the fastest growing segment of home schooling families, however, are Muslim (Basham, 2001). Many of the websites that provide information for families that home school their children are affiliated with Christian Right organizations. These

**Figure 10-5   Home Schooling Laws by State**

States differ in the level of regulation they require for students who are home schooled.

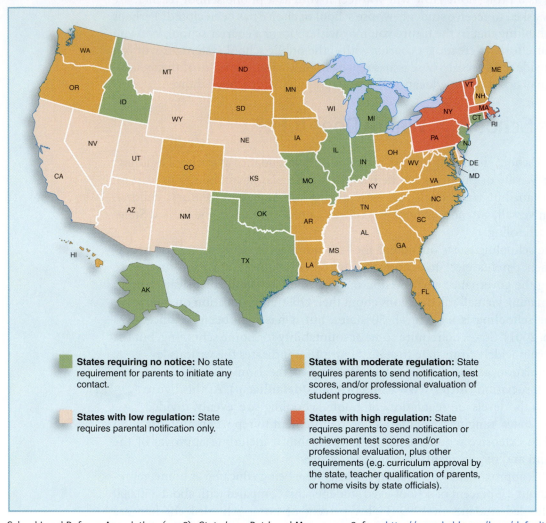

**States requiring no notice:** No state requirement for parents to initiate any contact.

**States with low regulation:** State requires parental notification only.

**States with moderate regulation:** State requires parents to send notification, test scores, and/or professional evaluation of student progress.

**States with high regulation:** State requires parents to send notification or achievement test scores and/or professional evaluation, plus other requirements (e.g. curriculum approval by the state, teacher qualification of parents, or home visits by state officials).

**Source:** Home School Legal Defense Association. (2008). *State laws*. Retrieved May 25, 2008, from http://www.hslda.org/laws/default.asp.

websites also provide information regarding religiously oriented curriculum materials. Several of these websites have strong political advocacy perspectives, which suggests that for a large proportion of families who home school, the decision to do so may be part of a larger political agenda.

Home schooling has spawned a large and lucrative industry in curriculum materials specifically developed for families that home school their children. In addition, the emergence of technology in education supports families that home school their children. The availability of online courses means that children can access more advanced curriculum materials from home. This has important implications, especially for high school students. Finally, the American Library Association (**www.ala.org**) maintains a section on its website especially devoted to helping librarians support home schooling.

## Why It Counts in a Diverse World

This chapter discusses the various levels of influence leveraged by those charged formally with governing our schools. You have learned about the growing influence of the federal government, the increasing influence of the state in both the administration of schools and in policy setting, and the relative role of local control through school boards. We have also described the role of the district superintendent and principal, as well as the changing nature of school governance and control through practices such as school choice.

What do issues of governance and finance mean for you as a classroom teacher? Without an understanding of the governance of education, teachers will be ignorant about the political processes that influence how schools operate. They will not be familiar with how resources come to the schools and the various sources of control over resources that can make a huge difference in how they work with students. Funding inequities may have special significance for you if you teach in an urban or rural school. Further, if you teach in a school with high numbers of English language learners, you might feel the impact of whether or not there is sufficient funding for the resources needed to support this group of learners. Without a clear understanding of school governance, teachers may not understand how new ideas are generated and communicated to those who set educational policy.

As a result, teachers may fail to understand their own potential role in helping to shape policies and practices that can improve their effectiveness with students. Ideas to improve education can come from the top down or the bottom up. Participating in the process of developing and implementing new ideas and helping them move toward adoption are critical aspects of the work of professional teachers.

# CHAPTER SUMMARY

Schools are governed by a combination of formal responsibilities and informal influences that affect school policies and teachers' abilities to do their jobs well. With the responsibility for governance comes the responsibility for funding the schools.

## Putting Governance into Perspective

Providing for education is not spelled out in the Constitution as a federal responsibility; therefore, the governance and administration of education reside with the states. Unlike national systems in other countries, where decisions about education are made by a national ministry of education, in the United States each of the 50 states has an education agency that governs decision making and that works with federal government education agencies as appropriate. In addition, there is a long tradition of local, citizen control of the schools through local school boards. These three levels of governance interact to influence a teacher's work. The organizational culture at each individual school also influences how the policies and practices of each level of governance are implemented on a daily basis.

## The Influence of Local Control of Schools on a Teacher's Work

Local school boards are elected as independent entities charged with setting policy and procedures for every school district in the United States. School boards also are charged with drawing up school budgets, and generate revenue through taxes to pay for the local schools. School superintendents are the heads of the districts, serve at the pleasure of the school boards, and work side by side with school board members to ensure that the schools are carrying out their responsibilities. School boards must carry out federal and state policies, but they also have a great deal of local influence on school programs and policies.

## Decision Making at the Building Level

Depending on the district, individual school buildings may have greater or lesser autonomy to make decisions. In many districts, individual schools have school councils, or school site-based management teams, which make decisions at the school level. In some locations, such councils have the authority to hire and fire school principals. Such teams may also have responsibility for setting the school's budget.

## How State Governance Influences a Teacher's Work

The state has a lead education agency and a chief state school officer that are charged with making policy for all of the state's schools. Decisions may include the development of academic standards, state testing policies, policies for school funding, and requirements for teacher licensure. Because each state has its own rules, teachers who move from state to state are not automatically licensed in their new state.

## The Federal Role in Governing Education

Until the middle of the twentieth century, the federal role in education was limited. Since then the federal level has exerted two major influences. The first is federal legislation designed to ensure equal treatment for all students. Legislation passed during Lyndon Johnson's administration established the first major funding for low-income students under the Elementary and Secondary Education Act. Other significant legislation includes the Individuals with Disabilities Education Act and Title IX, which mandates gender equity in education. Federal legislation may or may not be accompanied by sufficient funding allocations to implement the law.

The second mayor federal influence has been the result of rulings made by the U.S. Supreme Court. Two decisions that have had enormous influence on the schools are *Brown v. Board of Education* on separate but equal schooling and *Lau v. Nichols* on educating students whose first language is not English.

## Financing Education: How Dollars Make their Way to Schools, Teachers, and Students

Revenues to finance the public education system come from a combination of local, state, and federal dollars. Traditionally, most revenues have been generated from local property taxes, but this approach led to serious funding inequities among communities. Today the trend is toward equalizing school funding across districts by increasing the state's contribution to reduce local responsibility. The federal contribution is comparatively quite low. Once local school district budgets are developed, spending at the district level may be centralized or decentralized. In districts where spending is decentralized, individual school principals—sometimes with the input of teachers and other community members on local school governance councils—make budgetary decisions.

## Changing Views of the Governance and Control of Schools

Improving the quality of the public schools is high on the national agenda. One radical approach to school improvement is school choice. Rather than preserving the longstanding tradition of children attending their neighborhood schools, school choice advocates argue that parents who are unhappy with a neighborhood school should be able to choose another school for their children. School choice is also based on the belief that if public schools are faced with competition, they will be motivated to improve, and so an effective way to introduce competition is to allow students to choose either public or private schools.

Charter schools represent publicly funded efforts to give schools greater autonomy and freedom from bureaucratic restrictions. Vouchers are another means of providing choice to parents, in which public dollars follow individual students to private schools that their parents select. In some states, vouchers for education can be applied at either sectarian or parochial schools; using vouchers at parochial schools sets up a challenge to the philosophy of the separation of church and state.

School choice changes the nature of the control of schools by altering the basic funding mechanisms available to public schools. Home schooling is another alternative for parents who do not wish their children to participate in the public schools, but these families receive no direct funds.

## LIST OF CRITICAL TERMS

Local education agency (LEA) *(333)*

Site-based management *(339)*

State education agency (SEA) *(343)*

Elementary and Secondary Education
    Act (ESEA) *(346)*

Categorical aid *(347)*

Title IX *(348)*

Per pupil expenditure *(355)*

Centralized budgeting system *(358)*

Decentralized budgeting
    system *(358)*

Charter school *(360)*

Vouchers *(360)*

## EXPLORING YOUR COMMITMENT

1. *on your own...* As a small group, investigate the type of structure your state and surrounding states follow to govern education. Is the state board of education, as well as the chief state school officer, elected or appointed? What information is readily available about the positions of various members of the state board of education, the chief state school officer, and the governor?

2. *on your own...* Make a list of issues/information you would expect to find on the website of your state education agency. Then log onto its website. What kind of information is actually available there? How did what you found match with your prediction of what might be available? How would you account for the difference? How helpful is the website to you as a prospective teacher? What three new things did you learn from the website?

3. *on your own...* In small groups, pick one district in your area and identify the members of the local school board. What is their educational, employment, and community involvement background? Pick one issue that is important to your group, and interview one of the local school board members for his or her opinion about that issue.

4. *on your own...* For a two-week period, read the local newspaper, including the editorial page, and note the education issues that are covered. What proportion of the issues, if any, feature local education issues, what proportion state issues, and what proportion federal issues? What is the political stance of the paper toward these issues?

5. *in the field...* In the school where you are placed for your field experience, identify a teacher who is active in negotiating the teachers' contract (or in issues affecting teachers if you are not in a collective bargaining state). Talk to this person to identify three or four crucial issues directly affecting the conditions of teachers' work in the classroom, and, if applicable, that have been negotiated as part of the contract. What kinds of discussions went on in negotiations around those issues?

6. ***on the web...*** Log onto the website of the organization for state boards of education, the National Association of State Boards of Education (**http://www.nasbe.org**). What are the three most pressing issues that appear to be important to this organization? How would you account for their importance?

7. ***on your own...*** Find out when the next local school board election in your community is being held. How many seats are up for election? Who is now on the local school board, and which current members are planning to run for reelection? Try to find out two or three issues current members believe are important. Why are these issues so important? How do they match up to the issues you identified in Activity 6?

8. ***on the web...*** Go to the website of the American Library Association (**www.ala.org**) and locate the list of the 100 most frequently challenged books. Have you read any of the books on the list? Were you surprised to see any of the titles? Why or why not?

9. ***in the field...*** Interview a teacher in the school to which you are assigned to discuss the decision-making process in the school. Is it a top-down model where the principal makes all of the decisions? What input and influence do teachers themselves have? How much input and influence do the teachers want? If there is a school governance council, how many teachers are members of the council? How do they communicate the deliberations of the council to the rest of the school staff?

10. ***in the research...*** Read Zittleman, K. and D. Sadker. (2002). "Gender bias in teacher education texts." *Journal of Teacher Education, 53*, 68–80. How does this article assist you in thinking about how to improve your own teaching practice with regard to gender equity, which is required by Title IX legislation?

## GUIDELINES FOR BEGINNING TEACHERS

1. If your school has a library/media specialist, make an appointment with this person to discuss whether or not there is a history of censorship in the district. If there is, what was its source? What books specifically have been censored?

2. One way to gauge the relationship between the board and the superintendent is to attend a school board meeting and see what kinds of interactions take place. Superintendents usually give regular reports to school board members at each school board meeting. Are the members of the school board respectful to the superintendent? Does a lot of discussion of ideas and initiatives take place, or do board members listen politely and then move on? If you live in a large metropolitan area, you might be able to tune into school board meetings on the radio, or they might be broadcast on television through a local cable station.

3. Find out from your principal if any dollars are allotted directly to you to spend on instructional materials or field trips. If you work with a grade-level team, discuss whether or not you want to pool your dollars for specific purchases.

4. Talk to the building representative of the teachers' union to see which "conditions of work" issues are negotiated in the contract. Find out what other issues are, or will be, under negotiation in the next round of contract talks.

5. Learn the names of the members of the school board and their general positions on the issues.

## THE **INTASC** CONNECTION

The INTASC standard that most directly addresses issues of school governance is Standard 10. This standard states: *The teacher fosters relationships with school colleagues, parents, and agencies in the larger community to support students' learning and well-being.* Relevant indicators include following:

● The teacher understands schools as organizations within the larger community context and understands the operations of the relevant aspects of the system(s) within which she or he works.

● The teacher is willing to work with other professionals to improve the overall learning environment for students.

● The teacher acts as an advocate for students.

If you are in a state that follows a different set of teacher standards, find the state standards that most closely relate to the INTASC standards discussed here.

## READING ON...

Eadie, D. (2005). *Five habits of high minded school boards.* Lanham, MD: Scarecrow Education. This volume describes five basic traits found in effective school boards around the country.

Good, T. L., and J. S. Braden. (2000). *The great school debate: Choice, vouchers, and charters.* Mahwah, NJ: Lawrence Erlbaum Associates. A comprehensive yet readable analysis of the shift to new forms of school governance through school choice, vouchers, and charter schools.

Peterson, B., and M. Charney (Eds.) (1999). *Transforming teacher unions: Fighting for better schools and social justice.* Milwaukee, WI: Rethinking Schools. Explores the role of teachers' unions in contributing to educational reform.

Rofes, E., and L. Stulberg. (2004). *The emancipatory promise of charter schools.* Albany: State University of New York Press. Activist educators provide their perspectives on the potential of charter schools to reinvigorate discussions about school reform.

# CONTRIBUTING ACTIVELY TO THE PROFESSION

What goes on within the four walls of your classroom will certainly dominate your thinking as a teacher. But being a teacher no longer means working in isolation with the classroom door closed. Instead, a new conception of teaching is emerging, one in which teachers are taking responsibility not only for their classrooms, but for making a commitment and contribution to the profession of teaching itself.

Yet tensions still exist between the view of teaching as a profession that requires sophisticated professional knowledge and the view of teaching as a job based on technical skills alone. Chapter 11 addresses teaching as a profession imbued with great moral responsibility. The trust families place in teachers every day to treat their children well, to encourage them to learn, and to succeed in having them learn is a manifestation of the moral dimension of teaching. Aspiring teachers are reminded of the scope of their moral responsibility to their students and its critical importance. This chapter also includes a discussion of legal issues in teaching and their relationship to the classroom. Chapter 12 explores the tensions between teaching as a job and teaching as a profession more directly. It also describes the changing nature of the profession and the possibilities that exist today for teachers to stay close to their classrooms but still take on professional leadership roles. These roles are designed to help others in the profession and at the same time satisfy the growing expectations and needs of veteran teachers. This chapter also provide you with the opportunity to reflect on your growth as a teacher, to explore some emerging issues in education, and to begin thinking about searching and interviewing for a teaching position.

The decision to become a teacher is a decision to accept the full array of responsibilities with conviction and dedication. As you complete this section, you should begin to get a clearer sense of what it means to make a commitment to teaching as a profession rather than a job, with the students you teach at the center of that commitment.

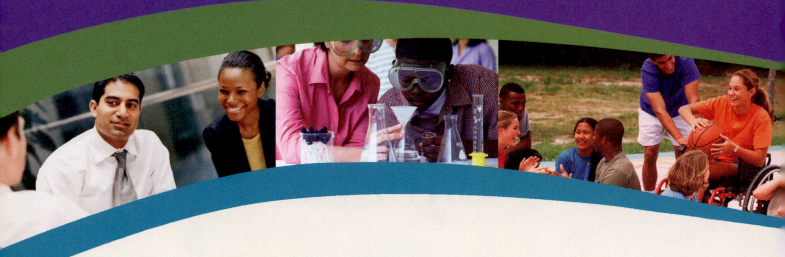

## Guiding Questions

- Why is trust so fundamental to the work of a teacher?

- What are the multiple dimensions of trust that teachers must consider?

- How do teachers create and maintain trusting relationships?

- How do teachers advocate for their students?

- What ethical considerations do teachers need to take into account in interacting with other teachers?

- How does a school function as an ethical community?

- What kinds of issues do teachers' codes of ethics address?

- What are some of the major legal issues that teachers need to take into account based on federal regulation and court cases?

- What legal issues relate to the use of technology in classrooms and schools?

- How do teachers balance the personal and the professional from an ethical perspective?

# Ethical and Legal Issues in the Work of Teaching

# 11

It's early spring at Darrell Jordan's high school. His first year has been going well, and he is feeling confident in his teaching. But in the past month he has begun to be concerned about one of his students, Melanie Bailey. It's not the quality of her work that Darrell is concerned about; she's doing well and continues to maintain an A- average in his Biology class. She participates regularly, does her homework and classwork, and seems to enjoy science.

But when he watches her in the hallway, the lunchroom, and at extracurricular activities he attends, he has noticed that Melanie's friends are changing. She has started hanging around with a group of students who do not do their work, who are not serious about school, and who are known as students who smoke marijuana regularly. Darrell has heard rumors that Melanie has started smoking marijuana with them on the weekends. He's concerned that this will have a long-term negative effect on Melanie, but he is not sure how to approach the problem, especially because he doesn't have any real evidence that Melanie is participating. He's wondering if he should talk with Melanie, talk with her parents, see them together, or just what to do. He doesn't want to cause problems for Melanie if no real problem exists.

He called Crystal, his mentor, to see what advice she had for him. Crystal asked him what he felt most comfortable doing. "Well," he said, "I really don't want to see Melanie get into bad habits. If she is smoking dope, it isn't affecting anything that she's doing for me. But the kids have been talking about her as if she's becoming one of the 'potheads.' I'm wondering if I should talk to her parents and see if they've noticed anything."

"So what would you gain—or lose—by talking to her parents?" Crystal asked.

"Well, I don't know what kind of relationship she has with her parents, and I don't really have any first-hand knowledge that she is involved. So it might cause a huge problem when there really isn't one at all."

"What other choices do you have?" Crystal continued.

"Well, I could talk with Monica, the guidance counselor, and see what she knows. Maybe someone has already talked with Melanie about this and knows more than I do. Then I can decide whether or not I need to talk with Melanie myself. I have a pretty

*Scratch a good teacher and you will find a moral purpose.*

Michael Fullan 1993, p. 10

good relationship with her. I'm just wondering if anyone she trusts has talked with her about drugs. I know she's heard it in classes, but that's not enough."

"I think you're right on that," Crystal said. "If she trusts you, you might have a chance of having her talk about what's going on. But I think it's a good idea to talk with Monica first and decide after that."

"I can see Monica right after school today. I'll keep you posted."

Teaching is a profoundly human endeavor. As a teacher, the adult professional in the classroom, you are responsible for the well-being and learning of each of your students every day that you teach, throughout your career. Teaching requires your commitment to put your students' needs first, on center stage, every single day. It is precisely because teaching is such a profoundly human endeavor that ethical and moral considerations are so critical to your preparation as a teacher. Good teachers do not just worry about whether they are prepared to "cover the content." Rather, they understand that teaching is centrally concerned with *creating a safe environment for their students so that they can learn*. The safety of that environment is communicated to students in countless ways every single day. Teachers are taking a moral stance that influences their students simply by virtue of the routine acts and decisions they make (Hansen, 2001). As you think about a career in teaching and all that it entails, you need to consider and take responsibility for the moral underpinnings of the profession. Furthermore, it is not enough to think of this responsibility as merely doing no harm to students. Instead, your commitment to teaching children and youth is a proactive, career-long commitment to work and advocate for their good and their well-being in the context of classrooms and schools. This is the moral dimension of teaching. For teachers, the moral should be universal (Fullan, 2004).

Teaching is wholly a human interaction, and human interactions are by definition complicated. The dilemma Darrell faces with Melanie illustrates just how challenging individual situations can be when teachers strive to balance the twin goals of helping students learn and protecting their overall well-being. It also demonstrates that in challenging interpersonal situations, the answer about what to do is not always clear-cut. If you have decided to become a teacher, you have likely already given a lot of thought to your commitment to your future students. You know you want to be in a profession that involves children or youth, you are excited about the idea of a career dedicated to helping students learn, and you are eager to gain the knowledge and professional skills that will get you there. But precisely how you will enact that commitment within the context of your classroom and your school is not always straightforward.

Your response to the situations you will encounter as a teacher and the ethical and moral decisions you will face may not always be self-evident, even though your moral stance toward teaching should be clear and deeply rooted. Christopher Clark (1990) sees the issue this way: "Overarching principles have been agreed on in our society and within the teaching profession—principles dealing with honesty, fairness, protection of the weak, and respect for all people. The real work of teaching, morally speaking, is carried out when a teacher rigorously struggles to decide how best to act in relation to those general principles" (p. 252).

How will you carry out your commitments as you perform your work and create safe learning environments for your students? This chapter addresses the moral and ethical considerations in teaching from three perspectives: within the classroom, where you have the greatest control; in the context of your relationships with your peers; and within your school. These three perspectives are important because you do not practice your profession in a vacuum. Decisions you make within your own classroom affect your students' well-being, but you will also be working in an organization where the decisions of others can affect students positively or negatively. The chapter concludes with a discussion of legal issues related to schools and classrooms. How might legal precedents and decisions in education shape your ethical stance? What constraints on your actions might legal issues pose? These are also important considerations for every teacher.

### Your turn... *to reflect*

Name five of the most important ethical issues you think teachers need to consider. In a small group, compare your list with your peers. Then as a group, try to put them in priority order. What issues are most important to the group? In reflecting on your list, what issues did you leave out?

## Trust: The Basic Moral Obligation of Teachers

The moral obligations of teachers derive from the simple fact that families entrust their children to teachers six hours a day, five days a week, for 180 days a year or more. That is a lot of time for students to spend in the care of teachers. Fundamentally, teachers have an obligation to do everything in their power to secure and maintain that trust. It is in gaining the trust of students and their families that teachers create a shared commitment to students' learning (Bryk & Schneider, 2002). Implicit in your job, then, is precisely *the ensuring of trust—trust between you and your students, between you and your students' families, and between you and your professional colleagues.*

Scholars who write about the moral dimensions of teaching uniformly raise the issue of trust. Consider the following observations:

One of the foremost ethical responsibilities teachers have is to develop a trusting relationship with students and their families. (Michael Newman/PhotoEdit)

> Parents entrust their children to teachers. School is mandatory, and that mandate settles on the shoulders of the teacher. The teacher, then, is obliged to care for children and be responsible for their empowerment. (Thomas, 1990, pp. 266–267)

> For a trusting relationship to exist, it is not enough that a school and its teachers be understood as "pro-kids." Teachers must be known by the parents and children as people they can trust. (Sockett, 1990, p. 233)

> Educators are people to whom we entrust our children or our selves. Educators are people to whom we entrust our chances in life. (Lagemann, 2004, p. 37)

> Trust, care, obligation, and responsibility are words that carry the burden of morality. Teaching is a moral enterprise because it is a social enterprise. (Thomas, 1990, p. 267)

Individually and collectively, these are weighty words. But it is precisely because teachers cannot separate their obligations to cultivate student learning from the students themselves and from their families that teaching is fundamentally a moral endeavor.

### Your turn... *to reflect*

Think back on a time when you (or one of your classmates) suffered unfair or demeaning treatment by a teacher. How did you feel (or how did you imagine your classmate felt)? What kinds of things did students say about this teacher? Was anything done about the teacher's behavior? What is the relationship of this type of negative teacher behavior to the issue of trust?

## The Multiple Dimensions of Trust

Ensuring trust means that teachers actively work to create classroom and school environments where students can thrive and learn. But what are the specific dimensions that go into building such trusting relationships? How does the question of trust play out across the span of a teacher's responsibilities to his or her students?

**Relationships with Students as a Dimension of Trust.** The first dimension of trust has to do with the quality of the human interaction between teachers and their students. Do teachers treat students respectfully on a day-to-day basis? Do they listen to their students? Do they genuinely want to know about their students' lives, their experiences, and what their students value? Do teachers extend this same level of respect to their students' families? Do they view *themselves* as learners about their students' lives—or do they just assume that the only learners in the room are the students?

This dimension of trust is intimately related to the issues of diversity that have been discussed throughout this book. What patterns might an outsider see if he or she observed you in relationship to your students and their families? Do you have trusting relationships with only some of your students or with all of them? Do you favor members of some racial and ethnic groups and not others? How do you determine whether you have established such relationships? What sources of feedback do you consider in gauging your success as a teacher who has developed positive relationships with all of his or her students?

When we talk about establishing relationships with students, we must understand that we are not talking about personal friendships. Obviously, the teacher–student relationship is not the same as a personal friendship. The goal for teachers is to support students as learners. To meet this goal, teachers need to create the conditions in which their students will want to learn. If teachers are not interested in their students as individuals—which also communicates that they are not interested in their students as learners—students are not likely to want to learn. If teachers do not connect their teaching to their students as individuals, their students are not likely to be as interested in learning as they would be with a teacher who makes those connections. If students experience humiliation at the hands of a teacher, or watch others endure the same treatment, they are not likely to want to be in that teacher's classroom at all. If students observe that their teacher does not listen to them, they will wonder why they are there in the first place.

You are not likely to feel the same way about all of your students or like all of your students equally. But as a teacher with a responsibility to all of your students, you have to figure out how to build a relationship with all of your students regardless of your initial feelings.

**Relationships with Families as a Dimension of Trust.** Family involvement is critical to a teacher's moral obligations because, as we noted above, families entrust the care of their children to you every day. In your classroom, your responsibilities focus on your students. But students live and learn within their families. Just as it is important for your students to feel comfortable in school so that they can be motivated to learn, it is also important for your students' family members to feel comfortable communicating with you about their child.

Good relationships with your students' families are necessary for your success as a teacher. When a teacher's behavior leads to distrust, parents and family members automatically enter into the dynamic because children let them know what is going on in school. When children are unnecessarily unhappy in school through the unprofessional actions of their teachers, their families also become unhappy, and justifiably so. In situations such as these, families may shut down communication with the school (Bryk & Schneider, 2002). Families expect their children to be treated respectfully.

How do teachers build trusting relationships with families? When you think about family involvement, what probably comes to mind first are the basic forms of school-to-family communication. For example, are family members attending open houses and conferences? Are they signing the forms, permission slips, and report cards that you send home? Each of these is important for your work as a teacher. But if parents and family members are not responsive, teachers (and school administrators) need to consider why and should ask questions such as the following:

- Have I made myself available to family members at convenient times for them?
- Have I contacted families at the start of the year to establish a good relationship so that they don't hear from me only when a problem arises?
- Do I speak with family members if they come to my classroom in the morning, or after school, or even during the day? Do I make them feel welcome even if I don't have the time at that moment to speak with them?
- Does the school staff treat family members as welcome guests when they come to school?
- Do I know the kind of work the family members of my students do?
- Do I know what language is spoken in the homes of my students?
- Do I listen well to my students' families, and do I show that I value their ideas and input?

In Chapters 6 and 7, we emphasized the need to value families, especially those whose background, race, ethnicity, or structure differs from that of the teacher. Families are more likely to participate in school if they feel that their children's teachers have a genuine interest in their children and are determined to create positive relationships with families. As a result, if any of the preceding questions do not have a positive answer, the trust of family members is not likely to follow.

The commitment to creating trust does not mean that teachers must avoid having difficult conversations or conferences with family members. Every teacher has worked with challenging students, and teachers must address these issues with families so that everyone can work together for the good of the students. Moreover, in the course of their careers, teachers do encounter some families that do not participate in their child's education. However, these situations are the exception, and in the context of a trusting relationship with the school and with their child's teacher, most families will be as supportive as possible in order to foster their children's success in school.

**Figure 11-1** **How Schools Build Supportive Relationships with Families—Selected Lessons Learned from a Synthesis of Research**

**Families are essential partners in education.**

- Programs that successfully connect with families and community invite involvement, are welcoming, and address specific parent and community needs.

- Parent involvement programs that are effective in engaging diverse families recognize, respect, and address cultural and class differences.

- Effective programs to engage families and community embrace a philosophy of partnership. The responsibility for children's educational development is a collaborative enterprise among parents, school staff, and community members.

- Parent and community involvement that is linked to student learning has a greater effect than more general forms of involvement.

- Families of all cultural backgrounds, education, and income levels encourage their children, talk with them about school, help them plan for higher education, and keep them focused on learning and homework. In other words, all families can, and do, have a positive influence on their children's learning.

**Source:** Henderson, A.T, & K.L. Mapp. (2002). *A new wave of evidence: The impact of school, family, and community connections on student achievement*. Annual Synthesis 2002. Austin, TX: Southwest Educational Development Laboratory.

# Philosophical Note
## Nel Noddings and the Ethic of Care

Nel Noddings, a professor of education at Stanford University, has developed a teaching philosophy that she calls an **ethic of care** (1992). This philosophy, which you read about briefly in Chapter 4, is an approach to organizing schools and teaching with the concept of care at the center of the profession.

Noddings developed the concept of the ethic of care out of a concern that students often do not engage deeply with school and with the content of their classes. Instead, they often view school as a site of competition. What would happen if schools were organized around understanding and meeting students' needs, that is, caring about them as people and as learners, rather than around achieving a score on a standardized test? What would this kind of care look like, and how would a teacher achieve it?

Noddings (1992) describes four essential attributes of a caring relationship in the context of education. First, teachers model caring in all of their relationships. As a basic professional commitment, teachers demonstrate caring relationships with their students and with the school staff. A teacher might reflect on his or her behavior toward students, especially those who are challenging, and ask him- or herself: How did I show this student that I cared about him today? Did I treat him respectfully? Did I humiliate him in any way? Was I unnecessarily sarcastic? Did I notice when he was doing things correctly and let him know? This aspect of care is basic to building trust.

Second, within an ethic of care, teachers engage in dialogue with their students. Dialogue is a central means by which teachers demonstrate their genuine interest. Noddings distinguishes between false dialogue, in which teachers already know what they want students to say, and real dialogue, in which teachers are genuinely seeking information and knowledge from their students that will help teachers understand them. In other words, an ethic of care depends on a real interchange of ideas and information so that teachers can better understand their students. Without dialogue, teachers will not really know how to respond to their students' needs. "Continuing dialogue," Noddings states, "builds up a substantial knowledge of one another that serves to guide our responses" (Noddings, 1992, p. 23).

Third, a teacher needs practice and experience to develop the capacity to function according to an ethic of care. This means that in an educational setting, creating purposeful opportunities to engage in caring relationships is essential.

Finally, caring involves what Noddings terms *confirmation.* "When we confirm someone, Noddings observes, "we spot a better self and encourage its development. We can only do this if we know the other well enough to see what he or she is trying to become" (Noddings, 1992, p. 25). In schools, teachers and administrators often attribute negative motives to students' bad behavior and poor decisions. When teachers practice confirmation, they instead try to understand what would motivate a student to behave in a particular manner from the perspective of that student's best reason for doing it. Confirmation does not mean that teachers should ignore misbehavior; rather, it means that they should approach correcting it from an understanding of students over time and from developing a caring relationship with them.

Noddings observes that these four attributes of caring do not constitute a recipe for teacher behavior. Rather, together they describe a way of being a teacher, a moral and ethical stance that communicates the notion that teachers are paying attention to their students' needs, that they are engrossed in understanding those needs, and that they are committed to responding to them. Noddings believes that it is possible to rethink the entire school curriculum, putting care at the center of the school's purpose and practice.

**Classroom Community as a Dimension of Trust.** The simple statement that "all children need to feel safe in their relations with teachers" (Noddings, 1992, p. 108) perhaps best defines the basis of a classroom community. Teachers who are serious about the moral obligations of teaching create classrooms in which students are welcome, feel a sense of belonging, and can thrive. Think of your classroom as a blank slate that contains desks, bookshelves, tables, and curriculum materials. As the teacher, you have the opportunity—and responsibility—to develop the tone of the classroom, the feeling students get when they enter, the sense they have that it is a place they want to be. Although the physical environment is not an unimportant issue, it is the tone you set as the teacher that has the greatest influence on the kind of classroom you will have. Your interactions with your students—and the quality of these interactions under your guidance—tell them whether the classroom is a trustworthy environment for them.

Do you welcome your students into the classroom each day? Do you talk with them informally about what's going on in their lives? Do you listen to them and encourage them to listen to each other? Do they have consistent routines so that they know what is expected of them? Is everyone treated fairly? Do students know you are genuinely pleased when they are learning? Are you excited about learning

In a strong classroom community, students can feel free to express their opinions and have those opinions respected by their peers and their teacher. (Media Bakery)

yourself, and do you share your own learning with them? These are some of the deliberate decisions you make as the teacher. If your students consistently observe that some students get your attention and others do not, that you do not listen to them or entertain their concerns, or you are not genuinely enthusiastic about teaching and learning, they will be less likely to trust your motives.

As we noted earlier, being a teacher who creates a healthy classroom environment should not be confused with being a teacher who is "friends" with his or her students. The teacher's job is to teach students and make sure they learn. But teachers do not teach only content; they teach content to real, live students who deserve their respect and consideration.

Particularly at the middle and high school levels, you need to make distinctions between when your students, who are increasingly sophisticated from a developmental perspective, are raising legitimate issues and when they may be trying to divert you from your teaching agenda. This has practical implications in two ways. First, some of your students may raise legitimate questions or issues that deserve more time than you can adequately give on a certain day. For example, if you are teaching about the role of strikes in labor unions and the teachers in your district are experiencing problematic contract negotiations, your students may raise this issue and want to discuss it at a time when you have not planned for such a substantial discussion. You can legitimize their interest in several ways: by anticipating this as an issue and including it in the first place, by scheduling a follow-up discussion, or by devoting a lunch hour to this topic as a drop-in session. Second, you may have students who wish to divert the class's (and your) attention by purposefully introducing topics that are not related to your goals. Teachers can best make distinctions between these two situations by getting to know their students well enough to tell when their interest is genuine.

**Your turn...** *to reflect*

What are three things you could do on the first day of class to build a trusting classroom environment? How might those activities differ from elementary to middle to high school?

### Knowledge of Content and Pedagogy as a Dimension of Trust.

Students and families trust teachers who know their material and can teach it well. After all, that is why families send their children to school. If teachers are not competent both in the content *and* in the best ways of teaching it to students in the grade to which they are assigned, how will students be able to learn?

This aspect of your moral responsibilities involves not only knowing the material you are to teach, but also being *prepared* to teach it well. When teachers are well prepared each day, students know it. When teachers are floundering, using valuable class time to get materials ready, students know this as well. As a professional, you demonstrate respect to your students and to the material you wish them to learn by being prepared for your work each day.

However, no amount of content or pedagogical knowledge or preparation for instruction can make up for a teacher's failure to understand the moral significance of his or her work. "Moral knowledge in teaching becomes ineffectual without technical skill. But technical skill and expertise may be damaging, or even dangerous without a moral vision informing their use" (Hansen, 2001, p. 848). Technical skills of teaching have meaning only when they are built on a foundation of trust and caring between students and teachers.

The educator Parker Palmer (1998) perhaps best sums up the need for teachers to create such relationships with their students:

> One student I heard about said she could not describe her good teachers because they differed so greatly, one from another. But she could describe her bad teachers because they were all the same: "Their words float somewhere in front of their faces, like the balloon speech in cartoons." With one remarkable image she said it all. Bad teachers distance themselves from the subject they are teaching—and in the process, from their students. Good teachers join the self and subject and students in the fabric of life. (p. 11)

## Creating and Maintaining Trusting Relationships

Through your daily behavior as a teacher you communicate to your students either that you are a committed professional who cares about them—or that you are not. Children and youth have a sixth sense about teachers and whether teachers are worthy of their own and their families' trust. After all, they spend more concentrated time with teachers than does anyone else in our society. Developing trusting relationships with students and their families is one of the moral obligations of teachers.

Creating a trusting relationship does not mean that your skills as a new teacher will be perfect or that you will have the same skills as a veteran, master teacher. Creating a trusting relationship also does not mean that you won't make mistakes, especially in complicated human interactions that are part of a teacher's daily life. What it does mean, however, is that you decide at the start of your career not to compromise on your fundamental commitment to your students. Your students will know if you can be counted on to act reasonably and be supportive.

Teachers also create trusting relationships when they set high expectations for their students and communicate those expectations clearly and consistently. In Chapter 7 we discussed different ways teachers communicate their expectations. Students know whether teachers believe they can learn and whether teachers are providing them with the instruction that will lead to new learning. They are far more likely to trust teachers who are actually teaching and challenging them—rather than teachers who convey the belief that they are not capable of real learning.

Teachers demonstrate respect for their students by providing them with work that is challenging, interesting, and meaningful.
(Bonnie Kamin/PhotoEdit)

**The Role of Reflection in Building Trust.** One hallmark of a professional teacher, emphasized throughout this book, is reflection—the ability to think about and inquire into your own practice, to learn from it, and to improve your teaching as a result. Reflection and subsequent action to improve practice is one way teachers take responsibility for the quality of their work. If you are committed to reflecting on your actions, you can learn from your mistakes and grow and develop professionally, as well as strengthen your teaching performance. When things do not go smoothly, reflection is critical to how well you create and maintain a safe, trusting environment in your classroom.

If you fail to build reflection into your professional habits and to take responsibility for the quality of your work, you may end up blaming students for your own shortcomings. For example, if your students are not meeting your expectations for behavior, do you get frustrated with them and begin to blame them for not staying on task, not being interested, or not listening to you? Or do you first ask yourself why this might be happening? Do you think about what you could do differently? In this situation you should consider whether your expectations were reasonable in the first place given your students' ages and skills. Have you clearly communicated your expectations for classroom behavior to your students? Have you thought about whether the work you are asking of them is interesting, stimulating, and important, or might it be consistently boring, unchallenging, or repetitive, which may cause them to "tune out"? Or perhaps you are inconsistent in how you are treating your students, giving some preferential treatment over others. In each of these cases, students would have some reason to feel distrustful toward their teacher.

A related example involves students' performance. If 90 percent of your students do poorly on a science test, do you blame the students for not learning, stating that "they just can't do it"? Or do you ask yourself how you taught and reviewed the material and what you could have done differently to ensure a better result?

**Critical Term**

**Blaming the victim.** Rather than taking responsibility for the quality of one's teaching, a weak teacher may blame the students —the "victims" of the teacher's poor teaching —instead.

**Blaming the victim** (i.e., the student) is not a healthy moral stance for a teacher, and when a teacher adopts this attitude, the trust between teachers and their students may be compromised. Students do not expect their teachers to be perfect, nor do they expect to be blamed for their teachers' own poor performance.

### Power, Teacher Maturity, and Trust Building.

The basic relationship of trust means that teachers place their students' needs at the center of their work. They work with their students' families as members of a team devoted to the students' growth and learning. As Christopher Clark (1990) notes, however, teachers must be mature individuals in order to be able to put their students' needs first.

Teachers have tremendous power over their students but must use this professional authority wisely, for the good of the students. When teachers put their own needs first and create a classroom atmosphere in which they make their personal power a priority over student learning, teachers have crossed an ethical boundary. Using their power and authority in this manner is not only a breach of professionalism, but a rejection of the moral obligation they accept upon entering the profession.

Teachers, of course, must have their own professional needs met to feel comfortable in their profession—in their classroom, school, and school district. Teachers also need ways to "let down" from the normal stresses associated with their work. To be successful with your students, you must balance your personal needs with your basic responsibility for working together effectively with your students within your classroom community.

## The Teacher as Advocate

The teacher also has a role as an advocate for his or her students. When teachers advocate for their students, they are putting their students first and are working to make sure that their schools also put their students first. Teachers can advocate for students directly, or they can help students learn to be their own advocates.

### Advocating Directly for Students.

Fiedler (2000) identifies the following characteristics of teacher advocates: (1) a willingness to take risks, (2) professional self-confidence, and (3) professional persistence. He also states that teacher advocates must have a strong sense of purpose, hope, and passion for their work

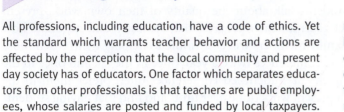

# REWARDS AND CHALLENGES

## The Day-to-Day Challenges of Teaching Ethically

Erika Stubbs
*Lawrenceville, New Jersey*

All professions, including education, have a code of ethics. Yet the standard which warrants teacher behavior and actions are affected by the perception that the local community and present day society has of educators. One factor which separates educators from other professionals is that teachers are public employees, whose salaries are posted and funded by local taxpayers. This distinction can challenge a teacher's ability to act ethically.

All teachers are taught to be fair and objective in situations dealing with students and parents. Parents and educators share the common thread of wanting what is ultimately best for their children. What a teacher believes is fair for the class as a collective of students does not always factor into parents' individual desires for their child. For example, in teaching students who are identified as gifted, I have learned that most parents brag when their child is identified for the program, yet often only ultimately care about the grades their child receives. I remember a specific situation where a student was constantly missing work. The parents wanted to be notified via email whenever the student had incomplete assignments so they could follow up at home. I felt that this was an unfair accommodation, as the child was capable of handling this responsibility. I voiced my opinion to the parents, but I did agree to email them. Though this was against my professional and ethical judgment, I compromised with the parents. I agreed to email them, but I would also penalize the student for the late assignments. Ultimately, the parents never followed up to ensure the work was done; the child earned the grade his work warranted. Just as teachers expect students to take responsibility for learning, we too have a responsibility to meet both students' needs and parental desires. There will be times that our ethics and better judgment will be questioned; we have to find a fair compromise that both enables us to work with parents and that allows us to maintain our ethical standard.

The bottom line on teachers' code of ethics is: remember to be accountable for your decisions, and to meet every new challenge with an open-mind. Teachers must be willing to compromise with parents, so that every possible outcome is win/win. But it is important to maintain your ethical standard as an educator even in the face of compromise; if that is lost, your will and commitment to education as a profession is also lost. ●

and their students. Being an advocate means that teachers see to it that their students are treated fairly and are given the resources they need.

Teachers who are strong advocates for their students are not passive when they see their students struggling, but rather take action to help them. For example, the teacher as advocate makes sure a specialist at school—for example, a school psychologist or social worker—follows up on any concerns that exist. Similarly, if a teacher suspects that a child needs a hearing test, the teacher either persists in making sure the district audiologist follows up or puts the family in touch with appropriate community services.

Teachers who advocate for their students also work to protect them from unfair actions. Let's say, for example, that an elementary classroom teacher finds that a music teacher is consistently denigrating a student who is working well in the regular classroom but is displaying poor behavior in the music classroom. Advocating for this student means (1) determining whether the problem appears to be due to the situation rather than the student's consistent negative behavior, (2) approaching the music teacher to discuss the situation,

One way teachers can build students' ability to advocate for themselves is to have students lead their own conferences with parents or guardians. (Digital Vision)

and (3) providing collegial support and suggestions to the music teacher about what is working in the regular classroom for this particular student. The regular classroom teacher might also begin following the student into music class with prior agreement to provide another perspective for the music teacher.

**Self-Advocacy for Students.** Self-advocacy refers to students' involvement in various aspects of decision making regarding their own education.

One example of self-advocacy is having students lead conferences with their parents or family members. Teachers who promote **student-led conferences** are committed to having their students talk about the quality of their own work, present samples of their work, set goals for their progress that semester, and negotiate how they, their teachers, and family members will contribute to helping them reach those goals. Schools typically hold conferences twice a year, once in the fall and once in the spring. Teachers who implement student-led conferences often prefer them in the spring, when students can present work done over time, and find that having students lead conferences improves parent and family motivation to attend (Flannery, 2004).

Student-led conferences allow students themselves to take greater responsibility for learning, self-assess their work, and set future goals (Bailey & Guskey, 2001; Juniewicz, 2003). Holding student-led conferences requires that teachers save student work for review, often in a portfolio, and help students select samples of work from that portfolio. This work should represent the student's progress and the new learning challenges that the student needs to work on. The teacher and student prepare for the conference together; in addition, teachers need to prepare parents and family members for this new form of conferencing (Bailey & Guskey, 2001; Flannery, 2004). Student-led conferences can be implemented at all grade levels. Figure 11-2 illustrates a planning document for student-led conferences in first grade.

**Critical Term**

**Student-led conferences.** An approach to parent-teacher conferences where students lead the conference by reviewing and assessing samples of their work to describe progress and set new goals.

---

**Figure 11-2    Sample Student-Led Conference Planner for First Grade**

Student-led conferences can be used at all grade levels as a way of increasing student involvement in the assessment of their own learning.

**Sample Conference Plan**

**I will do these activities for my family:**

❏ Read a book.

❏ Share my poetry journal and read at least one poem.

❏ Share my First Grade Log/Writing Journal.

❏ Share my writing portfolio and read some of my stories.

❏ Share the other work in my portfolio.

❏ Talk about how my work is quality work.

❏ Visit the math center and do a problem together.

❏ Share my handwriting work.

❏ Share and read my Friendship Book.

My Name: _____

**Source:** Bailey, J. M., and T. R. Guskey. *Implementing student-led conferences*, p. 33, copyright 2001 by Sage Publications. Reprinted by permission of Sage Publications, Inc.

Another kind of self-advocacy is related to working with students with disabilities, who often have to advocate throughout their lives for the services they need. This in an important kind of student advocacy. Participating in their own IEP conferences is one form of self-advocacy for students with disabilities, but it also includes learning about one's self and one's rights, communicating one's needs and beliefs, and showing leadership (Test, Fowler, Wood, Brewer, & Eddy, 2005).

All students need good communication skills in order to advocate for themselves. Students learn to be their own advocates, for example, through experiences in which they learn to argue skillfully for what they believe is right. If students believe something needs to be changed in their school or their community, teachers who provide students with the opportunity to write letters, give speeches, and visit with powerful leaders are teaching them how to advocate for themselves in the future.

# Ethical Considerations at the Teacher-to-Teacher Level

The overarching moral stance of teaching as a human interaction that requires teachers to place students at the center of their work is not negotiable. Being clear about your own moral stance will guide your actions in your own classroom. Ethical dilemmas are somewhat different; they require teachers to make decisions in situations that are often uncomfortable and in which there may not be one right response (Hansen, 2001). How will you respond to situations that you have not created but that affect your students nevertheless? What will you do in situations that seem to be beyond your control but that you believe are not serving your students well? For example, when you encounter a teacher who creates a negative environment in the classroom, will you be able to respond in a manner that is consistent with your principles? Or will you "cave in" to the status quo, to pressure from your co-workers? These are ethical considerations.

## A Case In Point
### Unwanted Advice

You are a new fourth grade teacher. You have had a successful first semester, and things seem to be going along well. You are happy at your school and have found a group of like-minded teachers in the fourth grade.

In the beginning of February, the principal informs you that in a few days you will receive a new student, Lynnette Taylor. The principal has also told you that Lynnette was a former student at the school, had transferred out of the district last year, and was now back. The next morning, one of your colleagues in the sixth grade approaches you and says in a sarcastic voice, "I heard that Lynnette Taylor is coming back. Good luck! I taught her brother and it was nothing but trouble." That afternoon at lunch, one of the third grade teachers sits down next to you and says, "So, Lynnette Taylor is going to be in your class. Want to hear the lowdown?"

This same kind of interaction occurs several times in the days preceding Lynnette's arrival, making you feel nervous about your new student and wonder how you could possibly work with her successfully. At the same time, you know you should not be swayed inappropriately or develop a set of beliefs and expectations about Lynnette before you even have a chance to meet her.

Situations such as these, which involve the behavior of your co-workers, are not easy to address. But as a teacher you will need to think about how you will respond in a way that maintains your commitment to your students, responds to your co-workers, and enables you to continue feeling comfortable in your working environment. In these situations, teachers need to be problem solvers as they interact with other adults in the building every day.

## The School as an Ethical Community

Taking a moral stance toward students is also the job of the school itself and represents its collective moral purpose (Fullan, 2004). The norms of professional behavior in a school—the daily practices and interaction patterns of its teachers and administrators—define the kind of community each school is and the moral purpose that guides it.

In the school where you teach, you may observe patterns of practice that result in inequities for students or signal that the school is not as focused as it could be on the students and their learning. How do you begin to participate in a conversation about those patterns—especially as a new, inexperienced teacher? What will you do when you are faced with practices you consider unethical? Is the school community strong enough to withstand what may be a difficult conversation about its moral stance? One place that may pose a challenge to ethical behavior in schools is the teacher's lounge, as shown in the next Case in Point.

### A Case In Point
#### In or Out of the Teachers' Lounge?

Kelly Anderson has accepted a position at a middle school in a small town near where she grew up. She was hired to teach mathematics to eighty seventh and eighth graders in Team C, a grouping of students in the school and one of four teams in the school. She had wanted to teach in this community for many years and was thrilled to get the job. The year has gotten off to a good start with her students and with the teachers in her team. They include Anna Smith, a language arts teacher; Jeff Holdner, a science teacher; Judy Ford, a special education teacher; and Emily Xiong, a social studies teacher. Anna has been teaching at the school for 10 years, Jeff for 5, Judy for 12, and Emily for 3 years. This is the second year the teachers have teamed together; Kelly is replacing a teacher who moved out of the area. Her team is considered a strong one, and these experienced teachers are known to be good role models for new teachers.

During the lunch hour, nearly all of the teachers eat in the teachers' lounge. There are comfortable chairs, large tables, beverage machines, newspapers and education-related reading material, and a bulletin board with professional announcements posted. Kelly usually sits with the teachers from her team and often also sits with the two other first-year teachers in the building. Among the teachers on Kelly's team, lunchtime talk usually focuses on their lives outside of school, local entertainment, sharing information about students, and school district politics. There is also a certain amount of "unloading"—that is, commenting on a particularly hard day in the classroom, a student who was troublesome, or an unnecessary disagreement among a few students.

Kelly had been warned about "lounge talk" in her teacher education program but was pleased to discover that the teachers in her team did not talk about students disrespectfully, even when those students were having a bad day and even when her colleagues were exasperated. But as the year progressed, Kelly began to notice that many teachers in other teams did indeed speak very negatively about not only the students but their students' families as well. Kelly frequently heard things such as "He's a hopeless case," "She's so lazy," "I wish that family would move," "Those parents just don't care about their kids," or "At the rate he's going, he won't amount to anything. Why try?" Kelly also noticed that the teachers in her team did not interact with the other teachers in the lounge, although they were cordial, served together on committees, and participated in other school functions together.

Kelly's own teammates seemed to be able to make a distinction between letting off steam about students and talking about them disrespectfully. But the general tone of teachers' lounge talk troubled Kelly and made her feel uncomfortable. She did not want to expose herself to teachers who had such negative attitudes, and yet she also wanted to continue to build her relationship with them. A few months into the school year, Kelly felt secure enough to raise the issue with the other teachers in her team. They understood what Kelly was talking about and shared their own discomfort with some of their colleagues, but seemed to be able to separate themselves from it. Their view was that the principal was inclined to ignore teacher talk in the lounge as a natural need to unwind. Apparently, no one had raised this concern publicly in the past. Instead, they stepped around the issue, which meant that the negative teacher talk continued.

Kelly believed that it was her obligation to raise her concerns, but she wanted to do it in a way that was effective. She was also nervous about doing so as a new teacher. She continued to voice her discomfort in discussions with the teachers in her team. She also scheduled a conference with the assistant principal, Ada Santiago, with whom she had developed a good working relationship, and she and the teachers in her team asked Ada to attend one of their team meetings to discuss the situation. At that meeting, Ada told them that the district was initiating an effort to help all schools to develop strong professional communities among the faculty, administration, and staff at every school. She suggested that as this concept was introduced and as the school discussed what it meant to be a member of a professional learning community, she could use the example of how professionals talk about their students as an indicator that the staff and teachers were trying to establish a professional, positive tone in the building. Kelly asked Ada how she might follow up on this if nothing changed in the teachers' lounge. Ada replied that she would first like to try linking the issue to the development of a more professional learning community and revisit the situation in a month's time.

**Your turn...** *to reflect*

As you read about Kelly's dilemma, would you have taken the same route? What alternatives did Kelly have? What alternatives might you have tried, and why?

For schools to improve their ability to help students learn, they must look at their own collective behavior, reflecting on their work in the same way we have encouraged you as an individual teacher to reflect on the quality of your teaching. Schools must therefore look at the patterns of practice across the whole school, or patterns of behavior that affect how the whole school community operates, and make decisions about what needs to change and how to make those changes. But schools must also be places where teachers feel comfortable taking the risks necessary to have such discussions and move ahead (Bryk & Schneider, 2002).

Consider the following practices. What ethical concerns does each situation signal? What patterns do they suggest that may have a harmful effect on students?

- The percentage of parents and family members who participate in fall conferences is low. The school sends out a single announcement about conferences. When turnout is low, teachers and administrators complain that "the parents just don't care."

- A teacher in your school is universally known to be ineffective with students. It appears to be a case of burnout in a male who used to be a model teacher. Each year he is assigned well-behaved students because "they won't act up." Your district does not have a peer assistance and review process to help teachers who are struggling, and your principal is unwilling to follow the procedures that exist to document teachers who are not effective.

- You teach in a school that is 70 percent white and 30 percent African American. In the school, 70 percent of the students in special education are African American and 30 percent are white.

- When assignments are made for the coming school year, experienced, more senior teachers always make sure their classes are filled with high achieving students. The new teachers always have classes of students with the greatest academic and behavior difficulties.

By noting patterns in the school, for example, whether students from all backgrounds are involved in specific high-visibility extracurricular activities, teachers can begin to ask important ethical questions about the kind of school community they are creating for all of their students.
(Elizabeth Crews/The Image Works)

Each of these situations presents real alternatives. But the problem has to be identified and acknowledged in order to be addressed. When the staff regularly looks at the school's progress as a whole, acknowledging such problems can become part of the regular work of the school. But the administration and teachers need to have an established forum in which to discuss such issues. This is more likely to occur when the culture of the school is trusting and is focused on improving the quality of its work.

# Ethical Behavior, Codes of Ethics, and Standards of Professional Practice

The National Education Association has developed a code of ethics for teachers, which appears in Figure 11-3. Unlike the Hippocratic oath that all doctors must take before they practice medicine, the NEA Code of Ethics is a suggested set of professional guidelines. It is not a requirement to which new teachers must formally commit before they are permitted to practice.

## The Role of Codes of Ethics for Teachers

The NEA Code of Ethics in Figure 11-3 encompasses two principles. The first addresses your commitments to students themselves—the human, interactive, moral side of teaching. The second focuses on your behavior with regard to the profession and to your colleagues.

Committing oneself to a code of ethics does not necessarily mean that a teacher has developed ethical habits in the daily practice of the profession. In fact, some scholars describe these codes not as codes of ethics but as *codes of practice* (Sockett, 1990), implying that it is what you do, not what you profess or promise to do, that matters. During the course of your teacher education program, your instructors will be seeking evidence *in your performance* that you have developed and that you carry out ethical professional practices both in your interactions with students and with your fellow professionals.

What is the relationship between the 10 INTASC standards and a code of ethics? In general, the purpose of standards is to set forth the practice of a competent beginning teacher, including both the technical skills you need to teach well (for example, mastering methods of instruction) and the moral stance you adopt in relation to your students, their families, and your professional peers. A code of ethics is focused more directly on your relationships with students and professional peers and the fundamental responsibility all teachers have to act in ethically sound, defensible ways. The code does not, however, focus on the technical skills teachers need to carry out those responsibilities.

## The Ethics of Recommending Candidates for Teaching

Professionals who prepare the nation's teachers bear a deep responsibility when they recommend students for a teaching license. As gatekeepers to the profession, teacher educators must consider whether you, as a prospective teacher, are committed to the moral obligations of teaching and can be counted on to handle ethical dilemmas professionally. But what does this actually mean in the course of your teacher education program? On what basis might your instructors make such a decision?

You will have many opportunities to learn, practice, and demonstrate the skills you will need as a teacher, both during your classes and in your early field experiences and student teaching or internship. You will plan and implement lessons and assess your students' learning accordingly. You will organize the classroom for instruction and demonstrate not only your knowledge of content, but also your ability to use effective, up-to-date methods of teaching. Elementary school teachers, for example, must be able to demonstrate the knowledge and skills to teach reading. High school English teachers must know how to structure a writing program in which students improve their ability to write for multiple purposes across

## Figure 11-3    NEA Code of Ethics

### Code of Ethics of the Education Profession
#### Preamble

*The educator, believing in the worth and dignity of each human being, recognizes the supreme importance of the pursuit of truth, devotion to excellence, and the nurture of the democratic principles. Essential to these goals is the protection of freedom to learn and to teach and the guarantee of equal educational opportunity for all. The educator accepts the responsibility to adhere to the highest ethical standards.*

*The educator recognizes the magnitude of the responsibility inherent in the teaching process. The desire for the respect and confidence of one's colleagues, of students, of parents, and of the members of the community provides the incentive to attain and maintain the highest possible degree of ethical conduct. The Code of Ethics of the Education Profession indicates the aspiration of all educators and provides standards by which to judge conduct.*

*The remedies specified by the NEA and/or its affiliates for the violation of any provision of this Code shall be exclusive and no such provision shall be enforceable in any form other than the one specifically designated by the NEA or its affiliates.*

### PRINCIPLE I
#### Commitment to the Student

The educator strives to help each student realize his or her potential as a worthy and effective member of society. The educator therefore works to stimulate the spirit of inquiry, the acquisition of knowledge and understanding, and the thoughtful formulation of worthy goals.

In fulfillment of the obligation to the student, the educator—

1. Shall not unreasonably restrain the student from independent action in the pursuit of learning.
2. Shall not unreasonably deny the student's access to varying points of view.
3. Shall not deliberately suppress or distort subject matter relevant to the student's progress.
4. Shall make reasonable effort to protect the student from conditions harmful to learning or to health and safety.
5. Shall not intentionally expose the student to embarrassment or disparagement.
6. Shall not, on the basis of race, color, creed, sex, national origin, marital status, political or religious beliefs, family, social or cultural background, or sexual orientation, unfairly—

a. Exclude any student from participation in any program
b. Deny benefits to any student
c. Grant any advantage to any student

7. Shall not use professional relationships with students for private advantage.
8. Shall not disclose information about students obtained in the course of professional service unless disclosure serves a compelling professional purpose or is required by law.

### PRINCIPLE II
#### Commitment to the Profession

The education profession is vested by the public with a trust and responsibility requiring the highest ideals of professional service.

In the belief that the quality of the services of the education profession directly influences the nation and its citizens, the educator shall exert every effort to raise professional standards, to promote a climate that encourages the exercise of professional judgment, to achieve conditions that attract persons worthy of the trust to careers in education, and to assist in preventing the practice of the profession by unqualified persons.

In fulfillment of the obligation to the profession, the educator—

1. Shall not in an application for a professional position deliberately make a false statement or fail to disclose a material fact related to competency and qualifications.
2. Shall not misrepresent his/her professional qualifications.
3. Shall not assist any entry into the profession of a person known to be unqualified in respect to character, education, or other relevant attribute.
4. Shall not knowingly make a false statement concerning the qualifications of a candidate for a professional position.
5. Shall not assist a noneducator in the unauthorized practice of teaching.
6. Shall not disclose information about colleagues obtained in the course of professional service unless disclosure serves a compelling professional purpose or is required by law.
7. Shall not knowingly make false or malicious statements about a colleague.
8. Shall not accept any gratuity, gift, or favor that might impair or appear to influence professional decisions or action.

*Adopted by the NEA 1975 Representative Assembly*

**Source:** National Education Association. *Code of ethics of the education profession.* Retrieved May 26, 2008, from http://www.nea.org/aboutnea/code.html.

multiple subject areas. These represent the pedagogical skills of teaching, and they are things many teacher education students can learn to do well through instruction and practice.

But making a commitment to care about, advocate for, and develop trustworthy relationships with your students—the moral stance of teaching—is *not* something you can learn in a teacher education program. On the contrary, these are commitments you bring with you to your professional preparation, and they are the basis on which you will build your professional practice. Instead, your program of teacher education provides the context in which you demonstrate the depth of your commitments and in which you can begin to address some of the ethical dilemmas of practice.

The language that is often used today to describe the moral stance teachers take is the term *dispositions*. This term gained prominence in the INTASC standards as a feature of teaching that goes along with the knowledge and skills a prospective teacher must demonstrate. Villegas (2007) defines dispositions as "tendencies for individuals to act in a particular manner under particular circumstances, based on their beliefs" (p. 373).

For example, teacher education can help you deepen your commitment to your future students' learning by ensuring that you have the knowledge and skills to carry out your profession well. It can broaden your perspective on what it means to teach and on what constitutes state-of-the-art instruction. It can provide increasing levels of responsibility within your field experiences so that you can strengthen your abilities and develop confidence. It can give you direct experiences with students whose racial, ethnic, language, and socioeconomic groups differ from your own so that you can strengthen your responsiveness to diversity.

But even the finest teacher education program cannot teach someone to *want* to be with children and youth each day and to be interested in who they are as human beings. Your professional program will provide you with multiple opportunities to demonstrate the technical skills of teaching, and, more importantly, the professional standards of ethical behavior. For example, your instructors may want to observe how you interact with your students. Are you genuinely interested in their well-being? Are you committed to supporting all of your students as learners, or are you interested in only certain categories and classes of students? Are you an active advocate for students?

**Your turn...** *to reflect*

Place yourself in the position of a teacher educator who is making a decision about whether a teacher education student, Sandra, is ready to be recommended for student teaching for the upcoming semester. In her required personal interview at the end of the semester before student teaching, you learn that although there were many Latino students in the fifth grade classroom where she was placed during early field experience, Sandra did not know her students' countries of origin. Is this an ethical problem? Why or why not?

Christopher Clark provides an appropriate summary of our discussion of the moral and ethical responsibilities of teachers: "What educators and parents fear most about bad teaching and celebrate most about good teaching are manifestations of fundamental moral virtues. Really bad teaching is 'bad' in a moral sense; really good teaching is 'good' in a moral sense. No amount of technical virtuosity in instruction can compensate for or excuse morally flawed, irresponsible behavior" (1990, pp. 263–264).

## Historical Note
### The Moral Context in Colonial Schools

In colonial America, the moral context for education differed significantly from that of today. Schools operated as close partners with the church, and the church permeated every aspect of society (Butts & Cremin, 1953, p. 20). The earliest education legislation itself (the Old Deluder Satan Act, see Chapter 5) ensured a link between religion and the purposes of education. As a result of this close connection, education was infused with the moral expectations of the church in multiple ways.

All teachers were required to be morally upstanding and sound in their religious faith in order to be appointed (Butts & Cremin, 1953). Ministers themselves were often teachers in these early schools. When teachers were not ministers, ministers could be found visiting schools and providing religious instruction to ensure that students were educated according to the tenets of Christianity.

Religion permeated the colonial curriculum. Textbooks were making their initial appearances, and few were available early on, so instructional materials often included catechisms and the Bible. Clifton Johnson (1963) describes several early textbooks, all of which included religious material as a means of providing moral instruction. Early English texts used in the colonies included the following:

- A New Guide to the English Tongue (1740). This popular speller included spelling words, religious reading, moral instruction, and fables.
- The Universal Spelling Book (1755). This work included "lessons moral and divine, fables and pleasant stories, and a very easy and approved Guide to English Grammar" (Johnson, 1963, p. 53).
- Watts' Compleat Spelling Book (1770). This text included, along with spelling words, moral instructions for each letter of the alphabet, as well as small portions of scripture.

One of the most famous early textbooks, however, and the first truly American textbook, which could be found in nearly every home along with the Bible, was The New England Primer. The Primer appeared at the end of the seventeenth century. It included spelling and syllable study, but most of its contents, according to Johnson, were religious and moral verses, prayers, and prose. Its subtitle read: "An Easy and Pleasant Guide to the Art of Reading, to Which is Added the Catechism" (Johnson, 1963, p. 75). Other primers that were published subsequently followed this same pattern. For an example of a primer see Figure 11-4.

The relative homogeneity of religious practice, especially in New England, enabled the early colonists to mesh religious, moral, and civic life, and this was nowhere more apparent than in the schools. The moral stance that was expected of teachers and the view of teaching as a moral enterprise were defined by this relationship.

| Figure 11-4 | Facsimile From an Early Primer |
|---|---|

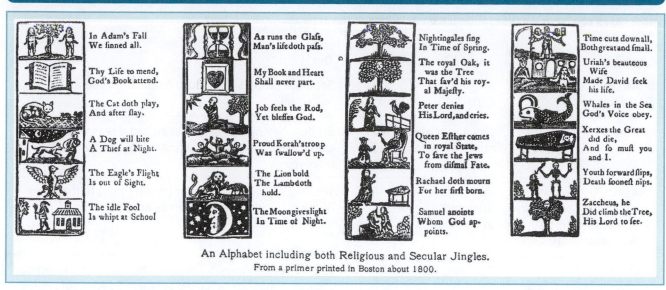

An Alphabet including both Religious and Secular Jingles.
From a primer printed in Boston about 1800.

**Source:** Johnson, C. (1963). *Old-time schools and schoolbooks.* New York: Dover Publications.

## How Legal Issues Influence Teachers' Ethical Practice

Ethical decisions about appropriate behavior by teachers are also influenced by legal decisions and legal precedents. Important legal decisions in the main have had as their purpose to ensure that specific groups of students are not discriminated against in the educational process. They include, for example, the 1954 *Brown v. Board of Education* decision that was designed to end the segregation of schools (Chapter 7), the Lau Remedies protecting the rights of students whose first language is not English (Chapter 10), and the Individuals with Disabilities Education Act (Chapter 8), which had its antecedents in state-level legal decisions. These decisions address the provision of equitable education for students who are often the most underserved in the schools, and as such they are directly related to issues of ethics in teaching. Legal decisions that seek equity in education often derive their power from the Fourteenth Amendment to the Constitution, which protects the individual rights of all citizens of the United States. The **Equal Protection Clause** of the Fourteenth Amendment proclaims that the states cannot "deny to any person within its jurisdiction the equal protection of the law."

The **Due Process Clause** of the Fourteenth Amendment adds that the states cannot "deprive any person of life, liberty, or property without due process of the law." For example, due process must be extended to families who seek appropriate educational opportunities for their children who have disabilities.

In this section we review several additional laws and decisions that directly relate to your daily interactions with students and families. Many of these issues were decided in the courts on the basis of the First Amendment to the Constitution, which includes the **Establishment Clause**, prohibiting the government from establishing religion and which is the source of the "separation of church and state"; the **Free Exercise Clause**, which guarantees religious freedom; and the **Freedom of**

### Critical Term
**Equal Protection Clause.** Clause of the Fourteenth Amendment of the Constitution stating that no person can be denied equal protection of the law.

### Critical Term
**Due Process Clause.** Clause of the Fourteenth Amendment to the U. S. Constitution stating that each citizen must have due process of the law.

### Critical Term
**Establishment Clause.** Clause of the First Amendment to the Constitution stating that the U.S. Congress cannot make laws that establish religion.

### Critical Term
**Free Exercise Clause.** Clause of the First Amendment to the Constitution stating that the U.S. Congress cannot make laws that prohibit the free exercise of religion.

## Table 11-1    Selected Major Education-Related Court Cases

Court cases can have a major influence on activities in the schools.

| Case/Year | Topic/Question | Decision |
|---|---|---|
| *Brown v. Board of Education*, 1954 | Are segregated schools equal? | Separate schools for African American students are not equal. |
| *New Jersey v. TLO*, 1985 | Can a school search a student's belongings? | Student belongings can be searched if reasonable cause exists that evidence related to a crime may be discovered. |
| *Tinker v. Des Moines Independent Community School District*, 1969 (Tinker Standard) | Can students wear armbands to protest war in Vietnam? | Wearing armbands does not pose a threat to the order of the schools and is allowed as an expression of students' beliefs. |
| *Bethel School District, No. 403 v. Fraser* (Fraser Standard) | Can lewd language be used in a school speech nominating a student for office? | Lewd or vulgar speech can be curbed in a school setting; a balance must be achieved between freedom of expression and the school's role in establishing the boundaries of what is socially acceptable. |
| *Hazelwood School District v. Kuhlmeier*, 1988 | Can the school censor articles in the school newspaper? | Censorship is allowed when school officials have reasons related to legitimate issues of education. |
| *Wallace v. Jaffree*, 1985 | Is prayer permitted in schools? | If purpose of moment of silence is to promote prayer, it may not be enacted. |
| *Lemon v. Kurtzman*, 1971 | Can government sponsor religious activity related to education? | No, with three criteria known as "The Lemon Test" Actions taken by the government must have a secular legislative purpose. Actions taken by the government must not have the primary effect of either advancing or inhibiting religion. Actions taken by the government must not result in an "excessive government entanglement" with religion. |

**Sources:** Haynes, C. C., S. Chaltain, J. E. Ferguson, D. L. Hudson, and O. Thomas. (2003). *The First Amendment in schools.* Alexandria, VA: Association for Supervision and Curriculum Development and the First Amendment Center; Imber, M., and T. Van Geel. (2001). *A teacher's guide to education law.* Mahwah, NJ: Lawrence Erlbaum Associates.

### Critical Term

**Freedom of Expression Clause.** Clause of the First Amendment to the Constitution stating that the U.S. Congress cannot make laws that abridge freedom of speech.

**Expression Clause,** which guarantees free speech and freedom of the press. Table 11-1 lists several court cases that have had a major influence on schools.

## Students' Rights to Free Expression of Opinions

The First Amendment guarantees the right of free expression. In relationship to this right, however, schools also have the responsibility to maintain an orderly school environment. The standard for students' free expression allows schools to restrict such expression if there is reasonable cause that the action will disrupt the school (Haynes et al., 2003; Valente, 1998). Thus, for example, if students wish to wear armbands or buttons to protest a governmental action, in general they must be allowed to do so. Each local school context differs, however, and what may lead to disruption in one school may not have the same effect at another. School administrators need to be able to justify their decisions based on the standards of disruption (or not) to the environment.

Speech that is considered lewd, vulgar, or offensive can also be regulated by school officials. One function of school, according to relevant court rulings, is to foster an understanding of what is deemed socially appropriate (Haynes et al., 2003). Such speech does not meet this standard. Schools may also take action against school-sponsored media, for example, a school newspaper, and censor certain of its contents (Haynes et al., 2003). But the lines are not clearly drawn in terms of what is considered to be appropriate, and school officials must consider each specific situation they encounter.

The right of students to express themselves freely in school is protected as long as it does not pose a serious disruption in school; these students were protesting the war with Iraq shortly before its start. (©AP/Wide World Photos)

The ethical issue in this regard is that school officials may not choose to censor speech or publications just because they do not agree with what is being said or written (Imber & Van Geel, 2001). Instead, they must view the situation through the lens of the school and the purposes and functions of school in our society in relationship to freedom of expression.

## Privacy and Confidentiality

The records that schools keep on their students have also been an object of legal consideration. The Family Educational Rights and Privacy Act, known as **FERPA** (also known as the Buckley Amendment), was enacted by Congress in 1974 (**http://www.ed.gov/policy/gen/reg/ferpa/index.html**). FERPA defines who may have access to student records. This act offers protection to students and their families, both allowing them to see formal records for themselves and ensuring that only appropriate people have access to these records. An important issue for you as a classroom teacher is that the informal, private notes you may keep on your students are not covered by FERPA. Rather, FERPA covers formal records that a school keeps about its students. Also, FERPA applies only to schools that receive federal funding. Schools that do not comply with FERPA and do not share records may be denied federal funds.

FERPA contains several major provisions:

**Critical Term**

**FERPA.** The Family Educational Rights and Privacy Act (also known as the Buckley Amendment) enacted by Congress in 1974, which governs who may see school records and under what conditions.

- Schools are required to allow parents and families to review school records within 45 days of a request. Schools need not provide free copies of these records.

- Parents and students may ask to have formal school records amended. If the school does not agree to amend the records, parents and families have the right to a hearing.

- In general, schools may not release student information without permission. Some general kinds of information, known as "directory" information, may be released if families are notified to this effect and have reasonable opportunity to decline having such information made available. Directory information may include a student's name, address, telephone number, date and place of birth, honors and awards, and dates of attendance. FERPA specifically identifies other conditions under which schools may release information about students' records.

- Each year schools must notify families of their rights under FERPA. Schools may decide how such notification takes place (e.g., parent handbook, letter, etc.).

How is the question of students' formal records related to the ethics of teaching? Before passage of FERPA, parents and families were not always permitted to see their own children's records, which meant that they were not able to fully understand the basis of decisions made using those records. Records on which decisions were made sometimes reflected subjective judgments and interpretations of students' performance and behavior among teachers, administrators, or other school professionals. Under FERPA, school personnel are reminded that they should carefully consider how they interpret specific situations and how they portray their students in writing and should base those portrayals on the most objective view of the situation possible.

The protections of FERPA, however, do not mean that school professionals and parents or families will always agree on decisions based on students' formal school records. That is why it includes a provision for a hearing—either to resolve such disagreements or to clarify that the family disagrees with the school's description in the records.

## Reporting Child Abuse and Neglect

Teachers have the moral and ethical obligation, as well as a legal obligation, to protect the well-being of children and youth. As we noted in Chapter 6, teachers are mandated reporters of suspected child abuse and neglect. This is an essential part of a teacher's commitment to ethical behavior and to advocating for children.

As a teacher, you must know the procedures within your school building and district for reporting suspected cases of abuse and neglect. Typically, a classroom teacher reports a concern to a principal or other designated person in the school. In this area of the law, it is preferable to err on the side of caution and make a report if your observations suggest that a problem may exist. It is not your obligation to prove that abuse or neglect has actually taken place; instead you are required to report *suspected* cases of abuse and neglect. Extensive information on child abuse and neglect is available at: **www.childwelfare.org**.

## Corporal Punishment

Over the centuries, methods of disciplining students in school have changed considerably, especially with regard to the practice of corporal punishment. The infamous paddle is no longer present in every classroom and principal's office, and the use of corporal punishment is on the decline generally (National Association of School Psychologists, 2002). However, among the industrialized countries of the world, only the United States, Australia, and Canada do not ban corporal punishment in the schools; on a state-by-state basis in the United States, 29 states do currently ban corporal punishment (Center for Effective Discipline, n.d.).

In states that do not expressly have laws against the use of corporal punishment, individual school district boards may ban its use. School districts that do permit it often have strict guidelines for the conditions under which it may be used (Imber & Van Geel, 2001). For example, in some districts this type of punishment can be administered only by school principals or with the express permission of the principal (Valente, 1998). According to the Center for Effective Discipline, corporal punishment is used most frequently in schools in the South, with schools in the states of Mississippi and Arkansas having the highest frequency reported. When such punishment is used, the test from a legal perspective is whether it is reasonable and does not constitute an excessive use of force (Valente, 1998).

From the perspective of a teacher's moral stance, your role is to create an environment where your students feel safe so that they can learn. The use of corporal punishment is inconsistent with this moral responsibility. Your job is to set specific expectations for your students' behavior, to be clear about those expectations, and to be consistent in enforcing them. You must also establish clear consequences for students' misbehaviors and enforce them consistently. Every teacher needs to establish the limits for what is acceptable behavior in his or her classroom and determine what will occur if students are unable to meet those expectations. There are many appropriate approaches to discipline in the classroom that do not rely on corporal punishment and that are effective in changing students' behavior. As a start, effective teachers set up classroom environments where students' misbehavior is minimized—because their classrooms are engaging, interesting, stimulating, safe places to begin with.

That said, some students are likely to "push your buttons" more than others. And some students will act out in ways that are inappropriate. On occasion students' actions will make you angry. Teachers, even the best teachers, cannot prevent all misbehavior. Understanding the motivations behind misbehaviors can help teachers overcome the desire to respond negatively to students who are irritating them. For example, according to Linda Albert (2003), who has created a cooperative approach to classroom discipline, students act out because they seek attention, power, and revenge, or because they want to avoid failure. Teachers who understand what is behind their students' misbehavior are in a better position to respond in a productive manner. When confrontations do occur in the classroom, Albert offers these guidelines:

● Focus on the behavior, not the student.

● Take charge of negative emotions.

● Avoid escalating the situation.

● Discuss misbehavior later.

● Allow students to save face. (2003, p. iv)

Teachers face ethical dilemmas when they know, for example, that a parent or family member might use corporal punishment if a student is having difficulties in school. Let's say, for example, that a student's homelife is chaotic, which makes it impossible for him or her to get homework completed. Is it ethical in this situation to punish the student for failing to turn in homework? Rather than subject the student to punishment, a teacher could make it possible for the student to complete the homework at school, perhaps before or after school, or at the lunch hour. At the same time, the teacher can take a proactive role in providing parent and family education programs on effective parenting and alternatives to corporal punishment. What other options might you consider if you face a situation such as this?

A random search of students' lockers is permissible because they are under the shared control of the school and the student. (Digital Vision)

## Search and Seizure

As a teacher, are you allowed to search your students' backpacks or desks if you suspect that a student has cigarettes, drugs, alcohol, or weapons? What if other students report to you that they believe a student has these items? What about locker searches—are such searches a violation of students' rights? From a legal perspective, protection against "search and seizure" comes under the Fourth Amendment to the Constitution. The standard applied in schools differs from the standard applied generally, however.

The courts' view of the situation is that schools have a responsibility to keep an orderly and safe environment. In some cases, searches are warranted to meet this expectation. The courts have ruled that a school may search a student's personal belongings if there are *reasonable grounds* to do so for that individual student and if the search is likely to yield useful results (Valente, 1998). School officials can also conduct random locker searches; the argument enabling this search is that lockers are not entirely personal possessions, but rather are under the joint control of students and the schools (Imber & Van Geel, 2001).

What is the ethical issue here? Schools must be safe places for all students, and sometimes searches are necessary to keep a school safe. But teachers must not search students' belongings without a compelling reason for doing so.

## Religion in the Schools

How does the role of religion play out in the public schools? While teachers may teach about religion, they must hold a neutral stance toward religion and not promote any specific religion (Haynes et al., 2003). As we noted in Chapter 10, teachers do not have to avoid discussing religion in the context of the curriculum, but they cannot teach about a particular religion with the purpose of showing preference for that religion, proselytizing for that religion, or presenting a negative view of other religions.

Teachers often raise questions about religion and schools with regard to celebrating holidays. Although teachers are permitted to teach about religious holidays, as with religion in general, they must hold a neutral stance toward those holidays and not *celebrate* them. This is often more of an issue at the elementary level than at the secondary level, especially in December when seasonal activities are widespread. The standard that is applied is whether the celebratory activities are part of an effort to educate students about the holidays or whether such activities actually promote religion or are part of a clearly secular, nondenominational seasonal program (Imber & Van Geel, 2001). In other words, the religious significance cannot dominate in a way that represents school-sponsored endorsement of that religion (Valente, 1998).

Another important issue with respect to religion and the schools is school prayer. The standard that the courts have used is whether prayer is being forced on students, who are essentially considered to be a "captive audience" in the schools. Prayer cannot be an official part of school or school-sponsored activities because then it is considered to be endorsed by the school—a violation of the First Amendment (Haynes et al., 2003). Thirty-four states permit or require a moment of reflection, prayer, silence or meditation (Colasanti, 2008), but if this is observed, neither the school nor the teacher can endorse it for purposes of religious proselytizing.

The general standard is clear: public schools cannot endorse any specific religion. Teachers and other school personnel must honor this requirement in their capacity as employees of the school and in their work with students.

## Your turn... *to reflect*

It is late November and you are visiting an elementary school as part of your teacher education program. Upon entering the school, you come up a flight of steps leading to a large central hallway. The entryway and the central hallway of the building have been decorated with Christmas decorations. The first thing you see upon entering the school, at the top of the stairs, is a large Christmas tree, and Christmas carols are playing in the hallways. The door to each room is decorated with a Christmas theme. Do you think this violates the Establishment Clause of the Constitution? Why or why not?

# Digging Deeper
## The Persistent Debate over Teaching Evolution

Court rulings and legal precedents do not protect the schools from continued wrangling over legal issues. A good example is the persistent debate over the teaching of evolution.

**Pro and Con:** Evolution is a longstanding theory in science and a standard topic of the biology curriculum. It provides an explanation for the origin of animal and plant species and is generally accepted by scientists as vital to the understanding of biology. The role of science education is to teach students to use rigorous scientific inquiry to understand natural phenomena—as well as to interest them in the further study of science. The view of the National Science Teachers Association, the professional organization for science teachers in the United States, is as follows:

> The National Science Teachers Association (NSTA) strongly supports the position that evolution is a major unifying concept in science and should be included in the K–12 science education frameworks and curricula. Furthermore, if evolution is not taught, students will not achieve the level of scientific literacy they need. This position is consistent with that of the National Academies, the American Association for the Advancement of Science (AAAS), and many other scientific and educational organizations. (National Science Teachers Association, 1996)

Arguments against the teaching of evolution are often supported by religious organizations associated with Christian fundamentalism. These arguments are based on the belief that the origin of the universe was a divine act. The term to describe this position is creationism. Supporters of this position have attempted to strike evolution from the science curriculum in the state of Kansas, and have had stickers placed (and subsequently removed) on science textbooks in the state of Georgia informing students that evolution is "only a theory." The term *intelligent design* (ID) was introduced into this debate several years ago. ID, which is described by its proponents as a new scientific theory, is based on the belief that some type of unnamed designer was responsible for the origin of the universe; the designer is not named specifically. The scientific community does not recognize ID as a valid scientific theory because its supporters have not "provided credible scientific evidence to support their claim" (American Association for the Advancement of Science, 2005).

In 1987, the U.S. Supreme Court struck down a Louisiana court's decision, *Edwards v. Aguillard*, regarding the Balanced Treatment for Creation-Science and Evolution-Science in Public School Instruction Act. This act was designed to require that one of these issues could not be discussed in schools without discussing the other; the Court argued that the specific purpose of the act was to promote religion (Haynes et al., 2003). The 2004 federal court decision, *Selman et al. v. Cobb County, Georgia*, ruled that disclaimer stickers stating that evolution is "just a theory" intrude on individual personal religious freedom. In December 2004, the American Civil Liberties Union filed and won the suit *Kitzmiller v. Dover (PA) Area School Board* on behalf of parents who believe that teaching ID in the schools promotes a specific religious view and is a violation of their First Amendment rights. Despite these rulings and cases, proponents of creationism and ID continue to press their case in local school districts.

**The Nuances:**  The nuances of this debate lie in the relationship between science and religion. The courts have made a clear distinction between the two in the context of the teaching of science, as has the scientific community. From a legal perspective, evolution is science and creationism is religion. From the perspective of the science community and science teachers, it is the teaching of science itself that is at stake when ideas that are not scientifically grounded, but rather religiously grounded, can replace those that have stood the test of scientific rigor, and when attempts are made to excise whole theories of science from the curriculum (American Association for the Advancement of Science, 2005).

Controversies exist within science itself about many phenomena, and teaching about controversies within science, based on the discipline of science and scientific rigor, is appropriate within the science curriculum. Teaching about religion as a historical phenomenon within the humanities is also appropriate. What differs in this situation is that the religious view of the origin of the world is being presented as science rather than as a religious perspective about a scientific theory. In essence, this means that a specific religious perspective is being sponsored by the school as an institution. The controversy, then, is not about competing scientific theories of the origin of the earth, which is what ID proponents advocate and refer to as "teaching about the controversy." Rather, the controversy is about pitting a religious explanation against a scientific one—which is not a controversy within science.

**Rethinking the Issue:**  Where then do these debates belong in relationship to teachers' ethical responsibilities?

As a result of the vehement beliefs that underlie this issue, science teachers in communities where ID is being introduced are often placed in challenging positions and find themselves having to confront passionate supporters of ID in their communities. As a result, some are downplaying the teaching of evolution altogether in order to avoid such conflicts (Cavanaugh, 2005). This weakens the science curriculum and fails to place the debates in their proper perspective.

Mark Terry (2004), a longtime science teacher, suggests that teachers themselves must be better educated about religion, history, and the humanities to be able to hold more informed discussions of these issues in the schools. As a science teacher who has worked within an integrated science and humanities curriculum, Terry has had the opportunity to teach both the science of evolution and the debates and controversies surrounding it as an issue within the humanities. The persistence of the debate over decades suggests that it will not be easy to find common ground; if common ground is not found, both the teaching of science and the teaching of the humanities will continue to challenge educators.

## Technology, The Internet, Fair Use, and Copyright Issues

The explosion of technology has led to the need for schools to address its use across a range of technology applications. For example, cell phone use in schools is an ongoing concern. Some states that once made decisions to ban cell phones to reduce their use for illegal purposes (e.g., drug sales or gang-related activity) have revised their policies following events such as 9/11 and shootings in high schools such as Columbine (Education Commission of the States, 2004).

In 2000, the United States Congress passed the Children's Internet Protection Act (CIPA) to provide guidance and regulations regarding access to content that is deemed offensive over the Internet in computers in schools and libraries. This act applies to schools and libraries that receive funds through a federal program known as E-Rate, which provides discounted rates for technology purchases for schools and libraries (for more information on E-rate, see **http://www.ed.gov/about/offices/list/oii/nonpublic/erate.html**). CIPA requires the following for any school or library that receives E-rate funding:

● Schools and libraries subject to CIPA may not receive the discounts offered by the E-Rate program unless they certify that they have an Internet safety policy and technology protection measures in place. An Internet safety policy must include technology protection measures to block or filter Internet access to pictures that: (a) are obscene, (b) are child pornography, or (c) are harmful to minors, for computers that are accessed by minors.

● Schools subject to CIPA are required to adopt and enforce a policy to monitor online activities of minors; and

● Schools and libraries subject to CIPA are required to adopt and implement a policy addressing: (a) access by minors to inappropriate matter on the Internet; (b) the safety and security of minors when using electronic mail, chat rooms, and other forms of direct electronic communications; (c) unauthorized access, including so-called "hacking," and other unlawful activities by minors online; (d) unauthorized disclosure, use, and dissemination of personal information regarding minors; and (e) restricting minors' access to materials harmful to them. (Federal Communications Commission, 2006)

Since Internet use is so widespread in the schools, policies protecting which sites can be accessed is essential. Legal considerations that govern the use of materials that are written by others or that are available on the Internet fall under the topics of **fair use** and copyright. Why are copyright and fair use issues of ethical behavior? According to Cathy Newsome (1997), "Teachers have a moral obligation to practice integrity and trustworthiness. Just as they expect students to refrain from cheating on tests and from taking others' belongings at school, teachers should honor the law when it comes to fair use and copyright. Thus, teachers not only should protect themselves from legal liability but should model honesty and truthfulness by knowing when and what may be copied for educational use."

**Critical Term**

**Fair use.** Laws allowing teachers to make limited numbers of copies for instructional purposes in the classroom.

All students should be familiar with the concept of copyright. Creative works that are protected by copyright cannot be reproduced without explicit permission from the author or creator. Works that are in the public domain can be copied without permission (for discussion of what is included in the public domain, see **http://www.education-world.com/a_curr/curr280a.shtml**). An exception exists for the use of copyrighted materials specifically for educational purposes, which is known as *fair use*. But this exception does not give teachers carte blanche to use copyrighted materials wherever and whenever they want. Instead, teachers must be familiar with the fair use restrictions so that they do not violate the copyright laws.

The *fair use* exception allows a teacher to copy and use no more than (1) 10 percent of works that are over 1000 words, (2) two pages or fewer of poetry, short essays, or (3) a single graph or cartoon for classroom use by an individual teacher (Imber & Van Geel, 2001). The idea is that teachers should not be constrained from using relevant materials to enhance their teaching, but these materials cannot replace textbooks, anthologies, or workbooks. Copies that are meant to be

The increased use of technology in schools means that teachers must be familiar with their legal obligations concerning the use of materials from the Internet. (Media Bakery)

temporary, or that are copied spontaneously, meet the fair use criterion (Newsome, 1997).

To read more about fair use and copyright issues and the Internet, go to the Learning and Leadership with Technology publication on the ISTE website at **www.iste.org** and locate the April 2005 issue.

Copyright and fair use also apply to the Internet. Teachers and students alike must cite Internet sources that they copy into their own documents. The easy availability of new resources on the Internet means that teachers must be especially careful about how they use and model the use of the Internet with their students. The International Society for Technology in Education's (ISTE) fourth standard specifically covers issues related to the ethical and legal use of technology, as well as issues of equity in the use of technology: (see Chapter 9 for the entire list of ISTE standards for teachers).

Teachers understand local and global societal issues and responsibilities in an evolving digital culture and exhibit legal and ethical behavior in their professional practices. Teachers:

    a.  advocate, model, and teach safe, legal, and ethical use of digital information and technology, including respect for copyright, intellectual property, and the appropriate documentation of sources.

    b.  address the diverse needs of all learners by using learner-centered strategies providing equitable access to appropriate digital tools and resources.

    c.  promote and model digital etiquette and responsible social interactions related to the use of technology and information.

    d.  develop and model cultural understanding and global awareness by engaging with colleagues and students of other cultures using digital-age communication and collaboration tools. (ISTE, 2008)

## Your turn... *to review*

1. What three clauses of the Constitution are most often involved in legal cases regarding education?
2. What is the major issue in education that FERPA addresses?
3. What does the term *fair* use refer to?

## The Personal versus the Professional as an Ethical Issue for Teachers

Like anyone else in our society, teachers have personal beliefs, and they do not leave these beliefs at the schoolhouse door each day. What is the appropriate relationship between a teacher's personal beliefs and his or her professional ethical responsibilities?

## Personal Beliefs and Inclusivity in Public Schools

By their very nature, public schools are meant to be inclusive institutions and to serve a special function in our society as the places where every child is supposed to be accepted and educated. With the exception of a very small percentage of selective public specialty schools (often, but not always, located in large cities), schools do not have entry criteria, and teachers generally have little say about which students they will and will not accept. Serving the public good, teachers are obliged to teach all the students who are assigned to their classrooms. This is as true in the city as it is in the country, in the suburbs, and in rural communities.

Accordingly, public schools are places where the potential for diversity is at its greatest. To be sure, other institutional and societal dynamics, for example, neighborhoods segregated by socioeconomic class, control and affect who attends which schools. But within any single public school system, any student who lives in the district and shows up at your classroom door is eligible to be educated—and every child must be welcomed both as an individual and as a learner under your care and guidance.

Public school teachers thus work in a world in which students are to be included rather than excluded. As a matter of professional ethics in such a world, teachers do not have the choice to teach some students but not all of them, to be interested in some students but not all of them, to interact with some students' families but not all of them. Ethical behavior for teachers requires believing that the learning of each student is as important as the learning of the next student.

What does this mean for you in your daily practice? Over the course of your teaching career, you are likely to encounter a wide range of students and families—wider than the range you might encounter if you chose to teach in a private secular or religious school. The varying family structures described in Chapter 6 mean that you may be teaching children whose families' values, religious beliefs, political beliefs, and cultural and social practices may differ from yours. In many communities, you may teach students who come from nontraditional families, multiracial families, or single-parent families, or students who live with grandparents or other extended family members. Increasingly, you may teach students from gay and lesbian families. While you may privately hold beliefs that differ from those of some of your students and their families, your job as a teacher is not to pass judgment on those differences. Rather, it is to create the conditions in which each of your students thrives and learns.

## Personal Beliefs and the Curriculum

What about teachers' rights to self-expression in school? The courts have clearly ruled that teachers, like students, do not leave their First Amendment rights with regard to free expression at the schoolhouse door. However, teachers also cannot operate as curricular free agents in schools. They must use standards of good judgment, and what is taught in the classroom is typically judged by whether it is reasonably related to the curriculum (Haynes et al, 2003). In general, the rule is that the classroom is not a public forum.

For example, teachers cannot refuse to teach the explicit curriculum because they may disagree with it. If they believe a novel in the English curriculum is objectionable and it is a required text with no substitute permitted, they will have to teach the text. They can hold substantial discussions about the pros and cons of the text and explore it in depth, but they cannot make an individual personal determination to avoid it. Related to the debate on evolution versus creationism addressed earlier, a teacher cannot unilaterally decide to ignore evolution if it is in the curriculum and instead teach only creationism. In contrast, teachers also cannot introduce anything they wish into the classroom. Unlike the "academic freedom" that governs college and university classrooms, public school teachers are subject to more stringent guidelines and are not free to control the curriculum (Imber & Van Geel, 2001). The courts have upheld firing a teacher who chose to show an R-rated film in her classroom, for example, judging that the action did not fall within the bounds of reasonableness (Imber & Van Geel, 2001). The challenge for teachers on a day-to-day basis in the classroom, then, is to strike a balance between freedom of expression and the reasonable, responsible practice of expression within the framework and purposes of schools (Strike, 1990).

## Why It Counts in a Diverse World

No one looks over a teacher's shoulder when he or she is alone in the classroom teaching. Until recently, it was rare for teachers to watch their peers teach at all. It is for this reason that teachers need to develop a strong internal sense of what it means to be ethical and to behave in an ethical manner—even when all of the answers are not neatly packaged.

Teachers make important judgments about students every day. These judgments affect how teachers interact with students and how students feel about being in school. Teachers also have authority and power over students for several hours each day. The basic question of teachers' ethical behavior, then, is transparent. Doing harm to students is not ethical, and teachers should not practice in a way that harms students in any way. Classrooms and schools are increasingly diverse places in terms of demographics, and teachers have the responsibility of ensuring that each of their students—and especially students whose backgrounds they might not be familiar with—experience their classrooms as safe and comfortable learning environments. In addition, teachers need to understand that when situations are complex, joint discussion and reflection will probably be needed to find appropriate responses and solutions. As teachers gain confidence and skills through practice, experience, and reflection, it becomes easier to address what may appear to be complex ethical dilemmas.

At the same time, because teaching is a human endeavor, problems come with the professional territory, and teachers address ethical issues and dilemmas throughout their careers. Being clear about your commitment to students from the start gives you the sound foundation you need to face a range of ethical decisions.

That said, on a day-to-day basis there will not always be clear-cut answers. So what should teachers be expected to do? What is the standard for their ethical behavior? Strike (1990) provides perhaps the most useful guideline: In cases where there is a clear right or wrong, teachers should do "the right thing," and when that is not clear, they must reflect carefully and act responsibly, always considering the best interests of students.

# CHAPTER SUMMARY

Ethical considerations are critical for teachers because teaching is essentially a human interaction. Teachers have a responsibility to create a safe environment for their students to help them thrive and learn.

## Trust: The Basic Ethical Obligation of Teachers

Students and their families need to be able to trust the teacher to treat students with respect and dignity. Teachers develop trusting relationships with students when they build personal relationships with them, create supportive and welcoming classroom communities, know their content and pedagogy, and maintain a reflective stance on the quality of the classroom they have created.

## Ethical Considerations at the Teacher-to-Teacher Level

Ethical issues arise between teachers as well as between teachers and students. When other teachers speak disrespectfully about students, or when teachers communicate low expectations for students, their well-being is not being placed at the center of teaching. Responding to other teachers when such practices occur requires problem-solving skills so that teachers can maintain their commitment to students and continue to work within the school community.

## The School as an Ethical Community

Practices that are accepted within a school can represent ethical or unethical behavior. These behaviors are often taken for granted. They may include the kind of talk that goes on in the teachers' lounge and remarks from teachers about parents and families. When such talk is negative, students are not well served. Similarly, ethical considerations come up when a school has a disproportionate percentage of racial and ethnic minority students in special education compared with the percentage of students in the school as a whole. These practices demonstrate how the school treats students and families and the degree to which students and their potential are respected.

## Ethical Behavior, Codes of Ethics, and Standards of Professional Practice

The National Education Association has a code of ethics for teachers. The INTASC standards also provide a set of professional expectations, including dispositions, for how teachers carry out their work. Teacher education instructors are responsible for deciding which of their students are recommended for certification and can be counted on to practice teaching from an ethical standpoint. As teacher education students move through their programs, their development is measured against these standards to determine whether they demonstrate ethical behaviors in their work.

## How Legal Issues Influence Teachers' Ethical Practice

Many legal decisions affect the ethical decisions teachers make. These decisions relate to the freedoms enumerated in the First and Fourteenth Amendments to the Constitution. Within the general protection of these freedoms, however, courts have ruled that the purposes of schooling and the need to maintain order within schools may require some limits on freedom of religion and speech in school. Teachers must honor the separation of church and state and may not promote any specific religion in school. Freedom of speech is also protected, but schools may curtail certain expressions, especially if they might disrupt the order of the school. Students' belongings may be searched only when the school has good reason to believe that such a search will turn up relevant evidence. In many states, corporal punishment is banned altogether; in those that permit it, there are usually specific circumstances under which it is permissible. A teacher's legal obligations also extend to following copyright laws and ensuring the privacy of student records.

## The Personal versus the Professional as an Ethical Issue for Teachers

A critical function of public schools is to provide an education to all students across all racial, ethnic, language, and socioeconomic groups. Teachers who work in public schools have an ethical responsibility to teach all students, to accept them as learners, and to foster their learning. Teachers may not always agree with or approve of the lifestyle of their students and their families, but their job is to teach the students, not to pass judgment on aspects of their lives with which they do not agree.

## LIST OF CRITICAL TERMS

Blaming the victim  (382)

Student-led conferences  (384)

Equal Protection Clause  (393)

Due Process Clause  (393)

Establishment Clause  (393)

Free Exercise Clause  (393)

Freedom of Expression Clause  (394)

FERPA  (395)

Fair use  (401)

## EXPLORING YOUR COMMITMENT

1. *in the field...*  Conduct a formal observation of the class you are assigned to and observe for indicators of trust between teachers and students, and between students and students. What do you see that suggests a healthy level of trust exists? What tells you otherwise?

2. *in the field...*  Identify a teacher in the school who teaches about religion or who brings in guest speakers to talk about religion. How does this individual maintain respect for the Establishment Clause?

3. *on your own...*  Prepare a short written reflection describing several teachers you had whom you considered to be trustworthy. What did they have in common? In what ways were they different?

4. *on the web...*  Individual states may have their own statements of ethical conduct for teachers. For example, the state of Alaska's ethics statement is available at **http://www.eed.state.ak.us/TeacherCertification/20AAC10.html**. Check the state in which you think you want to teach to see if you can locate an ethics statement. If not, select a similar statement from another state, or

review the Alaska ethics website. Then compare the statement with the NEA Code of Ethics. How are they similar? different? Which is more prescriptive? How might you account for the difference?

5. *on the web...* Many professional teacher organizations have their own codes of ethics. For example, the Council for Exceptional Children's Code of Ethics for special education teachers is located at **http://www.cec.sped.org/ps/code.html**. Review that code of ethics, or select another for a different professional organization (refer to list of websites in Chapter 12). Compare them with the NEA Code of Ethics to see how they are similar or different.

6. *on the web...* Locate a website about the teaching of evolution versus creationism. What is the nature of the discussion on the site you reviewed? To what extent does the site promote the teaching of evolution? creationism? intelligent design? How do these discussions help or hinder a reasoned discussion of the issue for teachers?

7. *on the web...* Locate specific descriptions of the project schools on the website for the First Amendment Schools Project at **http://www.firstamendmentschools.org**. Select either the elementary or the secondary sites and read each entry. What is it that these schools are emphasizing as part of their involvement? Is this a project you would support in your school? Why or why not?

8. *in the field...* Interview a teacher in the school to which you are assigned. Ask the teacher to describe the one or two most challenging ethical situations he or she has faced as a teacher. Ask the same questions of the principal. How did they resolve the issues?

9. *on your own...* Select a book on classroom management for teachers. Review the table of contents to determine if this book addresses issues of trust in the classroom. If it does, what is the emphasis? If it does not, how does the text describe the relationships between teachers and students? What perspective does the author take about the moral imperative of teaching?

10. *in the research...* The following article addresses ways in which male elementary teachers are constrained in demonstrating their care for students. Read Hansen, P., and J. A. Mulholland. (2005). "Caring and elementary education: The concerns of male beginning teachers." *Journal of Teacher Education, 56,* 119–131. How do the ways of caring these teachers enact match with how you see yourself demonstrating your care in the classroom?

## GUIDELINES FOR BEGINNING TEACHERS

1. Establish a relationship with each student's family at the beginning of the year by placing a phone call to them and meeting them. Call each family regularly with a general report and/or good news.

2. To establish a positive start to the year, send a postcard to students just before the first day of the year introducing yourself and welcoming them into your classroom.

3. Drive or walk around the community surrounding the school in which you will be teaching. What resources do you find there? How might those resources be connected to the curriculum or enhance the curriculum you will be teaching?

4. After you get settled into your classroom, set up a meeting with the union representative in your building/district to find out who can provide you with advice about legal developments and cases that affect you as a teacher.

5. Set up a class roster with room for brief notes about each student. Each week, make sure you pay special attention to five students in your classroom. Make a point of learning something new about what they are doing outside of school, what they are reading or listening to, what they are concerned about.

6. At the start of the year, set as a goal finding one thing about each of your students that you like and can say positive things about, and build on that throughout the year.

## THE **INTASC** CONNECTION

The INTASC standard that most directly addresses ethical and legal considerations is Standard 10. It states: *The teacher fosters relationships with school colleagues, parents, and agencies in the larger community to support students' learning and well-being.* Indicators include the following:

● The teacher values and appreciates the importance of all aspects of a child's experience.

● The teacher is concerned about all aspects of a child's well-being (cognitive, emotional, social, and physical), and is alert to signs of difficulties.

● The teacher is willing to consult with other adults regarding the education and well-being of his or her students.

● The teacher respects the privacy of students and the confidentiality of information.

● The teacher is willing to work with other professionals to improve the overall learning environment for students.

● The teacher establishes respectful and productive relationships with parents and guardians from diverse home and community situations, and seeks to develop cooperative partnerships in support of student learning and well-being.

● The teacher talks with and listens to the students, is sensitive and responsive to clues of distress, investigates situations, and seeks outside help as needed and appropriate to remedy problems.

● The teacher acts as an advocate for students.

● The teacher understands and implements laws related to students' rights and teachers' responsibilities (e.g., for equal education, appropriate education for handicapped students, confidentiality, privacy, appropriate treatment of students, reporting in situations related to possible child abuse).

Indicators for several other INTASC standards also address ethical considerations that have been discussed in this chapter. For example, Standard 2, which addresses child development, includes the following indicators:

● The teacher understands students' physical, social, emotional, moral, and cognitive development and knows how to address these factors when making instructional decisions.

● The teacher appreciates individual variation within each area of development, shows respect for the diverse talents of all learners, and is committed to help them develop self-confidence and competence.

Standard 3 focuses on understanding individual student differences and addresses how teachers build safe and welcoming communities in their classrooms for all students. Indicators include the following:

- The teacher makes students feel valued for their potential as people and helps them learn to value each other.

- The teacher creates a learning community in which individual differences are respected.

Standard 5 focuses on creating effective learning environments. A relevant indicator is:

- The teacher takes responsibility for establishing a positive climate in the classroom and participates in maintaining such a climate in the school as a whole.

Finally, Standard 9 focuses on the role of reflection in meeting one's basic commitments to students. Indicators include the following:

- The teacher is willing to give and receive help.

- The teacher is committed to seeking out, developing, and continually refining practices that address the individual needs of students.

If you are in a state that follows a different set of teacher standards, find the state standards that most closely relate to the INTASC standards discussed here.

## READING ON...

Haynes, C. C., S. Chaltain, J. E. Ferguson, D. L. Hudson, and O. Thomas. (2003). *The first amendment in schools.* Alexandria, VA: Association for Supervision and Curriculum Development and the First Amendment Center. A succinct, readable description of major court cases related to the First Amendment and their implications for teachers. This book also describes the First Amendment Schools Project, whose purpose is to identify and fund schools that make a commitment to educating students for their roles as citizens in a democratic society.

Jackson, P. W., R. E. Boostrom, and D. T. Hansen. (1998). *The moral life of schools.* San Francisco: Jossey-Bass. Through a careful observation of elementary and secondary school classrooms, the authors illustrate teaching as a daily moral enterprise.

Watson, M. (2003). *Learning to trust.* San Francisco: Jossey-Bass. Describes one teacher's approach to creating a caring classroom based on strong trusting relationships.

Zubay, B., and J. F. Soltis. (2005). *Creating the ethical school.* New York: Teachers College Press. Case studies of daily ethical dilemmas in schools.

## Guiding Questions

- What are the tensions between teaching as a profession and teaching as a job?

- How is teaching becoming a more collaborative and public form of work?

- What kinds of leadership roles are developing for teachers?

- What is teacher research and how does it contribute to teachers' professional development?

- What is the National Board for Professional Teaching Standards?

- What is the role of networking in supporting a teacher's professional development?

- How do teachers set professional development goals?

- What challenges are on the horizon in education?

- How do you prepare for and find your first teaching position?

# Becoming a Teacher: New Visions and Next Steps

# 12

Darrell Jordan continues to be excited about his job teaching as a high school science teacher in a suburban school in California. When he interviewed for his position, both the principal and the science department chairperson said that they had been considering some new approaches to professional development for the next year. They asked Darrell if he would be comfortable having the other science teachers observe his teaching, and vice versa, and also if he would be comfortable spending one staff meeting per month analyzing student work. This sounded a lot like what Darrell had been doing in his teacher education program, but he was a little nervous about giving feedback to teachers who had so much more experience than he had.

Darrell's mentor, Crystal Hanlon, helped him set up his classroom, and they established a good relationship from the time they spent together planning. Now it's October, and Darrell is getting ready for the first meeting with the entire science faculty to discuss student work. Crystal has come by to see him on one of her regular weekly visits.

"I know I shouldn't be worried about this," Darrell began. "I've had some practice talking about student work with the other student teachers last year. And I really like the other science teachers. But doing this with a bunch of teachers who have been here longer than me is a little different than doing it in my teacher education program."

"They've already agreed that talking together about student work will be a good way to think about how well the science curriculum is working," Crystal said. "So the teachers have been moving in this direction already for professional development."

"But thinking about it and doing it are two different things," Darrell said. "What if they think that as the new kid on the block, I really don't have anything valuable to contribute?"

"I think it may be just the opposite," Crystal replied. "They may be looking to you because as a new teacher, you have the latest knowledge on many things. Like you said, you've already had some experience analyzing student work in your program. One thing you might think about is starting with the work of an average student who's having some problems, but not really challenging ones. If you're willing to talk about the way you're teaching a concept that an average student is struggling with, I bet the other teachers will be right there with you, talking about different ways to teach the concept. The key is to keep focused on discussing the student's work and the curriculum."

*If we expect today's teachers to become tomorrow's accomplished teachers, we must devote equal energy to building career paths that offer them the satisfactions of a rewarding profession. This means recruiting good teachers, supporting them with mentoring, sustaining them with professional growth opportunities and recognition, and rewarding them with pay that recognizes the value they provide to our nation.*

National Commission on Teaching and America's Future, 2003, p. 111

As he thought about it, Darrell had one more idea. "Maybe I'll also talk with the department chair, Tom, before the meeting, and just let him know that I'd prefer to listen to one round of discussion before I present the work I'm going to bring."

"Great idea, " Crystal said. "Why don't we look at that student's work together now to help you get ready?"

Y ou are entering teaching at a time when improving the quality of the teaching force is a major national goal, and efforts are being made to give teaching the status it deserves. More than ever before, the over 3 million teachers in the United States are entering into professional dialogue about their work and their students' progress—much like the meeting Darrell Jordan is preparing for with his colleagues in the science department. Within the profession, expectations are higher than ever before, based on the understanding that teaching is complex and that teachers "must exercise trustworthy judgment based on a strong base of knowledge" in order to prepare students for their role in a complex society (Bransford, Darling-Hammond, & Le Page, 2005, p. 2). Outside of the profession, politicians, through the No Child Left Behind Act, have weighed in on discussions of what it means to be a highly qualified teacher by requiring that teachers not be assigned to teach in fields in which they are not certified. Although various interpretations of what it means to be a professional may differ among different constituencies, there is no doubt that the quality of teaching is a major concern in United States today.

Yet a curious tension still exists in this country between treating teaching as the *profession* that it certainly is and treating it as a *job*, and this tension has existed for well over a century. Although substantial progress has been made in advancing the goals that mark teaching as a real profession, questions continue, suggesting that society is still ambivalent about the status of teaching. This chapter addresses some of the sources of this ambivalence; explains current efforts to increase the stature of teaching as a profession; describes specific practices that you can expect to see, participate in, and benefit from in terms of what it means to be a professional teacher; and helps you prepare for your transition from student to teacher.

## Your turn... *to reflect*

Write down the five most important reasons you want to become a teacher. Compare your reasons with those of some of your peers. Which of these reasons would suggest to you and your peers that teaching is a job? Which would suggest that it is a profession?

# The Profession/Job Conflict

What exactly is the tension between thinking of teaching as a *profession* and thinking of it as a *job*? How did this conflict emerge, and what is its legacy?

## Defining the Tension

As it is commonly understood, a **profession** requires specialized knowledge, skills, and preparation to carry out the responsibilities associated with it. Professionals are expected to draw on their knowledge and skills to make judicious decisions about their work—usually without directives from a supervisor. Professionals also often have high status in a society, and it is not unreasonable to say they are sometimes revered for the work they do. Teaching is not merely a technical occupation, doing what one is told or what comes next in the manual. Rather, it is a complex intellectual act that requires teachers, on a daily basis, to make professional judgments that directly affect the lives of the students they teach. If these professional qualities characterize teaching, why is it that so many people have for so long viewed teaching as more of a job than a profession?

Part of the answer is historical. First, education was long dominated by a hierarchy in which administrators were traditionally male in a workforce that traditionally was (and continues to be) largely female. Even though the earliest teachers in the colonies were male, beginning in the nineteenth century teaching became "feminized," especially as large city school districts began to be organized centrally (Rury, 1989). Women sought teaching jobs because it was one of the few kinds of employment available at a time when the idea of women in the workplace was not acceptable. Although teachers were often well versed in their profession and drew on their specialized knowledge and skills daily to educate their students, their work was not necessarily valued in a hierarchy headed by male superiors. From a societal perspective, teaching was seen pejoratively as low-status "women's work." Today 76 percent of the teaching force is female and 24 percent is male (Johnson, 2008). There is no doubt that the politics of gender has played a role in diminishing the social status of teaching (Clifford, 1989), undermining its role as a profession.

Second, and connected to the high numbers of women in teaching, salaries have traditionally been, and continue to be, low relative to with the responsibilities teachers are expected to carry out. Teachers' salaries have improved over time, but they are still low relative to salaries in other professions in the United States. Table 12-1 indicates that for 2004–2005, the average teacher salary for the 50 states was $47,602; average salaries span the range from a low of $34,039 in South Dakota to a high of $57,760 in Connecticut. In addition, the average beginning teacher salary for 2005–2006 was $31,753, with a range of $24,872 in North Dakota to $39,259 in Connecticut. (Table 12-1 also presents beginning salaries in each state.) Therefore, especially at the start of a teacher's career, low salaries are still common, which reinforces the image of teaching as a lower status occupation. Since teachers continue to be in demand, new arrangements for teachers are developing in some locations, such as sign-up bonuses or mortgage assistance. But these financial supports do not close the gap between initial teaching salaries and those of other comparable white-collar entry-level professionals (American Federation of Teachers, 2007).

Finally, conflicts still exist about how much empowerment teachers should have to make decisions about the curriculum, how schools should be run, and what schools should emphasize. For example, when school districts and principals select curriculums that devalue teacher knowledge and suggest that "anyone can teach" if they only follow the highly prescriptive directions of that curriculum, teacher professionalism is denigrated. As Chapter 5 indicated, some curriculums are created precisely because teachers are not trusted to know what and how to teach; these curriculums prescribe exactly what teachers are supposed to do, complete with

Teachers who are true professionals bring a high level of knowledge and skill to their work. (Tom Stewart/Corbis Images)

## Table 12-1  Average and Beginning Teacher Salaries by State, 2004–2005

Wide variation exists in teacher salaries across the 50 states.

| Rank | State | 2004–2005 Average Teacher Salary | Rank | State | 2004–2005 Beginning Teacher Salary |
|---|---|---|---|---|---|
| 1 | Connecticut | $ 57,760 | 1 | Connecticut | $ 39,259 |
| 2 | California | 57,604 | 2 | Alaska | 38,657 |
| 3 | New Jersey | 56,635 | 3 | New Jersey | 38,408 |
| 4 | Illinois | 56,494 | 4 | Illinois | 37,500 |
| 5 | Rhode Island | 56,432 | 5 | New York | 37,321 |
| 6 | New York | 55,665 | 6 | Maryland | 37,125 |
| 7 | Massachusetts | 54,688 | 7 | Delaware | 35,854 |
| 8 | Michigan | 53,959 | 8 | Hawaii | 35,816 |
| 9 | Pennsylvania | 53,281 | 9 | California | 35,760 |
| 10 | Delaware | 52,924 | 10 | Michigan | 35,557 |
| 11 | Alaska | 52,467 | 11 | Massachusetts | 35,421 |
| 12 | Maryland | 52,330 | 12 | Colorado | 35,086 |
| 13 | Ohio | 49,438 | 13 | Pennsylvania | 34,976 |
| 14 | Oregon | 48,320 | 14 | Georgia | 34,442 |
| 15 | Hawaii | 47,833 | 15 | Rhode Island | 33,815 |
| 16 | Minnesota | 47,411 | 16 | Texas | 33,775 |
| 17 | Indiana | 46,591 | 17 | New Mexico | 33,730 |
| 18 | Georgia | 46,437 | 18 | Oregon | 33,699 |
| 19 | Washington | 45,722 | 19 | Ohio | 33,671 |
| 20 | Virginia | 45,377 | 20 | Florida | 33,427 |
| 21 | Vermont | 44,346 | 21 | Virginia | 33,200 |
| 22 | Colorado | 43,965 | 22 | Tennessee | 32,369 |
| 23 | New Hampshire | 43,941 | 23 | Minnesota | 31,632 |
| 24 | North Carolina | 43,343 | 24 | Wyoming | 31,481 |
| 25 | Nevada | 43,212 | 25 | Alabama | 31,368 |
| 26 | Wisconsin | 43,099 | 26 | Louisiana | 31,298 |
| 27 | Florida | 43,095 | 27 | Washington | 30,974 |
| 28 | South Carolina | 42,189 | 28 | Indiana | 30,844 |
| 29 | Tennessee | 42,076 | 29 | Kentucky | 30,619 |
| 30 | Arkansas | 41,489 | 30 | Arizona | 30,404 |
| 31 | Kentucky | 41,075 | 31 | Nebraska | 29,303 |
| 32 | Texas | 41,009 | 32 | Missouri | 29,281 |
| 33 | Maine | 40,935 | 33 | Oklahoma | 79,174 |
| 34 | Idaho | 40,864 | 34 | Arkansas | 28,784 |
| 35 | Wyoming | 40,487 | 35 | South Carolina | 28,568 |
| 36 | Nebraska | 39,441 | 36 | New Hampshire | 28,279 |
| 37 | New Mexico | 39,391 | 37 | Mississippi | 28,200 |
| 38 | Kansas | 39,351 | 38 | Nevada | 27,957 |
| 39 | Iowa | 39,284 | 39 | North Carolina | 27,944 |
| 40 | Arizona | 39,095 | 40 | Kansas | 27,840 |
| 41 | Missouri | 39,064 | 41 | Idaho | 27,500 |
| 42 | Louisiana | 39,022 | 42 | Iowa | 27,284 |
| 43 | Montana | 38,485 | 43 | West Virginia | 26,704 |
| 44 | West Virginia | 38,404 | 44 | Maine | 26,643 |
| 45 | Mississippi | 38,212 | 45 | Utah | 26,521 |
| 46 | Alabama | 38,186 | 46 | Vermont | 26,451 |
| 47 | Oklahoma | 37,879 | 47 | South Dakota | 26,111 |
| 48 | Utah | 37,006 | 48 | Montana | 25,318 |
| 49 | North Dakota | 36,449 | 49 | Wisconsin | 25,222 |
| 50 | South Dakota | 34,039 | 50 | North Dakota | 24,872 |
| **U.S. Average 2004–2005** | | **$ 47,602** | **U.S. Average** | | **$ 31,753** |

**Source:** American Federation of Teachers. (2007). "*Survey and analysis of teacher salary trends 2005.*" Retrieved June 2, 2008, from http://www.aft.org/salary/index.htm.

**Your turn...** *to reflect*

Role-play the following situation. You are at a party and you have just been introduced to a new acquaintance. You begin talking together, and you tell this person that you are studying to become a teacher. He or she says to you, "That's an easy job. You only work six hours a day and you have summers off." How will you respond?

scripts for what they should say and, in some cases, even specific gestures teachers must use as they move their students through the lessons. Poorly prepared teachers may require this level of guidance, but the use of such programs is just another way of saying that teaching does not require highly skilled, knowledgeable professionals who are called upon to make complex judgments about their students.

Historical, economic, and societal forces such as these have contributed to the undervaluing of teaching—and continue to raise questions among the public as to whether teaching is a job or a profession. The lack of full professional status for teaching, coupled with the demands of preparing students for work in a complex, global world, which makes teaching ever more demanding, fuels the work of organizations such as the National Commission on Teaching and America's Future (1996, 2003); the two major teachers' organizations, the National Education Association and the American Federation of Teachers; and many others.

## Enduring Myths about Teaching

Alongside the conflict about whether teaching is a job or a profession are a number of persistent, misleading myths about teaching and the work of teachers. As a prospective teacher you have no doubt heard some of these myths.

**Myth #1:** *Anyone can stand up in front of a roomful of children and teach; how hard could it be?* This myth is based on the belief that all teachers need to do to be effective in the classroom is to stand up and talk—and that students will absorb all of the information and learn simply from listening to what the teacher says. In reality, as we have argued throughout this book, teachers must do far more than simply stand up and talk to ensure student learning. Instead, teachers must have deep knowledge in their subjects and in pedagogy, be able to deal with the complexities of the classroom, and make sound professional judgments about what it means to prepare students for the future.

The fact that all some teachers do is to stand up and talk, moving from one chapter in the textbook to the next in rote fashion, does not mean that this approach to teaching works well. It is true that just about anyone can do that, but such actions do not represent good teaching.

**Myth #2:** *As long as you know the content students are supposed to learn, you can be an effective teacher.* Although teachers must of course understand the content they are responsible for teaching, knowledge of content alone does not insure the teacher's ability to motivate and engage children to learn that content. Teachers who know their content but cannot explain and present it well are ineffective in the classroom. Instead, as we noted in Chapter 3, along with knowing content, teachers also need to master pedagogy—the skills of instructing students about the content knowledge they possess in a way that results in learning.

Arguing that content knowledge alone is sufficient devalues the professional knowledge a teacher needs and in so doing also devalues the profession. Those who believe that knowing content is enough fail to understand the day-to-day work of teachers, the role of pedagogical content knowledge in teaching, and the critical nature of teacher–student interactions in the classroom.

**Myth #3:** *Teachers work only six hours a day.* The formal, "legal" teaching day is a contractual agreement between teachers as represented by their organizations and local boards of education (where collective bargaining exists). The exact determination is arrived at during the collective bargaining process between the teachers' union and the school district. Teachers are usually required to report to school before the students arrive and stay after they leave, but the exact times are specified locally. The myth of the six-hour day is just that; the formal workday for teachers in 2001 was 7.4 hours (National Education Association, 2003). According to the Bureau of Labor Statistics (2004), teachers commonly spend more than 40 hours per week working in their profession, either directly with students or communicating with parents and families, planning instruction, grading student work, and the like.

So, as you can see, the myth that teachers have a short, easy workday is not reflected in the world of teaching practice. In reality, a teacher's work schedule does not differ markedly from the typical 40-hour workweek. However, teachers in the United States actually spend more face-to-face time with children and youth than do their peers in other industrialized countries, especially those at the elementary level (Nelson, 1994).

Teachers often work consecutive hours every day and during every one of their working hours are responsible for the lives of many, many students. Teaching, in fact, is the only profession where a single adult is in continuous contact with large groups of children who must constantly be supervised. More importantly, these children and youth not only must be supervised but must be guided effectively, with professional knowledge and skill, to ensure their learning.

**Myth #4:** *Teachers have summers off.* Most teachers work a 10-month year (Bureau of Labor Statistics, 2004). It is not unusual for teachers to spend time during their summer breaks taking additional coursework, often at their own expense, or engaging in other activities related to improving their professional knowledge and skills. It is also becoming increasingly common, during this era of school reform and restructuring, for teachers to participate in professional development activities sponsored by their school districts in the summer months. Districts often try to set aside funds for these kinds of activities during the summer.

Furthermore, teachers must prepare for their new classes in the summer before school starts. Typically, districts have a paid day or two available to teachers so that they can prepare for the new school year. However, anyone who has taught can tell you that it takes far more than a few days to prepare for the new school year, and this preparation often takes place during teachers' summer breaks.

## Beyond the Myths: Teaching as a Profession

The myths associated with teaching do not accurately represent the real work teachers do every day to improve the lives of children and youth in our schools. Those who denigrate teaching as an easy occupation with undue benefits often do not have a realistic view of what good teaching entails.

Professional organizations continue to seek recognition, in terms of higher salaries, professional status, and improved working conditions, in order to enable teachers to do their work well. Most teachers are dedicated professionals who go above and beyond what is expected to provide an effective learning environment for their students. People in every profession need to be monitored and followed to improve their practice, and every profession requires policies and practices to dismiss those who are incompetent. The fact that some teachers may not carry out their responsibilities professionally is not an excuse to fault the entire profession. The recognition of teaching as a full-fledged profession is long overdue.

Compared with how society has viewed teaching traditionally, how is the work of teachers changing with regard to what it means to be a professional teacher? What efforts are currently being made to increase the stature of teaching as a profession? What new roles do teachers have? The National Commission on Teaching and America's Future (NCTAF) was established in 1996 for the purpose of ensuring that every child in America's schools has a caring, competent, and qualified teacher by the year 2006. The development of a "professionalization agenda" for teaching is based on the goal of increasing the status of the profession.

Part of this commitment lies not only in increasing support to new teachers, but in creating opportunities for teachers to grow throughout their careers, assigning them roles that challenge them and help support the profession. This commitment to the profession signifies a change in the way teachers and nonteachers alike think about teaching. One of NCTAF's three major strategies, designed to address the importance of career-long retention of teachers in the profession, is "building a professionally rewarding career for all teachers" (NCTAF, 2003, p. 111). Several of the developments and opportunities described in the balance of this chapter are designed to do just that.

## Teaching as a Collaborative and More Public Form of Work

The traditional view of a teacher's day is that it is spent within the classroom's four walls, with anywhere from 25 to 40 students for the entire day, and few if any breaks. This is the dominant organizational pattern of schooling, often called the "egg crate" model, in which teachers are isolated from one another. Whether teachers are alone with one class all day (the elementary model), or alone with consecutive classes of students for several class periods a day (the secondary model), the egg crate model, where what goes on within the four walls of a classroom occurs in private, has long dominated our image of teaching. In this model, teachers' classrooms are their kingdoms, so to speak, with little input from anyone except perhaps an annual visit from the principal to complete a required evaluation.

Analyzing students' work together provides teachers with the opportunity to learn from each other in a collaborative professional community. (Robin Sachs/ Photo Edit)

The profession has long been organized so that teachers do not work with each other during the school day, nor have teachers traditionally been encouraged to do so. It was assumed that teachers had little need to work with other teachers. Nothing in the structure or culture of schooling required that teachers work with each other or participate in joint professional conversations about their work to improve the quality of their teaching.

As a result of the current movement to reform teaching and learning that began in the 1980s, both researchers and practitioners in education began to realize the value of having teachers work together to examine the quality of their

work. This was seen as a crucial strategy for school reform and professional improvement (Little, 2001). Attention began to be paid to creating more collaborative environments in schools, recreating them as places where teachers could continue to learn as part of a community of peers and ultimately be empowered to take greater responsibility for the quality of the school.

For example, a school staff might decide, after reflecting on the data on achievement of their students, that they need to work on improving the mathematical problem-solving abilities of their students. Rather than hosting a single lecture on this topic, they might instead agree to send two staff members to intensive training in the new mathematics curriculum, work with them on their return to try out the new methods in two grade levels as a start, have teachers observe each other as they use the new curriculum, and provide friendly feedback and constructive criticism about the mathematics lesson. In this way, teachers in the building engage in a joint commitment to improve their skills as mathematics teachers, and all teachers are committed to watching their peers teach and giving them suggestions for improving their practice. A school might form two or three such groups, focusing on different areas of student need or interest among its staff.

You can see how this approach creates a more stimulating professional environment, one in which teachers are co-responsible for improving teaching and learning in the school. This shift signals a move from a culture of individual, external professional growth to a **culture of collaboration** within a school and/or a district, where teachers work as part of a professional community dedicated to continuous learning. In addition to focusing professional development, collaboration can provide moral support, reduce overload, and make the entire school organization more capable of responding to changes and challenges (Hargreaves, 1994).

Ann Lieberman and Lynne Miller (1999) talk about creating an *ethic of collaboration* among teachers. An ethic of collaboration does not mean that teachers will always agree. Furthermore, collaboration does not mean that everyone is always working on the same professional growth task. As with any other team, teachers draw on their different strengths to help their students, and the school, move ahead. "But," as Lieberman and Miller state, "when teachers have opportunities to work, plan, and be together, they can achieve enhanced individual goals in their classrooms even as they are accomplishing collective ones for the school" (1999, p. 64). As teachers work in more collaborative school communities, they create ways to learn from each other and to enhance teaching and learning from the inside out—rather than assuming that the only important new knowledge to improve their work comes from the outside into the school. This represents a radical change in thinking about how teachers go on learning and places greater responsibility within the profession of teaching itself.

## Opening the Classroom Doors for Observation and Feedback

Directly related to the notion of collaboration is the fact that teaching is beginning to be a more public profession within schools and districts; the doors of teachers' classrooms are increasingly being opened. Once the doors are open, teachers can learn directly from watching each other teach, which becomes an important source of professional growth and development. In a professional culture of teaching, one that prizes learning from one another, teachers who are especially strong can be models for teachers who need to develop strength in a

**Critical Term**

**Culture of collaboration.**
A culture within a school organization that supports teachers working together and learning from one another to improve teaching and learning.

particular area. If a whole staff decides to move in a new direction instructionally, teachers can coach and observe one another as they all work to implement new teaching methods.

In the brief example offered above, teachers decided to work on improving their teaching of mathematics problem solving and agreed to observe each other and provide feedback. Teachers who participated had to be comfortable having their peers watch them teach for the express purpose of getting constructive criticism and ideas from their peers. Teachers today are expected to learn about each other's teaching by watching each other teach—rather than only by receiving advice in the teachers' lounge, in a hallway conversation, or in a before- or after-school meeting.

Today classroom doors are open, with teachers supporting one another to improve the quality of their work. (Will Hart/ Photo Edit)

Another development that is making teaching more public is the reemergence of team teaching. Team teaching was popular during the 1960s but diminished substantially recently. Today its use is related to: (1) the development of middle schools, (2) teaming of general and special education teachers, and (3) the need for a strategy to reduce class size. When teachers team, they necessarily observe each other teaching, and teaming thus becomes a significant change in how teachers do their work. Teachers who team automatically have access to, and can benefit from, a built-in form of professional feedback from their teaching partner that was unavailable when all teachers taught alone. Team teaching, then, is inherently collaborative, and done well can help strengthen the culture of professional collaboration within a school.

Finally, technology has also contributed to teaching becoming a more public, shared form of work. Technology has made possible, for example, video hook-ups that enable teachers and students in one school to tune in to a live classroom in another school. In this way, teachers can watch each other teach and learn from each other at the same time their students are interacting with another classroom in another part of the country or the world. Often these hook-ups enable teachers from different schools to conference with one another after their students are gone for the day. Schools can also use simple technologies such as videotaping as formats for sharing how teachers are implementing new approaches, especially when the school schedule does not permit in-person visits among teachers. Schools can structure professional development sessions during which each teacher shares a videotape of his or her teaching in a specific area of the curriculum, and peers provide feedback and support.

Technology has also increased the teachers' capacity to share their work through multiple websites. For example, the Apple Learning Interchange (**http://edcommunity.apple.com/ali**) features lessons and units created and implemented by accomplished teachers that draw on technology as a tool for enhancing their instruction. These "exhibits" are accompanied by videoclips of teachers in action, working directly with their students, and are available for anyone to see. Such websites offer new resources to those who are studying to teach as well as to veteran teachers. Teachers who create personal webpages also have a ready vehicle for sharing their work with other teachers.

## Philosophical Note
### Collaboration *and* Autonomy for Teachers

The philosophy of collaboration is widely accepted today as an overarching professional stance for teaching. Collaboration represents a major change in the way teachers work, and learning to collaborate is now a regular feature of many teacher education programs. Teacher education students may work together in a classroom during early clinical experiences to learn to share responsibility, or students may observe and provide feedback to one another on their skills. We see collaboration embedded in how general education teachers conduct their work, as well as in how general and special education teachers work together to create more effective learning for students with disabilities.

In addition to working collaboratively, teachers may also want to put their own individual, personal stamp on their teaching. The traditional isolation of teachers probably provided too much autonomy, but it also allowed teachers to create highly personal ways of teaching. Teachers' passions and personal interests often motivate them to teach, and they may, as Andy Hargreaves (1994) has observed, value working solo as a way of focusing on their subject matter, as well as on the energy and care it takes to sustain effective personal interactions with their students. How does the philosophy of collaboration fit in with teachers' desires to put their own personal signature on their teaching? How does a philosophy of collaboration fit in with the individual nature of teachers' relationships with their students?

A philosophy of collaboration does not require that teachers do everything together, nor does it mean that all teachers must teach in the same way all the time. Rather, collaboration means that teachers work within the framework that they are part of a school organization and that they have an obligation to contribute actively to the well-being of that organization. Students do not simply attend one classroom; they attend a school that also affects how they view their learning. Within the philosophy of collaboration there should be room to honor the individuality of teachers and their need for autonomy. However, that autonomy exists within a larger school culture that can both acknowledge the individuality of teachers and expect teachers to share what they are doing for the good of their students.

## Collaboration: A Shared Resource for Professional Dialogue

In today's increasingly professional environment, teachers have both the opportunity *and* the obligation to work together on curriculum, school reform, teaching teams, effective education for students with disabilities, and much more. These various forms of collaboration provide a shared basis for teachers to talk about and work on their teaching practice. When teachers watch each other teach and then participate in reflective follow-up discussions, they learn from their work. When teachers meet to share their progress in implementing new methods, they are helping each other improve the quality of everyone's teaching. When teachers meet regularly to talk about their students' progress in a specific subject area, they are working out the real problems of teaching with their professional peers. Each of these professional development strategies enables teachers to develop a shared commitment to improving teaching and learning, a shared vocabulary of professional work, and a shared view of what it means to participate in career-long professional development.

The key to developing a successful collaborative culture in schools is for teachers to learn to work well with the other adults on their staff. Collaboration cannot succeed if teachers do not trust each other as colleagues, as sources of constructive feedback, or as observers in their classrooms; trust enables them to take new risks that can lead to improving their schools (Bryk & Schneider, 2002). True collaboration does not take place simply because teachers watch each other teach or work jointly on the curriculum. Rather, these opportunities to work together must be rooted in a school culture that values such collaborative work.

## Historical Note
### The Emergence of Teachers' Organizations in the United States

Two teachers' organizations dominate the landscape of American education: the National Education Association (NEA), founded in 1857 as the National Teachers' Association, and the **American Federation of Teachers (AFT)**, founded in 1916 as the Teachers' International Union of America. Originally, these organizations served fundamentally different purposes. Membership in the NEA, which was a freestanding, unaffiliated organization, included teachers, school administrators, and university faculty in education. Although its members were chiefly classroom teachers, who were largely female, its leadership was made up primarily of school superintendents and professors of education, who were mostly male (Johnson & Boles, 2001). This reflected the traditional division of labor in education according to gender. By contrast, membership in the AFT, which was affiliated with the American Federation of Labor (AFL), was open to classroom teachers only. Because most classroom teachers were female, the leadership of local AFT unions differed considerably from that of the NEA, with local activist women teachers often in the lead, pressing for grassroots teacher leadership and attention to teachers' concerns about classrooms. Three of these early leaders were urban teachers: Margaret Haley of Chicago, Florence Rood of St. Paul, and Mary Barker of Atlanta (American Federation of Teachers, n.d.).

The NEA considered itself early on an organization of professionals separate from the world of labor unions. Its relatively conservative membership emphasized the NEA's role in improving teaching as a profession and viewed working to improve teachers' conditions and the conditions of schooling as a goal (Johnson & Boles, 2001). Those who belonged to the NEA clearly stated that they were not members of a union, deliberately separating themselves from the U.S. labor movement.

In contrast, the AFT combined its concern for the welfare of teachers "in the trenches"—that is, salaries and working conditions for the classroom teachers who made up its membership—with a deep concern for improving the quality of education and educational conditions for students. Thus, both organizations were concerned about improving the profession of teaching, but they were not equally vocal about working to improve the conditions of teaching and learning.

The difference in their roots set up a dichotomy between the NEA and the AFT that lasted into the 1960s, and the difference was profound. Once teachers began to win the right to collective bargaining, the landscape of teacher organizations began to change significantly. The first collective bargaining agreement for teachers

**Critical Term**

**American Federation of Teachers (AFT).** A teachers' union affiliated with the American Federation of Labor with 1.4 million members.

Teachers' unions have played an important role in raising the visibility of the profession. (Corbis Images)

was negotiated in 1962 on behalf of the teachers of New York City; the bargaining agent was the United Federation of Teachers, the AFT affiliate in New York City. The NEA actually opposed collective bargaining until the 1960s, when it slowly began to change from an organization dominated by administrators to one that more closely represented teachers (**http://weac.org/historybook/ contents.htm**). As more and more states began to pass laws allowing teachers to engage in collective bargaining, the NEA eventually became more aligned with the goals of the AFT in terms of its support for collective bargaining for teachers.

Although there are clear historical differences between the NEA and the AFT and their roots differ substantially, today both consider themselves to be "teachers' unions," engage in collective bargaining, work to improve the conditions of teaching and learning in schools, and participate in substantial political activity on behalf of teachers and the schools. In addition, both organizations have active professional development units that provide resources and support to classroom teachers.

These similarities have led to periodic talks about merging these two organizations and uniting their political and professional strength. Today the NEA has 3.2 million members, and the AFT has 1.4 million members. You can view a video documentary of the AFT at **http://www.aft.org/about/history/history- chapters.htm**.

## Teacher Leadership

Teaching is starting to gain greater status as a profession as teachers take on formal leadership roles that did not exist within the traditional school structure. These new roles are based on the assumption that accomplished teachers have important knowledge about teaching and important contributions to make to the profession. One such role, discussed in Chapter 3, is having teachers serve as clinical faculty members in teacher education programs.

As indicated in Table 12-2, teacher leaders are, first and foremost, good classroom teachers who have credibility with their peers. In other words, leadership is not divorced from classroom practice. Instead, it is a deep knowledge of and skill in classroom practice that lays the foundation for the kinds of teacher leadership that are emerging today. These developments in teacher leadership are providing new career paths for veteran teachers who do not view school administration as a suitable goal or match for their skills and interests but who want to advance in their profession. The Center for Teaching Quality (**www.teachingquality.org**) is committed to promoting teacher leadership and links high quality, experienced teachers in conducting practical research and demonstrating the voices of practicing teacher leaders in educational policy making. Three forms of teacher leadership that are becoming more commonplace are mentoring, coaching, and peer review of teaching.

## Table 12-2 Qualities of Teacher Leaders

First and foremost, teacher leaders are good teachers of students in their classrooms.

| Who is a teacher leader as a teacher? | Who is a teacher leader as a leader? |
|---|---|
| • Has significant experience and excellence in their field of teaching | • Can influence school culture through relationships by building trust and rapport |
| • Has extensive knowledge of teaching, learning, and curriculum | • Is supportive of colleagues and promotes their professional growth |
| • Has a clear philosophy of education | |
| • Is creative and innovative; seeks challenges, risks, and lifelong learning; and is enthusiastic about teaching | • Is an effective communicator with good listening skills |
| • Assumes responsibility for actions | • Handles conflict, knows how to negotiate and mediate |
| • Is respected, valued, and viewed as competent by colleagues | • Is effective dealing with group process |
| • Is sensitive to others | • Can assess, interpret, and prioritize needs and concerns of teachers and the district |
| • Is flexible both cognitively and affectively | |
| • Is hardworking, manages workload, and has strong administrative skills | • Has the ability to diagnose organizations and the big issues within the organization |
| • Can build trust and rapport with colleagues | • Sees broad impact of decisions made by administrators and teachers |

**Source:** Adapted from York-Barr, J., and K. Duke. (2004). What do we know about teacher leadership? *Review of Educational Research, 74,* 255–316.

## Mentoring as Teacher Leadership

One robust example of teacher leadership is **mentoring** new teachers. As we noted in Chapter 3, once teacher education students complete their preservice programs, their knowledge and skills are still fragile, and they usually need support in order to gain confidence in their practice. To ensure their success and to help retain new teachers in the profession, the term *induction* describes a period of support to teachers in their first years of teaching. Mentors are accomplished veteran teachers who have demonstrated their knowledge and skills and who also can work well with novice teachers during this induction period to support their growth and development.

Induction is a broad term that refers to any kind of support that is provided to new teachers so they can have a successful start in their careers. Mentoring is a more specific term that refers to the help provided by an identified veteran teacher who has as part or all of his or her job supporting new teachers. Twenty-five states require all new teachers to participate in state-funded mentoring programs (Education Week, 2008). However, the fact that 25 states provide mentoring programs does not mean that they necessarily provide full funding for mentors, so the amount of time a new teacher has with a mentor can vary significantly from state to state and district to district.

An important study indicated that the more induction support new teachers have, the more likely they are to remain in teaching. Figure 12-1 indicates the various combinations of supports that were provided to the teachers in this study.

**Critical Term**

**Mentoring.** Providing expert, veteran teachers to support new teachers in the induction years so that they can gain confidence and strengthen their teaching skills, and stay in teaching.

**Figure 12-1    Predicted Probability of First-Year Turnover Depending on Level of Induction Support**

Turnover includes teachers who leave the profession and teachers who move to positions in other schools and districts.

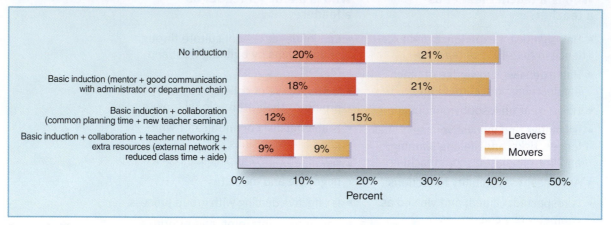

Source: Smith, T., & R. Ingersoll. (2004). "What are the effects of induction and mentoring on beginning teacher turnover?" *American Educational Research Journal*, 41, 681–714.

What do mentors do? Specifically what supports do they provide? According to the New Teacher Center located at the University of California at Santa Cruz, mentors "observe and coach the new teacher, offer emotional support, assist with short- and long-term planning, design classroom management strategies, teach demonstration lessons, provide curriculum resources, and facilitate communication with the principal. Advisors and new teachers keep an interactive journal to enhance communication, problem solve and reflect" (New Teacher Center, n.d.). It takes a highly skilled veteran teacher to provide high-quality support in these areas, and it is critical that mentors be able to respond to the needs of the beginning teachers they serve. Mentors themselves can benefit from participating with other mentors in a community of learners in order to ensure that their own practice is of the highest quality (Carver & Katz, 2004). Further, a single veteran teacher may not have expertise in all the different areas of support a new teacher requires, so shared responsibility for new teachers is also important.

Finally, mentoring is based on the idea of a staged entry into a teaching career rather than on the assumption that new teachers can readily take on all the responsibilities of veteran teachers. When the first years of teaching are acknowledged formally as induction, and when formal support is provided in the form of mentoring, the career of teaching begins to become differentiated, with defined levels of support and responsibility throughout the career. As we will see later in this chapter, such differentiation can begin to lead to differentiated salaries for teachers, thus creating a real career ladder within the ranks of the profession.

## Coaching as Teacher Leadership

Another emerging leadership role is teacher coaching. In some school districts, teachers are formally designated as teacher coaches for various content areas. Literacy coaches have as their job *not* to work directly with a class or special group of students to teach reading and writing, but rather to provide professional development for teachers on site in the schools to improve their teaching skills in literacy (Sturtevant, 2003).

The tasks of literacy coaches might include (1) modeling appropriate practices in literacy by demonstrating teaching in the classrooms of other teachers, (2) observing teachers and providing feedback, (3) analyzing samples of students' literacy work with a team of classroom teachers to identify how to support students who are struggling, (4) providing school-based expertise on topics relevant to the needs of the school's literacy program, or (5) following up on those workshops in the classrooms of participating teachers. Coaches work in classrooms to provide direct support and professional development not just to new teachers, but to any teacher who is developing or strengthening new approaches to literacy teaching. Coaching models such as these can exist in other content areas as well.

Coaches provide what is called **job-embedded professional development**. This means that the development of practicing teachers goes on within their classroom and their school as a regular part of their work. This approach contrasts with one-shot lectures that have in the past been provided as professional development for teachers. The coaching model is built on the assumption that to keep their practice current and to improve the quality of their teaching, novice and veteran teachers alike require ongoing professional development that is directly related to their daily work in classrooms. Instead of assuming that outside consultants are the main source of expertise, the coaching model recognizes that there is substantial expertise among expert, veteran practicing teachers that can be drawn on to help other teachers. Job-embedded professional development does not bypass the expertise of educators at universities and colleges. Instead, districts often partner with universities and colleges to offer courses and workshops that are directly connected to areas in which the school wishes to improve and in which coaches provide follow-up support.

### Critical Term

**Job-embedded professional development.** Providing support to teachers to develop their skills in the context of their classrooms with the support of other professionals who work directly in their classrooms demonstrating, observing, and providing feedback.

## Your turn... *to review*

1. Name one reason the profession of teaching has been undervalued.
2. What is one professional benefit of team teaching?
3. Identify at least two forms of teacher leadership and the professional development opportunities they provide.

## Peer Review of Teaching as Teacher Leadership

Another form of teacher leadership, **peer assistance and review**, refers to having skilled veteran teachers provide support for teachers who are having difficulty carrying out their responsibilities well. Coaching and mentoring exist to support the professional development of all teachers. In contrast, peer assistance and review extends the notion of teachers helping other teachers by adding the professional responsibility of intervening specifically with those who are not performing well and, if the situation does not improve sufficiently, to counsel them out of teaching. With the inception of these programs, the responsibility for monitoring the quality of the profession no longer resides exclusively with principals but with teachers themselves. This is another sign of increased professionalism in teaching (Anderson & Pellicer, 2001).

The process of nominating a teacher for intervention owing to poor performance is usually negotiated in the teachers' contract if collective bargaining applies. Typically, principals nominate teachers for participation. In the award-winning program founded in Columbus, Ohio, teachers may also refer themselves for this assistance (Columbus Education Association, 2001). In

### Critical Term

**Peer assistance and review.** Observation and review of experienced teachers who are having trouble carrying out their responsibilities, conducted by other teachers, as a way of monitoring the quality of the teaching force.

Peer assistance and review programs are designed to help experienced teachers who are struggling as they carry out their professional responsibilities. (Robin Sachs/ Photo Edit)

this program, teachers can refer other teachers but must do so through the union's building representative. By negotiating these programs carefully, safeguards are put into place to ensure that a referral is based solely on professional performance and is not made for personal reasons.

Peer assistance programs for struggling teachers represent the profession's serious commitment to taking responsibility for the quality of teaching. With peer assistance and review, greater control resides with the teachers themselves.

## Teacher Leadership and the New Teacher Unionism

Through these new leadership roles, teachers have made a leap forward in the effort to identify teaching as a real profession. This progress would be difficult to achieve, however, without the support of teachers' unions. Historically, teachers' unions were not comfortable having teachers evaluate each other by watching each other teach. However, several local unions eventually softened this position when they began to recognize that for teaching to gain the status of a profession, teachers themselves had to begin taking responsibility for improving its quality.

Programs such as mentoring, coaching, and peer assistance enable teachers to take leadership roles across the whole continuum of teacher learning throughout their careers—from supporting new teachers to making sure that poor teachers who cannot improve are given support and an opportunity to improve, and, if not, are not allowed to continue teaching.

Although not all teachers' unions have moved in this direction, the trend is clear. The *Teacher Union Reform Network*, or TURN, is a coalition of progressive teachers' unions that share ideas and serve as a resource nationally for unions wishing to move toward professionalization. TURN has a website that links the webpages of local unions involved in what is sometimes called the "new teacher

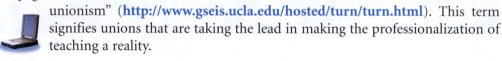

unionism" (**http://www.gseis.ucla.edu/hosted/turn/turn.html**). This term signifies unions that are taking the lead in making the professionalization of teaching a reality.

# Teachers as Researchers

Another way teachers demonstrate their professionalism is by gathering data systematically, analyzing it, and drawing conclusions that work to improve their own educational practice. In so doing, they may become wiser about what it means to teach (Feldman & Atkin, 1995).

Teachers who study their practice systematically are actually conducting research. Research conducted by teachers at the school level differs from traditional university-based research in several ways (Cochran-Smith & Lytle, 1993). First, research conducted by teachers is defined around problems and issues teachers see as important for themselves and the learning of their students, rather than having someone else decide what is important to study. Next, teacher research is conducted "in the heat of combat" (Corey, 1953, p. 142)— that is, right where teachers do their work and not at a distance from work, as university research may be. In addition, teachers conduct their research with few resources, little money, and no released time from their teaching responsibilities.

**Your turn...** *to reflect*

When you think of the term "research," what images come to mind? What purposes do you associate with the term as it pertains to teaching and the schools? Have you ever been involved in a research project in education? What was its purpose?

Finally, the results of research done by teachers are used in their own classrooms or schools, unlike university-based research which often has as its goal applying results across educational settings.

Having teachers conduct research on their own teaching is not a new concept. In the 1950s Stephen Corey (1953), a professor of education at Teachers College at Columbia University in New York City, was instrumental in promoting **teacher research**. Although teacher research languished from about 1960 to 1980, it began to enjoy a renaissance in the 1980s (Noffke & Stevenson, 1995). Today it is recognized as one of the most important ways to help teachers learn from their own practice over the life of their careers (Darling-Hammond & Hammerness, 2005). Teacher research also has an active following in England and in Australia, where some of the most prolific activities to support such work are taking place.

### How Do Teachers Conduct Their Own Research?

Just thinking about your own teaching or asking questions about it is different from actually studying it. It is only when teachers study teaching *systematically and intentionally* to reflect on and improve their practice, and when they share the results of their research with their peers, that they are engaging in teacher research (Cochran-Smith & Lytle, 1993). Table 12-3 illustrates three ways teachers can participate in systematic inquiry into, and a deeper understanding of, teaching.

The first, *action research*, perhaps most closely resembles what we think of as research. In this strategy, which can also be thought of as classroom or school studies, teachers pose specific questions, systematically implement new methods or new strategies, collect data in their classroom or school to provide insight into the question they want to answer, and analyze the data to determine whether the changes they have implemented improve their students' learning. Then they use their findings to improve their teaching skills. Data may include, for example, student work or videotapes of teachers teaching using a new approach. Action research is the specific form of teacher research Stephen Corey popularized in the 1950s and the form of teacher research that is so common in England and Australia.

In the second strategy, *oral inquiry*, teachers agree to prepare and present information about a particular student and work with a group of peers to deepen their understanding of the situation. The student's work and the teacher's analysis of that work in relation to his or her own teaching become the source of data for analysis, but the analysis takes place in a discussion format with other teachers, who bring their own insights to the discussion. Oral inquiry helps teachers gain a deeper understanding of the specific student or situation that is the focus of the discussion.

Finally, teachers can keep *journals* related to their work. Rereading one's journal allows teachers to look for patterns in their own teaching, to consider specific students who pose particular challenges, or to reflect on new methods or curriculum.

**Critical Term**

**Teacher research.** Research conducted by teachers in their own classrooms or school settings for the purpose of systematically studying their teaching and taking action to improve it.

## Table 12-3    Different Ways Teachers Can Inquire into Their Own Practice

Teachers can inquire into their practice in the following ways.

| Form of Inquiry into Teaching | Purpose | Benefit | Learning Potential for Teachers |
|---|---|---|---|
| **Action Research (classroom or schoolwide studies)** | Exploration of practice-based issues using data from observation, interview, or analysis of documents (e.g., curriculum, lesson plans) | Data collected about problem or issue as a basis for reflection, analysis, deeper understanding, and action | Refining/ improving methods of teaching |
| **Oral Inquiry** | Oral exploration into and examination of classroom/school issues and experiences; collaboration with peers | Shared insights with and learning from peers regarding student learning as a basis for deeper understanding and action | Solving/addressing specific problems of practice and student learning with peers |
| **Journals** | Accounts of classroom life over time; may be records of observation, analyses of experiences, or reflections and interpretations of practice | Written record that can be reviewed and analyzed as a basis for deeper understanding and action | Valuing own insights as a basis for improving practice |

**Source:**  Adapted by permission of the publisher from Cochran-Smith, M., and S.Lytle, *Inside outside: Teacher research and knowledge.* (New York: Teachers College Press, © 1993 by Teachers College, Columbia University. All right reserved.), p. 27.

Some teacher research is conducted to improve the conditions of education for those who are powerless in society—that is, from a social justice perspective. Although this type of teacher research relies on the same strategies and methods as teacher research in general, the questions teachers pose and the motivation they have are rooted in a deep social consciousness and a desire to make schools more democratic. When teacher research is viewed from the perspective of social justice, it "acknowledges . . . that educational (and other) lives are filled with injustices—and a moral and ethical stance that recognizes the improvement of human life as a goal" (Noffke, 1995, p, 4).

Teacher research is based on the belief that good teachers are continuously involved in a cycle of reflection, action, and improvement. Being involved in teacher research, then, does not mean that what teachers are doing before they begin their inquiries is wrong. Rather, teacher research is based on the assumption that teaching is complex and challenging, and that "understandings and actions emerge in a constant cycle, one that always highlights the ways in which educators are partially correct, yet in continual need of revision, in their thoughts and actions" (Noffke & Stevenson, 1995, p. 4). In the following Case in Point, a teacher uses action research to improve her writing program.

## A Case In Point
### Yolanda's Research on Teaching Writing in a Middle School Language Arts Class

Yolanda Rivera is a sixth grade middle school language arts teacher. She is in her third year of teaching in a middle school for grades 6–8. The school is located in a town of about 25,000 people located two hours from New York City. Her students represent a mix of racial and ethnic backgrounds, including students whose families are from Mexico, China, the Dominican Republic, Japan, and Vietnam, as well as a group of students who are African American. All of her students are fluent in English; many speak their family's native language as well.

In her first two years of teaching, Yolanda followed the district's language arts curriculum without much deviation. The writing curriculum in her district was based on providing predetermined prompts, or starters, to her students and also teaching them a five-paragraph approach to writing. Yolanda's students could write using this format, but she also noticed that this approach did not really motivate them and that their writing was flat. Because her students kept personal journals that they shared with her, she knew that they had a lot of important things to say and were curious about many important issues. These issues included immigration, bilingual education, and cultural issues between them and their parents. But her students did not delve into these issues in their formal writing assignments. Instead, they seemed to treat writing like an assignment to be gotten over with—rather than an opportunity to express their real opinions or describe their experiences in any depth.

The summer before Yolanda's third year of teaching, a group of veteran teachers from her school took a course in action research at a local university. They were required to carry out an action research project during the fall semester, and they invited other teachers in the building to participate. Yolanda thought this was a perfect opportunity to experiment with her writing curriculum to see if she could improve her students' motivation to write and the quality of their writing. She was familiar with other ways of teaching writing, but no one else in the building used them, and, as a new teacher, she had been reluctant to buck the status quo. She believed that the action research group would give her the confidence she needed to move beyond the existing writing curriculum. Another English teacher was also interested in working on writing, so they decided to work together to increase their students' motivation in writing by allowing them to write about topics they were interested in instead of set prompts, by modeling the writing process, and by introducing peer editing. Working with the group, Yolanda and her partner defined their action research project and identified the strategies they wanted to implement in their classrooms. They would compare students' writing from the past spring to the writing they would do in the fall.

The action research inquiry group met for an hour every two weeks. Yolanda was able to share and get feedback on her concerns about the students' current achievement as well as her plans for her action research project. She was also able to get regular feedback on her progress from her peer teachers in the action research group. As they analyzed the students' new writing, Yolanda and her partner observed major improvements in their students' interest. Their work was longer and more descriptive, and once they received feedback they eagerly got back to work. Students also began generating topics for future writing projects;

one student was selected to keep a class journal of potential topics. However, Yolanda noted that the students needed additional support on some of the grammatical aspects of their writing. So, for the third cycle of her action research project, she included several explicit mini-lessons on various grammatical structures that were causing her students the greatest difficulty.

Yolanda reported on her project at a midyear staff meeting in her building, where other members of her group also presented their work. The principal was so impressed that she encouraged others to join the group. The principal also said she would be willing to devote one staff meeting a month to working on action research projects instead of holding a typical staff meeting, where often teachers sat and listened to announcements and information. More importantly, the principal began talking to Yolanda and her partner about how they were teaching writing and asked them to share their work in a smaller group setting with the other language arts teachers in the building.

## Why Is Teacher Research a Sign of Increased Professionalism?

At this point you may be asking yourself why research conducted by teachers is so important. Why don't we just leave research to the professional researchers at the university level?

When teachers study their own teaching, they are agreeing to make inquiring into the quality of their work a regular part of their professional practice. Teachers who participate in their own research are saying that they want to take responsibility for improving the quality of their own work—which is one of the hallmarks of a profession. Rather than waiting for an administrator to observe them and tell them whether they are doing a good job, teachers who do research begin to take charge of improving their own work and, working collegially, that of their own school as well.

Teacher research also brings status to the profession because it is based on the assumption that teachers *themselves*, based on their own systematic study, have valuable knowledge to share with the larger education community about what constitutes good teaching and learning. When research takes place at the university alone, ownership of the research agenda—and the power associated with that ownership—also exists only within the university. Teachers are accordingly always seen as being in the position of receiving research-based information from university researches. Teacher research changes the balance of power, altering not only the perception others have of the profession, but also teachers' perceptions of their own status (Feldman & Atkin, 1995). Teachers can team with university-based researchers as partners, with research questions being defined by teachers themselves.

Finally, when teacher research is considered to be a legitimate form of professional development, administrators are challenged to create conditions in schools that support teachers conducting research. Districts might consider, for example, supporting action research teams as a sanctioned form of professional development. When a district chooses to sponsor such groups, it may decide to pay for substitute teachers so that those involved in research can meet to work on their studies, as well as to support the costs of printing and distributing the reports teachers prepare on the results of their work (Caro-Bruce & McCreadie, 1995).

The renaissance that teacher research is enjoying today indicates that teachers themselves can and do contribute important knowledge about teaching. The extent to which teacher research is considered a serious undertaking is reflected in the greater number of teachers presenting their research at academic meetings once dominated by university-based researchers. The Teachers Network at **www.teachersnetwork.org** includes a link to examples of teachers' action research under the "Teacher Research" link.

# Recognizing Accomplished Teaching through the National Board for Professional Teaching Standards

One of the most significant developments in improving society's views on teaching was the establishment, in 1987, of the **National Board for Professional Teaching Standards (NBPTS)**. The mission of the NBPTS is to "advance the quality of teaching and learning by: maintaining high and rigorous standards for what accomplished teachers should know and be able to do, providing a national voluntary system certifying teachers who meet these standards, and advocating related education reforms to integrate National Board Certification in American education and to capitalize on the expertise of National Board Certified Teachers" (NBPTS, 2008a). That is, the NBPTS provides a means of identifying "accomplished teachers" from among experienced teachers who volunteer to undergo a rigorous assessment of their teaching judged by their peers. The NBPTS defines "accomplished" by a set of specific standards for various levels and content areas of teaching, all based on five core propositions adopted by the NBPTS, listed in Table 12-4.

Teachers are eligible for National Board certification if they have a bachelor's degree and have successfully completed three years of teaching in a public or private school. Those who volunteer to be assessed for NBPTS certification prepare a portfolio based on analyses of videotaped segments of teaching and take a test of content knowledge for the area in which they seek to be certified. Once obtained, board certification is good for 10 years. The NBPTS offers certification in 25 areas of specialization in PK–12 teaching, including special education.

What makes National Board certification such a watershed concept in the educational system and in the profession of teaching? Perhaps its most important aspect is its delineation of levels of teaching skill. Historically, teaching has been a flat profession with no formal differentiation between highly skilled and less highly skilled classroom teachers in terms of title, pay, or recognition. Traditionally, the only way to move up in the profession was to leave the classroom and take a position in administration—either in central administration of a school district or in building administration as a principal. Or a teacher might decide to move into higher education, teaching at a university in a school or college of education. Needed was a career ladder that acknowledges and values teachers' high levels of expertise and draws on teachers' ability to provide leadership to other classroom teachers. The NBPTS serves this function.

To be sure, on an informal basis, both principals and other teachers have always known which teachers have well-honed expertise in which areas, and informally highly skilled teachers such as these have always provided invaluable assistance to their peers and to new teachers. But structurally and in terms of formal acknowledgment and pay, teachers wanting to "get ahead" were unable to do

**Critical Term**

**National Board for Professional Teaching Standards (NBPTS).** An organization that reviews representative work of experienced teachers to determine whether their work merits their gaining board certification as accomplished teachers.

**Table 12-4   Five Core Propositions of the National Board for Professional Teaching Standards**

These propositions describe the ways accomplished, Board-certified teachers practice the work of teaching.

| Core Proposition | NBPTS Teachers: |
|---|---|
| **Proposition 1:** Teachers are committed to students and their learning. | • are dedicated to making knowledge accessible to all students and believe all students can learn.<br>• treat students equitably, recognize the individual differences that distinguish their students from one another, and take account of these differences.<br>• understand how students develop and learn.<br>• respect the cultural and family differences students bring to their classroom.<br>• are concerned with their students' self-concept, motivation, and the effects of learning on peer relationships.<br>• are concerned with the development of character and civic responsibility. |
| **Proposition 2:** Teachers know the subjects they teach and how to teach those subjects to students. | • have mastery over the subject(s) they teach. They have a deep understanding of the history, structure, and real-world applications of the subject.<br>• have skill and experience in teaching subjects and are familiar with the skills, gaps, and preconceptions students may bring to the subject.<br>• are able to use diverse instructional strategies to teach for understanding. |
| **Proposition 3:** Teachers are responsible for managing and monitoring student learning. | • deliver effective instruction. They move fluently through a range of instructional techniques, keeping students motivated, engaged, and focused.<br>• know how to engage students to ensure a disciplined learning environment, and how to organize instruction to meet instructional goals.<br>• know how to assess the progress of individual students as well as the class as a whole.<br>• use multiple methods for measuring student growth and understanding, and clearly explain student performance to parents. |
| **Proposition 4:** Teachers think systematically about their practice and learn from experience. | • model what it means to be an educated person—they read, question, create, and are willing to try new things.<br>• are familiar with learning theories and instructional strategies and stay abreast of current issues in American education.<br>• critically examine their practice on a regular basis to deepen knowledge, expand their repertoire of skills, and incorporate new findings into their practice. |
| **Proposition 5:** Teachers are members of learning communities. | • collaborate with others to improve student learning.<br>• are leaders and actively know how to seek and build partnerships with community groups and businesses.<br>• work with other professionals on instructional policy, curriculum development, and staff development.<br>• can evaluate school progress and the allocation of resources in order to meet state and local education objectives.<br>• know how to work collaboratively with parents to engage them productively in the work of the school. |

**Source:** Reprinted with permission from the National Board for Professional Teaching Standards, *What teachers should know and be able to do*, www.npbts.org. All rights reserved.

so unless they left the classroom. The NBPTS makes it possible for accomplished teachers to put themselves to the test by participating in the process of National Board certification.

Thirty-eight states provide some form of financial incentive for teachers who achieve National Board certification (Education Week, 2008). Other incentives, though not financial, are substantial nevertheless. Incentives to obtain NBPTS certification include:

● **Salary supplements.** Salary supplements are a major incentive to teachers who achieve Board certification. These supplements can be provided by the state, the local school district, or both. They range widely from state to state and district to district; a full description of incentives by state is available on the NBPTS website. In North Carolina, for example, Board-certified teachers receive a 12 percent salary increment for each year of their 10-year license. In Kansas, teachers receive a stipend of $1000 each year they are certified. In Montana, teachers are given a one-time additional stipend of $3000.

● **Fee support.** Many states and local districts cover all or part of the fees required to participate in the certification process. The cost of participating in the process is currently $2500.

● **Renewal of teaching license.** In most states, teachers have to renew their licenses regularly as a means of ensuring that their skills are current. In many states, meeting the requirements of Board certification counts for the renewal of a teaching license or for required continuing education credits that a state might require.

● **License portability.** In the majority of states, plus the District of Columbia, Board-certified teachers can teach in these states in the area in which they are certified, no matter what state is the origin of their original teaching license. This is a very significant change in policy and practice in teaching.

These incentives signify an important shift in how the profession of teaching is conceptualized. When accomplished teachers receive different levels of pay for their work, the profession begins to be differentiated not only in terms of recognition (i.e., Board certification) but also in terms of salary. The concept of differential pay was never systematically implemented in teaching until the advent of financial incentives for those certified by the NBPTS. School districts are now experimenting with differential roles for Board-certified teachers, for example, asking them to voluntarily take positions to help turn around struggling schools and providing additional pay for doing so.

The NBPTS maintains an extensive website that provides information about board certification, which states offer which incentives, as well as a list of every teacher, by state, who has received this designation (**www.nbpts.org**). It holds an annual national conference for teachers who are certified, provides networking opportunities, and works with local colleges and universities to support candidates who are volunteering to take on the challenge of preparing their portfolios for National Board assessment.

In 1994, the first year that teachers could participate in these assessments, 86 teachers successfully completed the process and were certified by the NBPTS; in 2002, that number rose to about 24,000 teachers (NBPTS, 2008). Today the total number of teachers who are Board-certified stands at about 64,000 (NBPTS, 2008b). The states with the highest number of Board-certified teachers are North Carolina, Florida, and South Carolina, accounting for a total of approximately

38,000 NBPTS teachers. There is no question that the NBPTS has established itself as a major force for America's teachers today. As more states provide monetary rewards for teachers who achieve board certification, it is likely that more teachers will attempt to achieve this status. Early on in the history of the NBPTS the participation of teachers from racial and ethnic minority groups was quite low, but the organization created a diversity initiative that has resulted in increased numbers of Board-certified teachers who are African American, Asian, Hispanic, and American Indian teachers.

National Board certification has raised the visibility of teaching in a very real way, but it does have its critics. For example, should a teacher who has been teaching for only three years be eligible to apply for the designation of "accomplished" teacher? Is there a great enough distinction between the standards that have been developed for beginning teachers, as represented by INTASC, and the standards for the National Board? Is the NBPTS assessment process so writing-intensive that assesses a candidate's writing ability rather than teaching ability? Despite these criticisms, the National Board for Professional Teaching Standards is an important asset in increasing the status of the teaching profession.

## Digging Deeper
### Differentiated Pay for Teachers?

For teachers, moving up the salary scale has always been based on two things: (1) by staying in their jobs—or for providing years of service; and (2) by taking courses—sponsored either by a university or the local district—and gaining credits or advanced degrees. Neither of these approaches depends on the quality of a teacher's performance in the classroom. To increase accountability for teachers' performance, a trend that is gaining some visibility is differentiating pay teachers receive based on their performance. This "pay for performance" trend represents a radical change in the dominant philosophy of teacher compensation. Rather than having all teachers earn the same raises over time regardless of the quality of their teaching, the philosophy of differentiating teachers according to their performance calls for distinctions to be made among teachers and differential pay based on these distinctions. Seven states have programs or pilot programs tying pay to raising student achievement (Education Week, 2008), often called "merit pay". Programs that compensate teachers based on various aspects of their performance, rather than moving all teachers up the salary scale, are known as **differentiated compensation** for teachers.

**Pro and Con:** Advocates of differentiated compensation argue that spending money on teachers who are not effective, year after year, is not a wise use of resources. Furthermore, treating all teachers the same in terms of salary, when it is obvious that not all teachers are equally effective, fails to promote accountability or professionalism for teachers. Especially in an era of financial stress, paying for ineffective teaching is not deemed appropriate.

Opponents of differentiated compensation argue that there is no satisfactory way to determine the meritorious performance of teachers. Teachers work in school and district environments they do not control that may negatively affect their ability to perform well. For example, they may work for incompetent principals whose schools are not functioning well overall. They may be required to use a curriculum that is ineffective. They may have unusually challenging students in a particular year. They may team with an incompetent teaching partner. Under

**Critical Term**

**Differentiated compensation.** Pay for teachers based on various aspects related to the quality of their performance rather than only on years of service and course credits taken.

these circumstances, it may be difficult to perform well and receive a pay increase for good performance. Further, basing salary decisions only on test scores, as some states do, does not take into account these conditions.

**The Nuances:** Distinguishing between simplistic differentiation based solely on student achievement scores on standardized tests and more complex approaches to differentiated compensation is appropriate.

In creating a salary system that is differentiated, test scores need not be the sole measure of a teacher's meritorious performance—or even any measure of it. Instead, teachers' unions and school districts, which have to negotiate such differentiated compensation programs, can introduce multiple measures of teacher quality to begin to develop differentiated compensation systems. For example, the Columbus, Ohio, school district and the Columbus Education Association experimented with a program in which teachers could create action research projects for their own classrooms in specified areas of the curriculum that the district and the teachers' union decided needed attention. If the projects were successful in increasing students' achievement, teachers were eligible to receive additional pay. Columbus also experimented with a plan to award additional pay to the staff of an entire school if test scores increased, with built-in special considerations for schools with high populations of challenging students.

The Denver Public Schools and the Denver Classroom Teachers Association (DCTA) created a completely new approach to teacher compensation known as ProComp, or the Professional Compensation System for Teachers. This compensation system, approved by the DCTA in 2004, is considered to be a historic landmark in the field of teacher compensation. Teachers would receive differentiated salary levels for professional development study, advanced degrees, and tuition reimbursement; professional evaluation based on new teacher evaluation tools; market incentives, including teaching in fields that are hard to staff and in schools that are hard to serve; and student growth, including meeting annual objectives for students based on agreements between the principal and the teachers, test data for grades required to take state mandated standardized tests, and distinguished performance by a school (Denver Public Schools, 2005). Each of these aspects of the program is connected to a proposed salary increase.

**Rethinking the Issue:** New approaches to teacher salaries based on teacher performance need not be defined only as comparing test scores for individual teachers or individual schools. As the examples above illustrate, teachers' unions and school districts can develop plans that enable teachers to take much greater responsibility for the quality of their work and be compensated based on a variety of performances. However, teachers need to be vigilant that the use of standardized test scores in isolation is not the criterion for differential pay.

# The Role of Networking in Professional Growth and Development

A final form of professional development that is emerging as an important source of professional growth and reflection is teacher networking. Teacher networks link together teachers who have similar interests—in a particular content area or a particular interest area (e.g., multicultural education). They give teachers the opportunity to develop a professional community outside of their own school and district community as another source of support, stimulation, and feedback.

## Table 12-5    Selected National Professional Organizations and Websites

Professional organizations enable teachers to network with others who have similar interests in content areas or specific interest areas like technology.

| Organization Name | Website Contact |
| --- | --- |
| American Council on the Teaching of Foreign Languages | **www.actfl.org** |
| Association for Supervision and Curriculum Development | **www.ascd.org/portal/site/ascd** |
| International Council for Exceptional Children | **www.cec.sped.org** |
| International Reading Association | **www.reading.org** |
| International Society for Technology in Education | **www.iste.org** |
| National Art Education Association | **www.naea-reston.org** |
| National Association for Bilingual Education | **www.nabe.org** |
| National Association for the Education of Young Children | **www.naeyc.org** |
| National Association for Multicultural Education | **www.nameorg.org** |
| National Association for Music Education | **www.menc.org** |
| National Coalition of Education Activists | **www.nceaonline.org** |
| National Council for the Social Studies | **www.ncss.org** |
| National Council of Teachers of English | **www.ncte.org** |
| National Council of Teachers of Mathematics | **www.nctm.org** |
| National Science Teachers Association | **www.nsta.org** |
| Teachers of English to Speakers of Other Languages | **www.tesol.org** |

Teachers have always been able to join active professional organizations that focus on various content areas or different specialized areas of the curriculum. Several of these organizations are listed in Table 12-5. They offer rich resources, annual conferences, and regular publications for classroom teachers and university researchers alike, and have long provided a valuable source of professional development for teachers. These organizations tend to be large and can be overwhelming at first for a novice teacher, but they provide a good source of external professional contacts and networking. Such organizations often host smaller special interest groups within the organization where teachers with like interests can focus on a topic in depth.

Smaller formal, freestanding teacher networks that are not offshoots of large organizations have also emerged in the past few decades. These provide another, more personal and more intense way for teachers to develop their skills. Some of the more prominent networks are listed in Table 12-6. These intensive, more highly focused networks usually require teachers to attend a summer institute and then follow up in their classrooms once school begins (Murphy & Klein, 2003). The National Writing Project, for example, hosts regional networks of teachers who are committed to improving how writing is taught in the schools.

Active teacher networks can also develop locally. One longstanding local network that concentrates on supporting teachers' inquiry into their own practice is the Teachers' Learning Cooperative in Philadelphia. Members of this network meet in col-

**Table 12-6    Active Formal Teacher Networks, Focus, and Website Contacts**

**Formal teacher networks provide a combination of an onsite summer workshop and extensive communication and follow-up.**

| Teacher Network | Focus | Website |
|---|---|---|
| American Social History Project | Challenge traditional ways people learn about the past | **www.ashp.cuny.edu** |
| Bread Loaf Rural Teacher Network | English | **www.middlebury.edu/academics/blse** |
| Foxfire | Local culture and folklore | **www.foxfire.org** |
| Humanitas | Humanities and Arts | **www.lalc.k12.ca.us/humanitas** |
| Empire State Partnerships | Connecting schools and arts organizations | **www.espartsed.org** |
| Facing History and Ourselves | Finding meaning in history leading to participation and responsible decision making | **www.facinghistory.org** |
| National Writing Project | Writing across the curriculum | **www.nwp.org** |

**Source:** Adapted from Murphy, J. P., and E. J. Klein. (2003). Networking for teacher learning. *Teachers College Record, 105*, 1606–1621.

laboration with local faculty from the University of Pennsylvania. Their work is based on sharing rich, detailed descriptions of a specific student's work, a specific classroom practice, or new local initiatives that concern participants, and bringing the collective knowledge and expertise of the network's members to the issue (El-Haj, 2003).

Technology facilitates teacher networking and instant communication among teachers who would otherwise never be connected. Today teachers can share this process with other like-minded teachers across the country and indeed the world.

# Accountability and Control in the Profession of Teaching

For any profession, the question of control is crucial, because professions are largely defined by the degree to which they have control over their own work. Considerable tension has arisen in education today, however, between teachers wanting control over their profession and public accountability for the quality of teachers' work. Prominent examples of the demand for accountability are the standardized testing movement and the sanctions of the No Child Left Behind Act.

Should teachers have control over their profession, or should they be forced to take their direction from administrators and external agencies, regulators, and constituencies? The issue of control is crucial because without it, teachers may not be adequately valued in terms of the professional knowledge they possess and the ideas they may have for improving their schools and their students' learning. A longstanding tension exists, for example, between top-down control by building principals and teacher control. When teachers work in a top-down situation where their major responsibility is to follow the directives of the principal, the school board, and the state or federal government, their opinions about how a school should be organized and how students' education should be structured may not be heard or acknowledged. Ironically, however, it is teachers who have the most direct contact with students, and, as a result, usually possess the greatest knowledge about how students learn and what might be best for their own particular students in any given year or class.

Teachers are undoubtedly gaining greater control over some aspects of their profession. The movement toward teacher leadership is one illustration of this progress. Developments such as the National Board for Professional Teaching Standards represent a new view of teacher accountability and of the role of accomplished teachers in the schools. At the same time, the external pressure for accountability is perhaps greater than at any other time in recent memory. The cliché that with control comes the responsibility for accountability is something that teachers' unions are beginning to take seriously, especially with processes such as peer assistance and review of teaching. The trend toward teacher leadership is signaling an emerging level of trust in teachers to be major players in school reform. Structurally, however, traditional forms of control still exist, with administrators having the ability to rule with an "iron hand."

Realistically, tension between control and accountability in teaching will always be present. That tension is greater or lesser in any given era, depending on the political climate. However, sharing responsibility means that teachers' voices are heard and taken seriously. Teachers' wish to control their work environment should not be construed as just a matter of power. Rather, it should be based in a strong commitment to their students' well-being and learning, as well as a commitment to sharing power for the benefit of the students. Teachers and principals, teachers and state education officials, and teachers and politicians have an obligation to work together to improve students' learning and the quality of education provided in their school. Sharing both control *and* accountability is most likely to contribute to a work environment that is rooted in responsible professional behavior and consistent professional responsibility.

## Your turn... *to review*

1. What is action research and how can it help teachers improve their teaching?
2. What is the purpose of the National Board for Professional Teaching Standards?
3. Name two functions of professional organizations for teachers.

# Time to Grow, Time to Lead

One major impediment to teacher professionalism is the structure of the school day itself. When teachers are expected to be teaching every hour of the working day, there is little time to engage in professional development activities, especially at the elementary level, where planning periods are not typically built into the schedule. Time to watch each other teach and to confer after observations, time for special and general education teachers to plan together, time to learn new methods, time to analyze data related to how the school's students are doing and what needs to change—in short, *time to reflect about teaching*—are not part of the way schools are organized.

The National Commission on Teaching and America's Future considers the question of time to be one of the most important barriers to improving the quality of teaching systematically. Compared with Belgium, Japan, Italy, Australia, France, and Denmark, for example, the United States has the lowest proportion of teachers in relationship to other educational employees (National Commission on Teaching and America's Future, 1996). The assumption in these countries is that teachers must have time for professional growth and development as part of their regular work—not as an additional responsibility they must take on individually after working hours. The very structure of the education workforce, then, works against increasing the teachers' ability to carry out the complex tasks and professional obligations that serious teaching requires.

A related issue is creating teaching positions that enable teachers to both teach students and work with other teachers and staff in the building. When every teacher has full-time classroom responsibilities, his or her first priority must be the students. However, if teachers want to grow over the life of their careers, take on various leadership roles in the profession, and still stay close to the classroom, the structure of the profession needs to be rethought. In many mentoring programs, for example, mentors are either pulled from their classrooms or are retired teachers. Less common is the model where a teacher might mentor on a half-time basis in his or her own school and retain classroom teaching responsibilities on a half-time basis. This allows teacher leaders to model teaching for their mentees while preserving time to provide the level of intensive support new teachers require. Such arrangements require not only enough teaching staff to make these arrangements possible, but also agreements between districts and unions to make part-time teaching and part-time teacher leadership a reality.

Time is consistently identified as one of the most critical resources lacking in teachers' efforts to engage in high-quality, serious professional development. The need for time clashes with the fundamental structure of the school day as it currently exists in the American education system. However, with the advent of so many new and challenging leadership roles for teachers, it will be critical to restructure the system so that teachers can stay close to the classroom but also carry out their professional responsibilities.

Teacher leaders take responsibility for improving the quality of the profession in many ways, including helping their peers learn about new teaching methods. (Jeff Greenberg/ PhotoEdit)

# Reflecting on Your Views and Beliefs, Assessing Your Progress

By now you should be well on your way to thinking about what teaching means from "the other side of the desk"—that is, the teacher's side. You should have a better sense of teaching as a profession, its rewards and challenges, and the range of responsibilities teachers have at the classroom, school, and school district level. You should also have a better sense of what you will encounter during your professional studies to become a teacher. Your ideas about teaching should be changing, not necessarily because you have changed your mind about particular issues, but because your studies and experiences should be contributing to a broader and deeper understanding of what teaching entails. The questions and concerns you have about teaching today are probably different from those you had just a few months ago.

As emphasized throughout this book, to learn to teach well, teachers need to develop the habit of reflecting on teaching. Reflection is not an end in itself, but rather a route to assessing and understanding the quality of your teaching, identifying areas for improvement, and taking action to make those improvements or changes occur. Using this process is one important way to demonstrate your commitment to professional growth throughout your career. You can begin by identifying and setting specific goals to improve your own teaching each year—a habit that will be useful even while you are still learning to teach.

You began your initial study of teaching with a set of understandings, perspectives, and beliefs about teaching that developed, as we noted in Chapter 2, from a combination of your life experiences, prior beliefs, and commitments. Your own *apprenticeship of observation*, also described in Chapter 2, has influenced your views of teaching as well. Now that you have been thinking in greater depth about teaching, it is an appropriate time to consider how those early understandings, perspectives, and beliefs may have changed up to this point. Since the five professional development commitments that frame this book are ones that you will encounter throughout your career, you can use them as one way to structure how you think about your own developing beliefs about teaching. Such a self-assessment can form the basis for a portfolio entry (or multiple entries) related to the early stages of your preparation as a teacher.

Table 12-7 is one way of organizing your thoughts around each of these five commitments. It provides you with questions to stimulate your own reflective thinking. You might prepare a short written paragraph related to each commitment and use this analysis to begin to set new goals for the coming semester or year. It might be helpful if you consider what might have stimulated your thinking about a particular issue. Was it a specific experience you had? something you read? a conversation with a colleague, teacher, or professor? If your concerns and questions have changed, do you notice a pattern that shows what influences you most?

**Your turn...** *to reflect*

One thing you were asked to do at the start of this book, as you began thinking about learning to teach, was to identify your three greatest concerns or questions about becoming a teacher. Take a minute now to look back at that list and think about whether your concerns and questions have changed. If they have, what do you think accounts for the changes you notice? If your concerns or questions have not changed at all, what do you think accounts for this?

**Table 12-7    Assessing Your Changing Understandings and Beliefs about Teaching**

Self-assessment can be a tool for reflection throughout your teaching career.

| Five Career-Long Professional Development Commitments | "I began by thinking..." (entering beliefs and understandings) | "Now I see that..." or "Now I'm wondering about..." (changing beliefs and understandings) | What accounts for new perspectives, changes or complexity? What accounts for an absence of changes? | Next Steps/Goals |
|---|---|---|---|---|
| Learning from Multiple Sources of Knowledge Throughout Your Career | | | | |
| Using the Curriculum Responsibly | | | | |
| Crossing Your Own Familiar Borders to Embrace Diversity | | | | |
| Meeting the Needs of Individual Students in the Context of the Classroom and the School | | | | |
| Contributing Actively to the Profession | | | | |

Are your understandings more complex than they were? If you do identify changes, what do they tell you about yourself as a learner within the profession of teaching?

This type of analysis should help you discover patterns related to your own journey in learning to teach. You may find, for example, that you are more open to growth in some areas than in others. If this is the case, it is important to think about why. Are you simply more interested in one of these issues than the others? Are you resistant to thinking about particular issues, or do some make you uncomfortable? Do you have a deeply held conviction about a particular issue that you are not willing to change? If so, is there good evidence in the world of teaching and learning for holding onto that position? Are your reasons justifiable? Have you considered competing perspectives? As you assess your own patterns, have you given some of these issues more or less thought than others?

Each prospective teacher comes to his or her professional preparation with a different array of strengths and weaknesses, interests, beliefs, and preferences related to the work of teaching. But what teachers all have in common is the need to grow over the life of their career in order to continue to do their job well.

Working with your peers to assess the quality of your teaching is a career-long strategy that can lead to improvement. (Susan Van Etten/PhotoEdit)

## Reflection: An Enduring Habit

How do you make informed choices about charting your own course for a career of professional learning once you have completed your formal preparation? How will you identify areas to focus on for future growth?

One continuous source of new ideas will be your own professional reflection. Whether it is observing how well your students are doing, having others observe your teaching and providing you with feedback, writing about your teaching, or discussing various aspects of your teaching with your professional peers, a systematic consideration of the "data" you collect on your own work as a teacher is an important source of motivation, inspiration, and information to guide subsequent action for career-long growth and development. It allows you to target areas where you want to improve based directly on an understanding of what is going on in your own classroom and school with your own students.

Such areas might include, for example, academic content, building relationships with students or parents, classroom organization, classroom interaction, implementation of a social justice approach to teaching, or improvement of individual students' behavior. You may set a goal of changing grade levels and learning the curriculum for the new level at which you wish to teach. Whatever your focus, assessing the quality of your work through reflection is an important career-long strategy to help you set professional goals.

Adopting an attitude of reflection and action is one way to take responsibility for improving the quality of your work and for expanding your professional horizons. Reflection will encourage you to gain greater awareness of yourself as a teacher and the impact of your work on your students.

## Incorporating New Developments in Teaching and Learning

A different source of ideas and direction to help you set professional goals is regularly staying in touch with new developments in teaching and learning. Educational researchers are continuously studying how children learn and how well different methods of instruction work. The results of research are regularly reported in scholarly journals. These results, along with descriptions of applications in the classroom, are also reported in more practitioner-oriented, teacher-friendly journals in nearly every subject area, as well as in general educational journals such as *Educational Leadership* or journals and newsletters of the American Federation of Teachers or the National Education Association. Table 12-8 shows both the research journals for several professional organizations and their associated practitioner-oriented, more teacher-friendly journals.

Attending professional conferences is another way to come into contact with new ideas in teaching and learning and new approaches you may wish to try out in your classroom. Once you find an area within your teaching specialization that is especially interesting to you or an area in which you feel you could improve your skills, you can begin by attending state or regional meetings of content-oriented

**Table 12-8    Examples of Research and Practitioner Journals for Various Professional Organizations**

Professional organizations are a rich resource for teachers' ongoing professional development.

| Professional Organization | Research Journal | Practitioner Journals |
|---|---|---|
| Council for Exceptional Children | Exceptional Children | *Teaching Exceptional Children* |
| International Reading Association | Reading Research Quarterly | *The Reading Teacher, The Journal of Adolescent & Adult Literacy* |
| National Council of Teachers of English | Research in the Teaching of English | *Language Arts, Voices from the Middle, English Journal* (high school) |
| National Council of Teachers of Mathematics | Journal for Research in Mathematics Education | *Teaching Children Mathematics, Mathematics Teaching in the Middle School, Mathematics Teacher* (high school), *Online Journal for School Mathematics* |
| National Science Teachers Association | Journal of Research in Science Teaching (published by the National Association for Research in Science Teaching) | *Science and Children, Science Scope, The Science Teacher* |
| National Council for the Social Studies | Theory and Research in Social Education | *Social Education, Social Studies and the Young Learner* |
| The National Association for Music Education | Journal of Research in Music Education | *Music Educators Journal, Teaching Music* |
| National Art Education Association | Studies in Art Education: A Journal of Issues and Research | *Art Education* |
| Teachers of English to Speakers of Other Languages | TESOL Quarterly | *Essential Teacher* |

organizations such as the National Council for the Teachers of Mathematics or those in the various individual specialty areas such as the state branch of the Council for Exceptional Children, or the National Association of Bilingual Education. As you gain confidence and experience, you may eventually choose to share some aspect of your own teaching at such a conference and begin to develop a professional support network with other teachers who have similar interests.

Another way to guide your development as a professional is to consider new areas of teaching in which you have a special interest. Once you identify an area, you can begin to follow developments and set goals in those areas. For example, perhaps as a classroom teacher you find yourself increasingly interested in the climate of the school and decide to develop expertise in peer mediation and other similar programs. A new professional area of interest may be related to the subject you are preparing to teach. By developing an area of special expertise, you challenge yourself and you also become a valuable, knowledgeable resource for your peers.

As you plan for your own ongoing professional development, one of the areas you might consider is increasing the use of technology to enhance your students' learning of the curriculum. (Corbis Images)

## School or Districtwide Professional Development

Another source of professional goal-setting can develop from issues that your school or district consider important. When grade-level teachers or teachers and administrators schoolwide work together to reflect on the school's effectiveness as a whole and look at the data on student learning and school climate, they may identify content areas or problems that need to be addressed across all grades. Districts may develop projects to increase the quality of teaching and learning in a particular content area as well and commit its professional development dollars in that direction.

As a group, for example, your school can work to address teaching reading or to decrease tardiness or truancy. A staff may choose to set a goal of increasing the use of certain kinds of technology to support student learning and communication, for example, using handheld devices for collecting data in science. Within this theme, you can then select a specific goal that relates to your students and your classroom. If this focus is consistent with district goals, small grants may be available for which either individual teachers or schools can compete related to this goal.

## Setting Short- and Long-Term Goals

Based on the self-assessment you completed, using the chart in Figure 12-7, at this point you should be prepared to set some specific goals for the next stage of your development as a teacher. Furthermore, you now have some perspective on issues that may play a role in shaping your own professional development plans. You may also have started to think about some longer-term goals that you may begin to identify as you take your first job and encounter the daily responsibilities that teaching entails.

As these examples illustrate, teachers set both shorter- and longer-term goals depending on their circumstances, interests, and opportunities. Goals may be developed for a grading period, a semester, or an entire school year. A teacher might set a year-long goal of improving a skill or introducing a new subject area, or finding better ways to support a struggling learner in a specific subject. Another annual goal might be to build more active relationships with students' families and to sustain those relationships more effectively over the year.

An example of a longer-term goal would be seeking certification by the National Board for Professional Teaching Standards. This goal requires an intensive commitment and may constitute your primary professional development focus over a few years. Or you may make long-term plans to enter a graduate program to obtain a master's degree in a specialized area—for example, reading education or instructional technology, which may also take several years.

Before you set long-term goals, you should give yourself a chance to consider several areas of interest and get some classroom experience. Sometimes new teachers feel pressured to make a choice about a graduate program as soon as they begin their careers. For example, some new teachers decide to enter a graduate program

# REWARDS AND CHALLENGES

## Revisiting Why We Teach

Erika Stubbs
*Lawrenceville, New Jersey*

If you were to ask teachers to describe the professional development workshops they are presently involved in, the responses you may hear are: Differentiated Instruction, Clustering, Guided Reading, and Literature Circles; the list goes on and on. Districts spend thousands of dollars on workshops to enhance teachers' methods and practices to positively influence student learning.

One of the best professional development workshops I attended this year was given by a consultant hired to work with a group of our students. In the workshop we were asked, "Why did you decide to teach?" "What are you bringing to the table?" and "What is your purpose?" There was a dead silence. These questions required us to self-reflect on why we are educators. Though the questions seem simple enough, it was apparent that the thought process was complex as the teachers mulled silently. The responses shared were also simple; teachers want to affect students and their lives. We (teachers) are profound and insightful people, in a self-chosen profession. There is one reason we are teachers; we love children and we want to help them learn. The consultant challenged us to strengthen our connections with the students, to show them we care. He reminded us

that "students know who cares about them and who doesn't." We were reminded that students' extracurricular lives and environments directly influence what they are able to accomplish academically. Lack of essentials like food, shelter, clothing, and general care dictates learning circumstances and as teachers we need to remember this. I left the workshop with the charge to redirect my teaching: to remind myself why I teach.

As educators, we do have specific guidelines and requirements that drive our curriculum and ultimately direct what we teach. What teachers need to "professionally develop" is to focus on *how* we teach—the approaches we use. We need to stay fresh and current in an effort to connect to our students. We have to work to bridge the generation gap. We have to transform our teaching styles from curriculum-centered to student-centered. Whatever topic is the focus of our ongoing professional development, we need to keep motivation, enthusiasm, and dedication at the forefront. I truly believe that exceptional teaching practice includes putting students first, staying motivated, and renewing our commitments to affect change in someone's life. ●

in school administration the minute they begin classroom teaching. With the emerging focus on teacher leadership and the possibilities for teachers through developments such as the National Board for Professional Teaching Standards, becoming an administrator is no longer the only way to move ahead in the teaching profession. Take your time setting long-term goals, give yourself a chance to get some experience, and decide only when you are confident about the direction in which you want to go.

## Becoming an Informed Professional

Being a well-informed professional means becoming a careful observer of education and becoming knowledgeable—not only from the perspective of professional knowledge about pedagogy and content, but also from the perspective of political issues and developments related to education.

It is important that you as a committed educator be aware of what is happening in education not only in your community but also in your region, state, and nationally. In Chapter 10 we described how decisions at each of these levels can affect your work directly. As a beginning professional you should find it useful to acquire the habit of following developments in education in the print or electronic media—whether they describe events and activities in the local schools or policy developments at any level. This means reading the local newspaper or consulting **Education Week**, the major weekly professional newspaper in education (**www.edweek.org**), a publication to which your school may subscribe. At a minimum, you will want to keep informed about school board elections, the candidates' positions on the issues, and how those positions translate into policies at the school and classroom level in your district. It is also important to be aware of state and federal legislation that might affect you and your school, for example, the No Child Left Behind Act. During 2004, many newspapers ran stories commemorating the fiftieth anniversary of the *Brown v. Board of Education* decision and describing the current state of education for racial and ethnic minority students.

An additional way to get up-to-date information about education issues is through publications and communications from your local teachers' union. Unions publish local and state newsletters, and as a member you will receive national magazines that include coverage of political and other critical, timely educational issues.

At this point, you are likely to have more questions than answers about current educational issues. For some issues, it is enough to be aware of them; for others, you may wish to take action to influence the outcome of an election or a legislative initiative.

## Challenges on the Horizon in Education

One of the great rewards and opportunities of a career in teaching is that the field of education is never stagnant. Certainly, some of the major goals of education stay the same—making a commitment to your students and creating an environment in which they develop the knowledge and skills to become independent learners and to function effectively in the world. Teachers do not start with a blank slate each year and create their work from scratch. But the curriculum does change over time, as does the educational context on the local, state, and national level. Teachers must therefore be flexible and responsive to these changes over the course of a career. Furthermore, the social and political world within which teaching takes place changes, creating new demands but also providing new opportunities and challenges.

In every generation, issues emerge that make demands on teachers and how they do their work. For example, the 1960s were dominated by the integration of schools and bussing, following the *Brown v. Board of Education* decision of 1954. At the beginning of the twenty-first century, one dominant issue is accountability for student learning and closing the achievement gap, defined primarily as scores on standardized achievement tests. Teachers who are sound in their commitment to the profession consider the nature of the changes and their relationship to their core reasons for teaching.

What issues might be on the horizon during your career as a teacher? We are not referring here to fads (e.g., school uniforms) or issues that can be addressed relatively quickly (e.g., whether or not soda machines should be placed in schools). Global education, foreign language education, the resegregation of schools, and the future of public schooling itself are four examples of issues that have not been resolved within the American educational system. They are likely to have major implications for education during your career and may represent changes in how education is conceptualized and delivered. As such, during the span of your professional career, they may provide a wide array of interesting and challenging professional opportunities.

# Global Education

World history and current events have long been regular parts of the curriculum. However, studying world history and reporting on current events is not the same as being able to take one's place in an increasingly global society—one that is connected electronically and instantaneously and demands a more sophisticated level of interaction across cultures and countries, and a much higher level of understanding, than ever before (Diaz, Massialas, & Kanthopoulos, 1999; Ladson-Billings, 2004). "The world is at our doorstep, and we cannot help being aware of it," writes one advocate of global education (Urso, 1991, p. 100).

Globalization requires a broader view of the world and of the relationship between the United States and other countries. Global concerns are no longer just a function of the social studies curriculum. Global issues related to the environment, the development of nuclear capabilities, the international marketplace, or treating diseases across the globe span science and social studies (Diaz, Massialas, & Kanthopoulos, 1999). Both the National Council for the Social Studies (2005) and the National Science Teachers Association (1996) have drafted formal position statements on global education. In its position statement on this issue, the National Council for the Social Studies (2001) views *global education and international education* as complementary:

> … an effective social studies program must include global and international education. Global and international education are important because the day-to-day lives of average citizens around the world are influenced by burgeoning international connections. The human experience is an increasingly globalized phenomenon in which people are constantly being influenced by transnational, cross-cultural, multi-cultural and multiethnic interactions. The goods we buy, the work we do, the cross-cultural links we have in our own communities and outside them, and increased worldwide communication capabilities all contribute to an imperative that responsible citizens understand global and international issues. The increasing globalization in the human condition has created additional opportunities and responsibilities for individuals and groups to take personal, social, and political action in the international arena.

The position of the National Science Teachers' Association (1996) is clear about the need for teachers to take a global perspective on international science education:

> The global nature of our culture and existence becomes more apparent almost continuously. No longer can isolationism and ethnocentrism take precedence over concern for our planet and, ultimately, our own life quality and survival. Science and education can play a key role in developing such global awareness that leads to appropriate understanding, attitude, and action. Students must come to see themselves, their learning, and their past and future in a context which includes the entire spectrum of life on earth. Citizens educated in this manner should develop historical and cultural perspective, leading to mutual respect and mutual understanding of the ideas of others.

Taking a global perspective also implies that as a teacher you will be able to converse about current global issues with your students, respond to their questions, and provide guidance as they grapple with global issues—no matter what subject you teach. Imagine yourself in a classroom during the events of 9/11 or the war in Iraq. Would you have been ready to discuss the Middle East, or would you have known where to locate Afghanistan or Iraq on the world map? Students do not leave the issues of the day—which are increasingly global issues—at the classroom door. Although you are not expected to be an expert on every global issue, as a teacher you should be able to carry on an informed, educated conversation on current issues facing your students, your community, and the nation at large. The United Nations sponsors a website on global education at **www.un.org/pubs/cyberschoolbus**.

## World Languages Education

How will graduates of schools in the United States navigate their way through this global society? How will they compete in the international marketplace? In addition to studying global issues and developing an awareness of the global society, will they be able to speak other languages and interact personally and professionally across the world in an effective manner?

The United States has long been resistant to teaching languages other than English and does not generally view this skill or other international concerns as essential (Bales, 2004). But the new global arena demands such skills (Diaz, Massialas, & Kanthopoulos, 1999; Marcos & Peyton, 2000). In fact, among the developed countries, the United States lags in world language education, begins teaching languages later than other countries, (Christian, Pufahl, & Rhodes, 2004/2005), and is the only country that does not teach other languages throughout a student's schooling.

There has been a longstanding tradition of studying world languages for a few years starting in high school, but this kind of language education is designed primarily for those who intend to pursue college. World language education starting in the early grades is the exception rather than the rule, and it is generally not valued as part of universal schooling in the United States, especially when compared with other countries.

The goal of world language education, however, reaches far beyond merely speaking another language for purposes of global communication. Standards for the study of foreign languages were published in 1996 by a coalition of professional organizations concerned with language education. These standards appear in Figure 12-2 and include the "Five C's of Foreign Language Education": Communication, Cultures, Connections, Comparisons, and Communities.

The issue of world language education and the need to start it in the early grades is not new, and the professional language community has adopted a PK–12 view of language learning with the motto "Start Early—Stay Long" (Curtain &

The United States lags behind other developed countries in terms of world language education. (Corbis Images)

**Figure 12-2    Five Standards for World Language Education**

These standards show the connection between learning foreign languages and cultural learning.

1. COMMUNICATION
   Communicate in Languages Other Than English

2. CULTURES
   Gain Knowledge and Understanding of Other Cultures

3. CONNECTIONS
   Connect with Other Disciplines and Acquire Information

4. COMPARISONS
   Develop Insight into the Nature of Language and Culture

5. COMMUNITIES
   Participate in Multilingual Communities at Home and Around the World

**Source:** American Council on the Teaching of Foreign Languages. *National standards for foreign language education.* Retrieved June 2, 2008, from http://www.actfl.org/i4a/pages/index.cfm?/pageid=3392.

Dahlberg, 2004). Figure 12-3 describes various uses of videoprograms for teaching world languages at the elementary level. Yet education in world languages remains an unresolved issue in the American educational system.

What does the issue of world languages education mean for you as a classroom teacher? During the course of your career, your school (especially if it is an elementary school) or your district might consider changing its policies toward language instruction and request your opinions on the issue. You may also want to consider world language education as an area for your own growth and development, especially in relationship to student populations in your school whose first language is not English.

**Figure 12-3    Technology and Teaching World Languages in Elementary Schools**

Videos appear to be a practical approach to beginning world language instruction at the elementary level.

Recommendations for the use of videos include:

Video-based programs as a targeted supplement to the standards-based world languages curriculum

Video-based programs as the curriculum in the absence of a licensed teacher of that language

Video-based program implemented by a teacher who does not know the language being taught (teacher learns alongside students) with native speaker as a regular (e.g., weekly) resource

Follow-up activities to video-based program integrated into regular school curriculum world language learning as a schoolwide and districtwide activity, including language clubs

**Source:** Adapted from Rhodes, N., & I. Pufahl. (2003). *Teaching foreign languages to children through video.* CAL Digest EDO-FL-03-10, Updated October 2004. Washington, DC: Center for Applied Linguistics. Retrieved June 2, 2008, from http://www.cal.org/resources/digest/0310pufahl.html.

## Resegregation of Schools

How successful has the country been in ensuring that the schools whose students are primarily from racial and ethnic minority groups are equal to those of majority students in terms of the education they provide? Whole states, as well as whole school districts, now have majority populations of nonwhite students (Orfield & Lee, 2007). In many communities nationwide, urban schools have long had majority populations of nonwhite students and thus, schools that are segregated by race or ethnicity. Schools with predominantly low-income and racial and ethnic minority populations have typically lacked equivalent resources and have experienced lower levels of achievement than their majority population counterparts (Orfield & Lee, 2007).

Despite decades of desegregation efforts in the schools following the Brown decision, the achievement gap between white and nonwhite students persists. The issue of resegregation of schools challenges the education establishment to provide a quality education for all students.

In June of 2007, the Supreme Court ruled that race cannot be a used as a factor in assigning students to schools, even if such plans for school integration are voluntary. These cases, which refer to both Louisville and Seattle, increase the likelihood that separate schools, which historically have been unequal in terms of quality, will continue. As Orfield and Lee observed in their 2007 report on the resegregation of schools:

> The trends…are those of increasing isolation and profound inequality. The consequences become larger each year because of the growing number and percentage of nonwhite and impoverished students and the dramatic relationships between educational attainment and economic success in a globalized economy." (p. 3-4)

In addition, the teaching force appears to be segregated despite the fact that the majority of teachers are white. For example, Latino and Asian teachers are more likely to teach in schools where the population of English Language Learners is highest, and white teachers are less likely to teach in schools that are struggling to meet annual proficiency goals (Frankenberg, 2006).

Will schools with dominant minority student populations really have the same quality of teaching and learning as those with dominant majority populations? As states such as California become places where the majority of the population is "minority," will the schools provide an educational experience that ensures high levels of academic achievement for all students? Will urban schools—which have long had majority populations of racial and ethnic minority students—be supported to meet the challenge of ensuring that all students are able to learn at high levels? These questions remain unresolved for our educational system.

As you embark on your career, it is important to ask what the resegregation of schools means for you as a classroom teacher. If you teach in a majority nonwhite school, what resources will you draw on to ensure that your students achieve at high levels? If you teach in a school that is monocultural, how will you address issues of diversity and multiculturalism?

## The Future of Public Education

In theory one bedrock of the experiment in democracy in the United States is an educated citizenry that can participate in the democratic process from an informed perspective. Another is the function public education plays in leveling the playing field and enabling individuals of modest means to move up the economic ladder. Given the persistent achievement gap, it is clear that this promise has not ensured a high-quality education for all groups in our society. Nevertheless, public education is one of the few national institutions that has had the capacity to do so.

At the start of the twenty-first century, public education as we have known it in the United States has undergone a radical change. The long-term effect of charter schools and vouchers, discussed in Chapter 10, has already begun to alter the educational landscape profoundly, shifting resources away from public education and public schools.

The physical infrastructure of the public schools is also a very serious consideration. Today only 22 states regularly check on the physical facilities in which school takes place (Education Week, 2008). Facility maintenance has been deferred due to financial pressures, and problems include not only poor and obsolete buildings, but also environmental risk due to poor ventilation and mold, and thus poor air quality (American Federation of Teachers, 2006; Filardo, 2008). Technology infrastructure and science facilities are also major infrastructure considerations that require a public investment (Filardo, 2008). Such poor facility conditions are not conducive to learning.

What role will the public schools continue to play? What student populations will they eventually serve, and will the country accept the shift to a publicly funded system of public and private (and sometimes religious) schools? Whether the country will wish to invest in public education, raise teacher salaries, and support rebuilding the educational infrastructure by investing in the modernization of the public schools, including state-of-the-art technology for all schools, are issues that affect every teacher's work and every student's life.

As more and more schools become "majority minority" schools, how will the country ensure that these schools are of the highest quality? (Media Bakery)

# Finding Your First Teaching Position: Smart Preparation Pays Off

As you put your early experiences with learning to teach into perspective, searching for your first job may seem far off, but that time will arrive sooner than you think. Preparing to obtain a job as a teacher actually begins as soon as you start your professional program and continues through the application and interview process. There are four things you can do to prepare for getting a teaching job: (1) take your preparation seriously, (2) make your portfolio count, (3) be an informed applicant, and (4) prepare for your job interview.

## Take Your Preparation Seriously

The quality of your performance in both your classes and clinical experiences and your student teaching or internship is critical to your future in the profession. How you approach your preparation for teaching reflects how serious you are about your career choice and how motivated you are in pursuing it. Your professional education depends on a combination of your own commitment along with the knowledge, skills, and experiences that span formal university classes and clinical experience in the schools. Together these form the basis of your professional knowledge and provide you with guidance for your work in the classroom.

It is important for you, as someone who is learning to teach, to begin to master the full range of knowledge and skills you will need to help your students learn. The more confidence you gain during your preparation, the better able you will be to convey the depth of your knowledge and skill when the time comes to interview for a job. As you move through your professional program, with each successive experience you should begin to look and sound like someone who possesses professional knowledge and whose understanding of and commitment to what it means to teach is beginning to differ from that of a layperson. No one expects you to command the same knowledge as a seasoned professional teacher, but those who observe and work with you expect you to be curious about and interested in the work of teaching, to have a professional stance toward teaching, and to begin to display your professional knowledge.

As you move through your professional program, it is important to remember that from the minute you step into a classroom, whether it is simply to observe, to begin to teach lessons, or to student teach or begin an internship, the professionals with whom you work—from principals to teachers to school secretaries and building engineers—are judging you as a potential colleague. They are likely to ask themselves questions such as the following:

- Would I want this person to teach in my school? in the classroom next to mine?

- Can I see myself team teaching with this person?

- How does this person present him- or herself in the school?

- How does he or she interact with others?

- What kind of attitude does this person have?

- Does this person set an upbeat tone? or does this person talk negatively about colleagues or students? or both?

- Does this person seem to enjoy teaching, or does it seem like a chore—another experience to "get through" on the way to earning a degree? Is there a real sense of dedication, even at this early stage?

- Does this person volunteer to do his or her share of the school's work? Is he or she a team player?

- Will this person add to the school—or make it a less pleasant place to be?

In other words, you begin to gain a reputation in the various school buildings in which you are learning to teach. Your supervisors are asking themselves similar questions: Does this person have the skills to earn a teaching license? What evidence do I have that this is the case?

One more very important consideration is the attitude you bring to your professional studies. What you are asked to do in your professional program may not always appear to be immediately applicable or relevant to your conceptions of teaching, but in the end it should have prepared you for your future responsibilities. By keeping an open mind, the connections between what you are learning and what your responsibilities will be as a classroom teacher should become clearer over time.

## Make Your Portfolio Count

Another way to prepare for your eventual job search is to make sure your portfolio represents your commitment to teaching, and what you know and are able to do as a new professional. Your portfolio will contain several important documents that, taken together, can provide a picture of the kind of professional you are likely to be—in addition to the grades you have earned and the evaluations you have received along the way.

As we discussed in Chapter 3, the format and contents of a teaching portfolio differ from program to program and from state to state. Yet most portfolios include certain basic items: a resume, a personal statement or teaching philosophy, and several entries demonstrating your ability to plan and implement lessons and units (usually including lesson plans and an analysis of student work related to those lessons), to work effectively with families, and to participate in the profession. If your portfolio is in an electronic format, it may also include videoclips of your actual teaching.

Your portfolio should represent the best of your work. Putting together a portfolio is somewhat like editing a film. You will have many lessons and units to draw on as possible entries for your portfolio, but in the end, your portfolio will only be as good as the very best lessons and units you have taught—the ones that engaged your students the most and for which you can demonstrate that your students actually learned as a result of your teaching. If the connections to your students and their families are strong, and you have many good lessons, units, and experiences to draw on, you will be able to construct a portfolio that serves you well as a beginning professional. And, of course, remember that your portfolio must not contain any mistakes in grammar and spelling.

## Become an Informed Job Applicant

The application process and application forms differ from district to district, so one of the first things you need to do once you identify districts where you want to teach is to familiarize yourself with the specific process they use. A good place to begin is the district website, which usually provides information regarding openings and application procedures. If the process is not clearly spelled out, call the human resources department to find out exactly what you need to do.

You may be able to complete your initial application for teaching online. Some districts require letters of recommendation with your application; others will simply ask for names and contact information of references. With most applications you will attach your resume; your resume will be included in your portfolio, but it is a good idea to have several extra copies on hand to send with applications. Make sure your resume reflects the clinical experiences and student teaching or internship placements you have completed, as well as any other job-related experiences or special skills you bring to teaching.

In most cases, obtaining your legal state teaching certification is separate either from graduating or completing your teacher preparation program. Program faculty and administrators can help you complete your formal application to the state for certification. You may not have your formal teaching credential in hand at the time you actually apply for positions, so check with the program in which you are enrolled to see if they will prepare a letter attesting that you have successfully completed your program until such time as your legal credential arrives.

If you are moving across state lines to teach, you should check early on whether the state to which you are moving will recognize the teaching credential you obtain in the state where you are learning to teach. The best way to begin this process is to go directly to the state education agency's website for the state in which you intend to live and teach.

Usually some level of initial screening of applications takes place before individuals are invited to continue in the hiring process. What happens from that point on depends entirely on the individual district. In some districts, you may be required to complete a preliminary screening assessment before you can be interviewed for a particular position. In others, you may be asked to interview based only on a preliminary review of your application. You might interview with a centralized team that includes a building principal and/or teachers, as well as central office personnel. Or you might interview with a team at the individual school where there is an opening. There may or may not be parents or family members on the interview team. The best way to find out what to expect is to ask for information—politely and professionally. For example, it is appropriate to ask who the members of the interview team will be (by position, not by name) and approximately how long the interview is scheduled to take. In some instances, you may also be asked to prepare a demonstration of your teaching as part of your interview process.

## Prepare for Your Job Interviews

One of the most important things you can do to prepare for a job interview is to "do your homework." Become as familiar as you can with both the school district and the individual school in which you want to teach. Not only can the district website be helpful, but the individual school may also have a website. Learn as much as you can about the size and structure of the school (e.g., what grade levels does it include, do teachers team for certain subjects, are the upper elementary grades departmentalized, etc.?) and the curriculum (e.g., is there a school theme that drives curriculum decisions, or is the district committed to certain aspects of the curriculum—such as a strong emphasis on "science"?). If you have spent time at the school for clinical experience, student teaching, or an internship, you have a head start on the details of how the school operates. Communicating to the interview team that you have some familiarity with the school indicates how serious you are about wanting to work there.

When you go for a job interview, be prepared with specific questions about the district and the school.
(Media Bakery)

Most interview teams are looking for at least four things when they interview candidates for teaching positions. First, is the candidate enthusiastic about teaching? Second, is the candidate knowledgeable about the profession in general and the grade or subject for which he or she is interviewing in particular? Third, is there a good fit between the candidate's commitments, goals, philosophy, and interests and the needs of the school? Finally, is the candidate someone the team members would want as a colleague? As you think about and prepare for the interview process, think about how you will convey these things to the members of the interview team.

One of the most effective ways to present yourself as a candidate is to draw on specific examples from your experiences in schools and in your teacher preparation program. Interviewers tend to be less interested in general statements or platitudes and more interested in what you have actually accomplished. Even if an interview team asks about your beliefs or philosophies, which is fairly typical, be prepared to back up your answer with examples from your own work in schools. Also,

Set your sights high for the kind of teacher you want to be and make the choices along the way that will get you there. (Media Bakery)

make sure you highlight any special skills or talents you would bring to the position (for example, second languages, musical or other artistic skills, interest in sponsoring debate or other special interest clubs at the middle and high school levels, etc.).

During the interview process, referring to your portfolio gives you a chance to share specific examples of your work. The interviewer or team may not have the time to read every entry or review every example of lessons you have planned, samples of student work, or professional activities in which you have participated. It is up to you to use your portfolio strategically during the interview and be prepared to connect the questions you are being asked to various items in it. Before the interview, mark lessons and activities so that you can locate them easily. Depending on the circumstances, you may or may not wish to leave your portfolio with the interviewer or interview team for a brief period of time. Whether or not you do so, it is a good idea to prepare a small packet of materials from your portfolio that you can leave with the interviewers at the conclusion of the interview. This might include, for example, your resume, a brief biographical or philosophical statement, and a sample lesson plan or unit plan that you have taught, along with a personal assessment of or reflection on how well the lesson or unit actually resulted in student learning.

Often interviewers end by asking candidates if they have any questions. Asking informed questions communicates that you are serious about your interest in the position and the district. So it is a good idea to prepare two or three questions in advance. That way, if one question has been answered in the course of the interview, you will still have others to ask. Ideas for end-of-interview questions might include new directions in the curriculum, the school, or the district in general; laboratory or technology resources; what kind of special support the school provides for new teachers; what the administrator or teachers see as the school's greatest challenge; or what happens next in the hiring process. The more specific your questions are to the position you seek, the school, and the district, the more you communicate the depth of your interest.

## What Counts for You Now as a Teacher in a Diverse World?

Why are issues related to the status of the profession so important for you as you begin thinking about a career in the classroom? Probably the most critical reason is that the agenda to improve the status of teaching has career-long implications that can help teachers stay in the teaching force. When new teachers can expect support from knowledgeable veterans the minute they take their first positions, they are encouraged to remain in the field. When more experienced teachers can see the possibilities for using their knowledge and skills in the service of the larger profession—and not just within their classroom walls—they can see the possibility of growing throughout their career and giving back to the profession without having to leave the classroom. When teachers no longer feel that the only way they can progress in their careers is to distance themselves from the classroom by becoming administrators—but can instead be teacher leaders who use their well-honed classroom knowledge to improve the profession—they can begin to envision a career-long commitment.

Few other professions have the same rewards as teaching. The unique opportunity to shape the lives of your students is precisely what makes teaching such a significant career. It is also what makes teaching such a challenge. Although it is not the easiest of professions, teaching is undoubtedly one of the most important and one that affects the lives of nearly every single person in the country. And as a teacher in a diverse world, you will undoubtedly affect the lives of students for whom school will be essential to creating future opportunities in their lives. If you have made the choice to teach with your eyes open, if you have the passion to work with students and see them grow and learn, then you can expect a fulfilling professional life.

As you move on to the next stage of your professional preparation, keep in mind the balance between the rigors of your preparation and the rewards of teaching. You are poised to gain the knowledge and skills you will need to do your job at the highest level of professionalism and confidence. But professional knowledge and skills are only meaningful in the context of your own commitment to your students and their well-being, and to making school a meaningful place in which they can learn. Now flash forward to your first classroom. It is September, the first day of school. Your students and their families are wondering who this new teacher is and what kind of year it will be. Find the image of the teacher every student wants to have, the one who both respects them and teaches them well. Now put yourself into that picture, because teaching matters.

# CHAPTER SUMMARY

Teaching is in a state of evolution, progressing from being considered a job to being seen as the profession it is. Myths about teaching, such as the short teaching day, and the long summer vacation, are just that—myths—and do not capture the true essence of teaching as a profession.

## The Profession/Job Conflict

Historically, teaching was dominated by female teachers working under male administrators. Salaries reflected this division of labor, with female teachers being paid less than men and working under challenging conditions. Teaching was thought of as a job and as one "fit for a woman," at that. The knowledge teachers themselves had about their own professional practice was not recognized as such, and new knowledge about and inquiry into teaching and learning were usually sought outside the classroom and with little real regard for the teacher's day-to-day responsibilities. The current attempt to professionalize teaching is an effort to honor the expertise of teachers themselves.

## Teaching as a Collaborative and More Public Form of Work

Today teaching is a collaborative form of work. Teachers observe each other as they try to implement new approaches to curriculum or methods. If they team, they might regularly watch each other teach and provide feedback. A literacy or mathematics coach—a teacher—might observe a single class and provide ideas for improvement. Together a building staff might focus on improving science across the whole school. Today teachers are expected to work together with other adults, not just with students.

## Teacher Leadership

Various new roles for teachers are enabling them to envision a career-long commitment without having to "advance" into administration. They also help teachers take responsibility for the quality of the profession. These forms of teacher leadership are based on the assumption that teachers themselves possess critical, important knowledge about teaching that is a resource for other teachers.

Teacher leadership can take the form of mentoring new teachers to help them make the transition from initial preparation to the day-to-day demands of real practice. Mentors can support new teachers in all aspects of their jobs, providing them with the wisdom of their own years of practice. Teacher leadership can also take the form of coaching, in which accomplished teachers provide professional development for their peers—new and experienced alike—in specific content areas. A coach might observe a peer's lesson, provide feedback, and present model lessons in the classroom.

A final form of teacher leadership is peer review of teaching for those who are having serious difficulty carrying out their responsibilities. Peer review is a relatively new phenomenon, in which a group of teachers takes responsibility for observing peers who are having problems, providing support, and, when appropriate, making the recommendation for a teacher to be relieved of his or her duties if student learning and well-being are in jeopardy.

## Teachers as Researchers

Teachers can generate new knowledge about teaching and learning by conducting their own systematic study in their classrooms and schools. This is known as teacher research and has emerged as an important form of career-long professional growth and development for teachers. When teachers choose to inquire into the quality of their own teaching through research, they are exercising responsibility for the quality of the profession.

Systematic inquiry into the practice of teaching can take three forms. Teachers can conduct classroom studies, trying out new approaches and collecting data on their effectiveness; this is known as action research. They can participate in oral inquiries with colleagues about student work. Or they can keep journals that encourage them to reflect in writing on their teaching. Each form of research requires teachers to be reflective about their profession.

## Recognizing Accomplished Teaching through the National Board for Professional Teaching Standards

The goal of recognizing accomplished, professional teachers has been institutionalized with the creation of the National Board for Professional Teaching Standards, an organization that supports the voluntary certification of accomplished teachers. Five core propositions form the conceptual foundation for certification as an accomplished teacher. Teachers who seek board certification participate in a lengthy process of portfolio development and review, and also take a test of content knowledge.

In many states, certification by the National Board results in a salary increment. As a result, teachers can receive differential pay depending on the accomplishments they have made as teachers—as defined by National Board certification. The National Board has changed teaching from a flat career where everyone was seen as equal in accomplishment to one in which accomplished teachers can be recognized for the quality of their work.

## The Role of Networking in Professional Growth and Development

Networks of teachers with like-minded interests form an important external source of professional growth. These networks can be affiliated with large national organizations, or they can be smaller networks with specialty interests. Such organizations allow teachers to overcome isolation, especially if no one else in their building or district shares their interest.

Technology also plays an important role in teacher networking, facilitating teachers' connections across districts, states, and countries and enabling unprecedented wide-scale networking among teaching professionals.

## Accountability and Control in the Profession of Teaching

With increased professionalism comes accountability for the quality of teaching. There is an ongoing tension between the idea of accountability and external control of teaching. Balancing accountability and control is an ongoing challenge for the relationship between school districts, building principals, and teachers.

## Reflecting on Your Views and Beliefs

Reflection is a tool that helps you grow throughout your teaching career. It assists teachers in identifying areas for their own improvement and professional development. Professional reflection as a source of development can be initiated in multiple ways, including reading professional journals, focusing on schoolwide improvement areas, setting both short and long term professional goals, and being informed about the politics of education.

## Challenges on the Horizon in Education

Education is not a static field. Several challenges are on the horizon as you begin your career. One challenge is preparing students for taking up their lives in a global society that is characterized by instant communication and worldwide interdependence. A second is learning world languages so that global communication and understanding is even possible. A third is the resegregation of schools and the need to assure that schools with "majority minority" populations provide a high quality of education to its students. A final challenge is the very future of public education itself.

## Finding Your First Teaching Position

There are several steps you can take to secure your first teaching position. Taking your professional preparation seriously allows you to become a highly knowledgeable beginning teacher. Completing a portfolio that showcases your most successful decisions and results as a novice allows you to provide real examples of your skill during an interview. Learning everything you can about the districts to which you are applying shows your level of interest. Finally, preparing well for job interviews communicates how seriously you yourself are taking your desire to secure an exciting and challenging first teaching position.

## LIST OF CRITICAL TERMS

Profession (*412*)

Culture of collaboration (*418*)

American Federation of Teachers (AFT) (*421*)

Mentoring (*423*)

Job-embedded professional development (*425*)

Peer assistance and review (*425*)

Teacher research (*427*)

National Board for Professional Teaching Standards (NBPTS) (*431*)

Differentiated compensation (*434*)

## EXPLORING YOUR COMMITMENT

1. ***in the field...*** Interview a practicing teacher to find out what kinds of professional development activities he or she is involved in. How would you classify these activities in terms of the professional opportunities discussed in this chapter?

2. *on the web...* Select three school districts in the area in which you live or study. Go to the website of those districts and explore the way professional development is presented. What opportunities for professional development exist? Do they represent a wide range of opportunities?

3. *on your own...* Meet with a representative of one of the local teachers' unions or organizations. What professional development do they sponsor?

4. *on the web...* Visit the websites of the National Education Association (**www.nea.org**) and the American Federation of Teachers (**www.aft.org**). How do they address teaching as a profession? What surprised you, if anything, about how these two unions discuss teaching as a profession?

5. *on the web...* Check the National Board for Professional Teaching Standards website for incentives for the state in which you want to teach (**www.nbpts.org**). What incentives exist to encourage teachers to participate in this process? How would these incentives affect the way you think about your job as a teacher?

6. *on the web...* Explore the websites of at least three of the professional organizations listed in this chapter. Try to locate a chat room or a teacher discussion board on a topic in which you are interested. What topics were discussed? How did these discussions help you as a prospective teacher?

7. *on your own...* Interview a recent graduate of your teacher education program to discuss what his or her first year of teaching is/was like. In a brief written reflection, discuss how this interview may influence how you think about your own teacher education.

8. *in the field...* Attend a professional development meeting or session at your school. This may be a whole school session or a grade-level or department meeting. What was the topic? How was it connected to classroom practice? How involved were the teachers themselves? Did this session reflect a professional, intellectual approach to teaching or teaching as a technical job? Why or why not?

9. *on your own...* Compare the 10 INTASC standards with the five core principles of the National Board for Professional Teaching Standards. How are they alike? different? How do these differences, if any, imply a distinction between beginning and experienced teachers?

10. *in the research...* Kelly, L. M. (2004). "Why induction matters." *Journal of Teacher Education, 55,* 438–448. What is it about the induction program described in this article that appears to make it successful? Is it a program in which you would like to take part, and why?

## GUIDELINES FOR BEGINNING TEACHERS

1. Find out what kinds of professional development opportunities are available to you within your district, especially those for beginning teachers.

2. Visit your district's website or portal to see what kind of technology support is available to you. Districts may host online chats or interactive sessions on specific topics of interest.

3. Visit with representatives of your local teachers' union or organization to see what level of professional development activities they sponsor.

4. Retain your professional stance by avoiding conversations where other teachers are talking inappropriately about students, families, or other teachers. This may mean avoiding the teachers' lounge.

5. As you seek out experienced teachers within your building who can help you get started, be cautious and judicious about whom you align yourself with in the school. Not all experienced teachers may be the best professional models for you. Choose wisely.

6. Choose one professional publication that you will read regularly during your first year of teaching. It may be a journal that you receive from your union, or it may be a publication related to a professional organization in a specific area in which you are interested. Plan to add a new publication in your second year.

## THE INTASC CONNECTION

The INTASC standards that most directly address issues of the profession and the professional development of teachers are Standards 9 and 10. Standard 9 states: *The teacher is a reflective practitioner who continually evaluates the effects of his/her choices on others (students, parents, and other professionals in the learning community) and who actively seeks out opportunities to grow professionally.* Indicators include the following:

- The teacher is aware of major areas of research on teaching and of resources available for professional learning (e.g., professional literature, colleagues, professional associations, professional development activities).

- The teacher is committed to reflection, assessment, and learning as an ongoing process.

- The teacher recognizes his/her professional responsibility for engaging in and supporting appropriate professional practices for self and colleagues.

- The teacher uses classroom observation, information about students, and research as sources for evaluating the outcomes of teaching and learning and as a basis for experimenting with, reflecting on, and revising practice.

- The teacher seeks out professional literature, colleagues, and other resources to support his/her own development as a teacher.

- The teacher draws upon professional colleagues within the school and other professional arenas as supports for reflection, problem solving, and new ideas, actively sharing experiences and seeking and giving feedback.

Standard 10 states: *The teacher fosters relationships with school colleagues, parents, and agencies in the larger community to support students' learning and well-being.* Indicators include the following:

- The teacher is willing to work with other professionals to improve the overall learning environment for students.

- The teacher participates in collegial activities designed to make the entire school a productive learning environment.

If you are in a state that follows a different set of teacher standards, find the state standards that most closely relate to the INTASC standards discussed here.

## READING ON...

Lieberman, A., and L. Miller. (2004). *Teacher leadership.* San Francisco: Jossey-Bass. A concise discussion of teacher leadership that contains several portraits of teacher leaders in the schools.

Noffke, S. E., and R. B. Stevenson. (1995). *Educational action research: Becoming practically critical.* New York: Teachers College Press. An orientation to teacher research based on a critical, social justice philosophy of education. This volume contains case studies of action research projects that took place in diverse school and classroom settings.

Scherer, M. (2003). *Keeping good teachers.* Alexandria, VA: Association for Supervision and Curriculum Development. Practitioners offer a range of examples of supporting new teachers in the profession.

**Academic content standards.** Formal, public statements of what students should know and be able to do in each of the content areas at various points in their PK–12 education.

**Academic tracking.** Grouping students homogeneously by academic ability for purposes of instruction.

**Accountability.** Ensuring that teachers are held responsible for their students' learning; using student learning as the measure of a teacher's effectiveness.

**Achievement gap.** The gap between African American or Latino students and white middle-class students in terms of school achievement, usually reported based on the results of standardized tests.

**African American Vernacular English.** The language, or dialect of English, that is used by many African American people in the United States.

**Age-graded school.** A school with classrooms organized by age, with students moving up to a new grade each year with a new teacher.

**Alternate route.** Programs that place teachers in classrooms with little formal teacher preparation prior to taking on a job. Teachers instead learn to teach on the job, often with the support of an experienced mentor.

**American Federation of Teachers (AFT).** A teachers' union affiliated with the American Federation of Labor with 1.4 million members.

**Americans with Disabilities Act (ADA).** Federal legislation protecting the rights of children and adults with disabilities in society at large, rather than only in educational settings.

**Anecdotal recording.** Observing and recording the specific events that occur in a defined timeframe in the classroom, without making judgments or interpreting those events.

**Apprenticeship of observation.** The knowledge you have about teaching from the 12 years you spent in classrooms as a student—a term coined in 1975 by the sociologist Dan Lortie.

**Assistive technology.** Technology developed to give individuals with disabilities the ability to have access to the curriculum and other resources and to communicate easily and regularly.

**Blaming the victim.** Rather than taking responsibility for the quality of one's teaching, a weak teacher may blame the students—the "victims" of the teacher's poor teaching—instead.

**Block scheduling.** Organizing the high school schedule to allow for longer class periods that meet fewer times a week.

**Categorical aid.** Federal funding to school districts to support a specific category of federal education program.

**Centralized budgeting system.** A system in which budgetary decisions are made at the school district level with little budget authority at the local school level.

**Charter school.** A nonsectarian, publicly funded school that is usually not bound to the regulations of a typical public school or the restrictions of the collective bargaining agreement between a school district and a teachers' union.

**Child abuse.** The federal definition is "any recent act or failure to act on the part of a parent or caretaker which results in death, serious physical or emotional harm, sexual abuse or exploitation; or an act or failure to act which presents an imminent risk of serious harm."

**Child neglect.** Failing to provide for the basic needs of children, including physical, medical, educational, or emotional needs and, in many states, abandonment.

**Class size reduction.** Usually refers to funding to ensure small class sizes from kindergarten through third grade; funding may be federal or state, or both.

**Classroom as a culture.** The customs, practices, and traditions within a classroom that distinguish it from other organizations.

**Common school movement.** The movement to provide universal education and schools that would serve all children at public expense.

**Concept map.** A visual tool teachers can use to show an individual's ideas about a particular concept and how they relate to one another; concept maps can be used as a starting point for teaching new knowledge about that concept.

**Contextualized teaching and learning.** Teaching that draws on students' life experiences to make instruction meaningful and to motivate students to engage with learning in the classroom and the school.

**Cooperative learning.** A set of organizational strategies that combines social goals with academic goals for mixed-ability groups of students.

**Critical theory.** Analysis of education that focuses on understanding and changing structural inequities that systematically advantage certain groups of students over others.

**Culturally responsive teaching.** Teaching that is continuously responsive to the race, class, culture, ethnicity, and language of each student. It is based on the knowledge and active use of students' backgrounds and cultural experiences to create and implement curriculum, ensuring that all students are successful in school.

**Culture of collaboration.** A culture within a school organization that supports teachers working together and learning from one another to improve teaching and learning.

**Curriculum guide.** A document prepared at the state or local district level that provides detailed information to help teachers plan instruction.

**Curriculum potential.** Using textbooks and other instructional materials by interpreting their potential to meet the needs of a specific class of students.

**Dame Schools.** Education that was delivered in the homes of women, usually consisting of the basics of reading and writing.

**Decentralized budgeting system.** A system in which schools get a certain amount of money to spend each year and the school principal—sometimes in conjunction with a teacher or community advisory group—develops a local budget based on the individual needs and goals of the school.

**Deficit model.** Assuming, inaccurately, that students from low-income families or racial and ethnic minority families lack substantial, useful knowledge or resources upon which to build and support a student's education.

**Departmentalization.** An organizational structure where teachers with academic content expertise teach only the subjects in which they are experts, and students move from teacher to teacher and class to class during the school day. Departmentalization can take place for every subject, or a single teacher might teach two subjects (for example, language arts and social studies).

**Developmental delay.** A term used to describe children who are not reaching typical developmental milestones and who may, based on such a delay, be eligible to receive special education services.

**Developmental guidance.** Classroom program or curriculum that addresses personal and social aspects of learning and that sometimes includes career awareness.

**Differentiated compensation.** Pay for teachers based on various aspects related to the quality of their performance rather than only on years of service and course credits taken.

**Differentiated instruction.** Approaching instruction from the belief that students' abilities differ and that it is the teacher's responsibility to organize instruction to account for those differences on an ongoing basis.

**Due Process Clause.** Clause of the Fourteenth Amendment to the U. S. Constitution stating that each citizen must have due process of the law.

**Early intervention.** Special education services for young children from birth to age 5.

**Efficiency movement.** Schooling that was designed to prepare students for life in the world of work, with an emphasis on conformity, following directions, rote learning and memorization, and strict rules of comportment.

**Eight-Year Study.** A study in the period of the 1930s that compared the progressive approach to education with the traditional approach, and found that the progressive approach produced more intellectual curiosity and drive and higher levels of critical thinking and judgment.

**Elementary and Secondary Education Act (ESEA).** A major piece of federal legislation that provides federal direction to education and federal funds for schools, first passed in 1965.

**English-only rule.** Rule barring Mexican American children from speaking Spanish in public schools.

**English schools (academies).** Schools that followed a practical curriculum rather than a classical curriculum focused solely on Latin and Latin readings.

**English Language Learners (ELL).** Students whose first language is not English.

**Equal Protection Clause.** Clause of the Fourteenth Amendment of the Constitution stating that no person can be denied equal protection of the law.

**Essentialism.** A philosophy of education based on the assumption that students should learn the basic facts regarding the social and physical world.

**Establishment Clause.** Clause of the First Amendment to the Constitution stating that the U.S. Congress cannot make laws that establish religion.

**Ethic of care.** A philosophy of education based on the commitment to caring.

**Explicit curriculum.** The formal, official, public academic program of study that defines what students are expected to know as a result of being in school.

**Extrinsic motivation.** Motivation to do something because one receives a reward or one wishes to avoid a punishment.

**Fair use.** Laws allowing teachers to make limited numbers of copies for instructional purposes in the classroom.

**FERPA.** The Family Educational Rights and Privacy Act (also known as the Buckley Amendment) enacted by Congress in 1974, which governs who may see school records and under what conditions.

**Foundations of education.** The psychological, historical, philosophical, and sociological aspects of the field of education that are considered essential to the professional knowledge of all teachers.

**Free Exercise Clause.** Clause of the First Amendment to the Constitution stating that the U.S. Congress cannot make laws that prohibit the free exercise of religion.

**Freedom of Expression Clause.** Clause of the First Amendment to the Constitution stating that the U.S. Congress cannot make laws that abridge freedom of speech.

**Full-service schools.** Schools that include social and health services in the same building or complex, reducing the need for families to go to several locations to receive services.

**Funds of knowledge.** Knowledge students and families possess from their own cultural and community experiences that enables them to operate successfully in their own cultures and communities but that often is a mismatch with knowledge required to be successful in school and is often, therefore, devalued.

**Hidden curriculum.** The unstated outcomes of education that students experience and learn by spending time in schools. These outcomes may be intended or unintended, positive or negative.

**High-incidence disabilities.** Disabilities that occur with relative frequency in the population, for example, learning disabilities and speech and language impairments; often referred to as mild disabilities.

**Individualized Education Plan (IEP).** A legal document defining the educational program and related services for a specific student who has a disability.

**Individuals with Disabilities Education Act (IDEA).** Federal legislation protecting the rights of students with disabilities to receive a free, appropriate education that meets their needs.

**Induction.** The first three years of a teacher's career, which are recognized as years requiring special support to help consolidate the beginner's skills.

**Instructional technology.** Technology that supports students' learning the school curriculum.

**Intrinsic motivation.** Motivation to do something without external rewards or consequences.

**Job-embedded professional development.** Providing support to teachers to develop their skills in the context of their classrooms with the support of other professionals who work directly in their classrooms demonstrating, observing, and providing feedback.

**Latin Grammar school.** Early schools that followed a classical curriculum consisting mainly of Latin and Latin texts, with some Greek.

**Least restrictive environment (LRE).** Students with disabilities are to be educated in the learning environment that poses the fewest restrictions on their lives as students and that provides the most opportunities for interaction with nondisabled peers.

**Learned curriculum.** What students actually learn in relationship to the goals of the explicit curriculum—which is not always the same as those goals.

**License portability.** The ease with which a valid teaching license from one state is recognized in another state.

**Local education agency (LEA).** A term used to describe the local school district.

**Looping.** Keeping students of the same age together with the same teacher for more than one year; students move up with their teachers to the next grade.

**Low-incidence disabilities.** Disabilities that occur with relative infrequency in the population, for example, cerebral palsy or deafness.

**Magnet schools.** Schools with a unifying theme designed to attract students because of the special opportunities associated with the curriculum designed around that theme, often developed following Brown decision to retain middle-class students in inner-city urban schools.

**Making the familiar strange.** Looking at the familiar procedures, events, and interactions in the classroom from a more objective viewpoint and treating them as something you do not fully understand. This is a way of helping you begin to analyze and ask questions about why things happen the way they do in classrooms.

**Mentor.** A highly skilled, experienced teacher who has specific responsibility for supporting teachers during the induction phase of the career.

**Mentoring.** Providing expert, veteran teachers to support new teachers in the induction years so that they can gain confidence and strengthen their teaching skills, and stay in teaching.

**Misconceptions.** Ideas you may have about teaching that are not accurate but that may represent strongly held beliefs about teaching and so may be difficult for you to discard or replace.

**Multi-age classrooms.** Classrooms where students of various ages are enrolled in the same classroom and taught simultaneously by the same teacher.

**National Board for Professional Teaching Standards (NBPTS).** An organization that reviews representative work of experienced teachers to determine whether their work merits their gaining board certification as accomplished teachers.

**National Council for Accreditation of Teacher Education (NCATE).** The largest voluntary accreditation agency for teacher education programs nationwide.

**National Education Association.** The largest teachers' organization in the United States, with approximately 3.2 million members.

**No Child Left Behind Act of 2001.** Federal legislation applying to all schools that receive certain categories of federal funding, which increases accountability for the quality of teaching and learning through annual testing of students and which has sanctions for schools that do not perform adequately each year.

**Normal school.** The earliest schools that existed for the sole purpose of preparing teachers for their professional roles in the classroom.

**Null curriculum.** Everything that is not included in the explicit curriculum, and, thus, is not expected to be learned during a student's PK–12 education.

**Pedagogical content knowledge.** The ability to present academic content to students so they understand it well.

**Pedagogy.** The methods and activities teachers use to instruct their students.

**Peer assistance and review.** Observation and review of experienced teachers who are having trouble carrying out their responsibilities, conducted by other teachers, as a way of monitoring the quality of the teaching force.

**Peer mediation.** Structured programs of problem solving in which students are trained to work with their peers to solve problems between students.

**Peer tutoring.** Structured programs in which students are trained to tutor other students.

**Per pupil expenditure.** The average total amount of money that is spent per pupil each year, which varies greatly from state to state.

**Perennialism.** A philosophical orientation based on the assumption that all learning should be focused on unchanging principles or great ideas.

**Praxis tests.** A series of tests and assessments for teacher education students and beginning teachers developed by the Educational Testing Service; in many states, passing scores on the written tests are required to apply for a teaching license.

**Prior knowledge.** Knowledge about teaching that you already have before you enter your formal preparation, which affects how you think about teaching and what you learn about teaching as a profession.

**Profession.** Work that requires specialized knowledge, skills, and preparation in which individuals are expected to draw on their knowledge and skills to make judicious decisions—usually without directives from a supervisor.

**Professional development school.** A public school that works in close partnership with a school, college, or department of education as a site for the simultaneous preparation of new teachers and improvement of teaching and learning for PK–12 students.

**Professional knowledge base.** The body of professional knowledge teachers possess that distinguishes them from what laypersons know about how to carry out the professional responsibilities of teachers.

**Professional school.** A unit of a college or university that prepares students for the professions, in contrast to the liberal arts and sciences, which prepare students in the academic disciplines, or subject matter.

**Progressivism.** A philosophy of education developed by John Dewey based on the assumption that all learning is active, that learning is intellectual, social, and emotional, and that curriculum should begin with the child's interests and experiences.

**Project-based learning.** Studying a particular question, problem, or theme in depth over time that requires the use of several academic content areas.

**Reciprocity.** Formal recognition that a teaching license that is valid in one state allows a teacher to be eligible to teach in another state.

**Regularities of schooling.** A term coined by Seymour Sarason to describe the traditions and practices of schooling that are taken for granted and are not questioned—even though schooling could be organized and carried out in other ways.

**Resilience.** A characteristic of some children who are exposed to stressors from the social conditions of their lives but who appear to be invulnerable to the negative effects of those stressors.

**Scope and sequence.** Charts that lay out the various topics within a subject that will be included, as well as what level of that topic students will study at each grade level in a particular subject.

**Self-fulfilling prophecy.** A teacher's expectations about a student which may come true whether or not there is evidence to support that expectation.

**Site-based management.** Individual management of schools where principals share decision-making authority with teachers, staff, and community members.

**Social justice.** A curriculum orientation that organizes education around understanding the problems of society and working toward equity and justice in the society.

**Social reconstructionism.** A philosophy of education based on the belief that schools should aim to foster active participants in society through a study of social problems and an aim to create a more just society.

**State education agency (SEA).** The agency at the state level that makes educational policy and ensures that districts within the state comply with regulations governing education.

**Student-led conferences.** An approach to parent-teacher conferences where students lead the conference by reviewing and assessing samples of their work to describe progress and set new goals.

**Taught curriculum.** The curriculum that is delivered by teachers once they make decisions about how to teach the explicit curriculum.

**Teacher Education Accreditations Council (TEAC).** A group that accredits teacher education programs.

**Teacher expectations.** The expectations teachers set for what their students are capable of doing and achieving in the classroom. Teachers can treat students for whom they have set higher or lower expectations differently, often presenting lesser challenges for those whom they believe cannot achieve at high levels.

**Teaching portfolio.** A written or electronic compilation of documentation demonstrating that a teacher education student possesses the knowledge, skills, and dispositions to teach students well at the level of a beginning teacher.

**Teacher-proof curriculum.** Highly prescriptive curriculum or instructional materials that can be implemented without independent thinking or decision making on the part of the teacher.

**Teacher research.** Research conducted by teachers in their own classrooms or school settings for the purpose of systematically studying their teaching and taking action to improve it.

**Title IX.** Federal legislation designed to ensure equity between men and women in education.

**Transition services.** Special education services to help adolescents and young adults with disabilities make the transition from the school setting to the "real world" of work and living away from home, whether in a protected or a completely independent living or work situation.

**Universal design.** Design of architecture and learning environments that is based on a consideration of all individuals, including those with disabilities, from the outset rather than as an afterthought.

**Virtual schools.** Schools that are conducted partly or entirely online for students of traditional PK–12 school age.

**Vouchers.** An arrangement whereby parents can enroll their children in a private school and can apply a specific amount of public dollars toward the tuition for that school.

**White privilege.** The advantages white persons experience by virtue of being white, whether they seek the privileges out or not, compared with individuals from racial or ethnic minority groups.

**Year-round schools.** Schools with a calendar organized so that students attend over the course of the entire calendar year, with shorter vacations interspersed across the year.

Administration for Children and Families. (2006). *Summary: Child maltreatment 2006.* Washington, DC: Author. Retrieved April 3, 2008 from http://www.acf.hhs.gov/programs/cb/pubs/cm06/summary.htm.

Albert, L. (2003). *Cooperative discipline.* Circle Pines, MN: American Guidance Service.

American Association for the Advancement of Science. (2005). Dialogue on science, ethics, and religion. Retrieved April 3, 2005 from http://www.aaas.org/spp/dser/evolution/issues.shtml.

American Association for the Advancement of Science. (2008). *Evolution on the front line.* Washington, DC: Author. Retrieved May 15, 2008 from http://www.aaas.org/news/press_room/evolution

American Association of Colleges for Teacher Education. (1999, July). *Comparison of NCATE and TEAC processes for accreditation of teacher education.* Washington, DC: Author.

American Association of Colleges for Teacher Education. (2005). *Professional development schools at a glance.* Retrieved February 9, 2005, from http://www.aacte.org/Eric/pds_glance.htm.

American Educational Research Association. (2003, Fall). Class size: Counting students can count. *Research Points, 1* (2), 1-4.

American Educational Research Association. (2007). Time to learn. *Research Points, 5*(2). Retrieved May 23, 2008 from www.aera.net.

American Federation of Teachers. (2007). *Building minds, minding buildings: Turning crumbling schools into environments for learning.* Washington, DC: Author. Retrieved June 3, 2008 from www.aft.org.

American Federation of Teachers. (2007). *Survey and analysis of teacher salary trends 2005.* Washington, DC: Author. Retrieved April 1, 2005 from http://www.aft.org/salary/2002/download/AFT2005/SalarySurvey.pdf.

American Federation of Teachers. (2008). *Grade school teachers become labor leaders.* Retrieved June 18, 2008 from http://www.aft.org/about/history/index.htm.

American Library Association (2008). Banned books week. Retrieved May 24, 2008 from http://www.ala.org.

Anderson, C. W., and M. K. Fetters. (1996). Science education trends and special education. In Pugach, M. C. and C. L. Warger (Eds.), *Curriculum trends, special education, and reform* (pp. 53-67). New York: Teachers College Press.

Anderson, L. W., and L. S. Pellicer. (2001). *Teacher peer assistance and review.* Thousand Oaks, CA: Corwin Press.

Anderson, P., Aromaa, S., & D. Rosenbloom. ( 2007). *Prevention education: Survey and recommendations.* Albany, NY; Join Together. Retrieved May 6, 2008 from http://www.jointogether.org/aboutus/ourpublications/pdf/prevention-report.pdf

Anyon, J. (1981). Social class and school knowledge. *Curriculum Inquiry, 11* (1), 3-42.

Apple, M. W. (1979). *Ideology and curriculum.* London: Routledge & Kegan Paul.

Armstrong, J. (2005, January). *State strategies for redesigning high schools and promoting high school to college transitions.* Issue Brief. Denver, CO: Education Commission of the States. Retrieved July 30, 2008 from http://www.ecs.org.

Association of American Publishers. (2007). *Industry statistics.* Retrieved June 18, 2008 from http://www.publishers.org/main/industry/stats/indstats-01.htm.

Association of American Publishers. (n.d.). *School division: Interactive textbook adoptions/open territory map.* Retrieved June 18, 2008 from http://www.publishers.org/schooldiv/textbooks/textBK_01_Map.htm.

Association of Waldorf Schools of North America. (n.d.). Classroom and curriculum. Retrieved July 30, 2008 from http://www.whywaldorfworks.org.

Bailey, J. M., and T. R. Guskey. (2001). *Implementing student-led conferences.* Thousand Oaks, CA: Corwin Press.

Bales, S. N. (2004). How Americans think about international education and why it matters. *Phi Delta Kappan, 86,* 206-209.

Ball, E. W., and B. Harry. (1993). Multicultural education and special education: Parallels, divergencies, and intersections. *The Educational Forum, 57,* 430-436.

Banks, J. A. (1996). Transformative knowledge, curriculum reform, and action. In Banks, J. A. (Ed.), *Multicultural education, transformative knowledge, and action* (pp. 335-348). New York: Teachers College Press.

Banks, J., M. Cochran-Smith, L. Moll, A. Richert, K. Zeichner, P. LePage, L. Darling-Hammond, and H. Duffy. (2005). Teaching diverse learners. In Darling-Hammond, L. and J. Bransford (Eds.), *Preparing teachers for a changing world* (pp. 232-274). San Francisco: Jossey-Bass.

## 470   References

Banks, J. A. (1995). Multicultural education: Historical development, dimensions, and practice. In Banks, J. A. (Ed.), *Handbook of research on multicultural education* (pp. 3-24). New York: Simon and Schuster Macmillan.

Barton, A. C. (2003). *Teaching science for social justice.* New York: Teachers College Press.

Basham, P. (2001). *Home schooling: From the extreme to the mainstream.* Public Policy Sources #51. Vancouver, BC: Fraser Institute. Retrieved July 30, 2008 from http://www.fraserinstitute.org.

Beane, J. A., and M. W. Apple. (1995). The case for democratic schools. In Apple, M. W. and J. A. Beane (Eds.), *Democratic schools* (pp. 1-25). Alexandria, VA: Association for Supervision and Curriculum Development.

Bear, G. G., & J. Blank. (2008, March). *Fact sheet #2; Bullying prevention.* Muncie, IN: Consortium to Prevent School Violence. Retrieved April 4, 2008 from www.preventschoolviolence.org.

Bennett, K. P., and M. D. LeCompte. (1990). *The way schools work: A sociological analysis of education.* New York: Longman.

Ben-Peretz, M. (1990). *The teacher-curriculum encounter: Freeing teachers from the tyranny of texts.* Albany, NY: SUNY Press.

Berry, B., M. Hoke, and E. Hirsh. (2004). The search for highly qualified teachers. *Phi Delta Kappan, 85,* 684-689.

Bigelow, B., and R. Peterson. (Eds.). (1998). *Rethinking Columbus: The next 500 years.* Milwaukee, WI: Rethinking Schools.

Bill and Melinda Gates Foundation. Transforming high schools. Retrieved July 30, 2008 from http://www.gatesfoundation.org.

Black, S. (2000).Together again: The practice of looping keeps students together with the same teachers. *American School Board Journal, 187* (6), 40-43.

Blatt, B. (1984). Biography in autobiography. In Blatt, B. and R. J. Morris (Eds.), *Perspectives in special education: Personal orientations* (pp. 263-307). Glenview, IL: Scott Foresman.

Blatt, B., and F. Kaplan. (1966). *Christmas in purgatory: A photographic essay on mental retardation* (2nd ed.). Boston: Allyn & Bacon.

Bleakley, A., Hennessy, M., & M. Fishbein. (2006). Public opinion on sex education in U.S. schools. *Archives of Pediatrics and Adolescent Medicine, 160,* 1151–1156.

Boyd, D., Grossman, P., Lankford, H., Loeb, S., & J. Wyckoff.(2006). How changes in entry requirements alter the teacher workforce and affect student achievement. *Education Finance and Policy, 1* (2), 176–216.

Bransford, J., L. Darling-Hammond, and P. LePage. (2005). Introduction. In Darling-Hammond, L. and J. Bransford (Eds.), *Preparing teachers for a changing world* (pp. 1-39). San Francisco: Jossey-Bass.

Brantlinger, E. (1997). Using ideology: Cases of nonrecognition of the politics of research and practice in special education. *Review of Educational Research, 67,* 425-459.

Brown, K. (1996). Revisiting the Supreme Court's opinion in *Brown v. Board of Education* from a multiculturalist perspective.

In Lagemann, E. C. and L. P. Miller (Eds.), *Brown v. Board of Education: The challenge for today's schools* (pp. 44-53). New York: Teachers College Press.

Bryk, A. S., and B. Schneider. (2002). *Trust in schools: A core resource for improvement.* New York: Russell Sage Foundation.

Bryk, A. S., and Y. M. Thum. (1989). The effect of high school organization on dropping out: An exploratory investigation. *American Educational Research Journal, 26,* 353-383.

Bryson, K., and L. M. Casper. (1999, May). *Current population reports: Special studies/Co-resident grandparents and grandchildren* (Report p. 23-198). Washington, DC: U. S. Census Bureau.

Bulman, R.C. (2005). *Hollywood goes to high school: Cinema, schools and American culture.* New York: Worth Publishers.

Bureau of Labor Statistics. (2008). *Occupational outlook handbook, 2008-09 edition, teachers—preschool, kindergarten, elementary, middle, and secondary.* Washington, DC: U.S. Department of Labor. Retrieved July 30, 2008 from http://www.bls.gov/oco/ocos069.htm.

Butts, R. F., and L. A. Cremin. (1953). *A history of education in American culture.* New York: Henry Holt and Company.

California State Board of Education. *Grade four science content standards.* Sacramento, CA: Author. Retrieved July 30, 2008 from http://www.cde.ca.gov

Carnegie Forum on Education and the Economy. (1986). *A nation prepared: Teachers for the 21st century.* Washington, DC: Task Force on Teaching as a Profession.

Caro-Bruce, C., and J. McCreadie. (1995). What happens when a school district supports action research? In S. E. Noffke and R. B. Stevenson (Eds.), *Educational action research: Becoming practically critical* (pp. 154-164). New York: Teachers College Press.

Carter, K., and W. Doyle. (1996). Personal narrative and life history in learning to teach. In J. Sikula (Ed.), *Handbook of research on teacher education* (2nd ed.) (pp. 120-142). New York: Simon and Schuster/Macmillan.

Carver, C. L., and D. S. Katz. (2004). Teaching at the boundary of acceptable practice: What is a new teacher mentor to do? *Journal of Teacher Education, 55,* 449-462.

Cavanaugh, S. (2005, February 2). Teachers torn over religion, evolution. *Education Week, 1,* 18.

Cawley, J., S. Hayden, E. Cade, and S. Baker-Kroczynski. (2002). Including students with disabilities into the general education science classroom. *Exceptional Children, 68,* 423-435.

Center for Applied Special Technology. (2007). *About CAST.* Retrieved July 25, 2008 from http://www.cast.org.

Center for the Study and Prevention of Violence. (1998). *CSPV position summary: D.A.R.E. program.* Report PS 001. Boulder: University of Colorado. Retrieved February 28, 2005 from http://www.colorado.edu/cspv/publications/factsheets/positions/pdf/PS-001.pdf.

Center on Education Policy. (2005, March). *From the capital to the classroom: Year 3 of the No Child Left Behind Act.*

Washington, DC: Author. Retrieved July 30, 2008 from http://www.cep-de.org.

Child Welfare Information Gateway. (2007). *Foster care statistics.* Retrieved April 3, 2008 from http://www.childwelfare.gov/pubs/factsheets/foster.cfm.

Child Welfare Information Gateway. (2006). *Recognizing child abuse and neglect: Signs and symptoms factsheet. Washington,* DC: Author. Retrieved April 3, 2008 from http://www.childwelfare.gov/can.

Childhelp USA. (2006). *National child abuse statistics.* Scottsdale, AZ: Author. Retrieved March 5, 2005 from http://www.childhelpusa.org/abuseinfo_stats.htm.

Christian, D., I. U. Pufahl, and N. C. Rhodes. (2004/2005). Language learning: A worldwide perspective. *Educational Leadership, 62* (4), 24-30.

Cincinnati Federation of Teachers. (2003). *Professionalization: Peer assistance and evaluation.* Retrieved July 30, 2008 from http://www.cft-aft.org/paep.pdf.

Clark, C. (1990). The teacher and the taught: Moral transactions in the classroom. In Goodlad, J. I., R. Soder, and K. A. Sirotnik (Eds.), *The moral dimensions of teaching* (pp. 251-265). San Francisco: Jossey-Bass.

Clark, T. (2001, October). *Virtual schools: Trends and issues. A study of virtual schools in the United States.* Distance Learning Resource Network, WestEd. Retrieved July 30, 2008 from http://www.wested.org/online_pubs/virtualschools.pdf.

Clifford, G. J. (1989). Man/woman/teacher: Gender, family, and career in American educational history. In D. Warren (Ed.), *American teachers* (pp. 293-343). New York: Macmillan.

Coalition for Community Schools. (n. d.). *Frequently asked questions.* Retrieved June 18, 2008 from http://www.communityschools.org.

Cochran-Smith, M., and S. Lytle. (1993). *Inside outside: Teacher research and knowledge.* New York: Teachers College Press.

Cody, C. (1990). The politics of textbook publishing, adoption, and use. In Elliott, D. L. and A. Woodward (Eds.), *Textbooks and schooling in the United States* (pp. 127-145). The 89th yearbook of the National Society for the Study of Education (Part I). Chicago: University of Chicago Press.

Cohen, E. G. (1986). *Designing groupwork: strategies for the heterogeneous classroom.* New York: Teachers College Press.

Cohen, G., C. Miller, R. Stonehill, and C. Geddes. (2000, September). *The class-size reduction program: Boosting student achievement in schools across the nation.* Washington, DC: United States Department of Education. Retrieved July 30, 2008 from http://www.ed.gov/offices/OESE/ClassSize/class.pdf.

Cohen, S.S. (1974). *A history of colonial education, 1607–1776.* New York: John Wiley & Sons.

Colasanti, M. (2008, March). *School prayer, moment of silence, other policies concerning religion.* ECS StateNotes. Denver: Education Commission of the States. Retrieved May 25, 2008 from www.ecs.org.

Columbus Education Association. (2001). Peer assistance and review. Retrieved July 30, 2008 from http://www.ceaohio.org/professionaldevelopment

Comer, J. P. (1997). *Waiting for a miracle: Why schools can't solve our problems and how we can.* New York: Plume.

Commonwealth of Virginia, Department of Education. (2000). *Science standards of learning teacher resource guide, grade four.* Richmond, VA: Author.

Commonwealth of Virginia. (1995, June). *Grade eight standards of learning for Virginia public schools.* Richmond, VA: Commonwealth of Virginia Board of Education. Retrieved July 30, 2008 from http://www.knowledge.stateva.us/main/sol/sol.cfm.

Connelly, F. M., and M. Ben-Peretz. (1980). Teachers' roles in the using and doing of research and curriculum development. *Journal of Curriculum Studies, 12* (2), 95-107.

Constitution Society. (2008). *Northwest Ordinance of 1787.* Retrieved May 18, 2008 from http://www.constitution.org/liberlib.htm.

Cooper, B. S., L. D. Fusarelli, and E. V. Randall. (2004). *Better policies, better schools.* Boston: Pearson/Allyn & Bacon.

Corbett, D., and B. Wilson. (2002). What urban students say about good teaching. *Educational Leadership, 60,* 18-22.

Corey, Stephen, M. (1953). *Action research to improve school practice.* New York: Bureau of Publications, Teachers College, Columbia University.

Council of Chief State School Officers (1992). *INTASC membership. Model standards for beginning teacher licensing and development: A resource for state dialogue.* Washington, DC: Author.

Council of Chief State School Officers. (2007). *INTASC membership.* Retrieved July 30, 2008 from www.ccsso.org.

Crawford, J. (1991). *Bilingual education: History, politics, theory, and practice.* Los Angeles: Bilingual Education Services.

Cremin, L. A. (1988). *American education: The metropolitan experience, 1876-1980.* New York: Harper and Row.

Crocco, M.S. (2007). *Teaching the levees: A Curriculum for democratic dialogue and civic engagement.* New York: Teachers College Press.

Cuban, L. (2001). Why are teachers infrequent and restrained users of computers in their classrooms? In Woodward, J. and L. Cuban (Eds.), *Technology, curriculum and professional development* (pp. 121-131). Thousand Oaks, CA: Corwin.

Cuban, L. (1992). Curriculum stability and change. In P. W. Jackson (Ed.), *Handbook of research on curriculum* (pp. 216-247). New York: Macmillan.

Curtain, H., and C. A. Dahlberg. (2004). *Languages and children—making the match: New languages for young learners, grades K-8* (3rd ed.). Boston: Pearson Education.

D.A.R.E. America. (2005). *The new D.A.R.E. program.* Retrieved February 28, 2005 from http://www.dare.com/home/newdareprogram.asp.

Darling-Hammond, L. (1995). Inequality and access to knowledge. In Banks, J. A. (Ed.), *Handbook of research on multicultural education* (pp. 465-483). New York: Simon and Schuster Macmillan.

Darling-Hammond, L. (1997). *The right to learn: A blueprint for creating schools that work*. San Francisco: Jossey-Bass.

Darling-Hammond, L. (2001). Standard setting in teaching: Changes in licensing, certification, and assessment. In Richardson, V. (Ed.), *Handbook of research on teaching* (4th ed.) (pp. 751-776). Washington, DC: American Educational Research Association.

Darling-Hammond, L., and K. Hammerness. (2005). The design of teacher education programs. In L. Darling-Hammond & J. Bransford (Eds.), *Preparing teachers for a changing world* (pp. 390-441). San Francisco: Jossey-Bass.

Darling-Hammond, L . (2004). What happens to a dream deferred? In Banks, J. A. and C. A. M. Banks (Eds.), *Handbook of research on multicultural education* (2nd ed., pp. 607-630). San Francisco: Jossey-Bass.

Day, J. C. (2003, August). *School enrollment: 2000*. Census 2000 Brief. Report C2KBR-26. Washington, DC: United States Census Bureau.

Delpit, L. (1995). *Other people's children: Cultural conflicts in the classroom*. New York: The New Press.

Denver Public Schools. (2008). *Procomp: Professional compensation for teachers*. Denver: Author. Retrieved July 30, 2008 from http://denverprocomp.org/.

Dewey, J. (1916/1966). *Democracy and education*. New York: Free Press.

Diaz, C. F., B., G. Massialas, and J. A. Kanthopoulos. (1999). *Global perspectives for educators*. Boston: Allyn & Bacon.

Donovan, M. S., and C. T. Cross. (Eds.). (2002). *Minority students in special and gifted education*. Washington, DC: National Academy Press.

Donovan, M. S., J. D. Bransford, and J. W. Pellegrino. (Eds.). (2000). *How people learn: Brain, mind, experience, and school*. Washington, DC: National Academy Press.

Dounay, J. (2005, April). *Site-based decisionmaking: State level policies*. StateNotes. Denver, CO: Education Commission of the States. Retrieved May 27, 2008 from www.ecs.org.

Dryfoos, J. G. (1994). *Full-service schools: A revolution in health and social services for children, youth, and families*. San Francisco: Jossey-Bass.

Dwyer, K., D. Osher, and C. Warger. (1998). *Early warning, timely response: A guide to safe schools*. Washington, DC: U.S. Department of Education.

Dykeman, T. B., with D. Rogers. (2002). *The social, political and philosophical works of Catharine Beecher*. Bristol: The Thoemmes Continuum.

Easton, J. Q., and S. L. Storey. (1994). The development of local school councils. *Education and Urban Society, 26*, 220-238.

Eccles, T. S., and J. Templeton. (2002). Extracurricular and other after-school activities for youth. In Secado W. G. (Ed.), *Review of research in education*, Volume 26 (pp. 113-180). Washington, DC: American Educational Research Association.

Editorial Projects in Education Research Center. (2008). *National highlights: A special supplement to Education Week's Quality Counts 2008*. Retrieved April 26, 2008 from http://www.edweek.org/media/ew/qc/2008/18shr.us.h27.pdf.

Education Commission of the States. (1999). *Beginning teacher mentoring programs*. Retrieved January 27, 2005, from http://www.ecs.org/clearinghouse/13/15/1315.htm.

Education Commission of the States. (2004, September). *Pagers and cellular phones on school property*. StateNotes. Retrieved May 27, 2008 from www.ecs.org.

Education Commission of the States. (2005). *Accountability-sanctions-takeovers*. Retrieved March 27, 2005 from www.ecs.org.

Education Commission of the States. (2008a). *About ECS*. Retrieved July 25, 2008 from www.ecs.org.

Education Commission of the States. (2008b). *State Notes: States/Collective bargaining*. Policies for teachers. Retrieved July 25, 2008 from http://www.ecs.org/clearinghouse/79/27/7727.pdf.

Education Week. (2008, January 10). *Quality counts 2008: Tapping into Teaching*.

Educators for Social Responsibility. (2007). *Peer mediation programs, Grades 4-12*. Cambridge, MA: Author. Retrieved June 18, 2008 from http://www.esrnational.org.

Eisner, E. W. (1979). *The educational imagination: On the design and evaluation of school programs*. New York: Macmillan.

Eisner, E. W., and E. Vallance. (Eds.). (1974). *Conflicting conceptions of curriculum*. Berkeley, CA: McCutchan Publishing Company.

El-Haj, T. R. A. (2003). Practicing equity from the standpoint of the particular: Exploring the work of one urban teacher network. *Teachers College Press, 105*, 817-845.

Ellis, S. (1991, February 4). Little schoolhouse on the prairie. *Time* Magazine, pp. 64-69.

ERIC Clearinghouse on Disabilities and Gifted Education. (2003, Spring). *Paraeducators: Providing support to students with disabilities and their teachers*. ERIC Document ED 476 844.

Erickson, F. (1986). Qualitative methods in research on teaching. In M. Wittrock (Ed.), *Handbook of research on teaching* (3rd ed., pp. 119-161). New York: Macmillan.

Erickson, F. and J. Shultz. (1992). Students' experience of the curriculum. In Jackson, P. W. (Ed.), *Handbook of research on curriculum* (pp. 465-485). New York: Macmillan.

Esquith, R. (2007). *Teach like your hair's on fire*. New York: Viking.

Everhart, N. (2003). The impact of year-round schools on the school library media program. *Knowledge Quest, 32* (2), 47-49.

Evertson, C. M., and J. L. Green. (1986). Observation as inquiry and method. In M. Wittrock (Ed.), *Handbook of research on teaching* (3rd ed., pp. 162-213). New York: Macmillan.

Falk, B. (2000). *The heart of the matter: Using standards and assessments to learn*. Portsmouth, NH: Heinemann.

Federal Communications Commission. (2006). Children's Internet Protection Act. FCC Consumer Facts. Retrieved May 27, 2008 from http://www.fcc.gov/cgb/consumerfacts/cipa.html.

Feiman-Nemser, S., and M. Buchmann. (1985). Pitfalls of experience in teacher preparation. *Teachers College Record, 87* (1), 53-65.

Feldman, A., and J. M. Atkin. (1995). Embedding action research in professional practice. In S. E. Noffke and R. B. Stevenson (Eds.), *Educational action research: Becoming practically critical* (pp. 127-137). New York: Teachers College Press.

Fenstermacher, G. D., and J. F. Soltis. (1986). *Approaches to teaching.* New York: Teachers College Press.

Feretti, R. P., C. D. MacArthur, and C. Okolo. (2001). Teaching for historical understanding in inclusive classrooms. *Learning Disability Quarterly, 24,* 59-72.

Festritzer, C. E. (2000, February). *Alternative teacher certification: A state by state analysis 2000.* Washington, DC: National Center for Educational Information.

Fiedler, C. R. (2000). *Making a difference: Advocacy competencies for special education professionals.* Boston: Allyn & Bacon.

Fields, J., and L. M. Casper. (2001, June). *Current population reports: America's families and living structures 2000* (Report 20-537). Washington, DC: United States Census Bureau.

Filardo, M. (2008, April). *Good buildings, better schools.* Washington, DC: Economic Policy Institute. Retrieved June 3, 2008 from www.epi.org.

Finn, J. (2002). Small classes in American schools: Research, practice, and politics. *Phi Delta Kappan, 83,* 551-560.

Flannery, M. E. (2004). Turning the Tables. *NEA Today, 23* (3), 36-37.

Florio-Ruane, S. (1989). Social organization of classes and schools. In Reynolds, M. C. (Ed.), *Knowledge base for the beginning teacher* (pp. 163-172). Published for the American Association of Colleges for Teacher Education. New York: Pergamon Press.

Ford, A., L. Davern, and R. Schnorr. (2001). Learners with significant disabilities. *Remedial and Special Education, 22,* 214-222.

Frankenberg, E. (2006, December). *The segregation of American teachers.* A Report of the Civil Rights Project. Cambridge: Harvard University. Retrieved June 2, 2008 from http://www.civilrightsproject.ucla.edu.

Fuchs, D., and L. S. Fuchs. (1994). Inclusive schools movement and the radicalization of special education reform. *Exceptional Children, 60,* 294-309.

Fullan, M. (1993). *Change forces: Probing the depths of educational reform.* New York: Teachers College Press.

Fullan, M., A. Bertani, and J. Quinn. (2004). New lessons for districtwide reform. *Educational Leadership, 61,* 42-46.

Gabrieli, C., & W. Goldstein. (2008). *Time to learn.* San Francisco: Jossey-Bass.

Garmezy, N., and M. Rutter. (1983). *Stress, coping, and development in children.* New York: McGraw-Hill.

Gilman, D. A., and S. Kiger. (2003). Should we try to keep class sizes small? *Educational Leadership, 60* (7), 80-86.

Girod, G. R. (Ed). (2002). *Connecting teaching and learning.* Western Oregon University.

Gladden, R. M. (2002). Reducing school violence. In Secada, W. G. (Ed.), *Review of research in education,* Volume 26 (pp. 263-290). Washington, DC: American Educational Research Association.

Glesne, C. (2006). *Becoming qualitative researchers* (3rd ed.). Boston: Pearson Education, Inc.

Gonzalez, N., Moll, L.C., & C. Amanti. (2005). *Funds of knowledge: Theorizing practices in households, communities and classrooms.* Mahwah, NJ: Lawrence Erlbaum Associates.

Good, T. L, and J. S. Braden. (2000). *The great school debate: Choice, vouchers, and charters.* Mahwah, NJ: Lawrence Erlbaum Associates.

Greene, M. (1978). *Landscapes of learning.* New York: Teachers College Press.

Greenwood, C. R., and J. Delaquadri. (1995). Class wide peer tutoring and the prevention of school failure. *Preventing School Failure, 39* (4), 21-25.

Grimmett, P. P., and A. M. MacKinnon. (1992). Craft knowledge and the education of teachers. In Grant, G. (Ed.), *Review of research in education,* Volume 18 (pp. 385-456). Washington, DC: American Educational Research Association.

Guajardo, M. A., and F. J. Guajardo. (2004). The impact of Brown on the Brown of South Texas: A micropolitical perspective on the education of Mexican Americans in a South Texas community. *American Educational Research Journal, 41,* 501-526.

Guttman, A. (1987). *Democratic education.* Princeton, NJ: Princeton University Press.

Hackmann, D. (2004). Constructivism and block scheduling: Making the connection. *Phi Delta Kappan, 85,* 697-702.

Hakuta, K. (1986). *Mirror of language: The debate on bilingualism.* New York; Basic Books.

Hale, L. (2002). *Native American handbook: A reference handbook.* Santa Barbara, CA: ABC-CLIO.

Hampel, R. L. (2002). Historical perspective on small schools. *Phi Delta Kappan, 83,* 367-363.

Hansen, D. T. (2001). Teaching as a moral activity. In Richardson, V., (Ed.), *Handbook of research on teaching* (4th ed., pp. 826-857). Washington, DC: American Educational Research Association.

Hargreaves, A. (1994). *Changing teachers, changing times: Teachers' work and culture in the postmodern age.* New York: Teachers College Press.

Harry, B., & J. Klingner. (2006). *Why are so many minority students in special education?* New York: Teachers College Press.

Haynes, C. C., S. Chaltain, J. E. Ferguson, D. L. Hudson, and O. Thomas. (2003). *The First Amendment in schools.* Alexandria, VA: Association for Supervision and Curriculum Development and the First Amendment Center.

Heath, S.B. (1983). *Ways with words: Language, life and work in communities and classrooms.* New York: Cambridge University Press.

Heller, K. A., W. H. Holtzman, and S. Messick. (Eds.). (1982). *Placing children in special education: A strategy for equity.* Washington, DC: National Academy Press.

Henderson, A.T., & K. L., Mapp. (2002). *A new wave of evidence: The impact of school, family, and community connections on student achievement.* Annual Synthesis 2002. Austin, TX: Southwest Educational Development Laboratory. Retrieved May 25, 2008 from http://www.sedl.org/connections/resources/evidence.pdf.

Hendrie, C. (2004, January 21). In U.S. schools, race still counts. *Education Week, 23* (19), 1, 16-19.

Herbst, J. (1989). Teacher preparation in the nineteenth century. In Warren, D. (Ed.), *American teachers* (pp. 213-236). New York: Macmillan.

Hoffman, N. (1981). *Women's "true" profession: Voices from the history of teaching.* Old Westbury, NY: Feminist Press.

Holloway, J. (2000). The promise and pitfalls of site-based management. *Educational Leadership, 57* (7), 81-82.

Home School Legal Defense Association. (2008). *State laws.* Retrieved July 30, 2008 from http://www.hslda.org/laws/default.asp.

Hord, S. (2004). *Learning together, leading together.* New York: Teachers College Press.

Howard University School of Law. (2004). *Brown at 50: Fulfilling the promise.* Retrieved July 30, 2008, from http://www.brownat50.org.

Howard, G. R. (1999). *We can't teach what we don't know: White teachers, multiracial schools.* New York: Teachers College Press.

Huberman, M. (1993). *The lives of teachers.* Translated by Jonathan Neufeld. Teacher Development Series. New York: Teachers College Press.

Human Rights Watch. (2001). *Hatred in the hallways: Violence and discrimination against lesbian, gay, bisexual and transgender students in U.S. schools.* New York: Author. Retrieved July 30, 2008 from http://www.hrw.org/reports/2001/uslgbt/.

Humphrey, D.C., Wechsler, M.E., Bosetti, K.R., Park, J., & J. Tiffany-Morales. (2008, February). *Teacher induction in Illinois and Ohio: Findings and recommendations.* Menlo Park, CA: SRI International.

Iano, R. P. (2004). Inside the schools: Special education and inclusion reform. In Gallager, D. (Ed.), *Challenging orthodoxy in special education: Dissenting voices* (pp. 311-352). Denver, CO: Love Publishing Company.

IDEAdata.org. (2006). Data Tables for OSEP. *Data Table 1–4. Students ages 6 through 11 served under IDEA, Part B, by disability category and state: Fall 2006.* Retrieved May 11, 2008 from https://www.ideadata.org/arc_toc8.asp# partbCC.

Imber, M., and T. Van Geel. (2001). *A teacher's guide to education law* (2nd ed.). Mahwah, NJ: Lawrence Erlbaum Associates.

Ingersoll, R. (2001). Teacher turnover and teacher shortages: An organizational analysis. *American Educational Research Journal, 38,* 499-534.

International Society for Technology in Education. (2008). *National educational technology standards for teachers.* Retrieved July 25, 2008 from www.iste.org.

Irvine, J. J. (1990). *Black students and school failure: Policies, practices, and prescriptions.* New York: Praeger.

Jackson, P. (1968). *Life in classrooms.* New York: Holt, Rinehart, and Winston.

Johnson, C. (1963). *Old-time schools and school books.* New York: Dover Publications.

Johnson, D. W., and R. T. Johnson. (1987). *Learning together and alone: Cooperation, competition and individualization.* Englewood Cliffs, NJ: Prentice-Hall.

Johnson, S. M. (2004). *Finders and keepers: Helping new teachers survive and thrive in our schools.* San Francisco: Jossey-Bass.

Johnson, S. (2008, Winter). *The status of male teachers in public education today.* Education Policy Brief, 6 (4). Bloomington, IN: Center for Evaluation and Education Policy.

Johnson, S. M., and K. C. Boles. (2001). *The power of collective action: A century of teachers organizing for education.* In V. Richardson (Ed.), *Handbook of Research on Teaching* (4th ed., pp. 858-876). Washington, DC: American Educational Research Association.

Johnston, L. D., P. M. O'Malley, J. G. Bachman, and J. E. Schulenberg. (2008). *Monitoring the future national results on adolescent drug use: Overview of key findings.* (NIH Publication No. 08-6418). Bethesda, MD: National Institute on Drug Abuse. Retrieved June 18, 2008 from http://www.monitoringthefuture.org.

Johnston, L. D., O'Malley, P. M., Bachman, J. G., & J. E. Schulenberg. (2008, April). *Monitoring the Future national results on adolescent drug use: Overview of key findings, 2007* (NIH Publication No. 08-6418). Bethesda, MD: National Institute on Drug Abuse. National Institute on Drug Abuse NIH Publication No. 08-6418.

Juniewicz, K. (2003). Student portfolios with a purpose. *Clearing House, 77* (2), 73-77.

Kalkowski, P. (1995). *Peer and cross age tutoring.* School Improvement Research Series Close-Up #18. Portland, OR: Northwest Regional Educational Laboratory.

Katsiyannis, A. (2000). Paraeducators. *Remedial and Special Education, 21,* pp. 297-305.

Katz, L. G., D. Evangelou, and J. Hartman. (1990). *The case for mixed-age grouping in early education.* Washington, DC: National Association for the Education of Young Children.

Kirby, D. (2007). Emerging answers 2007: *Research findings on programs to reduce teen pregnancy and sexually transmitted diseases.* Washington, DC: The National Campaign to Prevent Teen and Unplanned Pregnancy.

Kirby, D. (2002, October). *Do abstinence-only programs delay the initiation of sex among young people and reduce teenage pregnancy?* Washington, DC: National Campaign to Prevent Teen Pregnancy. Retrieved June 18, 2008 from http://thenationalcampaign.org.

Kliewer, C. (2000). Review of The collected papers of Burton Blatt. *Journal of the Association for Persons with Severe Handicaps, 25*, 59-63.

Kosciw, J.G., & E.M. Diaz. (2008). Involved, invisible, ignored: *The experiences of lesbian, gay, bisexual, and transgender parents and their children in our nation's K-12 schools*. New York: GLSEN. Retrieved May 14, 2008 from www.glsen.org.

Kozol, J. (2007). *Letters to a young teacher.* New York: Crown.

Kridel, C., & Bullough, R.V. (2007). *Stories of the Eight-year Study: Reexamining secondary education in America*. Albany: State University of New York Press.

Ladson-Billings, G. (1994). *The dreamkeepers: Successful teachers of African-American children*. San Francisco: Jossey Bass.

Ladson-Billings, G. (2004). Landing on the wrong note: The price we paid for Brown. *Educational Researcher, 33* (7), 3-13.

Ladson-Billings, G. (2004). New directions in multicultural education: complexities, boundaries, and critical race theory. In Banks, J. and C. A. M. Banks (Eds.), *Handbook of research on multicultural education* (2nd ed., pp. 50-65). San Francesco: Jossey-Bass.

Lagemann, E. C. (2004, February 25). Toward a strong profession. *Education Week*, Vol. 23, no. 24, 48, 36-37.

Land, D. (2002). Local school boards under review: Their role and effectiveness in relation to students' academic achievement. *Review of Educational Research, 72*, 229-278.

Lawrence, J., and R. L. Lee. (1955). *Inherit the wind*. New York: Random House.

Le Tendre, G. K., B. K. Hofer, and H. Shimizu. (2003). What is tracking? Cultural expectations in the United States, Germany, and Japan. *American Educational Research Journal, 40*, 43-89.

Lee, H. (1960/2002). *To kill a mockingbird*. New York: Harper-Collins Perennial Classics Edition.

Leithwood, K., and T. Menzies. (1998). Forms and effects of school-based management: A review. *Educational Policy, 12*, 325-347.

LePage, P., L. Darling-Hammond, and H. Akar. (2005). Classroom management. In Darling-Hammond, L. and J. Bransford (Eds.), *Preparing teachers for a changing world* (pp. 327-357). San Francisco: Jossey-Bass.

Lieberman, A., and L. Miller. (1999). *Teachers—transforming their world and work*. New York: Teachers College Press.

Lieberman, A., and L. Miller. (2004). *Teacher leadership*. San Francisco: Jossey-Bass.

Little, J. W. (2001). Professional development in pursuit of school reform. In Lieberman, A. and L. Miller (Eds.), *Teachers caught in the action: Professional development that matters* (pp. 23-44). New York: Teachers College Press.

Lloyd, L. (1999). Multi-age classes and high ability students. *Review of Educational Research, 69*, 187-212.

Lortie, D. (1975). *Schoolteacher: A sociological study*. Chicago: University of Chicago Press.

Lowenthal, B. (2001). *Abuse and neglect: The educator's guide to the identification and prevention of child maltreatment*. Baltimore MD: Paul H. Brookes Publishing Co.

Lugaila, T., and J. Overturf. (2004, March). *Children and the households they live in: 2000*. Census 2000 Special Reports, Report CENSR-14. Washington, DC: U.S. Census Bureau. Retrieved July 30, 2008 from http://www.census.gov/population/www/cen2000/briefs.html.

Manlove, J., K. Franzetta, K. McKinney, A. R. Papillo, and E. Terry-Humen. (2004, January). *A good time: After school programs to reduce teen pregnancy*. Washington, DC: National Campaign to Prevent Teen and Unplanned Pregnancy. Retrieved July 30, 2008 from http://www.thenationalcampaign.org.

Marcos, K. M., and J. K. Peyton. (2000, April). *Promoting a language proficient society: What you can do*. ERIC Clearinghouse on Languages and Linguistics Digest EDO-FL-00-01. Center for Applied Linguistics. Retrieved July 30, 2008 from http://www.cal.org/resources/digest/0001promoting.html.

Massachusetts Department of Education. *Assistive technology guide for Massachusetts schools.* (2002, November). Malden, MA: Author. Retrieved May 13, 2008 from http://www.doe.mass.edu/edtech/assistive/ATguide.pdf.

Mayer, M. J. (2008, March.). Fact *Sheet # 1; Overview of school violence prevention*. Muncie, IN: Consortium to Prevent School Violence. Retrieved May 4, 2008 from www.preventschoolviolence.org.

McCaffrey, D. F., J. R. Lockwood, D. M. Koretz, and L. S. Hamilton. (2003). Evaluating value-added models for teacher accountability. Santa Monica, CA: RAND Corporation.

McDiarmid, G. W., D. L. Ball, and C. W. Anderson. (1989). Why staying one chapter ahead doesn't really work: Subject specific pedagogy. In Reynolds, M. C. (Ed.), *Knowledge base for the beginning teacher* (pp. 193-205). Published for the American Association of Colleges for Teacher Education. New York: Pergamon Press.

McFarland, W. (2001). The legal duty to protect gay and lesbian students from violence in school. *Professional School Counseling, 4* (3), 171-179.

McGhan, B. (2002). A fundamental educational reform: Teacher-led schools. *Phi Delta Kappan, 83*, 538-541.

McIntosh, P. (1989). White privilege: Unpacking the invisible knapsack. *Peace and Freedom*, (4th ed., pp. 877-904) July/August 1989, 10-12.

McLaren, P. (2003). *Life in schools: An introduction to critical pedagogy in the foundations of education* (4th ed.). Boston: Allyn & Bacon/Longman.

McMillen, B. J. (2001). A statewide evaluation of academic achievement in year-round schools. *Journal of Educational Research, 95* (2), 67-74.

Meier, D., and P. Schwartz. (1993). Central Park East Secondary School: The hard part is making it happen. In Apple, M. W. and J. Beane (Eds.), *Democratic schools* (pp. 26-40). Alexandria, VA: Association for Supervision and Curriculum Development.

Mergendoller, J., Markham, T., Ravitz, J., & J. Larmer. (2006). Pervasive management of project based learning. In C. M. Evertson, C. S. Weinstein (Eds.), *Handbook of classroom management: Research, practice, and contemporary issues* (pp. 583–615). Mahwah, NJ: Lawrence Erlbaum Associates.

Metz, M. H. (1986). *Different by design: The context and character of three magnet schools*. New York: Routledge & Kegan Paul.

Meyers, J., and B. K. Nastasi. (1999). Primary prevention in school settings. In Reynolds, C. R. and T. B. Gutkin (Eds.), *The handbook of school psychology* (pp. 764-799). New York: John Wiley & Sons.

Moll, L., and N. Gonzalez. (2004). Engaging life: A funds-of-knowledge approach to multicultural education. In Banks, J. A. and C. A. M. Banks (Eds.), *Handbook of research on multicultural education* (4th ed., pp. 877-904). San Francisco: Jossey-Bass.

Morocco, C. C., A. Hindin, C. Mata-Aguilar, and N. C. Clark-Chicarelli. (2001). Building a deep understanding of literature with middle-grade students with learning disabilities. *Learning Disability Quarterly, 24*, 47-59.

Motley, C. B. (1996). The Legacy of *Brown v. Board of Education*. In Lagemann, E. C. and L. P. Miller (Eds.), *Brown v. Board of Education: The challenge for today's schools* (pp. 37-53). New York: Teachers College Press.

Munby, H., T. Russell, and A. K. Martin. (2001). Teachers' knowledge and how it develops. In Richardson, V. (Ed.), *Handbook of research on teaching* (4th ed.) (pp. 877-904). Washington, DC: American Educational Research Association.

Murphy, J. P., and E. J. Klein. (2003). Networking for teacher learning. *Teachers College Record, 105*, 1606-1621.

Murray, F. M. (1989). Explanations in education. In Reynolds, M. C. (Ed.), *Knowledge base for the beginning teacher* (pp. 1-12). Published for the American Association of Colleges for Teacher Education. New York: Pergamon Press.

Murrell, P. C. (1998). *Like stone soup: The role of the professional development school in the renewal of urban schools*. Washington, DC: American Association of Colleges for Teacher Education.

National Association of School Psychologists. (2002). *Position statement on corporal punishment in schools*. Retrieved July, 30 2008 from http://www.nasponline.org/information/pospaper_corppunish.asp.

National Association of Year Round Education. *YRE statistics*. Retrieved July 30, 2008 from http://www.nayre.org.

National Board for Professional Teaching Standards. (2008a). *Mission and history*. Retrieved July 27, 2008 from www.nbpts.org.

National Board for Professional Teaching Standards. (2008b). *2007 National Board Certification Day*. Retrieved July 27, 2008 from www.nbpts.org.

National Campaign to Prevent Teen and Unplanned Pregnancy. (2008a). *Unplanned pregnancy and birth data*. Washington, DC: Author. Retrieved June 18, 2008 from http://www.thenational campaign.org.

National Campaign to Prevent Teen and Unplanned Pregnancy. (2008b). *Why it matters: Teen Pregnancy*. Washington, DC: Author. Retrieved June 18, 2008 from http://www.thenationalcampaign.org/why-it-matters.

National Campaign to Prevent Teen and Unplanned Pregnancy. (n.d.). Partners in progress: The education community and preventing teen pregnancy. Washington, DC: Author. Retrieved July 30, 2008 from http://www.thenationalcampaign.org.

National Catholic Education Association. (2008). *A brief overview of Catholic schools in America*. Washington, DC: Author. Retrieved May 18, 2008 from www.ncea.org.

National Center for Alternative Certification. (2007). *Alternative teacher certification: A state by state analysis*. Accessed 4.25.08 at http://www.teach-now.org/intro.cfm

National Center for Educational Information. (2005). *Alternative routes to teacher education*. Retrieved April 23, 2008 at www.ncei.com.

National Center for Education Statistics. (2002). *Digest of education statistics 2002*. Retrieved September 23, 2004 from http://nces.ed.gov/programs/digest/d02/tables/dt068.asp.

National Center for Education Statistics. (2004). *Digest of education statistics 2003*. Washington, DC: U.S. Department of Education. Retrieved March 30, 2005 from http://nces.ed.gov/pubs2005/2005025b1.pdf.

National Center for Hearth Statistics. (2005). *Teen births*. Fast stats A to Z. Hyatts ville, MD: Author.

National Center on Education and the Economy. (2006). *Tough choices or tough times: The report of the New Commission on the Skills of the American Workforce*. San Francisco: Jossey-Bass.

National Clearinghouse for Paradeducator Resources. (2008). Los Angeles: Rossier School of Education, University of Southern California. Retrieved July 30, 2008 from http://www.usc.edu/dept/education/CMMR/Clearinghouse.html.

National Commission on Excellence in Education. (1983). *A nation at risk: The imperative for educational reform*. Washington, DC: Author.

National Commission on Teaching and America's Future (NCTAF). (1996). *What matters most: Teaching for America's future*. New York: Teachers College, Columbia University.

National Commission on Teaching and America's Future. (1996). *What matters most: Teaching for America's future*. New York: Author.

National Commission on Teaching and America's Future. (2007). *State coalition network*. Washington, DC: Author. Retrieved May 25, 2008 from www.nctaf.org.

National Council for Accreditation of Teacher Education. (2001). *Standards for professional development schools*. Washington, DC: Author. Retrieved July 30, 2008 from http://www.ncate.org.

National Council for Accreditation of Teacher Education. (2008). *NCATE: Frequently asked questions*. Retrieved July 30, 2008, from www.ncate.org/public/standards.asp.

National Council for the Social Studies. (2001, May). *Preparing citizens for a global community*. Position Statement. Washington, DC: Author. Retrieved June 2, 2008 from http://www.socialstudies.org/positions/global.

National Council for the Social Studies. (2005). *What are global and international education?* Retrieved July 30, 2008 from http://www.socialstudies.org/positions/global/whatisglobal.

National Education Association. (2003, August). *Status of the American public school teacher 2000-2001*. Washington, DC: National Education Association Research. Retrieved July 30, 2008 from http://www.nea.org/edstats/images/status.pdf.

National Education Association. (2007, December). *Rankings and estimate: Rankings of the states 2003 and estimates of school statistics 2007*. Washington, DC: National Education Association Research. Retrieved July 30, 2008 from http://www.nea.org/edstats.

National Education Association. (2008, May). *Access, adequacy, and equity in education technology*. Washington, DC: National Education Association in Collaboration with the American Federation of Teachers. Retrieved June 15, 2008 from http://www.nea.org/newsreleases/2008/nr080610.html.

National School Boards Association. (2008). *About NSBA*. Retrieved June 16, 2008 from http://www.nsba.org/site/index.asp.

National Science Foundation. (2008). *Back to school: Five myths about girls and science*. Press Release 7-108. Retrieved May 25, 2008 from http://www.nsf.gov/news/news_summ.jsp?cntn_id=109939

National Science Teachers Association. (1996). *NSTA Position Statement: International Science Education and the National Science Teachers Association*. Washington, DC: Author. Retrieved June 2, 2008 from http://www.nsta.org/about/positions/international.aspx.

National Writing Project. (2008) *About the National Writing Project*. Retrieved July 30, 2008 from www.nwp.org.

National Youth Violence Prevention Resource Center. (2008). *School violence*. Rockville, MD: Author. Retrieved July 30, 2008 from www.safeyouth.org.

National Women's Law Center. (2008, February). *Budget woes: President's FY '09 budget seeks to lock in gains for the rich, cut services for women and families*. Washington, DC: Author. Retrieved May 24, 2008 from www.nwlc.org.

Neag Center for Gifted Education and Talent Development. (2008). Retrieved July 25, 2008 from http://www.gifted.uconn.edu.

Nelson, F. N. (1994). *Conditions of employment for teachers in the United States*. Washington, DC: American Federation of Teachers.

New Teacher Center. (n.d.). *Teacher induction*. Santa Cruz: University of California at Santa Cruz. Retrieved July 30, 2008 from http://www.newteachercenter.org.

Newsome, C. (1997). *A teacher's guide to fair use and copyright: Modeling honesty and resourcefulness*. Retrieved July 30, 2008 from http://home.earthlink.net/~cnew/research.htm.

Nichols, J. D., and G. W. Nichols. (2002). The impact of looping classroom environments on parental attitudes. *Preventing School Failure, 47* (1), 18-25.

Nieto, S. (1996). *Affirming diversity: The sociopolitical context of multicultural education* (2nd ed.). White Plains, NY: Longman.

Nieto, S. (2003). *What keeps teachers going?* New York: Teachers College Press.

Nieto, S. (2004). *Affirming diversity: The sociopolitical context of multicultural education* (4th ed.). New York: Pearson Allyn & Bacon.

Noddings, N. (1992). *The challenge to care in schools: An alternative approach to education*. New York: Teachers College Press.

Noddings, N. (2005, February 23). Rethinking a bad law. *Education Week*, p. 38.

Noffke, S. E. (1995). Action research and democratic schooling. In Noffke, S. E. and R. B. Stevenson (Eds.), *Educational action research: Becoming practically critical* (pp. 1-10). New York: Teachers College Press.

Noffke, S. E., and R. B. Stevenson. (Eds.). (1995). *Educational action research: Becoming practically critical*. New York: Teachers College Press.

Noguera, P. A. (2002). Beyond size: The challenge of high school reform. *Educational Leadership, 59* (5), 60-63.

North Central Regional Education Laboratory. (n.d.). *Small by design: Resizing America's high schools*. Retrieved July 30, 2008 from http://www.ncrel.org/policy/pubs/html/smbydes/index.htm.

Northeast and Islands Regional Education Laboratory at Brown University. (1997). *Looping: Supporting student learning through long-term relationships*. Retrieved July 30, 2002, from http://www.ncrel.org/sdrs/areas/issues/methods/instrctn/in5lk10.htm.

Novak, J., and B. Gowin. (1984). *Learning how to learn*. Cambridge: Cambridge University Press.

Orfield, G., & C. Lee. (2007). *Historical reversals, accelerating resegregation, and the need for new integration strategies*. A Report of the Civil Rights Project. Los Angeles: University of California Los Angeles. Retrieved June 2, 2008 from http://www.civilrightsproject.ucla.edu/.

Paine, L., D. Pimm, E. Britton, S. Raizen, and S. Wilson. (2003). Rethinking induction: Examples from around the world. In Scherer, M. (Ed.), *Keeping good teachers* (pp. 67-80). Alexandria, VA: Association for Supervision and Curriculum Development.

Paley, V. G. (2000). *White teacher*. Cambridge, MA: Harvard University Press.

Palmer, P. (1998). *The courage to teach*. San Francisco: Jossey-Bass.

Palincsar, A. S., S. J. Magnusson, K. M. Collins, and J. Cutter. (2001). Making science accessible to all: Results of a design experiment in inclusive classrooms. *Learning Disability Quarterly, 24,* 15-32.

Paltrow, J. (2004, October 10). School board considers censoring books, handing out Bibles, teaching creationism. *The Washington Post,* p. C04.

Pang, V. O., P. N. Kiang, and Y. K. Pak. (2004). Asian Pacific American students. In Banks, J. A. and C A. M. Banks (Eds.), *Handbook of research on multicultural education* (2nd ed., pp. 542-563). San Francisco: Jossey-Bass.

Pavan, B. N. (1992). The benefits of nongraded schools. *Educational Leadership, 50* (2), 22-25.

People for the American Way. (n.d.). *Back to school with the religious right.* Retrieved March 27, 2005 from http://www.pfaw.org/pfaw/general/default.aspx?oid=3655.

Perez, B., Skiba, R. J., & C. Chung. (2008). *Latina students and disproportionality in special education.* Education Policy Brief. Bloomington, IN: Center for Evaluation and Education Policy. Retrieved May 22, 2008 from http://www.indiana.edu/~ceep.

Perry, T., and L. Delpit. (Eds.). (1998). *The real Ebonics debate: Power, language, and the education of African-American children.* Boston: Beacon Press.

Pickett, A. L., M. Likins, and T. Wallace. (2003). *The employment and preparation of paraeducators: The state of the art.* New York: National Resource Center for Paraprofessionals, Center for Advanced Study in Education, City University of New York. Retrieved July 30, 2008 from http://www.nrcpara.org/resources/stateoftheart/index.php.

Pisha, B., and P. Coyne. (2001). Smart from the start: The promise of universal design for learning. *Remedial and Special Education, 22,* 197-203.

Planty, M., Hussar, W., Snyder, T., Provasnik, S., Kena, G., Dinkes, R., KewalRamani, A., and J. Kemp. (2008). *The Condition of Education 2008* (NCES 2008-031). National Center for Education Statistics, Institute of Education Sciences, U.S. Department of Education. Washington, DC.

Pollard, D. S., and C. S. Ajirotutu. (2000). *African-centered schooling in theory and practice.* Westport, CT: Bergin & Garvey.

Public Education Network (PEN). (2005). *Open to the public: Speaking out on "No Child Left Behind."* Washington, DC: Author. Retrieved July 30, 2008 from http://www.publiceducation.org/.

Pufahl, I., N. C. Rhodes, and D. Christian. (2001). *Foreign language teaching: What the United States can learn from other countries.* Washington, DC: Center for Applied Linguistics.

Pufahl, I., N. C. Rhodes, and D. Christian. (2001, September). *What we can learn from foreign language teaching in other countries.* CAL Digest EDO-FL-01-06. Washington, DC: Center for Applied Linguistics. Retrieved July 30, 2008 from http://www.cal.org/resources/digest/0106pufahl.html.

Pugach, M. C. (1998). *On the border of opportunity: Education, community and language at US-Mexico line.* Mahwah, NJ: Lawrence Erlbaum Associates.

Pugach, M. C., and B. L. Seidl. (1998). Responsible linkages between diversity and disability: A challenge for special education. *Teacher Education and Special Education, 21,* 319-333.

Pugach, M. C., L. M. Post, and A. Thurman. (2006). Engaging the university in the system-to-system reform of urban education through a community-wide partnership. In S. L. Percy, N. L. Zimpher, and M. J. Brukardt (Eds.), *Creating a new kind of university.* Bolton, MA: Anker Press.

Rau, W., P. J. Baker, and D. Ashby. (1999). The Chicago school reforms: Are they working? *Sociological Quarterly, 40,* 641-662.

Ravitch, D. (1996). 50 states, 50 standards. *The Brookings Review, 14* (3), 6-9.

Raymond, M., S. H. Fletcher, and J. Luque. (2001). *Teach for America: An evaluation of teacher differences and student outcomes in Houston, Texas.* Stanford, CA: Center for Research on Education Outcomes.

Reggio Emilia. (n.d.). *Reggio children.* Retrieved May 16, 2008 from http://zerosei.comune.re.it.

Reynolds, J. C., B. Barnhart, and B. N. Martin. (1998). Looping: A solution to the retention versus local promotion dilemma? *ERS Spectrum, 17* (2), 16-20.

Reynolds, M. C. (Ed.). (1989). *Knowledge base for the beginning teacher.* New York: Pergamon Press for the American Association of Colleges for Teacher Education.

Richardson, V. (1996). The role of attitudes and beliefs in learning to teach. In Sikula, J. (Ed.), *Handbook of research on teacher education* (2nd ed., pp. 102-119). New York: Simon and Schuster/ Macmillan.

Rohrbeck, C. A., J. W. Fantuzzo, M. D. Ginsberg-Block, and T. R. Miller. (2003). Peer-assisted learning interventions with elementary school students: A Meta-analytic review. *Journal of Educational Psychology, 95,* 240-257.

Rose, M. (1997, March 19). The prairie years. *Education Week, 16* (25), p. 36-42.

Rosebery, A., E. McIntrye, and N. Gonzalez. (2001). Connecting students' cultures to instruction. In McIntrye, E., A. Rosebery, and N. Gonzalez (Eds.), *Classroom diversity: Connecting curriculum to students' lives.* Portsmouth, NH: Heinemann.

Rosenholtz, S. (1989). *Teacher's workplace: The social organization of schools.* New York: Longman.

Roth, R. A (1996). Standards for certification, licensure, and accreditation. In Sikula, J. (Ed.), *Handbook of research on teacher education* (2nd ed., pp. 242-278). New York: Simon & Schuster Macmillan.

Rubenstein, W. B., Sears, R. B., & R. J. Sockloski. (2003 January). Some demographic characteristics of the gay community in the United States. Los Angeles: The Williams Project, UCLA School of Law. Retrieved April 23, 2008 from http://www.law.ucla.edu/WilliamsInstitute/home.html.

Rueda, R. (1989). Defining mild disabilities and language minority students. *Exceptional Children, 56,* 121-128.

Rufo-Lignos, P., and C. E. Richards. (2003). Emerging forms of school organization. *Teachers College Record, 105,* 753-781.

Rury, J. L. (1989). Who became teachers? In Warren, D. (Ed.), *American teachers* (pp. 9-48). New York: Macmillan.

Sailor, W. (2002). Devolution, school/community/family partnerships, and inclusive education. In Sailor, W. (Ed.), *Whole school success and inclusive education* (pp. 7-25). New York: Teachers College Press.

Sanders, W. L., and S. Horn. (1994). The Tennessee value-added assessment system (TVAAS): Mixed-model methodology in educational assessment. *Journal of Personnel Evaluation in Education, 8,* 299-311.

Sarason, S. (1982). *The culture of the school and the problem of change* (2nd ed.). Boston: Allyn & Bacon.

Sarason, S. B., and J. Doris. (1979). *Educational handicap, public policy, and social history: A broadened perspective on mental retardation.* New York: Free Press.

Sawyer, K. (2004). Creative teaching: collaborative discussion as disciplined improvisation. *Educational Researcher, 33* (2), 12-20.

Schofield, J. W. (1995). Improving intergroup relations among students. In Banks, J. A. (Ed.), *Handbook of research on multicultural education* (pp. 635-646). New York: Simon and Schuster Macmillan.

Sedlak, M. W. (1989). "Let us go and buy a school master." Historical perspectives on the hiring of teachers in the United States, 1750-1980. In Warren, D. (Ed.), *American teachers* (pp. 257-290). New York: Macmillan.

Shepard, L., K. Hammerness, L. Darling-Hammond, and F. Rust. (2005). Assessment. In Darling-Hammond, L. and J. Bransford (Eds.), *Preparing teachers for a changing world* (pp. 275-326). San Francisco: Jossey-Bass.

Shin, H. B., and R. Bruno. (2003, October). *Language use and English speaking ability: 2000.* Census 2000 Brief, Report C2KBR-29. Washington, DC: United States Census Bureau. Retrieved March 13, 2005 from http://www.census.gov/prod/2003pubs/c2kbr-29.pdf.

Silva, E. (2007, January). *On the clock: Rethinking the ways schools use time.* Washington, DC: Education Sector. Retrieved May 23, 2008 from www.educationsector.org.

Simel, D. (1998). Education for "bildung:" Teacher attitudes toward looping. *International Journal of Educational Reform, 7,* 330-337.

Simmons, T., and J. L. Dye. (2003, October). *Grandparents living with grandchildren: 2000.* Census 2000 Brief. Report C2KBR-31. Washington, DC: United States Census Bureau. Retrieved July 30, 2008 from http://www.census.gov/population/www/cen2000/briefs.html.

Sirotnik, K. A. (1991). Critical inquiry: A paradigm for praxis. In E. C. Short (Ed.), *Forms of curriculum inquiry* (pp. 243-258). Albany: State University of New York Press.

Sklar, K. K. (1973). *Catharine Beecher: A study in American domesticity.* New Haven and London: Yale University Press.

Skrtic, T. (1991). The special education paradox: Equity as the way to excellence. *Harvard Education Review, 61,* 148-206.

Sleeter, C. E., and C. A. Grant. (2002). *Making choices for multicultural education: Five approaches to race, class, and gender* (4th ed.). Hoboken, NJ: John Wiley and Sons.

Smith, T., & R. Ingersoll. (2004). What are the effects of induction and mentoring on beginning teacher turnover? *American Educational Research Journal, 41,* 681–714.

Sockett, J. (1990). Accountability, trust, and ethical codes of practice. In Goodlad, J. I., R. Soder, and K. A. Sirotnik (Eds.), *The moral dimensions of teaching* (pp. 224-250). San Francisco: Jossey-Bass.

Spring, J. (1998). *American education* (8th ed.). New York: McGraw-Hill.

Spring, J. (2004). *Deculturalization and the struggle for equality: A brief history of the education of dominated cultures in the United States.* Boston: McGraw-Hill.

Squire, J. R., and R. T. Morgan. (1990). The elementary and high school textbook market today. In Elliott, D. L. and A. Woodward (Eds.), *Textbooks and schooling in the United States* (pp. 107-126). The 89th yearbook of the National Society for the Study of Education (Part I). Chicago: University of Chicago Press.

Stacey, J., and T. J. Biblarz. (2001). (How) does the sexual orientation of parents matter? *American Sociological Review, 66,* 159-183.

Staples, A., and J. Pittman. (2003). Building learning communities. In Solomon, G., N. J. Allen, and P. Resta (Eds.), *Toward digital equity: Bridging the divide in education* (pp. 99-114). Boston: Allyn & Bacon.

State of Wisconsin Department of Public Instruction. *Wisconsin Model Academic Standards.* Retrieved February 13, 2005 from http://www.dpi.state.wi.us/dpi/standards/scia8.html.

Stecher, B., G. Bohrnstedt, M. Kirst, J. McRobbie, and T. Williams. (2001). Class-size reduction in California: A story of hope, promise, and unintended consequences. *Phi Delta Kappan, 82,* 670-674.

Steck-Vaughn Publishing Company. (2004). Retrieved July 30, 2008 from http://www.harcourtachievc.com.

Stiggins, R. J., Arter, J., Chappuis, J., & S. Chappuis. (2005). *Classroom assessment for student learning: Doing it right-using it well.* Princeton, NJ.

Stipek, D. J. (2002). *Motivation to learn: From theory to practice* (4th ed.). Boston: Allyn & Bacon.

Strike, K. A. (1990). The legal and moral responsibility of teachers. In Goodlad, J. I., R. Soder, and K. A. Sirotnik (Eds.), *The moral dimensions of teaching* (pp. 188-223). San Francisco: Jossey-Bass.

Sturtevant, E. G. (2003, July). *The literacy coach: A key to improving teaching and learning in secondary schools.* Washington, DC: Alliance for Excellent Education.

Sum, A., and P. Harrington. (2003, February). *Hidden crisis in the high school dropout problems of young adults in the U.S.* Washington, DC: The Business Roundtable. Retrieved July 30, 2008 from http://www.businessroundtable.org/ pdf/914.pdf.

Swanson, C. B. (2004, February). *Who graduates? Who doesn't? A statistical portrait of public high school graduation, Class of 2001.* Washington, DC: The Urban Institute. Retrieved May 10, 2008 from http://www.urban.org/url.cfm?ID=410934

Tanner, D., and L. N. Tanner. (1980). *Curriculum development: Theory into practice.* (2nd ed.). New York: Macmillan.

Terry, M. (2004). One nation, under the designer. *Phi Delta Kappan, 86,* 265-270.

Test, D. W., C. H. Fowler, W. M. Wood, D. M. Brewer, and S. Eddy. (2005). A conceptual framework of self-advocacy for students with disabilities. *Remedial and Special Education, 26,* 43-54.

Tharp, R. G., P. Estrada, S. Dalton, and L. A. Yamauchi. (2000). *Teaching transformed: Achieving excellence, fairness, inclusion, and harmony.* Boulder, CO: Westview Press.

The Center for Effective Discipline. (n.d.). *Discipline at school.* Retrieved July 26, 2008 from www.stophitting.com.

The crafy attacks on evolution. *The New York Times,* January 23, 2005, p. A16.

The Forum for Education and Democracy. (2008, April). *Democracy at risk: The need for a new federal policy in education.* New York: Author. Retrieved April 25, 2008 at http://www.forumforeducation.org/.

The Holmes Group. (1986). *Tomorrow's teachers.* East Lansing, MI: Author.

The Peak Group. (2002). *Virtual schools across America: Trends in K-12 online education, 2002.* Los Altos, CA: Author.

Thomas, B. R. (1990). The school as a moral learning community. In Goodlad, J. I., R. Soder, and K. A. Sirotnik (Eds.), *The moral dimensions of teaching* (pp. 266-295). San Francisco: Jossey-Bass.

Tillman, L.C., & J. Trier. (2007). "Boston Public" as public pedagogy; Implications for teacher preparation and school leadership. *Peabody Journal of Education, 82,* 121–149.

Tomlinson, C. A. (1999). *The differentiated classroom: Responding to the needs of all learners.* Alexandria, VA: Association for Supervision and Curriculum Development.

Tomlinson, C.A., & J. McTighe. (2006). *Integrating differentiated instruction and understanding by design: Connecting content and kids.* Alexandria, VA: Association for Supervision and Curriculum Development. Chapters 1 and 9 retrieved May 23, 2008 from www.ascd.org.

Trenholm, C., Devaney, B., Fortson, K., Quay, L., Wheeler, J., & M. Clark. (2007). Impacts of four Title V, Section 510 abstinence education programs: Final report. Washington, DC; Mathematica Policy Research Institute. Retrieved May 5, 2008 from http://www.mathematica-mpr.com/ publications/pdfs/impactabstinence.pdf.

Tyack, D., and K. Tobin. (1994). *American Educational Research Journal, 31,* 453-479.

University of Akron. (2006, March). *A longitudinal evaluation of the new curricula for the D.A.R.E Middle (7th Grade) and high school (9th Grade) Programs: Take charge of your life.* Year Four Progress Report. Carnevale Associates, LLC. Retrieved May 6, 2008 from http://www.dare.com/home/Resources/ documents/DAREMarch06ProgressReport.pdf

University of Pennsylvania Archives. (n.d.) Penn in the eighteenth century: Academy of Philadelphia curriculum. Philadelphia: University of Pennsylvania. Retrieved May 17, 2008 from (http://www.archives.upenn.edu/histy/features/1700s/acad_curric.html).

U.S. Census Bureau. (2005, August 11). *Texas becomes nation's newest "majority-minority" state, Census Bureau announces.* Washington, DCL Author. Retrieved May 10, 2008 from http://www.census.gov/Press-Release/www/releases/ archives/population/005514.html.

U.S. Census Bureau. (2008, April). *Public education finances 2006.* Washington, DC: Author. Retrieved July 30, 2008 from http://ftp2.census.gov/govs/ school/06f33pub.pdf.

U.S. Department of Commerce. (1999, September). *Minority population growth: 1995-2050.* Washington, DC: Author.

U.S. Department of Education. (1997, June). *Title IX: 25 years of progress.* Retrieved July 30, 2008 from http://www.ed.gov/ pubs/TitleIX/index.html.

U.S. Department of Education (2004, July). *Issue Brief: 1.1 million home-schooled students in the United States in 2003.* National Center for Education Statistics. NCES Report 2004-115. Washington, DC: Author. Retrieved July 30, 2008 from http://nces.ed.gov/ pubs2004/2004115.pdf.

U.S. Department of Education. (2004, October). *A guide to education and "No Child Left Behind."* Washington, DC: Author. Retrieved July 30, 2008 from http://www.ed.gov/nclb.

U.S. Department of Education. (n.d). *10 facts about education funding.* Retrieved July 30, 2008 from http://www.ed.gov.

U.S. Department of Education. (2003.). *About ED: Overview.* Retrieved July 30, 2008 from http://www.ed.gov.

U.S. Department of Education. (n.d.). *Mission statement.* Retrieved July 30, 2008 from http://www.ed.gov/about/ overview/mission/mission.html.

U.S. Department of Education. (2007a). *Twenty-fourth annual report to Congress on the implementation of the Individuals with Disabilities Education Act.* Retrieved July 30, 2008 from http://www.ed.gov/about/reports/annual/ osep/2005/parts-b-c/index.html.

U.S. Department of Education. (n.d.). *Educational technology fact sheet.* Retrieved July 30, 2008 from http://www.ed.gov/ print/about/offices/list/os/technology/facts.html.

U.S. Department of Education. (2006). *Internet access in U.S. public schools and classrooms: 1995–2005.* Washington, DC: National Center for Education Statistics.

U.S. Department of Education. (2007, June). *Description and employment criteria of instructional paraprofessionals. Issue Brief (NCES 2007-008)*. Washington, DC: Institute of Education Sciences, National Center for Education Statistics. Retrieved July 25, 2008 from http://nces.ed.gov/pubs2007/2007008.pdf.

U.S. Department of Education, National Center for Education Statistics. (2007b). *The condition of education 2007 (NCES 2007-064): Elementary/secondary education, Children with disabilities in public schools*. Washington, DC: U.S. Government Printing Office. Retrieved May 13, 2008 from http://nces.ed.gov.

U.S. Department of Education. (2007c). *Numbers and types of public elementary and secondary schools from the Common Core of Data: School year 2006–07*. NCES 2007-354. July 2007. Retrieved June 16, 2008 from http://nces.ed.gov.

U.S. Department of Education. (2008). *Overview-Budget Office, U.S. Department of Education*. Retrieved May 28, 2008 from http://www.ed.gov.

U.S. Department of Health and Human Services. Administration for Children and Families, Children's Bureau. Washington (2006a). *Child maltreatment 2006*. DC: Author. Retrieved June 18, 2008 from http://www.acf.hhs.gov/programs/cb/pubs/cm06.

U.S. Department of Health and Human Services. Child Welfare Information Gateway. (2007). *Foster care statistics*. Washington, DC: Author. Retrieved June 18, 208 from http://www.childwelfare.gov/pubs/factsheets/foster.cfm.

U.S. Office of Refugee Resettlement. (2005). *Annual ORR reports to Congress 2005*. Washington, DC: Administration for Children and Families. Retrieved May 10, 2008 from http://www.acf.hhs.gov/programs/orr/data/05arc2.htm&num;_Ref532807044.

Urso, I. (1991). Teacher development through global education. In Tye, K. (Ed.), *Global education: From action to thought* (pp. 100-108). The 1991 Association of Supervision and Curriculum Development Yearbook. Alexandria, VA: Association of Supervision and Curriculum Development.

Valente, W. D. (1998). *Law in the schools* (4th ed.). Upper Saddle River, NJ: Merrill Prentice Hall.

Veenman, S. (1995). Cognitive and noncognitive effects of multi-grade and multi-age classes: A best evidence synthesis. *Review of Educational Research, 65*, 319-381.

Villa, R. A., J. S. Thousand, and A. I. Nevin. (2004). *A guide to co-teaching*. Thousand Oaks, CA: Corwin Press.

Villegas, A. M., and T. Lucas. (2002). *Educating culturally responsive teachers: A coherent approach*. Albany: State University of New York Press.

Villegas, A. M. (2007). Dispositions in teacher education: A look at social justice. *Journal of Teacher Education, 58,* 370–380.

Walker, D. F., and J. F. Soltis. (1992). *Curriculum and aims*. (2nd ed.) New York: Teachers College Press.

Walker, V. Siddle. (1996). *Their highest potential: An African-American school community in the segregated south*. Chapel Hill: University of North Carolina Press.

Walser, N. (1998, January/February). Multi-age classrooms: An age-old grouping method is still evolving. *Harvard Education Letter, Research Online*. Retrieved July 30, 2008 from http://www.edletter.org/past/issues/1998-jf/multiage.shtml.

Warger, C. (2001, October). *Research on full-service schools and students with disabilities*. (ERIC Identifier: ED458749). Arlington VA: ERIC Clearinghouse on Disabilities and Gifted Education. ERIC/OSEP Special Project. Retrieved July 30, 2008 from http://www.ericdigests.org/2002-3/full.htm.

Warger, C. L. (2002, September). *Full service schools' potential for special education*. ERIC/OSEP Topical Brief (ED 473821). Alexandria, VA: Council for Exceptional Children. Retrieved May 5, 2008 from http://eric.ed.gov.

Weiss, J., and R. S. Brown. (2003). Telling tales over time: Constructing and deconstructing the school calendar. *Teachers College Record, 105*, 1720-1757.

Wells, J., and L. Lewis. (2006). *Internet access in U.S. public schools and classrooms: 1994-2005*. National Center for Education Statistics, Report 2007-020. Washington, DC: United States Department of Education. Retrieved May 22, 2008 http://nces.ed.gov/pubs2007.

Wisconsin Department of Public Instruction. (2002). *Wisconsin model academic standards for science*. Madison, WI: Author. Retrieved July 30, 2008 from http://www.dpi.wi.gov/standards/sciintro.html.

Wisconsin Education Association Council. *WEAC: A history*. Retrieved July 30, 2008 from http://weac.org/historybook/intro.htm.

Women's Sports Foundation. (2008). *2007 statistics—Gender equity in high school and college athletics*. Retrieved May 24, 2008 from www.womenssportsfoundation.org.

Woodward, J., and L. Cuban. (Eds.). (2001). *Technology, curriculum and professional development: Adapting schools to meet the needs of students with disabilities*. Thousand Oaks, CA: Corwin Press.

Woolfolk, A. (2001). *Educational psychology* (8th ed.). Boston: Allyn and Bacon.

Worthen, M.R. (2007). Commentary: Education policy implications from the Expert Panel on Electronic Media and School Violence. *Journal of Adolescent Health, 41*, S61–63.

Wright, S. S., S. Horn, and W. Sanders. (1997). Teacher and classroom content effects on student achievement: Implications for teacher evaluation. *Journal of Personnel Evaluation in Education, 11*, 57-67.

Yamauchi, L. A. (2003). Making school relevant for at-risk students: The Wai'anae High School Hawaiian studies program. *Journal of Education for Students Placed at Risk, 8*, 379-390.

Yinger, R. (1987, April). *By the seat of your pants: An inquiry into improvisation and teaching*. Paper presented at the annual meeting of the American Educational Research Association, Washington, DC.

York-Barr, J., and K. Duke. (2004). What do we know about teacher leadership? Findings from two decades of scholarship. *Review of Educational Research, 74,* 255-316.

Zeichner, K., and H. Conklin. (2005). Teacher education programs. In Cochran-Smith, M. and K. Zeichner, (Eds.), *Studying teacher education: The report of the AERA panel on research and teacher education.* Mahwah, NJ: Lawrence Erlbaum Associates.

## A

Adler, Mortimer, 119
Ajirotutu, C. S., 149
Akar, H., 293, 294
Albert, Linda, 397
Alexie, Sherman, 110–111
Amanti, C., 294
Anderson, C. W., 65, 274
Anderson, L. W., 425
Anderson, P., 193
Anyon, Jean, 175
Apple, Michael, 129, 309–310
Aristotle, 115
Armstrong, J., 305
Aromaa, S., 193
Arter, J., 296
Ashby, D., 339
Atkin, J. M., 426, 430
Aycock, J. C., 125

## B

Bachman, J. G., 192
Bagley, William, 78, 117
Bailey, J. M., 384
Baker, P. J., 339
Baker-Kroczynski, S., 274
Balistreri, Adriana, 25, 85, 115
Ball, D. L., 65
Ball, E. W., 278
Banks, James, 233, 235, 237, 294
Barker, Mary, 421
Barnard, Henry, 103
Barnhart, B., 299
Barton, A. C., 165
Basham, P., 363
Beane, James, 309–310
Bear, G. G., 188
Beecher, Catharine, 32–33, 112
Ben-Peretz, Miriam, 155, 156, 157
Bennett, K. P., 334
Berge, Z. L., 329
Berry, B., 62, 63
Bertani, A., 295
Black, S., 299
Blank, J., 188
Blatt, Burton, 249, 252–254
Bleakley, A., 191

Bohrnstedt, G., 302
Boles, K. C., 340, 421
Boostrom, R. E., 409
Bosetti, K. R., 295
Boss, S., 329
Boveda, Mildred, 153, 195
Boyd, D., 84
Braden, J. S., 370
Bransford, J., 4, 412
Brantlinger, E., 261
Bravmann, M. A., 165
Brewer, D. M., 385
Britton, E., 86
Brown, K., 308
Brown, Linda, 222
Brown, R. S., 309
Bruno, R., 211
Bryk, A. S., 190, 375, 377, 388
Bryson, K., 180
Bullough, R. V., 95, 113
Bulman, Robert, 30, 32, 49
Bush, George W., 347
Butts, R. F., 100, 102, 104, 178, 333, 343, 344, 392

## C

Cade, E., 274
Caro-Bruce, C., 430
Carter, Jimmy, 345
Carter, K., 49
Carter, Kathy, 19
Carter, Kenisha, 318–320
Carver, C. L., 424
Casper, L. M., 179, 180
Cawley, J., 274
Chaltain, S., 394, 409
Chappuis, J., 296
Chappuis, S., 296
Charney, M., 370
Christian, D., 448
Chung, C., 279
Clark, Christopher, 374, 382, 391
Clark, T., 329
Clark-Chicarelli, N. C., 274
Clifford, G. J., 413
Cochran-Smith, M., 426, 428
Cody, C., 160
Cohen, E. G., 321

Colasanti, M., 353, 398
Collins, K. M., 274
Comer, J. P., 294
Conklin, H., 83, 84
Connelly, F. M., 155, 156, 157
Cooper, B. S., 357
Corbett, D., 294
Corey, Stephen, 426, 427
Counts, George, 119
Coyne, P., 276
Crawford, J., 227, 228, 229, 230, 231
Cremin, Lawrence, 100, 102, 104, 146, 178, 210, 333, 343, 344, 346, 392
Cross, C. T., 265, 279
Cuban, Larry, 131–133, 135, 275, 303
Cubberley, Elwood, 107–108, 112
Cusick, P. A., 125
Cutter, J., 274

## D

Dalton, M. M., 216
Dalton, Mary, 30, 31, 32
Dalton, S., 291
Darling-Hammond, Linda, 60, 224, 293, 294, 295, 412, 427
Day, J. C., 179
Day, M., 286
Delpit, Lisa, 209, 213, 224, 226, 228, 229
Dewey, John, 97, 112–113, 117, 118, 146–147, 309
Diaz, C. F., 447, 448
Diaz, E. M., 189
Donovan, M. S., 4, 265, 279
Doris, J., 251, 277
Dounay, J., 339
Doyle, Walter, 19, 49
Dryfoos, J. G., 195, 196
Duke, K., 338, 423
Dwyer, K., 187, 188
Dye, J. L., 181, 182
Dykeman, T. B., 33

## E

Eadie, D., 370
Easton, J. Q., 339
Eccles, T. S., 199, 200
Eddy, S., 385

Edelman, Marian Wright, 167
Eisner, Eliot, 131–132, 135, 143, 145, 155, 170, 173, 236
El-Haj, T. R. A., 437
Eliot, Charles, 145
Ellis, Joe, 350–356
Emilia, Reggio, 149
Erickson, Frederick, 40–41, 170, 171
Escalante, Jaime, 30
Esquith, Rafe, 34, 155, 289
Estrada, P., 216, 291
Evangelou, D., 298
Evans, R., 206
Everhart, N., 308
Everston, C. M., 40

**F**

Falk, Beverly, 154, 295
Fantuzzo, J. W., 321
Feiman-Nemser, S., 49
Feldman, A., 426, 430
Fenstermacher, Gary, 78, 198–199
Feretti, R. P., 274
Ferguson, J. E., 394
Fetters, M. K., 274
Fiedler, C. R., 382
Fields, J., 179
Filardo, M., 451
Finchler, Judy, 35
Fishbein, M., 191
Flanagan, Kate, 234, 268
Flannery, M. E., 384
Florio-Ruane, Susan, 20, 21, 41
Fowler, C. H., 385
Frankenberg, E., 450
Franklin, Benjamin, 101
Freire, P., 206
Fuchs, D., 259, 260
Fuchs, L. S., 259, 260
Fullan, Michael, 4, 295, 304, 373, 374, 386
Fusarelli, L. D., 357

**G**

Gabrieli, C., 307, 308
Garmezy, N., 185
Gilman, D. A., 302
Ginsberg, M B., 329
Ginsberg-Block, M. D., 321
Girod, G. R., 73
Gitlin, A. D., 95
Gladden, R. M., 187
Glesne, C., 42
Goldstein, W., 307, 308
Gonzalez, N., 218, 294
Good, T. L., 370
Goodlad, J. I., 125
Goodlad, S. J., 125
Gowin, B., 22
Grant, C. A., 148, 233, 234, 236

Green, J. L., 40
Green, N. S., 165
Greene, Maxine, 1, 125
Griffin, G., 95
Grimmett, P. P., 35
Guajardo, F. J., 222
Guajardo, M. A., 222
Guskey, T. R., 384
Guttman, Amy, 309

**H**

Hackmann, D., 303
Haddon, M., 286
Hakuta, K., 230, 231
Hale, L., 110
Haley, Margaret, 421
Hall, G. Stanley, 112
Hamilton, L. S., 58
Hammerness, K., 295, 427
Hampel, R. I., 304
Hansen, D. T., 374, 385, 409
Hargreaves, Andy, 338, 418, 420
Harrington, P., 305
Harry, B., 278, 279, 286
Hartman, J., 298
Hayden, S., 274
Haynes, C. C., 394, 395, 398, 403, 409
Heath, Shirley Brice, 215
Heller, K. A., 279
Henderson, A. T., 378
Hendrie, C., 210
Hennessy, A., 191
Hindin, A., 274
Hirsh, E., 62, 63
Hofer, B. K., 224
Hoffman, N., 33
Hoke, M., 62, 63
Holloway, J., 339
Holtzman, W. H., 279
Hord, S., 4
Horn, S., 58
Horton, M., 165
House, David, 311, 345
Howard, Gary, 238
Huberman, Michael, 85–86
Hudson, D. L., 394, 409
Humphrey, D. C., 295
Humphrey, Hubert, 347
Hurston, Zora Neal, 337
Hutchins, Robert, 119

**I**

Iano, R. P., 251, 261
Imber, M., 395, 396, 398, 401, 404
Ingersoll, Richard, 82, 424
Irvine, Jacqueline Jordan, 212, 218

**J**

Jackson, Andrew, 103

Jackson, M. J. B., 125
Jackson, P., 135, 169, 409
Jefferson, Thomas, 101–102, 178
Johnson, Clifton, 340, 392, 393
Johnson, D. W., 321
Johnson, L. J., 270
Johnson, Lyndon, 345, 346
Johnson, R. T., 321
Johnson, S., 86, 413, 421
Johnson, S. M., 95
Johnston, L. D., 192
Joseph, P. B., 165

**K**

Kalkowski, P., 321
Kalyanpur, M., 286
Kanthopoulous, J. A., 447, 448
Kaplan, F., 253
Katsiyannis, A., 323
Katz, D. S., 424
Katz, L. G., 298
Kennedy, Robert, 253
Kiang, P. N., 352
Kiger, S., 302
Kirby, D., 191, 192
Kirst, M., 302
Klein, E. J., 436, 437
Kliewer, C., 253
Klingner, J., 279, 286
Kohl, H., 55
Koplow, L., 206
Koretz, D. M., 58
Kosciw, J. G., 189
Kozol, J., 190
Krauss, J., 329
Kridel, C., 113

**L**

Ladson-Billings, G., 220, 447
Lagemann, E. C., 375
Lancaster, Joseph, 107
Land, D., 334, 337
Larmer, J., 149
Lawrence, J., 143
Le Tendre, G. K., 224
LeCompte, M. D., 334
Lee, C., 450
Lee, Harper, 175
Lee, R. I., 143
Leithwood, K., 339
LePage, P., 293, 294, 412
Lieberman, Ann, 4, 338, 418, 462
Likins, M., 323
Linney, J., 206
Little, J. W., 418
Lloyd, L., 298
Lockwood, J. R., 58
Lortie, Dan, 20, 21
Lowenthal, B., 185

Lucas, T., 231, 232
Lugaila, T., 180, 181
Lyon, Mary, 112
Lytle, S., 426, 428

**M**

MacArthur, C. D., 274
MacKinnon, A. M., 35
Magnusson, S. J., 274
Manlove, J. K., 192
Mann, Horace, 103–104, 108
Mantle-Bronley, C., 125
Mapp, K. L., 378
Marcos, K. M., 448
Markham, J., 149
Marshall, Thurgood, 222
Martin, A. K., 39
Martin, B. N., 299
Maslow, Abraham, 199
Massialas, G., 447, 448
Mata-Aguilar, C., 274
Mayer, M. J., 187
Mayhew, Ira, 106
McCaffrey, D. F., 58
McCourt, Frank, 34
McCreadie, J., 430
McDiarmid, G. W., 65
McGhan, B., 339
McIntosh, Peggy, 237–238
McIntyre, E., 218
McLaren, P., 236
McMillen, B. J., 309
McRobbie, J., 302
McTigue, J., 312, 313
Meier, D., 329
Meier, Deborah, 306
Menzies, T., 339
Mergendoller, J., 149
Messick, S., 279
Metz, M. H., 149
Meyers, J., 185, 193, 198
Mikel, E. R., 165
Miller, Lynne, 4, 338, 418, 462
Miller, T. R., 321
Moll, L., 218, 294
Montessori, Maria, 149
Morgan, R. T., 160
Morocco, C. C., 274
Motley, C. B., 222
Munby, H., 39
Murphy, J. P., 436, 437
Murray, F. M., 35
Murrell, P. C., 75

**N**

Nastasi, B. K., 185, 193, 198
Nelson, F. N., 416
Nevin, A. I., 272
Newsome, Cathy, 401, 402

Nichols, G. W., 299
Nichols, J. D., 299
Nieto, Sonia, 55, 57, 212, 213, 221, 227,
    228, 229, 232, 235, 237
Noddings, Nel, 120, 348, 378–379
Noffke, S. E., 427, 428, 462
Noguera, P. A., 307
Novak, J., 22

**O**

Obidah, J. E., 246
Okolo, C., 274
O'Malley, Kevin, 35
O'Malley, P. M., 192
Orfield, G., 450
Osher, D., 187, 188
Overturf, J., 180

**P**

Pack, C., 206
Paine, L., 86
Pak, Y. K., 352
Paley, Vivian Gussin, 239
Palincsar, A. S., 274
Palmer, P. J., 55
Palmer, Parker, 381
Paltrow, J., 337
Pang, V. O., 352
Paterson, Russell, 10–11
Pavan, B. N., 298
Payne, Daniel, 109
Pedraza, Melissa, 45
Pellegrino, J. W., 4
Pellicer, L. S., 425
Pereira, Becky, 45
Perez, B., 279
Perry, Theresa, 226, 228
Peterson, B., 370
Peyton, J. K., 448
Phelps, Mrs. Lincoln, 111
Phillips, R., 206
Pickett, A. L., 323
Pimm, D., 86
Pincus, Marsha, 45
Pisha, B., 276
Pittman, J., 275
Pollard, D. S., 149
Post, L. M., 75
Pufahl, I. U., 448, 449
Pugach, M. C., 75, 228, 270, 278

**Q**

Quinn, J., 295

**R**

Raider-Roth, M., 206
Raizen, S., 86
Randall, E. V., 357
Rau, W., 339

Ravitch, D., 160
Ravitz, J., 149
Reynolds, J. C., 71, 299
Rhodes, N. C., 448, 449
Rice, J., 95
Richards, C. E., 334
Rofes, E., 370
Rogers, Carl, 199
Rohrbeck, C. A., 321
Rood, Florence, 421
Rose, M., 300
Rosebery, A., 218
Rosenbloom, D., 193
Rosenholtz, S., 4
Roth, R. A., 60
Rousseau, Jean Jaques, 199
Rubenstein, W. B., 182
Rueda, R., 278
Rufo-Lignos, P., 334
Rury, J. L., 413
Russell, T., 39
Rust, F., 295
Rutter, M., 185

**S**

Sailor, W., 259
Sanders, W. L., 58
Santayana, George, 98
Sarason, Seymour, 171–172, 251, 277, 303,
    309
Sawyer, K., 36
Scherer, M., 462
Schneider, B., 375, 377, 388
Schofield, J. W., 223
Schulenberg, J. E., 192
Schwartz, P., 306
Sears, R. B., 182
Secret, Carrie, 228
Sedlak, Michael, 82
Seidl, B. L., 278
Shepard, L., 295
Shimizu, H., 224
Shin, H. B., 211
Shultz, J., 170, 171
Silva, E., 308
Simel, D., 299
Simmons, T., 181, 182
Simpson, D. J., 125
Sirotnik, Kenneth, 175
Sizer, N. F., 329
Sizer, T. R., 329
Skiba, R. J., 279
Skinner, B. F., 112
Sklar, K. K., 33
Skrtic, T., 265
Sleeter, C. E., 148, 233, 234, 236
Sloan, G. D., 95
Smith, T., 424
Sockett, J., 375
Sockloski, R. J., 182

Soltis, Jonas, 78, 146, 198–199, 409
Spring, Joel, 110, 228, 246, 352
Squire, J. R., 160
Staples, A., 275
Stecher, B., 302
Stevenson, R. B., 427, 428, 462
Stiggins, R. J., 296
Stipek, D. G., 292
Storey, S. L., 339
Strike, K. A., 404
Stubbs, Erika, 383, 445
Stulberg, L., 370
Sturtevant, E. G., 425
Sum, A., 305
Swank, Hilary, 30–32

**T**

Tanner, D., 146, 147, 169
Tanner, L. N., 146, 147, 169
Taylor, D., 286
Taylor, Frederick, 107
Teel, K. M., 246
Templeton, J., 199, 200
Terry, Mark, 400
Test, D. W., 385
Tharp, R. G., 216, 219, 291
Thomas, B. R., 375
Thomas, O., 394, 409
Thompson, G. L., 246
Thornton, S. J., 165
Thousand, J. S., 272

Thum, Y. M., 190
Thurman, S., 75
Tillman, L. C., 33
Tobin, K., 303
Tomlinson, C. A., 312. 313
Trenholm, C., 191
Trier, J., 33
Tyack, D., 303

**U**

Unz, Ron, 230

**V**

Valente, W. D., 394, 396, 398
Valenzuela, A., 247
Vallance, E., 145
Van Geel, T., 395, 396, 398, 401, 404
Veenman, S., 298
Verturf, J. O., 180, 181
Villa, R. A.7, 272
Villegas, A. M., 231, 232, 391

**W**

Walker, D. F, 221
Walker, Decker, 146
Walker, V. Siddle, 247
Wallace, T., 323
Walser, N., 298
Warger, C., 187, 188, 195
Washington, Booker T., 109

Watson, M., 409
Weber, Lillian, 55
Wechsler, M. E., 295
Weiss, J., 308, 309
Wells, J., 314
Wessler, S. L., 206
Willard, Emma, 111
Williams, Robin, 32
Williams, T., 302
Wilson, B., 294
Wilson, Eleanor, 10
Wilson, S., 86
Windschitl, M. A., 165
Wlodkowski, R. J., 329
Wood, W. M., 385
Woodward, J., 275
Woolfolk, Anita, 221
Worthen, M. R., 189
Wright, S. S., 58

**Y**

Yamauchi, L. A., 216, 291, 299
Yinger, R., 35, 36
York-Barr, J., 338, 423

**Z**

Zeichner, K., 83, 84
Zubay, B., 409

## A

*A Nation at Risk: The Imperative for Educational Reform*, 67, 144

Abstinence education, 191

Abuse, child. *See* Child abuse and neglect

Academic content standards, 131, 136–138. *See also* Standardized testing
creation of, 137
differences in, 137–138
positive and negative uses of, 154
textbooks and, 158

Academic tracking, 222–225

Academies, development of, 100–101

Acceptable behavior, setting limits for, 396–397

Accountability, 134, 437–438

Accreditation, teacher education programs, 79–81
national accreditation, 79–80
standards and, 80–81

Achievement gap, 210

Action research, 427

Additive bilingualism, *231*

Adequate yearly progress (AYP), 347

Adoption states, textbooks and, 159–160

Advocacy
student self-advocacy, 384–385
teacher and, 382–384

Aesthetics, educational philosophy and, 116

African American children, 108–109

African American Vernacular English (AAVE), 226, 228–229

Afro-centric curriculum, 149

Age-graded classroom model, 296–298

Alcohol abuse, 192–193

Alternate route programs, 82–84

American Board for the Certification of Teacher Excellence (ABCTE), 77

American education
academy development and, 100–101
African American children and, 108–109
Catholic issue and, 104
common schools and, 103–104
contested control and, 102–103
current era and, 113–114
early colonial efforts, 99–100
efficiency movement and, 107
Eight-Year Study and, 113
for girls and women, 111–112
Hispanic American children and, 111
historical origins of, 98–114
Horace Mann and, 103–104
industrialization and, 107–108
Jeffersonian ideals and, 101–102
late nineteenth century and, 105–106
Native American children and, 109–110
religion and, 104
twentieth century and, 112–113

American Federation of Teachers (AFT), 340, 421–422

Americans with Disabilities Act (ADA), 254

Ancillary materials, textbooks and, 156

Anecdotal recording, 42

Apple Learning Interchange, 419

Application process, first job and, 453–454

Apprenticeship of observation, 20–23

Ashmun Institute, 109

Assistive technology, 270–272
categories of, 276
classroom integration of, 275–276
individual needs and, 277
text-to-speech software, 277
universal design and, 276–277

Association for Conflict Resolution, 194

Athletics, 199–200

Autobiographical knowledge, 23–27
family and, 23–24
personal commitments and, 24–27

Autonomy, teacher isolation and, 420

Axiology, 116

## B

Banned Books Week, 337

Basic skills, role in curriculums, 150–151

Beginning teachers. *See* Induction period

Behaviorism, 112

*Bethel School District No. 403 v. Fraser*, 394

Biases, textbooks and, 158

Bilingual education, 229–231. *See also* Diversity

Bill and Melinda Gates Foundation, 306

BioKIDS project, 314

Bisexual students or families, 189

Blaming the victim, 382

Block scheduling, 302–303

Book challenges, 336–337

*Boston Public*, 33

*Brown v. Board of Education*, 109, 221–222, 351, 394, 446

Bullying, 188–189

Butler Act, 143

## C

Categorical aid, 347

Catholic schools, 104

CD-ROMs, 317

Celebrating differences, 233–235. *See also* Diversity

Cell phones
communication with families and, 171
student's use of, 400

Censorship, 337, 395

Center for Effective Discipline, 396

Center for Safe and Responsible Internet Use, 189

Center for Teaching Quality, 422
Centralized budgeting systems, 358
Challenged books, 336–337
Charity schools, 108
Charter schools, 360–362
Child abuse and neglect, 185–186
    federal legislation and, 186
    reporting laws and, 185
    reporting of, 396
    signs of, 185–186
Child Abuse Prevention and
        Treatment Act (CAPTA), 186
Children's Internet Protection Act
        (CIPA), 401
Class size
    local school boards and, 334
    reduction of, 301–302
Classical curriculum debate, 105–106
Classroom community
    creating, 293–294
    trust and, 379–380
Classroom observation, 40–45
    etiquette and, 45
    objective observation, 44
    observing with a map, 41–42
    systematic observation, 42–44
Classroom organization. See also
        School organization
    differentiated instruction and,
        312–313
    instructional technology and,
        314–320
    Internet accessibility and, 314–315
    multimodal literacy and, 315–316
    virtual schools and, 320
Co-teaching, with students disabilities
        and, 271–272
Coaching, teacher leadership
        and, 425
Coalition for Community Schools,
        195–196
Codes of ethics, 389
Codes of practice, 389
Cognitive disabilities, 252–254
Collaboration
    culture of, 418
    ethic of, 418
    philosophy of, 420
    as shared resource, 420–421
    trust and, 421
    value of, 417–418
Collaborative professional learning
        communities, 4–5
Collective bargaining status by state,
        341

Colonial era, education during,
        99–100, 177–179
Colonial schools, moral context in,
        392
Committee of Fifteen on Elementary
        Education, 145
Committee of Ten on Secondary
        Education, 145
Common schools, 103–104, 111,
        177–179
Commonplace knowledge, 40–41
Community schools, 194–197
Compensation, differentiated, 434–435
Compulsory Education Act, 112
Concept maps, 22–23
Confidentiality, 395–396
Confrontations, classroom, 397
Content integration, 233–235
Content knowledge, 380–381
Contextualized teaching and learning,
        216–218
Cooperative learning, 321–322
Copyright laws, 401–402
Corporal punishment, 396–397
Council for Exceptional Children, 354,
        443
Creationism, 143, 399
Creativity, 10
Critical theory, 175–176
Culturally responsive teaching,
        231–232. See also Diversity
Culture of collaboration, 418
Current events, as hidden curriculum,
        175–176
Curriculum. See also Curriculum devel-
        opment; Hidden curriculum
    academic content standards and,
        131
    academic tracking and, 224
    accountability for learning, 134
    Afro-centric curriculum, 149
    basic skills and, 150–151
    dilemmas and, 136
    students with disabilities and,
        273–274
    dumbing down of, 174
    explicit curriculum, 131–132
    guides, 131
    learned curriculum, 132–134
    magnet schools and, 149
    null curriculum, 132, 135–136
    personal beliefs and, 403–404
    professional choices and, 130–131
    project-based learning and,
        148–149

social justice and, 148
    special curriculum identities,
        147–151
    standardized testing and, 145–146,
        152–155
    students with disabilities and,
        273–274
    taught curriculum, 132–133
    teacher's roles and, 157
    teaching with purpose and,
        145–155
    textbooks role in, 155–162
Curriculum development, 136–145
    academic content standards and,
        136–138
    comparison of, 139
    conceptual approach and, 141
    curriculum guides and, 138–141
    local district level and, 142–143
    local values and, 143
    national influences and, 143–145
    scope and sequence charts and, 140
    state level and, 138–141
Curriculum guides, 131, 138–141
Curriculum potential, 156–157
Cyberbullying, 188–189
Cyberschools, 320

D
Dame Schools, 99
Dead Poets Society, 32
Decentralized budgeting systems,
        358–359
Demands of teaching, 11–12
Democracy and Education, 309
Democracy at Risk: The Need for a New
        Federal Policy in Education, 84
Democratic schools idea, 309–310
Demographics, changing, 211–213
Department of Education, 345–346
Departmentalization, 296
Devaluation of students, 219–225
Developmental delay, 267
Developmental guidance, 194
Developmental portfolios, 72
Differentiated compensation, 434–435
Differentiated instruction, 312–313
Differentiated instruction, disabilities
        and, 269–270
Disabilities. See also Special education
    advocacy and, 252–254
    assistive technology and, 275–277
    best curriculum and, 273–274
    classroom integration and, 268–269
    co-teaching and, 271–272

differential instruction and, 269–270

diminishing differences and, 272–273

diversity issues and, 277–279

early intervention and, 257

expectations and, 265

federal mandates and, 254–257

flexibility with accommodations and, 269–270

high-incidence disabilities and, 262

historical treatment of, 251–252

inclusion movement and, 258–261

labeling and, 261–267

least restrictive environment and, 255–256

low-incidence disabilities and, 262

major principles of IDEA and, 255

referral process and, 271

response to intervention and, 271

self-advocacy and, 385

student numbers and, 262

teacher collaboration and, 270–272

teacher's role and, 267–274

transition services and, 258

Disability categorization

developmental delay identification and, 267

IDEA legislation and, 263

inequalities caused by, 264–265

limitations of, 264, 266

simplification of, 267

Dispositions, 391

Districtwide professional development, 444

Diversity. See also Family structures; Language diversity

academic tracking and, 222–225

assuring equity and, 237

celebrating difference and, 233–235

changing demographics and, 211–213

content integration and, 233–235

contextualized teaching and learning, 216–218

culturally responsive teaching and, 231–232

deficit model of, 213

devaluing students and, 219–225

embracing, 6

funds of knowledge and, 218–219

interpersonal relationships and, 220–221

language diversity, 226–231

monocultural schools and, 239–240

multiple perspectives and, 235–237

"not seeing color" responses and, 238–239

self-fulfilling prophecy and, 221

social reconstructionism and, 236

teacher expectations and, 219–222

understanding, 213–215

white privilege and, 237–238

Drug abuse, 192–193

Drug Abuse Resistance Education (DARE) program, 192

Due Process Clause of the Fourteenth Amendment, 393

Dumbing down, curriculum, 174

**E**

e-mail, communication with families and, 171

Early intervention, special education and, 257

*Early Warning, Timely Response: A Guide to Safe Schools*, 187–188

Education Commission of the States (ECS), 61, 344, 354

Education-related court cases, 394

*Education Week*, 446

Educational agendas, local school boards and, 336

Educational foundations, 63–64

*Educational Leadership*, 442

Educators for Social Responsibility, 194

*Edwards v. Aguillard*, 399

Efficiency movement, 107

Eight-Year Study, 113

Electronic communication, 317

Electronic journals, 319

Electronic portfolios, 72–73

Elementary and Secondary Education Act, 229, 346

Emotional maltreatment. See Child abuse and neglect

Empowerment conflicts, 413–415

English Language Learners (ELL), 226

English-only rules, 111

English speaking ability, 211–213

Enhancing Education Through Technology Program (ETTP), 358

Entering beliefs and images, 36–39

Epistemology, 116–117

Equal Protection Clause of the Fourteenth Amendment, 393

Essentialism, 78–79, 117, 145, 146–147

Establishment Clause of the First Amendment, 393

Ethic of care, 120, 378–379

Ethic of collaboration, 418

Ethical considerations

codes of ethics, 389

educational philosophy and, 116

legal issues and, 393–402

school as ethical community, 386–388

teacher recommendations and, 389–391

teacher-to-teacher level, 385–388

Ethical issues

personal beliefs and curriculum, 403–404

personal beliefs and inclusivity, 403

personal *vs.* professional, 402–404

Ethnic diversity. See Diversity

Ethnic festivals, 233

Etiquette of interviewing, 47

Etiquette of observing, 45

Evolution, teaching of, 143, 399–400

Expectations, communicating, 219–222

Explicit curriculum, 131–132

Extracurriculum, 199–200

Extrinsic motivation, 293

**F**

Facility maintenance, 451

Fair use, 401–402

Family background, teacher, 23–24

Family Educational Rights and Privacy Act (FERPA), 395–396

Family relationships, trust and, 377–379

Family structures

books representing diversity in, 184

caregivers and, 180–183

foster care settings and, 182

gay and lesbian familles and, 182

grandparents role and, 180–182

homelessness and, 182–183

legal rights and, 183

nuclear families and, 179

poverty rates and, 181

responding to, 183–185

state by state, 180

stress and, 184–185

Federal governance, 344–353

categorical aid and, 347

court decisions and, 351–352

Federal governance, *(continued)*
    disabilities and, 254–257
    educational funding and, 113
    Elementary and Secondary
        Education Act (1965), 346
    Head Start and, 347
    historical aspects of, 344–346
    legislation and, 346–351
    No Child Left Behind Act (2001),
        347–348
    paradox of, 351
    Title IX legislation and, 348–351
Feedback, importance of, 295
Field experience, PK-12 classrooms
    and, 65–66
Financing education. *See also*
    Governance
    decentralized budgeting systems
        and, 358–359
    federal and state sources and,
        358–359
    inequities in, 357–358
    per pupil expenditures and,
        355–356
    referendums and, *357*
First job search
    becoming informed applicant,
        453–454
    job interviews, 454–455
    making your portfolio count, 453
    taking preparation seriously and,
        451–452
Formal classroom observation, 40–45
Foster care, 182
Foundations, educational, 63–64
Fraser Standard, 394
Free Exercise Clause of the First
    Amendment, 393
Free expression of opinions, 394–395
Freedom of Expression Clause of First
    Amendment, 393–394
*Freedom Writers*, 30
Full-service schools, 194–197
Funds of knowledge, 218–219
Furniture arrangement, classroom,
    170–171

**G**

Gay and lesbian families, 182
Gender, historical roles and, 413
Gender equity, 348–350
G.I. Bill of Rights, 113
Gifted and talented students, 279–280
Girls and women, education for,
    111–112

Globalization, 447–448
Goal setting, 444–445
Good schools and classrooms. *See also*
    Classroom organization; School
    organization
    connecting to local community
        and, 294
    cooperative learning and, 321–322
    creating strong classroom commu-
        nity and, 293–294
    effective teaching communities
        and, 294–295
    extrinsic motivation and, 293
    high expectations and, 291–292
    intrinsic motivation and, 292
    motivating students and, 291–292
    paraprofessionals and, 322–324
    peer tutoring and, 320–321
    student and teacher assessment
        and, 295–296
    student engagement and, 292
    teacher knowledge and, 292
*Goodbye, Mr. Chips*, 32
Governance. *See also* Financing
    education
    booster groups and, 354
    changing views and, 359–363
    coalitions or partnerships and,
        354–355
    federal government influence and,
        344–353
    levels of authority and, 332–333
    local school boards and, 333–338
    national committees and, 354
    nation's earliest schools and,
        342–343
    policymaking and, 335–338
    principal's role and, 338
    shared decision making and, 339
    state governance, 343–344
    superintendent of schools and,
        334–335
    teachers' leadership roles and,
        339–340
    teacher's unions and, 340–342
Grandparents as caregivers, 180–182
*Great Books of the Western World*, 119

**H**

*Hazelwood School District v. Kuhlmeier*
    *(1988)*, 394
Head Start, 347
Health clinics, 195–196
Hidden curriculum
    benefits of, 172–173

    critical theory and, 175–176
    current events as, 175–176
    definition of, 169
    furniture arrangement and,
        170–171
    liabilities and, 173–174
    messages and, 172
    passive consumption and, 174
    power of, 169–176
    question of privilege and, 174–175
    regularities of schooling and,
        171–172
    school as culture and, 170–172
    societal context and, 176–179
    socioeconomic structure of society
        and, 175
    taking responsibility and, 173
High expectations, motivation and,
    291–292
High-incidence disabilities, 262
Hispanic American children, 111
Historical origins of American educa-
    tion. *See* American education
Holiday celebrations, religious impli-
    cations and, 398
Hollywood images of teaching, 30–33
Holmes Partnership, 354
Home schooling, 363–364
    laws by state, 364
    reasons for, 363
    religion as factor in, 363–364
Homelessness, 182–183
Humanism, 198–199

**I**

Inclusion movement, 258–261
Inclusivity, personal beliefs and, 403
Individual students, meeting needs of, 7
Individualized Education Plan (IEP),
    255
Individuals with Disabilities
    Education Act (IDEA), 254–255
    disability categories and, 255
    major principles of, 255
Induction period, teacher, 86–89
    guidelines and, 94
    mentoring and, 86–89
    support and, 423–424
    tenure and, 89
Industrialization, effects on education,
    107–108
*Inherit the Wind*, 143
Innovation, 303–304
Institutional life, cognitive disabilities
    and, 252–254

Instructional technology, 314–320
Intelligent design, 399
International Reading Association, 443
International Society for Technology
    in Education (ISTE), 318, 402
Internet
    accessibility to, 314–315
    cautions regarding, 318
    Children's Internet Protection Act,
        401
    cyberbullying and, 188–189
    legal issues and, 401–402
    multitasking and, 320
    virtual schools and, 320
Interpersonal relationships, diversity
    and, 220–221
Interstate New Teacher Assessment
    and Support Consortium
    (INTASC) standards
    academic content knowledge and,
        94
    accreditation and, 80
    classroom organization and, 328
    curriculum issues and, 164
    diversity issues and, 246
    educational history and philosophy
        and, 125
    ethical and legal considerations
        and, 408
    meeting standards, 12–13
    professional development and, 461
    professional growth and, 54
    school as social institution and, 205
    school governance and, 370
    structural changes and, 71
    students with disabilities and, 285
    ten basic standards, 13
Interviewing, 45–48
    etiquette of, 47
    question construction and, 46–47
Intrinsic motivation, 292
Invisibility of everyday life, 40

**J**

Jacob K. Javits Gifted and Talented
    Students Education Program,
    279
Jeffersonian ideal of education,
    101–102
Job-embedded professional develop-
    ment, 425
Job interviews, 454–455
Job search. See First job search
Journals, teacher research and, 427

**K**

Keeping Children and Families Save
    Act (2003), 186
*Kitzmiller v. Dover (PA) Area School
    Board*, 399

**L**

Language diversity. See also Diversity
    additive bilingualism and, *231*
    addressing in classroom, 226–231
    bilingual education and, 229–231
    building respect for, 229
    setting parameters and, 227–229
    unrealistic expectations and, 227
Language use, 211–213
Latin grammar schools, 99
*Lau v. Nichols*, 229, 351
Leadership, teacher. See Teacher lead-
    ership
Learned curriculum, 132–134
Learning, as career-long commitment,
    3–5
Least restrictive environment (LRE),
    255–256
Legal issues, 393–402
    corporal punishment, 396–397
    fair use and copyright, 401–402
    Internet and, 401–402
    major education-related court
        cases, 394
    privacy and confidentiality,
        395–396
    religion in schools, 398
    reporting child abuse and neglect,
        396
    search and seizure, 397–398
    student's right to free expression of
        opinions, 394–395
    technology and, 400–402
*Lemon v. Kurtzman*, 394
Lengthening school day and year,
    307–308
Lesbian and gay student or familes,
    189
Letters of recommendation, 453
License portability, 61
License renewal, 89
Literacy coaches, 423–424
Local community, connecting to, 294
Local district level, curriculum devel-
    opment and, 142–143
Local education agency (LEA). See
    Local school boards
Local school boards, 332–333

    book challenges by, 336–337
    member demographics and, 334
    policymaking and, 335–338
    political or educational agendas
        and, 336
    relationship with superintendent,
        335
    role of, 333–334
    taking control from, 337–338
Local values, curriculum development
    and, 143
Locker searches, 397–398
Logic, educational philosophy and,
    116
Long-term goals, 444–445
Looping, 299
Lounge talk, 386–387
Low-incidence disabilities, 262
Low teacher expectations, 219–222

**M**

*Mad Hot Ballroom*, 32
Magnet schools, 149
Making the familiar strange
    formal classroom observation and,
        40–45
    through interviewing, 45–48
Mandates, 12
*Marianthe's Story: Painted Words and
    Spoken Memories*, 35
Maturity, teacher, 382
Media images, 30–36
    movies and television and, 30–33
    print media, 34–35
*Mendez v. Westminster*, 111
Mental retardation. See Cognitive dis-
    abilities
Mentoring
    alternative route programs
        and, 83
    formal programs of, 86–89
    teacher leadership and, 423–424
Merit pay, 434–435
Misbehaviors, dealing with, 396–397
Misconceptions, role of, 37–38
*Miss Malarkey Doesn't Live in Room
    10*, 35
*Miss Nelson Is Missing*, 35
Mission schools, 109
Monitorial system, 107
Monocultural schools, 239–240
Montessori schools, 149
Moral knowledge, 380–381
Moral obligations, 375–385. See also
    Trust

Motivation
  extrinsic motivation, 293
  high expectations and, 291–292
  instructional technology and, 317
  intrinsic motivation, 292
  for teaching, 26–27
Mount Holyoke Seminary, 112
*Mr. Holland's Opus*, 32
Multi-age classrooms, 298
Multicultural literature, 235
Multimodal literacy, 315–316
Multiple perspectives, diversity and, 235–237
Multitasking, 9, 12
Multiyear grouping, 299
*Music of the Heart*, 30
Myths about teaching, 415–417

**N**

National accreditation, 79–80
National Art Education Association, 443
National Association for Music Education, 443
National Association of Bilingual Education, 443
National Association of State Directors of Teacher Education, 61
National Board for Professional Teaching Standards, 431–434, 438
  certification by, 431
  certification incentives, 433
  core propositions of, 432
  fee support and, 433
  license portability and, 433
  racial and ethnic minority groups and, 434
  salary supplements and, 433
  teaching license renewal and, 433
National Commission on Teaching and America's Future, 80, 354, 417, 439
National Council for Accreditation of Teacher Education, 61, 79–80
National Council for the Social Studies, 443, 447
National Council for the Teachers of Mathematics, 443
National Council of Teachers of English, 443
National Defense Act, 113
National Education Association, 25, 144–145, 340, 389–390, 421–422
National Education Technology Standards (NETS), 318

National level, curriculum development and, 143–145
National Parent Teacher Association, 354
National professional organizations and websites, 436
National Resource Center for Paraeducators, 322
National Science Foundation, 349
National Science Teachers Association, 443, 447
National Writing Project, 37, 436
Native American children, 109–110
Negative teacher talk, 386–387
Neglect, child. *See* Child abuse and neglect
Networking, 435–437
  formal teacher networks, 437
  national professional organizations, 436
New developments, incorporating, 442–443
*New Jersey v. TLO* (1985), 394
News media images, 34
No Child Left Behind Act
  adequate yearly progress and, 347
  basic principles of, 347
  criticism of, 348
  federal government role and, 12
  low-income students and, 152
  multiple data form use and, 296
  narrowing subjects offered and, 307
  principles and accountability under, 347–348
  reporting of school scores and, 34
  supporters and, 348
*No Dream Denied: A Pledge to America's Children*, 58
Nondiscriminatory evaluation, 255
Normal school movement, 67–69
Northwest Ordinance of 1787, 103
Null curriculum, 132, 135–136

**O**

Oberlin College, 112
Objective observation, 44
Observation. *See* Classroom observation
Observing with a map, 41–42
Offensive speech, 395
"Old Deluder Satan Act," 178, 342
One-room schools, 300–301
Open classrooms, 418–419
Open territory states, textbooks and, 159–160
Oral inquiry, teacher research and, 427

Organizations, teacher, 421–422

**P**

Paraprofessionals, 27–30
  career ladder for, 322
  role differentiation and, 323
  roles of, 322–324
Parent Teacher Organization, 354
Parochial schools, 362
Passive consumption, curriculum and, 174
Pay, differentiated, 434–435
Pedagogical knowledge, 64–65, 380–381
Pedagogical content knowledge, 65
Pedagogy, 64–65
Peer assistance and review, 425–426
Peer mediation, 193–194
Peer tutoring, 320–321
Per pupil expenditures, 355–356
Perennialism, 118–119, 147
Personal commitments, 24–27
Philosophy of education, 114–120
  aesthetics and, 116
  epistemology and, 116–117
  essentialism and, 117
  ethic of care and, 120
  ethics and, 116
  logic and, 116
  perennialism and, 118–119
  progressive view of education, 146–147
  progressivism and, 117–118
  social reconstructionism and, 119
  usefulness and, 120
  Western philosophical concepts, 115–117
Philosophy of teaching, 38–39
Physical abuse. *See* Child abuse and neglect
Physical infrastructure, 451
PK-12 classrooms, field experience in, 65–66
*Plessy v. Ferguson*, 221–222
Political agendas, local school boards and, 336
Population, school enrollments and, 179
Portfolios
  developmental, 72
  electronic, 72–73
  first job search and, 453
  showcase, 72
  standards-based teacher education and, 71–73
  value of, 73–74

Poverty rates, 181
Power, teacher, 382
Practical curriculum, 105–106
Praxis™ tests, 76–77
Preparation, finding first job and, 451–452
Preschool programs, students with disabilities and, 257
Presentation software, 319
Principal, role of, 338
Print media images, 34–35
Prior knowledge and experiences
  autobiographical knowledge, 23–27
  entering beliefs and images, 36–39
  media images and, 30–36
  as paraprofessionals, 27–30
  personal schooling experience and, 20–23
Privacy, 395–396
Private schools, 360–363
Profession/job conflict, 412–417
Profession, teaching as, 416–417
Professional commitment, 14–15
Professional Compensation System for Teachers (ProComp), 435
Professional conferences, 442–443
Professional contributions, 7–8
Professional development, networking and, 435–437
Professional development schools, 74–76
Professional knowledge base, 71
Professional organizations, national, 436
Professional schools, 62
Professionalism, teacher research and, 430–431
Professionalization agenda, 417
Progressivism, 117–118, 146–147
Project-based learning, 148–149
Public education
  contested control of, 102–103
  future of, 450–451

Q

Question construction, interviewing and, 46–47

R

Racial diversity. See Diversity
Reading your students, 10
Reciprocity agreements, 61
Recommendation letters, 453
Records access, 395–396
Reflection
  building trust and, 381–382

professional, 442
role of, 8
Reggio Emilia curriculum, 149
Religion in schools, 352–353
  colonial curriculum and, 392
  holiday celebrations and, 398
  home schooling and, 363–364
  legal issues and, 398
  school prayer and, 398
  teaching evolution and, 399–400
Research. See Teacher research
Resegregation of schools, 450
Resiliency, children, 185
Resource rooms, 272
Response to intervention (RTI), 271
Rewards of teaching, 9–10
Roberts v. City of Boston, 108

S

Salaries, 413–414
Salary scales, 434–435
School as ethical community, 386–388
School boards. See Local school boards
School board elections, 446
School choice, 360–363
School community, ethical considerations and, 386–388
School organization. See also Classroom organization
  age-graded classroom model, 296–298
  block scheduling and, 302–303
  class size reduction and, 301–302
  departmentalization and, 296
  historical aspects and, 300–301
  introducing change and, 303–304
  lengthening school day and year, 307–308
  looping and, 299
  multi-age classrooms and, 298
  organizing for democracy, 309–310
  small high schools movement, 304–307
  year-round schools, 308–309
School prayer, 398
School psychologist, 383
School quality. See Good schools and classrooms
School takeovers, 337–338
School taxes, local school boards and, 333
School violence, 187–190
  bullying and, 188–189
  early warning signs and, 188

lesbian, gay, bisexual, or transgendered students and, 189
  prevention strategies and, 187
  safety measures and, 188
Schools within schools concept, 306
Scope and sequence charts, 140
Scopes trial (1925), 143
Screenreading software, 277
Search and seizure, 397–398
Segregation, 108–109, 221–222
Self-advocacy, student, 384–385
Self-assessment, 440–441
Self-expectations, 15
Self-fulfilling prophecy, 221
Selman et al. v. Cobb County, Georgia, 399
Separation of church and state, 352–353
Serrano v. Priest, 357
Sex education, 191
Sexual abuse. See Child abuse and neglect
Short-term goals, 444–445
Shortages, teacher. See Teacher shortages
Showcase portfolios, 72
Sister Act II, 32
Site-based management, 339
Small high schools movement, 304–307
Small schools, benefits of, 189–190
Smith-Hughes Act, 113
Social dynamics, 193–199
  developmental guidance and, 194
  full-service schools and, 194–197
  peer mediation, 193–194
  redefining the environment, 193–197
  teacher's role in promoting competence, 198
Social issues and trends
  changing family structures, 179–185
  child abuse and neglect, 185–186
  drug and alcohol abuse, 192–193
  school size and, 189–190
  school violence, 187–190
  teen pregnancy, 191–192
Social justice curriculum, 148
Social reconstructionism, 119, 236
Social workers, 383
Societal context, hidden curriculum and, 176–179
Societal perspective on teaching, historical, 413

Socioeconomic structure, hidden curriculum and, 175
Special education. *See also* Disabilities; Disability categorization
co-teaching and, 271–272
diminishing differences and, 272–273
early intervention and, 257
historical treatment of, 251–252
resource rooms and, 272
teacher's role and, 267–274
transition services and, 258
Specialized schoolwide curriculums, 147–151
Spelman College, 109
Sports funding, 348
*Stand and Deliver*, 30
Standardized testing
accountability and, 438
curriculum and, 145–146, 152–155
positive and negative uses of, 154
Standards, accreditation and, 80–81
Standards-based teacher education
purpose of, 71
role of portfolios in, 71–73
State court decisions, 352
State Education Agency (SEA), 343–344
State governance, 343–344
State level, curriculum development and, 138–141
Stereotypes, about teaching, 34–35
Stress, family situations and, 184–185
Student assessment, 295–296
Student engagement, teacher knowledge and, 292
Student-led conferences, 384
Student relationships, trust and, 376
Subject matter content, teacher education and, 62–63
Summer months, 416
Superintendent of schools, 334–335
Systematic observation, 42–44

**T**

Taught curriculum, 132–133, 153
*Teach for America*, 83
Teacher assessment, 295–296
Teacher education
accreditation and standards, 80–81
after formal education, 85–89
connecting elements of, 66
deregulation and, 78
dimensions of high quality, 59
early history of, 67–69

essentialist view of, 78–79
field experience in PK-12 classrooms, 65–66
foundations of education, 63–64
increasing rigor in, 70–74
induction period and, 86–89
license portability and, 61
license renewal and, 89
national accreditation and, 79–80
normal school movement and, 67–69
pedagogical knowledge and, 64–65
professional development schools and, 74–76
professional schools and, 62
purpose of standards in, 71
reforming, 67–70
role of testing in, 76–79
shared responsibility and, 74–76
state requirements and, 60–61
subject matter content and, 62–63
teaching portfolios and, 71–73
Teacher Education Accreditation Council (TEAC), 79–80
Teacher expectations, 32
Teacher films, 30–33
Teacher guides, 156
Teacher isolation, autonomy and, 420
Teacher knowledge, student engagement and, 292
Teacher leadership, 422–426
coaching as, 425
forms of, 422–423
mentoring as, 423–424
new teacher unionism and, 426
peer review and, 425–426
personal qualities and, 423
roles and, 339–340
Teacher-led schools, 339–340
*Teacher Man*, 34
Teacher-proof curriculum, 155–156
Teacher recommendations, 389–391
Teacher research, 426–431
action research, 427
journals and, 427
oral inquiry, 427
professionalism and, 430–431
writing program improvement and, 428–430
Teacher shortages, 82–84
alternate routes and, 82–84
cyclical nature of, 82
Teacher-student ratio, 301–302
Teacher-to-teacher ethical considerations, 385–388

Teacher Union Reform Network (TURN), 426
*Teachers for a New Era*, 70
Teachers' Learning Cooperative in Philadelphia, 436–437
Teacher's lounge, 386–387
Teachers of English to Speakers of Other Languages, 443
Teacher's organizations, emergence of, 421–422
Teacher's unions
role of, 340–342
teacher leadership and, 426
TeachersCount, 10
Teaching career, five stages of, 85
Teaching communities, effective, 294–295
Teaching knowledge, sources of, 4
Teaching portfolios, 71–73
Teaching Tolerance, 235
Team teaching, 419
Technology
changing teacher's role and, 419
instructional, 314–320
legal issues regarding, 400–402
standards and, 318
teaching world languages and, 449
Teen pregnancy, 191–192
Tenure, 89
Testing in teacher preparation, 76–79
Text-to-speech software, 277
Textbook industry, 158–160
Textbooks
academic standards and, 158
adoption states and, 159–160
ancillary materials and, 156
biases and, 158
curriculum potential and, 156–157
open territory states and, 159–160
role in curriculum and, 155–162
teacher guides and, 156
teacher-proof curriculum and, 155–156
teacher's roles and, 157
*The Landry News*, 35
*The New England Primer*, 392
*There Are No Shortcuts*, 34
Time issues, 439
Tinker Standard, 394
*Tinker v. Des Moines Independent School District*, 394
Title IX legislation, 348–351
*To Kill a Mockingbird*, 175
*Tomorrow's Teachers*, 69–70, 74
*Tough Choices, Tough Times*, 358

Transgendered students or familles, 189

Transition services, special education and, 258

Transmission model of teaching, 146–147

*Troops to Teachers*, 83

Troy Academy, 111–112

Trust
  classroom community and, 379–380
  content knowledge and, 380–381
  creating and maintaining, 381–385
  ethic of care and, 378–379
  multiple dimensions of, 376–381
  pedagogical knowledge and, 380–381
  relationships with families and, 377–379
  relationships with students and, 376
  role of reflection and, 381–382
  teacher maturity and, 382
  teacher power and, 382

Turnover, first-year, 424

Tuskegee Normal and Industrial Institute, 109

**U**

Unfair actions, protection from, 383

Unions. *See* Teacher's unions

United Nations, 448

Universal Design of Learning (UDL), 276–277

Universal education, initial notion of, 178

Urban schools, alternative route programs and, 83

U.S. Supreme Court, 351–352

**V**

Video-based programs, 449

Video hook-ups, 419

Videoconferencing equipment, 319

Videotaping, 419

Violence. *See* School violence

Virtual schools, 320

Voluntary accreditation, 79–80

Vouchers, 113, 360–362

**W**

*Wallace v. Jaffree*, 394

*Ways with Words*, 215

Websites, professional, 436–437

*Welcome Back, Kotter*, 33

Western philosophical concepts, 115–117

White privilege, 237–238

Workdays, 416

Working portfolios, 72

World languages education, 448–449

Writing across the curriculum, 335

Writing programs, teacher research and, 428–430

**Y**

Year-round schools, 308–309

Youth development programs, 192